Fodor's 95 Ireland

PRAISE FOR FODOR'S GUIDES

"Fodor's guides . . . are an admirable blend of the cultural and the practical."

—The Washington Post

"Researched by people chosen because they live or have lived in the country, well-written, and with good historical sections . . . Obligatory reading for millions of tourists."

—The Independent, *London*

"Usable, sophisticated restaurant coverage, with an emphasis on good value."

—Andy Birsh, Gourmet restaurant columnist, quoted by Gannett News Service

"Packed with dependable information."

—Atlanta Journal Constitution

"Fodor's always delivers high quality . . . thoughtfully presented . . . thorough."

—Houston Post

"Valuable because of their comprehensiveness."

—Minneapolis Star-Tribune

Fodor's Travel Publications, Inc.
New York • Toronto • London • Sydney • Auckland

ISBN 0-679-02726-2

Fodor's Ireland

Editor: Caroline V. Haberfeld
Contributors: Georgina Campbell, Giuliano Davenport, Echo Garrett, Alannah Hopkin, Laura M. Kidder, Bevin McLaughlin, Hugh Oram, Andrew Sanger, Mary Ellen Schultz, Nancy van Itallie.
Creative Director: Fabrizio La Rocca
Cartographer: David Lindroth
Illustrator: Karl Tanner
Cover Photograph: Peter Guttman

Design: Vignelli Associates

Special Sales

Fodor's Travel Publications are available at special discounts for bulk purchases for sales promotions or premiums. Special editions, including personalized covers, excerpts of existing guides, and corporate imprints, can be created in large quantities for special needs. For more information, contact your local bookseller or write to Special Markets, Fodor's Travel Publications, 201 East 50th Street, New York, NY 10022. Inquiries from Canada should be directed to your local Canadian bookseller or sent to Random House of Canada, Ltd., Marketing Dept., 1265 Aerowood Drive, Mississauga, Ontario L4W 1B9. Inquiries from the United Kingdom should be sent to Fodor's Travel Publications, 20 Vauxhall Bridge Road, London SW1V 2SA, England.

MANUFACTURED IN THE UNITED STATES OF AMERICA
10 9 8 7 6 5 4 3 2 1

Contents

Foreword *vi*

Highlights '95 *viii*

Fodor's Choice *xii*

Introduction *xxvi*

1 Essential Information *1*

Before You Go *2*

Government Information Offices *2*
Tours and Packages *2*
When to Go *5*
Festivals and Seasonal Events *6*
What to Pack *9*
Taking Money Abroad *10*
Getting Money from Home *11*
Currency *11*
What It Will Cost *12*
Long-Distance Calling *12*
Passports and Visas *13*
Customs and Duties *13*
Traveling with Cameras, Camcorders, and Laptops *15*
Language *16*
Staying Healthy *16*
Insurance *17*
Car Rentals *18*
Rail Passes *19*
Student and Youth Travel *20*
Traveling with Children *22*
Hints for Travelers with Disabilities *23*
Hints for Older Travelers *24*
Hints for Gay and Lesbian Travelers *25*
Further Reading *25*

Arriving and Departing *27*

From North America by Plane *27*
From North America by Ship *30*
From Britain by Plane *31*
From Britain by Ferry, Car, and Bus *31*

Staying in the Irish Republic *33*

Getting Around *33*
Telephones *35*
Mail *36*
Tipping *36*
Opening and Closing Times *36*
Shopping *36*

Sports and the Outdoors *38*
Beaches *40*
Dining *40*
Lodging *42*

Staying in Northern Ireland *44*

Getting Around *44*
Telephones *45*
Mail *46*
Tipping *46*
Opening and Closing Times *46*
Shopping *46*
Sports and the Outdoors *46*
Dining *47*
Lodging *47*
Credit Cards *48*

Great Itineraries *48*

2 Portraits of Ireland *53*

"Bogland," by Seamus Heaney *54*
Ireland at a Glance: A Chronology *55*
"Irish Miles," by Frank O'Connor *59*
"The Stone Walls of Ireland," by Richard Conniff *63*

3 Irish Greens *69*
Golfing in Ireland, by Jonathan Abrahams

4 Dublin *77*

5 Dublin Environs *148*
County Wicklow, the Boyne Valley, and County Kildare

6 The Lakelands *174*

7 The Southeast *195*
Kilkenny Town, Wexford Town, Waterford City, Tipperary Town

8 The Southwest *232*
Cork City, Killarney, the Ring of Kerry, Dingle

9 The West *290*
Cliffs of Moher, the Burren, Galway City, County Mayo

10 The Northwest *333*
Yeats Country, Donegal Bay, the Northern Peninsulas

11 Northern Ireland *371*
Belfast, the Antrim Coast, Derry City, the Mountains of Mourne

Index *408*

Maps and Plans

Ireland *xviii–xix*
Ireland's Counties *xx–xxi*
Europe *xxii–xxiii*
World Time Zones *xxiv–xxv*
Dublin Exploring *80–81*
Tours 1 and 2: Dublin City Center *88–89*
Tour 3: Dublin West *98*
Tour 4: James Joyce's Dublin *103*
Tour 5: Dublin Southside *105*
Tour 6: Dublin Northside *110*
Dublin Shopping *115*
Dublin Dining *124–125*
Dublin Lodging *138–139*
Dublin Environs *151*
The Lakelands *178*
The Southeast *200–201*
Kilkenny Town *204*
Wexford Town *207*
Waterford City *211*
The Southwest *240–241*
Cork City *242*
Killarney Area *250*
The West *296*
Galway City *303*
Yeats Country and Around Donegal Bay *339*
Sligo Town *340*
The Northern Peninsulas *349*
Northern Ireland *380–381*
Belfast *382*

Foreword

We wish to express our gratitude to the staff of the Irish Tourist Board for their assistance in the preparation of this guide.

While every care has been taken to ensure the accuracy of the information in this guide, the passage of time will always bring change, and consequently, the publisher cannot accept responsibility for errors that may occur.

All prices and opening times quoted here are based on information available to us at press time. Hours and admission fees may change, however, and the prudent traveler will avoid inconvenience by calling ahead.

Fodor's wants to hear about your travel experiences, both pleasant and unpleasant. When a hotel or restaurant fails to live up to its billing, let us know and we will investigate the complaint and revise our entries where the facts warrant it.

Send your letters to the editors of Fodor's Travel Publications, 201 East 50th Street, New York, NY 10022.

Highlights '95 and Fodor's Choice

Highlights '95

Dublin On March 27, 1994, after almost 50 years of being required to stop over in Shannon on the way to Dublin, Aer Lingus and other transatlantic carriers were allowed to fly directly to Dublin from the United States. Aer Lingus is flying nonstop from New York, year-round with daily service, while Delta Airlines flies four times a week nonstop from Atlanta. These flights will probably attract a lot more business travelers who previously were flying to London and then on to Dublin.

The look of Dublin City Center continues to improve, with more pedestrian-only streets and a greater variety of shops. In the South City Center, **Grafton Street** looks resplendent with its new redbrick walkways for shoppers. The **Temple Bar** area on the south side of the Liffey has also been largely converted to a traffic-free area giving Dublin a revitalized "Left Bank." The North City Center is also changing; **O'Connell Street** now features recently planted trees, a fountain near the General Post Office, and a new James Joyce statue at the O'Connell Street corner of **North Earl Street,** which has also been pedestrianized.

The **National Gallery, Civic Museum,** and **Municipal Gallery** were all refurbished in 1991, during Dublin's term as the Cultural Capital of Europe. Several new museums also opened: Foremost is the **Irish Museum of Modern Art,** which is housed in the beautifully restored **Royal Hospital Kilmainham,** a fine late-17th-century building also open to the public. The **Dublin Writer's Museum** honors the city's rich literary past and the interiors of **Newman House** and **Number Twenty-Nine,** two typical late-18th-century family homes, have been fully restored in period detail.

Bloomsday, June 16, the day made famous by James Joyce's *Ulysses*, has become a festive annual occasion. Even those who have never read Joyce dress up in Edwardian attire and parade (preferably by horse-drawn carriage) around the areas detailed in the book. In the evening Joyce's works are celebrated at a series of lighthearted theatrical events, many of them in pubs associated with the author.

Dublin Environs The **Millmount Museum** in Drogheda was recently refurbished and is now one of the best exhibition halls in the country, with numerous relics of Drogheda's commercial and industrial past.

After thirty years of excavation, the site of the 18 megalithic passage-tombs at **Knowth** (dating from 3000 BC) is now open to the public. Many visit Knowth in conjunction with the completed excavation at **Newgrange,** one of the greatest—and most puzzling—megalithic tombs in Europe.

The Lakelands **Shannonbridge Bog Tour,** which takes visitors on an old works train for 8 kilometers (5 miles) across a raised peat bog, is a modest excursion, but it's been one of Ireland's most talked about attractions since opening in 1992. The wildlife, flora, and history of the bog—a site of international scientific interest—is discussed by the driver as the train makes its slow journey. **Strokestown Park House** in County Roscommon has opened a museum that gives an imaginative insight into the disastrous 1845 famine, whose 100th aniversary is commemorated this year.

Visitors familiar with the traditionally unpretentious accommodations available in this area will be pleasantly surprised by the opulence of the **Slieve Russell Country Club and Hotel** at Ballyconnell near Cavan; the 300-acre compound features a luxurious indoor leisure center with a 20-meter pool, 18-hole golf course, and 50 acres of lakes for anglers.

The Southeast Walkers and outdoor types will enjoy the scenery around the unspoilt little village of Graiguenamanagh on the banks of the River Barrow in County Kilkenny. **Hanora's Cottage,** a charming B&B in the neighboring County Waterford supplies guests with maps of the newly opened trails in the Comeragh Mountains, which can be explored on foot, horseback, or bicycle. Six new parkland golf courses opened recently in the area: the Jack Nicklaus–designed course at **Mount Juliet** in **Kilkenny,** 18-hole parkland courses adjoining the **Waterford Castle Hotel** and the **Dundrum House Hotel,** and new clubs that welcome visitors at Checkpoint and Dunganan, County Waterford, and St. Helen's, County Wexford.

The Irish National Heritage Park at Ferrycarrig, near Wexford Town, continues to enhance its attractions. This 35-acre open-air theme park, which covers Irish history from 9000 BC to AD 1100, is now handling up to 1,500 visitors per day. It has hired costumed crafts workers and students to bring a human dimension to its full-scale replicas of Irish life in the distant past.

The Southwest Cork City Center's pedestrian-only **Paul Street** area with its paved piazza has revitalized the whole area between Patrick Street and the river. Paul Street, French Church Street, and Carey's Lane are fast becoming the best addresses in town for lively moderately priced restaurants, adventurous fashion boutiques, specialty book shops, and top-quality crafts shops.

Sheen Falls Lodge, a luxury development on Kenmare Bay, is the newest upscale hotel in the region. It has a magnificent location beside a waterfall and is surrounded by 300 secluded acres of lawn, semitropical gardens, and forest. **Adare Manor,** an even grander recent arrival on the scene in County Limerick, is a vast, Gothic Victorian manor on a 1,000-acre estate. It recently added an 18-hole golf course to its sporting facilities, which already included fishing, horseback riding, and a fitness center. The hotel is an ideal touch-down point for transatlantic passengers arriving at Shannon, which is only 25 kilometers (16 miles) away. (*See* Dining and Lodging in Chapter 8, The Southwest.)

Where tourism is concerned, **Kinsale,** with its quaint narrow streets and fine restaurants, is the boom town of the Southwest, although Dingle, in the far west (favorite hideaway of actress Julia Roberts, among others), is equally attractive and offers a good choice of restaurants during its April-to-October high season. The completed **Dingle Way** walking trail loops from Tralee for 153 kilometers (95 miles) around the Dingle peninsula and back. And the **Kerry Way,** which starts in Killarney, now extends for 209 kilometers (130 miles) around the Ring of Kerry. The **Skellig Experience,** beside the road bridge to Valentia Island, combines an interpretative center telling of **Skellig Michael** (an ancient Christian monastery on a conical rock 13 kilometers/8 miles off the coast), with a 1½-hour cruise around the islands. The newly opened **Blasket Centre** near Dunquin explains the heritage and rugged lifestyle of the Blasket Islands.

The West Galway City now has two much-needed new hotels. **Glenlo Abbey** is a monastery overlooking Lough Corrib that has been converted into a small luxury hotel, while the newly built **Jury's Inn,** near the Spanish Arch in the very center of Galway, offers good-quality budget accommodations. The new **Connemara Airport,** serving the Aran Islands, has cut the journey time to the island to five minutes, and has also led to a significant price reduction. The first phase of a major renovation of its neglected docks was completed in Galway City in 1993, adding considerably to the cosmopolitan charm of the old Atlantic seaport.

The Northwest A steady process of upgrading, refurbishment, and expansion continues in the Northwest's **accommodations.** Now it's the norm rather than the exception for hotel rooms to have wall-to-wall carpets, a TV, and private bathrooms. Yet price increases have remained steady, with only a few rises since last year in this remote, rustic region. The modern Sligo Park Hotel, on the outskirts of Sligo Town, Mount Errigal Hotel in Letterkenny, Arnold's Hotel at Dunfanaghy, and the Hyland Central in the middle of Donegal Town have all benefited from recent improvements.

If you're interested in knitting, particularly the stitches and styles of traditional Irish handknits, you might like to consider a course at Ireland's National Knitting Centre, near Buncrana, County Donegal (tel. 077/62355 for details). The price, currently around £400 for a week, includes tuition, guest house accommodations, meals, tours, and entertainment. If you love Irish handknits but don't want to take a course, just pop into the centre's shop to pick up some bargains.

Northern Ireland A year of renewed turbulence, violence and political problems in Ireland's troubled British enclave has deterred many tourists. This is unfortunate, since incidents are almost invariably confined to the same few relatively small urban areas (tourist information offices can advise).

There's even more to draw visitors than last year, with the opening of new or expanded attractions at Armagh Planetarium, Portaferry Aquarium, Carrickfergus Castle, Dunluce Castle, and the Ulster-American Folk Park. Interpretative Centers combining fun with learning have been opened at Armagh, Navan, Lough Neagh's Oxford Island, Enniskillen Castle, and Belfast Castle. Meanwhile, work continues to transform Belfast's old waterfront district. If you want to watch its progress and learn the history of the city's docks, visit the new Lagan Lookout on Donegall Quay.

Fodor's Choice

No two people will agree on what makes a perfect vacation, but it's fun and helpful to know what others think. We hope you'll have a chance to experience some of Fodor's Choices yourself while visiting Ireland. For detailed information about each entry, refer to the appropriate chapters (given in the left-hand margin) within this guidebook.

Sights to Remember

Dublin
Sunset over the River Liffey
Deserted Georgian squares on a Sunday
Phoenix Park

Dublin Environs
Glendalough Valley
Greystones Harbour at dusk
Japanese Gardens, in Tully near Kildare Town

Lakelands
Birr Castle Demesne, Birr

Southeast
Ballyhack Village from Passage East
Lismore Castle Gardens
Mitchelstown Cave, Burncourt, Cahir

Southwest
The view of the Blasket Islands from Slea Head
Dusk over Killarney's Lower Lake as seen from Aghadoe Heights
The view of Fastnet Rock Lighthouse from Cape Clear Island

West
The view of the Aran Islands from the Cliffs of Moher
Clifden's twin spires nestled in the mountains above the sea
Salmon Weir Bridge, Galway

Northwest
Peat cutters in the bog country
Whitewashed single-story cottages with tied-on thatched roofs

Northern Ireland
Devenish Island viewed from Lough Erne's shore
The Giant's Causeway
Red, white, and blue curbstones in Protestant neighborhoods

Buildings and Monuments

Dublin
Bank of Ireland, College Green
National Library—the Reading Room
Royal Hospital, Kilmainham

Trinity College

Dublin Environs Castletown House, Celbridge

Church of Ireland cathedral and Round Tower, Kildare Town

Newgrange, west of Drogheda

Russborough House, Blessington

Lakelands Emo Court, Emo

Clonmacnoise Monastery, Co. Offaly

Shannonbridge bog railway tour

Southeast Brown's Hill Dolmen, Carlow Town

Kilkenny Castle, Kilkenny Town

Reginald's Tower, Waterford City

Rock of Cashel, Cashel

Monastic remains, Ardmore

Southwest Bunratty Castle, Bunratty

Charles Fort, Kinsale

Gallarus Oratory, Dingle Peninsula

Blarney Castle, Blarney

West Ashford Castle, Cong

Dún Aengus, Inishmore, Aran Islands

Kylemore Abbey, Connemara

Northwest Creevykeel megalithic court-cairn, near Cliffony

Donegal Castle, Donegal Town

Glenveagh Castle, Co. Donegal

Northern Ireland Belfast's Victorian pubs

Carrickfergus Castle, Carrickfergus

Castle Coole, near Enniskillen

Museums and Works of Art

Dublin Irish Museum of Modern Art, Kilmainham

Guinness Hop Store

Dublin Writers Museum

Treasury, at the National Museum

Dublin Environs Millmount Museum, Drogheda

Ledwidge Cottage and Museum, Slane

Southeast Irish National Heritage Park, Ferrycarrig

Southwest Bantry House, Bantry

Crawford Art Gallery, Cork

Hunt Collection, Limerick

Craggaunowen Project, Co. Limerick

West Dysert O'Dea Castle Archaeology Center, Corofin

Thoor Ballylee, Gort

Northwest Glebe Gallery, Church Hill

Sligo County Library and Museum, Sligo Town

Northern Ireland Ulster Museum, Belfast

Ulster Folk Museum, near Belfast

Scenic Drives and Views

Dublin East pier, Dun Laoghaire

Hill of Howth

Dalkey Coast Road

Dublin Environs Around the shores of Poulaphouca Reservoir, Co. Wicklow

Banks of Grand Canal, Co. Kildare

Hill of Tara, Co. Meath

Southeast Vee Gap scenic route, Co. Tipperary

Southwest Connor Pass, Dingle Peninsula

Scenic route from Allihies to Eyeries, Beara Peninsula

Tunnel road: Glengarriff–Kenmare–Killarney

West Atlantic drive around Achill Island

The Burren: Cliffs of Moher to Ballyvaughan via Doolin and Fanore (coast road), returning to Lisdoonvarna via Corkscrew Hill

Sky Road, Clifden

Northwest Killybegs to Glencolumbkille, Donegal Bay

Around Sheephaven Bay

The road along Errigal Mountain's south side

Northern Ireland The Glens of Antrim

Around Lower Lough Erne

Hotels

Dublin Shelbourne (*$$$$*)

Killiney Castle, Co. Dublin (*$$$*)

Hibernian (*$$*)

	The Towers (*$$*)
	Ariel House (*$*)
Dublin Environs	Kildare Hotel and Country Club, Straffan (*$$$$*)
	Rathsallagh House, Dunlavin (*$$$$*)
	Tinakilly House, Rathnew (*$$$$*)
	Ballymascanlon House, Dundalk (*$$*)
Lakelands	Slieve Russell Hotel and Country Club, Ballyconnell (*$$$$*)
	Hodson Bay Hotel, Athlone (*$$*)
Southeast	Cashel Palace Hotel, Cashel (*$$$$*)
	Mount Juliet, Thomastown (*$$$$*)
	Ferrycarrig, Wexford (*$$$*)
	Kelly's, Rosslare (*$$*)
	Newpark Hotel, Kilkenny Town (*$$*)
Southwest	Adare Manor, Adare (*$$$$*)
	Park Hotel, Kenmare (*$$$$*)
	Sheen Falls Lodge, Kenmare (*$$$$*)
	Longueville House, Mallow (*$$$*)
West	Cashel House Hotel, Cashel Bay (*$$$$*)
	Dromoland Castle, Newmarket-on-Fergus (*$$$$*)
	Ballynahinch Castle, Recess (*$$$*)
	Gregan's Castle Hotel, Ballyvaughan (*$$$*)
	Rock Glen Manor House, Clifden (*$$$*)
Northwest	Rathmullan House, Rathmullan (*$$$*)
	St. Ernan's House, Donegal Town (*$$*)
Northern Ireland	Culloden Hotel, Belfast (*$$$$*)
	Wellington Park Hotel (*$$$*)
	Londonderry Arms, Carnlough (*$$*)

Bed-and-Breakfasts

Dublin	Kilronan House (*$*)
	Montrose House (*$*)
Dublin Environs	Old Rectory Country House, Wicklow Town (*$$*)
	Lennoxbrook, Kells (*$*)
Lakelands	Gurthalougha House, Terryglass (*$$*)
	Ballycormac House, Borrisokane (*$*)

Southeast	Diamond Hill Country House, Waterford City (*$*)
Southwest	Bantry House, Bantry (*$$$*)
	Scilly House, Kinsale (*$$*)
	Kathleen's Country House, Killarney (*$*)
West	Currarevagh House, Oughterard (*$$$*)
	Ballinalacken Castle, Lisdoonvarna (*$*)
	Dun Aengus, Clifden (*$*)
Northwest	Coopershill, Riverstown (*$$$*)
	Markree Castle, Collooney (*$$$*)
	Bruckless House, Bruckless (*$$*)
	Temple House, Ballymote (*$$*)
	Woodhill Guest House, Ardara (*$*)
Northern Ireland	Ash-Rowan Guest House, Belfast (*$$*)
	Jamestown House, Ballinamallard (*$$*)
	Camera House, Belfast (*$*)

Restaurants

Dublin	Restaurant Patrick Guilbaud (*$$$$*)
	The King Sitric (*$$$*)
	Les Frères Jacques (*$$$*)
Dublin Environs	Rathsallagh House, Dunlavin (*$$$$*)
	Tinakilly House, Rathnew (*$$$$*)
	Roundwood Inn, Roundwood (*$$$*)
	Tree of Idleness, Bray (*$$$*)
Lakelands	Crookedwood House, near Mullingar (*$$$*)
	Moorhill Country House, Tullamore (*$$*)
Southeast	Chez Hans, Cashel (*$$$$*)
	Marlfield House Hotel, Gorey (*$$$$*)
	Waterford Castle, Waterford (*$$$$*)
	Dwyers of Mary Street, Waterford (*$$*)
	The Granary, Wexford (*$$*)
Southwest	Arbutus Lodge, Cork (*$$$*)
	Clifford's, Cork (*$$$*)
	Shiro Japanese Dinner House, Durrus (*$$$*)
West	Drimcong House, Moycullen (*$$$*)
	Claire's, Ballyvaughan (*$$*)

Noctan's, Galway (*$$*)

The Orchid Room, Sheedy's Spa View, Lisdoonvarna (*$$*)

Northwest Cromleach Lodge, Castlebaldwin (*$$$*)

Restaurant St. John's, Fahan (*$$–$$$*)

Northern Ireland Roscoff, Belfast (*$$$–$$$$*)

Restaurant 44, Belfast (*$$$*)

After Hours

Dublin Irish music session at O'Donoghue's

National Concert Hall

A play at the Abbey, the Gate, or the Project Arts Centre

Dublin Literary Pub Tour

Southeast Portholes Bar, Hotel Rosslare, Rosslare

Seanachie Pub, Ballymacart

T&H Doolans Bar, Waterford City

Southwest Gleneagles, Killarney

O'Flaherty's Pub, Dingle

West Abbeyglen Castle Hotel, Clifden

Murray's Piano Bar, Hotel Salthill, Galway

West County Hotel, Ennis

Northwest Abbey Hotel, Donegal Town

Hargadon's Pub and Sligo Park Hotel, Sligo Town

Nancy's and Peter Oliver's pubs, Ardara

Northern Ireland Grand Opera House, Belfast

Irish music sessions at the Rotterdam, Maddens, and Pat's Bar, Belfast

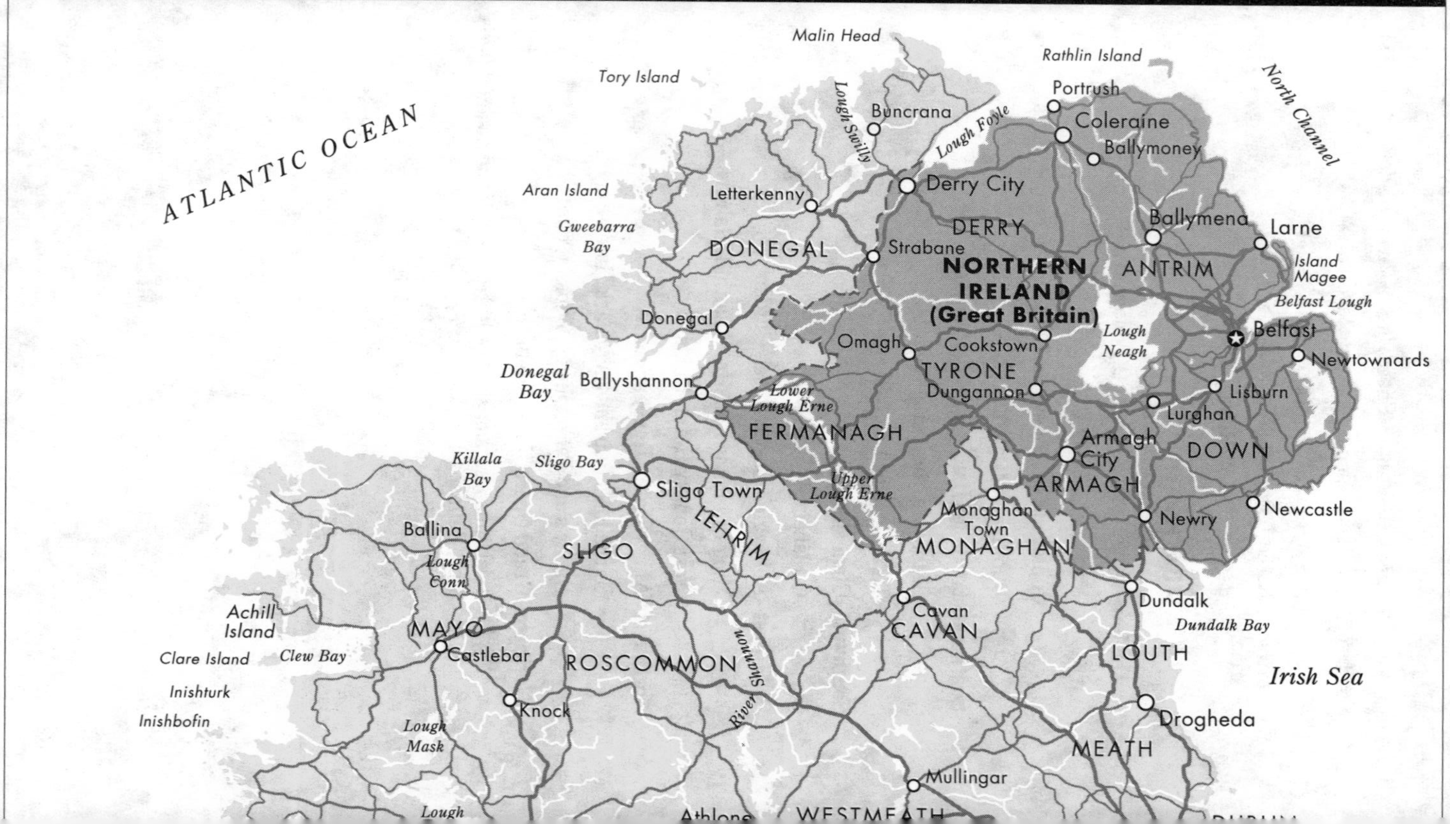
ATLANTIC OCEAN
North Channel
Irish Sea
Malin Head
Tory Island
Rathlin Island
Aran Island
Gweebarra Bay
Donegal Bay
Killala Bay
Sligo Bay
Clew Bay
Dundalk Bay
Belfast Lough
Island Magee
Lough Swilly
Lough Foyle
Lough Neagh
Lower Lough Erne
Upper Lough Erne
Lough Conn
Lough Mask
Lough
River Shannon
Achill Island
Clare Island
Inishturk
Inishbofin
NORTHERN IRELAND (Great Britain)
DONEGAL
DERRY
ANTRIM
TYRONE
FERMANAGH
ARMAGH
DOWN
MONAGHAN
CAVAN
LOUTH
MEATH
LEITRIM
SLIGO
MAYO
ROSCOMMON
Buncrana
Portrush
Coleraine
Ballymoney
Derry City
Letterkenny
Strabane
Ballymena
Larne
Donegal
Omagh
Cookstown
Belfast
Newtownards
Ballyshannon
Dungannon
Lisburn
Lurghan
Armagh City
Sligo Town
Monaghan Town
Newry
Newcastle
Ballina
Dundalk
Cavan
Castlebar
Knock
Drogheda
Mullingar

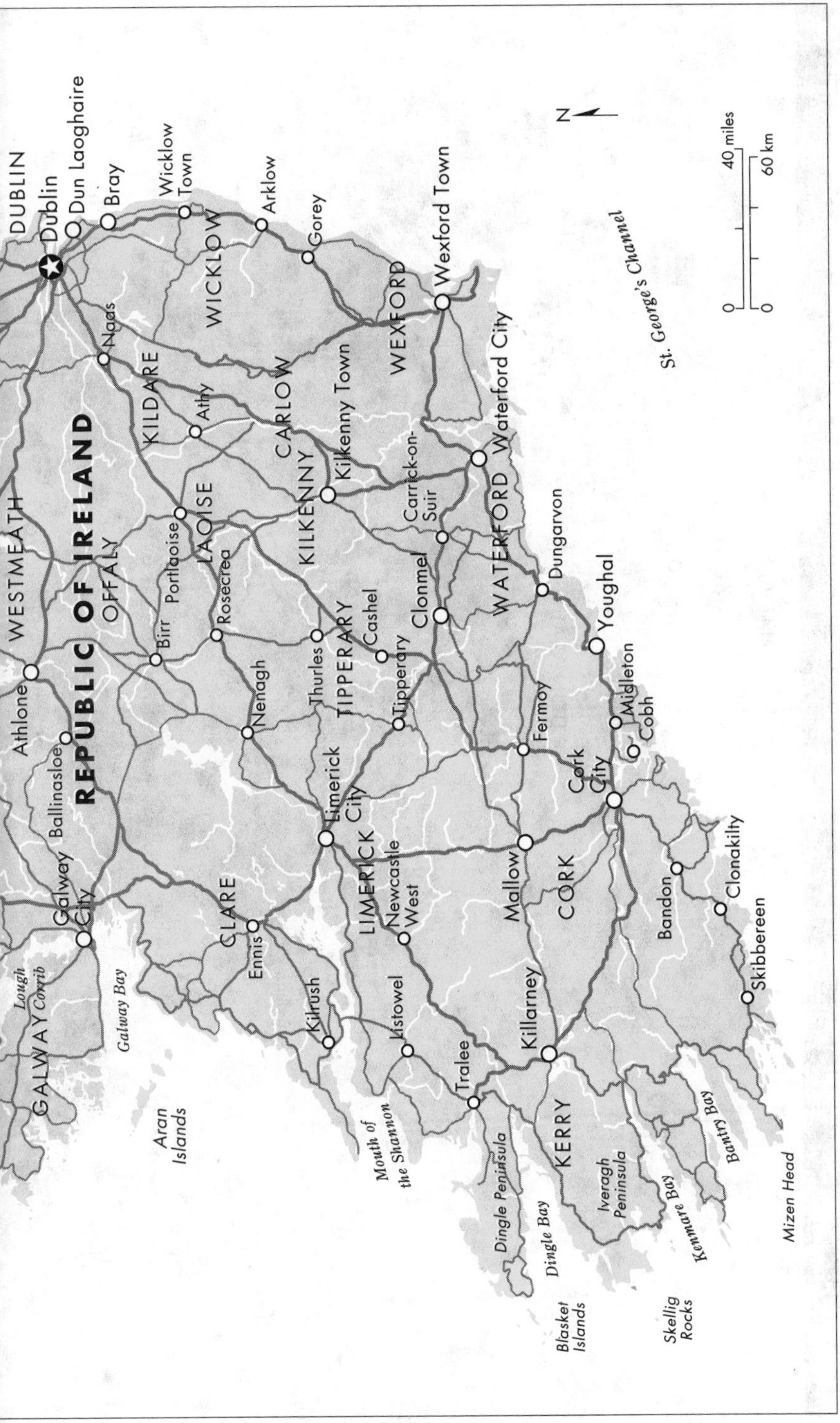
DUBLIN
Dublin
Dun Laoghaire
Bray
Wicklow Town
Arklow
Gorey
Wexford Town
WICKLOW
WEXFORD
Naas
KILDARE
Athy
CARLOW
Kilkenny Town
Waterford City
REPUBLIC OF IRELAND
WESTMEATH
OFFALY
LAOISE
Portlaoise
KILKENNY
Carrick-on-Suir
WATERFORD
Dungarvon
Rosecrea
Birr
Athlone
TIPPERARY
Thurles
Cashel
Clonmel
Tipperary
Nenagh
Youghal
Midleton
Cobh
Fermoy
Cork City
Ballinasloe
Limerick City
LIMERICK
Newcastle West
Mallow
CORK
Clonakilty
Bandon
Skibbereen
Galway City
CLARE
Ennis
Kilrush
Listowel
Killarney
Tralee
KERRY
GALWAY
Lough Corrib
Galway Bay
Aran Islands
Mouth of the Shannon
Dingle Peninsula
Dingle Bay
Iveragh Peninsula
Kenmare Bay
Bantry Bay
Mizen Head
Blasket Islands
Skellig Rocks
St. George's Channel
N
0
40 miles
0
60 km

Ireland's Counties

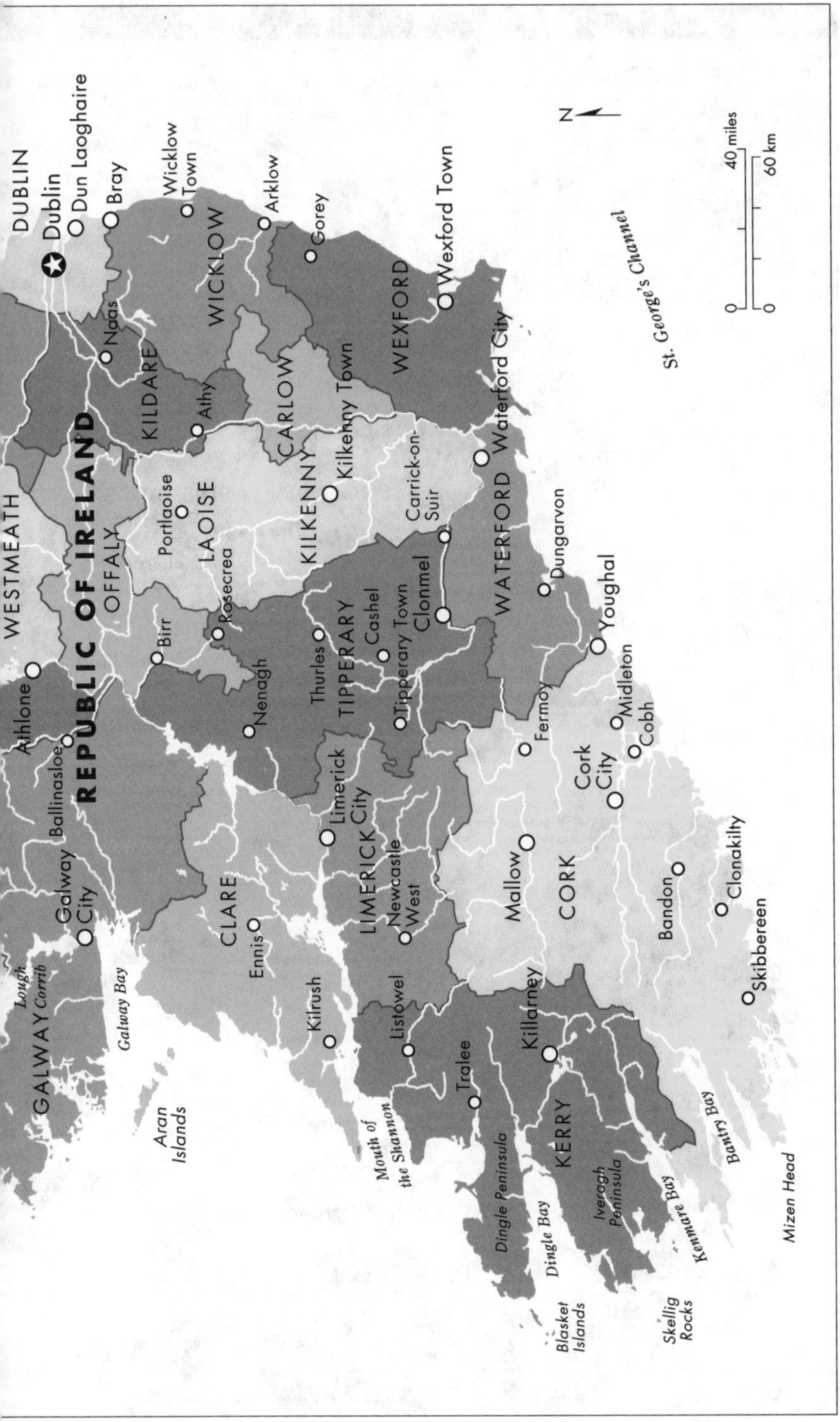

REPUBLIC OF IRELAND
DUBLIN
Dublin
Dun Laoghaire
Bray
Wicklow Town
Arklow
Gorey
Wexford Town
WICKLOW
WEXFORD
Naas
KILDARE
Athy
CARLOW
Kilkenny Town
Waterford City
WESTMEATH
OFFALY
Portlaoise
LAOISE
KILKENNY
Carrick-on-Suir
WATERFORD
Dungarvon
Youghal
Athlone
Birr
Rosecrea
Nenagh
Thurles
Cashel
TIPPERARY
Tipperary Town
Clonmel
Midleton
Fermoy
Cobh
Cork City
Ballinasloe
Galway City
Limerick City
LIMERICK
Newcastle West
Mallow
CORK
Clonakilty
Bandon
Skibbereen
GALWAY
Lough Corrib
Galway Bay
CLARE
Ennis
Kilrush
Listowel
Killarney
Tralee
KERRY
Aran Islands
Mouth of the Shannon
Dingle Peninsula
Dingle Bay
Iveragh Peninsula
Kenmare Bay
Bantry Bay
Mizen Head
Blasket Islands
Skellig Rocks
St. George's Channel
N
0
40 miles
0
60 km

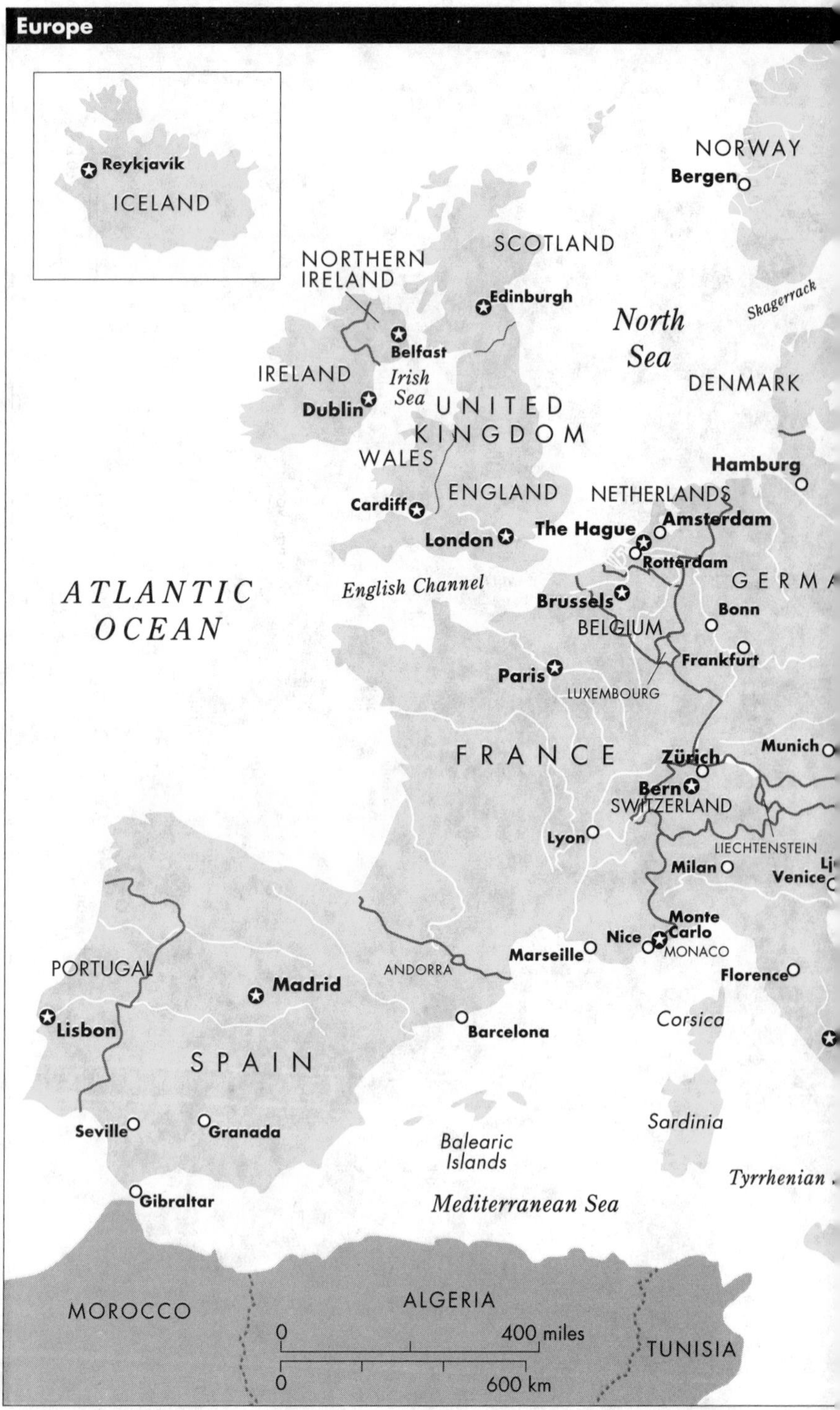
Europe
Reykjavík
ICELAND
NORWAY
Bergen
SCOTLAND
NORTHERN IRELAND
Edinburgh
Skagerrack
North Sea
Belfast
IRELAND
Irish Sea
DENMARK
Dublin
UNITED KINGDOM
WALES
Hamburg
ENGLAND
NETHERLANDS
Cardiff
Amsterdam
The Hague
London
Rotterdam
ATLANTIC OCEAN
English Channel
GERMA
Brussels
Bonn
BELGIUM
Frankfurt
Paris
LUXEMBOURG
FRANCE
Zürich
Munich
Bern
SWITZERLAND
Lyon
LIECHTENSTEIN
Milan
Venice
Monte Carlo
Nice
Marseille
MONACO
PORTUGAL
ANDORRA
Madrid
Florence
Lisbon
Barcelona
Corsica
SPAIN
Seville
Granada
Sardinia
Balearic Islands
Tyrrhenian
Gibraltar
Mediterranean Sea
MOROCCO
ALGERIA
0
400 miles
TUNISIA
0
600 km

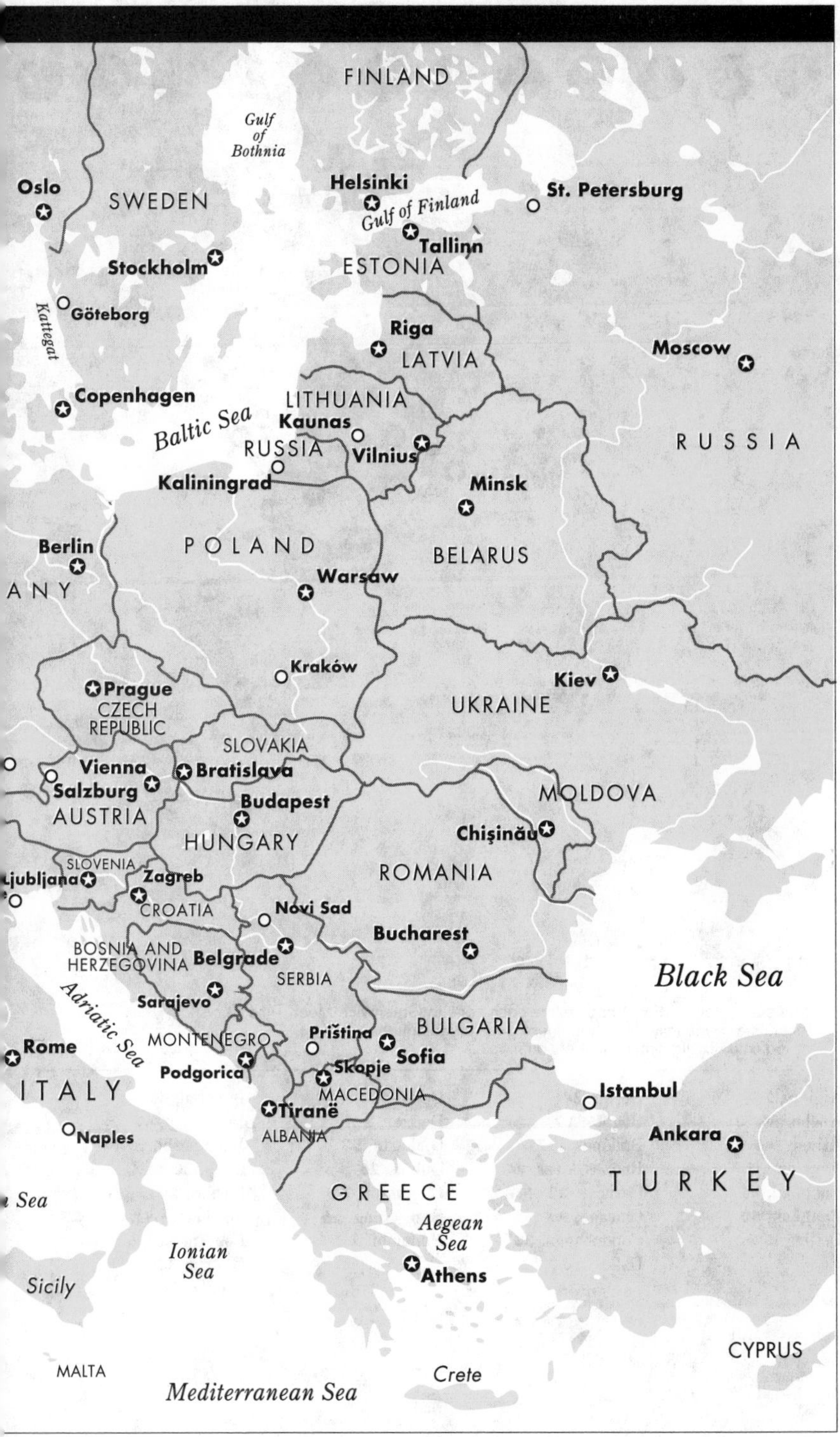
FINLAND
Gulf of Bothnia
Oslo
SWEDEN
Helsinki
Gulf of Finland
St. Petersburg
Tallinn
Stockholm
ESTONIA
Kattegat
Göteborg
Riga
LATVIA
Moscow
Copenhagen
LITHUANIA
Baltic Sea
Kaunas
RUSSIA
Vilnius
RUSSIA
Kaliningrad
Minsk
Berlin
POLAND
BELARUS
Warsaw
ANY
Kraków
Kiev
Prague
CZECH REPUBLIC
UKRAINE
SLOVAKIA
Vienna
Bratislava
Salzburg
Budapest
MOLDOVA
AUSTRIA
HUNGARY
Chişinău
SLOVENIA
Ljubljana
Zagreb
ROMANIA
CROATIA
Novi Sad
Bucharest
BOSNIA AND HERZEGOVINA
Belgrade
Black Sea
SERBIA
Adriatic Sea
Sarajevo
BULGARIA
MONTENEGRO
Priština
Rome
Sofia
Podgorica
Skopje
ITALY
MACEDONIA
Istanbul
Tiranë
ALBANIA
Ankara
Naples
GREECE
TURKEY
Sea
Aegean Sea
Ionian Sea
Athens
Sicily
CYPRUS
MALTA
Crete
Mediterranean Sea

World Time Zones

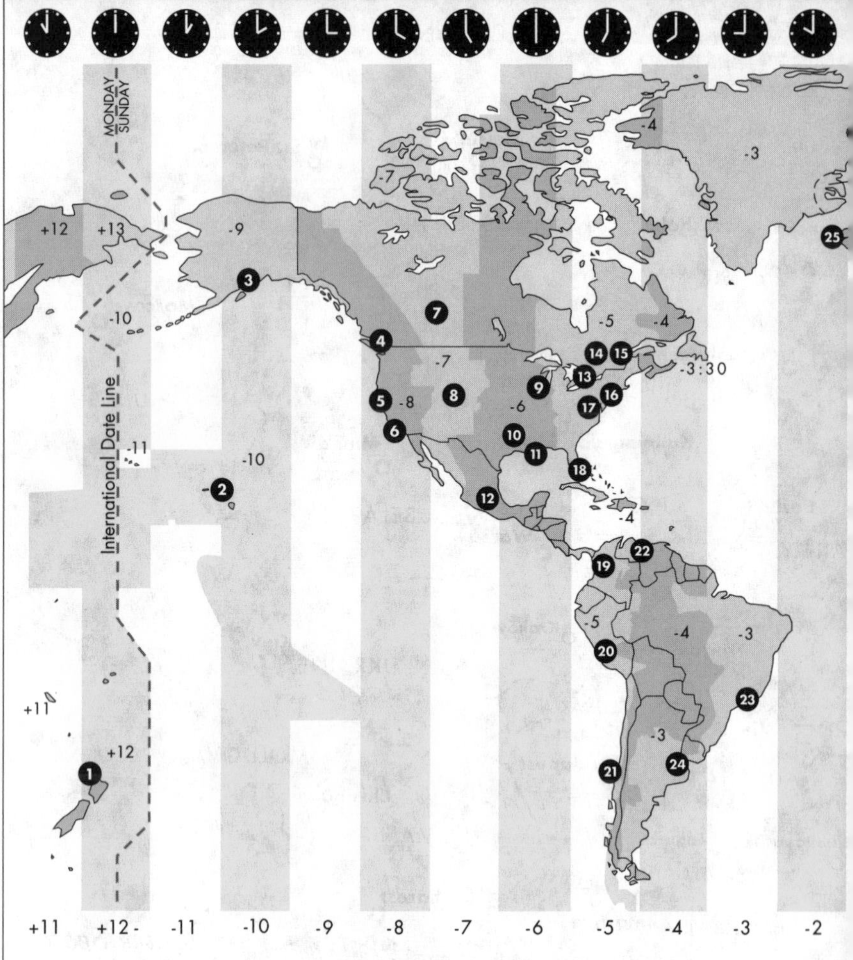

Numbers below vertical bands relate each zone to Greenwich Mean Time (0 hrs.).
Local times frequently differ from these general indications,
as indicated by light-face numbers on map.

Algiers, **29**
Anchorage, **3**
Athens, **41**
Auckland, **1**
Baghdad, **46**
Bangkok, **50**
Beijing, **54**
Berlin, **34**
Bogotá, **19**
Budapest, **37**
Buenos Aires, **24**
Caracas, **22**
Chicago, **9**
Copenhagen, **33**
Dallas, **10**
Delhi, **48**
Denver, **8**
Djakarta, **53**
Dublin, **26**
Edmonton, **7**
Hong Kong, **56**
Honolulu, **2**
Istanbul, **40**
Jerusalem, **42**
Johannesburg, **44**
Lima, **20**
Lisbon, **28**
London (Greenwich), **27**
Los Angeles, **6**
Madrid, **38**
Manila, **57**

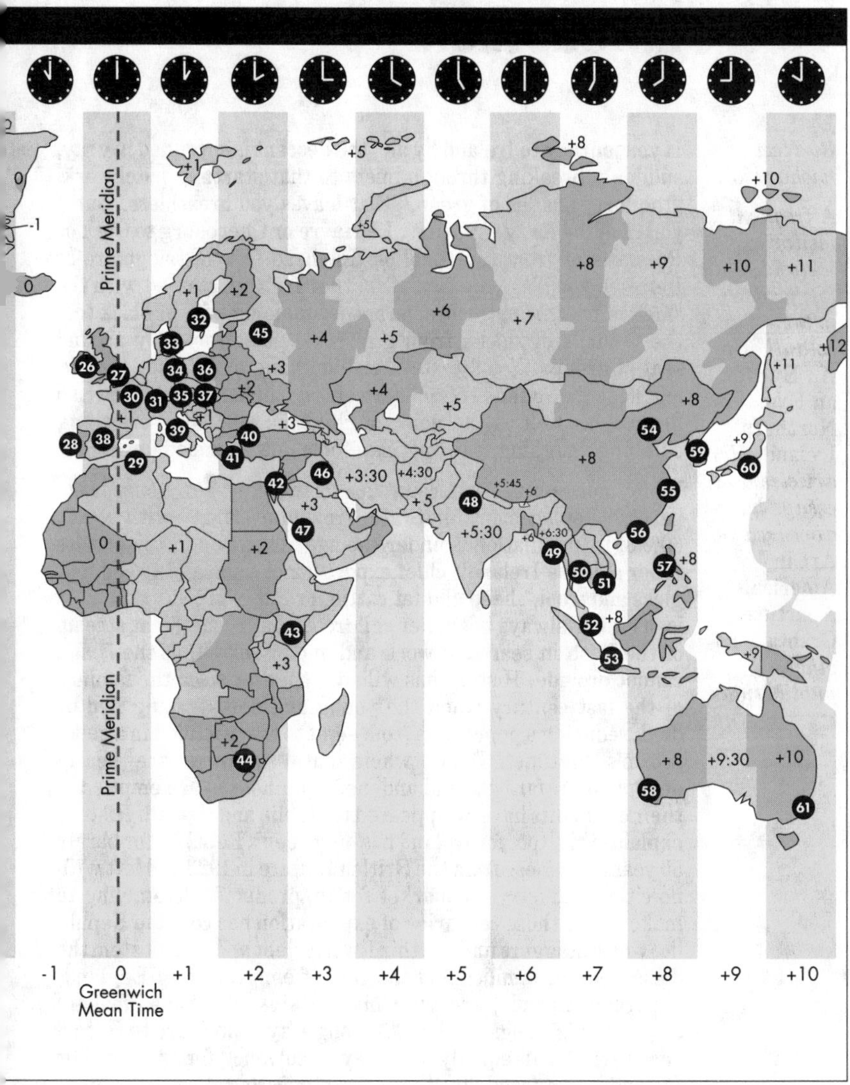

Mecca, **47**
Mexico City, **12**
Miami, **18**
Montréal, **15**
Moscow, **45**
Nairobi, **43**
New Orleans, **11**
New York City, **16**
Ottawa, **14**
Paris, **30**
Perth, **58**
Reykjavík, **25**
Rio de Janeiro, **23**
Rome, **39**
Saigon (Ho Chi Minh City), **51**
San Francisco, **5**
Santiago, **21**
Seoul, **59**
Shanghai, **55**
Singapore, **52**
Stockholm, **32**
Sydney, **61**
Tokyo, **60**
Toronto, **13**
Vancouver, **4**
Vienna, **35**
Warsaw, **36**
Washington, D.C., **17**
Yangon, **49**
Zürich, **31**

Introduction

By Nan Richardson

A frequent visitor to Ireland, Nan Richardson is the co-author of An Eye for an Eye: Northern Ireland. *Her articles and essays have appeared in* Art in America, Aperture, Granta, *and other publications.*

If you journey to Ireland by air, the descent is shrouded in gray, suddenly breaking through mists to that startling patchwork, "the forty shades of green," that leaves you breathless. But if you take the ferry (from say, Le Havre or Cherbourg to Cork or Rosslare; or from Liverpool or Holyhead to Dun Laoghaire or Belfast), you'll see the face of another Ireland, stained with the smell of peat from the braziers, the steaming pots of black tea, the tendrils of smoke from cigarettes passed silently around seated groups. You'll taste the sharp tang of golden whiskey, and hear the sounds of Gaelic-accented English that is the Irish brogue, as well as the noise of children: wheeling, crawling, climbing, laughing, bawling, like some untrammeled force.

While more prosperous countries of the EU vainly encourage barely a replacement birthrate, Ireland overflows with youth: 60% of its population is under the age of 25. But all this has its sober side, as Ireland's chief export is not linen and tweed, cut glass and wool, sheep and fat cattle, or music and literature. It is, as it has always been, her children, joining the great stream of the Irish in search of work and opportunity that the island cannot provide. History has willed it so, ever since the famines of the last century when the young and not-so-young fled or died, reducing a population from eight to three million in a generation's lifetime. Today whole rural counties are nearly depopulated, farms are abandoned, and houses are emptied—their occupants have disappeared to Dublin and beyond. History explains this, too, for Ireland has only been a Republic for barely 50 years, cut loose from the British Empire in 1923 and left with no cities, industry, or market for its products. Scrambling to make up for those centuries of exploitation has cost the Republic, which staggers under a third-world debt and cannot stem the dissolution of families and the tide of emigration to England, Australia, Canada, and the United States. The ballad makers sing émigrés' songs, such as "A Long Way from Clare to Here," and it will be an equally long way to solvency for Ireland. For Ireland is two-faced, like the Janus-stones and sheela-na-gigs of its pre-Christian past; it's a complex place where the mystic lyricism of Yeats, the hard Rabelaisian passions of Joyce, and the spare, aloof dissection of Beckett grew not only from a rich and ancient culture but also from 20th-century upheavals.

A Friendly People

Simple customs tell a lot. Hospitality in Ireland is counted among the greatest of virtues, a legacy from Celtic times when anyone not offering the traveler food and drink was shamed; the country is justly legendary even now for the friendliness of its people. "You are welcome," people say in greeting the moment you cross the threshold of the poorest house, while total strangers will take you home for tea or supper and strike up conversations with ease and curiosity, entertaining you perhaps with an account of their second cousin's memorable fortnight in America (a fortnight's worth of stories if you have the time!).

Time, in fact, is one of the greatest luxuries of Ireland. On a fine day, along a lushly green country lane, you may pass a bicycle abandoned against a tree; looking for its owner, you'll find him reclining in the feathery hedgerows or on the long grass, contemplating fast-moving clouds like some philosopher-king. "Oh the dreaming, the dreaming, the heart-scalding bitter, maddening dreaming," cried the playwright George Bernard Shaw, but to knowing travelers in the stressed and industrialized world, this haven of dreamers is a pearl of great price, sought after and kept secret. Not long ago, in a bar in Crossmaglen, a village in Armagh, a rugged farmer in oilskins and thornproof, chores over and done with (or just put on hold) turned an amused and quizzical eye as I fretted at the lateness of my appointment. "All that rushing about—and what for?" he reprimanded. "Give us a wee one there," he signaled the barman with a lift of his pipe, and pushed his glass to mine to toast the sentiment, "Life's for the living!" And, he concluded with another swallow, "Never put off for tomorrow a drink you can have today."

Much of the real beauty of Ireland is hidden on the back roads. If America is known for its car culture, Ireland is known for its cow culture, ever since the days of the "Tuigne na Cuailnge," or "The Cattle Raid of Cooley," the 8th-century epic that is the Iliad of Ireland, describing a marital dispute between the two leaders, King Ailill and Queen Maeve, over who had the finest herds in the land. Equal down to the last cow, Maeve had one item that Ailill lusted after: a giant brown bull; to win the wager, the king kidnapped the bull one night, kicking off a 50-year internecine war. Although Irish wealth today is not exactly measured in sirloin pound, the moo-cows seem to own the country lanes, staring haughtily and curiously at interloping motorists, lazily drooping timothy from their soft maws. In the end, with persuasion from harried livery equipped with frisky dogs and long-knobbed sticks, they'll share the road—but all in their time.

Somehow this may help explain why Ireland is what anthropologists call a "lived" culture, one that doesn't put much stock in the outward monuments of achievement; where the most potent history is oral, where storytelling is an art, and where people will travel miles for the "crack," the Irish synonym for a rousing good time. Ireland teaches you patience, reminds you of the rhythms of the natural world, and convinces you, reassuringly, of the essential well-being of man. French traveler LaTocnaye wrote in his journals in 1644, after a tour of the island, that "the Irish are very fond of strangers," and Oliver Goldsmith, later in the 18th century, observed, "The natives are peculiarly remarkable for their gaiety and the levity of their dispositions; English transplanted here lose their serious melancholy and become gay and thoughtless, more fond of pleasure and less addicted to reasoning."

The Price of a Pint

Hospitality finds its logical institution in the local pub, the center of social life in Ireland. Even a small town such as Dingle in County Kerry (population 1,000) boasts 52 watering holes, open day and night. Protocol dictates that you enter and greet everyone, taking a seat alone until invited (as you inevitably are) to join a table. Then the ancient custom of rounds begins, with the newcomer offering to buy the first set of drinks, and when the pints are barely half-full (half-empty from an Irish perspective), another imbiber stands the round, and so on, in turn. With a few companions, this makes it nearly obligatory to spend an afternoon in the pub. Similarly, if you're smoking, custom demands that you offer the pack to fellow socializers before you light up yourself. Women are often exempted from these rituals, if, indeed, they are allowed to join in at all, for in rural areas the sight of a woman drinking is still frowned upon, and if they do darken a publican's door they head for the "lounge," a slightly dressed-up version of the same establishment to drink glasses, never pints, even if they have a powerful thirst. Of course, "strangers," female or other, can be non-conformist with impunity.

These social and equitable customs help explain why 10% of Irish personal spending goes to alcohol like some unholy tithe and why these dark village pubs with their scratched wooden counters, dusty tiled floors, and the yeasty smell of Guinness have a feeling of sanctity and remove from worldly cares not unlike a church. It may also explain, incidentally, the historic Irish reputation for wit and bellicosity. The rumor of bellicosity, however, is ill-founded: "The only people in Europe who have never set out to conquer," my friend, a Dublin photographer claimed with pride, but wit flows untapped from unexpected sources. It might come from the use of a borrowed language, perhaps from the need of a subject people for subterfuge, but nuance and irony are the rules of conversation, and anything less would be considered flat-footed. Irish expertise in double-think and forked tongue makes for a universally acknowledged aptitude for legal affairs, a gift for words of imagination and persuasiveness that you can find in the crossroads *shebeen* (pub) much as in Dublin's Leinster House, where the Irish *Dail* (or legislature) sits.

The Grand Tour

You are never very far from anywhere in Ireland, but each of its 32 counties have their special character and history, and fierce loyalty from their sons and daughters. Dublin is the millennium-old capital, once a Celtic settlement by the ford of the River Liffey, later a Norse encampment for raiding Viking and Danish pirates, and finally the citadel-seat of the British colonizer's power for centuries. Today it is a graceful mix of fine Georgian buildings, a lively waterfront, wrought-iron canals and bridges, an army of booksellers, 800-odd pubs, and a rich cultural life. Ireland chooses to exempt artists from taxes, designating them national resources of sorts, and filmmakers, painters, and writers are part of the local scenery, along with the "rale Dubs," or "jackeens,"—the breezy natives born in the heart of the city between the Grand and Royal canals that divide North and South Dublin into two worlds. Although it can be a sophisticated city, with sushi bars, French restaurants, and bold theater, it hasn't lost any of its simple pleasures, like waking to the tinkling of glass bottles with round silver caps, delivered to the stoop by a milkman dressed all in white; afternoon tea at Bewley's with scones slathered with Kerry Gold butter; soda farls heaped with clouds of whipped cream; waitresses in black dresses and starched aprons; or breakfast "the like of which you'll never see again," my landlady promised (though everywhere in Ireland seemed to be competing in this category). The silver pots of dark tea, the wheaten bread and toast in gleaming racks, the eggs, oatmeal, rashers (bacon), and sausages all done up with doilies, send you out into the permeating mists that the Irish ironically call "soft weather," fortified and content.

Nearby, the scenic Wicklow mountains and rich Boyne valley are home to the wealthier class. The ancestral homes of the dwindling members of the Anglo-Irish ascendancy dot the landscape throughout the country, and lords and baronets down on their luck have turned hoteliers and welcome guests to castle holidays with adaptable grace. County Limerick is famed as horse country. County Tipperary's rolling green flatlands and Galtee mountains are known for champion greyhounds and the stud farms that have turned out winners for generations. The Rock of Cashel, seat of the Kings of Munster for 700 years (where St. Patrick said his first mass in Ireland) is here, along with Cahir Castle, one of the few places that managed to resist Cromwell's hordes, now restored to its former impressiveness.

The coast of County Wexford was the original beachhead of Ireland named by the Vikings after the consort of their one-eyed god Odin; it still bears the stamp of its fearless, seagoing settlers, in its steep pathways and fine seafood. Wexford is a quick trip to Kilkenny, the finest medieval city in Ireland and known for its artisans. Also nearby is Waterford City, where the crystal of the same name is produced, at the delta of three great rivers—the Nore, Barrow, and Suir. Waterford City has one of the oldest forts in Ireland, Reginald's Tower, built in 1013 and named for the Viking warrior who founded the city. But while the Southeast has its charm, for scenery, generally speaking, go to the counties in the West: from Cork and Kerry to Clare and Galway, from Sligo up to Donegal.

County Donegal, in the far northwest, is among the wildest, most ruggedly beautiful places in the world, with its long rocky coastline, white beaches, turbulent surf, and impressive mountains and plateaus, full of legendary lore of giants and witches, fairies, and *pishogues*. Irish is widely spoken here, and the music is famous; traditional groups, such as Clannad and De Dannaan, named after the prehistoric followers of the goddess Dana, are local heroes, and when Enya, daughter of local musicians, hit the top of the charts in Europe and the United States with her Irish-New Age instrumentals, the roof flew off Leo's pub in Gweedore, where spontaneous sessions for the music-loving community are regular happenings.

Galway City is a port and university town, bustling and businesslike, and the departure point for the Aran Islands, celebrated by playwright J.M. Synge in *Riders to the Sea* and Robert Flaherty in his classic documentary film *Man of Aran*. Just to the west of Galway City lies Connemara, loved by painters, who flock there in summer, by writers (from Yeats to Gogarty to Joyce), and by all seekers of silence and beauty. It, too, is a Gaeltacht (Irish-speaking area), celebrated for its simplicity of lifestyle and genuinely warm natives. Connemara is also known for its ponies, descendants of the Andalusian horses that swam to shore from the Spanish fleet and bred with the local Celtic stock (direct descendants of the original Ice Age horse of 20,000 BC).

At the southwestern end of the Republic is County Kerry, full of soft accents and magic places. For centuries, summer travelers here have been thrilled by the surfeit of natural beauty as they've gazed at the black rocks and green waves glistening at Slea Head on the Dingle Peninsula or at the Blasket Islands, where St. Brendan the Navigator was said to have set sail in a wooden *curragh* (boat) to discover the Americas in the 7th century. Sea birds reel and wild donkeys graze among the fuschia hedges awash in crimson velvet flowers, and the fields explode with deep yellow gorse, may-blossom, and honeysuckle against a dark blue sky. County Kerry's special events and attractions include Killorgin's annual three-day Puck Fair in midsummer (when a large billy goat is crowned king and garlanded with flowers, a residue of an old pre-Christian fertility rite) and Killarney, with its lakes, parklands, and jumping-off places for a drive around the Ring of Kerry.

Nearby Cork (from the Gaelic "corcaigh," meaning marshes) has always been called "The Rebel County," and a quick tour of all the monuments will tell you why. Michael Collins, the general who won independence for Ireland was assassinated here, and Terence McSweeney, a former mayor of Cork, died on hunger strike here, to name a couple. A Venice-like port city of canals and bridges, and a bustling mercantile center, Cork was once home to writers Sean O'Faolain and Frank O'Connor, and is today a city of sport. Its team is always in the championship finals of hurling, that fast and furious ancient game that makes soccer look like kick-the-can, and the city is one of the few places where they still play the traditional, two-thousand-year-old game of bowls that the Irish giant Cuchulain used to excel at. If your taste runs to less athletic entertainment, visit the exquisitely restored village of Kinsale, or the attractive historical and arts centers of West Cork, helped along by an influx of discriminating French and German settlers in this part of Ireland for the last 20 years.

Taking the main road from Dublin to Belfast is a reminder—as you pass bristling watchtowers, sandbagged forts and warpainted soldiers in camouflage who check your papers—that, as another song goes, "one of Ireland's four green fields are still in strangers' hands." While Munster, Leinster, and Connaught are in the south, six of the nine counties of Ulster remained part of Britain in 1921. Today Northern Ireland is definitely worth a trip, and the reward for a little courage is great: Here you have the beauty of the Antrim Coast from Carncastle to Bushmills; the Giant's Causeway; the rich farmlands and lakelands of Fermanagh; and the austere beauty of the Mourne Mountains. People are as friendly and helpful here as they are in the Republic, and, probably because of their history, perhaps a little sharper and wittier. Northern Ireland is also fascinating for any follower of history and politics, for you get an unforgettable glimpse of the winds of time changing, a scene not unlike the last days of the Raj, as Britain's first colony erodes to be her last.

Digging up the Past

That sense of otherness that few destinations on this scale, or this accessible, can provide, cannot only be attributed to its evergreen climate and leisurely pace of life but also to the palimpsest of history and legend dug deep under Ireland's rich grassy surface. Its tumultuous past is in evidence everywhere, from the Neolithic tombs and defenses of Newgrange in County Meath and Dun Aengus on Inishmore Island, 5,000 years older than the pyramids of Giza, to the numerous other antiquities and archeological sites, registered and unregistered—standing stones and court graves, mottes and dolmens, raths and cairns, holy wells and mass stones, round towers and Celtic crosses.

The legacy of the first-known Scandinavian settlers in Ireland and the later influx of Bronze Age Celts from Central Europe was an agrarian society based on a democratic kingship, a justice system known as the Brehon laws, and an artisan caste proficient in gold and precious metals. Christianity followed in the 4th century, and while European culture flickered and died in the Dark Ages, priests nurtured knowledge in beehive huts and stone monasteries. About AD 800, Viking longboats scourged the island's coasts, leaving the mark of bright red hair behind on their Irish descendents. Brian Boru, last of the High Kings to sit at Tara, won the Battle of Clontarf against Danish armies in 1014, only to have his successors lose Ireland in 1169 to the Norman Strongbow, opening the door to 800 years of rebellion.

By 1609, the last of the Irish chieftains sailed for exile, making way for the "Plantation" of 200,000 Scottish Lowlanders on native Irish lands. Britain's Oliver Cromwell, "the Avenger," reinforced those Protestant claims, beheading thousands of men, women, and children in his devastating marches. In their wake came the "Penal Code," forbidding the Irish Catholics to practice their religion, exercise law, or own land, vote, and hold office. The crushing blow was the famine that struck after 1845, reducing the once-populous island from eight to three million inhabitants, through death or emigration, creating the first wave of the Irish diaspora and setting the stage for the ultimate uprising, on Easter morning, 1916, when Irish Nationalists proclaimed a republic. England's vengeance on the patriots galvanized the country to the bitter war of independence that ended in the partitioning of Ireland into 26 counties in the South and six in the North, a political struggle that continues today. Like many facets of history in Irish life, this conflict is subtle, often below the surface, and invisible to the casual observer.

Ireland Today

Present-day Ireland encourages creativity that goes beyond history and tradition. In the music field, internationally known talents have emerged, such as the rock bands U2, Hothouse Flowers, The Pogues, and In Tua Nua; top-of-the-charts singers Sinead O'Connor, Van Morrison, Christy Moore, and Chris de Burgh; and folk musicians Sean Keane, Maggie Barrie, Liam Og O'Flynn, Paddy Reilly, Billy Bragg, and Mary Black. Theater is bursting with talent that often takes the centuries-old route across the water to London, with actors such as Richard Branagh, Brenda Fricker, Stella McCusker, Gabriel Byrne, and Daniel Day-Lewis, not to mention playwrights Brian Friel, Hugh Leonard, John Boyd, Graham Reid, Anne Devlin, John B. Keane, and the late Stewart Parker.

Contemporary filmmakers Pat O'Connor, Jim Sheridan, and Joe Comerford often draw from a rich source of narrative writing provided by novelists Neil Jordan, William Trevor, James Plunkett, Bernard McLaverty, Thomas Kinsella, Edna O'Brien, Benedict Kiely, and John McGahern. Irish poetry is alive and well in the hands of Seamus Heaney, Derek Mahon, Paul Muldoon, Seamus Deane, Tom Paulin, and Medh McGuckian.

While literature is certainly Ireland's single greatest contribution to the arts, with the shadow of giants like Jonathan Swift, Oscar Wilde, Patrick Kavanagh, Brendan Behan, George Bernard Shaw, and others still casting a shadow, the country shows hidden strengths in other creative fields. In the visual arts, the legacy of Irish Impressionists Jack Yeats and Paul Henry, gave way to painters such as Tom Carr, David Crone, Felim Egan, Jack Pakeham, James Coleman, and Louis de Brocquy, whose subject matter is metaphor, "the secret logic of ambivalence." Meanwhile, a younger generation of artists, including Rita Duffy, Micky Donnelly, Fergus and Diarmuid Delargy, sculptor Ailish O'Connell, and others confront issues of social and political contradiction in their work. In its capacity for regeneration, irrepressible vitality, mordant wit, eerie spirituality, and culturally ingrained generosity, Ireland often seems to move backwards in time to the Tir-na-Og—the mythical land of the ever-young, an alternative world of fairies, pishogues, and hidden supernatural forces that remains alive in the Irish imagination.

1 Essential Information

Before You Go

Government Information Offices

Irish Republic Contact the **Irish Tourist Board,** known as Bord Fáilte (pronounced "Board Falcha"), for information on all aspects of travel to and around Ireland.

In the United States 345 Park Ave., New York, NY 10154, tel. 212/418–0800 or 800/223–6740, fax 212/371–9052.

In Canada 160 Bloor St., Suite 934, Toronto, Ont. M4W 1B9, tel. 416/929–2777, fax 416/929–6783.

In the United Kingdom 150 New Bond St., London W1Y 0AQ, tel. 0171/493–3201, fax 0171/493–9065.

Northern Ireland Contact the **Northern Ireland Tourist Board** (NITB) office. Where there is no NITB office, the **British Tourist Authority** (BTA) can usually supply information.

In the United States **NITB,** 551 5th Ave., Suite 701, New York, NY 10176, tel. 212/922–0101 or 800/326–0036, fax 212/922–0099; **BTA,** 2580 Cumberland Pkwy., Suite 470, Atlanta, GA 30339, tel. 404/432–9635, fax 404/432–9641; 875 N. Michigan Ave., Chicago, IL 60611, tel. 312/787–0490, fax 312/787–7746; World Trade Center, Suite 450, 350 Figueroa St., Los Angeles, CA 90071, tel. 213/628–3525, fax 213/687–6621.

In Canada **BTA,** 111 Avenue Rd., Suite 450, Toronto, Ont. M5R 3J8, tel. 416/925–6368, fax 416/961–2175.

In the United Kingdom **NITB,** Ulster Office, 11 Berkeley St., London W1X 6BU, tel. 0171/493–0601; 38 High St., Sutton Coldfield, B72 1UP, tel. 0121/354–1431; or, contact the head office at 59 North St., Belfast BT1 1NB, tel. 01232/246609, fax 01232/240969.

U.S. Government Travel Briefings The U.S. Department of State's **Overseas Citizens Emergency Center** (Room 4811, Washington, DC 20520; enclose SASE) issues Consular Information Sheets, which cover crime, security, political climate, and health risks as well as embassy locations, entry requirements, currency regulations, and other routine matters. Travel Warnings, which counsel travelers to avoid a country entirely, are issued in extreme cases. For the latest information, stop in at any U.S. passport office, consulate, or embassy; call the interactive hotline (tel. 202/647–5225, fax 202/647–3000); or, with your PC's modem, tap into the Bureau of Consular Affairs' computer bulletin board (tel. 202/647–9225).

Tours and Packages

Should you buy your travel arrangements to Ireland packaged or do it yourself? There are advantages either way. Buying packaged arrangements saves you money, particularly if you can find a program that includes exactly the features you want. You also get a pretty good idea of what your trip will cost from the outset. Generally, you have two options: fully escorted tours and independent packages. Escorted tours are most often via motorcoach, with a tour director in charge. They're ideal if you don't mind having limited free time and traveling with strangers. Your baggage is handled, your time rigorously scheduled, and most meals planned. Such tours are therefore the most hassle-free way to see a destination, as well as generally the least expensive. Independent packages allow plenty of flexibility. They generally include airline travel and hotels, with certain options available, such as sightseeing, car rental, and excursions. Such packages are usually more expensive than escorted tours, but your time is your own.

While you can book directly through tour operators, you will pay no more to go through a travel agent, who will be able to tell you about tours and packages from a number of operators. Whatever program you ultimately choose, be sure to find out exactly what is included: taxes, tips, transfers, meals, baggage handling, ground transportation, entertainment, excursions, sports or recreation (and rental equipment if necessary). Ask about the level of hotel used, its location, the size of its rooms, the kind of beds, and its amenities, such as pool, room service, or programs for children, if they're important to you. Find out the operator's cancellation penalties. Nearly everyone charges them, and the only way to avoid them is to buy trip-cancellation insurance (*see* Trip Insurance, *below*). Also ask about the single supplement, a surcharge assessed to solo travelers. Some operators do not make you pay it if you agree to be matched up with a roommate of the same sex, even if one is not found by departure time. Remember that a program that has features you won't use may not be the most cost-wise choice for you.

Fully Escorted Tours

Escorted tours are usually sold in three categories: deluxe, first-class, and tourist or budget class. The most important differences are the price, of course, and the level of accommodations. Some operators specialize in one category, while others offer a range.

Contact **Abercrombie & Kent** (1420 Kensington Rd., Oak Brook, IL 60521, tel. 708/954–2944 or 800/323–7308), **Maupintour** (Box 807, Lawrence, KS 66044, tel. 913/843–1211 or 800/255–4266), and **Tauck Tours** (11 Wilton Rd., Westport, CT 06881, tel. 203/226–6911 or 800/468–2825) in the deluxe category; **Aer Lingus** (tel. 800/223–6537), **American Airlines Fly AAway Vacations** (tel. 800/321–2121), **Brendan Tours** (15137 Califa St., Van Nuys, CA 91411, tel. 818/985–9696 or 800/421–8556), **Brian Moore International Tours** (116 Main St., Medway, MA 02053, tel. 508/533–6683 or 800/982–2299), **British Airways** (tel. 800/247–9297), **Caravan Tours** (401 N. Michigan Ave., Suite 3325, Chicago, IL 60611, tel. 312/321–9800 or 800/227–2826), **CIE Tours International** (108 Ridgedale Ave., Morristown, NJ 07960, tel. 201/292–3438 or 800/243–8687), **Collette Tours** (162 Middle St., Pawtucket, RI 02860, tel. 401/728–3805 or 800/832–4656), **Delta Dream Vacations** (tel. 800/872–7786), **European Travel Management** (237 Post Rd. W, Westport, CT 06880, tel. 203/454–0090 or 800/992–7700), **Globus** (5301 S. Federal Cir., Littleton, CO 80123, tel. 303/797–2800 or 800/221–0090), and **Trafalgar Tours** (21 E. 26th St., New York, NY 10010, tel. 800/854–0103 or 212/689–8977) in the first-class category; and **Cosmos Tourama,** a sister company of Globus (at the same number) in the budget category.

Most itineraries are jam-packed with sightseeing, so you see a lot in a short amount of time (usually one place per day). To judge just how fast-paced the tour is, review the itinerary carefully. If you are in a different hotel each night, you will be getting up early each day to head out, travel to your next destination, do some sightseeing, have dinner, and go to bed; then you'll start all over again. If you want some free time, make sure it's mentioned in the tour brochure; if you want to be escorted to every meal, confirm that any tour you consider does that. Also, when comparing programs, be sure to find out if the motorcoach is air-conditioned and has a restroom on board. Make your selection based on price and stops on the itinerary.

Independent Packages Independent packages, which travel agents call FITs (for foreign independent travel), are offered by airlines, tour operators who may also do escorted programs, and any number of other companies from large, established firms to small, new entrepreneurs.

Contact **Aer Lingus** (*see above*), **Brian Moore International Tours** (*see above*), **British Airways** (*see above*), **Celtic International Tours** (161 Central Ave., Albany, NY 11206, tel. 518/463–5511 or 800/833–4373), **CIE Tours** (*see above*), **Delta Dream Vacations** (*see above*), **DER Tours** (11933 Wilshire Blvd., Los Angeles, CA 90025, tel. 213/479–4140 or 800/937–1234), **Destination Ireland** (250 W. 57th St., Suite 2511, New York, NY 10107, tel. 212/977–9629 or 800/832–1848), or **Irish American International Tours** (Box 465, Springfield, PA 19064, tel. 215/543–0785 or 800/633–0505) for starters. Their programs come in a wide range of prices based on levels of luxury and options—in addition to hotel and airfare, sightseeing, car rental, transfers, admission to local attractions, and other extras. Note that when pricing different packages, it sometimes pays to purchase the same arrangements separately, as when a rock-bottom promotional airfare is being offered, for example. Again, base your choice on what's available within your budget for the destinations you want to visit.

Special-Interest Travel Special-interest programs may be fully escorted or independent. Some require a certain amount of expertise, but most are for the average traveler with an interest and are usually hosted by experts in the subject matter. When the program is escorted, it enjoys the advantages and disadvantages of all escorted programs; because your fellow travelers are apt to be passionate or knowledgeable about the subject, they can prove as enjoyable a part of your travel experience as the destination itself. The price range is wide, but the cost is usually higher—sometimes a lot higher—than for ordinary escorted tours and packages, because of the expert guiding and special activities.

Bed-and-Breakfasts **Brendan Tours** (*see above*) offers tours throughout Ireland with stays in family-owned bed-and-breakfast inns and country houses throughout Ireland. The **Irish Tourist Board** (*see above*) will send you a book called *Be Our Guest*, and the **Northern Ireland Tourist Board** (*see* Government Information Offices, *above*) provides *Where to Stay*, both listing hotels, guest houses, and bed-and-breakfast accommodations throughout the island.

Biking **Backroads** (1516 5th St., Suite Q333, Berkeley, CA 94710, tel. 510/527-1555 or 800/245–3874) offers an inn-to-inn bike trip that includes a stay at Dromoland Castle.

Cruises **EuroCruises** (303 W. 13th St., New York, NY 10014, tel. 212/691–2099 or 800/688–3870) and **Le Boat, Inc.** (Box E, Maywood, NJ 07507, tel. 201/342–1838 or 800/922–0291) both offer a variety of water-travel alternatives.

Culture **Backroads** (*see above*) leads you along the 130-mile Kerry Way, following ancient routes linking the area's early Christian settlements. **Lynott Tours** (Empire State Bldg., 350 5th Ave., Suite 1619, New York, NY 10118, tel. 212/760–0101 or 800/221–2474) customizes self-drive and chauffeur-driven tours that focus on topics such as history, literature, and architecture.

Golf **Abercrombie & Kent** (*see above*) will custom-design golf programs for individual travelers. **Aer Lingus** (*see above*) also offers golf packages. **Value Holidays** (10224 N. Port Washington Rd., Mequon, WI 53092, tel. 414/241–6373 or 800/558–6850) organizes golf vacations for groups of two or more travelers at some of Ireland's most famous courses. **Adventure Golf Holidays** (815 North Rd., Westfield, MA 01085, tel. 413/568–2855 or 800/628–9655) specializes in golf vacations to Europe, including Ireland, as does **Irish Links Tours & Travel** (2701 Summer St., Suite 200, Stamford, CT 06905, tel. 203/363–2088 or 800/824–6538), **ITC Golf Tours** (4134 Atlantic Ave., Suite 205, Long Beach, CA 90807, tel. 310/595–6905 or 800/257–4981), and **PerryGolf** (8302 Dunwoody Pl., Suite 305, Atlanta, GA 30350, tel. 404/641–9696 or 800/344–5257).

Hiking **Butterfield & Robinson** (70 Bond St., Toronto, Ont., Canada M5B 1X3, tel. 416/864–1354 or 800/387–1147) takes in lush countryside, rugged islands, and the western coastline. **Hiking Holidays** (Box 750, Bristol, VT 05443, tel. 802/453–4816) offers an inn-to-inn hiking trip that includes exploration of historic sites, castles, and ruins of the Dingle Peninsula, Killarney, and the Burren.

Horseback Riding **FITS Equestrian** (685 Lateen Rd., Solvang, CA 93463, tel. 805/688–9494 or 800/666–3487) threads the hills and valleys of Ireland on horseback.

Sports **Destination Ireland** (*see above*) and **Lismore Tours** (106 E. 31st St., New York, NY 10016, tel. 212/685–0100 or 800/547–6673) specialize in equestrian and golf packages to Ireland and the United Kingdom. They also offer escorted and independent hiking, garden tours, castle and manor house, and walking tours.

When to Go

Summer remains the most popular time to visit Ireland, and for good reason. The weather is pleasant, the days are long (daylight lasts until about 10 PM in late June), and the countryside is green and beautiful. But there will be crowds in popular holiday spots, and prices for accommodations are at their peak. As British and Irish school vacations overlap from late June to mid-September, families, backpacking students, and other vacationers descend on popular coastal resorts in the South, West, and East. Unless you are determined to enjoy the short (July and August) swimming season, you would be well advised to take your vacation in Ireland outside these months.

Fall and spring are good times to travel, although the weather can be unpredictable. Seasonal hotels, restaurants, and accommodations usually close from early or mid-November until mid-March or Easter. During this off-season, prices are considerably lower than in summer, but your selection of hotels and restaurants is limited, and many minor attractions also close. St. Patrick's Week in March gives a focal point to a spring visit, but some American visitors may find the saint's-day celebrations a little less enthusiastic than the ones back home. Dublin, however, welcomes American visitors on March 17 with a parade and the Lord Mayor's Ball. If you're planning an Easter visit, don't forget that most theaters close from Thursday to Sunday of Holy Week (the week preceding Easter), and all bars and restaurants, except those serving hotel residents, close on Good Friday.

If you want to feel like the only tourist in town, try a winter visit. Many hotels arrange special Christmas packages with entertainment and outdoor activities. Horse races and hunting trips abound, although mid-November to mid-February is either too cold or too wet for all but the keenest golfers. There are cheerful open fires in almost all hotels and bars, and with extra time on their hands, people tend to take an added interest in visitors.

Climate What follows are average daily maximum and minimum temperatures for some major cities in Ireland.

Dublin

Jan.	47F	8C	**May**	59F	15C	**Sept.**	63F	17C
	34	1		43	6		49	9
Feb.	47F	8C	**June**	65F	18C	**Oct.**	58F	14C
	36	2		49	9		43	6
Mar.	50F	10C	**July**	68F	20C	**Nov.**	50F	10C
	38	3		52	11		40	4
Apr.	56F	13C	**Aug.**	67F	20C	**Dec.**	47F	8C
	40	4		52	11		38	3

Cork

Jan.	49F	9C	**May**	61F	16C	**Sept.**	65F	18C
	36	2		45	7		50	10
Feb.	49F	9C	**June**	67F	19C	**Oct.**	58F	14C
	38	3		50	10		45	7
Mar.	52F	11C	**July**	68F	20C	**Nov.**	52F	11C
	40	4		54	12		40	4
Apr.	56F	13C	**Aug.**	68F	20C	**Dec.**	49F	9C
	41	5		54	12		38	3

Belfast

Jan.	43F	6C	**May**	59F	15C	**Sept.**	61F	16C
	36	2		43	6		49	9
Feb.	45F	7C	**June**	65F	18C	**Oct.**	56F	13C
	36	2		49	9		45	7
Mar.	49F	9C	**July**	65F	18C	**Nov.**	49F	9C
	38	3		52	11		40	4
Apr.	54F	12C	**Aug.**	65F	18C	**Dec.**	45F	7C
	50	4		52	11		38	3

Information Sources For current weather conditions and forecasts for cities in the United States and abroad, plus the local time and helpful travel tips, call the **Weather Channel Connection** (tel. 900/932–8437; 95¢ per minute) from a touch-tone phone.

Festivals and Seasonal Events

Irish Republic

January At least six major **horse races** are held at centers such as Thurles (Co. Tipperary), Naas (Co. Kildare), Leopardstown (Co. Dublin), and Gowran Park (Co. Kilkenny). The **Point-to-Point** season opens; these are small but exciting steeplechases, held in a different spot every Sunday until mid-May. The **Garden Leisure Exhibition** is held at the Royal Dublin Society.

February International classical music stars feature in the **Celebrity Concert Series** at Dublin's National Concert Hall. The **Dublin Film Festival** starts at the end of the month, providing 10 days of the best in world cinema, plus lectures and seminars on all aspects of filmmaking. In Naas, County Kildare, one of the most important racehorse auctions in Ireland, the **Punchestown Bloodstock Sales,** is held. There's an **international rugby match** at Lansdowne Road, Dublin, in the middle of the month.

March **St. Patrick's Day** is celebrated March 17, with a parade in Dublin featuring guest bands from the United States and a festival of traditional Irish music, the Dublin **Feis Ceoil.** In mid-March Limerick hosts an international festival featuring competitions for marching bands, concert bands, drill- and dance-team groups.

April Easter provides one of the biggest events of the racing calendar, the two-day **Irish Grand National** race at Fairyhouse, County Meath, about 19 kilometers (12 miles) from Dublin. The leadership of the Gaelic Football League is decided in the capital at Croke Park. The **Pan Celtic Week** in Tralee is an international celebration of Celtic music, dance, and song. About sixty choirs raise their voices in the **Cork International Choral Festival.**

May This month the **County Wicklow Gardens Festival** includes flower festivals, musical evenings, and garden tours. Genealogical seminars on Irish Origins are held in Dublin, Kilkenny, and Tipperary. This is the height of the flowering season and the best time to take **The Burren Flora Tour,** a guided botanical walk. Festivals include the **Fleadh Nua,** with traditional music, song, and dance, at Ennis, County Clare; a **Maytime Festival** at Dundalk; and a **Walking Festival** in Kenmare.

June **Listowel Writers' Week** provides a mix of friendly workshops, readings, lectures, and plays. One of the richest and most exciting horse races in the world, the **Budweiser Irish Derby,** is run 48 kilometers (30 miles) from Dublin at the Curragh, headquarters of Irish racing. The **Festival of Music in Great Irish Houses**—a delightful series of classical music concerts—is held in different stately homes around the country. **Bloomsday,** June 16, is celebrated in Dublin with readings and dramatizations of James Joyce's *Ulysses,* preceded by fancy-dress breakfasts and pilgrimages around the city. **The Murphys Irish Open Golf Championship** is played on the Jack Nicklaus–designed course at Mount Juliet in County Kilkenny.

July Golf enthusiasts flock to Lahinch in County Clare for **The South of Ireland Amateur Open. Galway** swings during its **Arts Festival,** the largest in Ireland, which includes theater, parades, film, and rock music, as well as international art exhibits. There is an **International Coarse Angling** competition at Belturbet, County Cavan. On the last Sunday in July many thousands of pilgrims, some in bare feet, climb the rocky slopes of Croagh Patrick (765 meters/2,510 feet) in County Mayo to honor St. Patrick. The **Killarney Horse Racing Festival** attracts large crowds mid-month.

August The **Kerrygold Dublin Horse Show,** held in the second week of August, draws the best of Irish bloodstock and a highly fashionable crowd. **The Summer Show of Flowers** is held in conjunction with the Horse Show. **The Yeats International Summer School** in Sligo is the oldest and most famous of the 15 summer schools taking place around the country this month. **Puck Fair** is a robust and entertaining occasion held at mid-month at Killorglin, County Kerry. At the end of the month in the same county, the *Rose of Tralee* is selected from among women of Irish descent from around the world; the competition coincides with the **Tralee Races.** The **Connemara Pony Show** at Clifden, County Galway, attracts a cosmopolitan crowd. **Kilkenny Arts Week** at the end of the month is renowned for interesting classical music events.

September In Galway, the oyster season opens with appropriate celebrations. The **Hurling and Gaelic Football finals** are played at Croke Park in Dublin. The **Matchmaking Festival** in Lisdoonvarna, County Clare, is the traditional place for bachelor farmers to seek a wife; this informal tradition has become popular with American husband-seekers. The **Cork Film Festival,** the **Sligo Arts Week,** and the **Waterford International Festival of Light Opera** all start at the end of September and run into October.

October **The Dublin Theater Festival** is a fortnight of drama with up to 40 Irish and international productions. The **Ballinasloe October Fair** in County Galway is one of the biggest and oldest horse and cattle fairs in Europe. Cork swings on the last weekend of October when the town and its environs are taken over by the **Guinness International Jazz Festival. The Wexford Opera Festival** runs for the last two weeks of the month and the first week of November. It assembles international singers, directors, and conductors, all of whom present unfamiliar operatic gems in a tiny Georgian theater, the Theater Royal.

November The hunting season starts in November, continuing through April. The Irish Rugby Football season gets under way with games between the four provinces: Connacht, Leinster, Munster, and Ulster (in Northern Ireland). **Irish Birdwatching Tours** offer guided tours of Ireland's rich birdlife throughout the country.

December On **St. Stephen's Day,** December 26, the traditional *Wren Boys* in blackface and fancy dress still demand money and sing in the street, but these days most of the proceeds go to charity. If you miss them on the 26th, you can catch them at the **Wren Boy Festival** in Bunratty Folk Park on the 30th and 31st.

Northern Ireland

March The **Belfast Musical Festival** sponsors speech, drama, and music competitions for young people (Balmoral, Belfast). **St. Patrick's Day celebrations** include parades and pilgrimages at sites associated with the saint (Downpatrick, Newry, and Cultra). The **Horse Plowing and Heavy Horse Show** is an old-time plowing competition held for over 100 years at Fair Head, Ballycastle.

April The **Circuit of Ireland International Motor Rally,** with a 1,040-kilometer (650-mile) course, serves as a qualifying round for the **European Rally Championship.**

May Belfast Civic Festival and Lord Mayor's Show lasts 21 days and includes concerts, competitions, and exhibitions, starting on the second Saturday in May with floats and bands in the streets of Belfast. The **Belfast Marathon** is held. Anglers compete in the **P&O European Ferries Classic Fishing Festival** (Fermanagh Lakeland). The **Ballyclare Horse Fair** has horse dealing in the old style on the village street. The **Royal Ulster Agricultural Society Show** includes international show-jumping and sheep-shearing competitions, parades, bands, and fashion shows (Balmoral, Belfast).

June At the **Belfast Midsummer Jazz and Blues Festival,** international players join local talent (Culloden Hotel, Belfast). The **Black Bush Amateur Golf Tournament** is played over four days using four courses (close to the Giant's Causeway, County Antrim). At the **Fiddle Stone Festival,** fiddlers from all over Ireland converge on the pretty village of Belleek.

July The **City of Belfast International Rose Trials** has over 100,000 roses in a riverside park (Dixon Park, Belfast). The **Northern Ireland Open Amateur Golf Championship** is held on the famous Royal Portrush links (County Antrim). **Battle of Boyne** festivities celebrate this 17th-century battle, in which the Protestant William of Orange defeated the Catholic James II (Belfast and other large towns). **Ulster Steam Traction Engine Rally** has vintage cars and field sports at Shane's Castle, Antrim.

August On the **Feast of the Assumption** on the 15th of the month, Hibernians in green sashes march to the music of Gaelic pipers (various Ulster cities). **Oul' Lammas Fair,** on the last weekend of the month, has sheep and pony trading and about 100 stalls selling everything from antiques to ropes and ladders (Ballycastle).

September The **Belfast Folk Festival** provides a weekend of Irish folk talent in the center of Belfast. **Opera Northern Ireland** starts its autumn season at the end of the month in the Grand Opera House in Belfast.

October The **Ulster Antiques and Fine Art Fair** takes place at the Culloden Hotel in Belfast on the first weekend of the month.

November The **Belfast Festival** at Queen's University is a major arts festival featuring drama, ballet, cinema, and music from classical to jazz and folk.

December The **New Year Viennese Ball** is held, with music by Johann Strauss from the Ulster Orchestra (Belfast City Hall).

What to Pack

Clothing In Ireland you can experience all four seasons in one day, so pack accordingly. Even in July and August, the hottest months of the year, a heavy sweater and a good waterproof coat or umbrella are essential. You should bring at least two pairs of walking shoes: It can and does rain at any time of the year, and shoes can get soaked in minutes.

The Irish are generally informal about clothes. In the more expensive hotels and restaurants most people dress formally for dinner, and a jacket and tie are required in bars after 7 PM, but very few places operate a strict dress policy. Younger travelers should note that old or tattered blue jeans are forbidden in certain bars and discos.

Miscellaneous Bring an extra pair of eyeglasses or contact lenses in your carry-on luggage. If you have a health problem that requires a prescription drug, pack enough to last the duration of the trip or have your doctor write a prescription using the drug's generic name, because brand names vary from country to country. Always carry prescription drugs in their original packaging to avoid problems with customs officials. Don't pack them in luggage that you plan to check in case your bags go astray. Pack a list of the offices that supply refunds for lost or stolen traveler's checks.

Electricity The electrical current in Ireland is 220 volts, 50 cycles alternating current (AC); the United States runs on 110-volt, 60-cycle AC current. Unlike wall outlets in the United States, which accept plugs with two flat prongs, outlets in Ireland take plugs with three prongs.

Adapters, Converters, Transformers To use U.S.-made electric appliances abroad you'll need an adapter plug. Unless the appliance is dual-voltage and made for travel, you'll also need a converter. Hotels sometimes have 110-volt outlets for low-wattage appliances marked "For Shavers Only" near the sink; don't use them for a high-wattage appliance like a blow-dryer. If you're traveling with an older laptop computer, carry a transformer. New laptop computers are auto-sensing, operating equally well on 110 and 220 volts, so you need only the appropriate adapter plug. For a copy of the free brochure "Foreign Electricity Is No Deep Dark Secret," send a SASE to adapter-converter manufacturer Franzus Company (Customer Service, Dept. B50, Murtha Industrial Park, Box 142, Beacon Falls, CT 06403, tel. 203/723–6664).

Luggage *Regulations* Free airline baggage allowances depend on the airline, the route, and the class of your ticket; ask in advance. In general, on domestic flights and on international flights between the United States and foreign destinations, you are entitled to check two bags—neither exceeding 62 inches, or 158 centimeters (length + width + height), or weighing more than 70 pounds (32 kilograms). A third piece may be brought aboard; its total dimensions are generally limited to less than 45 inches (114 centimeters), so it will fit easily under the seat in front of you or in the overhead compartment. In the United States the Federal Aviation Administration (FAA) gives airlines broad latitude to limit carry-on allowances and tailor them to different aircraft and operational conditions. Charges for excess, oversize, or overweight pieces vary.

If you are flying between two foreign destinations, note that baggage allowances may be determined not by piece but by weight, which generally allows 88 pounds (40 kilograms) of luggage in first class, 66 pounds (30 kilograms) in business class, and 44 pounds (20 kilograms) in economy. If your flight between two cities abroad *connects* with your transatlantic or transpacific flight, the piece method still applies.

Safeguarding Your Luggage

Before leaving home, itemize your bags' contents and their worth in case they go astray. To minimize that risk, tag them inside and out with your name, address, and phone number. (If you use your home address, cover it so that potential thieves can't see it.) Put a copy of your itinerary inside each bag, so that you can easily be tracked. At check-in, make sure that the tag attached by baggage handlers bears the correct three-letter code for your destination. If your bags do not arrive with you, or if you detect damage, file a written report with the airline before you leave the airport.

Taking Money Abroad

Traveler's Checks

Traveler's checks are preferable in metropolitan centers, although you'll need cash in rural areas and small towns. The most widely recognized are **American Express, Citicorp, Diners Club, Thomas Cook,** and **Visa,** which are sold by major commercial banks. Both American Express and Thomas Cook issue checks that can be countersigned and used by you or your traveling companion. Typically the issuing company or the bank at which you make your purchase charges 1% to 3% of the checks' face value as a fee. Some foreign banks charge as much as 20% of the face value as the fee for cashing travelers' checks in a foreign currency. Buy a few checks in small denominations to cash toward the end of your trip, so you won't be left with excess foreign currency. Record the numbers of checks as you spend them, and keep this list separate from the checks.

If you are traveling to western Europe or Japan, buy some checks in the currency of the country you are visiting; banks will cash them with no fee, and you can use them as readily as cash in many hotels, restaurants, and shops.

Currency Exchange

Banks offer the most favorable exchange rates. If you use currency exchange booths at airports, rail and bus stations, hotels, stores, and privately run exchange firms, you'll typically get less favorable rates, but you may find the hours more convenient.

You can get good rates and avoid long lines at airport currency-exchange booths by getting a small amount of currency at **Thomas Cook Currency Services** (630 5th Ave., New York, NY 10111, tel. 212/757–6915 or 800/223–7373 for locations in major metropolitan areas throughout the United States) or **Ruesch International** (tel. 800/424–2923 for locations) before you depart. Check with your travel agent to be sure that the currency of the country you will be visiting can be imported.

Getting Money from Home

Cash Machines Many automated-teller machines (ATMs) are tied to international networks such as **Cirrus** and **Plus.** You can use your bank card at ATMs to withdraw money from an account and get cash advances on a credit-card account if your card has been programmed with a personal identification number, or PIN. Check in advance on limits on withdrawals and cash advances within specified periods. Ask whether your bank-card or credit-card PIN will need to be reprogrammed for use in the area you'll be visiting. Four digits are commonly used overseas. Note that Discover is accepted only in the United States. On cash advances you are charged interest from the day you receive the money from ATMs as well as from tellers. Although transaction fees for ATM withdrawals abroad may be higher than fees for withdrawals at home, Cirrus and Plus exchange rates are excellent, because they are based on wholesale rates only offered by major banks. They also may be referred to abroad as "a withdrawal from a credit account."

Plan ahead: Obtain ATM locations and the names of affiliated cash-machine networks before departure. For specific foreign Cirrus locations, call 800/424–7787; for foreign Plus locations, consult the Plus directory at your local bank.

Wiring Money You don't have to be a cardholder to send or receive a **MoneyGram from American Express** for up to $10,000. Go to a MoneyGram agent in retail or convenience stores or American Express travel offices, pay up to $1,000 with a credit card and anything over that in cash. You are allowed a free long-distance call to give the transaction code to your intended recipient, who needs only to present identification and the transaction reference number to the nearest MoneyGram agent to pick up the cash. MoneyGram agents are in more than 70 countries (call 800/926–9400 for locations). Fees range from 3% to 10%, depending on the amount and how you pay.

You can also use **Western Union.** To wire money, take either cash or a cashier's check to the nearest agent or call and use MasterCard or Visa. Money sent from the United States or Canada will be available for pick-up at *any* one of 25,000 agent locations in 100 countries within minutes (call 800/325–6000 for the one nearest you; 800/321–2923 in Canada). Fees range from 4% to 10%, depending on the amount you send.

Currency

The unit of currency in the Irish Republic is the pound or punt, pronounced *poont.* It is divided into 100 pence (abbreviated 100p). **In this guide, the £ sign refers to the Irish pound; the British pound is referred to as the pound sterling and is written U.K.£.**

Irish notes come in denominations of £100, £50, £20, £10, and £5. Coins are available as £1, 50p, 20p, 10p, 5p, 2p, and 1p. £1 coins are not exchangeable outside the Republic of Ireland. Dollars and British pounds are accepted only in large hotels and shops geared to tourists. Elsewhere you will be expected to use Irish currency.

At the time of writing (July 1994), the punt stood at around US$1.61, Canadian $2.16, and U.K.£1.07; however, these rates will inevitably change both before and during 1995, making it advisable to keep a sharp eye on the exchange rate during your trip.

The unit of currency in Northern Ireland is the pound sterling, divided into 100 pence. Notes come in denominations of U.K.£50, U.K.£20, U.K.£10, and U.K.£5, and coins of U.K.£1, 50p, 20p, 10p, 5p, and 1p. At the time of writing (July 1994), the pound sterling stood at around US$1.60, Canadian $2.16, and £0.98.

What It Will Cost

The strength of the punt in comparison with the pound sterling is making some headway in reducing Ireland's high cost of living. Dublin, far more expensive than the rest of the country, is reputed to be one of Europe's most expensive cities for the business traveler. However, the independent traveler does not have to spend a fortune. A modest hotel in Dublin costs about £90 a night for two; this figure can be reduced to under £70 by staying in a registered guest house, and reduced to under £35 by staying in a suburban bed-and-breakfast (*see* Lodging, *below*). As far as food goes, lunch, consisting of a good one-dish plate of bar food at a pub, costs around £5; a sandwich at the same pub, about £1.80. Dinner in Dublin is more expensive; a fancy restaurant, though not an absolutely top spot, charges about £20 per person, excluding drinks and tip. On the other hand, theater and entertainment in most places are inexpensive—about £12 for a good seat, and double that for a big-name pop-music concert. For the price of a few drinks and (in Dublin and Killarney) a small entrance fee of about £1.50, you can spend a fun and memorable evening at a *seisún* (pronounced *say-shoon*) in a music pub. Entrance to most public galleries is free, but stately homes and similar attractions normally charge about £2.50 per person.

Northern Ireland is generally inexpensive compared with both the rest of the United Kingdom and the Republic of Ireland. By comparison, the lower level of taxation in Northern Ireland makes dutiable goods such as gasoline, alcoholic drinks, and tobacco cheaper. The cost of accommodations and restaurant meals is also less expensive.

Sample Prices Just about everything is more expensive in Dublin, so add at least 10% to these sample prices, which apply in the rest of the country: cup of coffee, 65p; pint of beer, £2; soda, 95p; ham sandwich, £1.80; and 1-mile taxi ride, £3.

Long-Distance Calling

AT&T, MCI, and Sprint have several services that make calling home or the office more affordable and convenient when you're on the road. Use one of them to avoid pricey hotel surcharges. **AT&T** Calling Card (tel. 800/225–5288) and the AT&T Universal Card (tel. 800/662–7759) give you access to the service. With AT&T's USA Direct (tel. 800/874–4000 for codes in the countries you'll be visiting) you can reach an AT&T operator with a local or toll-free call. **MCI**'s Call USA (MCI Customer Service, tel. 800/444–4444) allows that service from 85 countries or from country to country via MCI WorldReach. From MCI ExpressInfo in the United States you can get weather, news and stock quotes 24-hours a day. MCI PhoneCash (tel. 800/925–0029) is available through American Express and through several convenience stores and retailers nationwide. **Sprint** Express (tel. 800/793–1153) has a toll-free number travelers abroad can dial using the WorldTraveler Foncard to reach a Sprint operator in the United States. The Sprint operator can offer international directory assistance to 224 countries in the world. All three companies offer message delivery services to international travelers, and they have added debit cards so that you don't have to fiddle with change.

Passports and Visas

If your passport is lost or stolen abroad, report the loss immediately to the nearest embassy or consulate and to the local police. If you can provide the consular officer with the information contained in the passport, he or she will usually be able to issue you a new passport promptly. For this reason, keep a photocopy of the data page of your passport separate from your money and traveler's checks. Also leave a photocopy with a relative or friend at home.

U.S. Citizens All U.S. citizens, even infants, need a valid passport to enter Ireland and Northern Ireland for stays of up to 90 days in the Republic, 180 days in the North. Tourists may be asked to show onward/return tickets. You can pick up new and renewal application forms at any of the 13 U.S. Passport Agency offices and at some post offices and courthouses. Although passports are usually mailed within four weeks of your application's receipt, allow five weeks or more from April through summer. Call the Department of State Office of Passport Services' information line (tel. 202/647–0518) for fees, documentation requirements, and other details.

Canadian Citizens Canadian citizens need a valid passport to enter Ireland and Northern Ireland for stays of up to 90 days. Application forms are available at 23 regional passport offices as well as post offices and travel agencies. Whether for a first or subsequent passport, you must apply in person. Children under 16 may be included on a parent's passport but must have their own to travel alone. Passports are valid for five years and are usually mailed within two weeks of an application's receipt. For fees, documentation requirements, and other information in English or French, call the passport office (tel. 514/283–2152 or 800/567–6868).

U.K. Citizens Citizens of the United Kingdom do not need a passport to enter Ireland.

Customs and Duties

On Arrival *Irish Republic* Two categories of duty-free allowance exist for travelers entering the Irish Republic: one for goods obtained outside the European Union (EU), on a ship or aircraft, or in a duty-free store within the EU; and the other for goods bought in the EU, with duty and tax paid.

In the first category, you may import duty-free: (1) 200 cigarettes or 100 cigarillos or 50 cigars or 250 grams of smoking tobacco; (2) 2 liters of wine, and either 1 liter of alcoholic drink over 22% volume or 2 liters of alcoholic drink under 22% volume (sparkling or fortified wine included); (3) 50 grams of perfume and ¼ liter of toilet water; and (4) other goods to a value of £34 per person (£17 per person for travelers under 15 years of age); you may import 12 liters of beer as part of this allowance.

In the second category, you may import duty-free a considerable amount of liquor and tobacco—800 cigarettes, 400 cigarillos, 200 cigars, 1 kilogram of pipe tobacco, 10 liters of spirits, 90 liters of wine, and 100 liters of beer. You'll need a truck!

Goods that cannot be freely imported include firearms, ammunition, explosives, drugs (e.g., narcotics, amphetamines), indecent or obscene books and pictures, oral smokeless tobacco products, meat and meat products, poultry and poultry products, plants and plant products (including shrubs, vegetables, fruit, bulbs, and seeds), domestic cats and dogs from outside the United Kingdom, and live animals from outside Northern Ireland.

Northern Ireland Two levels of duty-free allowance exist for people entering Northern Ireland: one for goods bought outside the EU or for goods bought in a duty-free shop in an EU country; the other for goods bought in an EU country but not in a duty-free shop.

In the first category you may import duty-free: (1) 200 cigarettes or 100 cigarillos or 50 cigars or 250 grams of tobacco (if you live outside Europe these allowances are doubled); (2) 1 liter of alcoholic drink over 22% volume, or 2 liters of alcoholic drink under 22% volume (fortified or sparkling wine, or 2 liters of table wine); (3) 2 more liters of still table wine; (4) 60 milliliters of perfume and ¼ liter of toilet water; and (5) other goods to the value of U.K.£32.

In the second category, you may import duty-free a considerable amount of liquor and tobacco—800 cigarettes, 400 cigarillos, 200 cigars, 1 kg of pipe tobacco, 10 liters of spirits, 90 liters of wine, and 50 liters of beer.

No animals or pets of any kind may be brought into Northern Ireland without a six-month quarantine. Other items that may not be imported include fresh meats, plants and vegetables, controlled drugs, and firearms and ammunition.

Returning Home

U.S. Customs If you've been out of the country for at least 48 hours and haven't already used the exemption, or any part of it, in the past 30 days, you may bring home $400 worth of foreign goods duty-free. So can each member of your family, regardless of age; and your exemptions may be pooled, so one of you can bring in more if another brings in less. A flat 10% duty applies to the next $1,000 worth of goods; above $1,400, the rate varies with the merchandise. (If the 48-hour or 30-day limits apply, your duty-free allowance drops to $25, which may not be pooled.) Please note that these are the *general* rules, applicable to most countries, including Ireland and Northern Ireland.

Travelers 21 or older may bring back 1 liter of alcohol duty-free, provided the beverage laws of the state through which they reenter the United States allow it. In addition, 100 non-Cuban cigars and 200 cigarettes are allowed, regardless of your age. Antiques and works of art more than 100 years old are duty-free.

Gifts valued at less than $50 may be mailed to the United States duty-free, with a limit of one package per day per addressee, and they do not count as part of your exemption (do not send alcohol or tobacco products or perfume valued at more than $5). Mark the package "Unsolicited Gift" and write the nature of the gift and its retail value on the outside. Most reputable stores will handle the mailing for you.

For a copy of "Know Before You Go," a free brochure detailing what you may and may not bring back to the United States, rates of duty, and other pointers, contact the **U.S. Customs Service** (Box 7407, Washington, DC 20044, tel. 202/927–6724).

Canadian Customs Once per calendar year, when you've been out of Canada for at least seven days, you may bring in C$300 worth of goods duty-free. If you've been away less than seven days but more than 48 hours, the duty-free exemption drops to C$100 but can be claimed any number of times (as can a C$20 duty-free exemption for absences of 24 hours or more). You cannot combine the yearly and 48-hour exemptions, use the C$300 exemption only partially (to save the balance for a later trip), or pool exemptions with family members. Goods claimed under the C$300 exemption may follow you by mail; those claimed under the lesser exemptions must accompany you on your return.

Alcohol and tobacco products may be included in the yearly and 48-hour exemptions but not in the 24-hour exemption. If you meet the age requirements of the province through which you reenter Canada, you may bring in, duty-free, 1.14 liters (40 imperial ounces) of wine or liquor *or* two dozen 12-ounce cans or bottles of beer or ale. If you are 16 or older, you may bring in, duty-free, 200 cigarettes, 50 cigars or cigarillos, and 400 tobacco sticks or 400 grams of manufactured tobacco. Alcohol and tobacco must accompany you on your return.

An unlimited number of gifts valued up to C$60 each may be mailed to Canada duty-free. These do not count as part of your exemption. Label the package "Unsolicited Gift—Value under $60." Alcohol and tobacco are excluded.

For more information, including details of duties on items that exceed your duty-free limit, ask the Revenue Canada Customs and Excise and Taxation Department (2265 St. Laurent Blvd. S, Ottawa, Ont., K1G 4K3, tel. 613/957–0275) for a copy of the free brochure "I Declare/Je Déclare."

U.K. Customs You can expect tight security coming into Great Britain from both the Irish Republic and Northern Ireland. Customs regulations are the same for Great Britain and Northern Ireland. For details, *see* On Arrival for Northern Ireland, *above*. Further information can be obtained by contacting **HM Customs and Excise** (Dorset House, Stamford St., London SE1 9PY, tel. 0171/928–3344).

Traveling with Cameras, Camcorders, and Laptops

Film and Cameras If your camera is new or if you haven't used it for a while, shoot and develop a few test rolls of film before you leave. Store film in a cool, dry place—never in the car's glove compartment or on the shelf under the rear window.

Airport security X-rays generally aren't harmful to film with ISO below 400. To protect your film, carry it with you in a clear plastic bag and ask for a hand inspection. Such requests are honored at U.S. airports and are up to the inspector abroad. Don't depend on a lead-lined bag to protect film in checked luggage—the airline may increase the radiation to see what's inside. Call the Kodak Information Center (tel. 800/242–2424) for details.

Camcorders and Videotape Before your trip, put camcorders through their paces, invest in a skylight filter to protect the lens, and check all the batteries. Most newer camcorders are equipped with batteries that can be recharged with a universal or worldwide AC adapter charger (or multivoltage converter) usable whether the voltage is 110 or 220. All that's needed is the appropriate plug.

Videotape is not damaged by X-rays, but it may be harmed by the magnetic field of a walk-through metal detector, so ask for a hand check. Airport security personnel may ask you to turn on the camcorder to prove that it's what it appears to be, so make sure the battery is charged. Note that rather than the National Television System Committee (NTSC) video standard used in the United States and Canada, Ireland and Northern Ireland use PAL/SECAM technology. You will not be able to view your tapes through the local TV set or view movies bought there in your home VCR. Blank tapes bought in Ireland can be used for NTSC camcorder taping, but they are pricey.

Laptops Security X-rays do not harm hard-disk or floppy-disk storage, but you may request a hand check, at which point you may be asked to turn on the computer to prove that it is what it appears to be. (Check your battery before departure.) Most airlines allow you to use your laptop aloft except during takeoff and landing (so as not to interfere with navigation equipment). For international travel, register your foreign-made laptop with U.S. Customs as you leave the country. If your laptop is U.S.-made, call the consulate of the country you'll be visiting to find out whether it should be registered with customs upon arrival. Before departure, find out about repair facilities at your destination, and don't forget any transformer or adapter plug you may need (*see* Electricity in What to Pack, *above*).

Language

Irish (also known as Gaelic), a Celtic language related to Scottish Gaelic, Breton, and Welsh, is the official national language. Though English is technically the second language of the country, it is in fact the everyday language of the majority of the population. Nowadays all Irish speakers are fluent in English.

Irish-speaking communities are found mainly in sparsely populated rural areas along the western seaboard, on some but not all offshore islands, and in small pockets in West Cork and County Waterford. Irish-speaking areas are known as Gaeltacht. While most road signs in Ireland are given in both English and Irish, within Gaeltacht areas the signs are often in Irish only. A good touring map will give both Irish and English names to places within the Gaeltacht. The most important Irish words a visitor needs to recognize are *Fir* and *Mná*, used frequently outside public toilets: *Fir* is Men and *Mná* is Women.

Staying Healthy

Shots and Medications
Assistance Companies

Pretrip medical referrals, emergency evacuation or repatriation, 24-hour telephone hot lines for medical consultation, dispatch of medical personnel, relay of medical records, cash for emergencies, and other personal and legal assistance are among the services provided by several organizations specializing in medical assistance to travelers. Among them are **International SOS Assistance** (Box 11568, Philadelphia, PA 19116, tel. 215/244–1500 or 800/523–8930; Box 466, Pl. Bonaventure, Montréal, Qué. H5A 1C1, tel. 514/874–7674 or 800/363–0263); **Medex Assistance Corporation** (Box 10623, Baltimore, MD 21285, tel. 410/296–2530 or 800/874–9125); **Near Services** (450 Prairie Ave., Suite 101, Calumet City, IL 60409, tel. 708/868–6700 or 800/654–6700); and **Travel Assistance International** (1133 15th St. NW, Suite 400, Washington, DC 20005, tel. 202/331–1609 or 800/821–2828). Because these companies will also sell you death-and-dismemberment, trip-cancellation, and other insurance coverage, there is some overlap with the travel-insurance policies discussed under Insurance, *below*.

Publications *The Safe Travel Book*, by Peter Savage ($12.95, Lexington Books, 866 3rd Ave., New York, NY 10022, tel. 212/702–4771 or 800/257–5755, fax 800/562–1272), is packed with handy lists and phone numbers to make your trip smooth. *Traveler's Medical Resource*, by William W. Forgey ($19.95, ICS Books, Inc., 1 Tower Plaza, 107 E. 89th Ave., Merrillville, IN 45410, tel. 800/541–7323), is also a good, authoritative guide to care overseas.

Insurance

For U.S. Residents Most tour operators, travel agents, and insurance agents sell specialized health-and-accident, flight, trip-cancellation, and luggage insurance as well as comprehensive policies with some or all of these features. Before you make any purchase, review your existing health and homeowner policies to find out whether they cover expenses incurred while travelling.

Health-and-Accident Insurance Specific policy provisions of supplemental health-and-accident insurance for travelers include reimbursement for $1,000 to $150,000 worth of medical and/or dental expenses caused by an accident or illness during a trip. The personal-accident, or death-and-dismemberment, provision pays a lump sum to your beneficiaries if you die or to you if you lose one or both limbs or your eyesight; the lump sum awarded can range from $15,000 to $500,000. The medical-assistance provision may reimburse you for the cost of referrals, evacuation, or repatriation and other services, or it may automatically enroll you as a member of a particular medical-assistance company (*see* Staying Healthy, *above*).

Flight Insurance Often bought as a last-minute impulse at the airport, flight insurance pays a lump sum—when a plane crashes—either to a beneficiary if the insured dies or sometimes to a surviving passenger who loses eyesight or a limb. Like most impulse buys, flight insurance is expensive and basically unnecessary. It supplements the airlines' coverage described in the limits-of-liability paragraphs on your ticket. Charging an airline ticket to a major credit card often automatically entitles you to coverage and may also embrace travel by bus, train, and ship.

Baggage Insurance In the event of loss, damage, or theft on international flights, airlines' liability is $20 per kilogram for checked baggage (roughly $640 per 70-pound bag) and $400 per passenger for unchecked baggage. On domestic flights, the ceiling is $1,250 per passenger. Excess-valuation insurance can be bought directly from the airline at check-in for about $10 per $1,000 worth of coverage. However, you cannot buy it at any price for the rather extensive list of excluded items shown on your airline ticket.

Trip Insurance **Trip-cancellation-and-interruption insurance** protects you in the event you are unable to undertake or finish your trip, especially if your airline ticket, cruise, or package tour does not allow changes or cancellations. The amount of coverage you purchase should equal the cost of your trip should you, a traveling companion, or a family member get sick, forcing you to stay home, plus the nondiscounted one-way airline ticket you would need to buy if you had to return home early. Read the fine print carefully; pay attention to sections defining "family member" and "preexisting medical conditions." **Default** or **bankruptcy insurance** protects you against a supplier's failure to deliver. Such policies often do not cover default by a travel agency, tour operator, airline, or cruise line if you bought your tour and the coverage directly from the firm in question. Tours packaged by one of the 33 members of the United States Tour Operators Association (USTOA, 211 E. 51st St., Suite 12B, New York, NY 10022, tel. 212/750–7371), which requires members to maintain $1 million each in an account to reimburse clients in case of default, are likely to present the fewest difficulties.

Comprehensive Policies Companies supplying comprehensive policies with some or all of the above features include **Access America, Inc.** (Box 90315, Richmond, VA 23230, tel. 800/284–8300); **Carefree Travel Insurance** (Box 310, 120 Mineola Blvd., Mineola, NY 11501, tel. 516/294–0220 or 800/323–3149); **Tele-Trip** (Mutual of Omaha Plaza, Box 31762, Omaha, NE 68131, tel. 800/228–9792); **The Travelers Companies** (1 Tower Sq., Hartford, CT 06183, tel. 203/277–0111 or 800/243–3174); **Travel Guard International** (1145 Clark St., Stevens Point, WI 54481, tel. 715/345–0505 or 800/826–1300); and **Wallach and Company, Inc.** (107 W. Federal St., Box 480, Middleburg, VA 22117, tel. 703/687–3166 or 800/237–6615).

U.K. Residents Most tour operators, travel agents, and insurance agents sell specialized policies covering accident, medical expenses, personal liability, trip cancellation, and loss or theft of personal property. You can also buy an annual travel-insurance policy valid for every trip (usually of less than 90 days) you make during the year in which it's purchased. Make sure you will be covered if you have a preexisting medical condition or are pregnant.

For advice by phone or a free booklet, "Holiday Insurance," that sets out what to expect from a holiday-insurance policy and gives price guidelines, contact the **Association of British Insurers** (51 Gresham St., London EC2V 7HQ, tel. 0171/600–3333; 30 Gordon St., Glasgow G1 3PU, tel. 0141/226–3905; Scottish Providence Bldg., Donegall Sq. W, Belfast BT1 6JE, tel. 01232/249176; call for other locations).

Car Rentals

If you are renting a car in the Irish Republic and intend to visit Northern Ireland, make this clear when you get your car. Similarly, if renting in Northern Ireland and crossing the border, make sure that the rental insurance applies.

All major car-rental companies are represented in Ireland and Northern Ireland, including **Alamo** (tel. 800/327–9633); **Avis** (tel. 800/331–1084, 800/879–2847 in Canada); **Budget** (tel. 800/527–0700); **Dollar** (tel. 800/800–6000); **Hertz** (tel. 800/654–3001, 800/263-0600 in Canada); and **National** (tel. 800/227–3876), known internationally as InterRent and Europcar. In Irish cities, unlimited-mileage rates range from $35 per day for an economy car to $92 for a large car; weekly unlimited-mileage rates range from $189 to $425; rates are a little better in the North, with some weekly rates as low as $149. These prices do not include tax, which is 12.5% in Ireland, 17.5% in Northern Ireland.

Requirements Your own driver's license is acceptable. An International Driver's Permit, available from the American or Canadian Automobile Association, is a good idea.

Extra Charges Picking up the car in one city and leaving it in another may entail substantial drop-off charges or one-way service fees. The cost of a collision or loss-damage waiver (*see below*) can be high, also. Some rental agencies will charge you extra if you return the car *before* the time specified on your contract. Ask before making unscheduled drop-offs. Be sure the rental agent agrees *in writing* to any changes in drop-off location or other items of your rental contract. Fill the tank before you turn in the vehicle to avoid being charged for refueling at what you'll swear is the most expensive pump in town. In Ireland manual transmissions are standard and air-conditioning is a rarity and often unnecessary. Asking for an automatic transmission or air-conditioning can significantly increase the cost of your rental.

Cutting Costs Major international companies have programs that discount their standard rates by 15%–30% if you make the reservation before departure (anywhere from 24 hours to 14 days), rent for a minimum number of days (typically three or four), and prepay the rental. More economical rentals may come as part of fly/drive or other packages, even bare-bones deals that only combine the rental and an airline ticket (*see* Tours and Packages, *above*).

Several companies operate as wholesalers. They do not own their own fleets but rent in bulk from those that do and offer advantageous rates to their customers. Rentals through such companies must be arranged and paid for before you leave the United States. Among them are **Auto Europe** (Box 7006, Portland, ME 04112, tel. 207/828–2525 or 800/223–5555, 800/458–9503 in Canada); **Europe by Car** (mailing address, 1 Rockefeller Plaza, New York, NY 10020; walk-in address, 14 W. 49th St, New York, NY 10020, tel. 212/581–3040, 212/245–1713, or 800/223–1516; 9000 Sunset Blvd., Los Angeles, CA 90069, tel. 213/272–0424 or 800/252–9401 in CA); **Foremost Euro-Car** (5658 Sepulvada Blvd., Suite 201, Van Nuys, CA 91411, tel. 818/786–1960 or 800/272–3299); and **The Kemwel Group** (106 Calvert St., Harrison, NY 10528, tel. 914/835–5555 or 800/678–0678). You won't see these wholesalers' deals advertised; they're even better in summer, when business travel is down. Always ask whether the prices are guaranteed in U.S. dollars or foreign currency and if unlimited mileage is available. Find out about any required deposits, cancellation penalties, and drop-off charges, and confirm the cost of any required insurance coverage.

Insurance and Collision Damage Waiver Until recently standard rental contracts included liability coverage (for damage to public property, injury to pedestrians, and so on) and coverage for the car against fire, theft, and collision damage with a deductible. Due to law changes in some states and rising liability costs, several car rental agencies have reduced the type of coverage they offer. Before you rent a car, find out exactly what coverage, if any, is provided by your personal auto insurer. Don't assume that you are covered. If you do want insurance from the rental company, secondary coverage may be the only type offered. You may already have secondary coverage if you charge the rental to a credit card. Only Diner's Club (tel. 800/234–6377) provides primary coverage in the United States and worldwide.

In general if you have an accident, you are responsible for the automobile. Car rental companies may offer a collision damage waiver (CDW), which ranges in cost from $4 to $14 a day. You should decline the CDW only if you are certain you are covered through your personal insurer or credit card company.

Rail Passes

The **EurailPass,** valid for unlimited first-class train travel through 17 countries, including the Republic of Ireland but not Northern Ireland or Britain, is an excellent value if you plan on traveling throughout Ireland and on the Continent. Standard passes are available for 15 days ($498), 21 days ($648), one month ($728), two months ($1,098), and three months ($1,398). **Eurail Saverpasses** valid for 15 days cost $430 per person, for 21 days $550, for one month $678 per person; you must do all your traveling with at least one companion (two companions from April through September). **Eurail Youthpasses,** which cover second-class travel, cost $578 for one month, $768 for two; you must be under 26 on the first day you travel. **Eurail Flexipasses** allow you to travel first class for 5 ($348), 10 ($560), or 15 ($740) days within any two-month period. **Eurail Youth Flexipasses,** available to those under 26 on their first travel day, allow you to travel second class for 5 ($255), 10 ($398), or 15 ($540) days within any two-month period. Apply through your travel agent or **Rail Europe** (226–230 Westchester Ave., White Plains, NY 10604, tel. 914/682–5172 or 800/848–7245; or 2087 Dundas East, Suite 105, Mississauga, Ont. L4X 1M2, tel. 416/602–4195), **DER Tours** (Box 1606, Des Plaines, IL 60017, tel. 800/782–2424, fax 800/282–7474), or **CIT Tours Corp.** (342 Madison Ave., Suite 207, New York, NY 10173, tel. 212/697–2100 or 800/248–8687; 310/670–4269 or 800/248–7245 in the western United States). If you plan to include travel in Great Britain, you might consider the **BritIreland Pass,** which allows you 5 days' unlimited travel within 15 days ($399 first class, $269 standard) or 10 days within a month ($629 first class, $419 standard). You *must* purchase your BritIreland Pass before you leave home. It is available from most travel agents or from the British Travel International office (1500 Broadway, New York, NY 10036, tel. 212/575–2667 or 800/677–8585).

The **Irish Explorer Rail & Bus Pass,** for use on Ireland's railroads, bus system, or both, covers all the state-run and federal railways and bus lines throughout the Republic of Ireland. It does not apply to the North or to transportation within the cities. An eight-day bus *or* rail ticket is $96. An eight-day ticket for use on buses *and* trains during a 15-day period is $136.

Also available is the **Go as You Please Rambler Card** that combines eight days of travel on bus and rail with seven nights' accommodations in your choice of private homes or first-class hotels. The home-stay program is $345 per person, with extra nights available for $22 each. The pass with first-class hotel accomodations costs from $455 to $515 per person, depending upon time of travel. Additional nights are available for $43 per night.

The **Emerald Isle Card** offers unlimited bus and train travel anywhere in Ireland and Northern Ireland, valid within cities as well. A 15-day pass gives you eight days of travel over a 15-day period; it costs $168, $84 for children. A pass for 15 days of travel over a 30-day period costs $288, $144 for children.

For more information on the Irish Explorer Rail & Bus Pass or Emerald Isle tickets, or to book in advance, contact **CIE Tours International** (108 Ridgedale Ave., Morristown, NJ 07960, tel. 201/292–3438 or 800/243–8687).

In Northern Ireland, **Rail Runabout** tickets, entitling you to seven days' unlimited travel on scheduled rail services April–October, are available from main Northern Ireland Railway stations. They cost UK£25 for adults, UK£12.50 for children under 16 and senior citizens. Interrail tickets are also valid in Northern Ireland; tickets for eight days of unlimited travel cost UK£55 for adults, UK£27.50 for children under 16 and senior citizens; tickets for 15 days cost UK£80 for adults, UK£40 for children and senior citizens.

Student and Youth Travel

Travel Agencies

Council Travel Services (CTS), a subsidiary of the nonprofit Council on International Educational Exchange, specializes in low-cost travel arrangements abroad for students and is the exclusive U.S. agent for several discount cards. Also newly available from CTS are domestic air passes for bargain travel within the United States. CIEE's twice-yearly *Student Travels* magazine is available at the CTS office at CIEE headquarters (205 E. 42nd St., 16th Floor, New York, NY 10017, tel. 212/661–1450) and in Boston (tel. 617/266–1926), Miami (tel. 305/670–9261), Los Angeles (tel. 310/208–3551), and at 43 branches in college towns nationwide (free in person, $1 by mail). **Campus Connections** (1100 E. Marlton Pike, Cherry Hill, NJ 08034, tel. 800/428–3235) specializes in discounted accommodations and airline fares for students. The **Educational Travel Centre** (438 N. Frances St., Madison, WI 53703, tel. 608/256–5551) offers low-cost domestic and international airline tickets, mostly for flights departing from Chicago, and rail passes. Other travel agencies catering to students include **TMI Student Travel** (1146 Pleasant St., Watertown, MA 02172, tel. 617/661–8187 or 800/245–3672), and **Travel Cuts** (187 College St., Toronto, Ont. M5T 1P7, tel. 416/979–2406).

Discount Cards For discounts on transportation and on museum and attractions admissions, buy the **International Student Identity Card** (ISIC) if you're a bona fide student or the **International Youth Card** (IYC) if you're under 26. In the United States the ISIC and IYC cards cost $16 each and include basic travel-accident and illness coverage and a toll-free travel assistance hot line. Apply to **CIEE** (*see above*, tel. 212/661–1414; the application is in *Student Travels*). In Canada the cards are available for $15 each from **Travel Cuts** (*see above*). In the United Kingdom they cost £5 and £4 respectively at student unions and student travel companies, including Council Travel's London office (28A Poland St., London W1V 3DB, tel. 0171/437–7767). You will find it well worthwhile to have the card endorsed with the **CIEE Travelsave Stamp** (£7), which entitles holders to discounts of at least 25% on standard passenger rates, and up to 50% off mainline rail fares, provincial bus journeys, B&I Ferry services to the United Kingdom, and Aran Island boats. Travel stamps are available from the **Union of Students International Travel (USIT)** (19 Aston Quay, Dublin 2, tel. 01/679–8833 or 01/778117, fax 01/778908; Market Parade, Cork, tel. 021/270900, fax 021/272469; 36–37 George's St., Waterford, tel. 051/72601, fax 051/71723; Central Buildings, O'Connell St., Limerick, tel. 061/415064, fax 061/416472). Ask USIT about other student discounts, which include "standby" theater tickets and cultural discounts. They also have details of self-catering accommodations available on Irish university campuses (Dublin, Cork, Limerick, Galway) during university vacations.

Hostelling A **Hostelling International** (HI) membership card is the key to more than 5,000 hostels in 70 countries; the sex-segregated, dormitory-style sleeping quarters, including some for families, go for $7 to $20 a night per person. Membership is available in the United States through **Hostelling International-American Youth Hostels** (HI-AYH, 733 15th St. NW, Suite 840, Washington, DC 20005, tel. 202/783–6161), the United States link in the worldwide chain, and costs $25 for adults 18 to 54, $10 for those under 18, $15 for those 55 and over, and $35 for families. Volume 1 of the *AYH Guide to Budget Accommodation* lists hostels in Europe and the Mediterranean ($13.95, including postage). HI membership is available in Canada through **Hostelling International-Canada** (205 Catherine St., Suite 400, Ottawa, Ont. K2P 1C3, tel. 613/748–5638) for $26.75, and in the United Kingdom through the **Youth Hostel Association of England and Wales** (Trevelyan House, 8 St. Stephen's Hill, St. Albans, Herts. AL1 2DY, tel. 0727/855215) for UK£9.

Tour Operators **Contiki** (300 Plaza Alicante, #900, Garden Grove, CA 92640, tel. 714/740–0808 or 800/266–8454) specializes in package tours for travelers 18 to 35.

Traveling with Children

The Irish love children and will go to great lengths to make them welcome. Many hotels offer baby-sitting facilities, and most will supply a cot, given advance warning. The Irish Tourist Board's *Accommodation Guide* (£4) lists hotels, guest houses, and bed-and-breakfasts indicating those that are "family friendly" with special facilities for children. Most hotel restaurants and many pub restaurants have a children's menu, and can supply a high chair if necessary. Unlike Great Britain, Irish licensing laws allow children under 14 into pubs—although they may not consume alcohol on the premises until they are 18—a boon if you are touring by car, as pubs make an ideal lunch or tea break. Children are usually expected to leave by about 7 PM. While most attractions and bus and rail journeys offer a rate of half-price or less for children, look for "family tickets" which may work out cheaper.

Publications *Newsletter* ***Family Travel Times,*** published 10 times a year by **Travel With Your Children** (TWYCH, 45 W. 18th St., New York, NY 10011, tel. 212/206–0688; annual subscription $55), covers destinations, types of vacations, and modes of travel. TWYCH also publishes *Cruising with Children* ($22) and *Skiing with Children* ($29).

Books *Great Vacations with Your Kids,* by Dorothy Jordon and Marjorie Cohen ($13; Penguin USA, 120 Woodbine St., Bergenfield, NJ 07621, tel. 800/253–6476), and *Traveling with Children—And Enjoying It,* by Arlene K. Butler ($11.95 plus $3 shipping per book; Globe Pequot Press, Box 833, 6 Business Park Rd., Old Saybrook, CT 06475, tel. 800/243–0495, or 800/962–0973 in CT), help plan your trip with children, from toddlers to teens. *Innocents Abroad: Traveling with Kids in Europe,* by Valerie Wolf Deutsch and Laura Sutherland ($15.95 or $4.95 paperback, Penguin USA, *see above*), covers child- and teen-friendly activities, food, and transportation.

Tour Operators **Grandtravel** (6900 Wisconsin Ave., Suite 706, Chevy Chase, MD 20815, tel. 301/986–0790 or 800/247–7651) offers tours for people traveling with their grandchildren. The catalogue, as charmingly written and illustrated as a children's book, positively invites armchair traveling with lap-sitters aboard.

Getting There *Airfares* On international flights, the fare for infants under age 2 not occupying a seat is generally either free or 10% of the accompanying adult's fare; children ages 2 to 11 usually pay half to two-thirds of the adult fare. On domestic flights, children under age 2 not occupying a seat travel free, and older children currently travel on the "lowest applicable" adult fare.

Baggage In general, infants paying 10% of the adult fare are allowed one carry-on bag, not to exceed 70 pounds or 45 inches (length + width + height) and a collapsible stroller; check with the airline before departure, because you may be allowed less if the flight is full. The adult baggage allowance applies for children paying half or more of the adult fare.

Safety Seats The FAA recommends the use of safety seats aloft and details approved models in the free leaflet **"Child/Infant Safety Seats Recommended for Use in Aircraft"** (available from the FAA, APA–200, 800 Independence Ave. SW, Washington, DC 20591, tel. 202/267–3479); Information Hot Line, tel. 800/322–7873). Airline policy varies.

U.S. carriers allow FAA-approved models bearing a sticker declaring their FAA approval. Because these seats are strapped into regular passenger seats, airlines may require that a ticket be bought for an infant who would otherwise ride free.

Facilities Aloft Some airlines provide other services for children, such as children's meals and freestanding bassinets (only to those with seats at the bulkhead, where there's enough legroom). Make your request when reserving. Biannually the February issue of *Family Travel Times* details children's services on three dozen airlines ($12; *see above*). "Kids and Teens in Flight" (free from the U.S. Department of Transportation's Office of Consumer Affairs (R-25, Washington, DC 20590, tel. 202/366-2220) offers tips for children flying alone.

Hints for Travelers with Disabilities

Only in the last few years has Ireland made any progress in providing facilities for the disabled such as ramps and accessible toilets. Public trasportation also lags behind. But, visitors with disabilities will often find that what is lacking in technology is compensated by the helpful attitude of the general public.

Organizations The **National Rehabilitation Board** (25 Clyde Rd., Dublin 4, tel. 01/668-4181, fax 01/660-9935) is the statutory body with responsibility for people with disabilities in Ireland. They publish two free guides: The *Accommodation Guide for Disabled Persons*, which has descriptions of establishments that are suitable for wheelchair users with the assistance of one helper, and *Dublin: A Guide for Disabled Persons*, which tells you about facilities and concessions for people with disabilities in Ireland. The **Irish Wheelchair Association** (Aras Chuchulain, Blackheath Dr., Clontarf, Dublin 3, tel. 01/833-8241, fax 01/833-3273) can help if you need to borrow or repair a wheelchair.

Several organizations provide travel information for people with disabilities, usually for a membership fee, and some publish newsletters and bulletins. Among them are the **Information Center for Individuals with Disabilities** (Fort Point Pl., 27-43 Wormwood St., Boston, MA 02210, tel. 617/727-5540 or 800/462-5015 in MA between 11 AM and 4 PM, or leave message; TTY 617/345-9743); **Mobility International USA** (Box 10767, Eugene, OR 97440, tel. and TTY 503/343-1284, fax 503/343-6812), the U.S. branch of an international organization based in Britain (*see below*) that has affiliates in 30 countries; **MossRehab Hospital Travel Information Service** (tel. 215/456-9603, TTY 215/456-9602); the **Travel Industry and Disabled Exchange** (TIDE, 5435 Donna Ave., Tarzana, CA 91356, tel. 818/344-3640, fax 818/344-0078); and **Travelin' Talk** (Box 3534, Clarksville, TN 37043, tel. 615/552-6670, fax 615/552-1182).

In the United Kingdom Important information sources include the **Royal Association for Disability and Rehabilitation** (RADAR, 12 City Forum, 250 City Rd., London EC1V 8AF, tel. 0171/250-3222), which publishes travel information for people with disabilities in Britain, and **Mobility International** (228 Borough High St., London SE1 1JX, tel. 0171/403-5688), an international clearinghouse of travel information for people with disabilities.

Travel Agencies and Tour Operators **Flying Wheels Travel** (143 W. Bridge St., Box 382, Owatonna, MN 55060, tel. 507/451-5005 or 800/535-6790) is a travel agency that specializes in domestic and worldwide cruises, tours, and independent travel itineraries for people with mobility problems.

Publications Several free publications are available from the U.S. Consumer Information Center (Pueblo, CO 81009): "New Horizons for the Air Traveler with a Disability" (include Dept. 608Y in the address), a U.S. Department of Transportation booklet describing changes resulting from the 1986 Air Carrier Access Act and from the 1990 Americans with Disabilities Act; and the Airport Operators Council's "Access Travel: Airports" (Dept. 5804), which describes facilities and services for people with disabilities at more than 500 airports worldwide.

Travelin' Talk Directory (*see* Travelin' Talk, *above*) was published in 1993. This 500-page resource book ($35 check or money order with a money-back guarantee) is packed with information for travelers with disabilities.

Twin Peaks Press (Box 129, Vancouver, WA 98666, tel. 206/694–2462 or 800/637–2256) publishes the *Directory of Travel Agencies for the Disabled* ($19.95), listing more than 370 agencies worldwide. Add $2 for shipping.

Hints for Older Travelers

The Irish Tourist Board has a free booklet, "Golden Holidays," that lists places that offer price reductions for one- to seven-night stays for the over 55s. These are mostly higher-end hotels, but the packages can mean significant savings.

Organizations The **American Association of Retired Persons** (AARP, 601 E St. NW, Washington, DC 20049, tel. 202/434–2277) provides independent travelers who are members of the AARP (open to those age 50 or older; $8 per person or couple annually) with the Purchase Privilege Program, which offers discounts on lodging, car rentals, and sightseeing, and arranges group tours, cruises, and apartment living through AARP Travel Experience from American Express (400 Pinnacle Way, Suite 450, Norcross, GA 30071, tel. 800/927–0111 or 800/745–4567).

Two other organizations offer discounts on lodgings, car rentals, and other travel products, along with such nontravel perks as magazines and newsletters: the **National Council of Senior Citizens** (1331 F St. NW, Washington, DC 20004, tel. 202/347–8800; membership $12 annually) and **Mature Outlook** (6001 N. Clark St., Chicago, IL 60660, tel. 800/336–6330; $9.95 annually).

Note: For reduced rates, mention your senior-citizen identification card when booking hotel reservations, not when checking out. At restaurants, show your card before you're seated; discounts may be limited to certain menus, days, or hours. If you are renting a car, ask about promotional rates that might improve on your senior-citizen discount.

Educational Travel The nonprofit **Elderhostel** (75 Federal St., 3rd Floor, Boston, MA 02110, tel. 617/426–7788) has offered inexpensive study programs for people 60 and older since 1975. Held at more than 1,800 educational and cultural institutions, courses cover everything from marine science to Greek myths and cowboy poetry. Participants generally attend lectures in the morning and spend the afternoon sightseeing or on field trips; they live in dormitory-type lodgings. Fees for two- to three-week international trips—including room, board, and transportation from the United States—range from $1,800 to $4,500.

Publications *The 50+ Traveler's Guidebook: Where to Go, Where to Stay, What to Do,* by Anita Williams and Merrimac Dillon ($12.95, St. Martin's Press, 175 5th Ave., New York, NY 10010), is available in bookstores and offers many useful tips. "The Mature Traveler" (Box 50820, Reno, NV 89513, tel. 702/786-7419; $29.95), a monthly newsletter, contains many travel deals.

Hints for Gay and Lesbian Travelers

Organizations The **International Gay Travel Association** (Box 4974, Key West, FL 33041, tel. 305/292-0217 or 800/999-7925 or 800/448-8550), which has 700 members, will provide you with names of travel agents and tour operators who specialize in gay travel. The **Gay & Lesbian Visitors Center of New York Inc.** (135 W. 20th St., 3rd Floor, New York, NY 10011, tel. 212/463-9030 or 800/395-2315; $100 annually) mails a monthly newsletter, valuable coupons, and more to its members.

Tour Operators and Travel Agencies The dominant travel agency in the market is **Above and Beyond** (3568 Sacramento St., San Francisco, CA 94118, tel. 415/922-2683 or 800/397-2681). Tour operator **Olympus Vacations** (8424 Santa Monica Blvd., #721, West Hollywood, CA 90069, tel. 310/657-2220) offers all-gay-and-lesbian resort holidays. **Skylink Women's Travel** (746 Ashland Ave., Santa Monica, CA 90405, tel. 310/452-0506 or 800/225-5759) handles individual travel for lesbians all over the world and conducts two international and five domestic group trips annually.

Publications The premier international travel magazine for gays and lesbians is **Our World** (1104 N. Nova Rd., Suite 251, Daytona Beach, FL 32117, tel. 904/441-5367; $35 for 10 issues). **Out & About** (tel. 203/789-8518 or 800/929-2268; $49 for 10 issues, full refund if you aren't satisfied) is a 16-page monthly newletter with extensive information on resorts, hotels, and airlines that are gay-friendly.

Further Reading

History For two intriguing studies of Irish culture and history, consult Constantine FitzGibbon's *The Irish in Ireland* and Sean O'Faolain's *The Irish: A Character Study*, which traces the history of Ireland from Celtic times. J.C. Beckett's *The Making of Modern Ireland*, a concise introduction to Irish history, covers the years between 1603 and 1923. *Modern Ireland*, by R.F. Foster, spans the years between 1600 and 1972. An up-to-date analysis of the making of modern Ireland can be found in *Ireland 1912–1985 Politics and Society*, by J. J. Lee. For an acclaimed history of Irish nationalism, try Robert Kee's *The Green Flag*.

Special-Interest Readers can choose from several volumes on a specific region. Peter Somerville-Large's *Dublin* is packed with anecdotes relating to the famed Irish city. *Georgian Dublin*, by Desmond Guinness, the founder of the Irish Georgian Society, explores the city's architecture, with photographs and plans of Dublin's most admirable buildings. The most up-to-date work on the Aran Islands is Tim Robinson's award-winning *The Stones of Aran: Pilgrimage*. Robinson has also written a long introduction to the Penguin edition of J.M. Synge's 1907 classic, *The Aran Islands*. Tomas Ó Crohán's *The Islandman* provides a good background on Dingle and the Blasket Islands.

Autobiography Several autobiographical accounts by both Irish natives and foreign visitors offer unique perspectives on Ireland. Deborah Tall's *The Island of the White Cow* chronicles five years spent with an Irish professor on an island off the coast of Connemara. In *An Only Child* and *My Father's Son,* Frank O'Connor, a well-known fiction writer, recounts his years as an Irish revolutionary and later as an intellectual in Dublin during the 1920s. Niall Williams and Christine Breen, an American-Irish couple who started anew by moving to the County Clare countryside, recount their experiences in *O Come Ye Back to Ireland* and *When Summer's in the Meadow.* In *Round Ireland in Low Gear,* Eric Newby, a British travel writer, writes of his bicycle journey with his wife around the Emerald Isle. Christy Brown's *My Left Foot,* recently made into an award-winning film, is the autobiographical account of an artist crippled with cerebral palsy.

Fiction Ireland has a long, impressive history of great novelists and story writers. For a literary history exploring the influence of Ireland's changing landscape on its writers, look at *A Writer's Ireland,* by William Trevor. Samuel Beckett fills his story collection *More Pricks than Kicks* with Dublin characters; if you enjoy literary gamesmanship, you may also want to try Beckett's trilogy—*Molloy, Malone Dies,* and *The Unnamable.* James Joyce, one of the most acclaimed writers of the 20th century, is renowned for *Ulysses,* a classic, linguistically innovative work, which follows a group of Dublin characters through the course of a single day; shorter introductions to Joyce's writing include *A Portrait of the Artist as a Young Man* and *Dubliners,* a story collection.

If you're drawn to tales of unrequited love, turn to Elizabeth Bowen's stories and her novel, *The Last September,* set in Ireland during the Irish Civil War. Coming-of-age novels include *Under the Eye of the Clock,* a somewhat autobiographical work by Christopher Nolan, which takes as its subject a handicapped youth discovering the pleasures of language, and *Fools of Fortune,* by William Trevor, which treats the loss of an ideal childhood, brought about by a changing political climate.

Thomas Flanagan's *The Year of the French* is a historical novel about the people of County Mayo, who revolted in 1798 with the help of French revolutionaries. *A Nest of Simple Folk,* by Sean O'Faolain, follows three generations of an Irish family between 1854 and 1916. Leon Uris's *Trinity* covers the years 1840–1916, as seen through the eyes of British, Irish Catholic, and Ulster Protestant families. Jennifer Johnston, admired for her verbal economy, sets her best novels (including *The Captains and the Kings, The Gates,* and *How Many Miles to Babylon*) in the declining world of the Anglo-Irish "big house" in the early 20th century. In *No Country for Young Men,* Julia O'Faolain writes of two Irish families struggling to overcome the effects of the Irish Civil War. In John McGahern's prize-winning novel *Amongst Women,* modern-day Ireland attempts to reconcile itself to the upheavals of the early years of this century. For a more contemporary look at life in urban Ireland, try the phenomenally successful Roddy Doyle: **The Snapper** and the **Commitments** were recently filmed; his latest, **Paddy Clarke Ha Ha Ha** is sure to follow.

If you prefer reading more magical novels, take a look at James Stephens's *A Crock of Gold,* a charming and wise fairy tale written for adults, and Flann O'Brien's *At Swim-Two-Birds,* a surrealistic tale full of Irish folklore.

Edna O'Brien writes often about romantic relationships in a trilogy of short novels titled *The Country Girls* and a collection of stories called *A Fanatic Heart.* Other superbly crafted story collections, full of acute observations of Ireland's social and political landscape, include Benedict Kiely's *The State of Ireland,* Mary Lavin's *Col-*

lected Stories, Frank O'Connor's *Collected Stories*, and William Trevor's *Stories*.

Theater Ireland claims a range of fine playwrights as well. Samuel Beckett, who moved from Ireland to Paris and began writing in French, is the author of the comic modernist masterpiece *Waiting for Godot*, among many other plays. *The Importance of Being Ernest* is perhaps the most acclaimed work of Oscar Wilde, a major proponent of "art for art's sake" and a dramatist, poet, and wit of the late 19th century. Among the many plays of George Bernard Shaw, who grew up in Dublin, are *Arms and the Man*, *Major Barbara*, *Pygmalion*, and *Saint Joan*.

The history of Irish theater includes a good number of controversial plays, such as J.M. Synge's *The Playboy of the Western World*, which was considered morally outrageous at the time of its opening in 1907, and is appreciated today for its poetic language. Sean O'Casey wrote passionately about social injustice and working-class characters around the time of the Irish Civil War in such plays as *The Plough and the Stars* and *Juno and the Paycock*. *The Quare Fellow*, by Brendan Behan, challenged accepted mores in the 1950s and at the time could only be produced in London. Behan is also well known for his play *The Hostage* and for *Borstal Boy*, his memoirs. Two more recently recognized playwrights are Hugh Leonard (*Da* and *A Life*) and Brian Friel (*Philadelphia, Here I Come!*, *The Faith Healer*, and *Dancing at Lughnasa*), whose work often illuminates Irish small-town life.

Poetry The most celebrated Irish poet is William Butler Yeats, whose poems often describe the Irish landscape, including the Sligo and Coole countryside. A favorite poet among the Irish is Patrick Kavanagh, whose distinguished career was devoted to writing exceptionally about ordinary lives. *The Collected Poems* of Derek Mahon and Seamus Heaney's *Selected Poems* are both highly recommended. Mahon won the Irish Times–Aer Lingus Literary prize in 1993 and is currently based in New York. Heaney is considered one of the most compelling Irish poets since Yeats; Northern Ireland serves as the setting for many of his recent poems.

Periodical *Ireland of the Welcomes* (United States and Canada: Box 2745, Boulder, CO 80322; Europe and elsewhere: Box 84, Limerick, Ireland), a magazine published six times a year by the Irish Tourist Board, features articles on aspects of Irish culture and travel, including driving tours.

Arriving and Departing

Flights are either nonstop, direct, or connecting. A **nonstop** flight requires no change of plane and makes no stops. A **direct** flight stops at least once and can involve a change of plane, although the flight number remains the same; if the first leg is late, the second waits. This is not the case with a **connecting** flight, which involves a different plane and a different flight number.

From North America by Plane

Irish Republic *Airports and Airlines* The main point of arrival for transatlantic flights is **Shannon Airport** (tel. 061/471444) on the west coast, 25½ kilometers (16 miles) west of Limerick City. Shannon is a small airport, with only one terminal building. As of this year, not all transatlantic flights touch down at

Shannon; almost half fly nonstop to Dublin. The Shannon–Dublin flight takes 30–40 minutes.

Dublin Airport (tel. 01/705–2222) is 10 kilometers (6 miles) north of the city center. Most of the flights it handles come from Europe, the United Kingdom, or inside Ireland. It has just one terminal building, but the well-stocked duty-free shop boasts an unusual concession: Books can be sold prior to their official launch, so you can pick up the latest work by your favorite author even before it's been reviewed in the papers.

Only three airlines have regularly scheduled flights from the United States: **Aer Lingus** (tel. 212/557–1110 or 800/223–6537), **Aeroflot** (tel. 202/429–4922 or 305/871–3611), and **Delta** (tel. 404/715–5000 or 800/221–1212). **Aer Lingus** flies from New York or Boston to Shannon and Dublin. **Aeroflot** flies from Washington, DC, Chicago, and Miami to Shannon. **Delta** flies from Atlanta to Shannon or Dublin. A number of charter flights operate from the United States and Canada between May and September. No direct commercial flights are scheduled from Canada.

Flying Time From Boston, a transatlantic flight to Shannon takes five hours and 35 minutes; from New York, 6½ hours; from Chicago or Washington, DC, 7½ hours; from Miami, nine hours. For flights continuing to Dublin, there is a 45-minute stopover at Shannon and then a 40-minute onward flight.

Northern Ireland *Airports* No scheduled transatlantic flights are available to Belfast, although some charter flights can be found in the summer. For details, check with your travel agent. Otherwise, pick up a connecting flight to Belfast in Shannon, Dublin, London, or Manchester. Two airports serve Belfast: **Belfast International Airport at Aldergove** (tel. 01232/229271), 24 kilometers (15 miles) from the city, handles all international traffic; **Belfast Harbour Airport** (tel. 01232/57754), 6½ kilometers (4 miles) from the city, handles local and United Kingdom flights only. In addition, **Eglinton,** Derry's airport, receives flights from Manchester and Glasgow in the United Kingdom (Loganair).

Cutting Costs The Sunday travel section of most newspapers is a good source of information for deals. When booking, particularly through an unfamiliar company, call the Better Business Bureau and your local or state Consumer Protection Bureau to find out whether any complaints have been registered against the company, pay with a credit card if you can, and consider trip-cancellation and default insurance (*see* Insurance, *above*). A helpful resource is *Airfare Secrets Exposed*, by Sharon Tyler and Matthew Wonder (Universal Information Publishing, $16.95), available in bookstores.

Promotional Airfares Less expensive fares, called promotional or discount fares, are round-trip and involve restrictions, which vary according to the route and season. You must usually buy the ticket—commonly called an APEX (advance purchase excursion) when it's for international travel—in advance (seven, 14, or 21 days are usual), although some of the major airlines have added no-frills, inexpensive flights to compete with new bargain airlines on certain routes.

With the major airlines the cheaper fares generally require minimum and maximum stays (for instance, over a Saturday night or at least seven and no more than 30 days). Airlines generally allow some return date changes for a $25 to $50 fee, but most low-fare tickets are nonrefundable. Only a death in the family would prompt the airline to return any of your money if you cancel a nonrefundable ticket. However, you can apply an unused nonrefundable ticket toward a new ticket, again with a small fee. The lowest fare is subject to availability, and only a small percentage of the plane's total seats will be sold at that price. Contact the U.S. Department of Transportation's Office of Consumer Affairs (I–25, Washington, DC 20590, tel. 202/366–2220) for a copy of "Fly-Rights: A Guide to Air Travel in the U.S." *The Official Frequent Flyer Guidebook*, by Randy Petersen (4715-C Town Center Dr., Colorado Springs, CO 80916, tel. 719/597–8899 or 800/487–8893; $14.99, plus $3 shipping and handling) yields valuable hints on getting the most for your air-travel dollars. Also new and helpful is *202 Tips Even the Best Business Travelers May Not Know*, by Christopher McGinnis, president of the Travel Skills Group (Box 52927, Atlanta, GA 30355, tel. 404/659–2855; $10 in bookstores.)

Consolidators Consolidators or bulk-fare operators—"bucket shops"—buy blocks of seats on scheduled flights that airlines anticipate they won't be able to sell. They pay wholesale prices, add a markup, and resell the seats to travel agents or directly to the public at prices that still undercut the airline's promotional or discount fares (higher than a charter ticket but lower than an APEX ticket, and usually without the advance-purchase restriction). Moreover, some consolidators sometimes give you your money back. Carefully read the fine print detailing penalties for changes and cancellations. If you doubt the reliability of a company, call the airline once you've made your booking and confirm that you do, indeed, have a reservation on the flight.

The biggest U.S. consolidator, C.L. Thomson Express, sells only to travel agents. **UniTravel** (Box 12485, St. Louis, MO 63132, tel. 314/569–0900 or 800/325–2222) is a well-established consolidator that sells to the public.

Charter Flights Charters usually have the lowest fares and the most restrictions. Departures are limited and seldom on time, and you can lose all or most of your money if you cancel. (The closer to departure you cancel, the more you lose, although sometimes you will be charged only a small fee if you supply a substitute passenger.) The charterer, on the other hand, may legally cancel the flight for any reason up to 10 days before departure; within 10 days of departure, the flight may be canceled only if it becomes physically impossible to operate it. The charterer may also revise the itinerary or increase the price after you have bought the ticket, but if the new arrangement constitutes a "major change," you have the right to a refund. Before buying a charter ticket, read the fine print for the company's refund policy and details on major changes. Money for charter flights is usually paid into a bank escrow account, the name of which should be on the contract. If you don't pay by credit card, make your check payable to the escrow account (unless you're dealing with a travel agent, in which case, his or her check should be payable to the escrow account). The U.S. Department of Transportation's Office of Consumer Affairs (*see above*) can answer questions on charters and send you its "Plane Talk: Public Charter Flights" information sheet.

Charter operators may offer flights alone or with ground arrangements that constitute a charter package. You must typically book charters through your travel agent.

Discount Travel Clubs Travel clubs offer members unsold space on airplanes, cruise ships, and package tours at as much as 50% below regular prices. Membership may include a regular bulletin or access to a toll-free hot line giving details of available trips departing from three or four days to several months in the future. Most also offer 50% discounts off hotel rack rates, but double-check with the hotel to make sure it isn't offering a better promotional rate independent of the club. Clubs include **Discount Travel International** (114 Forrest Ave., Suite 203, Narberth, PA 19072, tel. 215/668–7184; $45 annually, single or family); **Entertainment Travel Editions** (Box 1014, Trumbull, CT 06611, tel. 800/445–4137; price ranges $28–$48); **Great American Traveler** (Box 27965, Salt Lake City, UT 84127, tel. 800/548–2812; $29.95 annually); **Moment's Notice Discount Travel Club** (425 Madison Ave., New York, NY 10017, tel. 212/486–0503; $45 annually, single or family); **Privilege Card** (3391 Peachtree Rd. NE, Suite 110, Atlanta GA 30326, tel. 404/262–0222 or 800/236–9732; domestic annual membership $49.95, international, $74.95); **Travelers Advantage** (CUC Travel Service, 49 Music Sq. W, Nashville, TN 37203, tel. 800/548–1116; $49 annually, single or family); and **Worldwide Discount Travel Club** (1674 Meridian Ave., Miami Beach, FL 33139, tel. 305/534–2082; $50 annually for family, $40 single).

Publications The newsletter "Travel Smart" (40 Beechdale Rd., Dobbs Ferry, NY 10522, tel. 800/327–3633; $44 a year) has a wealth of travel deals in each monthly issue. The monthly "Consumer Reports Travel Letter" (Consumers Union, 101 Truman Ave., Yonkers, NY 10703, tel. 800/234–1970) is filled with information on travel savings and indispensable consumer tips.

Enjoying the Flight Fly at night if you're able to sleep on a plane. Because the air aloft is dry, drink plenty of fluids while on board. Drinking alcohol contributes to jet lag, as do heavy meals. Bulkhead seats, in the front row of each cabin—usually reserved for people who have disabilities, are elderly, or are traveling with babies—offer more legroom, but trays attach awkwardly to seat armrests, and all possessions must be stowed overhead.

Smoking Since February 1990, smoking has been banned on all domestic flights of less than six hours' duration; the ban also applies to domestic segments of international flights aboard U.S. and foreign carriers. On U.S. carriers flying to Ireland and other destinations abroad, a seat in a no-smoking section must be provided for every passenger who requests one, and the section must be enlarged to accommodate such passengers if necessary as long as they have complied with the airline's deadline for check-in and seat assignment. If smoking bothers you, request a seat far from the smoking section.

Foreign airlines are exempt from these rules but do provide no-smoking sections, and some nations, including Canada as of July 1, 1993, have gone as far as to ban smoking on all domestic flights; other countries may ban smoking on flights of less than a specified duration. The International Civil Aviation Organization has set July 1, 1996, as the date to ban smoking aboard airlines worldwide, but the body has no power to enforce its decisions.

From North America by Ship

The days are long gone when almost all transatlantic liners made Cobh in County Cork their first or last European port of call. The only regular visitor these days is Cunard's superliner, the *Queen Elizabeth 2*. For the last several years, she has called at Cobh in mid-July and mid-September en route to New York (a four-day trip). Confirmation of her 1995 schedule will be available early in 1995 from **Cunard** (555 5th Ave., New York, NY 10017, tel. 212/661–7777 or 800/528–6273). Inclusive tours that coincide with the sailings are offered by **O'Connor Fairways Tours** (800 2nd Ave., New York, NY 10017, tel. 212/661–0550 or 800/288–7609). Rates for the four-day crossing start at around $2,650 per person, including one-way economy-class airfare.

From Britain by Plane

Irish Republic *Airports and Airlines* The major carriers are **Aer Lingus, Ryanair,** and **British Midland Airways.** There are 12 flights every day to Dublin from Heathrow, operated by Aer Lingus. **British Airways** also operates frequent daily flights to Dublin from Gatwick. In addition, flights to Dublin leave from Birmingham, Bristol, East Midlands, Liverpool, Manchester, Leeds/Bradford, Newcastle, Edinburgh, and Glasgow. **Virgin** has flights to Dublin from London City Airport most days. There are at least two flights daily from Heathrow to Shannon, and three flights daily to Cork. There are also flights to Cork from Birmingham, Manchester, and Plymouth, and to Dublin, Cork, Knock, Shannon, and Waterford from Luton or Stansted (near London). Flying time to most Irish airports is around one hour.

The wide range of fares reflects the number of flights available—and the competition: Most fares offer good value. Contact in Britain: **Aer Lingus** (tel. 0181/899–4747); **British Midland Airways** (tel. 0171/589–5599); **Loganair** (tel. 0141/889–3181); **Manx Airlines** (tel. 0800/626627); **Ryanair** (tel. 0171/435–7101); **SAS** (tel. 0171/734–4020); **Virgin** (tel. 01293/747146).

Northern Ireland *Airports and Airlines* Frequent flights are scheduled daily to Belfast from Heathrow, Gatwick, and 17 other U.K. airports. Flights take about 1¼ hours from London. British Airways' and British Midland Airways' shuttle services from London are walk-on, no-reservation flights, and the airlines claim that no passenger is turned away; another plane would be employed if necessary. **Belfast International Airport at Aldergrove** is Northern Ireland's principal air arrival point. **Belfast Harbour Airport** receives flights from U.K. provincial airports and from Luton. **Eglinton Airport,** a few miles from Derry City, receives flights from Manchester and Glasgow. Call 01504/261911, 01504/44100, or 01504/43813 for a taxi into town.

British Airways and **British Midland Airways** (*see above*) operate most flights into Belfast, but cheaper flights may be available from **Brittania** (tel. 01582/405737) or **Loganair** (*see above*).

From Britain by Ferry, Car, and Bus

By Ferry *Irish Republic* Getting to Ireland by train/ferry is simple, though slow. There are two principal routes: to Dublin from Holyhead on the Isle of Anglesea, and to Rosslare from Fishguard or Pembroke in Wales. Two companies sail the Dublin route: **B&I** (tel. 0171/491–8682) and **Stena Sealink** (tel. 01223/647047), whose ferries go to Dun Laoghaire, a few miles south of Dublin. Buses into Dublin from the docks meet all the ferries. Total journey time from London is around 11 hours.

B&I operates the Pembroke–Rosslare route; Stena Sealink operates the Fishguard–Rosslare route. To connect with the Fishguard sailings, take one of the many direct trains from London (Paddington). A connecting train at Rosslare will get you to Waterford by about 8:30 PM, to Cork by about midnight. For the Pembroke sailings, you have to change at Swansea. Sailing time for both routes is 4½ hours.

Swansea Cork Ferries (tel. 01792/456116) operate a service between Swansea and Cork from April to December. The crossing takes 12 hours, but easy access by road to both ports make this longer sea route a good choice for motorists heading for the Southwest.

The cost of your trip can vary substantially. It's worth spending time with a travel agent and comparing prices carefully; flying is sometimes cheaper, and fares to Dublin are cheapest. Book well in advance at peak periods. Students and others under 26 should take advantage of the cheap fares offered by **Eurotrain.**

Northern Ireland Car ferries run to Northern Ireland from the Scottish port of Stranraer. Trains leave London (Euston) for Stranraer Harbour several times a day. **Sealink Ferries** crosses the water to the port of Larne, where you pick up a train to Belfast. The whole trip is around 13 hours. Much faster and more convenient is the **SeaCat** (tel. 01304/240241), a huge car-ferry catamaran that crosses from Stranraer right into Belfast in just 1½ hours. There is also a nine-hour crossing from Liverpool to Belfast, operated by **Belfast Ferries** (tel. 01519/226234). Trains leave London (Euston) for Liverpool throughout the day.

If you're traveling from Dublin, you can take the Belfast–Dublin Express, which goes nonstop between the two cities in two hours. Six trains run daily in both directions (only three on Sundays).

By Car
Irish Republic All ferries on *both* principal routes to Ireland—Holyhead–Dublin and Fishguard/Pembroke–Rosslare—take cars. Fishguard and Pembroke are relatively easy to reach by road. The car trip to Holyhead, on the other hand, is sometimes difficult: Delays on the A55 North Wales coastal road are not unusual. For reservations and information, *see* From Britain by Ferry, *above.*

Northern Ireland Car ferries to Belfast leave from the Scottish port of Stranraer and the English city of Liverpool; those to Larne leave from Stranraer and Cairnryan. For more information, *see* From Britain by Ferry, *above.*

Many roads from the Republic into Northern Ireland have been closed, but a score of legitimate crossing points exist. There's an army checkpoint, with relatively few formalities, at all approved frontier posts. The fast N1/A1 connects Belfast to Dublin (161 kilometers/100 miles); there are sometimes border delays on this road.

By Bus
Irish Republic Numerous bus services run between Britain and Ireland. Those traveling with young children should beware the long hours and possible delays. All bus services use either the Holyhead–Dublin or Fishguard/Pembroke–Rosslare ferry routes.

Services are operated by **National Express** (tel. 0171/724–0741), the consortium of bus companies, and **Slattery's** (tel. 0171/482–1604), an Irish bus operator. Supabus, as the National Express buses are known, has services from all major British cities to more than 90 Irish destinations. Slattery's has services from London, Manchester, Liverpool, and North Wales to Dublin, Tralee, Listowel, Ennis, and Galway.

Northern Ireland Buses to Belfast run from London and from Birmingham, making the Stranraer–Larne crossing. For reservations and information, contact **National Express.**

Staying in the Irish Republic

Getting Around

By Plane Ireland is not a large country, so air travel does not play a big role in internal travel, although a recent increase has led to the development of provincial airports, some of which now have regular daily flights from the United Kingdom. They can be very useful to vacationers. See relevant regional chapters for details on airports at Kerry, Sligo Town, Galway, Knock, Waterford, and Derry City (for Donegal). Several flights daily are scheduled between Shannon, Dublin, and Cork, with a flying time of 30–40 minutes between each city. There is also a regular air service to all three of the Aran Islands from Connemara Airport. Operated by Aer Arann, the flights take six minutes, weather permitting (*see* Chapter 9, The West).

By Car A car is the ideal way to explore Ireland, a country of small back roads and predominantly rural attractions. Roads are generally good, although four-lane two-way roads are the exception rather than the rule. Most National Primary Routes (designated by the letter "N") have two lanes with generous shoulders on which to pass. In general, traffic is light, especially off the national routes, but it's wise to slow down on the smaller, often twisty roads. The general speed limit in Ireland is 96 kph (60 mph) on the open road and either 48 kph (30 mph) or 64 kph (40 mph) in urban areas. Beware of high speeds on the back roads; you may find a herd of cattle or a donkey and a cart around the next corner.

Road signs are generally in both English and Irish (Gaelic). The Republic is currently undergoing a slow changeover from miles to kilometers. As a general rule, distances on the new *green* signposts (which cover most of the National Primary Routes) are in kilometers. Most white signposts are older, and they give the distance in miles. (The *new* white signposts, however, give the distance in kilometers!)

Because of the coexistence of both old and new signs, the route number is not always referred to on the signpost, particularly on National Secondary Roads (also N-numbered routes) or Regional roads (R-numbered routes). In these cases, the name of the next town on your itinerary is more important to know than the route number: Neither small local signposts nor local people refer to roads by their relatively new official numbers.

The Irish, like the British, drive on the left-hand side of the road. Safety belts must be worn by the driver and front passenger, and children under 12 must travel in the back. It is compulsory for motorcyclists and their passengers to wear helmets.

Traffic signs are the same as in the rest of Europe, and roadway markings are standard. Note especially that a continuous white line down the center of the road prohibits passing. Barred markings on the road and flashing yellow beacons indicate a crossing, where pedestrians have the right of way. At a junction of two roads of equal importance, the driver to the right has the right of way.

Despite the relatively light traffic, parking in towns can be a problem. Signs with the letter *P* indicate that parking is permitted; a stroke through the *P* warns you to stay away or you'll be liable for a fine of £15 to £40. In Dublin and Cork, parking lots are your best bet, but check the rate first in Dublin; they can vary wildly.

Drunk-driving laws are strict. Ireland has a Breathalyzer test, which the police can administer anytime. If you refuse to take it, the odds are you'll be prosecuted anyway. As ever, the best advice is not to drink if you're going to be driving.

By Train Ireland's train services are operated by the state-owned **Irish Rail (Iarnrod Éireann),** the rail division of **CIE (Coras Iompair Éireann).** They are generally reliable, reasonably priced, and comfortable. All the principal towns are easily reached from Dublin, though services between provincial cities are roundabout. If you want to go to Cork City from Wexford, for example, you have to go via Limerick Junction. It is often quicker, though perhaps less comfortable, to take a bus.

Most mainline trains have two classes: standard and superstandard. Round-trip tickets are usually cheapest. For information on long-term passes, *see* Rail Passes in Before Yo Go, *above*.

By Bus Long-distance bus services are operated by Irish Bus **(Bus Éireann),** a subdivision of CIE. Bus Éireann also provides local services in Cork, Galway, Limerick, and Waterford. Expressway bus services, with the most modern buses, cover the major routes throughout the country.

Buses are a cheap and flexible way of exploring the countryside. Outside the peak season, services are limited, and some routes (e.g., Killarney–Dingle) disappear altogether. There is often only one service a day on the express routes—and one a week to some of the more remote villages! To ensure that your proposed bus journey is feasible, buy a copy of Bus Éireann's timetable—50p from any bus terminal.

Many of the destination indicators on bus routes are in Irish, so make sure you get on the right bus. Asking someone to translate is often the best way to avoid a mishap.

By Ferry Ferries provide two very useful shortcuts. If you're traveling from County Kerry to County Clare and the West of Ireland, you can take the ferry from Tarbert (in County Kerry), leaving every hour on the half hour. Going the other way, ferries leave from Killimer (in County Clare) every hour on the hour. The boat takes 30 minutes to cross the Shannon Estuary. It costs £5 per car, £1 for foot passengers.

A 10-minute car ferry crosses the River Suir between Ballyhack in County Wexford and Passage East in County Waterford. It saves you a boring drive through New Ross on the N25 and also introduces you to two pretty fishing villages, Ballyhack and Arthurstown. It operates continuously during daylight hours and costs £3 per car, 80p for foot passengers.

The Cork Harbour Crossing is a scenic route that allows those traveling from west Cork or Kinsale to Cobh and the east coast to bypass the city center. The five-minute car ferry runs from Glenbrook (near Ringaskiddy) in the west to Carrigaloe (near Cobh) in the east and operates continuously from 7:15 AM to 12:45 AM daily. It costs £3 per car, 60p for foot passengers.

Many, but not all, of Ireland's offshore islands can be reached by ferry. There are regular services to the Aran Islands from Galway City, Rossaveal in County Galway, and Doolin in County Clare. Ferries also sail to Inishbofin off the Galway coast and Arranmore off the Donegal coast, and to Bere, Sherkin, and Cape Clear islands off the coast of

County Cork. The islands are all small enough to explore on foot, so the ferries are for foot passengers and bicycles only. Other islands—the Blaskets and the Skelligs in Kerry, Rathlin, and Tory off the Donegal coast—can be reached by private arrangements with local boatmen (*see* relevant regional chapters). Full details on ferries to the islands are available in *Islands of Ireland* (£1.50) from the Irish Tourist Board.

Telephones

Public pay phones are in all towns and villages. They can be found in street booths and in bars and shops, some of which display a sign saying "You can phone from here." There are currently at least three different models of pay phones in operation; read the instructions or ask for assistance. A local call costs 20p for three minutes; long-distance calls within Ireland are around 60p for three minutes. If you have trouble getting through, dial 10 for operator assistance; however, if the operator has to connect your call it will cost at least one-third more than direct dial. Do not make calls from your hotel room unless it's absolutely necessary. Practically all hotels add 200% to 300% to the cost of a call. Dublin is changing to seven-digit numbers; a six-digit number should be intercepted and the extra digit announced. If not, check by dialing 1190. Certain Galway City numbers will also be changed in '94-'95; if you do not get through the first time, call 1190.

International calls can be made from only the most up-to-date pay phones. Most towns and villages have this facility in the post office; in Cork City and Dublin, the general post offices are located on Oliver Plunkett Street and O'Connell Street, respectively.

International dialing codes can be found in all telephone directories. The international prefix from Ireland is 16. Calls to the United States cost about £4.50 for three minutes, less after 10 PM and on Saturdays, Sundays, and bank holidays. Calls to Canada cost the same.

AT&T and **MCI** both have direct calling systems in Ireland. AT&T's **USADirect** allows you to call collect or charge calls from abroad to your AT&T calling card. From Ireland, dial 1800/550000 to reach an operator; rates are $1.71 for the first minute and $1.09 for each additional minute, plus a $2.50 service charge. From Northern Ireland, dial 0800/890011; rates are $1.51 for the first minute, 99¢ for each additional minute, plus the service charge. For more information, tel. 412/553–7458, ext. 314 (collect from outside the United States), or 800/874–4400. MCI charges nearly identical rates and works the same way as AT&T; dial 1800/551001 in Ireland, 0800/890222 in Northern Ireland. For more information, call 800/950–5555, or in Ireland 800/551001 (MCI) or 800/550000 (AT&T).

For calls to Great Britain, dial 0044 before the exchange code, and drop the initial zero of the local code. Calls to Britain cost about £2.10 for three minutes, about one-third less after 6 PM and on Saturdays, Sundays, and public holidays.

For operator assistance, dial 10. To call the international operator, 114. The international operator covers collect calls, person-to-person calls, and calls to ships.

For international telegrams, dial 196; for audio conference calls, dial 114. To find out the time, dial 1191. For directory inquiries within Ireland and Northern Ireland, dial 1190; within Britain dial 1197.

Mail

Postal Rates Airmail rates to the United States and Canada are 52p for letters, 38p for postcards. Mail to all European countries goes by air automatically, so airmail stickers or envelopes are not required. Rates are 32p for letters, 28p for postcards. These rates may change before or during 1995, so be sure to check them.

Receiving Mail Mail can be held for collection at any post office free of charge for up to three months. It should be addressed to the recipient "c/o Poste Restante." In Dublin, use the General Post Office (O'Connell St., Dublin 1, tel. 01/872–8888).

Tipping

In some hotels and restaurants a service charge of around 12%—rising to 15% in some plush spots—is added to the bill. If in doubt, ask whether service is included. In places where it is included, tipping is not necessary unless you have received particularly good service. But if there is no service charge, add a minimum of 10% to the total.

Tip taxi drivers about 10% of the fare displayed by the meter. Hackney cabs, who make the trip for a prearranged sum, do not expect tips. There are few porters and plenty of baggage trolleys at airports, so tipping is usually not an issue; if you use a porter, 50p is the minimum. Tip hotel porters about 50p per large suitcase. Hairdressers normally expect about £1. You don't tip in pubs, but for waiter service in a bar or hotel lounge or a Dublin lounge bar, leave about 20p.

Opening and Closing Times

Most shops are open from 9 to 5:30 or 6, Monday–Saturday. Once a week—normally Wednesday, Thursday, or Saturday—they shut at 1 for the afternoon. These times do *not* apply to Dublin, and they can vary from region to region, so it's best to check locally. Larger shopping malls usually stay open late once a week—generally until 9 PM—on Thursday or Friday.

Banks are open from 10 to 4, Monday–Friday. In small towns they may close from 12:30 to 1:30. They remain open until 5 one afternoon per week; again, the day of week varies locally. Pubs are open Monday–Saturday from 10:30 AM to 11:30 PM May–September, closing at 11 the rest of the year. The famous Holy Hour, which required city pubs to close from 2:30 to 3:30, was abolished in 1988, and afternoon opening is now at the discretion of the owner or manager; few bother to close. On Sundays, the pubs are open from 12:30 to 2 and from 4 to 11. All pubs are closed on Christmas Day and Good Friday, but hotel bars are open for guests.

Shopping

Few visitors leave Ireland without purchasing at least a tweed hat or a hand-knitted Aran jersey, and if not one of these, then a linen tablecloth or a piece of Waterford crystal. All these items are reasonably priced investments that, given a little care, will last a lifetime.

The range of Irish-made goods available in the shops is no longer limited to the ethnic and the traditional: High-fashion garments and household goods combining traditional materials with the very best modern designs have added new dimension to the market.

The best selection of shops and the most sophisticated goods are found in Dublin—especially if high fashion and antiques are among your tastes. Cork City offers less choice but quite a few surprises, and Galway features crafts galleries and offbeat boutiques.

Most crafts shops sell a mix of goods drawn from all over the country. If you're after something a little different, keep an eye open for signs indicating "craft workshops": There are at least 20 of them around the country. In each of these workshops, you'll find independent craftspeople selling directly from their studios. Crafts workshops have helped increase the variety and quality of Irish souvenirs.

U.S. and Canadian visitors get a refund of the **value added tax** (VAT), which currently accounts for a hefty 21% of the purchase price of many goods and 12.5% of those that fall outside the luxury category. Apart from clothing, most items of interest to visitors, right down to ordinary toilet soap, are rated at 21%. Most crafts outlets and department stores operate a system called Cashback, which enables U.S. and Canadian visitors to collect VAT rebates in the currency of their choice at Dublin or Shannon Airport on departure. Otherwise, refunds can be claimed from individual stores after returning home. Forms for the refunds must be picked up at the time of purchase, and the form must be stamped by customs before leaving Ireland. Most major stores deduct VAT at the time of sale if goods are to be shipped overseas; however, there is a shipping charge.

Antiques Top-quality antiques shops are concentrated around Dublin's Grafton Street area, but it's still possible to pick up modestly priced pieces of 18th- and 19th-century silver, 19th-century pewter, and antique period furniture elsewhere in the country. Try Cork City, Castlecomer, Kilkenny, Galway City, and Limerick.

Crystal Irish lead crystal is justifiably world famous. The best known of all, Waterford Glass, is on sale all over Ireland in department stores and crafts shops. The demand is so great that substantial export orders can take weeks or even months to fill. Check out the lesser known crystals—Cork, Dublin, Kinsale, Tipperary, Tyrone, and Galway crystal—and the less formal uncut glass from Jerpoint and Stoneyford.

Drinkables Irish whiskey has an altogether different taste from Scotch whisky, and a different spelling, too. Well-known brands include Powers, Paddy, Jameson, and Bushmills. There are also two excellent Irish liqueurs: Irish Mist, which contains whiskey and honey, and Bailey's Irish Cream, a concoction of whiskey and cream, sometimes drunk on ice as an aperitif.

Edibles Smoked salmon can vary greatly in taste and quality. Make sure it's wild salmon, not farmed, and if the label tells you what sort of wood it was smoked over, opt for oak chips. A cheaper but also delicious alternative is smoked trout. Whole farmhouse cheeses like St. Killian's—a Camembert-like pasteurized cheese—are becoming popular gifts. More exotic and more expensive are the handmade farmhouse cheeses, each from an individual herd of cows. Milleens, Durrus, and Gubbeen are all excellent, though strong when ripe. A milder alternative is the Gouda-like Coolea cheese, found in most duty-free shops.

Jewelry Dublin and Cork City are the best spots for antique jewelry, but do not despair if the prices there are beyond your resources. Beautiful modern reproductions of such Celtic treasures as the Tara brooch are on sale for a fraction of the antique price. Other good buys include Claddagh friendship rings and beautiful pieces made by modern silversmiths using polished Connemara marble.

Knitwear Aran sweaters were developed by the women of the Aran Isles to provide a working garment that was warm, comfortable, and weatherproof. The religious symbols and folk motifs woven into distinctive patterns once enabled local people to identify one another's families and localities. Even today, no two Arans are alike: If you want to buy a handknit, take your time and wait till you find one that really takes your fancy. After all, it should last the rest of your life. Cheaper and less durable Arans are described as "hand-loomed," which is just another way of saying "machine-made," so be sure you are getting what you want. There is a wealth of other types of sweaters: classic blue fisherman's rib sweaters, homespun hand-dyed handknits, picture sweaters, and sophisticated mohair garments.

Linen A pure linen blouse, like an Aran sweater, can last forever. Designs are classic, so they will not date. Linen handkerchiefs for men make useful gifts. Damask tablecloths and crochet-linen place mats make ideal wedding gifts.

Rugs, Shawls, and Blankets Crafts shops sell fleece floor rugs made of goat- or sheepskin. Handwoven shawls made from unspun, undyed wool are even more luxurious than mohair, though not as easy to find. Lightweight woolen blankets in traditional plaids are always popular gifts.

Tableware The Arklow pottery in County Wicklow is famous for its fine china, sold at all major department stores. Belleek, on the border with Northern Ireland, produces delicate bone china, which is widely collected. Tableware by Ireland's many ceramic artists, with striking modern designs, can be a real bargain, especially if four or six place settings are ordered at once.

Tweeds The best selection of traditional tweeds is still found in the specialist tweed shops of Counties Galway and Donegal. Weavers can also be found at work in Kerry, Dublin, County Wicklow, and elsewhere in Connemara. Tweeds vary a good deal in type, from rugged-looking garments to clothes with jewellike colors that have been popularized by Avoca Handweavers.

Sports and the Outdoors

Participant Sports
Bicycling The combination of numerous side roads and very light traffic makes Ireland an attractive destination for cyclists. The less energetic can concentrate their itinerary on the relatively flat central area of the country; those who brave the mountains of the West and Southwest will be rewarded by magnificent scenery and a wonderfully varied coastline.

Boardsailing and Dinghy Sailing Boardsailing has caught on in the last 10 years. There are numerous locations suitable for the sport: inland lakes, river estuaries, and sheltered harbors. Dinghies can be hired at most of Ireland's sailing schools, which will also teach you how to sail them in five-day courses. Bring your own wet suit, if possible; you'll need it, even in July and August.

Cruising Fully equipped boats are rented by the week on the Shannon and the Grand Canal. It's a simple and relaxing holiday, allowing you to explore lesser-known, but beautiful, corners of Ireland. Boats can accommodate up to eight people and have showers, toilet, and well-equipped galleys. Prices start at about £190 per week.

Fishing Ireland is well known as a game-angling resort: Wild Atlantic salmon, wild brown trout, and sea trout abound in the rivers, lakes, and estuaries, and offshore is the deep-sea challenge. Coarse fishing (for all fish that are not trout or salmon) is also available. The salmon season is normally from January 1 to September 30, but dates vary from one district to another. The best period for sea trout is June to late September.

Permits are necessary on privately owned waters or club waters: the latter will cost £5–£15 a day for salmon, £2–£10 for trout. There is no closed season for coarse angling. Besides the permit for the use of a certain stretch of water, those who wish to fish for salmon and sea trout by rod and line must also have a state national license (£25 annually, or £10 for 21 days), available in some tackle shops or from the **Central Fisheries Board** (Balngowan House, Mobhi Boreen, Glasnevin, Dublin 9, tel. 01/837–9206). No license is required for brown trout, rainbow trout, or coarse fish, including pike. Sea angling is available on rocks and piers around the coast. A day of offshore fishing from an open launch costs about £20 per head.

Golf There are nearly 250 golf courses in Ireland, from world-famous championship courses to scenic nine-hole courses. About 50 of these courses have opened in the last two years. Choose between the challenging links of the Atlantic coast, the more subtle layouts on the eastern seaboard, and the mature parklands of the inland courses. Killarney's two courses are unmatched for scenery; Arnold Palmer says **Portmarnock** (near Dublin) is among the world's best. He himself designed the course at **Tralee,** and there's a second 18-hole course at **Ballybunion** designed by Robert Trent Jones. The historic **Royal Dublin** on the shores of Dublin Bay is another course not to be missed. For a more detailed description of courses around the country, *see* Chapter 3, Irish Greens.

Greens fees average about £15 but can be as much as £55 at the most prestigious places.

Hiking The Irish Tourist Board provides free information sheets on long-distance paths, set up throughout the country over the last few years with the consent of local landowners. Routes are indicated by trail markers and signposts. Most are between 30 and 60 kilometers (18 and 37 miles), with the exception of the **Wicklow Way,** the first to be opened and still one of the best, which is 137 kilometers (85 miles) long. Alternatively, you can plan your own walks with the help of a good touring map: Ireland is an excellent walking country, with its mild climate and virtually traffic-free byroads.

Horseback Riding Several riding stables offer all-inclusive holidays combining long days in the saddle with home-cooked food and bed-and-breakfast accommodations. Most stables charge about £10 for an hour's ride, a little more if tuition is included.

Jogging Early risers are amazed to find that no one in rural Ireland drives much before 8 AM, turning the place into a jogger's paradise. Phoenix Park is the place to go in Dublin; most hotels are a 10- to 15-minute jog from the park. The many long sandy beaches around the country are popular with runners, but you may find yourself sharing space with a string of racehorses: Beaches are favorite spots for practice gallops.

Sailing There are several companies around the coast offering bare-boat charters to experienced skippers, but cruises must be booked well in advance. The coastline is endlessly varied and remarkably uncrowded compared with, say, the southern coast of England. Formalities are minimal, harbor dues are low, and facilities are extremely simple.

Tennis Tennis has gained in popularity over the last few years, but it's not really suited to the rainy Irish climate. More than 100 hotels and guest houses have hard or grass courts—usually just one or two—and the cities and larger towns have public courts. Fees are low, but finding equipment to rent can be difficult.

Spectator Sports

Gaelic Games Gaelic football and hurling are played in most parts of the Republic. Gaelic football is an extremely fast and rough form of football (closer to rugby than American football), which involves two teams of 15 who kick and run around a field with a round, soccerlike ball. The rules are complicated, but the skill and speed of the players make it exciting and impressive to watch, even if you don't quite understand what is going on. Hurling, considered by many to be the fastest field game in the world, also involves two teams of 15 who use a three-foot wooden stick with a broad base to aggressively catch and hurl a leather-covered ball toward goalposts; the game can result in several injuries. Gaelic games are organized by the Irish Gaelic Athletic Association (GAA) and can be observed free of charge at local GAA fields and sports centers around the Republic. Inter-provincial games and All-Ireland finals are played in July and August at the GAA stadiums in Cork and Dublin. Croke Park in Dublin is the setting for the end of the annual All-Ireland finals. Tickets for these matches can be hard to obtain, but the events are televised.

Horse Racing There is a horse race somewhere in Ireland almost every day of the year. The flat season runs from March to November; steeplechases are held throughout the year. Several courses—about 28 of them altogether—are within easy reach of Dublin. Irish classics are run at the Curragh in County Kildare, and the **Irish Grand National** is at Fairyhouse in County Meath. Some of the best meetings are held in the summer at smaller courses: Killarney in mid-July, Galway in late July–early August, Tramore in mid-August, Tralee in late August, and Listowel at the end of September.

Beaches

Ireland has over 3,200 kilometers (2,000 miles) of coastline, with an abundance of beaches—or strands, as they are called locally. Some are small rocky coves with shingle where you can enjoy utter privacy; others, like Tramore, County Waterford; Courtown, County Wexford; Salthill, near Galway; and Bundoran in County Donegal are long sandy beaches fronting bustling resort towns. The Irish like their beaches kept simple, so you will not find much in the way of facilities outside the resort towns. At most, there might be a public toilet, or an isolated hotel or bar, but don't count on it. If bathing is unsafe there will probably be a notice to that effect, or a red flag. You should not assume that bathing is safe in the absence of any warnings: Ask locally to make sure. Few people swim outside the months of July and August, but beaches remain popular with walkers and runners throughout the year.

Dining

The quality and variety of Ireland's restaurants has improved greatly in the past 15 years. The soggy vegetables and overcooked meat that once characterized Irish hotel and restaurant food are becoming increasingly obsolete. A new generation of imaginative chefs has begun to capitalize on what are some of the best raw materials in the world for gourmet cooking.

Lavish hospitality has always been a characteristic of Irish society, and the generous portions offered in Irish hotels and restaurants prove the point. Breakfast starts with fruit juice, followed by cereal or porridge, and then a *fry* consisting of bacon, sausage, egg, and tomato, with local variations such as potato cakes or black pudding. This is accompanied by toast or soda bread (whole-meal bread made with bicarbonate of soda and buttermilk instead of yeast), orange marmalade, and a pot of tea or coffee.

Many people find that this is enough to keep them going until tea-time or early dinner. Others tide themselves over with a one-dish pub lunch—an open smoked-salmon sandwich or a bowl of Irish stew (mutton, potatoes, onions, and sometimes carrots and parsley, simmered together).

Most towns have at least one restaurant of some sort. In less commercial areas, such as the midland counties, the best bet is usually the local hotel. Irish pubs have taken over the role filled elsewhere by cafés and coffee shops. Most pubs serve tea, coffee, sandwiches, and bar food—a one- or two-course meal served informally at your table or collected from the buffet (referred to as a "carvery")—a popular and money-saving alternative to a formal restaurant meal. In general, the best bar food is found in those attached to a formal restaurant or hotel. Requests for tea, coffee, and food (and the presence of small children) are generally not welcome in the evenings, when the main business becomes alcoholic drinks.

Many Irish people eat their main meal at midday, so most restaurants are open at lunchtime—from 12:30 to 2:30. Dinner service begins at around 6, but 7:30 to 8:30 is the most popular time to eat. Reservations are advisable on weekends and during the peak season at many small Irish restaurants. In all but the fanciest spots, informal dress is acceptable—casual but neat. This does not include beachwear, shorts, skimpy or tattered T-shirts, or torn or cutoff jeans.

Ireland is renowned for its dairy products, its meat, and its seafood. The dominant school of cooking, best described as Irish with a French accent, combines classic French and traditional Irish cooking, and includes some nouvelle cuisine influence as well. Irish cream and butter are blended with wine and herbs to produce light sauces that complement rather than dominate the excellent meat and fish. Steak, which appears on nearly all menus, is usually a reliable option. A juicy, charbroiled sirloin needs no embellishment—but if you want it rare, be sure to ask. Lamb and pork are both of high quality. Lamb is at its best from March to September, which is also the best time for seafood—lobster, crab, prawns, fresh salmon, trout, mussels, scallops, sea urchin, sole, brill, monkfish, turbot, skate, and, except in summer, oysters. The coast is never more than an hour and a half away, so you can expect all seafood to be freshly caught and high in quality.

Winter travelers can look forward to sampling the game. Venison, from mountainous areas like Kerry and Wicklow, is a famous specialty beginning in October; the pheasant season starts on November 1 and lasts for three months. Quail, woodcock, wild duck, rabbit, and hare all appear frequently on the menus of the better restaurants—either roasted or in pâtés and pies.

A number of exceptionally good Irish cheeses have been developed recently, notably Cashel Blue, St. Killian, Coolea, Milleens, Gubbeen and Durrus. Many fruits and vegetables are still imported, but outside Dublin the best places limit themselves to the locally grown seasonal crop, often homegrown by organic methods. The more old-fashioned restaurants offer at least two kinds of potatoes, sometimes more: chipped (french-fried), boiled, sautéed, mashed, and *dauphinois* (sliced in a gratin dish), to name a few. But usually the Irish like their potatoes plainly boiled in their jackets, piled high on a serving dish and bursting open. Peel one on your side plate, smother it with butter, and you'll understand why.

Nowadays most restaurants have a license to serve alcoholic drinks. There are two kinds of licenses: A wine license allows a restaurant to serve wine and wine-based drinks such as sherry and vermouth; however, it cannot serve spirits or beer of any sort. Restaurants with a full license can serve the full range of liquors and beers.

To help visitors on a budget, more than 360 restaurants participate in a tourist menu scheme. Up to three three-course menus are available at set prices—£7, £8.50, and £12. The Irish Tourist Board's *Tourist Menu* (75p) gives full details on participating restaurants. Some places limit this menu to lunchtime and early evening.

Lodging

Accommodations in Ireland range from deluxe renovated castles and stately homes to thatched cottages and farmhouses. Room standards are rising all the time, especially in the middle and lower price ranges. Pressure on hotel space reaches a peak from June to September, but it's always a good idea to reserve in advance. Many Irish hotels can be booked directly from the United States. Ask your travel agent for details. The **Irish Tourist Board's Central Reservations Service** in Dublin (14 Upper O'Connell St., Dublin 1, tel. 01/874–7733, fax 01/874–3660) makes reservations in hotels and other accommodations; local tourist offices do the same. **Tel-A-Bed Ireland** (tel. 01/284–1765, fax 01/284–1751) is a computerized advance booking service for credit card holders. There is a £3 booking fee.

The Irish Tourist Board (ITB) has an official grading system and publishes a list of "approved accommodations," which includes hotels, guest houses, bed-and-breakfasts, farmhouses, hostels, and camping parks. For each accommodation, the list gives a maximum charge that no hotel may exceed without special authorization. Prices must be displayed in every room, so if the hotel oversteps its limit, do not hesitate to complain to the hotel manager and/or the ITB.

Ideally, visitors should sample a range of accommodations. The very expensive country-house hotels and renovated castles offer a unique combination of luxury and history. Less impressive, but equally charming, are the provincial inns and country hotels with simple but adequate facilities. Many visitors, seeking to meet a wide cross section of Irish people, prefer a different B&B every night. Others enjoy the simplicity of self-catering for a week or two in a thatched cottage.

Guest Houses Some guest houses, particularly in Dublin, are hard to distinguish from hotels, and they're cheaper as well; however, less is expected in terms of public rooms, bars, restaurants, and front-desk service, so, in general, guest houses are not for the business traveler. Most are owner-run with good standards of cleanliness and hospitality; they're often ideal for vacationers. They must have at least five bedrooms, but in Dublin and major cities they're often much bigger; many offer private bathrooms, and TV and direct-dial phones in the bedrooms. The larger guest houses are sometimes built above an existing bar or restaurant. Others are part of a large family home. The cost at these places may or may not include an optional evening meal.

Bed-and-Breakfasts This is a well-established and well-regulated form of accommodation in Ireland. B&Bs are classified by the Irish Tourist Board as either town homes, country homes, or farmhouses. Town and country B&Bs are listed in the ITB's illustrated *Town & Country Homes—Guest Accommodation* (£2.50). Many now have at least one bedroom with a bathroom, but don't expect this as a matter of course. B&Bs often charge an extra 50p–£1 for a bath or shower. If this is taken in the family bathroom, you should ask first whether you can use the facility. Many travelers do not bother booking a B&B in advance. They are so plentiful in rural areas that it's often more fun to leave the decision open, allowing yourself a choice of final destinations for the night.

Farm Vacations Many Irish farms offer holidays with part board or full board on a weekly basis. These are listed in the ITB's illustrated publication *Farm Holidays in Ireland* (£2). You will notice at once from the booklet that very few Irish farmhouses are picturesque: They are more likely to be modern bungalows or undistinguished two-story houses than creeper-clad Georgian mansions—though exceptions do exist. Room and part board—breakfast and an evening meal—costs from £165 per week.

Cottages In more than 100 locations there are clusters of holiday cottages for rent. Although often built in the traditional style, they have central heating and all the other conveniences of modern life. A three-bedroom cottage equipped for six adults is around £250 per week in mid-season. It is essential to reserve in advance. The ITB's publication *Self-Catering* lists individual properties and clusters of traditional cottages available by the week. For information on booking, contact the ITB.

Home Exchange You can find a house, apartment, or other vacation property to exchange for your own by becoming a member of a home-exchange organization, which then sends you its annual directories listing available exchanges and includes your own listing in at least one of them. Arrangements for the actual exchange are made by the two parties to it, not by the organization.

For more information, contact the **International Home Exchange Association** (IHEA, 41 Sutter St., Suite 1090, San Francisco, CA 94104, tel. 415/673–0347 or 800/788–2489). Principal clearinghouses include: **Homelink International** (Box 650, Key West, FL 33041, tel. 800/638–3841), with thousands of foreign and domestic listings, publishes four annual directories plus updates; the $50 membership includes your listing in one book. **Intervac International** (Box 590504, San Francisco, CA 94159, tel. 415/435–3497) has three annual directories; membership is $62, or $72 if you want to receive the directories but remain unlisted. **Loan-a-Home** (2 Park La., Apt. 6E, Mount Vernon, NY 10552, tel. 914/664–7640) specializes in long-term exchanges; there is no charge to list your home, but the directories cost $35 or $45 depending on the number you receive.

Apartment and Villa Rentals If you want a home base that's roomy enough for a family and comes with cooking facilities, a furnished rental may be the solution. It's generally cost-wise, too, although not always—some rentals are luxury properties (economical only when your party is large). Home-exchange directories do list rentals—often second homes owned by prospective house swappers—and some services search for a house or apartment for you (even a castle if that's your fancy) and handle the paperwork. Some send an illustrated catalogue and others send photographs of specific properties, sometimes at a charge; up-front registration fees may apply.

Among the companies are **At Home Abroad** (405 E. 56th St., Suite 6H, New York, NY 10022, tel. 212/421–9165); **Europa-Let** (92 N. Main St., Ashland, OR 97520, tel. 503/482–5806 or 800/462–4486); **Property Rentals International** (1 Park West Cir., Suite 108, Midlothian, VA 23113, tel. 804/378–6054 or 800/220–3332); and **The Invented City** (*see* IHEA, *above*).

Camping This is the cheapest way of seeing the country, and facilities for campers and caravaners are improving steadily. An abundance of coastal campsites compensates for the shortage of inland ones. All are listed in *Guest Accommodation* (£4), available from the ITB. Rates start at about £4 per tent, £6 per caravan overnight.

Youth Hostels **An Oíge** (The Irish Youth Hostels Association, 39 Mountjoy Sq., Dublin 1, tel. 01/363111) has a chain of 40 youth hostels ranging from a castle in Kilkenny to cottages at Killary Harbour on the edge of the Atlantic. You must have an International Youth Hostel card to stay in an Irish youth hostel, and it is advisable to book in advance if you're traveling in summer. Charges for adults are £5.90 per night in city hostels, around £4.50 in rural hostels. All have a curfew and are closed between 10 AM and 5 PM.

Another 93 hostels are linked together in the **Association of Independent Hostels.** These budget accommodations range from small cottages to rambling old mansions, each with an informal, friendly atmosphere. Some hostels have private rooms and all offer self-catering kitchens and hot showers. There is no late-night curfew at independent hostels, and no daytime closing rules either. Many have a small shop and offer evening meals of wholesome (often vegetarian) home-cooked food. For a copy of a leaflet listing Independent Hostels and their facilities and locations, write to **Patrick O'Donnell, Dooey Hostel** (Glencolumcille, County Donegal, tel. 073/30130).

Staying in Northern Ireland

Getting Around

By Car The road network in Northern Ireland is excellent and, outside Belfast, uncrowded. Road signs and traffic regulations conform to the British system. The speed limit is 48 kph (30 mph) in towns, 96 kph (60 mph) on country roads, and 112 kph (70 mph) on two-lane roads and motorways.

There are plenty of parking lots in the towns (usually free except in Belfast), and visitors are advised to use them. Control zones in town centers, where parking is prohibited, are indicated by yellow signs: CONTROL ZONE. NO UNATTENDED PARKING. An unattended car in a control zone is treated as a security risk.

If you are crossing into the Republic, be sure to use an approved road. Crossing the border on the clearly marked unapproved roads is strictly prohibited. Approved roads connect the following towns on either side of the border (the Northern Ireland town is first; the Republic town, second):

Newry–Greenore, Newry–Dundalk (via Killeen).

Armagh–Dundalk (via Newtown Hamilton).

Crossmaglen–Carrikmacross.

Armagh–Castleblayney, Armagh–Monaghan.

Roslea–Monaghan.

Enniskillen–Clones, Derrylin–Belturbet, Enniskillen–Swanlinbar.

Enniskillen–Manorhamilton, Enniskillen–Ballyshannon (via Belleek).

Kesh–Pettigo.

Castlederg–Castlefin, Strabane–Lifford.

Derry–St. Johnston.

Derry–Bridgend, Derry–Muff, Derry–Newton Hamilton.

Posts are normally staffed from 8 AM to 8 PM, and some are staffed until midnight. On both sides of the border, formalities are quick and friendly; a lengthier stop is more likely at a checkpoint a mile or so from either side of the border. North of the frontier you may be stopped by either the army or the police. Have your passport or driver's license handy.

By Train The state-owned **Northern Ireland Railways** has three main rail routes, all operating out of Belfast's **Central Station** (tel. 01232/230310). These are north to Derry, via Ballymena and Coleraine; east to Bangor along the shores of Belfast Lough; and south to Dublin and the Irish Republic.

Other than on the Dublin line, all trains are one class only, with reasonably priced fares similar to those in the Republic. The Belfast–Dublin nonstop express takes about two hours.

For information on long-term passes, *see* Rail Passes in Before You Go, *above*.

By Bus All services are operated by the state-owned **Ulsterbus** company. Services are generally good, with particularly useful links to those towns not served by train. In addition, there is a **Freedom of Northern Ireland** ticket costing U.K.£25 for seven days' unlimited travel. A one-day ticket costs U.K.£15. Ulsterbus also operates a wide range of bus tours. (For details, *see* Essential Information in Chapter 11.)

Telephones

Northern Ireland is part of the United Kingdom telephone system. A local call costs 10p.

If you are dialing Northern Ireland from the Republic, codes are different than they would be otherwise. For example, the code for Belfast is 01232 from anywhere within the United Kingdom including Northern Ireland, or indeed from anywhere in the world, but from the Republic of Ireland it's 0184. This is explained in detail in phone directories on both sides of the border. In the Republic, you can find the appropriate code for a Northern Ireland number either in the phone directory or by dialing 10. For all operator services in Northern Ireland, dial 100. (For details on international dialing, *see* Telephones in Staying in Ireland, *above*.)

Mail

Postal Rates Airmail rates to the United States and Canada are 39p for letters and 33p for postcards (not over 10 grams). To the rest of the United Kingdom and the Irish Republic, rates are 24p for first-class letters and 18p for second class. These rates may well increase before or during 1995.

Tipping

Northern Ireland follows Great Britain, rather than the rest of Europe, in keeping tipping to a minimum. In restaurants, check the bill to see if service is included. If it isn't, tip about 10% if you're satisfied with the service you've received. Taxi drivers don't normally expect tips, but again, tip about 10% of the fare if you think it's appropriate.

Opening and Closing Times

Shops in Belfast are open 9 to 5:30, Monday–Friday, with a late closing on Thursday, usually at 9 PM. Elsewhere, shops close for the afternoon once a week, usually Wednesday or Thursday, but it's best to check locally. In addition, most smaller shops close for an hour or so at lunch.

Bank hours are 9:30 to 12:30 and 1:30 to 3, Monday–Friday. All banks are closed on Saturdays.

Post offices are open 9 to 5:30, Monday–Friday, and 9 to 1 on Saturday. Some close for an hour at lunch.

Pubs in Northern Ireland are open from 11:30 AM to 11 PM Monday–Saturday, and 12:30 PM to 2 PM and 7 PM to 10 PM on Sundays. Sunday opening is at the owner's or manager's discretion.

Shopping

The range of Irish-made goods is roughly similar to that available in the Republic (*see* Staying in the Irish Republic, *above*). Most Irish linen is made in Northern Ireland; other items of interest include delicate Belleek porcelain, Carrickmacross lace, musical instruments (such as harps and bagpipes), Tyrone crystal, and silver jewelry and ornaments using polished Mourne granite. Keep an eye out also for traditionally woven tweeds and wall hangings—as well as clothing—designed by handweavers. Bushmills whiskey is made in County Antrim.

Sports and the Outdoors

Fishing With a long coastline (750 kilometers, 466 miles) on the Atlantic and the Irish Sea, Northern Ireland offers plenty of choices for shore angling and offshore excursions. Rivers and lakes, including large *loughs* such as Strangford, Neagh, and Erne, add to the variety.

To game fish in Northern Ireland, you need a rod license. The **Foyle Fisheries Commission** (FFC, 8 Victoria Rd., Londonderry BT47 2AB, tel. 01504/42100) distributes licenses for game fishing in the Foyle area, and the **Fisheries Conservancy Board** (FCB, 1 Mahon Rd., Portadown, Craigavon, Co. Armagh BT62 3EE, tel. 01762/334666) handles all other regions. A license costs between U.K.£5 and U.K.£10 for 15 days. You must also obtain a permit from the owner of the waters in which you plan to fish. Most of the waters are owned by the **Department of Agriculture** (Fisheries Division, Stormont, Belfast BT4 3PW, tel. 01232/63939) which charges about U.K.£10 for a 15-day permit, U.K.£3.50 for a daily one. If you plan to fish outside the jurisdiction of the Department of Agriculture, you must obtain a permit from one of the local clubs. For more information, and for Department of Agriculture permits and FFC and FCB rod licenses, contact the Northern Ireland Tourist Bureau (NITB).

Some of the same regulations apply to coarse fishing (for all fish that are not trout or salmon). A rod license is required by the FCB, though the cost is much less than that of the game-fishing license; the FFC requires no license for coarse fishing. In addition, you need a permit from the owner of the waters in which you plan to fish.

Golf Northern Ireland has 60 golf courses in a territory the size of Connecticut, including some of the most challenging and scenic golf courses in the world. In Newcastle, the **Royal County Down Golf Club,** which features two 18-hole courses, is considered one of the finest courses in the world. Visitors are welcome. In general, greens fees are modest (about U.K.£10 per day), and reductions are made for groups. There are plenty of caddies, but motorized carts are not available.

Hiking For serious hikers there is the challenge of the 790-kilometer (491-mile) **Ulster Way,** a footpath that travels through spectacular coastal scenery.

Horseback Riding and Pony Trekking These are popular sports throughout the area, particularly in the forest parks and the Glens of Antrim. Several Northern Ireland hunting clubs welcome visitors and will provide a mount if you have an introduction to the master of the hunt. This can be arranged through the NITB.

Sailing Two of the best places for sailing are Strangford Lough and Ballyholme Bay, Bangor. Lough Erne is a popular inland sailing spot; you can rent a craft at Kesh in County Fermanagh for sailing there.

Dining

Visitors can choose from a number of pleasant restaurants in Northern Ireland, mainly in the middle and lower price range. *Where to Eat* (U.K.£2.50), published by the Northern Ireland Tourist Board, contains a comprehensive list of places. Prices are notably lower than in the Republic, and there are often surprising differences in the style and presentation of food.

Lodging

Hotels and other accommodations in Northern Ireland are similar to those in the Republic of Ireland. The NITB publishes a complete list—called *Where to Stay* (U.K.£3.50)—of hotels, guest houses, farmhouses, bed-and-breakfasts, self-catering accommodations, youth hostels, and camping and trailer parks; prices and full information are included. There is more of a choice in the middle and lower price ranges than at the top.

Information on the nine hostels in Ulster is provided by **The Youth Hostel Association of Northern Ireland** (56 Bradbury Pl., Belfast, tel. 01232/324733). All hostels should be booked in advance for July and August.

Credit Cards

The following credit card abbreviations are used throughout this guide: AE, American Express; D, Discover; DC, Diners Club; MC, MasterCard (known as Access in Ireland and Northern Ireland); V, Visa. It's a good idea to call ahead to check current credit card policies.

Great Itineraries

Introduction to Scenic Ireland (One Week)

Although Ireland is not a large country, a week allows only enough time for a quick overview. A car is essential for this itinerary.

Day 1: Arrive in Shannon. Have a look at Bunratty Castle and Folk Park before heading south for Killarney. Take a break in Rathkeale for a tour of Castle Matrix.

Day 2: In Killarney, take a full-day organized tour through the Gap of Dunloe and on the Killarney lakes by jaunting car (pony and trap) and boat.

Day 3: Choose between the lush subtropical vegetation of the Ring of Kerry or the rugged mountains of the Dingle Peninsula. Both options involve a full-day trip, either by car or organized excursion from Killarney.

Day 4: Head for Galway City by crossing the Shannon estuary on the ferry from Tarbert to Killimer. Follow the coast road through Kilkee, Ennistymon, and Ballyvaughan past the spectacular Cliffs of Moher and into the extraordinary limestone landscape of the Burren.

Day 5: After a walk around Galway City, drive through the famous blue and purple Connemara landscape to Castlebar; then continue on to Sligo and "Yeats Country."

Day 6: Set off early for Dublin. After a lunch in one of Dublin's famous pubs, spend the afternoon on a walking and shopping tour of the City Center.

Day 7: Take the time to see the famous *Book of Kells* in Trinity College's Old Library (closed Sunday) before heading for the airport.

An Extended Tour of Scenic Ireland (Two Weeks)

The scenic contrasts within Ireland are remarkable. The classical splendor of the great buildings in and around Dublin, the rural simplicity of the West Coast, the lush vegetation of the Southwest, the ruggedness of Counties Sligo and Donegal, and the neatness of the Antrim Coast are all just a few hours' drive from one another. Listen for the astonishing variety of accents that you'll hear along the way—proof that there is no such thing as a "typical" Irish accent.

Day 1: Walk around Dublin City Center, taking time to see the *Book of Kells* at Trinity College and the State Apartments at Dublin Castle.

Day 2: Visit Boyne Valley by car or by organized tour, stopping at the Hill of Tara, Slane Castle, and the megalithic tombs at Newgrange, Knowth, and Dowth.

Day 3: Take a trip to County Wicklow, either by car or organized tour, taking in such sights as Powerscourt Estate, Glendalough, Mount Usher Gardens, and Russborough House at Blessington.

Day 4: Drive to Cork City via Kildare Town (stopping there perhaps to look at the National Stud or the Japanese Gardens) and the Rock of Cashel.

Day 5: Walk around Cork City and visit Kinsale, stopping there overnight to sample one of the latter's many fine restaurants.

Day 6: Proceed to Killarney with a short detour to Blarney if you wish to kiss the famous stone. Spend the afternoon riding around the Muckross Estate in a jaunting car.

Day 7: Either take a tour through the Gap of Dunloe by jaunting car and on the lakes by boat, or drive around the Ring of Kerry, one of Europe's premier scenic routes.

Day 8: Head north from Killarney, traveling up the West Coast toward Galway City. Cross the Shannon estuary by ferry from Tarbert to Killimer and follow the coast road through Kilkee, Ennistymon, and Ballyvaughan past the Cliffs of Moher to the extraordinary limestone landscape of the Burren.

Day 9: If the weather is fine, head for Rossaveale and take a day trip to the middle Aran Island, Inishman—or fly there from Connemara Airport. If the weather is unsuitable for visiting the Aran Islands, take a driving tour through the famous Connemara landscape, following the coast road to Clifden and returning to Galway City on the inland Maam Cross road.

Day 10: Head for Westport; for an unforgettable view of Clew Bay and its many islands, climb the mountain of Croagh Patrick. If the weather is unsuitable, take a drive to Achill Island, which is connected to the mainland by a highway.

Day 11: Drive through "Yeats Country" in County Sligo to Donegal Town, turning left at Donegal Town to visit Donegal tweed country—Ardara, Gweedore, and Dunfanaghy.

Day 12: Head through Letterkenny toward Derry City. Before crossing the border to Northern Ireland, stop at the Grianan of Aileach, a huge stone fort dating from 1700 BC. Drive through Derry City to the Causeway Coast, stopping overnight in Portrush or Bushmills.

Day 13: Spend the morning climbing over the Giant's Causeway and then drive through the Glens of Antrim to Belfast.

Day 14: Leave Belfast, and return over the border to the Republic, through Newry and Bundalk to Dublin.

Ireland by Rail (One Week)

All too many travelers who use Shannon as their gateway to Europe miss the opportunity of taking a quick look around Ireland before continuing their journey. This tour starts in Shannon and ends in Dublin, where you can either proceed by plane to mainland Europe or take a ferry to the United Kingdom. While not as flexible as travel by rental car, rail travel in Ireland is a less expensive alternative (especially on a rail pass). Your range of destinations can be extended by taking local buses and organized excursions.

Day 1: The bus from Shannon Airport to Limerick passes Bunratty Castle and Folk Park (both worth a look). Take a walk around old Limerick City and visit St. John's Castle and the city walls.

Day 2: Proceed by train to Killarney. After lunch, take either a half-day excursion to the Gap of Dunloe or (in bad weather) an organized orientation tour.

Day 3: Take an organized tour to either the Ring of Kerry or the Dingle Peninsula.

Day 4: Travel to Cork City by train. Explore the city on foot either before or after an organized excursion to Blarney Castle or a ride on the regular bus to the lovely port of Kinsale.

Day 5: Take the train to Kilkenny City and spend the day exploring this historic place.

Day 6: Get an early train to Dublin and allow a full day to explore the City Center on foot. Spend an evening at one of the traditional music pubs.

Day 7: Head for the airport or the ferry in the Dublin vicinity.

Great Irish Houses and Castles (8–12 Days)

Although it is physically possible to accomplish this tour in eight days, we suggest you allow three or four more days, if possible, to relieve the somewhat hectic pace. The itinerary is best undertaken between June and September, when the maximum number of houses are open to the public. Outside these months, you may often find that it is possible to view a house by phoning a day or so in advance and making an appointment, even if the house is officially closed. This tour will appeal to those with an interest in history, architecture, or interior decoration. You might wish to stay at one of the grand and often historic country-house hotels along the way.

Day 1: The Dublin Castle State Apartments and the Royal Hospital, Kilmainham, are the two must-sees in Dublin. A walk along the inner city stretch of the River Liffey provides excellent views of two of architect James Gandon's Georgian masterpieces, the Custom House and the Four Courts. South of the river, Georgian domestic town architecture at its best can be seen at Merrion Square and on the continuation of its east side, Fitzwilliam Street.

Day 2: Head north of Dublin to visit Slane Castle, Newbridge House, and Malahide Castle.

Day 3: Castletown House in Celbridge, County Kildare, is one of Ireland's most magnificent Georgian structures; it serves as the headquarters of the Irish Georgian Society, which works hard to preserve Ireland's Georgian heritage. Russborough House near Blessington, County Wicklow, has a good European art collection.

Day 4: Take the main road to Cork City, turning off at New Inn just beyond Monasterevin to visit Emo Court. You will pass the Rock of Cashel en route to Cahir, with a castle in the town center that is worth visiting.

Day 5: Riverstown House and Dunkathel House are both situated near the village of Glanmire, just outside the city on the Dublin road.

Day 6: A short detour from the main Killarney road will lead you to Blarney Castle and Blarney House. Muckross House in Killarney, a mid-Victorian manor house, is one of the least interesting on the tour, but it should be seen for its attractive location.

Day 7: From Killarney, head north to the Shannon estuary, on whose shore you will find Glin Castle, the ancestral home of the FitzGeralds. Take the Rathkeale road to Limerick in order to visit Castle Matrix; also stop at Cratloe Woods, on the other side of Limerick City, the only remaining 17th-century "longhouse" still inhabited. Stay overnight in or near Limerick City or Ennis.

Day 8: If you have enough time, visit Knappogue Castle and Bunratty Castle in the morning before heading for the airport.

2 Portraits of Ireland

Bogland

for T. P. Flanagan

By Seamus Heaney

Born in County Derry, Seamus Heaney is one of Ireland's most respected living poets. A new edition of his Selected Poems *appeared in 1990.*

We have no prairies
To slice a big sun at evening—
Everywhere the eye concedes to
Encroaching horizon,

Is wooed into the cyclops' eye
Of a tarn. Our unfenced country
Is bog that keeps crusting
Between the sights of the sun.

They've taken the skeleton
Of the Great Irish Elk
Out of the peat, set it up
An astounding crate full of air.

Butter sunk under
More than a hundred years
Was recovered salty and white.
The ground itself is kind, black butter

Melting and opening underfoot,
Missing its last definition
By millions of years.
They'll never dig coal here,

Only the waterlogged trunks
Of great firs, soft as pulp.
Our pioneers keep striking
Inwards and downwards,

Every layer they strip
Seems camped on before.
The bogholes might be Atlantic seepage.
The wet centre is bottomless.

Ireland at a Glance: A Chronology

ca. 6000 BC Mesolithic (middle Stone Age) hunter-gatherers migrate from Scotland to the northeastern Irish coast.

ca. 3500 BC Neolithic (new Stone Age) settlers (origins uncertain) bring agriculture, pottery, and weaving. They also build massive megaliths—stone monuments with counterparts in England (Stonehenge), Brittany (Carnac), and elsewhere in Europe.

ca. 700 BC Celtic tribes begin to arrive via Britain and France; they divide Ireland into "fifths" or provinces, including Ulster, Leinster, Connaught, Meath, and Munster.

ca. AD 100 Ireland becomes the center of Celtic culture and trade without being settled by the Romans.

432 Traditional date for the arrival of St. Patrick and Christianity; in fact, Irish conversion to Christianity began at least a century earlier.

ca. 500–800 Golden Age of Irish monasticism; as many as 3,000 study at Clonard (Meath). Irish missionaries carry the faith to barbarian Europe; art (exemplified by the *Book of Kells*, ca. 700) and Gaelic poetry flourish.

795 First Scandinavian Viking invasion; raids continue for the next 200 years. Viking towns founded include Dublin, Waterford, Wexford, Cork, and Limerick.

1014 Vikings decisively defeated at Clontarf by Irish troops under King Brian Boru of Munster. His murder cuts short hopes of a unified Ireland.

1066 Normans (French descendents of Viking invaders) conquer England and set their sights on Ireland as well.

1169 Dermot MacMurrough, exiled king of Munster, invites the Anglo-Norman adventurer Richard FitzGilbert de Clare ("Strongbow") to help him regain his throne, beginning a pattern of English opportunism and bad decisions by the Irish.

1172 Pope Alexander III confirms Henry II, king of England, as feudal lord of Ireland. Over the next two centuries, Anglo-Norman nobles establish estates, intermarry with the native population, and act in a manner similar to the neighboring Celtic chieftains. Actual control by the English crown is confined to a small area known as "the land of peace" or "the Pale" around Dublin.

1366 Statutes of Kilkenny attempt belatedly to enforce ethnic divisions by prohibiting the expression of Irish language and culture and intermarriage between the Irish and English, but Gaelic culture prevails, and the Pale continues to contract. Constant warfare among the great landowners keeps Ireland poor, divided, and isolated from the rest of Europe.

1477–1513 Garret Mor ("Gerald the Great") FitzGerald, eighth earl of Kildare, dominates Irish affairs as lord deputy (the representative of the English crown).

1494 Henry VII removes Kildare from office (he is soon reinstated), and initiates Statute of Drogheda (Poyning's Law), which is in force until 1782—Irish Parliament can only meet by consent of the king of England.

1534–40 Henry VIII's break with the Catholic Church leads to insurrection in Ireland, led by Garret Mor's grandson Lord Offaly ("Silken Thomas"). He is executed with five of his brothers.

1541 Parliament proclaims Henry VIII king of Ireland (his previous status was merely a feudal lord). Irish magnates reluctantly surrender their lands to him as their overlord. Hereafter, a constant English presence is required to keep the peace; no single Irish family replaces the FitzGeralds.

1558–1603 Reign of Queen Elizabeth I; her fear of Irish intrigue with Catholic enemies of England leads to expansion of English power, including the Munster "plantation" (colony) scheme and the division of Ireland into English-style counties.

1580–88 Edmund Spenser, an administrator for the Crown in Ireland, writes *The Faerie Queene*.

1591 Trinity College, Dublin, is founded.

1595–1603 Rebellion of Hugh O'Neill, earl of Tyrone (Ulster). Defeats England at Yellow Ford (1598), but assistance from Spain is inadequate; Tyrone surrenders at Mellifont six days after Queen Elizabeth's death.

1607 The Flight of the Earls, and the beginning of "the Troubles." The earl of Tyrone and his ally Tyrconnell flee to Rome; their lands in Ulster are confiscated and opened to Protestant settlers, mostly Scots.

1641 Charles I's policies provoke insurrection in Ulster and, soon after, Civil War in England.

1649 August: British leader Oliver Cromwell, having defeated Charles and witnessed his execution, invades Ireland, determined to crush Catholic opposition. Massacres at Drogheda and Wexford.

1652 Act of Settlement—lands of Cromwell's opponents are confiscated, and owners are forced across the Shannon to Connaught. Never fully carried out, this policy nonetheless establishes Protestant ascendancy.

1678 In the wake of the Popish Plot to assassinate King Charles II, Catholics are barred from British parliaments.

1683 Dublin Philosophical Society founded, modeled on the Royal Society of London.

1689 Having attempted, among other things, to repeal the Act of Settlement, King James II (a Catholic) is deposed and flees to Ireland. His daughter Mary and her husband William of Orange assume the throne.

1690 James is defeated by William III at the Battle of the Boyne.

1704 First laws of the Penal Code are enacted, restricting Catholic landowning; later laws prohibited voting, education, and military service among the Catholics.

1775 American War of Independence begins, precipitating Irish unrest. Henry Grattan (1746–1820), a Protestant barrister, enters the Irish Parliament.

1778 Land clauses of Penal Code are repealed.

1782 Grattan's Parliament—Grattan asserts independence of Irish Parliament from Britain. Britain agrees, but independence is easier to declare than to sustain.

1798 Inspired by the French Revolution and dissatisfied with the slow progress of Parliament, Wolfe Tone's United Irishmen rebel but are defeated.

1800 The Irish Parliament votes itself out of existence and agrees to Union with Britain, effective January 1, 1801.

1823 Daniel O'Connell (1775–1847), "the Liberator," founds the Catholic Association to campaign for Catholic Emancipation.

1828 O'Connell's election to Parliament (illegal, because he was a Catholic) leads to passage of Catholic Emancipation Act in 1829; later, he works for repeal of the Union.

1845–48 Failure of potato crop leads to famine; thousands die, others migrate.

1848 "Young Ireland," a radical party, leads an abortive rebellion.

1856 Birth of George Bernard Shaw, playwright (d. 1950).

1858 Fenian Brotherhood founded in New York by Irish immigrants with the aim of overthrowing British rule. A revolt in 1867 fails, but it compels Gladstone, the British prime minister, to disestablish the Anglican Church (1869) and reform landholding (1870) in Ireland. The government also increases its powers of repression.

1865 Birth of William Butler Yeats, the great Irish poet (d. 1939).

1871 Isaac Butts founds parliamentary Home Rule Party, soon dominated by Charles Stewart Parnell (1846–91, descendant of English Protestants), who tries to force the issue by obstructing parliamentary business.

1881 Gladstone's second Land Act opposed by Parnell, who leads a boycott (named for Captain Boycott, its first victim) of landlords.

1882 Phoenix Park murders—British officials murdered by Fenians. Prevention of Crime bill that follows suspends trial by jury and increases police powers. Acts of terrorism increase. Parnell disavows all connection with Fenians. Birth of James Joyce, novelist (d. 1941).

1886 Gladstone introduces his first Home Rule Bill, which is defeated. Ulster Protestants fear Catholic domination and revive Orange Order (named for William of Orange) to oppose Home Rule.

1890 Parnell is named co-respondent in the divorce case of Kitty O'Shea; his career is ruined.

1893 Second Home Rule Bill passes Commons but is defeated by Lords. Subsequent policy is to "kill Home Rule with kindness" with land reform, but cultural nationalism revives with founding of Gaelic League to promote Irish language. Yeats, John Synge (1871–1909), and other writers find inspiration in Gaelic past.

1898 On the anniversary of Wolfe Tone's rebellion, Arthur Griffith (1872–1922) founds the Dublin newspaper the *United Irishman*, preaching *sinn fein* ("we ourselves")—secession from Britain; Sinn Fein party founded 1905. Socialist James Connolly (executed 1916) founds the *Workers' Republic*.

1904 Abbey Theatre opens in Dublin.

1912 Third Home Rule Bill passes Commons but is rejected by Lords. Under new rules, however, Lords' veto is null after two years. Meanwhile, Ulster Protestants plan defiance; the Ulster Volunteers recruit 100,000. Radical Republicans such as Connolly, Patrick Pearse, and others of the Irish Republican Brotherhood (IRB) preach insurrection and recruit their own volunteers.

1914 Outbreak of war postpones implementation of Home Rule until peace returns. Parliamentarians agree, but radicals plan revolt.

1916 Easter Uprising—IRB stages insurrection in Dublin and declares independence; the uprising fails, but the execution of 15 leaders by the British turns public opinion in favor of the insurgents. Yeats writes "a terrible beauty is born."

1919 January: Irish Parliamentarians meet as the *Dail Éireann* (Irish Assembly) and declare independence. September: Dail suppressed; Sinn Fein made illegal.

1920–21 War breaks out between Britain and Ireland: the "Black and Tans" versus the Irish Republican Army (IRA). Government of Ireland Act declares separate parliaments for north and south and continued ties to Britain. Elections follow, but the Sinn Fein majority in the south again declare themselves the Dail Éireann under Eamonn de Valera (1882–1975), rejecting British authority. December 1921: Anglo-Irish Treaty grants the south Dominion status as the Irish Free State, allowing the north to remain under Britain.

1922 De Valera and his Republican followers reject the treaty; civil war results. The Irish Free State adopts a constitution; William T. Cosgrave becomes president. In Paris, James Joyce's *Ulysses* is published.

1923 De Valera is arrested and the civil war ends, but Republican agitation and terrorism continues.

1932 De Valera, who had founded the *Fianna Fáil* party in 1926, is elected president.

1932–36 Tariff war with Britain.

1938 New constitution creates Republic of Ireland with no ties to Britain.

1969 The annual Apprentice Boys' march in Londonderry, Northern Ireland, leads to rioting between Catholics and Protestants. British troops, called in to keep the peace, remain in Northern Ireland to this day.

1972 Republic of Ireland admitted to European Economic Community. Troubles continue in the north—January 30, British troops shoot 13 unarmed demonstrators on "Bloody Sunday." Stormont (the Northern Parliament) is suspended and direct rule from London is imposed. Acts of terrorism on both sides leads to draconian law enforcement by the British.

1986 Anglo-Irish Agreement signed, giving the Republic of Ireland a stronger voice in northern affairs.

1992 Ireland approves European Union.

Irish Miles

By Frank O'Connor

Born in County Cork, Frank O'Connor (1903–66), a pseudonym for Michael O'Donovan, was a Republican rebel and one of Ireland's best-loved fiction writers. The essay reprinted here is taken from the first chapter of Irish Miles, *a chronicle of a bicycle trip around Ireland taken by O'Connor, his wife, and a friend.*

Exploring the Boyne Valley in the early days of our married life, before we yet knew what we were looking for and when anything from a High Cross to a keep could lure us off our road, Célimène and I came on the prehistoric necropolis of Newgrange. Prehistory or High Crosses, all were the same to us. It was a showery day, and after cycling a mile and a half in the rain to find the caretaker so kindly provided by the Board of Works, we found he had already gone back to the tombs with a couple of military officers. We returned. The rain cleared off as quickly as it had begun, and the blue plains of Meath sparkled and steamed all round us, and there in the heart of them was the great tumulus, overgrown with grass and bushes, and surrounded by its circle of monoliths. The two officers were there, but the caretaker had gone off to find some candles—the Board of Works, as we learned later, hasn't yet heard of electric light and will probably drop dead when it does. Dwarfed by the tall stones with their mysterious patterns, the two young men, one plump and cheery, the other slim and good-looking, looked damned unhistoric. Somehow you could never imagine them turning into spirals and trumpets in the National Museum or being lectured on as a style or period. We nodded to one another and tried not to look too self-conscious, but all the same the atmosphere was rather like that of a doctor's waiting room. The slim officer broke the silence in a rather startling way.

"I wonder would you consider it—what's the word?—if I said this was Egyptian?"

"It's been called a lot of things in its time," I replied, so taken aback that I broke into a Belfast accent which made the other officer hoot with delight. He obviously thought I was a great card.

"Up the Six Counties!" he said.

"No, but I mean it," the first officer went on eagerly—he was a different type entirely; clever and highly strung. "I understand that all these spirals and things are really sun symbols."

"I think you'd be quite safe in calling them anything," said I. "You couldn't very well be contradicted."

"Oh, yes," he said, by no means satisfied with the reply. "I read that in a book somewhere. I wish I could remember the name of it. It's the same thing as you find in the pyramids."

We were interrupted by the caretaker bringing back the bits of sacred candle, which looked as if they might be contemporary, and we solemnly lit them and crawled after him through the depths of the hillside, under the great half-human shoulders of crude stone, giving ourselves a crick in the neck while we tried to study the patterns on them. In the central chamber we were able to stand, and the officer flicked his torch rapidly up the walls to the roof. I knew I ought to feel moved, but while I tried to remember that this was the heart of Irish prehistory, I found myself watching the shadows which the candlelight threw on the young, warm, eager faces. The second officer didn't seem to be altogether sure of himself, and waited for me to make another joke just to reassure him that history didn't apply to him. Personally, at that moment I very much doubted if it did. I felt sure he would get out of it somehow. But his friend was absolutely determined on the point.

"It was the Milesians who built this, wasn't it?" he asked, looking about him.

"It's supposed to have been the Tuatha De Danann," said I. "Whoever the blazes the Tuatha De Danann were."

"That's right," he said quickly. "They were priestly johnnies, weren't they?"

"At any rate, the people who came after them adopted them as gods," said I.

"That's just the same thing that happened in Crete," he said. "Crete was a daughter-civilization of Egypt. It was started by a priestly caste, just like the Tuatha De Danann, and then the Dorians came and booted them out. The Dorians were soldiers. That's how civilization began. It's all in a book I read once, but I can't remember the name of it. Can you?"

"No," I said firmly, "I can't."

"But that's what happened here all right," he said with conviction. "The Milesians were a military caste; they came from the Mediterranean, and booted out the priestly johnnies and took over the show."

I was just on the point of suggesting that I didn't notice any shortage of priestly johnnies, but decided that, having once talked in a Belfast accent, the less I had to say about the clergy the better. The other officer mightn't understand that I was joking.

"That's how civilization began," the first officer continued eagerly, "with priests and soldiers. It all centres on the Mediterranean. The first time it happened was on the banks of the Nile. A lot of priestly johnnies learned to calculate the time of the Nile floods so that they could have three crops of wheat instead of one. It's all in that book I've been telling you about if only I could remember the name."

I was just as glad he couldn't. I shouldn't have been able to believe in its existence. History simply vanished before the pair of them with their eagerness and good looks. I had no doubt it must be subjective. We left them with real regret, and cycled on uphill through a wooded glen, and downhill again into a secluded valley. This was Mellifont, Honey Fountain, St. Malachy's first settlement in his attempt to Europeanize the Irish Church. A French master-builder had supervised its erection, but his monks and the Irish monks didn't agree on the principles of architecture, so after some time they returned to France. But he must, I believe, have been still in Ireland at the time of the consecration and seen all the famous figures of the tragedy that led up to the Norman invasion. They were all there: O'Connor, the last Irish king; his ruffianly lieutenant, O'Rourke, with his middle-aged wife Darvorgilla, and her lover-to-be, Diarmuid MacMurrough, prince of Leinster, a ruffian even more abominable than her husband. A pretty gang of thieves they were, and Brother Robert of Citeaux must have had a rare time showing them the marvels of this new type of architecture. Up to this, they had seen nothing but the little churches of out-of-the-way monasteries which they were so fond of burning, but this great type of Cistercian architecture with its massive walls and vaulted roofs must have posed them some nice problems in arson. Not that we saw much of it. There was a ruined tower on the right, a tiny, ruined parish church on the side of the hill, an old mill where they sold picture postcards, and the octagon of a lavabo in beautiful European Romanesque. They were cutting the hay, and perhaps if we had come a day later we might have seen a bit more of the layout, but now there was nothing to assist us except a big blue notice board, the contents of which I had to read to Célimène, who fondly believed that there ought to be something to guide us. It ran:

Abstract of a Letter of the Lord Abbot of Mount St. Joseph, Roscrea, dated June 10th, 1929, to Very Rev. Francis Canon—, P.P. Mellifont.

"'Mellifont Abbey Items.

"'3,000,000 Masses celebrated, Community assembled in Choir 1,160,000 times to say Divine Praises, 4 Bishops, 2 of them Archbishops of Armagh, 25 Abbots and 3,000 Monks buried in Monastery. These Items—'"

"'Items is good'," interrupted Célimène.

"'These Items'," I continued firmly, "'have been Drawn Up by a Young Monk who was asked to make a *Special* Study of your Questions.'"

"Is he in the Board of Works too?" asked Célimène.

"His father was a labouring man in regular employment," I added.

"Is that there?" she asked in surprise, screwing up her eyes to look at the board.

"No," I said. "I just made it up."

That sprightly pair of lads had cast a spell on the day. We went on to Monasterboice, skipping back a couple of centuries to the days of the Culdees. They were making the hay there, too. We looked for a while at the beautiful old crosses, and then had our lunch and fell fast asleep propped up against a grave. We might of course have dreamed of some old abbot or stonecutter, in which case this chapter would have been much more exciting, but the fact is that we didn't dream at all. There was no history on us, and in the cool of the evening we cycled under awnings of blue shadow into the little village of Slane. It was dark on the steep road down to the river, with its great avenue of trees and Gothic gateway. By the bridge was a handsome old mill and mill-house, and the great span of the slow, sedgy Boyne. On the far bank a few country boys were playing pitch-and-toss by the light of an electric torch.

We went back and stood in the square. In the whole square there are only four houses; four three-story houses set back a little from the four corners, with flanking walls leading to pavilions in the shape of coach houses, each facing onto a different road. There were two wrought-iron lanterns in each roadway. That was all; four houses, eight coach-houses, sixteen arches, eight lanterns; and even then the lanterns are now only stumps, the arches hidden with shrubbery. One house belongs to the police, another to the doctor, while the parish priest's house has had its roof raised, and its little Georgian panes replaced by stained glass.

But it is clear that the architect had another story in mind when he found the solution to the problem of his square. I feel sure it was a love story, and that from one of the small-paned Georgian windows he intended some woman to look out night after night on the eight lanterns that shut in her little world, and the carriages that rolled in and out of it with their officers, duellists and squireens from Trim and Drogheda. Was she married, and, if so, for whom did he intend the other two houses? Was it perhaps one of the four-sided comic intrigues that 18th-century dramatists delighted in? The sense of the past swooped down and enveloped us. Below on the riverbank it all began, ages and ages ago, with priestly johnnies and soldier johnnies, and all the trouble they started hasn't yet come to an end.

I feel sure the architect's tale had a happy ending, for though the Gothic gateway under the trees may have been in existence, it had not yet set the fashion for unhappy love, Shelley's poetry and Robert Emmet's speech from the dock. Wolfe Tone, rationalism and married love were still the rage, and I fancy the architect saw a carriage waiting one night on the road down to the river, a coach-house door opening quietly, and a young woman tripping out with lifted skirts. Then a few whispered words, and the carriage rattled over the bridge in the direction of Dublin.

So, at least I fancy, but it is all hard to read, and it is only when darkness falls, and the four old houses cease to whisper correct, serious, official things to one another about the decline in morals and the decay of children's teeth, compulsory Irish and the licensing of dogs, that the old wrought-iron lanterns seem to glow again, the four houses become a string quartet, and the tune they play is a Boccherini minuet or a Mozart serenade, melancholy and gay.

The Stone Walls of Ireland

By Richard Conniff

Author Richard Conniff is a former managing director of Geo *magazine.*

The walls look as though they have been there forever: mottled with lichen and bearded with moss; woven together with vines, hedges, and trees; running, in more than one place, straight across a shallow stream bed, as if the wall were there before the water; emerging, in other places, from the low tide mark, as if the walls splashed ashore with the first settlers in Ireland, 8,000 years ago.

"All the people are dead now who was building walls," a man known locally as the Kaiser assured me one afternoon in County Kerry. It was the sort of remark you heard everywhere in Ireland: The walls were built "centuries ago, I suppose." Even "thousands and thousands of years ago." Or "in olden times." And what did he himself do for a living, I asked the Kaiser. Well, he built walls.

Long ago, of course? Not at all, he said. There was the one in Ballyferriter, built a year or two ago to "close up" around a man's house, and another outside the church. There was a fine new wall across from the pub in Ventry. There was the wall he was going to be building soon around Paudy O'Shea's new pub. And of course there was Sean Moran's wall on the Conor Pass Road in Dingle—I must've heard about it—a wall of such magnificence that people stopped their cars dead in the middle of the road to admire it: "You'd *have* to stop to look at it," he said, as if to explain away their poor driving habits. "You'd be blind if you didn't." He would show it to me himself, in fact.

The following Saturday, as arranged, we headed off around the tip of the Dingle Peninsula, stopping at a number of places not listed, including Sean Moran's wall—a structure of double thickness, six feet in height, around a field where sheep grazed. "The best wall around, I'd say, in Kerry," the Kaiser ventured, on his own craftsmanship. "There are no sheep going to be coming out of there soon. Or cattle."

As we drove, he talked about his craft. The common stone in the area was red sandstone, which breaks away in relatively flat tablets well suited to construction. "There's a bed for every one," the Kaiser explained. "You put it there and say, 'Get in it.'" It was sound material for a wall like, well, Sean Moran's. He'd set the stones there so snugly, he said, that "you couldn't pass a blade of grass across it with a pliers. Sean Moran'll be dead and rotting before it falls down. You'd travel a long time before you saw the likes of that again. You'd travel all Ireland, I suppose."

This essay is taken from Irish Wall, *published by Stewart, Tabori & Chang, Inc., New York.*

He lamented the tendency to use barbed wire and electric fencing, which give no shelter for the crops or the animals. Some farmers even bulldozed stone walls to make bigger fields. Sean Moran, of course, would need no wiring. One local man so admired the towering wall at Moran's place that he went out every day with his dog and gazed at it for a half-hour at a time, until one day the dog (gone mad with boredom) got away from him and was killed (doubtless by a driver who was looking at the wall instead of the road). "A lot of people came out to look at it when it was built. Thousands of people. All Dingle came." The wall achieved its rightful status as a conversation piece; it became that estimable thing in Irish country life—a "talking point." For its builder, anyway.

The Kaiser complained about a local farmer who wanted a wall built. "He told me, 'My cattle don't wear glasses looking at the wall. I don't want no fancy work.' The man had red trousers on and a white jacket and he only wanted a plain wall. 'Something thrown up. No fancy work.' And then he put in this big white stone that looks like the arse of a tank in there." Sean Moran's wall, by contrast, was a subtle masterpiece. "You don't see the likes of that in Connemara, do you? You'd travel the world. 'Tis a job forever and ever. And no cement."

Any comparison with Sean Moran's wall is of course invidious, but in that regard it was like a number of others we passed that day on the Dingle Peninsula: dry stone walls, built "forever and ever," of a sort that would make even a modern wall builder think the craft was one practiced mostly long ago, in days gone by. At the end of the peninsula, for instance, the ancient fort of Dunbeg walls off a small promontory from attack by land. The final line of defense is a massive stone barrier stepped up on the inside with walkways for men fighting with their backs to the Atlantic. No one really knows who built it, or against what foe. Farther on toward Slea Head, the slopes are dotted with beehive huts, monastic dwellings huddled together within small stone circles built high to shut out the world. Around the forts and these anchoritic retreats, the land is of a sort to keep monks and other farmers thin. But it is also well walled, and the field walls, too, look as if they have been there forever. Some of them are sod and stone. The grass grows sideways on them, and they look like yard-high ridges—elongated fins—of lawn. Elsewhere the walls are densely packed piles of flat sandstone. They run up to the mountaintops, enclosing fields pitched at an angle of 30 degrees. The scenery, out to the Blasket Islands, is spectacular, but it's the slope that takes your breath away.

If these walls appear ancient, it may be with good reason. A few Irish walls are as modern as Sean Moran's, and many are of far more recent vintage than a passerby would surmise. But archeologists have established that the building of walls in Ireland goes back to the Neolithic Age. They have found walls running *underneath* a prehistoric burial cairn in County Down. There, and all along the coast from Kerry to Antrim, farmers cutting turf have stumbled onto field walls—whole systems of walls, in some cases—hidden for millennia by the peat blanket. These subterranean walls run, in one case, from the waterline to a point 600 feet above sea level. At another site, the buried farm has much the shape of a modern one, with half-acre tillage plots, fields of 3 or 4 acres, and a long straight fence more than a mile long, apparently separating one family's holdings from another's. The blanket peat that hid these old fields began to build up around 1000 BC, as a result of early land clearing and deforestation. The walls beneath this blanket are thus probably 3,000 to 4,000 years old and are compounded of stone and sod, in the same manner as walls built on the present surface within the last century. In some places, the old walls emerge from the turf and continue on the surface as present-day boundaries. Like modern countrymen, prehistoric farmers doubtless cast a cool, appraising eye on one another's fields from across such walls.

But while the Irish landscape abounds in prehistoric and Early Christian antiquities, the walls generally do not date back that far, and the sense of continuity between modern walls and those of prehistoric farmers is an illusion. Most walls in Ireland went up no earlier than the agricultural revolution. The network of walls and hedges that we think of as timelessly defining the Irish countryside was, in fact, cast over the landscape like a web beginning in about 1750. Before that, much, if not most, of Ireland was, in effect, a great unfenced cow pasture. "Their fields lie open and unclosed," declared *Advertisements for Ireland* in 1623. Where proper fields existed, an anonymous writer added a few years later, they were "no better fenced than a midwife's toothless gums." In Donegal, in the middle of the 19th century, a landlord declared: "We suppose it would not be believed that in this district, until very lately, fences were altogether unknown."

Indeed, the Irish seem to have had something close to a split personality on the subject of walls. Scattered across the landscape by their pastoral, cattle-herding way of life, with nothing like the security of a town or village nearby, early Irish farmers commonly walled themselves in. The strongest farmers put up their houses within raths or ring-forts, a form associated with Celtic settlers of the first millennium AD. Thirty thousand of these raths survive around Ireland, visible, in the words of a Kerry farmer, as "old roundish rings of mouldy stone and sods." These grassy corrugations in the earth are all that remain even of Tara, once the seat of power over much of Ireland.

The raths are so well preserved partly because grazing was always more important in Ireland than the plow, but also because farmers regarded the raths as "fairy forts" and would not touch them. In Ulster in 1958, for example, a Land Commission work crew was building a fence in the course of rearranging land holdings in a congested district. "But an ancient rath lay in the path of the fence," a local newspaper reported. "The workmen refused to dig holes in the rath. They said they would die soon if they lifted a sod. A Land Commission supervisor suggested that two of the oldest men in the locality might have no fear of death. Two men, one of 97, the other 95, were asked and indignantly refused. They said that life was 'as sweet as the fairy music they often heard from the rath.'" Such caution has given the Irish landscape the quality of a palimpsest, with the earthworks of earlier civilizations still visible in the modern fields. But that is changing. Unfearing bulldozers now frequently level raths, and at Tara the raths sometimes serve as a sort of makeshift dirt bike course. Carrot-haired boys on fat-wheeled bicycles rise and disappear over the humpy landscape as if pedaling over waves.

The raths were once a place for a farmer to drive his livestock, to protect his wealth from hit-and-run cattle raiders. What field walls existed seem mostly to have been huddled around these refuges and around monastic sites. They formed the tillage plots of the "infield." But beyond them, in the "outfield," Irish farmers seem to have felt something like an abhorrence for walls. The occasional crop planted in a portion of the outfield would necessarily be enclosed, to keep the animals from trampling it. But the enclosure would be wicker, with stakes driven into the ground and rods woven around them. When the crop came in, the fence came down. The rods served as fuel in winter, and the outfield survived as open range. . . .

As English landlords and settlers took over [in Ireland] during the 17th century, widespread fencing of the land began almost immediately. Their methods had obvious and impressive advantages. In County Meath, for example, 5,000 acres of "waste sheep walk" were drained, limed, and fenced off into arable fields of 10 acres each, for settlement by French and English Protestants.

These fences were elaborate affairs. An 18th-century visitor described them as typically consisting of an earthen embankment between drainage ditches 6 feet wide and 5 feet deep. The bank was usually planted with hedges and with trees for lumber. (In Ireland, for unknown reasons, the word "ditch" came to apply to the raised bank, rather than to the trenches from which it was formed. The word is now used to denote almost any form of raised boundary, including an unmortared—but not a mortared—stone wall; a mortared stone wall is known as a "wall." By the same logic, the word "moat" or "mote" refers in Ireland not to a water-filled trench around a castle, but to the raised and fortified platform enclosed by the trench; it derives from the Norman French word for "mound." The traveler in Ireland must therefore be prepared to hear about people climbing ditches and walking, like Christ, on moats. These are merely lexical differences, not miracles.)

The single most important benefit of enclosing the countryside was that it made the livestock farming for which Ireland was best suited more systematic and productive. Confining the movement of cattle within an enclosed field meant that the grass would be grazed more thoroughly and the manure concentrated in a field that could subsequently be planted with crops. With cattle no longer wandering freely over the open outfield, more land came under cultivation. Crop rotation was possible, along with the use of hay and roots as winter fodder.

Unfortunately for the Irish, the countryside that was being fenced in had been their common grazing ground. Not only were their ancient ways being supplanted by new and foreign methods, they were themselves being forced out, especially in the fertile lowlands. They responded, in places, by hacking down the landlords' hedges to burn for winter fuel. Later, in the 18th century, secret societies like the Ribbonmen vented their anger at a variety of grievances by mutilating the landlords' livestock. In Munster, the Whiteboys burned the alien settlers' crops and leveled walls across former common grazing ground. By then, however, the walls had already wrought a singular, irreversible change in Irish life: They had made the herder obsolete. . . .

But if enclosure ended one way of life, it also began another, drawing out the latent Irish mania for walls. . . . The walls entered not just every field, but every life and every aspect of life. They became drying racks, clotheslines, coat hooks, scratching posts, hiding places for poteen, and dumps for weapons. They served as shelter for outdoor classrooms—the so-called hedge schools—when formal education of Catholics was for a time outlawed. The walls were a place for lovers to hide, and also for eavesdroppers. They were instruments of spite and weapons for assault, but they were also children's playthings. (Outside Mullingar, for instance, children running small stones across the resonant coping stones have worn a long groove in a "musical wall"; the groove is generations old, but it is also still fresh.) They were a source of entertainment and of "divilment," which was and is a national sport.

As boundaries, the walls became manifestations of the Irish fondness for small fiefdoms and the gleeful cultivation of petty divisions, but they were at times also instruments of self-destructive generosity by enabling the land to be further and further subdivided. For peasant and landlord alike, the walls were a way of showing wealth, power, craftsmanship. As such, like Sean Moran's wall, they were talking points. They were also objects of delight entirely on their own. If the walls closed off the Irish from certain wilder, more naturalistic feelings, still they had a beauty of their own, to which the Irish were hardly blind. (*Tarry Flynn*, Patrick Kavanagh's novel of country life in County Monaghan, is, for example, shot through with walls and hedges. One moment the excitable protagonist is counting the stones in a wall as an exercise in self-control; the next he is suffused with lyrical feelings: "The snails climbing up the stones of the fences and the rushes and thistles in the meadow beyond seemed to be putting a quilt of peace around his heart.")

Finally, of course, the walls had something to do with the business of farming. They were a place to put stones when the fields were being picked clean. They were a way to mark field boundaries. And they were barriers to keep cattle in the pasturage and donkeys out of the cabbages. Indeed, building good walls quickly became synonymous with sound farming in Ireland. It was something that got into the blood. The story is told of County Galway farmers who had complained all their lives about the miserable land, where stones grew like mushrooms and walls divided farms less into fields than into cubicles. In time, the Land Commission relocated them to the rich, wide fields of County Meath. They complained then, of course, that they hadn't enough stones to build a decent fence. There is a saying, still repeated in parts of Ireland: "You can tell a farmer by his ditches."

3 Irish Greens

Golfing in Ireland

by Jonathan Abrahams

Jonathan Abrahams is the associate editor at Golf Magazine *and is the author of* ClubSmarts: How to Buy Golf Clubs that Work.

Ask most golfers where to find the golf vacation of a lifetime—a variety of breathtaking courses, beautiful settings, history seeping into every shot—and they'll likely point you in the direction of Scotland. Unless, of course, they've been to Ireland.

Indeed, Ireland's neighbor to the Northwest gets more world attention when it comes to golf. It hosts most of the British Open Championships, and in many circles is considered the birthplace of the game. But Ireland doesn't lag far behind when it comes to golf history. Its oldest course dates back to 1881, and with close to 300 championship layouts, the Emerald Isle offers more golf per square mile than any place in the world. And if you ask a local how Ireland's courses stack up against Scotland's, he'll fix you with a steely stare before defending his homeland on his life. Then he very well may buy you a pint of the local stout.

But you don't have to be a native to have such passion for the golf courses of Ireland (not to mention the stout). Golfers the world over who are "in the know" have long sung the praises of Irish golf. Tom Watson, winner of five British Opens, lists not any Scottish course, but Ballybunion as his favorite, as does the legendary writer Herbert Warren Wind, who is credited with putting Irish golf on the map when he penned, "To put it simply, Ballybunion revealed itself to be nothing less than the finest seaside course I have ever seen." And although Ballybunion is generally considered the prize jewel of the Emerald Isle, it is indicative of the quality of courses found throughout the country.

So what makes Irish golf great? Architecture, perhaps the essence of a golfing experience, is one appropriate place to begin.

Connoisseurs of golf in America hold such courses as Cypress Point and Pebble Beach in the highest regard because their designers used the spectacular lay of the land to create a beautiful, challenging, but fair layout. These are two of the few true linksland courses in the states—there just isn't that much coastline available, and courses are designed more for the developer to build homes or resorts on than for the golfer.

In Ireland, however, there are many such courses. Golf was never a game for the idle rich, so high-priced resorts were never in demand. Instead, golf is, and always has been, a game for the local townspeople. The great architects were enthusiastic local golfers who wanted a place to play in their village. They designed courses not to challenge the world's best players, but to provide a fair test for all levels of golfers and to make the most of the landscape. It just so happened that most of the landscape was spectacular: Ireland is one of those remarkable places where mountains and sea meet, so there is no need to manipulate the land. Nature—the scraggly coast of a linksland or rolling hills of heather—dominates the courses here, not the other way around.

There is also something to be said for the sense of history that comes with playing golf on a land that is, most assuredly, "Old World." Only 10 minutes from the airport in Shannon is the charming nine-hole course at Adare, complete with a green nestled in the ruins of a 14th-century abbey. When you play Lahinch, one of the greats of the Southwest, you play in the shadows of the Cliffs of Moor. Every step you take on an Irish golf course is a step back in history. Where in America can you find something comparable to the "Mass Hole" at Waterville, a par-3 built over a large hollow where Catholic priests used to hold services in secret, because praying was a capital offense at the time?

The land is spread out and largely unsettled, not nearly as developed as Scotland. There are great courses nestled in remote areas nowhere near any transportation hub, so the hordes of golf tour buses that traverse Scotland are few and far between here. You can drive for miles on a seemingly endless two-lane highway, enveloped by the sea of meadow and the smell of burning peat, then suddenly descend on such a hidden jewel as Waterville and have the course to yourself.

And you will be welcomed: There isn't a friendlier face than that of an Irish host, who treats a shared round of golf (or stout) as the forging of a lasting bond. A tour of the links usually winds up in the 19th hole, the local pub, which may easily stretch into dinner. Although pride runs deep here, there isn't any of the resentment or jealousy toward tourists that is sometimes found in Europe. They actually like Americans!

But the best part of Irish golf is what perhaps makes it most different from golf in America: simplicity. The game is remarkably unspoiled on the Emerald Isle, where you're far more likely to see goats grazing on a fairway than an electric cart roaming in the rough. Caddies are the staple here, and although they are famous for their slightly twisted advice ("It's a slightly straight putt." You've got a strong crosswind against you."), they add a flavor lost to most of the world that hearkens back to the game's roots.

It's great stuff. But there are a few things you should know before you set out to conquer the courses of the Emerald Isle. Golf is a different game here, so be sure to address the following as you prepare:

- **The Weather Factor.** Pack heavy. You see all different kinds of weather in Ireland, from high winds to rain and sleet to beautiful sunshine, and you may see it all in one round. There are no rain checks here. You play unless it's lightning, so pack your sweaters and rain gear, especially if you're planning your trip for the off-season months of the spring and fall.

- **The Sunday Bag Factor.** If you don't have a golf bag that's light enough for you to carry for 18 holes, invest in one before your trip. There are almost no electric carts in Ireland, so you usually have the option of a caddy, caddy car (pull cart), or carrying your own bag. Many courses have caddies but will not guarantee their availability since they're not employed by the course directly, so it's conceivable that you may be left with only one option: toting your bag yourself. To be safe, make sure you have a carry-all, or Sunday bag.

- **The Private Club Factor.** Unlike America, most private golf clubs in Ireland are happy to let visitors play their course and use their facilities. It's important to remember, however, that the course is indeed there for the members first and the majority of the club's concerns lie with them. Preferred days for visitors are listed below, but it's always a good idea to call in advance and make sure that the club will make time for you.

- **The Northern Ireland Factor.** Some of the best and most beautiful courses are in Northern Ireland, a far less populated area than the Republic. Don't let media coverage from urban Belfast scare you away. Also, keep in mind that the region is under British rule, so all currency is in U.K. pounds.

And finally, a reality check. Ireland's best courses rank with the best of the world, but after that there's a bit of a drop off. Of the 300-odd courses, only 25 or so are worth crossing an ocean to play. Others are good, but nothing you can't find at home. Of that 25, all are happy to have visitors play, except Royal Belfast, in Northern Ireland. It's the oldest club in Ireland, and it's exclusive: If you belong to a club in America, they must write a letter of introduction to Royal Belfast to secure your playing privilege. The remaining 24 courses are listed below.

Northeast

County Louth Golf Club (Baltray). Like many Irish courses, County Louth is better known as its hometown, Baltray, a village sandwiched by the Boyne Estuary to the west and the Irish Sea to the east. Long hitters will love the atypical layout, a par-73 that features five par-5's, but beware the well-protected, undulating greens. *Tel. 041/22329. 18 holes. Yardage: 6,783. Par 73. Fees: weekdays, £27; weekends, £33. Visitors: Mon. and Wed.–Fri. Facilities: practice area, caddies (book in advance), caddy carts, catering.*

The Island Golf Club. Talk about exclusive: Until 1960, the only way to get to this club was by boat. It was about as remote as you could be and still be only 24 kilometers (15 miles) from Dublin (near Donabate), but things have changed. The Island has opened its doors and revealed a fine links course that rolls in and around sandhills, with small, challenging greens. *Tel. 01/843-6205. 18 holes. Yardage: 6,625. Par 71. Fees: weekdays, £27; weekends, £30. Visitors: Mon., Tues., and Fri. Facilities: practice area, catering.*

Portmarnock Golf Club. Across an estuary from the easternmost point of Ireland, Portmarnock is perhaps the most famous of Ireland's "Big Four." (Ballybunion, Royal County Down, and Royal Portrush are the others.) Largely because of its proximity to Dublin, this links course has hosted numerous major championships, most recently the 1991 Walker Club. Known for its flat fairways and greens, it provides a fair test for any golfer who can keep it out of the heavy rough. *Tel. 01/846–2968. 27 holes. Yardage: 7,051, 3,449. Par 72, 36. Fees: weekdays, £40; weekends, £50. Visitors: Mon., Tues., and Fri. Facilities: practice area, caddies (book in advance), caddy carts, catering.*

Royal Dublin Golf Club. Generally, links courses are in remote, even desolate areas (therein the charm), but this equally charming one is only 6 kilometers (3½ miles) from the center of Dublin, on Bull Island, a bird sanctuary. It's the second-oldest club in Ireland and is routed in the old tradition of seaside links: The front nine goes out in a line (wind helping), and the back nine comes back in a line (wind against). Don't expect to make a comeback on the way home if you've struggled going out. *Tel. 01/833–6346. 18 holes. Yardage: 6,763. Par 73. Fees: weekdays, £35; weekends, £45. Visitors: Mon., Tues., Thurs., and Fri. Facilities: practice area, caddies, caddy carts, catering.*

St. Margaret's Golf Club. Not all of the worthwhile golf in Ireland is played on links courses that are a century old. St. Margaret's is a parkland (inland) course that opened in 1992 and immediately received high praise from Ireland's golfing inner circle. If, after getting blown around on the seaside links, you long for a taste of Western golf, this is your haven. *Tel. 01/864–0400. 18 holes. Yardage: 6,965. Par 72. Fees: weekdays, £25; weekends and holidays, £30. Visitors: daily. Facilities: practice area, caddies, caddy carts, club rental, catering.*

Southwest

Ballybunion Golf Club. Put simply, one of the finest courses in the world. The Old Course was a virtual unknown until Herbert Warren Wind sang its praises in 1968, and today Ballybunion is universally regarded as one of golf's holiest grounds. On the shore of the Atlantic next to the southern entrance of the Shannon, it has the huge dunes of Lahinch without the blind shots. No pushover, but every hole is a pleasurable experience. Watch out for "Mrs. Simpson," a double fairway bunker on the first hole, named after the wife of Tom Simpson, the architect who remodeled the course in 1937. The New Course opened in 1985, designed by Robert Trent Jones. *Tel. 068/27611. 36 holes. Yardage: 6,593 (Old), 6,216 (New). Par 71, 72. Fees: Old Course, £35; New Course, £25, both courses £50. Visitors: weekdays. Facilities: practice area, caddies, caddy carts, catering.*

Cork Golf Club (Little Island). If you know golf-course architecture, you know the name of Alister MacKenzie, who designed Cypress Point in California and Augusta National in Georgia. One of his few designs in Ireland is Cork, better known as Little Island. There's water on this parkland course, but it's not the tempermental ocean; instead, Little Island is in Cork Harbour, a gentle bay of the Irish Sea. Little known, but one of the Emerald Isle's best. *Tel. 021/353451. 18 holes. Yardage: 6,687. Par 72. Fees: weekdays, £23; weekends, £26. Visitors: Mon.–Wed. and Fri. Facilities: practice area, caddies, caddy carts, club rental, catering.*

Dooks Golf Club. On the second tier of courses in Ireland's southwest, Dooks does not quite measure up to the world-class tracks. It is nonetheless a completely worthwhile day of golf if you're touring the area. Built in the old tradition of seaside links, it's shorter and a bit gentler, although the greens are small and tricky. An excellent way to take a breath. *Tel. 066/67370. 18 holes. Yardage: 6,010. Par 70. Fees: £15. Visitors: weekdays. Facilities: caddy carts, catering.*

Killarney Golf & Fishing Club. Freshwater fishing is the sport here, for Killarney is an inland town, set among a stunning mixture of mountains, lakes, and forests. There are two golf courses, the Killeen Course, host of the 1992 Irish Open, and Mahony's Point, set along the shores of Lough Leane. Killeen is longer; Mahony's puts a premium on accuracy. Despite the abundance of seaside links, many well-traveled golfers name Killarney their favorite place to play in Ireland. *Tel. 064/31034. 36 holes. Yardage: 7,056 (Killeen), 6,705 (Mahony's). Par 73, 72. Fees: £26. Visitors: Mon.–Sat. Facilities: practice area, caddies, caddy carts, catering.*

Lahinch Golf Club. The original course at Lahinch was designed by Old Tom Morris, who, upon the unveiling in 1892, called it "as fine a natural course as it has ever been my good fortune to play over." That was when blind shots (when you can't see your target) were in vogue, and there are many here, where towering sandhills dominate every hole. Only a course with as much charm as this one could get away with that in today's modern game. *Tel. 065/81003. 18 holes. Yardage: 6,613. Par 72. Fees: weekdays, £25; weekends, £30. Visitors: daily. Facilities: practice area, caddies, caddy carts, catering.*

Tralee Golf Club. Tralee is perhaps what all modern-golf-course architects *wish* they could do in the States: Find unspoiled seaside linksland and route a course on it that's designed for the modern game. This is an Arnold Palmer–Ed Seay design that opened in 1984, and the setting is as classic as it gets with plenty of cliffs, craters, dunes, and the gale-blowing ocean. Don't let the flat front nine lull you to sleep—the back nine can be a ferocious wake-up call. *Tel. 066/36379. 18 holes. Yardage: 6,738. Par 71. Fees: weekdays, £25;*

weekends, £30. Visitors: weekdays. Facilities: practice area, caddies, catering.

Waterville Golf Club. Here's what you should know about Waterville before you play: The first hole of this course is aptly named "Last Easy." At 7,184 yards from the tips, Waterville is the longest course in Ireland or Britain, and it is generally regarded as their toughest test. Now the good news: The scenery is so majestic you may not care that your score is approaching the yardage. Six holes run along the cliffs by the sea, surrounding the other 12, which have a tranquil, if not soft, feel to them. *Tel. 0667/4102. 18 holes. Yardage: 7,184. Par 72. Fees: £30. Visitors: weekdays. Facilities: practice area, caddies, caddy carts, buggies, catering.*

Northwest

Carn Golf Course (Belmullet). This is a newer, Eddie Hackett–designed links course that takes advantage of its location, far to the west on the shores of Blacksod Bay. From the elevated tees and greens you have a view of a string of Atlantic islands: Inishkea, Inishglora, and Achill. *Tel. 097/81051. 18 holes. Yardage: 6,608. Par 72. Fees: £12. Visitors: daily. Facilities: practice area, caddies, caddy carts, catering.*

Connemara Golf Club. The local club for the small town of Clifden, Connemara is a links course where you can get carried away not only by the golf, but by the surrounding scenery as well. The Atlantic Ocean and Ballyconneely Bay are immediately to the west and the Twelve Bens Mountains are to the east. The course starts flat, then rises into the hills for the final, challenging six holes. *Tel. 095/23502. 18 holes. Yardage: 7,174. Par 72. Fees: £16. Visitors: Mon.–Sat. Facilities: practice area, caddies, caddy carts, catering.*

County Sligo Golf Club (Rosses Point). A century old this year, the course at Sligo is one of the grand old venues of Ireland, having hosted most of the country's major championships. At 6,565 yards, this links course isn't particularly long; however, it still manages to have seven par-4s of 400 yards or more. Typical of Ireland's hidden jewels, Rosses Point clings to cliffs above the Atlantic. The third tee offers views of the ocean, the hills, and the unusual mountain Benbulben, which looks like a giant Irish arroyo. *Tel. 071/77186. 18 holes. Yardage: 6,565. Par 71. Fees: weekdays, £15; weekends, £20. Visitors: Mon., Tues., Thurs., and Fri. Facilities: practice area, caddies (summer only), caddy carts, club rental, catering.*

Donegal Golf Club (Murvagh). On the shores of Donegal Bay and approached through a forest, this windswept links is shadowed by the Blue Stack Mountains, with the Atlantic Ocean as a backdrop. The greens are large, but the rough is deep and penal, and there's a constant battle against erosion by the sea. Legendary golf writer Peter Dobreiner called it "hauntingly beautiful," perhaps recalling his experience on the par-3 fifth, fittingly called "The Valley of Tears." *Tel. 073/34054. 18 holes. Yardage: 7,153. Par 73. Fees: weekdays, £13; weekends, £16. Visitors: daily. Facilities: practice area, caddies, caddy carts, catering.*

Enniscrone Golf Club. Eddie Hackett designed this course on the shores of another bay, this time Killala. Hackett may be the Pete Dye of Ireland, due in part to the fact that he's blessed with wonderful land: Enniscrone's setting is a natural for good golf—a combination of flatlands, foothills, and of course, the Atlantic. It's not overly long on the scorecard, but the persistent winds can add yards to almost every hole. It's also one of the few clubs in Ireland with electric carts, or as they call them, buggies. *Tel. (0)96/36297. 18 holes. Yardage: 6,682. Par 72. Fees: £15. Visitors: weekdays, weekends by ap-*

pointment. Facilities: practice area, caddies (weekends and holidays), caddy carts, buggies, club rental.

Westport Golf Club. Twice the host of the Irish Amateur Championship, this inland course lies in the shadows of religious history. Rising 2,500 feet above Clew Bay, with its hundreds of islands, is Croagh Patrick, a mountain that legend connects with St. Patrick. The mountain is considered sacred, and attracts multitudes of worshippers to its summit every year. All the prayers might pay off at the 15th, where your drive has to carry the ball over 200 yards of ocean. *Tel. 098/25113. 18 holes. Yardage: 6,667. Par 73. Fees: weekdays, £15; weekends, £18. Visitors: weekdays. Facilities: practice area, caddies, caddy carts, catering.*

Northern Ireland

Ballycastle Golf Club. Pleasure comes first here, with challenge as an afterthought: It's beautiful (five holes wind around the remains of a 13th-century friary), short (less than 6,000 yards) and conveniently located right next to Bushmills, the world's oldest distillery at nearly 400 years. *Tel. 012657/62536. 18 holes. Yardage: 5,882. Par 71. Fees: weekdays, U.K.£13; weekends, U.K.£18. Visitors: daily. Facilities: practice area, caddy cars, catering.*

Castlerock Golf Club. Where else in the world can you play a hole called "Leg o' Mutton"? Not in America, that's for sure. It's a 200-yard par-3 with railway tracks to the right and a burn to the left—just one of several unusual holes at this course, which claims, year-round, to have the best greens in Ireland. True or not, the finish is spectacular: from the elevated 17th tee, where you can see the shores of Scotland, to the majestic 18th, which plays uphill to a plateau green. *Tel. 01265/848314. 27 holes. Yardage: 6,499, 2,678. Par 73, 35. Fees: weekdays, U.K.£15, U.K.£7; weekends, U.K.£25, U.K.£10. Visitors: Mon.–Thurs. Facilities: practice area, caddies (book in advance), caddy cars, catering.*

Malone Golf Club. Fishermen may find the 22-acre lake at the center of this parkland layout distracting: It's filled with trout. The golf, however, is just as well stocked; large trees and well-manicured, undulating greens combine to provide one of the most challenging inland tests in Ireland. Bring your power game—there are only three par 5s, but they're all over 520 yards. *Tel. 01232/612758. 27 holes. Yardage: 6,642, 3,138. Par 71, 36. Fees: Mon., Thurs., and Fri. U.K.£25 (men), U.K.£18 (women), U.K.£8.50 (children). Visitors: Mon., Thurs., and Fri. Facilities: practice area, catering.*

Portstewart Golf Club. One hundred years old this year, Portstewart may scare you with its opening hole, generally regarded as the toughest starter in Ireland. Picture a 425-yard par-4 that descends from an elevated tee to a small green tucked between the dunes. The greens are known for uniformity and speed, and seven of the holes have recently been redesigned to toughen the course. Also, if you want a break from the grand scale of championship links, there's the Riverside 9 and the Old Course 18, 27 holes of downsized, executive-style golf. *Tel. 01265/832015. 45 holes. Yardage: 6,784 (championship course), 4,733 (Old Course), 2,662 (Riverside). Par 72, 64, 32. Fees: weekdays, U.K.£22, U.K.£7, U.K.£10; weekends, U.K.£27, U.K.£10, U.K.£15. Visitors: Mon., Tues., and Fri. Facilities: practice area, caddies, caddy cars, catering.*

Royal County Down. This is perhaps the most beautiful course in Ireland. Catch it on the right day at the right time and you may think you're on the moon; Royal County Down is a links course with a sea of craterlike bunkers and small dunes. Actually, for better players, every day is the right one. Harry Vardon labeled it the toughest course on the Emerald Isle, and, if you can't hit your driver long and straight, you might find it the toughest course in the world. A true masterpiece. *Tel. 013967/22419. 36 holes. Yardage: 6,969 (Championship course), 4,087 (No. 2). Par 71, 65. Fees: weekdays, U.K.£43, U.K.£53 all day (Championship), U.K.£8 (No. 2); weekends, U.K.£55, U.K.£65 all day (Championship), U.K.£12 (No. 2). Visitors: Tues., Thurs., and Fri. Facilities: practice area, caddies, caddy cars, catering.*

Royal Portrush. The only club outside Scotland and England to have hosted a British Open, Portrush is perhaps the most understated of Ireland's "Big Four." The championship Dunluce course is named for the ruins of a nearby castle, and is a sea of sandhills and curving fairways. The Valley course is a less-exposed, tamer track. Both are conspicuous for their lack of bunkers. The Dunluce course, in a poll of Irish golf legends, was voted the best course in Ireland. *Tel. 01265/822311. 36 holes. Yardage: 6,530 (Dunluce), 6,054 (Valley). Par 72, 70. Fees: weekdays, U.K.£37.50 (Dunluce), U.K.£15 (Valley); weekends, U.K.£40 (Dunluce), U.K.£20 (Valley). Visitors: weekdays. Facilities: practice area, catering.*

4 Dublin

By Hugh Oram

Updated by Giuliano Davenport

Dublin, of all the capital cities in Europe, is the most intimate in scale and easiest to explore. Although one of its names in Irish (Gaelic), *Dubhlinn*, means "dark pool," most visitors to the city find it a friendly, lighthearted place. Its setting is definitely an added attraction: It is looped around the edge of Dublin Bay, and to the immediate south of the city rise the Wicklow Mountains, 620 meters (2,000 feet) high. From many neighborhoods of the city's southern suburbs, these mountains appear to block off the ends of the streets. From north to south, Dublin stretches 16 kilometers (10 miles), and from its center, immediately adjacent to the port area and the River Liffey, the city spreads westward for an additional 10 kilometers (6 miles); in total, it covers 28,000 acres.

As recently as 1600, Dublin was little more than a large village, with a population of 15,000. Much of its huge growth in population has occurred during this century; the capital has become the center for government offices and many new service industries. As a result, many people from other parts of Ireland have settled in here. Greater Dublin, with its one million residents, now claims nearly one-third of the population of the whole Irish Republic. Yet the city hardly ever seems too crowded, except for a few jam-packed pedestrian-only streets.

The population of Dublin is remarkably heterogeneous, reflecting the many invasions and settlements of the city over the years. From 1880 onwards, Jewish people fled the pogroms of eastern Europe and came to live in Ireland, and until the 1950s, the capital had a substantial Jewish population. (Much of the younger Jewish population has left the city to live in Israel and other countries.) Over the past decade, a large number of Middle Easterners and many American, Dutch, German, and Japanese immigrants have settled here.

Dublin first became a crossroads in Ireland some 1,500 years ago. Four of the main thoroughfares that traversed the country led to the site of present-day Dublin. Today, the area where the city's first inhabitants, members of the Gaelic order, built their dwellings is known as the Liberties; sections of the first town walls, dating back nearly 1,000 years, can still be seen off Thomas Street.

In 837, Norsemen from Scandinavia carried out the first outside attack on Dublin, arriving in a fleet of 60 long ships. Four years later, the Vikings built their first port here and used it for raiding large tracts of the countryside. Despite the resistance of the Irish against Viking rule, the Norsemen made Dublin one of the principal centers of their empire, from Russia in the east to Ireland in the west and Iceland in the north. The power of the Scandinavians was finally broken by the Irish at the Battle of Clontarf in 1014, which took place north of Dublin. Native rule, however, was short-lived. The Anglo-Normans landed in County Wexford, in southeast Ireland, in 1169; a mere two years later, King Henry II of England finally subdued some of the Irish chieftains and granted Dublin its first charter.

Through the Middle Ages, the city developed as a trading center, though fraught with political difficulties; the last remaining relic of medieval trade in Ireland can be seen nearly opposite the Christ Church Cathedral, in Tailor's Hall. In 1651, English soldier Oliver Cromwell occupied and ransacked Dublin. Not until the 18th century did Dublin reach a period of glory, when a golden age of enlightened patronage by wealthy members of the nobility turned the city into one of Europe's most prepossessing. Still, until the early 19th century, social and economic power rested exclusively in Protestant hands.

New streets and squares, such as Merrion and Fitzwilliam squares, were constructed with a classical dignity and elegance. Handel, the German-born English composer, wrote much of his great oratorio, the *Messiah,* in Dublin, where it was first performed in 1742. Many other crafts, such as bookbinding and silver making, flourished to cater to the needs of the often-titled and usually wealthy members of society. Ireland was granted a certain measure of political autonomy by the British, and in the new government buildings (now the Bank of Ireland) in College Green, opposite Trinity College, the independent parliament met for the first time in 1783.

However, this period of glory was short-lived; in 1800, the Act of Union brought Ireland and Britain together in a common United Kingdom, and the seat of political power and patronage moved from Dublin to London. Dublin quickly lost its cultural and social sparkle, as many members of the nobility moved to London. The 19th century proved to be a time of political turmoil and agitation, although Daniel O'Connell, a lord mayor of Dublin, won early success with the introduction of Catholic emancipation in 1829.

During the late 1840s, Dublin escaped the worst effects of the famine, caused by potato disease, that blighted much of southern and western Ireland. New industries, such as mineral-water manufacturing, were established, and with an emerging Victorian middle class introducing an element of genteel snobbery to the city, Dublin began its rapid outward expansion. Until the mid-19th century, Dublin extended little beyond St. Stephen's Green, but with the sudden demand for additional housing by the newly wealthy, many new suburbs were established, such as Ballsbridge, Rathgar, and Rathmines on the south side, and Clontarf and Drumcondra on the north side.

At the same time, Dublin's cultural activity blossomed, particularly in literature. Two main literary movements grew up side by side. In 1893, Douglas Hyde, later the first president of Ireland, founded the Gaelic League (Conradh na Gaelige) with the aim of restoring the Irish language. At the same time, W.B. Yeats played a pivotal role in the Irish literary renaissance; with the foundation of the Abbey Theatre in 1904 and the coming to prominence of other playwrights like Sean O'Casey and J.M. Synge, Irish literature thrived. The cultural ferment of Dublin in the first decade of this century inevitably had its political apotheosis in the uprising of 1916, which lasted a week, damaging many buildings in the central O'Connell Street area of the city. In 1919, the war aimed at winning independence from Britain began in County Tipperary and lasted for three years. Dublin was comparatively unscathed during this period, but during the Civil War, which followed the setting up of the Irish Free State in December 1921, more harm came to a number of the city's historic buildings, such as the Four Courts and the Custom House, which both burned down. The capital had to be rebuilt during the 1920s. After the Civil War was over, Dublin entered a new era of political and cultural conservatism, which continued until the late 1950s.

In the 1960s, an era of economic optimism pervaded the city, with many new internationally oriented businesses established. Much of this enthusiasm waned again during the recessionary years of the 1970s, but then in the 1980s the city became a world center for rock music, with artists such as Bob Geldof, Chris de Burgh, and U2.

Dublin Exploring *(Boxes Refer to Detail Maps)*

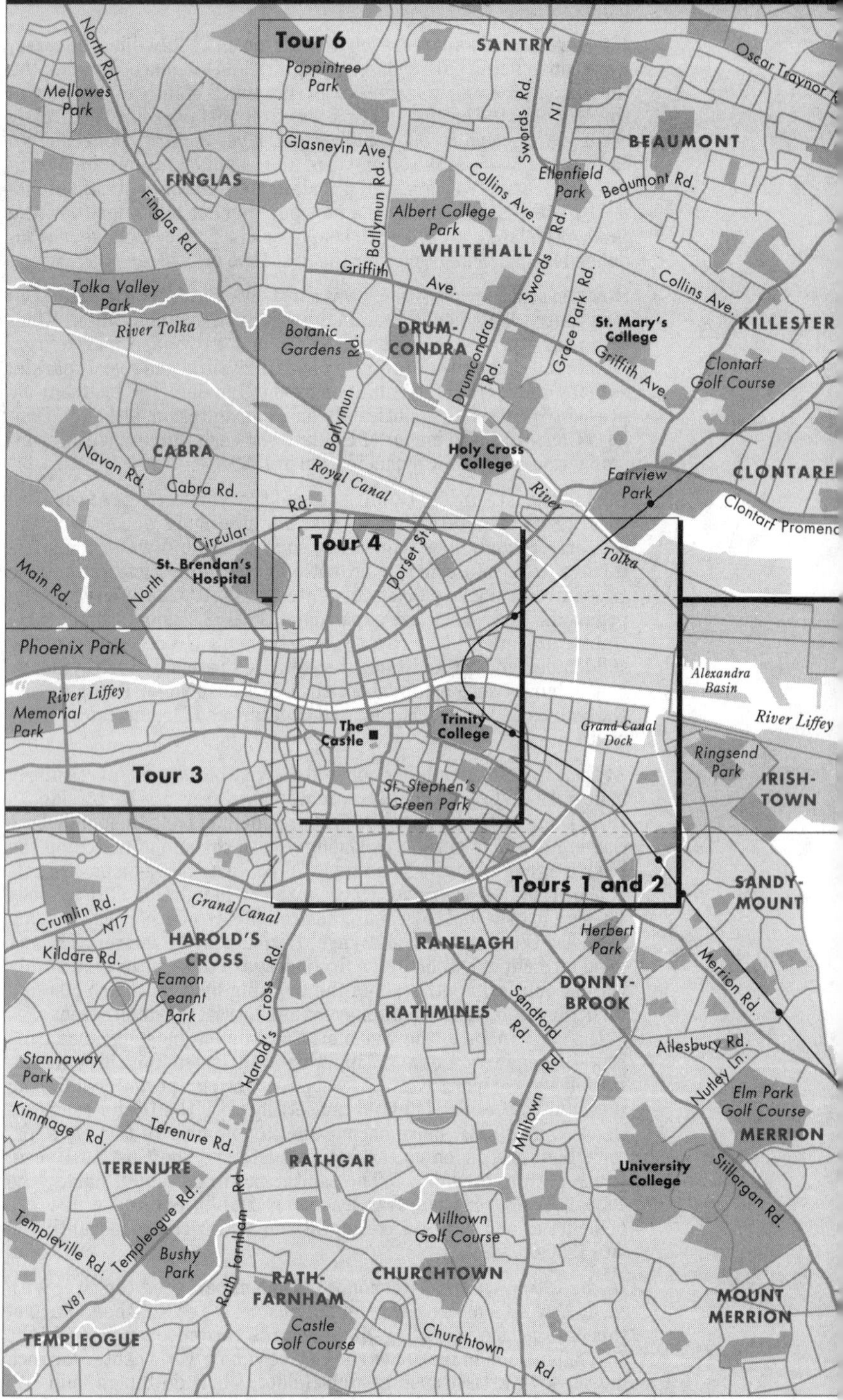

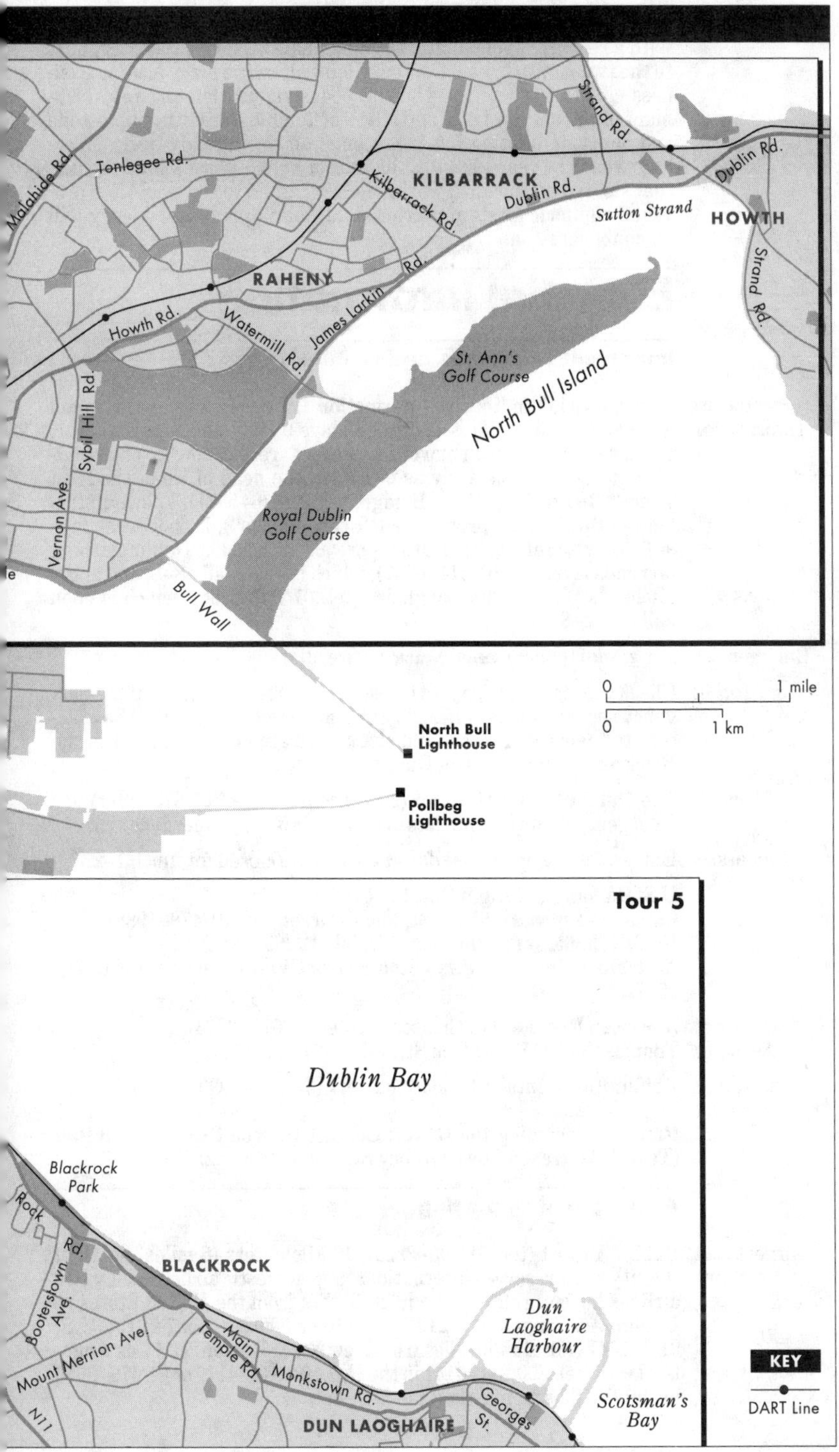
Malahide Rd.
Tonlegee Rd.
Strand Rd.
Dublin Rd.
KILBARRACK
Kilbarrack Rd.
Dublin Rd.
Sutton Strand
HOWTH
Strand Rd.
RAHENY
Rd.
Howth Rd.
Watermill Rd.
James Larkin
St. Ann's
Golf Course
North Bull Island
Sybil Hill Rd.
Vernon Ave.
Royal Dublin
Golf Course
Bull Wall
North Bull
Lighthouse
Pollbeg
Lighthouse
0
1 mile
0
1 km
Tour 5
Dublin Bay
Blackrock
Park
Rock
Rd.
BLACKROCK
Booterstown
Ave.
Mount Merrion Ave.
Main
Temple Rd.
Monkstown Rd.
Dun
Laoghaire
Harbour
Georges
St.
Scotsman's
Bay
DUN LAOGHAIRE
N11
KEY
DART Line

With the 1990s, a new spirit of economic enterprise is underway with a recently opened international financial services center, next to the two-centuries-old Custom House, drawing many leading business clients to the city. And the pedestrianization and refurbishment of the narrow lanes and alleys of Temple Bar with cobblestone and old-style lighting has brightened up this already lively inner-city area. The year 1992 was the year of *The Commitments*, the film that showed off modern, working-class Dublin to the world and provoked euphoric levels of patriotism. Dublin's pride and energy will no doubt carry on.

Essential Information

Important Addresses and Numbers

Tourist Information The main Dublin **Tourist Information Office** (14 Upper O'Connell St., tel. 01/874–7733) is open weekdays 9–5:30 and Saturday 9–1. Because the office is in one of the busiest areas of town, you are advised to go there as early as possible. The head office of the **Irish Tourist Board** (Baggot St. Bridge, tel. 01/676–5871), known in Ireland as **Bord Fáilte** (pronounced "Board Falcha"), is open weekdays 9–6. Tourist Information Offices are also located at Dublin Airport (arrivals level, tel. 01/844–5387), which is open daily 8–8, and at St. Michael's Wharf (Dun Laoghaire, tel. 01/280–6984), which is open daily 7 AM–8 PM.

Emergencies For **gardai** (police), **ambulance,** or **fire,** dial 999.

Medical Check the main newspapers to see which public hospitals offer emergency services on any given day. For minor ailments, hotels have access to their own doctors and also to private hospitals, such as the Blackrock Clinic, south of Dublin.

Dentists The **Dublin Dental Hospital** (20 Lincoln Pl., tel. 01/679–4311) has emergency facilities and lists of dentists offering emergency care.

Embassies Embassies are open weekdays 9–5, but are closed for lunch 1–2.

U.S. Embassy (42 Elgin Rd., tel. 01/688–8777).
Canadian Embassy (65 St. Stephen's Green, tel. 01/478–1988).
British Embassy (31 Merrion Rd., tel. 01/269–5211).
Australian Embassy (Fitzwilton House, Wilton Terr., tel. 01/676–1517).

Travel Agencies **American Express** (116 Grafton St., tel. 01/677–2874).
Thomas Cook (118 Grafton St., tel. 01/677–1721).

Lost and Found **Dublin Bus:** Contact its headquarters (59 Upper O'Connell St., tel. 01/873–4222).
Railways, including the DART: Contact **Iarnrod Éireann/Irish Rail** (Travel Centre, 35 Lower Abbey St., tel. 01/836–6222).

Arriving and Departing

Airport and Airlines **Dublin Airport** (tel. 01/705–2222), 10 kilometers (6 miles) north of the city center, serves international and domestic airlines. Only two airlines have regularly scheduled flights from the United States to Dublin: **Aer Lingus** (tel. 212/557–1110 or 800/223–6537 in the U.S; 01/844–4747 in Dublin) flies from New York, Boston, and Los Angeles; **Delta** (tel. 800/241–4141 in the U.S.; 01/844–4170 or 01/676–8080 in Dublin) flies from Atlanta to Dublin.

Flying to Ireland from Britain has never been easier, with five airlines serving destinations in Ireland from 19 British airports. The major carriers are Aer Lingus, Ryanair, and British Midland Airways. There are daily services to Dublin from all major London airports; Aer Lingus operates 12 flights from Heathrow Airport, with British Midland operating an additional 10 flights; Ryanair operates several flights from Luton and Stanstead airports, British Airways flies from Gatwick Airport, and Virgin Atlantic Cityjet flies from London City Airport. In addition, flights to Dublin leave from Birmingham, Bristol, East Midlands, Liverpool, Luton, Manchester, Leeds/Bradford, Newcastle, Edinburgh, and Glasgow. Aer Lingus operates flights from Dublin to Cork, Kerry, Shannon, Galway, Knock in County Mayo, and Sligo.

For reservations and information in Dublin, contact: **Aer Lingus** (tel. 01/844–4747), **Ryanair** (tel. 01/844–4411), or British Midland (tel. 01/842–2011).

Major European carriers such as Air France, Lufthansa, Sabena, SAS, and Alitalia run direct services to Dublin from most European capital cities and major regional airports, especially those in Germany.

When you arrive at Dublin Airport, currency can be exchanged at the Bank of Ireland in the arrivals hall or at the bank branch in the main check-in area. Just before you leave the arrivals hall, the **Tourist Information Office** (tel. 01/844–5387) will answer any questions relating to Dublin.

Between Airport and City Center

By Bus **Dublin Bus** (tel. 01/873–4222) operates a shuttle service between Dublin Airport and the city center with departures outside the arrivals gateway; pay the driver inside the coach. The single fare is £2.50. Service runs all day, from 7:30 AM to 11 PM, at intervals of about 30 minutes, to as far as **Busaras** (tel. 01/830–2222), the main provincial bus station in the city center. Journey time from the airport to the city center is normally 30 minutes, but it may be longer in heavy traffic.

By Taxi A taxi is a quicker alternative than the bus to get from the airport to Dublin center. A line of taxis waits by the arrivals gateway; the fare for the 30-minute journey to any of the main city-center hotels is about £12. It's advisable to ask about the fare before leaving the airport.

By Car Renting a car in Dublin is extremely expensive, with high rates and a 12½% local tax. Gasoline is also expensive by U.S. standards, at around 60p a liter. Peak-period car-rental rates begin at around £200 a week for the smallest models, like a Ford Fiesta. Dublin has many car rental companies, and it pays to shop around and to avoid "cowboy" outfits. Some reliable car rental firms in the Dublin vicinity are: **Avis** (Hanover St., tel. 01/677–4010; Dublin Airport, tel. 01/844–4466), **Budget** (151 Lower Drumcondra Rd., tel. 01/379802; Dublin Airport, tel. 01/844–5919), **Hertz** (Leeson St. Bridge, tel. 01/660–2255; Dublin Airport, tel. 01/842–9333), and **Murray's Rent-a-Car** (Baggot St. Bridge, tel. 01/668–1777; Dublin Airport, tel. 01/844–4179).

Getting Around

Traveling around Dublin by public transport is comparatively easy, although a car is useful for getting around the outlying suburbs. The city center, with its maze of one-way streets and parking restrictions, is best negotiated on foot.

By Train An electric railway system, the **DART** (Dublin Area Rapid Transit; tel. 01/836–6222) connects Dublin with Howth to the north and Bray to the south on a fast, efficient line. There are 25 stations on the route, which is the best means of getting to seaside destinations such as Howth, Blackrock, Dun Laoghaire, Dalkey, Killiney, and Bray. The service starts at 6:30 AM and runs until 11:30 PM; at peak periods, 8–9:30 AM and 5–7 PM, trains arrive every five minutes. At other times of the day, the intervals between trains are 15 to 25 minutes.

Tickets can be bought at stations, but it is also possible to buy weekly (£10) rail tickets, as well as weekly (£14) or monthly (£55) "rail-and-bus" tickets, from the **Irish Rail Travel Centre** (35 Lower Abbey St., tel. 01/836–6222). Individual fares begin at 60p and range up to £2.90. There are heavy penalties for traveling the DART without a ticket.

Diesel train services run from Connolly Station (Amiens St.) to more distant locations like Malahide, Maynooth, Skerries, and Drogheda to the north of Dublin, and Wicklow and Arklow on the south side. New trains are due to come into service on this route in 1995.

By Bus Dublin offers an extensive network of buses, but due to heavy traffic, bus service is not always reliable. Fares begin at 55p and have to be paid to the driver on entry to the bus, another cause of delays. Some bus services run on cross-city routes, but most buses start in the city center. Buses to the north of the city begin in the Lower Abbey Street/Parnell Street area, while those to the west begin in Middle Abbey Street and in the Aston Quay area. Routes to the southern suburbs begin at Eden Quay and in the College Street area. A number of services are links to DART stations, and another regular bus route connects the two main provincial railway stations, Connolly and Heuston. For Dublin Bus information, call 01/873–4222.

By Taxi The taxi service in Dublin is comparatively inexpensive, with a pick-up charge of £2 and a further charge of about £1.50 a mile thereafter. Many taxi stands, where a cab may be found at most times of the day and night, are located throughout the city center and suburbs, and are listed in the Dublin telephone directory. Alternatively, you may phone a taxi company and ask for a cab to meet you at your hotel, but this may cost up to £4 extra. Although the taxi fleet in Dublin is large, the cabs are nonstandard and some cars are neither spacious nor in pristine condition. Local taxi companies include **VIP Taxis** (tel. 01/478–3333), **Metro** (tel. 01/668–3333), and **Mercs and Perks** (tel. 01/842–1341).

By Car Dublin's notoriously complicated one-way traffic system and its high levels of congestion during the morning and evening rush hours make driving in the city center difficult at best; if you are not familiar with the city, stick with public transportation, which gets you to all points of interest.

Opening and Closing Times

Dublin is gradually becoming a 24-hour city, even though the bus and DART train services close down for the night at 11:30 PM. (A few lines run through till dawn on the weekends.) Many taxis run all night, so there is no problem getting around. Many of the clubs on the Leeson Street strip stay open until 4 AM or later. Even Sunday, once a day of sabbatical rest in Dublin, is lively in Continental style. Many smaller city-center shops and boutiques are open on Sundays; department stores are also occasionally open on Sundays.

Banks are open weekdays 10–12:30 and 1:30–3. Many branches now stay open until 4 PM each weekday, and all remain open on Thursdays until 5. Some banks stay open at lunchtime. Most branches now have automatic cash dispensers.

Post offices are open weekdays 9–1 and 2–5:30. On Saturdays, they are open 9–12:30. Main post offices are open Saturday afternoons, too. The General Post Office (GPO) on O'Connell Street, which has foreign exchange and general delivery facilities, is open Monday–Saturday 8–8. On Sunday, it is open 10:30–6:30.

Museums are normally open Tuesday–Saturday and also Sunday afternoon. Monday is the usual closing day.

The city's main **stores** are open Monday–Saturday 9–5:30 or 9–6. Department stores are closed on Sunday. Smaller specialty stores open on Sunday as well, usually 10–6.

Crime

Crime, often drug related, is a problem in Dublin, so visitors should watch over their wallets, handbags, and other personal possessions. Great care should be taken when parking a car not to leave any valuables inside, even under a raincoat on the back seat or in the trunk. Certain areas demand caution: The city center is where pedestrians and motorists should be especially careful. Another danger area for parking cars is in the vicinity of the Guinness Brewery Hop Store and Irish Whiskey Corner (*see* Tour 3: Dublin West, *below*). Side streets off O'Connell Street can also be dangerous, especially at night.

Guided Tours

Orientation Tours

Bus Éireann (tel. 01/836–6111) provides a four-hour city sightseeing tour that covers the main sights in the city center, including St. Patrick's Cathedral, Trinity College, the Royal Hospital, and Phoenix Park. The company also features day tours to country destinations out of the main bus station, Busaras, in Dublin.

Dublin Bus (tel. 01/873–4222) offers a three-hour city-center tour, taking in sights similar to the Bus Éireann tour (*see above*). Hourly departures for the 'Heritage Tour,' a one-hour city-center tour, allow visitors to hop on and off at any of the main sites. Tickets are available from the driver or Dublin Bus. During the summer, these tours run daily, using open-topped buses weather permitting. The company also conducts a north-city coastal tour, going to Howth, and a south-city tour, traveling as far as Enniskerry.

Gray Line Tours (tel. 01/661–9666) runs city-center tours that cover the same sights as the Bus Éireann and Dublin Bus itineraries (*see above*).

Special-Interest Tours

DART Train

Guided tours of Dublin using the DART system are organized by **Views Unlimited** (8 Prince of Wales Terrace, Bray, tel. 01/286–0164 or 01/286–2861).

Horse-Drawn Carriage Tours

Horse-drawn carriage tours are available around Dublin and in Phoenix Park. For tours of the park, contact the **Office of Public Works** (tel. 01/661–3111). Carriages can be hired at the Grafton Street corner of St. Stephen's Green, without prior reservation.

Pubs Highly enjoyable evening tours of the literary pubs of Dublin, where "brain cells are replaced as quickly as they are drowned," are offered by **Colm Quilligan** (tel. 01/454–0228).

Walking Tours **Historical Walking Tours of Dublin** (tel. 01/845–0241 or 01/535–730) provide an excellent introduction to Dublin. The Bord Fáilte Approved Tour assembles at the Front Gate of Trinity College on Saturday and Sunday at noon and 3 PM from March through May and 11 AM, noon, and 3 PM daily from May through September. **Eamonn MacThomais** offers entertaining walking tours of the Liberties and Literary and Georgian Dublin; tours begin at 2 PM on weekends at the statue of Molly Malone's barrow, Grafton Street. Tourist Information Offices also provide leaflets describing walking tours that follow signposted itineraries.

Exploring Dublin

Highlights for First-Time Visitors

Book of Kells at Trinity College (*see* Tour 1)
Chester Beatty Library (*see* Tour 5)
Guinness Brewery Hop Store (*see* Tour 3)
Howth Peninsula (*see* Tour 6)
Hugh Lane Municipal Art Gallery (*see* Tour 2)
Merrion Square (*see* Tour 1)
National Gallery of Ireland (*see* Tour 1)
Phoenix Park (*see* Tour 3)
Royal Hospital, Kilmainham (*see* Tour 3)
St. Stephen's Green (*see* Tour 1)

Tour 1: South City Center

Numbers in the margin correspond to points of interest on the Tours 1 and 2: Dublin City Center map.

A good place to start your tour of Dublin is the city-center area south of the River Liffey; it contains a majority of the city's historic buildings and monuments. Let's begin south of O'Connell Bridge and Westmoreland Street at College Green, once a Viking meeting place
1 and burial ground. East of College Green stands **Trinity College,** the sole college of Dublin University, Ireland's oldest, dating from 1592, when it was founded by England's Queen Elizabeth I on the site of the confiscated Priory of All Hallows. For centuries, Trinity was the preserve of the Protestant church, and it is only within the past 30 years that final prohibitions barring Catholics from studying there have been lifted. Among the distinguished alumni of the college are Jonathan Swift, Thomas Moore, Sheridan LeFanu, George Berkeley, Oscar Wilde, J.M. Synge, Bram Stoker, and Samuel Beckett. Trinity served as a stand-in for an English university in the popular 1983 movie *Educating Rita*.

Trinity's grounds cover 40 acres, and most of its buildings were constructed in the 18th and early 19th centuries. The extensive West Front, with a classical portico in the Corinthian style, faces onto College Green; recently restored, it was built between 1755 and 1759, possibly the work of Theodore Jacobsen, architect of London's Foundling Hospital. Statues of orator Edmund Burke and dramatist Oliver Goldsmith are positioned close to the front gate. Parliament Square, the cobbled quadrangle that is the visitor's first introduction to the grounds, also dates from the 18th century. On the right of the square, you'll find the Theatre, or Examination Hall, which features an impressive organ retrieved from an 18th-century Spanish ship and a gilded oak chandelier from the old House of Commons; concerts are sometimes held here. The Chapel, which stands on the left of the quadrangle, has stucco ceilings and fine woodwork. Both the Theatre and the Chapel were designed by Scotsman William Chambers in the late-18th century. The looming Campanile, or bell tower, erected in 1853, dominates the center of the square. *College information, tel. 01/677–2941. Grounds open daily 8 AM–10 PM.*

Beyond the right-hand corner of the second quadrangle, called Library Square, the new **Colonnades Gallery,** inside the Old Library, houses Ireland's most valuable collection of ancient volumes and priceless manuscripts; the most famous of these is the Book of Kells, a splendidly illuminated version of the Gospels, designed by unknown monks, perhaps in Kells, County Meath, in the 9th century. The 680-page book was rebound in four volumes in 1953, and two of these are usually displayed at a time, with pages turned periodically. The **Old Library,** known as the "Long Room," is a staggering 65 meters (213 feet) long and 13 meters (42 feet) wide. It has a high-pitched barrel-vaulted ceiling and contains approximately 200,000 of the 3 million volumes in Trinity's collection. Since the 1801 Copyright Act, the college has received a copy of every book published in Britain and Ireland, and a great number of these publications must be stored in other parts of the campus and beyond. The carved Royal Arms of Queen Elizabeth I, above the library entrance, is the only surviving relic of the original college buildings. The souvenir shop on the ground floor sells books, clothing, jewelery, and postcards. *Tel. 01/702–1016. Admission: £2.50 adults, £2 children 12–18, senior citizens, and students, free to children under 12. Open Mon.–Sat. 9:30–5:30, Sun. noon–5.*

At the east end of the Old Library stands the **New Berkeley Library,** built in 1967. The small open space in front of the library contains a spherical brass sculpture designed by Arnaldo Pomodoro. Behind the Old Library, you'll find the concrete Arts and Social Sciences Buildings, with an entrance on Nassau Street; this complex houses the **Douglas Hyde Gallery of Modern Art,** which concentrates on contemporary art exhibitions and has its own bookshop. *Tel. 01/677–2941, ext. 1116. Admission free. Open Mon.–Wed. 11–6, Thurs. 11–7, Fri. 11–6, Sat. 11–4:45.*

In the Thomas Davis Theatre in the Arts Building, Trinity recently introduced the **Dublin Experience,** an elaborate audiovisual presentation devoted to the history of the city over the past 1,000 years. *Tel. 01/702–1688. Admission: £2.75 adults (£5 with Old Library), £2.25 students and senior citizens (£4 with Old Library), £1.50 children under 18. The show runs every hour on the hour. Open May–Oct., daily 10–5. Tours of the college grounds are available at the main College Green entrance. Trinity Tours, tel. 01/602–2320. Admission: £3.50 adults, £3.25 children June–Sept.*

Directly opposite the front entrance of Trinity College in College Green stands one of Dublin's most striking buildings, now serving as
2 a branch of the **Bank of Ireland.** This grand structure, with a facade incorporating Corinthian pillars into its Ionic porticos, was first designed by Sir Edward Lovett Pearce to house the Irish Parliament, which resided here for 17 years; when the Parliament was abolished in 1803 under the Act of Union, the building was bought by the Bank of Ireland. Today the main banking hall is set in the old Court of Requests where citizens' petitions were heard. The former House of Lords, which may be viewed by small groups upon request, features

Bank of Ireland, **2**
Bewley's Café, **8**
Carmelite Church, **6**
City Hall, **4**
Dublin Castle, **5**
Dublin Civic Museum, **7**
Dublin Writers Museum, **30**
Garden of Remembrance, **27**
Gate Theatre, **29**
Genealogical Office, **12**
GPO (General Post Office), **31**
Heraldic Museum, **13**
Hugh Lane Municipal Art Gallery, **26**
Leinster House, **15**
Mansion House, **11**
Merrion Square, **22**
Mountjoy Square, **24**
National Gallery of Ireland, **21**
National Library, **14**
National Museum, **16**
Natural History Museum, **20**
Number Twenty-Nine, **23**
Olympia Theatre, **3**
Pro-Cathedral, **32**
RHA Gallagher Gallery, **19**
Rotunda Maternity Hospital, **28**
Royal Irish Academy, **10**
St. Ann's Church, **9**
St. Francis Xavier, **25**
St. Stephen's Green, **17**
Shelbourne Hotel, **18**
Trinity College, **1**

Tours 1 and 2: Dublin City Center

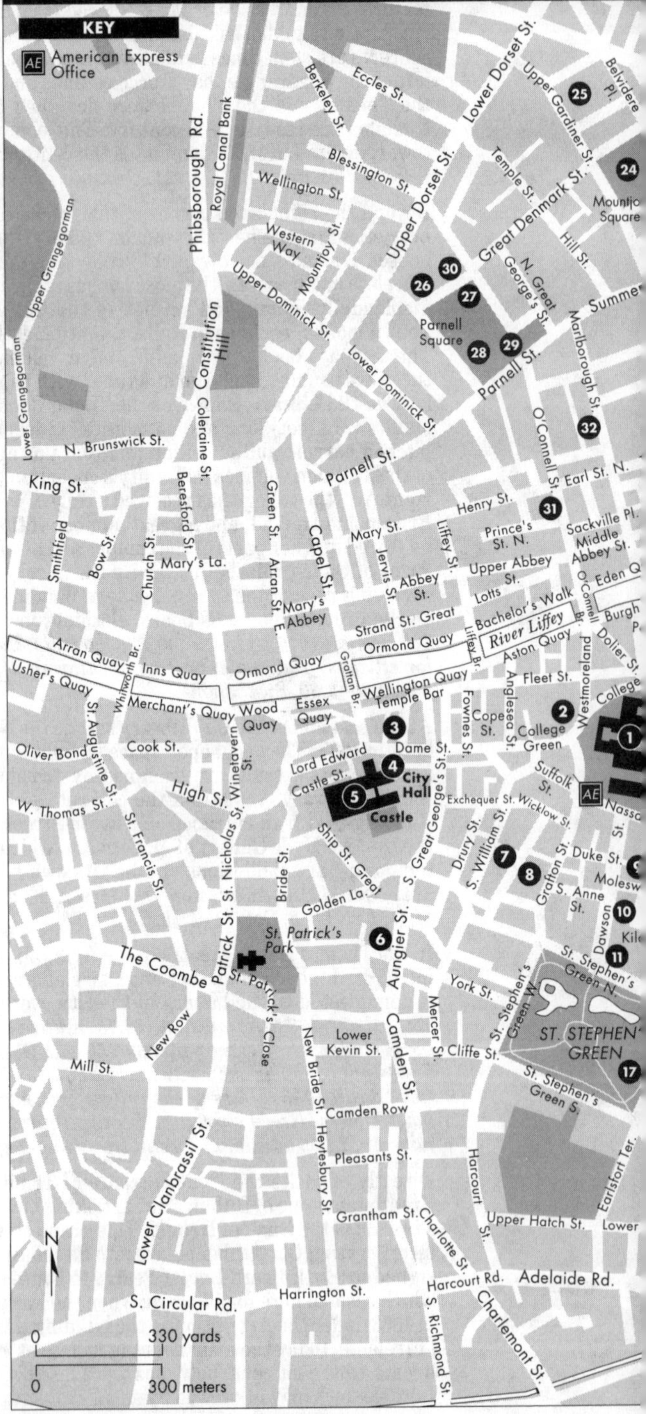

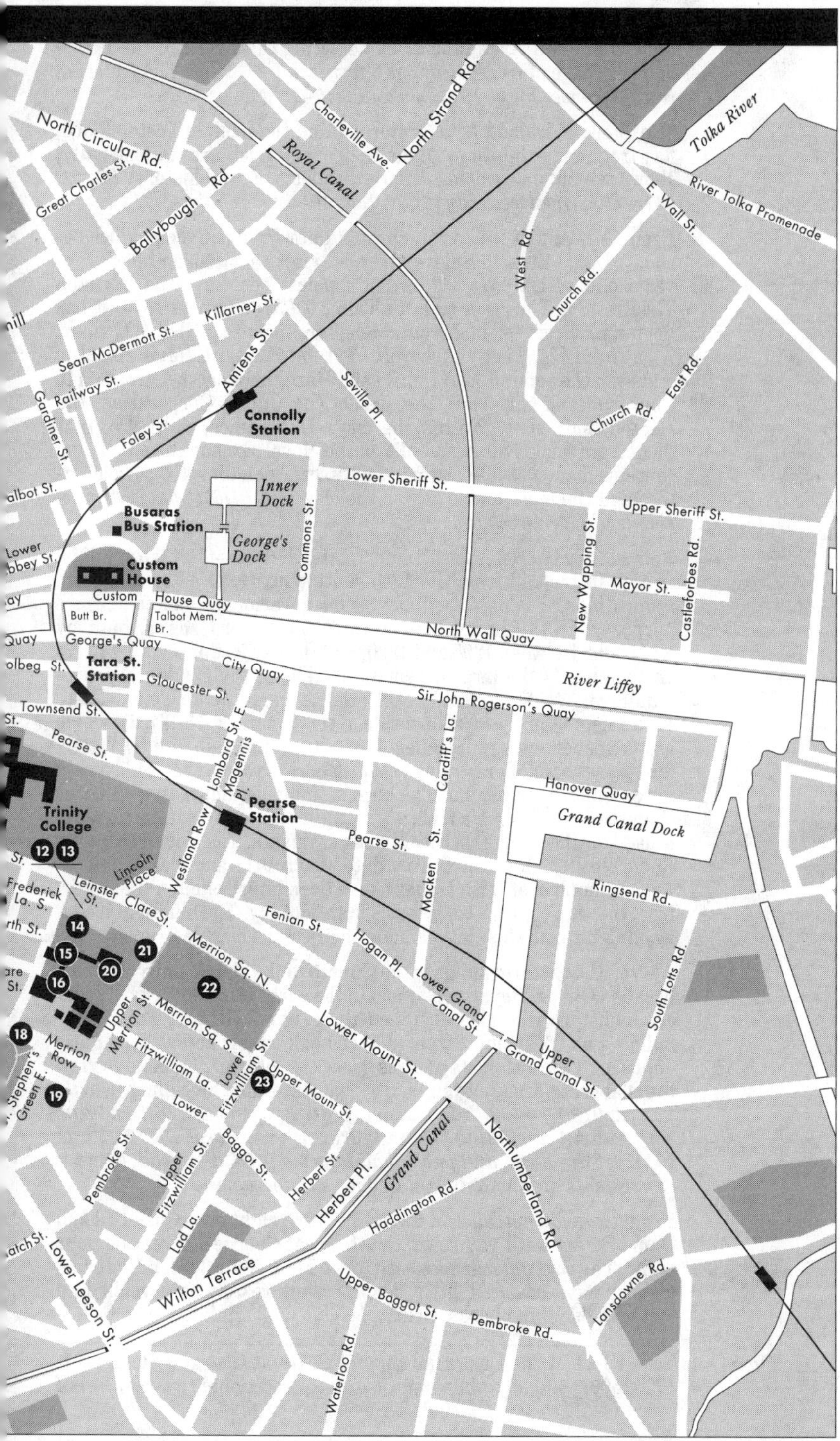

North Circular Rd.
Great Charles St.
Ballybough Rd.
Royal Canal
Charleville Ave.
North Strand Rd.
Tolka River
River Tolka Promenade
E. Wall St.
West Rd.
Church Rd.
East Rd.
Killarney St.
Sean McDermott St.
Railway St.
Amiens St.
Seville Pl.
Connolly Station
Foley St.
Gardiner St.
Talbot St.
Lower Sheriff St.
Upper Sheriff St.
Inner Dock
Busaras Bus Station
George's Dock
Commons St.
Custom House
Lower Abbey St.
Custom House Quay
New Wapping St.
Mayor St.
Castleforbes Rd.
Butt Br.
Talbot Mem. Br.
North Wall Quay
George's Quay
Tara St. Station
City Quay
River Liffey
Gloucester St.
Townsend St.
Sir John Rogerson's Quay
Pearse St.
Lombard St. E.
Magennis Pl.
Cardiff's La.
Hanover Quay
Grand Canal Dock
Trinity College
Pearse Station
Westland Row
Pearse St.
Macken St.
Ringsend Rd.
Lincoln Place
Leinster St.
Frederick La. S.
Clare St.
Fenian St.
Hogan Pl.
South Lotts Rd.
Merrion Sq. N.
Lower Grand Canal St.
Upper Merrion St.
Merrion Sq. S.
Lower Mount St.
Upper Grand Canal St.
Merrion Row
Fitzwilliam La.
Lower Fitzwilliam St.
Upper Mount St.
Northumberland Rd.
Grand Canal
Lower Baggot St.
Pembroke St.
Upper Fitzwilliam St.
Herbert St.
Herbert Pl.
Haddington Rd.
Lad La.
Lower Leeson St.
Wilton Terrace
Upper Baggot St.
Pembroke Rd.
Lansdowne Rd.
Waterloo Rd.
12
13
14
15
16
18
19
20
21
22
23

a coffered ceiling, an exquisite 18th-century Waterford glass chandelier, and two large tapestries depicting the Battle of the Boyne and the Siege of Derry. *College Green, tel. 01/677–6801. Admission free. Open weekdays 10–12:30 and 1:30–4.*

The Bank of Ireland **Arts Center,** behind the bank in Foster Place, has frequent exhibitions of contemporary Irish art. Occasionally, shows are put on covering different aspects of local history. *Tel. 01/671–1671. Open weekdays 10–5, Sat. 10–5.*

From the Bank of Ireland, turn right onto College Green, which becomes Dame Street. Before the road rises, a cast-iron portico reveals one of Dublin's oldest and busiest theaters, the **3** **Olympia Theatre** (*See* The Arts and Nightlife, *below*). Built in 1879, it has been a platform for many notable actors including Gladys Cooper, Alec Guinness, Peggy Ashcroft, Tyrone Power, George Formby, and even the comic duo of Laurel and Hardy. Follow the street up to Cork Hill and **4** **City Hall,** the seat of the Dublin Corporation, the elected body that governs the city. This edifice, with its great domed entrance hall, was built as the Royal Exchange in 1769 and contains many notable historical artifacts, including 102 royal charters and the mace and sword of the city. *Tel. 01/679–6111. Admission free. Open weekdays 9–5.*

5 Behind City Hall (west) is **Dublin Castle,** the seat of British administration in Ireland from the 13th century to 1922. After extensive renovations, it is now used mostly for government and conference purposes. In the Lower Castle Yard, the Record Tower, built by King John between 1208 and 1220, and the earliest of several towers on the site, is the largest remaining relic of the original Norman buildings. Guided tours are offered around the principal State Apartments (on the southern side of the Upper Castle Yard), which are furnished with rich Donegal carpets and illuminated by Waterford glass chandeliers; today these elaborate rooms are used largely for ceremonial occasions. The largest and most impressive of these chambers, St. Patrick's Hall, with its gilt pillars and painted ceiling, is used for the inauguration of Irish presidents. The Round Drawing Room, in Bermingham Tower, dates from 1411 and was rebuilt in 1777; a number of Irish leaders have been imprisoned in the tower, from the 16th century to the early 20th century. The blue oval Wedgwood Room contains Chippendale chairs and a marble fireplace.

Also on the castle grounds is the **Church of the Holy Trinity** (formerly called Chapel Royal), designed in the early 19th century by Francis Johnston, who also designed the original General Post Office building on O'Connell Street. Carved oak panels and stained glass depicting viceroys' coats of arms grace the interior. Look up to view the elaborate array of fan vaults that decorate the ceiling. *Castle St., tel. 01/677–7129. Admission to State Apartments: £1.50 adults, 75p children, including guided tour. Open weekdays 10–12:15 and 2–4:45; Sat., Sun., and public holidays 2–4:45. Call ahead, because apartments are sometimes closed for state occasions.*

From the main entrance of the castle, turn right onto Cork Hill and Dame Street until you reach South Great George's Street on your right. The covered markets here (open Mon.–Sat. 9–6), a Victorian legacy, have changed little despite their restoration; you'll find many stalls selling books, prints, fashion, and trinkets.

Time Out Take a look at the **Long Hall Pub** (51 S. Great George's St., tel. 01/475–1590), one of Dublin's most ornate traditional taverns, full of lamps, woodwork, mirrors, and chandeliers, all at least 100 years old. The pub serves sandwiches, beers, and whiskeys.

South Great George's Street eventually turns into Aungier Street. 6 The inside of the **Carmelite Church** on Whitefriar Street, off Aungier Street, contains an unusual bequest from an early 19th-century pope, Gregory XVI. He gave the prior of the church, in recognition of the latter's work, the remains of St. Valentine, the patron saint of lovers, who was martyred in Rome about AD 269. *Tel. 01/475–8821. Admission free. Open daily 8–8.*

Return to the market area on South Great George's Street; behind the shops on the right, approached by a pedestrian walkway, is the 7 **Dublin Civic Museum.** In the 18th century, the building housed the City Assembly Hall, precursor of City Hall. The museum's small, esoteric collection includes Stone Age flints, Viking coins, old maps and prints of the city, and the sculptured head of British admiral Horatio Nelson, which used to top Nelson's Pillar, beside the General Post Office on O'Connell Street (*see below*); the column was toppled by an explosion in 1966 on the 50th anniversary of the Easter Rising. Often the museum runs exhibitions relating to the city. *South William St., tel. 01/679–4260. Admission free. Open Tues.–Sat. 10–6, Sun. 11–2.*

From the museum, walk east, to Clarendon Street and the entrance of **Powerscourt Townhouse** (*see* Shopping, *below*), an enclosed courtyard that houses a small but charming mall where you can indulge in the many shops of high-quality Irish craft work and numerous food stalls. The mall exit leads to the Catholic **Church of St. Theresa's** and Johnson's Court. Beside the church, a pedestrian lane leads onto Grafton Street.

Part of Dublin's most famous chain of coffee houses, dating from 8 1840, **Bewley's Café** on Grafton Street with its dark wood and marble tables is renowned for its stained-glass windows by Harry Clarke (1889–1931), Ireland's most distinguished early 20th-century artist in this medium. The café, which serves reasonably priced tea, coffee, meals, and desserts, is a fine place in which to observe Dubliners of all ages and occupations. On the first floor, a small museum deals with Bewley's history. (Other branches of Bewley's are located at South Great George's and Westmoreland streets.) *Tel. 01/677–6761. Open weekdays 10–6.*

9 Cross Grafton Street and walk east along South Anne Street to **St. Ann's Church** (Church of Ireland) on Dawson Street. Its plain neo-Romanesque granite exterior, designed in 1868, belies its rich, 18th-century Georgian interior, with polished wood balconies and ornate plasterwork. *Dawson St., tel. 01/676–2186. Admission free. Open weekdays 10–3 and Sun. for services. Closed Sat.*

10 Steps away from the church is the **Royal Irish Academy,** which houses old scientific texts, a large collection of ancient Irish manuscripts, including the 11th–12th century Book of the Dun Cow and 18th-century poet Thomas Moore's library. *19 Dawson St., tel. 01/676–2570. Admission free. Open weekdays 10:30–5:15.*

11 To the right of the Academy is the **Mansion House,** home to the mayor of Dublin and host to many interesting exhibitions, held in the large circular hall. The residence dates from 1710 when it was built for Joshua Dawson, who later sold the property to the government on condition that "one loaf of double refined sugar of six pounds weight" be delivered to him every Christmas. This illustri-

ous street, with his namesake, holds the August Antiques Fair every year, a favorite among Dubliners.

From Dawson Street, walk along Molesworth Street, where you'll pass the **Freemasons Hall** (tel. 01/676–1337), a large 18th-century building with a pillared portico. At the end of the street, turn left onto Kildare Street. At 2 Kildare Street, the full records of the
12 **Genealogical Office** can help people who are searching for Irish ancestors. *Tel. 01/661–8811. Open weekdays 9:30–5:30.*

13 At the same address, you'll find the **Heraldic Museum,** founded in 1911 and once located in Dublin Castle. It now displays a collection of family coats of arms. *2 Kildare St., tel. 01/661–4877. Open weekdays 10–12:30 and 2–4:30.*

14 West of the museum stands the **National Library.** Its main Reading Room opened in 1890 to contain the collections of the Royal Dublin Society. Beneath its dramatic domed ceiling, countless authors have researched and written their books over the years. The library accommodates an important collection of first editions and works by Irish writers, including ones by Swift, Goldsmith, Yeats, Shaw, Joyce, and Beckett. Virtually every book ever published in Ireland is kept here, as well as an unequaled selection of old maps and an extensive collection of Irish newspapers and magazines. *Kildare St., tel. 01/661–8811. Admission free. Open Mon. 10–9, Tues. and Wed. 2–9, Thurs. and Fri. 10–5, Sat. 10–1.*

15 Next to the library you'll find the impressive **Leinster House** (Kildare St., tel. 01/678–9911), constructed in 1745 as a lavish town house for the duke of Leinster and now the seat of the Dáil Éireann (House of Representatives) and the Seanad Éireann (Senate), which constitute the National Parliament. The public is admitted to the Dáil visitors' gallery only with an introduction from a member of the House; local Tourist Information Offices can make arrangements.

16 The **National Museum** is west of Leinster House. Extensively renovated in recent years, the museum features several rooms devoted to artifacts from prehistoric Ireland, including carved stones, weapons, and jewelry. The Treasury collection, including some of the museum's most renowned pieces, is open permanently. Among the priceless relics on display are the 8th-century Ardagh Chalice, a two-handle silver cup with gold filigree ornamentation; the bronze-coated iron St. Patrick's Bell, the oldest surviving example (5th–8th centuries) of Irish metalwork; the 8th-century Tara Brooch, an intricately decorated piece made of white bronze, amber, and glass; and the 12th-century bejeweled oak Cross of Cong, covered with silver and bronze panels. Another room is devoted to the 1916 Easter Rising and the War of Independence (1919–1921); displays include uniforms, weapons, banners, and a piece of the flag that flew over the General Post Office during Easter Week, 1916. Other exhibits showcase Irish glass, lace, and instruments, including pipes, harpsichords, and 17th- and 18th-century harps.

In contrast to the convoluted late-Victorian architecture of the main museum building with its balustrades and fancy ironwork, the design of the **National Museum Annexe** (around the corner on Merrion Row, just past the Shelbourne Hotel) is purely functional; it houses temporary shows of Irish antiquities. *National Museum, Kildare St., tel. 01/661–8811; Annexe, 7–9 Merrion Row, tel. 01/660–1117. Admission free, except for certain exhibitions. Open Tues.–Sat. 10–5, Sun. 2–5.*

Across from the National Museum, at 30 Kildare Street, a plaque records that Bram Stoker, creator of the 19th-century classic horror story *Dracula*, once lived here, quite peacefully.

Time Out Right opposite the main museum entrance, **Cunningham's** (35A Kildare St., tel. 01/676–2952), a cozy tearoom and snack bar, serves all kinds of tantalizing sandwiches and salads.

17 At the south end of Kildare Street lies **St. Stephen's Green,** a verdant city-center square, with extensive lakeside paths. It was an open common until 1663, but the houses and buildings that now stand on its four sides were not constructed until the late 18th century. (Unfortunately, several of these old structures have been modernized without charm.) Lord Ardiluan, a member of the Guinness brewery family, paid for the space to be laid out as a public park in 1880. The green features flower gardens, formal lawns, a Victorian bandstand, and an ornamental lake that is home to many waterfowl. Among the park's many statues are a memorial to Yeats by Henry Moore, and the Three Fates, a dramatic group of bronze female figures watching over Man's destiny by a fountain.

To see inside one of the fine Georgian houses on the green, head for the **Newman House** on the south side. It was in these two houses that the Catholic University of Ireland was established in 1850, with Cardinal John Henry Newman as its first rector. James Joyce describes turn-of-the-century life at this university in *A Portrait of the Artist as a Young Man.* University College, which no longer uses these houses, restored them to their original 18th-century splendor. No. 85, the smaller of the two, has exuberant baroque plasterwork inside, while the style of No. 86 is quite different, containing rococo plasterwork, floral swags, and musical instruments. Built in 1765, they are furnished and decorated in period style. The Iveagh Gardens, at the back of Newman House, are a delightful and little-known oasis. *85–86 St. Stephen's Green, tel. 01/475–7255. Admission: £1 adults, 75p children, students, and senior citizens. Open June–Sept., Tues.–Fri. 10–4:30, Sat. 2–4:30, Sun. 11–2.*

On the north side of the green—referred to in the 18th century as the Beaux Walk—you'll find the imposing Victorian-era redbrick
18 **Shelbourne Hotel** (27 St. Stephen's Green, tel. 01/676–6471), where in a first-floor suite the Irish Free State's constitution was drafted in 1921. A center for Dublin's high society, the Shelbourne is a friendly place despite its grandeur, and nonguests can stop here comfortably for a drink or meal (*see* Lodging, *below*).

Next to the Shelbourne Hotel is the **Huguenot Cemetery,** the last such burial ground in Dublin, which was used in the late 17th century by French Protestants who had fled persecution in their native land. The gates to the cemetery are rarely open, but you can observe its grounds from the street.

Across the road from the Huguenot Cemetery, in Ely Place, is the
19 Royal Hibernian Academy's exhibition hall, known as the **RHA Gallagher Gallery.** This old institution is now housed in one of Dublin's newest spaces, a large, well-lit building; it holds adventurous exhibitions of the best in contemporary art, both from Ireland and abroad. *Ely Pl., off St. Stephen's Green, tel. 01/661–2558. Admission free. Open Mon.–Wed. and Fri.–Sat. 11–5, Thurs. 11–9, Sun. 2–5.*

From the corner of Merrion Row and Lower Baggot Street, turn left
20 onto Upper Merrion Street, where the **Natural History Museum**

houses a collection of mounted mammals and birds, with examples of extinct species, including skeletons of prehistoric giant deer. Beside the museum are the current Government Offices, recently restored and dramatically illuminated at night. *Merrion Sq. W, tel. 01/661–8811. Admission free. Open Tues.–Sat. 10–5, Sun. 2–5.*

21 The **National Gallery of Ireland,** on Merrion Square West, owes its existence to William Dargan (1799–1867), who was responsible for building much of Ireland's railway network in the 19th century (he is honored by a statue on the front lawn). The building was designed by Francis Fowke, who was also responsible for London's Victoria and Albert Museum. Rated as one of the best smaller public museums in Europe, the National Gallery contains more than 2,000 paintings, with a large number representing the Irish School, including the work of Jack B. Yeats, the brother of W. B. Yeats and considered by many to be one of Ireland's finest painters. The collection also includes work by French Impressionists, a small selection of Dutch masters (including some fine Rembrandts), and exceptional paintings from the 17th-century French, Italian, and Spanish schools. *Merrion Sq. W, tel. 01/661–5133. Admission free. Open Mon.–Wed. and Fri.–Sat. 10–5:30, Thurs. 10–8:30, Sun. 2–5.*

22 Across from the gallery, you'll come to **Merrion Square,** created in the late 18th century after the construction of the surrounding homes. This oasis of lawns and flower beds takes you away from the roar of city traffic. During the famine years of 1845–1847, soup kitchens were established here to feed starving refugees. The square has formerly been the home of several distinguished Dubliners, including Oscar Wilde's parents, Sir William and "Speranza" Wilde (No. 1), Irish national leader Daniel O'Connell (No. 58), and authors W.B. Yeats (Nos. 52 and 82) and Sheridan LeFanu (No. 70). Visitors can walk past the houses and read the plaques on the house facades, which identify the former inhabitants. Until 50 years ago, the square was a fashionable residential area, but today most of the houses are used for commercial purposes. At the south end of Merrion Square, on Upper Mount Street, stands St. Stephen's Church. Known locally as the "pepper cannister" church because of its spire, parts of the design were inspired by Wren's churches in London.

At the southeast corner of Merrion Square is another carefully refurbished and fully furnished 18th-century home, less grand than
23 Newman House. **Number Twenty-Nine,** as it's known, depicts the elegant lifestyle of the Dublin middle-class between 1790 and 1820, when the house was owned by a wine merchant's widow. The National Museum of Ireland has re-created the period's style with authentic furniture, paintings, carpets, curtains, painting, wallpapers, and even bellpulls. The house is refurbished from basement to attic showing everything from the kitchen, nursery, and servant's quarters to the formal living areas. *29 Lower Fitzwilliam St., tel. 01/676–5831. Admission: free. Open Tues.–Sat. 10–5, Sun. 2–5.*

Tour 2: North City Center

The northern part of the city center beyond the River Liffey—a mixture of densely thronged shopping streets and run-down sections of once genteel homes—is less attractive today than the south city center. But during the 18th century, most of the upper echelons of Dublin society lived in the Georgian houses around Mountjoy Square and shopped along Capel Street, which was lined with pricey shops that sold fine furniture and silver. However, with the construction of Merrion Square on the south side (completed in 1764) and the nearby Fitzwilliam Square (completed in 1825), the city's fashionable social center switched decisively and permanently from north to south of the River Liffey. Although some of the illustrious inhabitants in the north city center clung to their houses, this area gradually became more run-down over time.

24 Off Upper Gardiner Street, **Mountjoy Square,** built in the mid-18th century, once had four sides of elegant terraced houses, but today only the northern side remains intact. Irishman Brian Boru, who led his soldiers to victory against the Vikings in the Battle of Clontarf in 1014, was said to have pitched camp before the confrontation on the site of Mountjoy Square. Playwright Sean O'Casey once lived here at No. 35 and used the square as a setting for *The Shadow of a Gunman.*

25 A block and a half north of the square stands the Jesuit **St. Francis Xavier,** one of the city's finest churches in the classical style, begun in 1829, the year of Catholic Emancipation, and completed three years later; the building is designed in the shape of a Latin cross, with a distinctive Ionic portico and an unusual coffered ceiling. The striking faux-green marble high altarpiece, decorated with lapis lazuli, came from Italy. The church appears in James Joyce's story "Grace." *Upper Gardiner St., tel. 01/836–3411. Admission free. Open daily 8–6.*

A walk west from Mountjoy Square along Gardiner Street and Great
26 Denmark Street leads you to Parnell Square and the **Hugh Lane Municipal Art Gallery,** built originally as a town house for the earl of Charlemont in 1762 and named after an art benefactor who drowned on the *Lusitania,* which was sunk off the County Cork coast in 1915. The small museum features an impressive collection of paintings and sculpture by 19th- and early 20th-century French and Irish artists and strikingly displayed stained-glass work by Harry Clarke and Evie Hone. *Parnell Sq., tel. 01/874–1903. Admission free. Open Tues.–Fri. 9:30–6, Sat. 9:30–5, Sun. 11–5.*

27 The **Garden of Remembrance,** which faces the gallery, was opened in 1966 to commemorate all those who died fighting for Irish freedom. The garden has a large plaza at its entrance; steps lead down to the fountain area, which has a sculpture by contemporary Irish artist Oisin Kelly based on the mythological Children of Lir, who were turned into swans. Most of the remainder of Parnell Square is occu-
28 pied by the **Rotunda Maternity Hospital** (Parnell St., tel. 01/873–0700), founded in 1745 as the first of its kind in Ireland or Britain. The hospital, with a three-story tower and copper cupola, was designed on a grand scale by architect Richard Cassels (1690–1751). Its exquisite chapel features elaborate plasterwork, appropriately honoring motherhood, executed by Bartholomew Cramillion in 1757–1758.

29 Parnell Square is also the site of the **Gate** (Cavendish Row, tel. 01/874–4045), one of Dublin's main theaters. For five decades, from the 1930s to the 1970s, Michàel MacLiammóir and Hilton Edwards staged many startling and memorable productions here by Irish playwrights and introduced Dublin audiences to foreign writers. Orson Welles and James Mason both performed here early in their careers. Today the Gate continues to mount exciting plays, particularly by young Irish dramatists.

30 The **Dublin Writers Museum,** well worth a visit, opened in 1991 to celebrate Ireland's literary achievements past and present. Besides

exhibits relating to Irish writers, the museum has a writers' center where authors can meet informally. There is also a café and restaurant in the basement. *8–11 Parnell Sq., tel. 01/872–2077. Admission: £2.25 adults, 70p children. Open Mon.–Sat. 10–5, Sun. and public holidays 1–5.*

Completed in 1864, the **Abbey Presbyterian Church,** beside the Writers Museum, is popularly known as Findlater's Church, after Alex Findlater, the noted Dublin grocer, who endowed it. The exterior is distinguished by its soaring spire. The interior, although fit with stained glass windows and ornate pews, retains its stark Presbyterian atmosphere. Climb the small staircase that leads to a balcony for an interesting perspective of the interior.

Parnell Square leads to the top (north) end of **O'Connell Street,** Dublin's most famous thoroughfare. Previously known as Sackville Street, its name was changed in 1924, two years after the setting up of the Irish Free State. After the devastation of the 1916 Easter Rising, the street had to be almost entirely reconstructed, a job that took until the end of the 1920s. The main attraction of the street, Nelson's Pillar, a Doric column towering over the city center and a marvelous vantage point, was blown up by an unknown group in 1966, the year that the 50th anniversary of the Easter Rising was celebrated.

31 At the corner of Henry and O'Connell streets, you'll see the massive **General Post Office,** with the original facade and Ionic portico designed by the neoclassical architect Francis Johnston in the early 1800s. The building was destroyed during the Easter Rising and was then rebuilt in its original style; it reopened in 1929. Inside the main concourse of the building, the bronze sculpture depicts the dying Cuchulainn, a leader of the Red Branch Knights in Celtic mythology. The 1916 Proclamation and the names of its signatories are inscribed on the green marble plinth. *O'Connell St., tel. 01/872–8888. Open Mon.–Sat. 8–8, Sun. 10:30–6:30.*

32 From the GPO, cross O'Connell Street and walk down Cathedral Street to Marlborough Street and the Catholic **Pro-Cathedral,** built between 1815 and 1825. Although the severely classical church design is on a suitably epic scale, the building was never granted full cathedral status, nor has the identity of its architect ever been discovered. The church's facade with its six-pillared portico is based on the Temple of Theseus in Athens; the interior is modeled after the Grecian-Doric style of St. Philippe du Roule of Paris. The Pro-Cathedral has been used over the years for important state funerals. A Palestrina choir, in which the great Irish tenor John McCormack began his career, sings in Latin here every Sunday at 11. The cathedral also holds a large and impressive wooden model of the building itself. Check if the crypt, a dusty and macabre place where Church dignitaries as well as ordinary Dublin folk are buried, is open. *Marlborough St., tel. 01/874–5441. Admission free. Open daily 8–6.*

Time Out **Café Kylemore** (1 Upper O'Connell St., at North Earl St., tel. 01/872–2138) offers a plain menu, but its neo-Viennese decor is charming, with many unusual prints on the walls. **Conway's** (Parnell St., near Upper O'Connell St., tel. 01/873–2687), founded in 1745, is reputed to be Dublin's second-oldest pub. Among its antique furnishings is a real gem: a 130-year-old eight-day grandfather clock.

Tour 3: Dublin West

Numbers in the margin correspond to points of interest on the Tour 3: Dublin West map.

If you follow the River Liffey upstream from the north city center, keeping to the north bank, the streets along the quays lead you to
33 the classical edifice of the **Four Courts,** the seat of the Irish Law Courts. Built between 1786 and 1802 on the site of a 13th-century Dominican Abbey, this massive structure was designed by architect James Gandon, who was also responsible for another Dublin landmark, the **Custom House,** downstream on the same side of the River Liffey. In 1922, during the Irish Civil War, the Four Courts was almost totally destroyed by shelling, and the adjoining Public Records Office was gutted, many of its priceless legal documents destroyed, including innumerable family records; restoration to the building's original style took 10 years. Today the stately Corinthian portico and the circular central hall are worth viewing. The upper rotunda of the Four Courts' distinctive lantern dome provides a good view of the city. *Inns Quay, tel. 01/872–5555. Admission free. Open weekdays 10–4.*

Around the corner from the Four Courts on Church Street is the An-
34 glican **St. Michan's Church,** dating from 1685 and on the site of an 11th-century Danish church. The church, which is architecturally undistinguished except for its 37-meter (120-foot) bell tower, features an 18th-century organ, supposedly played by Handel, and the Stool of Repentance, the only one still in existence in the city; parishioners who were termed "open and notoriously naughty livers" used it to do public penance. St. Michan's main claim to notoriety, however, is down in the vaults, where the totally dry atmosphere has preserved a number of corpses in a remarkable state of mummification. They lie in open caskets, and strong-hearted visitors can shake hands with a former religious crusader or nun. Most of the preserved bodies are thought to have been Dublin tradespeople. *Church St., tel. 01/872–4154. Admission: £1.20 adult, 50p children. Open Apr.–Oct, Mon.–Fri. 10–12:45 and 2–4:45, Sat. 10–12:45; Nov.–Mar., Mon.–Sat. 10–12:45.*

From St. Michan's, turn left from Church Street onto Mary's Lane
35 and continue through to the **Irish Whiskey Corner.** Jameson's Whiskey Distillery was built here in 1791. After local distilleries merged in 1966 to form Irish Distillers, part of the old Jameson's complex was converted into the new group's head office and one of the bonded warehouses was turned into a whiskey museum. Visitors can watch a short audiovisual history of the industry, which actually had its origins 1,500 years ago in Middle Eastern perfume making. Mementos of whiskey making on display include antique posters and a large scale model of an old distillery; you can also view a reconstruction of a former warehouse, where the colorful nicknames of former barrel makers are recorded. In the Ball o' Malt bar, you're invited to taste the different blends of Irish whiskey and compare them against bourbon and scotch. *Bow St., tel. 01/872–5566. Guided tour: £3. Tours weekdays 11 AM and 3:30 PM.*

From the whiskey museum, turn left on Bow Street and make a left onto King Street; proceed to Blackhall Place and then make a left
36 onto Arbour Hill, the location of **Arbour Hill Cemetery,** where the leaders of the 1916 Easter Rising are buried. A total of 14 Irishmen were executed by the British; these included Patrick Pearse, who led the rebellion, and James Connolly, a labor leader wounded in the battle. The burial ground is a simple but formal area, with the

Tour 3: Dublin West

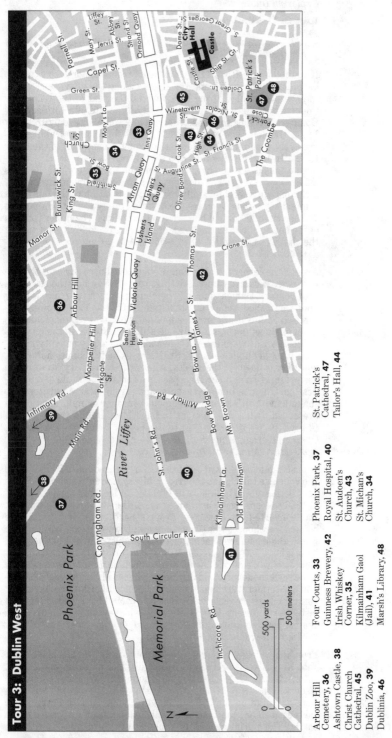

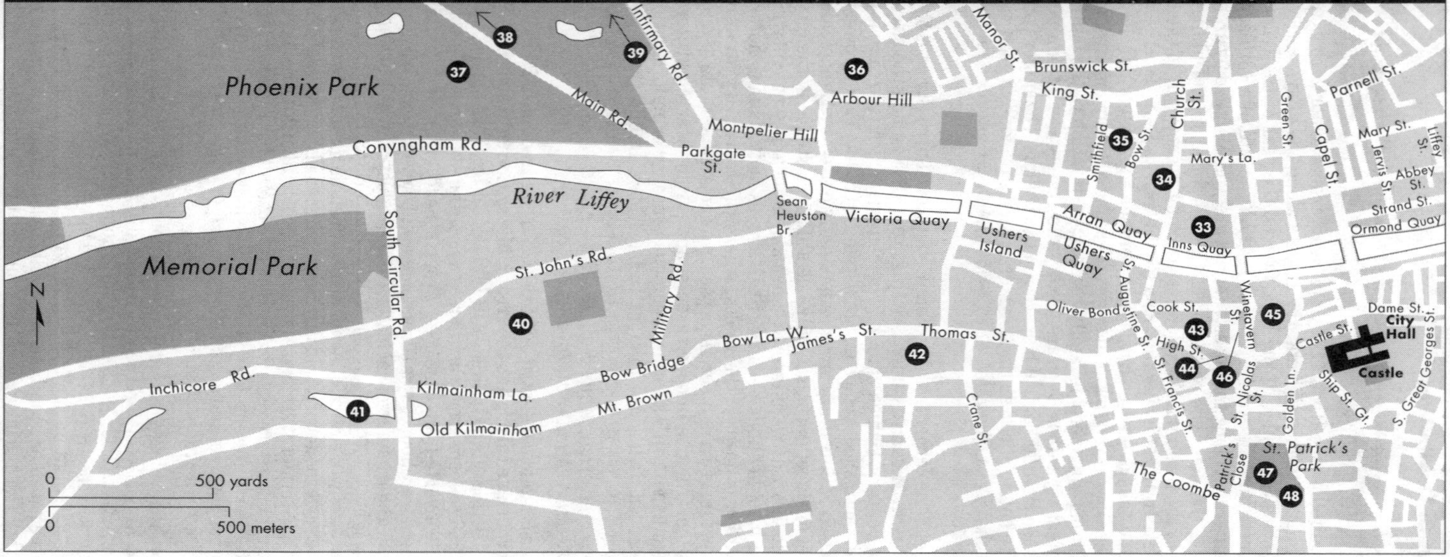

Arbour Hill Cemetery, **36**
Ashtown Castle, **38**
Christ Church Cathedral, **45**
Dublin Zoo, **39**
Dublinia, **46**
Four Courts, **33**
Guinness Brewery, **42**
Irish Whiskey Corner, **35**
Kilmainham Gaol (Jail), **41**
Marsh's Library, **48**
Phoenix Park, **37**
Royal Hospital, **40**
St. Audoen's Church, **43**
St. Michan's Church, **34**
St. Patrick's Cathedral, **47**
Tailor's Hall, **44**

names of the dead leaders carved in stone beside an inscription of the proclamation they issued during the uprising. *Arbour Hill. Admission free. Open Mon.–Sat. 9–4:30, Sun. 9:30–12.*

Walk south toward the quays and then west along Parkgate Street, a distance of 1 kilometer (½ mile).

Time Out **Ryans Pub** (Parkgate St., tel. 01/677–6097) is one of Dublin's last genuine late-Victorian-era pubs; it has changed little since its last (1896) remodeling. Its dark-mahogany bar counters and old-fashioned lamps and snugs (small drinking alcoves) create a restful setting.

At the end of Parkgate Street, opposite the bus depot, entrance
37 gates lead to the 1,752 attractive acres of **Phoenix Park,** Europe's largest public park, with lakes, woods, gardens, and expansive playing fields. The main road that bisects the park for 4 kilometers (2½ miles) was laid out by Lord Chesterfield, a lord lieutenant of Ireland, in the 1740s; old-fashioned gas lamps that line both sides of the road were recently renovated. By the entrance to the park is the People's Garden, a charming and colorful flower garden laid out in 1864.

Among the park monuments worth noting are the Phoenix Column, erected by Lord Chesterfield in 1747, and the 60-meter (198-foot) obelisk, built in 1817 to commemorate the Duke of Wellington, the Irish general who defeated Napoleon for the British. A much more recent edifice marks the visit to Ireland by Pope John Paul II in 1979, when he addressed more than a million people here. Often, wild deer can be seen grazing in the many open spaces of the park, especially near here. Both the president of Ireland and the U.S. ambassador have official residences in the park, but neither building is open to the public. The Garda Siochana (police) has its headquarters here; a small museum contains many relics of Irish police history, including old uniforms. *Park: tel. 01/677–1156, ext. 2250. Admission free. Open weekdays 9–5, but phone in advance to confirm.*

38 **Ashtown Castle,** a medieval fortified castle that probably dates from the 1600s, has been restored and now includes a visitor center with information on the interesting history of Phoenix Park and its varied flora and fauna. *Tel. 01/677–0095. Admission: £1.50 adults, 60p children. Open daily Mar.–May, 10–1 and 2–5, June–Sept., 9:30–6:30, Oct. 2–5; Nov.–Feb., on request.*

39 **Dublin Zoo** may be found on the northern fringes of Phoenix Park; founded in 1830, it is the third-oldest public zoo in the world. Many animals from tropical climes are housed in barless enclosures, while Arctic species swim the lakes close to the reptile house. The zoo is one of the few places in the world where lions will breed in captivity. Some 700 lions have been bred here since the 1850s, including the famous MGM film lion. The children's corner features goats, guinea pigs, and lambs. *Tel. 01/677–1425. Admission: £5 adults, £1.50 children. Open daily 9:30–sunset.*

Return to the main park entrance and walk east on Parkgate Street to the Sean Heuston Bridge; cross the River Liffey to the Heuston Railway Station, continue past the station's main entrance, cross St.
40 John's Road, and walk on Military Road to the **Royal Hospital** on Kilmainham Lane. Built in the late 17th century to house military pensioners, it is a replica of Les Invalides in Paris. After the founding of the Irish Free State in 1922, the building fell into disrepair, but over the last 15 years, a huge restoration program has returned

the entire edifice to what it once was. The structure consists of four galleries around a courtyard with a grand dining hall and a chapel with a stucco ceiling and fine wood carvings. Today the Royal Hospital offers a series of musical events and houses the **Irish Museum of Modern Art,** a survey of 20th-century Irish and international art that includes the prestigious Gordon Lambert collection of Irish contemporary art and the Sidney Nolan collection, featuring recent works by the Irish-Australian artist. The international collection includes work by Picasso and Miro and op art; among the Irish artists featured are Richard Deacon, Richard Gorman, Dorothy Cross, Sean Scully, Matt Mullican, Louis Le Brocquy, and James Colman. *Kilmainham La., tel. 01/671–8666. Royal Hospital: Admission free, but individual shows may have separate charges. Open Tues.–Sat. 10–6, Sun. noon–5:30; guided tours every 30 mins; closed Mon. Museum of Modern Art: Admission to permanent collection free; small charge for special exhibitions. Open Tues.–Sat. 10–5:30, Sun. noon–5:30.*

41 Immediately beyond the front gates of the Royal Hospital grounds lies **Kilmainham Gaol** (Jail), a grim, forbidding structure where leaders of the 1916 Easter Rising, including Patrick Pearse and James Connolly, were held before being executed in the prison yard. In the 19th century, other inmates here were the revolutionary Robert Emmet and Charles Stewart Parnell, a leading politician. You can visit the cells, a chilling sight, while the guided tour and a 30-minute audiovisual presentation relate a graphic account of Ireland's political history over the past 200 years from a nationalist viewpoint. *Inchicore Rd., tel. 01/453–5984. Admission: £1.50 adults, 60p children. Open May–Sept., daily 11–6; Oct.–Apr., Mon.–Fri. 1–4, Sun. 1–6.*

42 From the jail, turn right (east) onto Old Kilmainham, which turns into Mount Brown, James's Street, and then Thomas Street (a 1½-kilometer/1-mile walk). Here you'll reach the vast **Guinness Brewery** complex, the largest stout-producing brewery in the world, where a 19th-century **Hop Store** has been skillfully converted into a museum and exhibition space for art shows. An elaborate audiovisual presentation details Guinness's history since the brewery was established on this spot in 1759. The show ends with the curtain rising on the kind of old-fashioned pub, with mahogany decor, mirrors, and snugs, that has become hard to find in modern Dublin. A complimentary half-pint of Guinness is included in the admission price and a souvenir shop sells the best of Guinness memorabilia: posters, bar towels, beer mats, and garments. *Guinness Hop Store, Crane St., tel. 01/453–6700. Admission: £2. Open weekdays 10–3; show every 20 min. Parking available.*

43 Return to Thomas Street and continue east for 1 kilometer (½ mile) in the direction of the south city center. Thomas Street becomes Cornmarket and then High Street, where you'll find the Catholic **St. Audoen's Church,** with an elegant classical interior, completed in 1847, and a striking Corinthian pillared portico, added at the end of the 19th century. The church provides a well-produced audiovisual presentation, which tells the story of ancient Ireland before the arrival of the Vikings 1,200 years ago. St. Patrick and the Celtic gods figure prominently in the show. *High St., tel. 01/679–1855. Admission: £1.50. Open daily 10–4:30.*

44 An alley below the church takes you to the 13th-century archway of the only remaining stretch of Dublin's medieval city wall. South of the church across the road stands **Tailor's Hall,** built in 1706–07; the only surviving guildhall or crafts workers' center in Dublin, the

structure is now the headquarters of An Taisce, the Irish National Trust, committed to restoring ancient buildings. Visitors can request to see the exquisite 18th-century interior, especially the main hall with its lofty ceiling, tall Queen Anne windows, and a carved balcony for musicians. The basement bar has an authentic early 18th-century stone fireplace. *Back La., tel. 01/454–4794. Admission free. Open weekdays 9–5.*

If you return to High Street and walk east, the street quickly be-
45 comes Christ Church Place, where you'll reach **Christ Church Cathedral,** one of two Protestant cathedrals in Dublin, built on the site of a Viking wooden church founded in 1038; this church was replaced by a new stone church in 1173, constructed by the Norman invader Strongbow, who is said to be buried here. The cathedral was largely reconstructed from 1871 to 1878 in early Gothic style. Remains from the 12th-century building include the north wall of the nave, the west bay of the choir, and the transepts, featuring fine stonework with pointed arches and supporting columns. *Christ Church Pl., tel. 01/677–8099. Admission free. Open May–Sept., Mon.–Sat. 10–5, Sun. between church services; Oct.–Apr., Tues.–Fri. 10–12:45 and 2:15–4:30, Sun. between services.*

46 **Dublinia,** an entertaining and informative reconstruction of everyday life in medieval Dublin, using the latest audiovisual and computer techniques, is in the old Synod Hall, directly across from Christ Church Cathedral. The main exhibits are seen in the Great Hall. Other features include a scale model of what Dublin was like around 1500 and a medieval maze. *St. Michael's Hill, tel. 01/679–4611. Admission: £3.95 adults, £2.90 children. Open May–Oct., Mon.–Sat. 9–5, Sun. 10–4; Nov.–Apr., by appointment.*

Next, walk west from Christ Church Place to Nicholas Street, which turns south into the nearby incline of Patrick Street; this leads you
47 to **St. Patrick's,** the national cathedral of the Church of Ireland. Sir Benjamin Guinness, of the brewing family, paid for its renovation in the 1860s. The original building, dedicated in 1192, was an unsuccessful attempt to assert supremacy over Christ Church Cathedral. In the present-day St. Patrick's, a memorial to Jonathan Swift, the author of *Gulliver's Travels,* is located in the south aisle; Swift was dean of the cathedral between 1713 and 1745. Other interesting tributes include the 17th-century Boyle Monument with its numerous painted figures of family members and the monument to Turlough O'Carolan, the last of the Irish bards and one of the country's finest harp players. To the immediate north side of the cathedral is a small park, with statues of many of Dublin's literary figures. *Patrick St., tel. 01/475–4817. Admission: £1 adults, 40p students. Open Apr.–Oct., Mon.–Fri. 9–6, Sat. 9–5, Sun. 10–4:30; Nov.–Mar., Mon.–Fri. 9–6, Sat. 9–4, Sun. 10:30–4.*

48 Near the cathedral entrance is **Marsh's Library,** the oldest public library in Ireland, founded and endowed in 1701 by Narcissus Marsh, the Archbishop of Dublin. Housed in a modest two-story brick Georgian building approached through a small garden, the library stores a priceless collection of 200 manuscripts and 25,000 16th- to 18th-century books; many of these rare volumes are locked inside cages, as are any readers who wish to look at them. In recent years, the library has been restored with great attention to its original architectural details, especially in the book stacks. *St. Patrick's Close, off Patrick St., tel. 01/454–8511. Admission free. Open Mon., Wed.–Fri. 10–12:45 and 2–5, Sat. 10:30–12:45.*

Tour 4: James Joyce's Dublin

Numbers in the margin correspond to points of interest on the Tour 4: James Joyce's Dublin map.

James Joyce (1882–1941), one of Ireland's greatest 20th-century writers, set his major achievements (*Dubliners, A Portrait of the Artist as a Young Man, Ulysses,* and *Finnegans Wake*) in Dublin; he never wrote about another place. He was, however, unsentimental about his native city, and at one time referred to it as the Center of Paralysis. Joyce spent the first 22 years of his life in Dublin and the last 36 in self-imposed exile, in several locations including Trieste, Paris, and Zurich. Yet he knew and remembered Dublin in such incredible detail that he used to claim that if the city were destroyed, it could be rebuilt in its entirety from his written works, particularly *Ulysses*.

Begin your tour of Joyce's Dublin in the very heart of the city, on
49 **Prince's Street,** next to the GPO. The office of the old and popular *Freeman's Journal* newspaper (published 1763–1924) was located here, but the building was destroyed during the 1916 Easter Rising. The central character of *Ulysses,* Leopold Bloom, a newspaper advertisement canvasser, worked at the *Freeman's Journal* office. Next, travel northward up O'Connell Street and Parnell Square,
50 into Dorset Street, before turning right, then left into **Eccles Street.** No. 7 no longer exists, but the site is revered by Joycean scholars, since this was the fictional home of Bloom. Cross Dorset Street and walk down Temple Street into Great Denmark Street, where you'll
51 find **Belvedere College** (tel. 01/677–4795), a well-preserved 18th-century mansion where Joyce studied between 1893 and 1898. You can visit the interior during term time (September–June, excluding holidays). The entrance lobby, the classrooms, the rich Venetian plasterwork, and the staircase with bronze Apollo medallions are worth a look.

52 The **James Joyce Cultural Centre,** off Great Denmark Street at 35 North Great George's Street (tel. 01/873–1984), is a center for Joycean studies and events related to the author. Though not open to the general public, visitors may phone to hear of lectures and other events organized by the center. The restored 18th-century Georgian town house, once the dancing academy of Professor Denis J. Maginni, has a library and archives. Turn left at the foot of North Great George's Street and continue through to Parnell Street before turning right into the much redeveloped Lower Gardiner Street. Retrace your steps in the direction of the Custom House, with its green cupola dominating the foot of the street. Take the second turn
53 left, into Railway Street; No. 82 was the site of **Bella Cohen's Brothel,** a key location in Bloom's travels around Dublin on June 16, 1904. This immediate area contained many such houses of ill repute in the early years of this century. From here, return to the city center and travel westward along the quays, toward the Guinness Brewery.
54 The **New Ormond Hotel** (Upper Ormond Quay, tel. 01/872–1811), an afternoon rendezvous spot for Leopold Bloom, has been restored in recent years, and plaques in the Siren Suite Ballroom and Malachy's Bar note their connections with Joyce's writings. On Bloomsday, June 16 of each year, special Joyce-related events are organized at the hotel.

Return once more to the city center, eastward along the quays to O'Connell Bridge; walk south on Westmoreland and Grafton streets
55 to the **Bailey Restaurant** (tel. 01/677–3055) on Duke Street, which will be on your left off Grafton. Inside the restaurant, the actual

Tour 4: James Joyce's Dublin

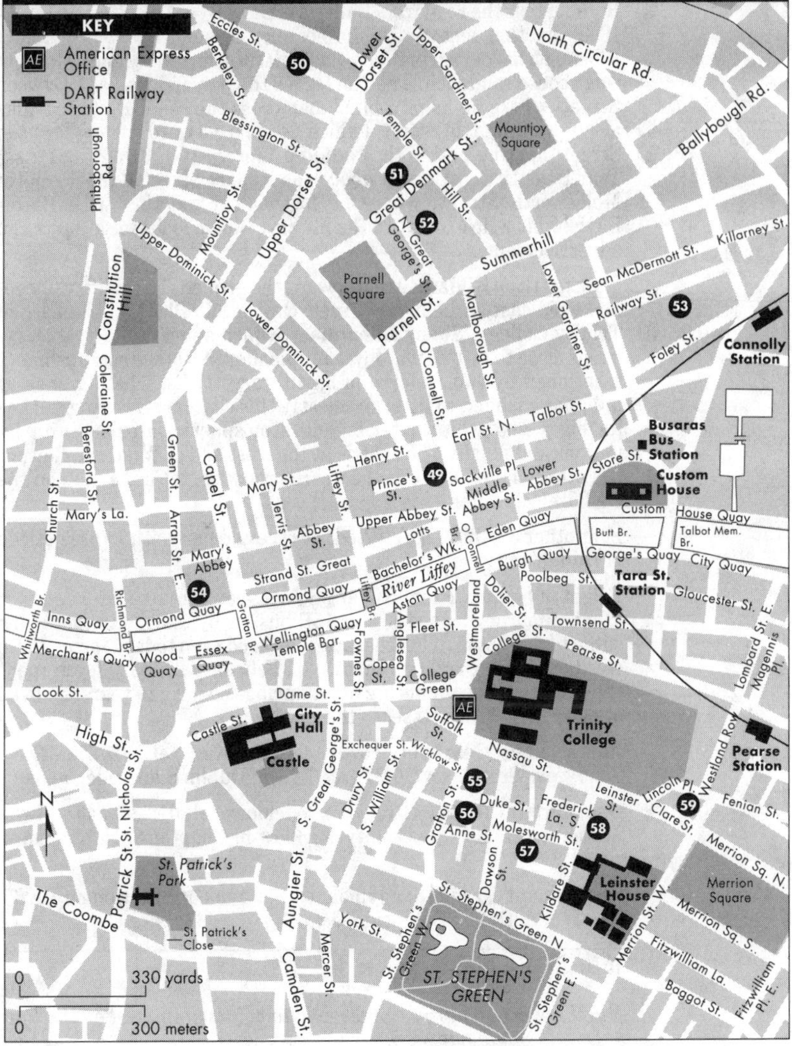

Bailey Restaurant, **55**

Bella Cohen's Brothel, **53**

Belvedere College, **51**

Davy Byrne's Pub, **56**

Eccles Street, **50**

James Joyce Cultural Centre, **52**

Molesworth Street, **57**

National Library, **58**

New Ormond Hotel, **54**

Prince's Street, **49**

Sweny's Pharmacy, **59**

door from No. 7 Eccles Street (*see above*) is carefully preserved.
56 Right across the road from Bailey's is **Davy Byrne's Pub** (tel. 01/671–1298), another historic Dublin hostelry frequented by Joyce; here Bloom, on his peregrinations, has a glass of burgundy and a Gorgonzola cheese sandwich. Then he leaves the pub and walks to Dawson Street, where he helps a blind man cross the road. He then walks
57 along **Molesworth Street** (which leads eastward) from Dawson
58 Street; next he enters the **National Library** (tel. 01/661–8811; *see* Tour 1: South City Center, *above*), on Kildare Street at the far end of Molesworth Street, where he has a near meeting with Blazes Boylan, his wife's lover. In the library, Bloom looks for a copy of an advertisement.

Walk north on Kildare Street toward the grounds of Trinity College, and head east on Leinster Street. On Lincoln Place, at the back of
59 Trinity College, **Sweny's Pharmacy,** which appears in *Ulysses*, remains close to its original Joycean splendor. No other establishment mentioned by James Joyce in his literary works, whether shop or pub, has changed so little since early this century. Sweny's still has its black and white exterior and atmospheric interior, with its potions and phials. The shop is at the west end of Westland Row, at the other end of which is the Pearse railway station, a stop on the DART electric line.

Four other destinations related to Joyce and his writings are outside of Dublin's city center:

Brighton Square. From Kildare Street, you can take a 5-kilometer (3-mile) journey by the 15A or 15B bus, or by taxi, to the southern suburb of Rathgar, a genteel neighborhood even today. James Joyce was born at 41 Brighton Square, on February 2, 1882. Joyce spent the first two years of his life here; during the next 20 years, he lived at more than 20 addresses in the city.

James Joyce Martello Tower (Sandycove, tel. 01/280–9265). Sandycove Station on DART (*see* Tour 5: Dublin Southside, *below*).

One Martello Terrace (Bray, Co. Wicklow, tel. 01/286–8407). Bray Station on DART (*see* County Wicklow in Chapter 5, Dublin Environs).

Sandymount Strand (Sandymount). Sandymount Station on DART (*see* Tour 5: Dublin Southside, *below*).

Tour 5: Dublin Southside

Numbers in the margin correspond to points of interest on the Tour 5: Dublin Southside map.

South of City Center

Take the 47A bus from Hawkins Street in the city center to the suburb of Rathfarnham, where you may explore the 50-acre **St. Edna's**
60 **Park,** which features a charming small-scale lake and nature trails. St. Edna's 18th-century house has been turned into a museum commemorating Patrick Pearse, leader of Dublin's 1916 Easter Rising. In the early years of this century, the house was a progressive boys' school, which Pearse and his brother Willie founded. The museum preserves Pearse family memorabilia, documents, and photographs. *Grange Rd., Rathfarnham, tel. 01/934208. Admission to park free. Open daily 8:30–sunset. Admission to museum free. Open daily 10–1 and 2–6; Oct.–Mar., closing time varies from 3:30 to 5:30. Call ahead.*

Leaving the park, turn on to Grange Road and walk up the hill for about 1 kilometer (½ mile), turning left at the T junction and contin-

Tour 5: Dublin Southside

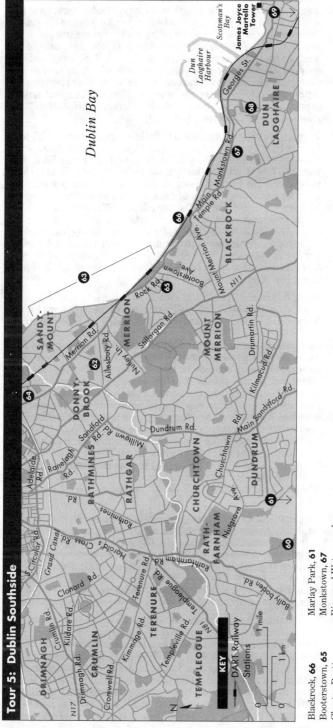

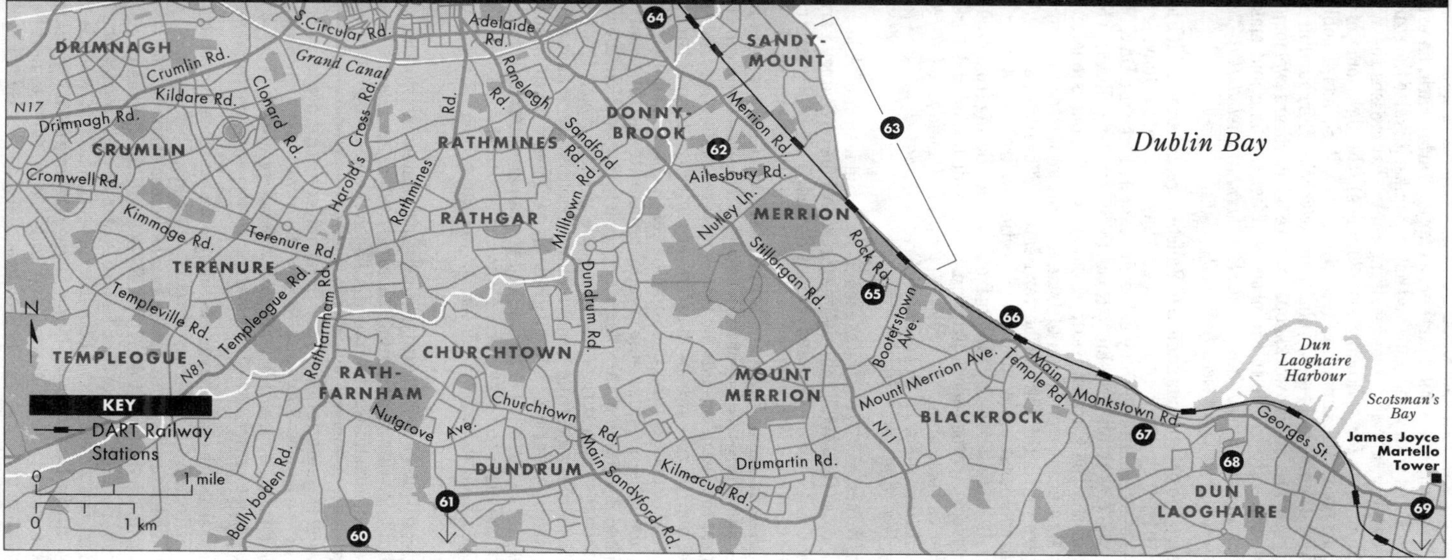

Blackrock, **66**
Booterstown, **65**
Chester Beatty Library, **62**
Dalkey, **69**
Dun Laoghaire, **68**
Marlay Park, **61**
Monkstown, **67**
Ringsend Waterways' Centre, **64**
Sandymount Strand, **63**
St. Edna's Park, **60**

61 uing ½ kilometer (¼ mile) farther, as far as **Marlay Park,** an extensive parkland with woodlands and nature walks; it is also the start of Wicklow Way, a well-defined walking route that crosses the Wicklow Mountains for 48 kilometers (30 miles), through some of the most rugged landscapes in Ireland. Marlay Park has a cobbled courtyard, home to brightly plumaged peacocks. Surrounding this courtyard are crafts workshops, where visitors are welcome to watch the craftspeople in the process of bookbinding and making jewelry and furniture. *Grange Rd., Rathfarnham, tel. 01/494–2834. Admission free. Open weekdays 9:30–5.*

Ballsbridge

To reach the prestigious suburb of Ballsbridge, take the DART local train to Sydney Parade; the No. 7 or 8 bus from Eden Quay; or the No. 45 bus from Burgh Quay in the city center. From the DART station, walk west on Ailesbury Road to Shrewsbury Road, where
62 you'll reach the **Chester Beatty Library,** which houses one of the most significant collections of Islamic and Far Eastern art in the Western world. Sir Alfred Chester Beatty (1875–1968), a Canadian mining millionaire, donated the collection to Ireland. Among the library's exhibits are clay tablets from Babylon dating from 2700 BC, Japanese color wood-block prints, Chinese jade books, and Turkish and Persian paintings. *20 Shrewsbury Rd., Ballsbridge, tel. 01/269–2386. Admission free. Open Tues.–Fri. 10–5, Sat. 2–5. Conducted tours, Wed. and Sat. 2:30.*

Next, return east from the museum, walk the length of Ailesbury Road, cross the DART railway line, and continue on Sydney Parade
63 Avenue until you reach **Sandymount Strand.** This beach stretches for 5 kilometers (3 miles) from Ringsend to Booterstown. It was cherished by James Joyce and his beloved from Galway, Nora Barnacle, and figures as one of the settings in *Ulysses*. When the tide recedes, the beach extends for 1½ kilometers (1 mile) from the foreshore, but the tide sweeps in again very quickly. A small park lies between the main Strand Road and the beach. You can take a bracing walk along the 1½-kilometer (1-mile) breakwater at Ringsend, approached by passing the electricity-generating station. Poolbeg Lighthouse stands at the end of this seawall walk. About ½ kilometer (¼ mile) inland from Sandymount Strand is the village of the same name, built round a large green that is lined with small shops. Some of the stores sell antiques, and you can also stop for a drink at one of the plain but cozy pubs. From the green, the No. 3 bus will take you back to the city center, or you can return by the DART train.

64 **Ringsend Waterways' Centre,** an imaginative new information center, built on stilts on an islet of the canal system, details the history of Ireland's inland waterways, developed 200 years ago. Cross the gangplank and immerse yourself in the working models, including a lock, and the descriptions of the flora and fauna that are an integral part of the canals. *Ringsend Basin, tel. 01/661–3111. Admission: £1.50 adults, 60p children. Open June–Sept., daily 9:30–6:30; Mar.–May and Oct., 10–1 and 2–5; Nov.–Feb., by appointment.*

Outer Southern Suburbs

The outer southern suburbs of Dublin offer a choice of attractions with historical and literary associations, enough for several day trips. These destinations can be reached most easily by the DART local train or by car, taking the R118 from the corner of Lower
65 Merrion Street and Merrion Square. Near **Booterstown,** along the R118 on the way south to Blackrock, lies the largest wildlife preserve in the Dublin area. Many fairly rare migratory species of birds, such as curlews, herons, and kingfishers, come to nest here; information boards along the road describe these birds for visitors.

Also on this main road you'll pass Glena, the house where Athlone-born John McCormack, the world-famous tenor, died in 1945.

66 Continue on 3 kilometers (2 miles) to **Blackrock,** a bedroom community with a popular shopping center, fine sea views, and swimming. Idrone Terrace, above the DART railway station, provides a view across the bay to Howth Peninsula. The old-fashioned lamps on the terrace were recently renovated.

67 **Monkstown,** 3 kilometers (2 miles) south beyond Blackrock on Temple and Monkstown roads (the R119) to Dun Laoghaire, boasts two architectural curiosities. The first is a strange-looking **Anglican Parish Church** in the main square, built in 1833. Its architect, John Semple, was inspired by two entirely different styles, the Gothic and the Moorish, which blend into an unlikely composite of towers and turrets. The church is only open during Sunday services. About 1 kilometer (½ mile) south of town you'll find the well-preserved ruins of **Monkstown Castle,** a 15th-century edifice with a keep, a gatehouse, and a long wall section, all surrounded by greenery.

68 Once a Protestant stronghold of the old ruling elite, **Dun Laoghaire** (pronounced "dunleary"), a further 2½ kilometers (1½ miles) beyond Monkstown along Monkstown Crescent (the R119), was once called Kingstown, after the British monarch, King George IV, disembarked for a fleeting visit in 1821. The town reverted to its original Irish name 99 years later. In some of the neo-Georgian squares and terraces behind George's Street, the main thoroughfare, a little of the community's former elitist elegance can still be felt.

Dun Laoghaire has long been known for its great harbor, enclosed by two piers, each 2½ kilometers (1½ miles) long. The harbor was constructed between 1817 and 1859, using granite quarried from nearby Dalkey Hill; the west pier has a rougher surface and is less favored for walking than the east pier, which features a bandstand where musicians play during summer. The workaday business here includes passenger-ship and freight services sailings to Holyhead in north Wales, 3½ hours away. A recent addition is the car and passenger "Sea Cat," a hydrofoil that takes 4½ hours to make the journey. Dun Laoghaire, however, is also a yachting center with the members-only Royal Irish, National, and Royal St. George yacht clubs, all founded in the 19th century, lining the harbor area.

The first railway in Ireland was built from Westland Row (now Pearse Station) in Dublin to Dun Laoghaire, opening in 1834. Much of the original station's entrance and booking hall has been converted into the fine but expensive **Restaurant na Mara** (Railway Station, Harbour Rd., tel. 01/280–6767), a fish restaurant owned and run by the Irish Rail company.

The former Mariners' Church, west of the harbor and across from the Royal Marine Hotel and the People's Park, now houses the **National Maritime Museum.** The former nave of the church makes a strangely ideal setting for such exhibits as the French longboat captured at Bantry, County Cork, in 1796, as part of an aborted French invasion. A particularly memorable exhibit is the old optic from the Baily Lighthouse on Howth Head, across Dublin Bay; the herringbone patterns of glass reflected light across the bay until 20 years ago. *Haigh Terr., Dun Laoghaire, tel. 01/280–0969. Admission: £1. Open May–Sept., Tues.–Sun. 2:30–5:30.*

From the harbor area, **Marine Parade** leads alongside Scotsmans Bay for 1¼ kilometers (¾ mile), as far as the **Forty Foot Bathing**

Pool, once a male-only preserve but now sometimes used by brave women.

A few steps away stands the **James Joyce Martello Tower,** originally built in 1804 as one of a series along Ireland's east coast, when Napoleon's invasion seemed imminent. Its first civilian tenant in 1904 was Oliver St. John Gogarty, a medical student who was known for his poetry and ready wit; Joyce spent time with Gogarty at the tower, and described it in the first chapter of *Ulysses*, using his friend as a model for the character of Buck Mulligan. The tower now houses a Joyce Museum, founded in 1962 thanks to Sylvia Beach, the first publisher of *Ulysses*, in Paris. The exhibition hall contains first editions of most of Joyce's works. Joycean memorabilia include his waistcoat, embroidered by his grandmother, and a tie that he gave to Samuel Beckett. The gunpowder magazine stores the Joyce Tower Library, including a death mask made of Joyce on January 13, 1941. *Tel. 01/280–8571 or 01/280–9265. Admission: £1.50. Open Apr.–Oct., Mon.–Sat. 10–1 and 2–5, Sun. 2:30–6; rest of year, by appointment.*

From the James Joyce Tower at Sandycove, walk the short distance to the main Sandycove road and continue for 1 kilometer (½ mile) to
69 the next seaside village, **Dalkey.** Along Castle Street, its main thoroughfare, you'll observe substantial stone remains, resembling small turreted castles, of two 15th- and 16th-century fortified houses. From the center of the village, walk up the coastal Coliemore road as far as Coliemore Harbour, where small boats during the summer make the 15-minute crossing to **Dalkey Island,** which is uninhabited except for a herd of goats. The island, covered in long grass, has its own Martello tower. Return to the mainland and continue up the hill to Vico Road, where you'll have astounding bay views (similar to those near Italy's Bay of Naples) as far as Bray in County Wicklow. On Dalkey Hill is Torca Cottage, home of the writer George Bernard Shaw from 1866 to 1874. Return to Dalkey Village by Sorrento Road.

Tour 6: Dublin Northside

Numbers in the margin correspond to points of interest on the Tour 6: Dublin Northside map.

Glasnevin Dublin's northern suburbs remain predominantly working class and largely residential but they do offer a few places worth an extra trip. To reach the suburb of **Glasnevin,** drive from the north city center by Lower Dorset Street, as far as the bridge over the Royal Canal. Turn left, go up Whitworth Road, by the side of the canal, for 1 kilometer (½ mile); at its end, turn right onto Prospect Road and then left onto the Finglas road, the N2. You may also take the No. 40 or 40A bus from Parnell Street, next to Parnell Square, in the north city center.

70 **Glasnevin Cemetery,** on the right-hand side of the Finglas road, is the best-known burial ground in Dublin; it contains the graves of many distinguished Irish leaders, including Eamon De Valera, a founding father of modern Ireland and a former Irish *taoiseach* (prime minister) and president. Other notables interred here include late-19th-century poet Gerard Manley Hopkins and Sir Roger Casement, an Irish rebel hanged for treason by the British in 1916. The cemetery is freely accessible all day.

71 From the eastern side of the cemetery, enter the **National Botanic Gardens,** which date from 1795 and feature more than 20,000 different varieties of plants, a rose garden, and a vegetable garden. The

main attraction is the curvilinear range of greenhouses, more than 124 meters (400 feet) long, designed and built by a Dublin ironmaster, Richard Turner, between 1843 and 1869. The Palm House, with its striking double dome, was built in 1884 and houses orchids, palms, and tropical ferns. In recent times, these buildings have become run-down, but an extensive restoration program is under way. Visitors here can stroll along the River Tolka. *Glasnevin Rd., tel. 01/837–4388. Admission free. Open summer, Mon.–Sat. 9–6, Sun. 11–6; winter, Mon.–Sat. 10–4:30, Sun. 11–4:30.*

Marino Casino To reach the Casino in the suburb of Marino by car, take the Malahide road from Dublin's north city center for 4 kilometers (2½ miles). You can also take the No. 20A or 24 bus to the Casino from Eden Quay in the north city center.

72 The **Casino** is one of Dublin's most exquisite, yet also most underrated, architectural landmarks; a former summerhouse that has never had anything to do with gambling, it rests on part of what was once Lord Charlemont's estate. The main grand mansion was demolished in 1921, but the delightful small-scale Palladian-style casino, built between 1762 and 1771 from a plan by William Chambers, was luckily saved. Although it remained in a decayed state for years, it has now been fully restored, complete with ornate fireplaces and authentic period furnishings in the 16 rooms. Outside, four stone lions grace the terrace, while on the roof, gracious urns hide the chimneys. *Malahide Rd., Marino, tel. 01/833–1618. Admission: £1. Open June–Sept., daily 10–6:30.*

North Bull Island To reach North Bull Island from Dublin's north city center by car, take the Clontarf road for 4 kilometers (2½ miles) to the causeway that leads out to Bull Wall, a walkway that stretches for 1½ kilometers (1 mile) seawards, as far as the North Bull Lighthouse. Bull
73 Wall also extends on the southern end of **North Bull Island,** a 5-kilometer- (3-mile-) long island created in the last century by the action of the tides. With its vast beach and dunes, it serves as a nature conservancy area.

The most northerly causeway from the island, halfway along the inland side, leads to the main James Larkin Road, which at this point
74 fronts **St. Anne's Park.** The green area features extensive rose gardens, with many prize species, and woodland walks. The park is freely accessible all day.

Howth From Dublin, you can easily get to Howth by the DART train, which takes about 30 minutes, or by the No. 31B bus from Lower Abbey Street in the city center. By car, take the Howth road from the north city center for 16 kilometers (10 miles) to Howth.

75 **Howth,** a fishing village set at the foot of a long peninsula, was an island inhabited as long ago as 3250 BC. Its name is derived from the Norse *hoved,* meaning head. The village served as the point for the sea crossing to Holyhead in north Wales between 1813 and 1833, but it was then superseded by the newly built harbor at Kingstown (now Dun Laoghaire), on the other side of Dublin Bay. Today, Howth Harbour is home to an extensive fishing fleet, and it also features a new marina. Both arms of the harbor pier form extensive walks. **Ireland's Eye,** an island with a prominent craglike profile, is separated from the harbor by a channel nearly 1½ kilometers (1 mile) wide. In calm weather, local boatmen make the crossing to the island, where visitors will find an old stone church on the site of a 6th-century monastery and also a Martello tower dating from nearly two centuries ago.

Tour 6: Dublin Northside

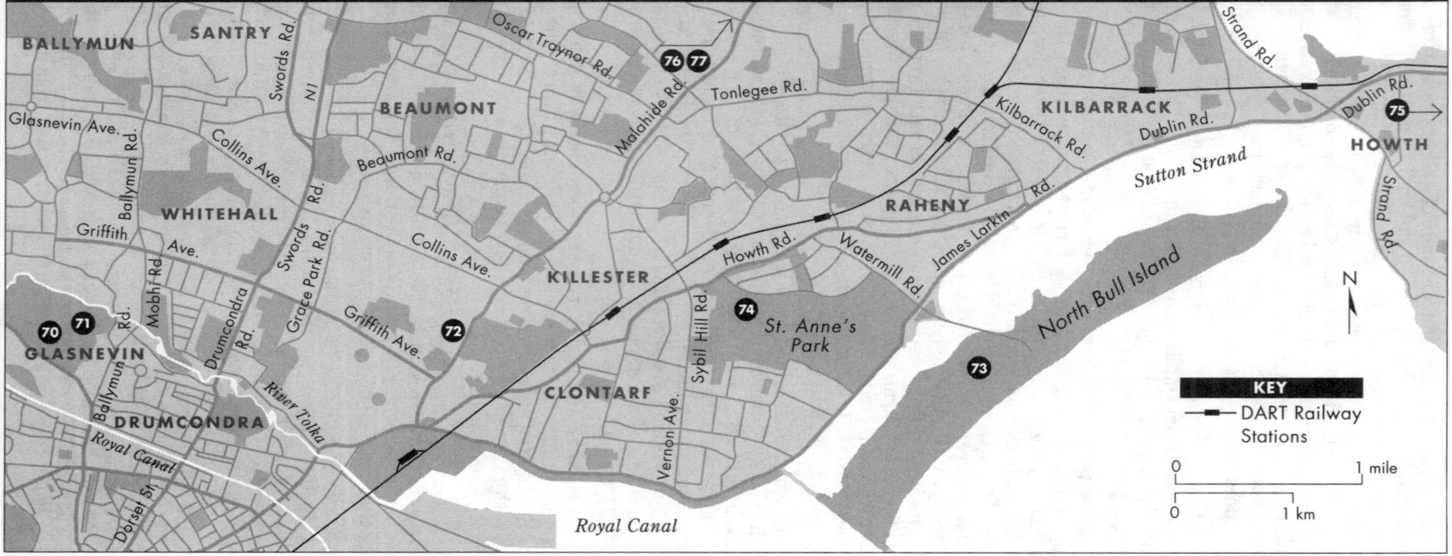

Casino, **72**
Glasnevin Cemetery, **70**
Howth, **75**
Malahide Castle, **76**
National Botanic Gardens, **71**
Newbridge House, **77**
North Bull Island, **73**
St. Anne's Park, **74**

At the King Sitric Restaurant on the East Pier (*see* Dining, *below*), a 2½-kilometer (1½-mile) cliff walk begins, leading to the white **Baily Lighthouse,** which was built in 1814. At times, the cliff path is narrow, with sheer drops to the sea, but the views out over the Irish Sea are very rewarding. From the car park above the lighthouse, you'll have access to perhaps the best views in the Dublin area, over the entire bay as far south as Dun Laoghaire, Bray, and the north Wicklow coast. Much of Dublin can also be seen.

North of the lighthouse at Howth Summit, you can take a local bus to complete the circuit of the peninsula. The 5½-kilometer (3½-mile) journey takes about 10 minutes. Just before the DART station at Howth, disembark for the **Transport Museum.** The star of the collection here is the open-topped Hill of Howth tram. Until 1959, a tram service ran from the railway station in Howth, over the summit and back down to the station. Volunteers have spent several years restoring the tram, which stands alongside other unusual vehicles, such as old horse-drawn bakery vans. *Tel. 01/848–0831 or 01/847–5623. Admission: £1 adults, 50p children. Open Easter–Sept., daily 10–6, Oct.–Easter, Sat., Sun., and public holidays noon–5. Last admission 30 min before closing time.*

Next door to the museum lie the **Howth Castle Gardens,** at the rear of the Deerpark Hotel. The rambling castle, which dates from 1654 and has been much altered in the intervening centuries, is not open to the public. However, visitors can revel in the beautiful gardens. A formal garden with high beech hedges was laid out in the early 18th century, and the rhododendron garden boasts many rare varieties, which can be seen in full flower during April, May, and June. The grounds also feature the ruins of a tall, square 16th-century castle and a Neolithic dolmen (a prehistoric free-standing structure made from boulders). *Tel. 01/832–2624. Admission free. Open daily 8–sunset.*

Malahide To reach Malahide by car from Dublin, drive from the north city center on the R107 for 14½ kilometers (9 miles). You can also get to Malahide by taking a train from Connolly Station, Dublin, which runs every hour and takes about 20 minutes. A bus to Malahide also leaves from Talbot Street, near Connolly Station; while service is more frequent (every 15 minutes), the ride takes about an hour.

Southwest of **Malahide** village, where work to add a big new marina
76 is near completion, stands **Malahide Castle,** which was occupied by the Anglo-Irish and aristocratic Talbot family from 1185 until 1976, when it was sold to the Dublin County Council. The great expanse of parkland around the castle includes a botanical garden with more than 5,000 species and varieties of plants, all clearly labeled. The castle itself is a combination of styles and periods; the earliest section, the three-story tower house, dates from the 12th century. The medieval Great Hall is the only one in Ireland that is preserved in its original form, while the National Portrait Gallery features many fine portraits of the Talbot family and 18th- and 19th-century Irish notables. Other rooms are well-furnished with authentic 18th-century pieces. Also in the Castle is the Fry Model Railway museum (*see* What to See and Do with Children, *below*), featuring rare handmade models of the Irish railway. *Malahide, Co. Dublin, tel. 01/845–2655. Admission: £2.50 adults, £1.25 children. Open Mon.–Fri. 10–5, Sat., Sun., and public holidays 11–5.*

If you're driving, continue from Malahide through Swords on the coastal road (the R106) for 8 kilometers (5 miles), turning off the N1
77 road as signposted to **Newbridge House** in Donabate. (You can also

travel from Malahide to Donabate by train, which takes about 10 minutes. From the Donabate train station, the walk to the Newbridge House grounds takes 15 minutes.) This 18th-century mansion, now publicly owned, features its original furnishings, and its drawing room is considered to be one of the best examples of Georgian domestic design in Ireland. The kitchens of the house are furnished with their original utensils, while in the courtyard, visitors find crafts workshops and some examples of old-style transportation, such as coaches. Beyond the walled garden are innumerable acres of parkland and an animal farm. *Donabate, Co. Dublin, tel. 01/843–6534. Admission: £2.50 adults, £1.25 children. Open Apr.–Oct., weekdays 10–5, Sun. and bank holidays 2–6; Nov.–Mar., Sun. and bank holidays 2–5.*

Dublin for Free

Bank of Ireland (College Green, tel. 01/677–6801) (*see* Tour 1: South City Center, *above*).

Dunsink Observatory, north of Phoenix Park, is one of the oldest in the world, dating from 1783. A small museum section features astronomical instruments. As the location is isolated, visitors are recommended to either drive there or take a taxi. *Castleknock, Dublin, tel. 01/838–7911. Open Mar.–Aug., 1st and 3rd Sat. of the month, 8–10 PM.*

Four Courts (Inns Quay) (*see* Tour 3: Dublin West, *above*).

Lunchtime concerts are presented free during the summer by brass bands and other musical ensembles in the bandstand in the heart of St. Stephen's Green (*see* Tour 1: South City Center, *above*) and in other parks around the city, such as Herbert Park in Ballsbridge.

Marlay Park Craft Courtyard (Grange Rd., Rathfarnham, tel. 01/494–2834) (*see* Tour 5: Dublin Southside, *above*).

Rathborne's Candle Factory (East Wall Rd., tel. 01/743515 or 01/874–9222), Ireland's oldest candle-making firm, dates from 1488. You can make an appointment to watch the candle-making process.

Tower Design Centre (Pearse St., tel. 01/677–5655) (*see* Shopping, *below*).

What to See and Do with Children

Dublin Zoo (Phoenix Park, tel. 01/677–1425) (*see* Tour 3: Dublin West, *above*).

Fry Model Railway is a museum on the grounds of Malahide Castle, 16 kilometers (10 miles) north of the city, offering a unique collection of models of Irish trains from their introduction in 1834 until the present day. They are displayed on an authentic layout built by a master craftsman, Tom Tighe, and feature city landmarks such as the River Liffey and the Hill of Howth. An hourly train runs from Dublin's Connolly Station to Malahide. *Tel. 01/845–2337. Admission: £2.50 adults, £1.25 children. Open Mon.–Fri. 10–5, Sat., Sun., and bank holidays 11–5.*

Lambert Puppet Theatre (Clifton La., Monkstown, Co. Dublin, tel. 01/280–0974) stages regular puppet shows and also has a puppetry museum. Visitors can take the DART train from the city center to the Monkstown and Seapoint stations.

Marlay Park (Grange Rd., Rathfarnham, tel. 01/494–2834), on the southern fringes of the city, provides a free ride for children every Saturday 3–6 PM, on the model steam railway. The No. 47B bus from Hawkins Street in the city center stops outside the park (*see* Tour 5: Dublin Southside, *above*).

Museum of Childhood, in a large 19th-century house, has a fascinating collection of dolls and toys. *20 Palmerstown Park, Rathmines, tel. 01/497–3223. Admission: £1 adults, 75p children under 12. Open July–Aug., Wed. and Sun. 2–5:30; rest of year, Sun. 2–5:30. Closed Oct.*

The **National Wax Museum** is Ireland's only such museum, accommodating more than 100 wax replicas. A favorite with many children is the Chamber of Horrors. *Granby Row, tel. 01/872–6340. Admission: £3.50 adults, £2 children. Open Mon.–Sat. 10–5:30, Sun. noon–5:30.*

Newbridge House (Donabate, Co. Dublin, tel. 01/843–6534) features Tara's Palace, a doll's house that was made to raise funds for children's charities. The palace has 25 rooms, all fully furnished in miniature. The exterior of the doll's house is based on the facades of three great Irish houses—Carton, Castletown, and Leinster (*see* Tour 6: Dublin Northside, *above*).

Shopping

Dublin's central shopping area, from O'Connell to Grafton streets, is the best place in Ireland for concentrated general and specialty shopping, at prices competitive with most other European countries. The big department stores stock the internationally renowned fashion lines and accessories, while alongside them stand small, owner-managed boutiques that make shopping in the city a personalized and pleasurable event. Prices can be higher in the smaller shops, but the department stores are less likely to stock specifically Irish crafts lines.

Shopping in central Dublin can mean pushing through crowds, especially in the afternoons and on weekends. Most large shops and department stores are open Monday–Saturday 9–6. While department stores are closed on Sundays, most smaller specialty shops stay open Sunday 10–6. Shops with later closing hours are noted below.

Shopping Districts

O'Connell Street The main thoroughfare of the city offers perhaps too many fast-food outlets, but it also has some worthwhile stores. One of Dublin's largest department stores, Clery's, faces the GPO, and on the same side of the street as the post office is Eason's, a large book, magazine, and stationery store.

Henry Street Running westward from O'Connell Street, this street features Arnotts department store and a host of smaller specialty stores selling records, footwear, and fashion. Henry Street's continuation, Mary Street, has a branch of Marks & Spencer.

Grafton Street Dublin's main shopping street is now closed to vehicles for most of the day. Two substantial department stores face each other here, while the rest of the street is taken up by smaller shops, many of them branches of international chains, such as The Body Shop, Bally Shoes, Next, and Principles. Smaller streets off Grafton Street, especially Duke Street, South Anne Street, and Chatham Street, have interesting crafts and fashion shops.

Francis Street The new hub of Dublin's antiques trade, this street and surrounding areas such as the Coombe offer a concentration of shops where you can browse at will. The smaller shops are more specialized. With a whole network of dealers, if what you want cannot be found, you will be quickly passed along the line to someone who carries what you seek. This area in the Liberties, the oldest part of the city, has largely replaced the quays upstream from O'Connell Bridge as the chief source of antiques.

Specialty Shopping Centers

Blackrock (Blackrock, Co. Dublin) is technically outside of Dublin's city center, but it deserves special mention as one of the most customer-friendly shopping centers around. It's built on two levels, looking onto an inner courtyard, with the giant Superquinn Center, cafés, and restaurants. Blackrock can be reached conveniently on the DART train line.

Powerscourt Townhouse (S. William St.), a fashionable town house built in 1771, housed a wholesale textile company for many years until it was updated nearly 15 years ago. The interior courtyard has been thoroughly refurbished and roofed over; on the dais at ground-floor level, live piano music is often heard. Two floors of galleries have a maze of small crafts shops interspersed with coffee shops and restaurants.

Royal Hibernian Way (between S. Anne and Duke Sts., off Dawson St., tel. 01/679–5915), a small development, stands on the former site of the two-centuries-old Royal Hibernian Hotel, a coaching inn that was demolished in 1983. The stylish shops are small in scale and include a branch of Leonidas, the Belgian chocolate firm.

St. Stephen's Green Centre (NW corner of St. Stephen's Green), Dublin's largest and most ambitious shopping center, resembles a giant greenhouse, with ironwork in the Victorian style. On three floors overlooked by a vast clock, the 100 mostly small shops sell a variety of crafts, fashions, and household goods.

Tower Design Centre (Pearse St., tel. 01/677–5655) is the most imaginative of Dublin's crafts centers, fashioned from an 1862 sugar-refinery tower. Taken over in 1978 by Ireland's Industrial Development Authority, the tower now houses more than 35 separate crafts firms. On the ground floor, visitors can stop at workshops devoted to heraldry, stained glass, and Irish pewter; the sixth floor features hand-painted silks, handknits, and silver jewelry.

Department Stores

Arnotts has two stores; its main one on Henry Street (tel. 01/872–1111) has three levels. On the top floor, the exhibition hall often has unusual art shows with a Dublin theme. The other store on Grafton Street (tel. 01/872–1111) concentrates exclusively on fashion.

Brown Thomas (Grafton St., tel. 01/679–5666) is Dublin's most elegantly decorated department store, with many international fashion labels on sale.

Clery's (O'Connell St., tel. 01/878–6000) has four floors of merchandise; the ground floor has a *bureau de change*.

Eason's (O'Connell St., tel. 01/873–3811) is a multipurpose store with four floors. The basement, with its rows of souvenirs, and the ground floor, with an especially large book section, are particularly worth browsing in.

Marks & Spencer has its main store on Mary Street (tel. 01/872–8833) with a larger range of fashions and foods than its three-story shop on Grafton Street (tel. 01/679–7855).

Switzers (Grafton St., tel. 01/677–6821) remains a middle-of-the-road department store; the ground floor carries a good selection of Royal Doulton porcelain, Wedgwood china, and Waterford crystal.

Dublin Shopping

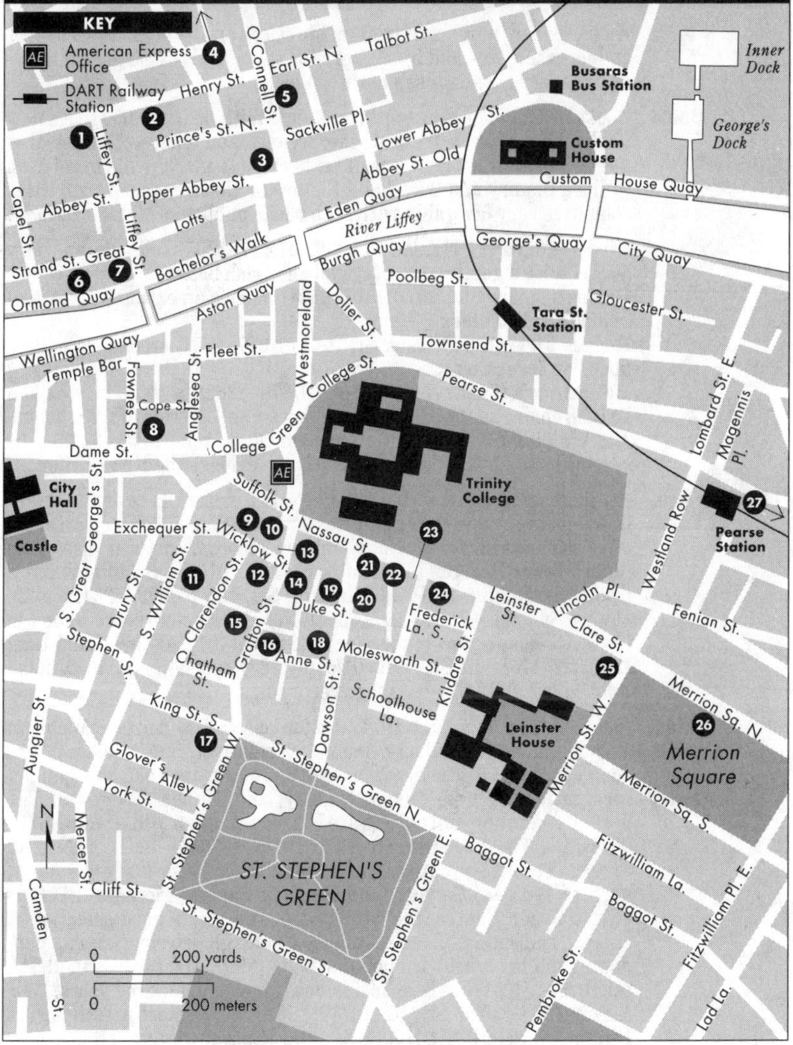

Arnotts, Grafton St., **10**
Arnotts, Henry St., **2**
Blarney Woollen Mills, **23**
Brown Thomas, **14**
Claddagh Records, **8**
Clery's, **5**
Dublin Woollen Company, **7**
Eason's, **3**
Fred Hanna's, **22**
Gael Linn, **26**
Greene's, **25**
HMV, **15**
Hodges Figgis, **19**
Kevin & Howlin, **21**
The Kilkenny Shop, **24**
Marks & Spencer, Grafton St., **16**
Marks & Spencer, **1**
McDowell, **4**
Powerscourt Townhouse, **11**
Royal Hibernian Way, **18**
St. Stephen's Green Centre, **17**
Switzers, **12**
Tierneys, **17**
Tower Design Centre, **27**
Tower Records, **9**
Waterstone's, **20**
The Winding Stair, **6**
Weir & Son, **13**

Specialty Shops

An increasing number of Irish-made crafts and souvenir lines reflect an increasing demand by visitors for specifically Irish goods. Some newer specialty shops sell nothing else.

Books Books are ideal presents from Ireland. With nearly 1,000 titles now published a year in Ireland, the breadth and choice of material is quite impressive. The range of texts is particularly wide in relation to Irish history and travel and the production quality of such titles compares very favorably with such books published outside Ireland.

Fred Hanna's (27 Nassau St., tel. 01/677–1255) sells old and new books, with a good choice of travel and Irish books.
Greene's (Clare St., tel. 01/676–2544) carries an extensive range of secondhand volumes.
Hodges Figgis (54 Dawson St., tel. 01/677–4754) stocks 1½ million books on three floors.
Waterstone's (7 Dawson St., tel. 01/679–1260), a large branch of a British chain, has two floors featuring a fine selection of Irish books.
The Winding Stair (40 Lower Ormond Quay, tel. 01/873–3292) sells second-hand books and has a café that overlooks the River Liffey.

CDs, Records, Tapes An increasing amount of Irish-recorded material, covering traditional folk music, country and western, rock, and even a smattering of classical music, is now available on records, compact discs, and tapes. **Tower Records** (6 Wicklow St., tel. 01/671–3250) now has a branch in Dublin. **HMV** (65 Grafton St., tel. 01/679–5334; and 18 Henry St., tel. 01/873–2899) is one of the larger record shops in town. **Claddagh Records** (2 Cecilia St., tel. 01/679–3664) and **Gael Linn** (26 Merrion Sq., tel. 01/676–7283) specialize in traditional Irish music and Irish-language recordings.

China, Crystal, Ceramics, and Jewelry Ireland is synonymous with Waterford crystal, which is available in a wide range of products, including relatively inexpensive items such as ashtrays or sets of glasses. But other lines are now gaining recognition, such as Cavan, Galway, and Tipperary crystal. The best city-center retail outlets are **Blarney Woollen Mills** (tel. 01/671–0068) and **The Kilkenny Shop** (tel. 01/677–7066), both on Nassau Street. The above outlets are also good for Irish-made ceramics, such as Belleek, Galway, and Donegal Parian. **Tierneys** (St. Stephen's Green Centre, tel. 01/878–2873) carries a good selection of crystal and china. The legendary Claddagh jewelry (rings, pendants, and brooches) are popular buys. **McDowell** (3 O'Connell St., tel. 01/874–4961) has been in business for over a hundred years. **Weir & Sons** (96 Grafton St., tel. 01/677–9678) is the most prestigious of Dublin's jewelers. At **Dublin Crystal** (Carysfort Ave., Blackrock, Co. Dublin, tel. 01/288–7932), visitors can watch the crystal being cut.

Irish Tweeds Suits and other garments, such as skirts for women and jackets for men, come ready-made in this durable and popular cloth. It can also be bought by the length for making your own clothes. The tweed on sale in Dublin comes from two main sources, Donegal and Connemara; labels inside the garments guarantee their authenticity. The following are the largest retailers of Irish tweeds in the city: **Dublin Woollen Company** (Metal Bridge Corner, tel. 01/677–5014); **Kevin & Howlin** (31 Nassau St., tel. 01/677–0257); **Blarney Woollen Mills** (College Park House, Nassau St., tel. 01/671–0068); and **The Kilkenny Shop** (Nassau St., tel. 01/677–7066).

Outdoor Markets

Dublin has a number of open-air markets, selling mostly men's and women's fashions. **Moore Street** is open from Mondays to Saturdays, 9–6; stalls lining both sides of the street sell fruits and vegetables. The traditional Dublin repartee here is renowned in the city. Other open markets are only open at the weekends. A variety of bric-a-brac is sold at the **Liberty Market** on Meath Street, open on Fridays and Saturdays, 10–6, and Sundays, 12–5:30. The indoor **Christchurch Market,** opposite St. Audeon's Church, is open Saturdays and Sundays, 10–5; come here for antiques and bric-a-brac.

Hotel Shops

Several of the leading hotels have shops. The **Berkeley Court** (Lansdowne Rd., Ballsbridge, tel. 01/660–1711) features a crafts shop and boutique that is open all year, adjoined by a branch of Weir's, the Grafton Street jewelers. The Irish gift shop and boutique in the adjacent **Jury's** (corner Lansdowne Rd. and Pembroke Rd., tel. 01/660–5000) stocks a wide selection of Irish tweeds and crystalware. The **Burlington** (Upper Leeson St., tel. 01/660–5222) has a small crafts shop with pottery and jewelry.

Sports and the Outdoors

Participant Sports

Bicycling Dublin streets have no special lanes for bicycles, but the flat countryside to the north and the west of Dublin and the mountains to the south are ideal territories for cycling. Bicycles can be rented for around £35 a week, with an equivalent amount charged for deposit. Nearly 20 firms in the Dublin region rent bicycles; Tourist Information Offices have a full list. Some of the best firms include **Joe Daly** (Lower Main St., Dundrum, tel. 01/298–1485), **McDonald's** (38 Wexford St., tel. 01/475–2586), **C. Harding** (30 Bachelor's Walk, off O'Connell St., tel. 01/873–2455), **Mike's Bike Shop** (Dun Laoghaire Shopping Center, tel. 01/280–0417), and **Ray's Bike Shop** (Milltown Center, Milltown, tel. 01/283–0355).

Cycling is not recommended in the city center as traffic is heavy. And though Dublin has no bicycle paths, Phoenix Park and some suburbs, especially Ballsbridge, Clontarf, and Sandymount, are pleasant for cycling once you're off the main roads. To the immediate south of Dublin, the Dublin and the Wicklow Mountains provide plenty of challenging terrain. Care should always be taken in securing your bicycle when it's left unattended.

Bowling Bowling continues to be a popular sport in Dublin; two kinds are played locally. The sedate, outdoor variety is played at a dozen outdoor areas; among the most attractive of these are **Herbert Park** (Ballsbridge, tel. 01/269–5637) and **Moran Park** (Dun Laoghaire, tel. 01/280–1179). The city has six indoor bowling centers: **Crumlin Super Bowl** (Crumlin Rd., tel. 01/455–9659), **Dundrum Bowl** (Dundrum, tel. 01/298–0209), **Leisure-plex Coolock** (Ballinteer Rd., tel. 01/848–5722), **Stillorgan Bowl** (Stillorgan, tel. 01/288–1656), **The Strand Bowl** (149 Strand Rd., tel. 01/674–1868), and **XL Bowl** (Palmerstown, tel. 01/626–0700).

Fitness Centers Two major fitness centers in the Dublin vicinity are **Fitzwilliam** (Appian Way, tel. 01/660–3988), a privately owned club offering a swimming pool, 10 tennis courts, six squash courts, a gym, and a sauna; and **RiverView Sports Club** (Beech Hill, Clonskeagh, tel. 01/283–0322), with a full gymnasium and sauna facilities. Both clubs offer temporary memberships.

Golf The Dublin region is an idyllic place for golfers, with a total of 30 18-hole courses and around 15 nine-hole courses, with several more in the development stage. Major 18-hole courses include **Deer Park** (Howth, tel. 01/832–2624), with appealing views of the water; **Elm Park** (Donnybrook, tel. 01/269–3438), in a south city suburb location, but with a rural ambience; **Foxrock** (Torquay Rd., tel. 01/289–3992), in an exclusive residential area; **Newlands** (Clondalkin, tel. 01/459–2903), an inland course west of Dublin; **Portmarnock** (Portmarnock, tel. 01/846–2968), one of Ireland's premier courses, situated above a beach northeast of Dublin city center and host to several international tournaments; **St. Margaret's** (St. Margaret's, Co. Dublin, tel. 01/864–0400), a championship parkland course 10 minutes north of the airport, is one of the area's newest courses; **Sutton** (Sutton, tel. 01/432–3013), a seaside course north of Dublin; and **Woodbrook** (Bray, tel. 01/282–4799), south of Dublin city center, with stunning mountain views and sea breezes.

Horseback Riding Few places could be more agreeable for horseback riding than the greater Dublin area. Stables on the city outskirts give immediate access to suitable riding areas. In the city itself, the Phoenix Park provides excellent quiet riding conditions away from the busy main road which traverses it. Outside Dublin, Counties Dublin, Kildare, Louth, Meath, and Wicklow all have unspoiled country territory ideal for horseback riding.

About 20 riding stables in the greater Dublin area have horses for hire by the hour or the day, for novices and experienced riders. A few of these stables also operate as equestrian centers with full tuition facilities. Some major stables in the vicinity include **Castleknock Riding Center** (Castleknock, tel. 01/820–1104), and **Riding and Driving Club** (Willow Rd., Dundrum, tel. 01/298–6112).

Jogging Joggers can enjoy running in Dublin's 40 parks and open squares and along the footpaths of the city's main roads after 6 PM, when traffic has become less heavy. The south city center around Merrion Square is ideal for the sport, but only after business hours and during weekends.

Squash Dublin has about 10 privately owned squash centers; **Squash Ireland** (tel. 01/280–1515) runs four main centers in various city locations.

Swimming Dublin has 12 public pools, but only two can be recommended to visitors, at **Townsend Street** (off Tara St., tel. 01/677–0503) and **Williams Park** (Rathmines, tel. 01/961275). **Fitzwilliam** (Appian Way, tel. 01/660–3988), a private fitness club, features a fine pool, and offers temporary memberships. Privately owned pools open to the public for a small fee are located at **Dundrum Family Recreation Center** (Meadowbrook, Dundrum, tel. 01/298–0183), **Fitzpatrick's Killiney Castle Hotel** (Killiney, tel. 01/285–1533), **Jury's Hotel** (Ballsbridge, tel. 01/660–5000), **St. Vincent's** (Navan Rd., tel. 01/838–4906), and **Terenure College** (Templeogue Rd., tel. 01/490–8822). For hardier spirits, there is year-round sea swimming at the **Forty Foot Bathing Pool** in Sandycove, County Dublin. Traditionally open only to men, it now admits women.

Tennis Tennis is one of Dublin's most popular participant sports, and some public parks have excellent tennis facilities that are open to visitors. Among these are **Bushy Park** (Terenure, tel. 01/490–0320), **Herbert Park** (Ballsbridge, tel. 01/668–4364), and **St. Anne's Park**

(Dollymount, tel. 01/831–3697) St. Anne's Park); these parks each have six courts. Several private tennis clubs are open to visitors, such as **Donnybrook** (Brookvale Rd., tel. 01/269–2838), with six courts; **Fitzwilliam** (Appian Way, tel. 01/660–3988), with eight outdoor and two indoor courts; and **Kilternan Tennis Centre** (Kilternan Golf and Country Club Hotel, Kilternan, tel. 01/295–3729), with four outdoor and four indoor courts. For more information, contact the **Irish Lawn Tennis Association** (22 Upper Fitzwilliam St., tel. 01/661–0117).

Spectator Sports

Football Although football, the equivalent of soccer in the U.S., is the country's latest big-time sport following some impressive international wins, facilities for watching it are not so ideal. **Dalymount Park,** north of the city center, is the main center for international matches.

Gaelic Games The traditional games of Ireland, including Gaelic football and hurling, still attract a large following with intensely exciting big national matches, full of roaring crowds as they cheer on their county teams; games are held at **Croke Park,** the main stadium, just north of the city center. For details of matches, contact the **Gaelic Athletic Association** (Croke Park, tel. 01/836–3222).

Horse Racing Horse racing is one of the great sporting loves of the Irish; nothing attracts the crowds like a race meeting. The sport is closely followed, with keen interest in betting, but the social side of attending racing is also important to Dubliners. The main course in Dublin is **Leopardstown** (tel. 01/289–3607), an ultramodern course on the south side. In the greater Dublin region, other courses include **Fairyhouse** (Co. Meath, tel. 01/825–6167) and **Curragh** (tel. 045/41205), west of Dublin, a setting for classic races on the vast Curragh plain.

Rugby International rugby matches are staged at the vast **Lansdowne Road Stadium,** normally during the winter and spring. Local matches are played every weekend, also during the winter and spring. For details, contact the **Irish Rugby Football Union** (62 Lansdowne Rd., tel. 01/668–4601).

Beaches

The immediate Dublin area has two main beaches. On the north side of the city lies **Bull Island,** created over the years by the action of the tides and offering an almost 3-kilometer- (2-mile-) long stretch of fine sand. The No. 30 bus from Lower Abbey Street stops by the walkway to the beach. The main beach for swimming on the south side of the city is situated at **Killiney,** 13 kilometers (8 miles) south of the city center; this shingly beach stretches for 3 kilometers (2 miles). The DART train station is right by the beach. Much nearer the city center, **Sandymount Strand** is a long expanse of fine sand where the tide goes out nearly 3 kilometers (2 miles), but it is not suitable for swimming or bathing because the tide races in so fast. The strand also can be reached easily by the DART train.

Dining

By Georgina Campbell

A resident of Howth in County Dublin, Georgina Campbell is the food writer for Dublin's The Sunday Press *and the author of* Classic Irish Recipes, *and* Meals for All Seasons, The Best of Contemporary Irish Cooking.

Until recently, most Irish people thought of going out for a meal as a treat reserved for special occasions, such as birthdays and anniversaries, and the most likely dining choice was usually the local hotel restaurant. During the last two decades, however, Ireland has experienced a gastronomic revolution. A new interest in dining out has paved the way for smaller, more individualized restaurants to do well, often in the well-tried French tradition of family ownership, with a chef-patron overseeing every detail. Many of these chefs have studied abroad and been influenced by recent trends; a disproportionately high number of recommended restaurants can be described as French. Nevertheless, although nouvelle cuisine will undoubtedly have a long-term effect on presentation, regional food is making a comeback, which is a positive trend. Traditional Irish dishes used to be thought too ordinary for restaurant menus, but talented young chefs are now keen to revive them, and, indeed, to demonstrate the goodness of Irish ingredients in any way possible. The Green movement is also on Ireland's side, with the potential of unpolluted Irish produce at last being properly valued.

Not many restaurants in Dublin have yet had the courage to specialize entirely in traditional Irish food, but two establishments reviewed below that concentrate on Irish cuisine—Oísins and Gallagher's Boxty House—are interesting and good in their own fashion. Meanwhile, even what is probably the smartest Dublin restaurant, Restaurant Patrick Guilbaud, at least makes an occasional gesture (albeit more Gallic than Gaelic) toward regional specialties.

The hotels, conscious of having lost their dining business to smaller restaurants, are fighting back, creating elegant restaurants, such as the Aisling at the Shelbourne, the Kish at Jury's, the Berkeley Room at the Berkeley Court, the Russell Room at the Westbury, and the Alexandra at the Conrad/Hilton. Yet despite the improved standards at these places, they still tend to lack atmosphere and generally aren't worth the price compared to the independent restaurants. Getting good value for your money is, in fact, a big problem when dining in Ireland. In a comparable British city, lively ethnic restaurants provide above-average meals at reasonable prices, but the ones in Dublin tend to be at the top end of the market. Still, good and less expensive restaurants are starting to fill in the gaps.

Situated as it is beside the sea and with easy access to fresh fish from all around the coast, Dublin offers several places to eat where seafood is the specialty. These restaurants feature not only the traditional cockles and mussels (although these dishes are reappearing on menus) but also wild salmon and oysters from the clear Atlantic waters off the west coast; deep-sea fish trawled off the Donegal coast and the Irish Sea; and lobsters, crabs, and more unusual creatures, such as sea urchins, from rocky coastal waters. Pork, bacon, lamb, and beef still provide the backbone for such traditional dishes as Dublin coddle, Irish stew, and corned beef with cabbage, but game, such as venison and quail, has also increased in popularity. The biggest culinary success story of the last decade has to be the growth of the farmhouse cheese industry: Whenever you see Irish farmhouse cheese on the menu, make a point of trying it; you'll now find dozens of cheeses from which to choose.

Dining hours in Dublin are much the same as elsewhere in Europe, with the main rush at lunchtime from 1 to 2 and at dinner from 8 to 9. VAT (value added tax) will automatically be added to your bill—a

12.5% tax on food, a 25% tax on drinks. Check to see, however, if service has been included before paying. If so, it can be paid with a credit card and there is no need to leave a tip. If not, it is more considerate to the staff to pay the main bill by card but leave the tip (10%–15%) in cash.

Highly recommended restaurants are indicated by a star ★.

Category	Cost*
$$$$	over £20
$$$	£15–£20
$$	£10–£15
$	under £10

**per person, without tax (12.5%), service, or drinks*

City Center

$$$$ **L'Ecrivain.** Set in a basement in the heart of Georgian Dublin, this traditional French restaurant is within pleasant walking distance of St. Stephen's Green. Derry Clarke, the owner-chef, has steadily built up its reputation as one of the city's best and most enduring eating places and he and the younger members of his staff have won numerous prizes at international culinary competitions. It's a small and cozy restaurant (seating only 34), but the menu and wine list are both generous and wide-ranging. The table d'hôte menus, especially at dinner, provide excellent variety and value—quality seasonal ingredients are cooked with care and imagination. Try one of the unusual first course salads followed, perhaps, by game when in season. Dessert is a specialty; save room for it. *112 Lower Baggot St., tel. 01/661–1919, fax 01/661–0617. Reservations advised (required on weekends). Jacket required; jacket and tie suggested. AE, DC, MC, V. Closed Sat. lunch, Sun.*

$$$$ **Number 10.** This elegant restaurant in the basement of the lovely Longfield's Hotel comprises two Georgian town houses that have been converted into a small hotel and decorated with period furnishings. Imagination has been used to create a bower-like antechamber in what was once a coal bunker. The main dining room is decorated in warm neutral colors and glows in the light of an open fire. Tables are set with white linen cloths and napkins and fine modern crystal. Although the place is a popular lunch spot for the local business community, the atmosphere is best at dinner, especially when there is a violinist—on Saturdays all year and on additional evenings in summer. The cuisine combines French-influenced post-nouvelle cooking with the increasingly popular traditional Irish style. A warm salad of lardons of bacon and croutons makes a good appetizer, to be followed, perhaps, by chicken in a creamy smoked salmon sauce or Barbary duck with brandy and green peppercorn sauce. The delicious desserts include simple choices like a puff pastry cream slice with fresh strawberries, and more sophisticated offerings, such as a vanilla and cassis bavarois with a fresh fruit coulis. *Fitzwilliam St. Lower, tel. 01/761060. Reservations advised; weekend reservations required. Dress: casual but neat; jacket and tie suggested weekends. AE, DC, MC, V. Closed Sat.–Sun. lunch.*

$$$$ ★ **Restaurant Patrick Guilbaud.** Discreet to the point of austerity, the modern and quiet ambience features pink and gray decor and large hanging plants. The formality of the service attracts the local business community, as does the air of professional calm combined with

absolute reliability; corner tables are often in demand for meetings. Officially, the cuisine is "classic and nouvelle French," yet in keeping with the current revival of interest in regional food, a selection of homemade black pudding, sweetbreads, and *crúbeens* (pigs' trotters) served with a pepper and red wine sauce, appears on the menu alongside more predictable dishes, such as casserole of Dublin Bay prawns and lobster served with aromatic butter. *46 James Pl., Lower Baggot St., tel. 01/676–4192, fax 01/660–1546. Reservations advised. Jacket and tie suggested. AE, DC, MC, V. Closed Sun., Mon., bank holidays.*

$$$ **Chapter One.** This restaurant beneath the Dublin Writers Museum has vaults, arches, old stone walls, and a warm, soothing decorative scheme in sophisticated shades and discreet patterns. Now a sister restaurant to The Old Dublin (*see below*), its decor and atmosphere echo the theme of the museum above. Although large, the restaurant consists of a network of small rooms linked by arches, creating an intimate atmosphere, even at quiet times. Short but imaginative set menus might start with warm salad of calves liver, flavored with strips of bacon and served on a bed of tossed salad, or blinis and gravlax. As an entrée, sample slices of pork fillet served on delicious little potato cakes, stuffed chicken breast with whiskey sauce, or pan-fried lamb cutlets with vegetables in a rosemary sauce; the food is well cooked, the ingredients fresh. Desserts are attractive and tempting, but don't overlook the farmhouse cheese selection. *18/19 Parnell Square, tel. 01/873–2266, fax 01/873–2330. Reservations accepted; weekend reservations advised. Dress: jacket and tie suggested. AE, DC, MC, V. Closed Sat. lunch, Sun., holidays.*

$$$ **The Commons Restaurant.** On the south side of St. Stephen's Green, this airy restaurant has French doors that open onto a pleasant paved courtyard used for summer aperitifs and occasional al fresco lunches. The elegantly modern cream and deep blue decor is enhanced by thick Oriental rugs. Competently prepared food is served from an international menu with classical French and Middle-Eastern influences. Start off, perhaps, with avocado in a yogurt-lime dressing, or sweetbreads with port and leaf spinach. Main courses lean toward fish, and game in season, but other favorites include lamb cutlets roasted in garlic and thyme, or beef medallions grilled to your liking with shallot sauce. *85/86 St. Stephen's Green, tel. 01/475–2597, 01/478–0530, or 01/478–0539. Reservations required for dinner, advised for lunch. Dress: casual but neat. AE, DC, MC, V. Lunch weekdays; dinner Mon.–Sat. Closed Sun., bank holidays.*

$$$ **Cooke's Cafe.** One of the most fashionable places to see and be seen, this stylish restaurant exudes a smart Continental atmosphere: Outside, there are pavement tables under a chic dark-green awning; inside, colorful trompe l'oeil walls and windows on two sides make up for its small size. Owner-chef John Cooke confidently creates lively "new age" Italian/Californian-influenced menus presented (albeit sometimes rather slowly) with panache. Dishes such as lobster and shrimp bisque garnished with crème fraîche; angel hair pasta with tomato, basil, and Parmesan cheese; and crunchy Caesar salad can be accompanied by an outstanding selection of homemade breads, offered with an olive oil and herb dip, a speciality of the house. Typical main courses, all served on enormous white plates, include lobster salad (a veritable mountain of mixed greens, threaded through with asparagus, red onion, tomato, potato, basil, and an amazingly generous amount of lobster meat); rigatoni with a highly complementary Gorgonzola cream sauce with sun-dried tomatoes and black olives; and duck confit served with *puy* lentils (small, dark green lentils) and pancetta. For dessert, try the fresh strawberry tart or a big, deep almond amaretto cake. *14 S. William*

St., tel. 01/679–0536. Reservations required. Dress: casual but neat. AE, DC, MC, V. Closed bank holidays.

$$$ **The Grey Door.** This establishment, just off Fitzwilliam Square and only a five-minute walk from St. Stephen's Green, is right in the heart of Georgian Dublin and takes its style from the elegance of the restored terraced building it occupies. The menu offers a unique combination of classical Scandinavian and Russian cuisine—the owners call it "the food of the Tsars." The restaurant, which is richly furnished with antiques and gleaming cut glass, is suitably sumptuous. Although the building is large (there is a less expensive, informal restaurant, Blushes Bistro, in the basement and a beautiful private dining room upstairs), the ground-floor restaurant is small and intimate, with tables in the front half of the room grouped around a magnificent Georgian fireplace, complete with open fire. Specialties include gravlax served with a light mustard sauce and dill potatoes, and beef Novgorod, a center-cut fillet, pan-fried and served on sauerkraut, fried barley, vegetables, garlic butter, and sour cream. The extensive wine list includes a good selection in the £11–£16 range; house wines are £11. Accommodation is also available in seven well-appointed rooms. *23 Upper Pembroke St., tel. 01/676–3286, fax 01/676–3287. Reservations advised. Dress: casual but neat. AE, DC, MC, V. Closed Sat. lunch, Sun., holidays.*

$$$ **Le Mistral.** Solid stone walls, pillars, and vaults create an atmospheric background in this classically appointed basement restaurant, with its old kitchen range still in place. Head chef Serges Mangin, hailing from Toulouse, is creating quite a stir in Dublin dining circles with his imaginative and well-presented food. The sunny flavors of Provence predominate the menu, which is especially strong on seafood. Start, perhaps, with fricassee of fresh mussels and *calamaris du pecheur* (a flavorful cross between a soup and a stew, with lots of mussels and pieces of tender squid), followed by attractively browned medallions of roast monkfish or simply grilled Mediterranean snapper. Hot desserts are a specialty and include an especially good *pithiviers* (freshly baked to order and filled with a moist almond mixture) served with a light crème anglaise. *16 Harcourt St., tel. 01/478–1662. Reservations advised. Dress: jacket suggested for lunch, jacket and tie for dinner. AE, DC, MC, V. Lunch weekdays; dinner Mon.–Sat. Closed Sun., bank holidays, Christmas week.*

$$$ ★ **Les Frères Jacques.** Housed in a late-Victorian corner house next door to the Olympia Theatre, this restaurant offers something special, exemplified by the Gallic charm of *le patron* and the nostalgic prints of Paris and Deauville on the green-papered walls. The French waiters, dressed in white Irish linen and black bow ties, are all very proper, yet the atmosphere is far from stiff; romantic souls will enjoy the piano player who performs in the evening. Expect traditional French cooking, with the emphasis on the changing seasons. You'll find a good choice of game in season. Fish lovers can dive into such delights as fresh turbot stuffed with mushroom duxelles, served with basil sauce; also recommended is the *magret de canard*—roast breast of duck, served with a ginger and grapefruit sauce. Chocolate marquise, well laced with rum and served with two sauces, provides a suitably dramatic ending. *74 Dame St., tel. 01/679–4555, fax 01/679–4725. Reservations advised. Dress: casual but neat. AE, MC, V. Lunch weekdays; dinner Mon.–Sat. Closed Sun., holidays.*

$$$ **Oísin's Irish Restaurant.** A restaurant that demonstrates the goodness of traditional Irish cuisine at its best is a rare treat, not to be missed. Although true to their origins, all the old favorites at Oísins have actually been improved by a lightness of touch that is utterly

Ayumi-Ya Japanese Steakhouse, **28**
The Bad Ass Café, **11**
Bewley's, **6**
Burdock's, **9**
Caesar's, **10**
Chapter One, **1**
The Commons Restaurant, **22**
Cooke's Cafe, **16**
Cornucopia Wholefoods, **13**
Eastern Tandoori, **17**
Elephant & Castle, **3**
Gallagher's Boxty House, **4**
Gotham Café, **19**
The Grey Door, **25**
Il Primo, **24**
The Imperial Chinese Restaurant, **14**
The Kilkenny Kitchen, **18**
Le Caprice, **12**
L'Ecrivain, **29**
Les Frères Jacques, **7**
Mitchells Cellars, **21**
Le Mistral, **23**
Number 10, **27**
Oísin's Irish Restaurant, **26**
The Old Dublin, **8**
Paddy Kavanagh's, **31**
Pasta Fresca, **20**
The Periwinkle Seafood Bar, **15**
Pigalle, **2**
Pizzeria Italia, **5**
Restaurant Patrick Guilbaud, **30**

Dublin Dining

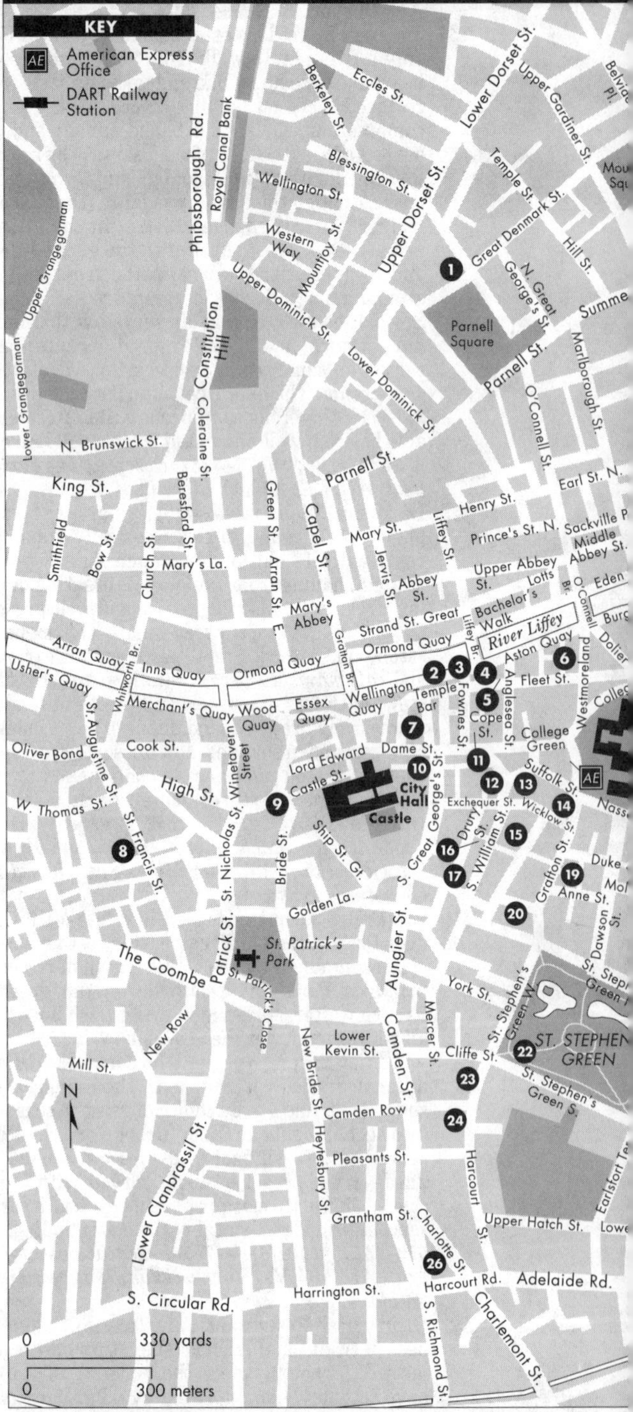

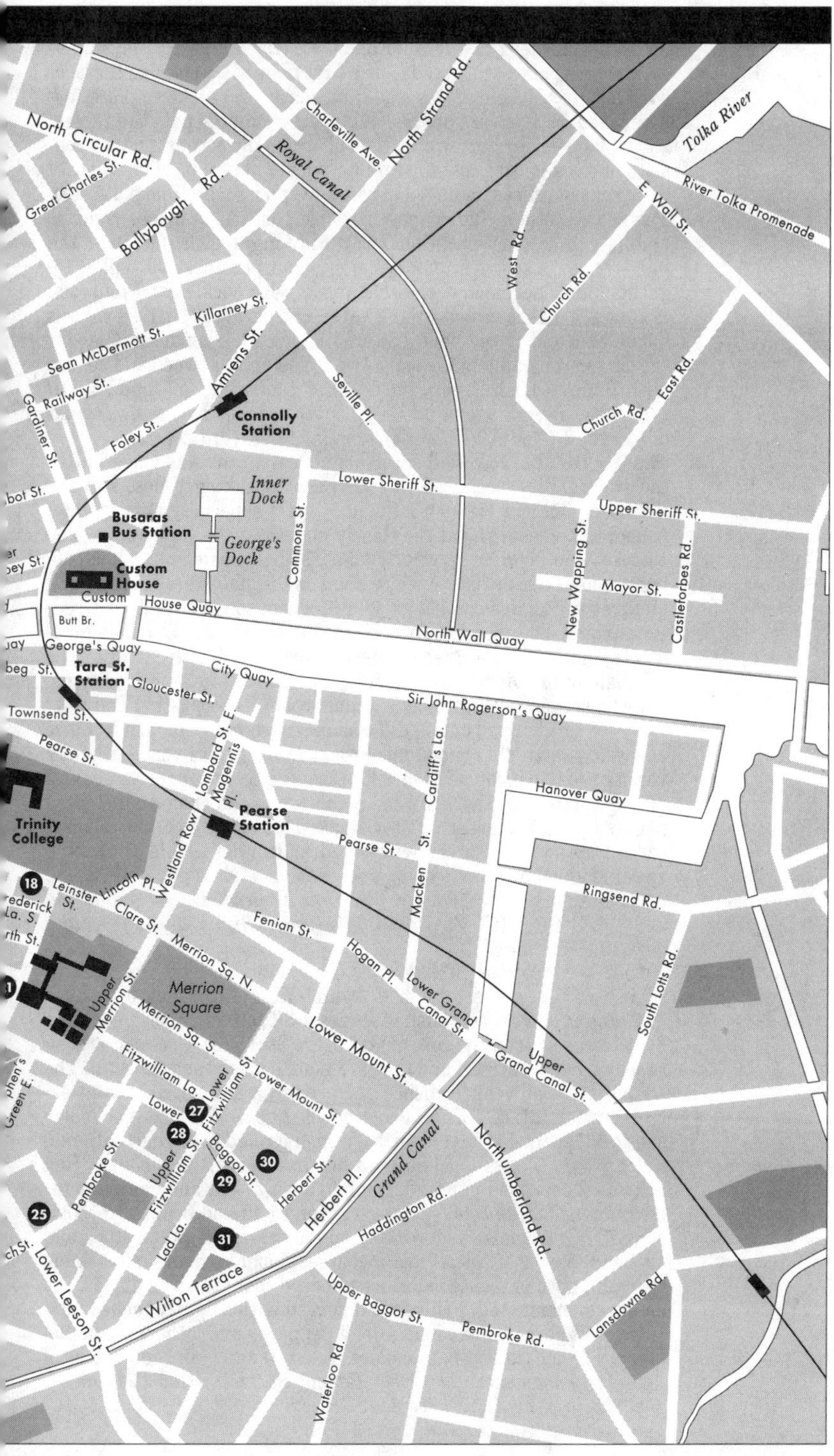
North Circular Rd.
Great Charles St.
Ballybough Rd.
Charleville Ave.
North Strand Rd.
Royal Canal
Tolka River
River Tolka Promenade
E. Wall St.
West Rd.
Church Rd.
East Rd.
Killarney St.
Sean McDermott St.
Amiens St.
Railway St.
Gardiner St.
Foley St.
Seville Pl.
Connolly Station
Lower Sheriff St.
Upper Sheriff St.
Inner Dock
George's Dock
Busaras Bus Station
Commons St.
New Wapping St.
Castleforbes Rd.
Mayor St.
Custom House
Custom House Quay
Butt Br.
North Wall Quay
George's Quay
Tara St. Station
Gloucester St.
City Quay
Townsend St.
Sir John Rogerson's Quay
Pearse St.
Lombard St. E.
Magennis Pl.
Cardiff's La.
Hanover Quay
Trinity College
Westland Row
Pearse Station
Macken St.
Ringsend Rd.
18
Leinster St.
Lincoln Pl.
Clare St.
Fenian St.
Merrion Sq. N.
Hogan Pl.
Lower Grand Canal St.
South Lotts Rd.
Merrion Square
Upper Merrion St.
Merrion Sq. S.
Lower Mount St.
Upper Grand Canal St.
Fitzwilliam La.
Lower Fitzwilliam St.
Lower Mount St.
27
28
Upper Fitzwilliam St.
Baggot St.
30
29
Pembroke St.
Herbert St.
Grand Canal
Northumberland Rd.
Herbert Pl.
Haddington Rd.
25
31
Lad La.
Wilton Terrace
Lower Leeson St.
Upper Baggot St.
Pembroke Rd.
Lansdowne Rd.
Waterloo Rd.

modern. Up-to-date sauces add interest to otherwise familiar dishes; garnishes provide color and a variety of texture pleasing to the modern palate. Situated on the first floor of a Victorian terrace, with a little bar below, this small, intimate, and relaxing place features modern Irish art on the walls, pottery on the polished tables, and a piano player performing the old airs in the corner. Dinner consists of a six-course menu, starting with a house specialty—tasty little sausage slices flambéed in *poítin* (a spirit made from potatoes). The next course includes appetizer-size portions of dishes, such as Dublin coddle (the traditional Saturday-night dish, for after the pub—bacon, sausages, onion, carrot, and potatoes, all boiled together) and, perhaps, a chowder made with cockles and mussels. Among the main courses are Irish stew and other specialties, such as baked ham and spiced beef. If you want a truly Irish dessert, go for the carrageen pudding, a cold sweet based on a seaweed and served with Bailey's Irish Cream. *31 Upper Camden St., tel. and fax 01/475–3433. Reservations advised. Dress: casual but neat. Dinner only. AE, DC, MC, V. Closed Christmas week, Easter week.*

$$$ **The Old Dublin.** This well-established restaurant was named after the surrounding area, which goes back to Viking times, and the Scandinavian and Russian influences seem especially appropriate. A doorman greets you at the clearly marked, well-lit entrance. The elegant, comfortable interior comprises a series of cozy, low-ceilinged rooms with pristine white linen, well-upholstered chairs, and pictures set against a background of warm tones of pink and red, candlelight, and glowing fires in marble fireplaces. Lunch is table d'hôte, but the dinner menu is cleverly organized with extras on the main menu broadening the choices. Specialities include traditional borscht served with piroshki (a mushroom-filled pastry) and blini served with chopped onion, dill cucumber, sour cream, and a choice of salted salmon, herrings, mushroom salad, or prawns. Authentic versions of much-copied dishes like chicken Kiev or beef Stroganoff may surprise, but there are many more unusual choices, including planked sirloin Hussar, a steak baked between two oak planks, served on an oak platter with salad and sweet pickle. Tempting sweets follow, or there's a good cheeseboard. *90/91 Francis St. tel. 01/542028, fax 01/541406. Reservations advised. Dress: casual but neat. AE, DC, MC, V. Closed Sat. lunch, Sun., holidays, and 3 days at Christmas.*

$$ **Ayumi-Ya Japanese Steakhouse.** This more casual, city-center branch of the well-established Ayumi-Ya in Blackrock opened in 1992 and is now an established success. Situated in a basement in a busy business area and convenient to St. Stephen's Green, it is easily seen from the street, and the basement is bright and cheerful. The simple but well-cooked dishes are prepared and served by an extremely helpful staff. Specialties include *kushi-yaki* (food cooked on skewers), teriyaki (food marinated then grilled over charcoal), and *teppan-yaki* steaks (cooked on a hot iron plate). Try *ebifari* (big prawns, deep-fried in breadcrumbs), a very light and crisp starter served with a *wakame* (seaweed) green salad and bean curd. Next comes fragrant miso soup, based on traditional seaweed stock and soybean paste. Typical main courses include beef and salmon teriyaki, both presented sizzling on board-mounted iron dishes, the chunks of marinated, grilled meat served with a lightly cooked mixture of vegetables—onion, sweet peppers, and others—complemented by a light soy-based sauce. Fresh fruit is offered in place of dessert. *Basement, 132 Lower Baggot St., tel. 01/6620233 or 01/6620223. Reservations accepted. Dress: casual but neat. AE, MC, V. Closed Sat. lunch, Sun.*

$$ **Caesar's.** The friendly, efficient staff and good food make for a warm atmosphere at this unpretentious Italian restaurant, with its rows of white-clothed tables. This is a good place for a late meal after visiting the Olympia Theatre across the road. Fresh pasta is made on the premises daily; fresh fish (especially prawns) and veal are other specialties. Favorite dishes include veal parmigiana or prawns with garlic and wine, served, perhaps, with spaghetti alla carbonara as a side dish. Across the road, you'll find a sister restaurant, Nico's (53 Dame St., tel. 01/677–3062), which is run on the same lines but also serves lunch. *18 Dame St., tel. 01/679–7049. Reservations advised. Dress: casual but neat. AE, DC, MC, V. Dinner only. Closed Sun., holidays.*

$$ ★ **Eastern Tandoori.** This popular Indian restaurant makes few concessions to European tastes; although it's on the ground floor of a modern office block in the very center of town, the decor is traditional Indian, with beautiful brasses, wall plaques, and lanterns (all imported from India). The staff wears traditional waistcoats and shirts, and Indian music plays in the background. The menu includes an extensive vegetarian choice, but no European alternatives for the faint-hearted. The cuisine tends to be aromatic rather than burning hot; chicken is a specialty—try, for instance, tandoori *makhan* chicken (spring chicken marinated in yogurt, herbs, and spices, first cooked over charcoal, then in butter with tomatoes and cream, and served topped with nuts). Or sample the hotter *pasanda* (lean pieces of chicken, lamb, or beef, cooked in an almond sauce with fresh cream, highly spiced, and also served with nuts). A second branch of Eastern Tandoori opened on Main Street, Malahide in 1992 (tel. 01/845–4154 or 01/845–4155). *34 South William St., tel. 01/671–0428 or 01/671–0506. Reservations advised. Dress: casual but neat. AE, MC, V.*

$$ **Elephant & Castle.** American visitors may be familiar with its Irish cousin of the same name in New York. Traditional American food in a similar tradition is served in this lively and cheerful restaurant. Bare tables and generally sparse decor contribute to a clatter that heightens the overall noise level. When the service is up to scratch, the turnover tends to be quick, and the slightly Bohemian Left Bank location attracts a young crowd. The food is varied and colorful, and portions are generous. The huge bowls of mixed leaf salad are a positive adventure, and the cosmopolitan contributions ranging from spicy nachos to ginger-laced stir-fries demonstrate the menu's eclectic and highly flavored nature. Seasoning is perhaps a bit strong for sophisticated palates, and main courses tend to be filling—but this suits the typically voracious clientele: Nobody ever leaves hungry. *18 Temple Bar, tel. 01/679–3121. No reservations. Dress: casual but neat. AE, DC, MC, V.*

$$ **The Imperial Chinese Restaurant.** In a city belatedly developing a wide choice of ethnic restaurants, this has long been (and remains) the preferred choice for the local Chinese community, especially at lunchtime on Sundays. Occupying two floors on a busy street very close to the fashionable Grafton Street shopping area, this recently refurbished eatery presents a restful and elegant facade, with deep blue carpets, warm pink walls, a fountain, and an arch, which breaks up the main ground-floor seating area and allows a more intimate dining experience. Although, like other Chinese restaurants, the Imperial offers a number of interesting set menus, the specialty of the house is dim sum (little heart), myriad small portions of steamed and deep-fried meats and vegetables. *12A Wicklow St., tel. 01/677–2580. Reservations accepted; weekend reservations advised. Dress: casual but neat. AE, MC, V. Closed 2 days at Christmas.*

$$ **Le Caprice.** Situated right in the city center, this Italian restaurant features white linen–covered tables and lots of bric-a-brac and busy decorations. The place also has a reputation for a real party atmosphere later in the evening if the pianist is in the right mood, or if musicians from the nearby National Concert Hall happen to be among the guests and an impromptu session gets going. The menu includes several old favorites, traditional Continental dishes such as prawn cocktail, deep-fried scampi, roast duckling à l'orange, and so on. Go, instead, for the Italian dishes, such as tortellini *alla panna* (cooked in broth, drained, and heated in cream) or *melanzane parmigiana* (a sort of pie made of eggplant, interspersed with layers of mozzarella cheese and tomato sauce) and finish up with *cassata*, the classic Sicilian ice cream with candied fruit. *12 St. Andrew's St., tel. 01/679–4050. Reservations accepted. Dress: casual but neat. AE, DC, MC, V. Dinner only. Closed New Year's Day, Good Friday, Easter Sunday, Dec. 24–26.*

$$ **Pigalle.** Housed in a very old building at the archway leading to Ha'penny Bridge, this charming restaurant built up a strong local following within six months of opening in 1988; it's located in an interesting area of antiques shops, galleries, unusual boutiques, and restaurants (now dubbed Dublin's Left Bank). The place features pleasantly old-fashioned decor, a relaxed atmosphere, and good food. Moroccan by birth, the owner-chef trained in the south of France. The menu is unashamedly French. It changes daily, but typical dishes include *le gâteau aux asperges fraîches* (fresh asparagus tart), *filet de truite saumonée à l'oseille et au muscadet* (fillet of sea trout with sorrel and muscadet), or *magret de canard au calvados et aux pommes* (duck breast with calvados and apples). Try to get the window table overlooking bustling Crown Alley. *14 Temple Bar, tel. 01/671–9262 or 01/679–6602. Reservations advised; weekend reservations required. Dress: casual but neat. MC, V. Lunch and dinner Mon.–Sat. Closed Sun., 1 wk at Christmas.*

$ **The Bad Ass Café.** This lively restaurant in the Left Bank area between the Central Bank and Ha'penny Bridge is set in a converted warehouse and retains a distinctly barnlike atmosphere, with primary colors used inside and out. Bulbs and floor alike are bare, but there's plenty to watch—notably the old-fashioned cash shuttles whizzing around the ceiling. Although the food (pizzas, burgers, etc.) is unexceptional, the Bad Ass can be great fun and is popular with all age groups. Children will enjoy the special Kidz Bizz menu. *9–11 Crown Alley, tel. 01/671–2596. Reservations only for groups of 8 or more. Dress: casual. AE, MC, V. Open daily 11:30 AM–11:00 PM (last orders). Closed Jan. 1, Good Friday, Dec. 25–26.*

$ **Bewley's.** This famous chain of coffeehouses is dear to the nation's heart; recent threat of closure provoked an unprecedented emotional response, even from respected national figures. Although no longer under family ownership, Bewley's now seems safe, and a massive restoration program is complete: Branches have now returned to their original style, with dark mahogany trim, stained-glass windows, bentwood chairs, and the much-loved waitresses in black dresses with white aprons and headbands. Specialties include the traditional Irish breakfast (eggs, bacon, sausage, black-and-white pudding, tomatoes, and mushrooms) and a wide range of home-baked breads, cakes, and pastries, which can be washed down with Bewley's own teas or coffees—the shops have 11 blends of tea and 15 of coffee from which to choose. *Westmoreland St., Grafton St., South Great George's St., and suburban branches, tel. 01/677–6761 (head office). No reservations, except in Grafton St. Dress: casual. AE, DC, MC, V. Open daily 7:30 AM–7 PM. Closed Dec. 25–26.*

$ **Burdock's.** In the heart of Viking Dublin, next door to the Lord Edward Pub, Dublin's most famous take-out fish-and-chipper is determinedly old-fashioned. Joining the inevitable queue is part of the fun. As your meal should be consumed as quickly as possible, the traditional place to sit and eat is on the steps of St. Patrick's Cathedral. *Werburgh St., tel. 01/540306. No credit cards. Closed Sun. and bank holidays.*

$ **Cornucopia Wholefoods.** Vegetarian restaurants often provide the best value for the money, and this spot, recently refurbished to offer proper sit-down service, albeit simply furnished, is no exception. The food remains as popular as ever. The menu includes red lentil soup, avocado quiche, vegetarian spring roll, and vegetarian curry, all of them regular favorites. *19 Wicklow St., tel. 01/677–7583. No reservations. Dress: casual. No credit cards. Closed Sun.*

$ **Gallagher's Boxty House.** In a late-Victorian building behind the Central Bank, right in the heart of the thriving Temple Bar area, this highly original restaurant features a lovely country ambience, with lots of dark-green decor complementing the antique pine furniture and trim, the stone floors, and the handmade pottery; everything is Irish made. The main dish, Boxty, is a traditional Irish potato bread or cake that has been cleverly adapted by the Gallaghers to make a potato pancake that is thin enough to wrap around all kinds of fillings, such as bacon and cabbage, chicken with leeks, and smoked fish. Other recommended dishes include bacon and cabbage with parsley sauce and champ (potato mashed with scallions, milk, and butter), followed by brown bread and Bailey's ice cream or gooey bread and butter pudding. Expect to share a table. *20 Temple Bar, tel. 01/677–2762. No reservations. Dress: casual. V. Closed Christmas and Good Friday.*

$ **Gotham Café.** Taking over the premises of the Independent Pizza Company (which still retains its original operation in Drumcondra), this stylish little place just off Grafton Street is very much in tune with the latest vogue for buzzing restaurants with strong Italian/ New York leanings. Zipped-up pasta is typically served with a hot chilli sauce and Creole sausage and special pizzas come gourmet style, with very inventive toppings reminiscent of Bernadette O'Shea's wonderful New Age pizzas up in Truffles of Sligo. It's all great fun and there's a wine license, too. *8 S. Anne St., tel. 01/679–5266. Dress: casual. MC, V. Open Mon.–Sat. 11 AM–midnight, Sun. from noon. Closed Good Friday, Dec. 24–26.*

$ **Il Primo.** Nothing has been wasted on the decor at this spartan little upstairs Italian restaurant just a few hundred yards from St. Stephen's Green. Bare boards and tables, simple (but comfortable) old-fashioned wooden-armed office chairs, stainless steel cutlery, and paper napkins all indicate economy—the (rather good) pictures are even for sale. Lovely, large, modern crystal wine glasses, however, give a hint of the good things to come: The generosity here is evident on your plate. Sound, middle-of-the-road Irish-Italian cuisine changes seasonally. Typical offerings include a starter of warm spinach salad—wilted in a balsamic vinegar dressing and shallots, then served with Parma ham and new potatoes—followed by a creamy delicious risotto—with chunky chicken breasts, a scattering of chicken livers, and some wild mushrooms. Pizzas are sizzling, aromatic, and inexpensive, and there's a choice of salads. Desserts include homemade ice cream, and the Italian cheeses are superb. *16 Montague St. (off Harcourt St.), tel. 01/478–3373. Reservations advised. Dress: casual but neat. AE, DC, MC, V. Closed Sun., holidays.*

$ **The Kilkenny Kitchen.** Uniquely situated in a modern shop specializing in the best of Irish craftsmanship and overlooking Trinity College, this tweed-carpeted self-service restaurant decorated with natural wood showcases wholesome home cooking in the traditional style. The menu includes a house quiche (combining Irish bacon, herbs, and fresh vegetables), a good traditional Irish stew, casseroles, and an imaginative selection of salads. The choice of Irish farmhouse cheeses and the home-baked scones, bread, and cakes are all tempting. Lunchtime is busy; expect to share a table. *6 Nassau St., tel. 01/677–7066. No reservations. Dress: casual. AE, DC, MC, V. Open Mon.–Sat. 9–5. Closed Sun., public holidays.*

$ **Mitchells Cellars.** Situated comfortingly in the vaulted basement of a wine shop, this place hasn't really changed since the early '70s: It still has the same bustling lunchtime crowd, the quarry-tiled floor, whitewashed walls, red and white lampshades hanging over pine tables, waitresses neatly dressed in navy and white—and much the same menu. Country French–influenced home cooking dominates the menu, which includes soups and pâtés, quiche lorraine and salads, beef braised in Guinness, and chocolate and brandy meringue. The restaurant's perennial popularity may be attributed to its attachment to the revered wine merchants upstairs (there's usually something interesting on the wine list at the right price) and to its location just off St. Stephen's Green. Get here early, or expect a line. *21 Kildare St., tel. 01/668–0367. No reservations. Dress: casual but neat. AE, DC, MC, V. Lunch only. Closed Sun.; Sat. in June, July, and Aug.; bank holidays; Dec. 24–28.*

$ **Paddy Kavanagh's.** Tucked away in a lane behind the Bord Fáilte (Tourist Board) head office, Paddy Kavanagh's isn't a place you're likely to come across by chance, but it's very popular with local office workers. This informal, friendly place in an old building has been transformed into an atmosphere well-suited to the restaurant's reputation for good home cooking—the decor features country tones of dark green and terra-cotta and plenty of natural wood. The main dishes tend to be fairly traditional and homey; fish pie is a typical specialty. Tasty vegetarian alternatives and an unusually wide range of salads are also on the menu. This weekday place opens early, with breakfast from 8 AM; it closes following afternoon tea. *6 Pembroke Row, tel. 01/676–5056. Limited reservations accepted for lunch. Dress: casual but neat. No credit cards. Open Mon.–Thurs. 8–5, Fri. 8–4. Closed weekends, bank holidays, Christmas week.*

$ **Pasta Fresca.** Situated on one of Dublin's most interesting thoroughfares, just off Grafton Street, this stylish little Italian restaurant and delicatessen has recently been doubled in size, but still squeezes a surprising number of people into a fairly small area. Antipasto *misto* (assorted sliced Italian meats) makes a good appetizer—or go for a single meat like prosciutto (Italian cured ham), or carpaccio *della casa* (wafer-thin slices of beef fillet, with fresh Parmesan, olive oil, lemon juice, and black pepper). The main courses consist mainly of Pasta Fresca's own very good versions of well-known dishes such as spaghetti *alla bolognese,* cannelloni, and lasagna *al forno.* The pasta is freshly made each day. You'll find lines at lunchtime. *3–4 Chatham St., tel. 01/679–2402. Reservations accepted; weekend reservations advised. Dress: casual but neat. MC, V. Open Mon.–Sat. 8 AM–11 PM. Closed Sun., public holidays.*

$ **The Periwinkle Seafood Bar.** This informal daytime restaurant is located in what was once the stable area of Lord Powerscourt's town house (now imaginatively converted into Dublin's most attractive shopping center); it features the original low arched ceiling and even the cauldron that was once used to prepare the horses' bran mash. The modern quarry-tiled floor, pine tables, and chunky pottery complement the old building's architecture; the kitchen is open, with a gray marble counter the only barrier. Expect home cooking with a leaning toward Cordon Bleu: The emphasis is on freshness, quality, and simplicity. Sample the seafood chowder, served with homemade brown bread, or the toasted crab claws in garlic butter, cheese, and breadcrumbs. *Unit 18, Powerscourt Townhouse Centre, South William St., tel. 01/679–4203. No reservations. Dress: casual. No credit cards. Open 10:30–5. Closed Sun., Christmas, Easter, bank holidays.*

$ **Pizzeria Italia.** This tiny, one-room pizza-bar and restaurant sports the colors of the Italian flag everywhere, from the striped awning over the door to the red, white, and green paper napkins which sprout with cheerful insouciance from stemmed glasses on every surface. Posters advertising famous Italian food products cover one wall and slightly unbelievable travel posters another. It is all delightfully cheap and cheerful, the staff are efficient and humorous, and everybody, whether perched on stools around the edge or eating off the one central table, loves the buzz, the crush, and—above all—the delicious, herby aromas. There's a good selection of starters and light snacks from stuffed zucchini or peppers, garlic mushrooms and mussels in a tomato sauce to homemade soups, and oh-so-garlicky garlic bread. For the main course, pizzas and classic pasta dishes predominate, of course, but there's also a good choice of steaks at very reasonable prices, plus spare ribs, *pollo caccciatore* (chicken cooked in red wine with mushrooms, onion, tomato, garlic, and oregano) and a very good crème caramel to go with the cappuccino. *23 Temple Bar, tel. 01/677–8528. No reservations. Dress: casual. No credit cards. Closed Sun., Mon., 2 wks in June, 2 wks from Dec. 24, and public holidays.*

Suburbs and County Dublin

$$$$ ★ **Le Coq Hardi.** This successful restaurant, close to the city center and most of the major hotels, is consistently popular with the business community. Rosewood furniture, gilt-framed pictures and mirrors, Irish linen, Newbridge silver, and Rosenthal china create a reassuring, clublike atmosphere. The house style is classical French, with some concessions to *cuisine moderne* in the choice and presentation of vegetables. Specialties include "smokies," an appetizer made with Scottish smoked haddock, marbled with tomato, double cream, and Irish cheese and baked "en cocotte" (in an ovenware dish), and *coq* Hardi, which is chicken filled with potatoes, mushrooms, and special herbs, wrapped in bacon, oven-baked, and finished with Irish whiskey. The outstanding wine list concentrates on the great wines of Bordeaux, Burgundy, Loire, and Champagne; bear in mind, however, that there are very few selections under £20. *35 Pembroke Rd., Ballsbridge, tel. 01/668–9070, fax 01/668–9887. Reservations required. Jacket required; tie advised. AE, DC, MC, V. Lunch weekdays; dinner Mon.–Sat. Closed Sun., bank holidays, 1 wk at Christmas, and 2 wks in Aug.*

$$$$ **Restaurant Na Mara.** Railway buffs will adore this elegant seafood restaurant overlooking Dun Laoghaire harbor. Designed in the classical style by the renowned early 19th-century architect John Mulvany, it was part of a prestigious new terminal for the Dublin–Kingstown (Dun Laoghaire) railway, completed in 1850. Run as a restaurant since 1965, the building is meticulously maintained and is, truly, a feast for the eyes. The lofty scale of both the bar-reception area and the main restaurant is highlighted by magnificent draperies, clever lighting, interesting pictures, and well-spaced luxuriously appointed tables (complete with Wedgwood plates depicting the station). But any tendency to over-formality is offset by the warmth of the predominating soft peaches and creams. While sea-

food is the speciality of the house, typically in classical dishes with a modern twist such as paupiette of sole with scallop mousse, served with tagliatelle of courgette (zucchini), sorrel, and tomato sauce, there is always at least one non-seafood offering—mousseline of duck livers with essence of wild mushroom to start, perhaps, with breast of guinea fowl with a black pudding farce and tarragon *jus.* Flambéed dishes are something of a speciality, including desserts like crêpes suzette and banana flambée, which bring a touch of old-style glamor to the Dublin dining scene. *Dun Laoghaire Harbour, Co. Dublin, tel. 01/280–0509. Reservations advised. Dress: jacket and tie suggested. AE, DC, MC, V. Closed Sun., bank holidays, Good Friday, 1 wk at Christmas.*

$$$–$$$$ **Clarets.** Behind its deep wine-purple public face, the soft-toned decor inside this highly regarded restaurant creates a soothing background. The dining area is cleverly divided into two levels and an irregular shape with plenty of corners and partitions creates an unusual amount of privacy in what is basically one large room. Well-appointed tables and comfortable chairs complete the thoughtfully planned, somewhat understated interior. Owner/chef Alan O'Reilly is well-known for his creative use of seasonal ingredients (including game), and he works hard to provide variety with frequently changing menus and occasional special theme evenings. Food is imaginative in concept and presentation: An appetizer of mousseline of seafood with a light ginger sauce and a fleuron of puff pastry may be followed by a selection of excellent homemade breads, including some particularly tasty basil bread and sesame seed rolls. Mixed-leaf salad is served dramatically in a filo basket, with quails' eggs hidden inside—witty and delicious. Pigeon in a rich port sauce is wrapped first in cabbage, then filo pastry, and baked. A typical main course is steamed supreme of turbot served with a grain mustard sauce and garnished with leeks, courgettes, and carrots in addition to a good selection of side vegetables. For dessert, look out for their excellent tangy lemon tart, but leave room to round off the meal with coffee and imaginative petits fours. *63–65 Main St., Blackrock, Co. Dublin, tel. 01/288–2008. Reservations advised. Dress: casual but neat. AE, DC, MC, V. Closed Sun., Mon., and 1 wk at Christmas.*

$$$–$$$$ **Ernie's Restaurant.** This long-established single-story restaurant in Donnybrook, only a few minutes by taxi from the city center, is built around a large tree and fountain that are particularly pretty when lit up at night. Almost as famous for the late Ernie Evans' personal collection of original paintings—which cover virtually all the available wallspace—as for the food, the dining room offers a welcoming atmosphere, with distinctive blue Irish linen tablecloths and sparkling crystal on the tables. The restaurant is still owned by the Evans family. The cuisine is basically classic French, with concessions to traditional Irish—dishes like *moules à la marinière* (mussels cooked with chopped shallot, bouquet garni, and white wine) or fillets of sole Bonne Femme (fillets baked with chopped mushrooms, parsley, and white wine) are typical. A seasonal vegetarian platter, willingly made to order, is a nice touch in an establishment where high-quality ingredients, attention to detail, and consistency are still the hallmarks. *Mulberry Gardens, Donnybrook, tel. 01/269–3260. Reservations advised; weekend reservations required. Jacket and tie suggested. AE, DC, MC, V. Closed Sun., Mon., bank holidays, 1 wk at Christmas.*

$$$ **Abbey Tavern.** In the fishing port of Howth, 14 kilometers (9 miles) north of the city center, this Old World tavern is only a five-minute walk from the DART station. The ancient building's original stone walls, flagged floors, and old gaslights are more effective than any-

thing a decorator might conceive; blazing turf fires add to the historic atmosphere. The upstairs restaurant specializes in fish dishes, with the traditional Irish and Continental cuisine. Sole Abbey—fillet of sole stuffed with prawns, mushrooms, and herbs—is a house specialty, and fresh Dublin Bay prawns can be cooked to order. Traditional Irish music is offered in a different part of the building. *Abbey St., Howth, tel. 01/839–0307. Reservations advised; weekend reservations required. Jacket suggested. AE, DC, MC, V. Dinner only: Apr.–Sept., daily; Oct.–Mar., closed Sun. eves.*

$$$ **Ayumi-Ya Japanese Restaurant.** This is Dublin's first Japanese restaurant, in a small shopping complex 8 kilometers (5 miles) from the city center. Customers have a choice of seating at regular tables; on the floor, Japanese-style; or at teppan-yaki tables (offered by reservation). Japanese decorations and porcelain are used throughout and the waiting staff wear kimonos or Japanese-style shirts. The Japanese proprietor-chef is a qualified dietician and has won numerous awards for her cuisine. Choices include sushi and sashimi (a selection of ultrafresh, thinly cut raw fish), tempura (a deep-fried selection of prawns, vegetables, and fish), beef teriyaki, and teppan-yaki, which the chef cooks right at the tables; Ayumi-Ya is the only restaurant in Ireland offering this iron-grill style of cooking. *Newpark Centre, Newtownpark Ave., Blackrock, tel. 01/283–1767. Reservations advised; weekend reservations required. Dress: casual but neat. AE, DC, MC, V. Dinner only. Closed Dec. 24–26, Jan. 1–2 and Good Friday.*

$$$ **Beaufield Mews.** A 10-minute taxi ride from the city center, this 18th-century coach house with stables still has its original cobbled courtyard and is even said to be haunted by a friendly monk. Inside it's all black beams, old furniture, and bric-a-brac, including stable artifacts. The most desirable tables overlook the courtyard or the garden, or are, less predictably, "under the nun" (the nun in question is a 17th-century portrait). The traditional food makes use of the best of seasonal ingredients; you'll find old favorites like roast duckling à l'orange but also fresh wild salmon steaks simply grilled or poached and served with hollandaise sauce. The menu also includes game in season—venison and pheasant are specialties—and homemade ice cream. *Woodlands Ave., Stillorgan, tel. 01/288–6945. Reservations required. Dress: casual but neat. AE, DC, V. Dinner only (other meals by arrangement). Closed Sun., Mon., bank holidays.*

$$$ **Bon Appetit.** Owner-chef Patsey McGuirk brought a loyal following from his previous city-center restaurant of the same name when he moved, in 1989, to this substantial Georgian terraced building in Malahide, only a 10-minute drive from Dublin Airport and a half-hour from the city center. The striking floral decor in warm shades of pink creates a cozy traditional atmosphere, an impression heightened by the staff of black-jacketed waiters. Patsey's wife, Catherine, manages the front of the house. The traditional Continental menu includes such entrées as escargots and mushrooms in garlic and cream sauce, and a generous choice of desserts. Especially recommended are sole McGuirk, boned sole stuffed with prawns and turbot and baked with white wine and cream, and duckling Montmorency served with black cherries and a cherry brandy and orange sauce. *9 James's Terr., Malahide, tel. 01/845–0314. Reservations advised. Dress: casual but neat. AE, DC, MC, V. Lunch weekdays; dinner Mon.–Sat. Closed Sun., bank holidays, Christmas week.*

$$$ ★ **The King Sitric.** This well-known seafood restaurant is a main attraction in the fishing port of Howth, north of the city center; it's in a Georgian house on the harbor front, with the yacht marina and port on one side, and with sea views from the upstairs seafood bar, where

informal lunches are served in summer. The restaurant consists of a series of rooms on the ground floor, furnished traditionally with antiques and white linen; try to get a table in the middle, near the kitchen. The menu makes little concession to non–fish eaters, although there's usually some alternative, such as chicken Kiev or some game, when in season. But who could resist fish that is so utterly fresh? Lobster, caught just yards away in Balscadden Bay, is the big treat; it's best at its simplest, in butter sauce. Crab is equally fresh and scrumptious here, dressed with mayonnaise or Mornay sauce. *Calmar frites* (deep-fried squid) is a special starter served with fresh tomato or tartar sauce. For dessert, don't miss the house specialty, meringue Sitric (hollow meringues, filled with homemade vanilla ice cream, covered with dark chocolate sauce, and scattered with flaked almonds). *East Pier, Howth, Co. Dublin, tel. 01/823–6729. Reservations advised; weekend reservations required. Jacket advised; jacket and tie suggested. AE, DC, MC, V. Private dining by arrangement. Closed Sun., bank holidays, and at Christmas and Easter, 10 days each.*

$$$ ★ **Roche's Bistro.** About a 15-minute drive out of Dublin and handy to the airport, Roche's is part of an old terraced house in the main street of a pretty coastal town. Orla Roche is a Francophile, and it shows—the particular brand of relaxed Gallic charm and good country French cooking found here is rare in Ireland. The small and cozy place, with white walls covered with French prints and antique copper utensils, has cheerful blue-and-white-check tablecloths and an open coal fire in winter. The cooking is done in full view of clients, in a minuscule kitchen behind the bar. Seafood figures strongly on the wide-ranging menu. You might start with a mousseline of scallops (scallops pureed with egg white, Noilly Prat, cream, and grated orange zest, cooked in a mold and served with orange beurre blanc) and follow with breast of duck with cassis. *12 New St., Malahide, tel. 01/845–2777. Reservations accepted; weekend reservations advised. Dress: casual but neat. AE, DC, MC, V. Lunch July–Dec., Mon.–Sat., dinner year-round, Thurs.–Sat. Closed bank holidays, 2 wks in Jan.*

$$–$$$ **The Hibernian Hotel.** This little gem of a "country town house" hotel, named after a once-famous Dublin hotel, is continuing the tradition of old-fashioned service with a reputation for all-round excellence, including good food, since the day it opened. The dining room can be glimpsed from the hall, through a cozy sitting room—a bright but warm scheme of terra-cotta and cream accented by green, elegantly appointed tables with fully upholstered high-backed chairs and windows dressed with sumptuous tassled draperies. Beyond it, a muslin-draped conservatory provides summer dining. Imaginative "cuisine moderne" is tempered by tradition to create a lively house style in dishes like duo of black and white pudding with black peppercorns and parsley, followed, perhaps, by *magret* of French duck with rosemary and roast garlic or steamed fillet of John Dory on a bed of red onion. If you can resist the delectable desserts, round off your meal with a selection from a well-balanced board of French and Irish farmhouse cheeses. *Eastmoreland Pl., Ballsbridge, Dublin 4, tel. 01/668–7666. Reservations required. Dress: casual but neat. AE, DC, MC, V. Closed Sat. lunch, Good Friday, and 2 days at Christmas.*

$$–$$$ **Roly's Bistro.** Since opening in 1992, this big two-story, air-conditioned brasserie-style restaurant has become the capital's most fashionable eating place. Aside from being run by Roly Saul and award-winning chef Colin O'Daly, the crowd, the buzz, the quality of the food and, above all, the surprisingly reasonable prices make it a small wonder that Roly's Bistro has been a runaway success since the doors opened. Set lunch menus are surprisingly long on choice at the price, while the evening à la carte menu offers a very wide selection, typically ranging from a wild mushroom soup with sorrel, or *tian* (tower) of crab with pink grapefruit served cold to start through main courses like roast guinea hen with grapes and lime sauce, rabbit and pigeon pie with red cabbage, or shellfish bake, an aromatic combination of scallops, prawns, and mussels with tomato and basil. Vegetables include traditional dishes such as colcannon (potato with kale, onion, and herbs), and desserts range from comfort food like apple rice meringue to elegant concoctions of various chocolate mousses served on a coffee sauce, or an irresistible crême brulée with contrasting homemade praline ice cream served in a glass beside it. A limited selection of cheese, including Long Clawson Stilton and an Irish farmhouse cheese such as Milleens or Gubbeen, changes regularly. *7 Ballsbridge Terr., Ballsbridge, Dublin 4, tel. 01/668–261. Reservations required. Dress: casual but neat. AE, MC, V. Closed Sat. lunch (brunch only), Dec. 25–26, Good Friday.*

$$ **China-Sichuan Restaurant.** This restaurant has the distinction of being state-owned by the Szechuan Province of the People's Republic of China; the ingredients (and the chefs) are supplied directly by China. The establishment is in an ordinary terraced building about a 15-minute drive from the city center. The focal point here is a giant ceramic water-lily fountain. Traditional scarlet lanterns and velvet-covered booths set in private areas help create an intimate ambience. Recommended specialties include duck skin stuffed with seafood, and whole steamed sole. Desserts are unexceptional. *4 Lower Kilmacud Rd., Stillorgan, tel. 01/288–4817. Reservations required. Jacket and tie suggested. AE, MC, V. Closed Sun., bank holidays, Good Friday, and 3 days at Christmas.*

$$ **De Selby's.** Named after a character in James Joyce's writings, this family restaurant is very close to the shopping center in the middle of Dun Laoghaire town. Situated in a Victorian terraced building, the restaurant is in one large room, but the space has been divided to create a more intimate atmosphere. A strikingly fresh cream-and-aquamarine color scheme complements the varnished wooden tables and chairs; the many paintings on display by young local artists are for sale. Good, reasonably priced food of this type is rare in the Dublin area: De Selby's specializes in fresh seasonal food with the emphasis on fish and steak, including delicious homemade burgers. The warm salad of chicken livers and mixed leaves makes a delicious starter, and the pasta entrées are also recommended. Seafood pasta and rack of lamb are house favorites. *17–18 Patrick St., Dun Laoghaire, tel. 01/284–1761 or 01/284–1762. Reservations accepted. Dress: casual. AE, DC, MC, V. Open every day except Dec. 24, 25, 26 and Good Friday.*

$$ **The Old Schoolhouse.** Although it's a half-hour drive from the city center, this attractively converted Victorian schoolhouse is only a five-minute drive from the airport. The stone-walled garden makes a delightful setting for alfresco dining in summer; guests can relax in the reception/lounge area of the recently added conservatory. Inside, you'll find an informal atmosphere, with old pine furniture and local pottery complementing the original wood floors and paneled walls. Traditional Irish home cooking is served, with the emphasis on fresh fish and steaks. Recommended dishes include the lemon sole stuffed with crab, or Irish potato cakes with crispy bacon. A vegetarian option is always available, such as mushrooms in garlic butter, followed by spinach roulade and salad. A garden room downstairs allows private dining for 14. *Coolbanagher, Swords, tel. 01/840–4160. Reservations advised. Dress: casual but neat. AE, DC,*

MC, V. Closed Sat. lunch, Sun., Christmas week, and public holidays.

Lodging

Dublin's city center and the immediate southside of the city offer a number of first-class hotels. Rates for these hotels are reasonable by international standards, although suites, usually a bedroom and a sitting room, are increasingly popular but very expensive, at around £500 a night plus 15% service charge. Service charges range from 15% in expensive hotels to zero in moderate and inexpensive ones. Be sure to inquire at time of booking. Some city-center hotels are in drab parts of town, such as Upper O'Connell Street. For travelers with their own cars, unless staying at a hotel with secure parking facilities, it is worth considering a location out of the city center, such as Dalkey and Killiney, where the surroundings are more pleasant.

The city also has a good choice of less expensive accommodations, with many moderately priced and inexpensive hotels offering basic but agreeable rooms. Bed-and-breakfast establishments, long the mainstay of the economy end of the market, have upgraded their facilities and now provide rooms with their own bathrooms or showers, as well as multichannel color televisions and direct-dial telephones, for around £20 a night per person.

A new development in Dublin is the renting of apartments and houses to visitors; the travelers usually cook their own meals. Most of these apartments and houses provide maid service that is responsible for daily cleaning. These apartments and houses are well decorated and furnished, offering travelers total freedom to come and go as they please.

Bord Fáilte publishes a complete *self-catering* guide; these recommended properties can be booked through any Tourist Information Office (*see* Important Addresses and Numbers in Essential Information, *above*).

Category	Cost*
$$$$	over £100
$$$	£75–£100
$$	£50–£75
$	under £50

**All prices are per person for a standard double room, including 12.5% local sales tax (VAT) but excluding service charge.*

Highly recommended hotels are indicated by a star ★.

City Center

$$$$ ★ **Shelbourne.** This grand old Dublin hotel may have an imposing redbrick-with-white-trim exterior, but you'll find it far from unfriendly. Its guest book contains names ranging from the Dalai Lama to Laurel and Hardy to Richard Burton to Peter O'Toole. (In the 19th century, writer William Makepeace Thackeray stayed here for six shillings and eight pence a day.) The blazing open fire in its bustling lobby, flanked by two huge rose brocade sofas, is proof that the hotel has not lost its grandeur. The Shelbourne first opened in

1824, in modest houses facing St. Stephen's Green; over the years, the buildings were expanded considerably, but also became run-down until, between 1986 and 1988, £7 million was lavished on a tip-top refurbishment. No two bedrooms are the same size or shape, but all have fine, carefully selected furniture and luxurious drapes, with splendid antiques in the older rooms. Rooms at the front of the hotel face lovely St. Stephen's Green, with the Dublin mountains in the distance; it's the only side of the hotel with good views. Although the back rooms face a service yard, you'll find them far quieter. The impressive suites have separate sitting rooms and dressing areas; the largest, with a mini-network of interconnecting rooms, is named in honor of the late Princess Grace of Monaco, who visited in the 1960s and 1970s. On the ground floor, the Horse Shoe Bar is a small, popular rendezvous spot; tea in the adjoining lounge, with its deep, comfortable armchairs and views of the green, is a real Dublin tradition. The distinguished Aisling Restaurant serves a varied, expensive menu with excellent seafood appetizers and such entrées as crab, duck, grilled salmon, and veal. *St. Stephen's Green, Dublin 2, tel. 01/676–6471, fax 01/661–6006. 164 rooms, 22 suites. Facilities: 2 restaurants, bar, lounge, gift shop/newsagent, parking. AE, DC, MC, V.*

$$$ **Berkeley Court.** This quietly elegant hotel, in the verdant residential district of Ballsbridge, attracts both local and foreign celebrities with its efficient service. Although the glass-and-concrete exterior is designed in a modern blocklike style, the vast, recently renovated lobby is attractive, with plush carpeting, roomy sofas, white tiles, and antique planters. The large bedrooms are decorated in light pastel shades, with antiques or reproductions of period furniture; bathrooms feature marble tiling. The Berkeley Room restaurant offers table d'hôte and à la carte menus; the more informal Conservatory restaurant, with hanging plants and large windows, serves grilled food and snacks. The hotel is a 10-minute cab ride from the city center. *Lansdowne Rd., Dublin 4, tel. 01/660–1711, fax 01/661–7238. 207 rooms, including 20 suites. Facilities: 2 restaurants, 2 shops, hairdresser, barbershop, Jacuzzis in suites, indoor pool, tennis court. AE, DC, MC, V.*

$$$ **Conrad.** Rising seven stories, the Conrad is well placed opposite the National Concert Hall and within a two-minute walk of St. Stephen's Green. Although gleaming light marble graces the large, formal lobby, bedrooms, furnished with sand-colored decor and natural wood furniture, offer uninspiring views of the adjacent tower blocks, and are rather cramped. The air-conditioning/heating systems can also be quite noisy. The suites, however, are spacious enough, with stylish, dark furniture in the sitting area. On the first floor, guests have a choice of two restaurants: The airy Plurabelle serves informal lunches and evening meals, and the more enclosed Alexandra room, with heavy wood paneling and drapes, has formal menus emphasizing elaborately prepared fish, fowl, and meat dishes. In the basement, the Alfie Byrne Bar, named in honor of Dublin's lord mayor for most of the 1930s, has a black bar counter in the center of the room that some may find a bit gloomy. *Earlsfort Terr., Dublin 2, tel. 01/676–5555, fax 01/676–5076. 179 rooms, 9 suites. Facilities: 2 restaurants. AE, DC, MC.*

$$$ **Davenport.** This lavishly fitted new (1993) hotel, at the back of Trinity College, was quite successfully converted from a dilapidated 1860s church. The neo-classical facade has been incorporated into the hotel's impressive four-story lobby. The reasonably spacious guest rooms and larger suites are well fitted in tasteful deep colors and functional furniture. The hotel restaurant, Lanyon's, serves breakfast, lunch, and dinner and is decorated in a traditional Geor-

Ariel House, **19**
Berkeley Court, **18**
Burlington, **13**
Conrad, **10**
Davenport, **3**
Dublin International Youth Hostel, **1**
Grafton Plaza, **6**
Hibernian, **14**
Isaac Tourist Hostel, **2**
Jury's Christchurch Inn, **5**
Jury's/The Towers, **17**
Kilronan House, **12**
Lansdowne, **15**
Montrose House, **16**
Mount Herbert, **20**
Shelbourne, **8**
Stauntons on the Green, **9**
Stephen's Hall, **11**
Temple Bar, **4**
Westbury, **7**

Dublin Lodging

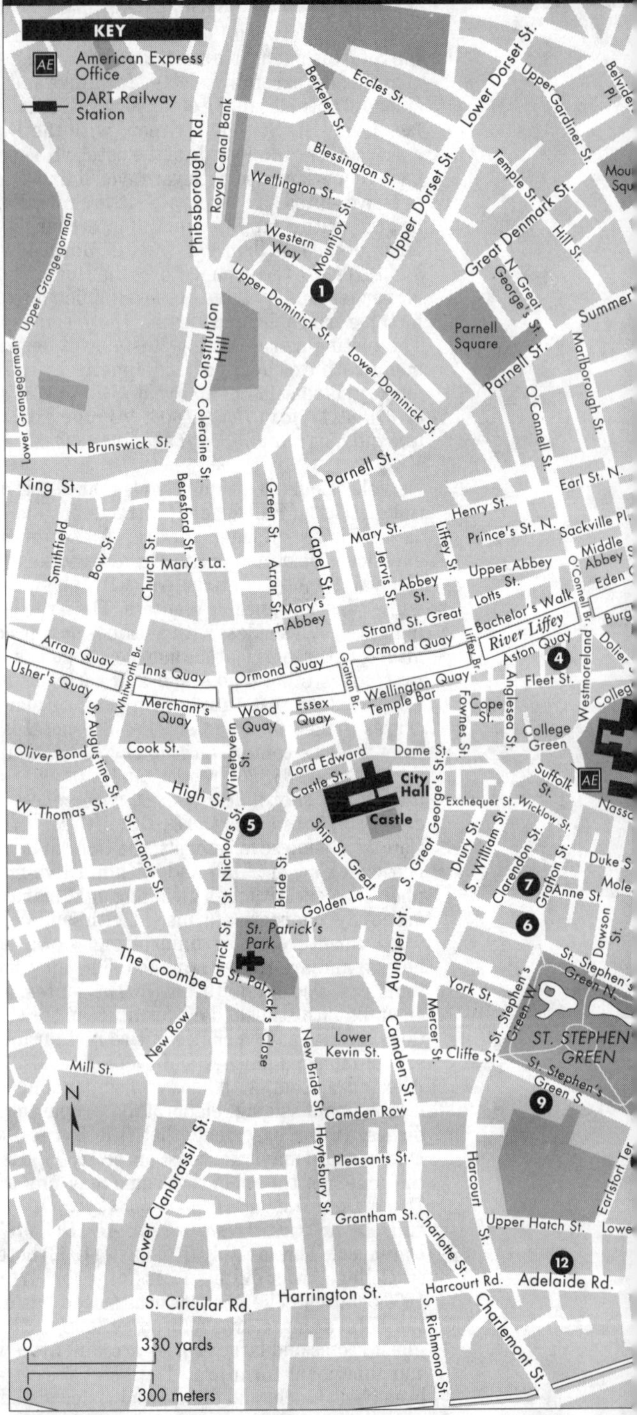

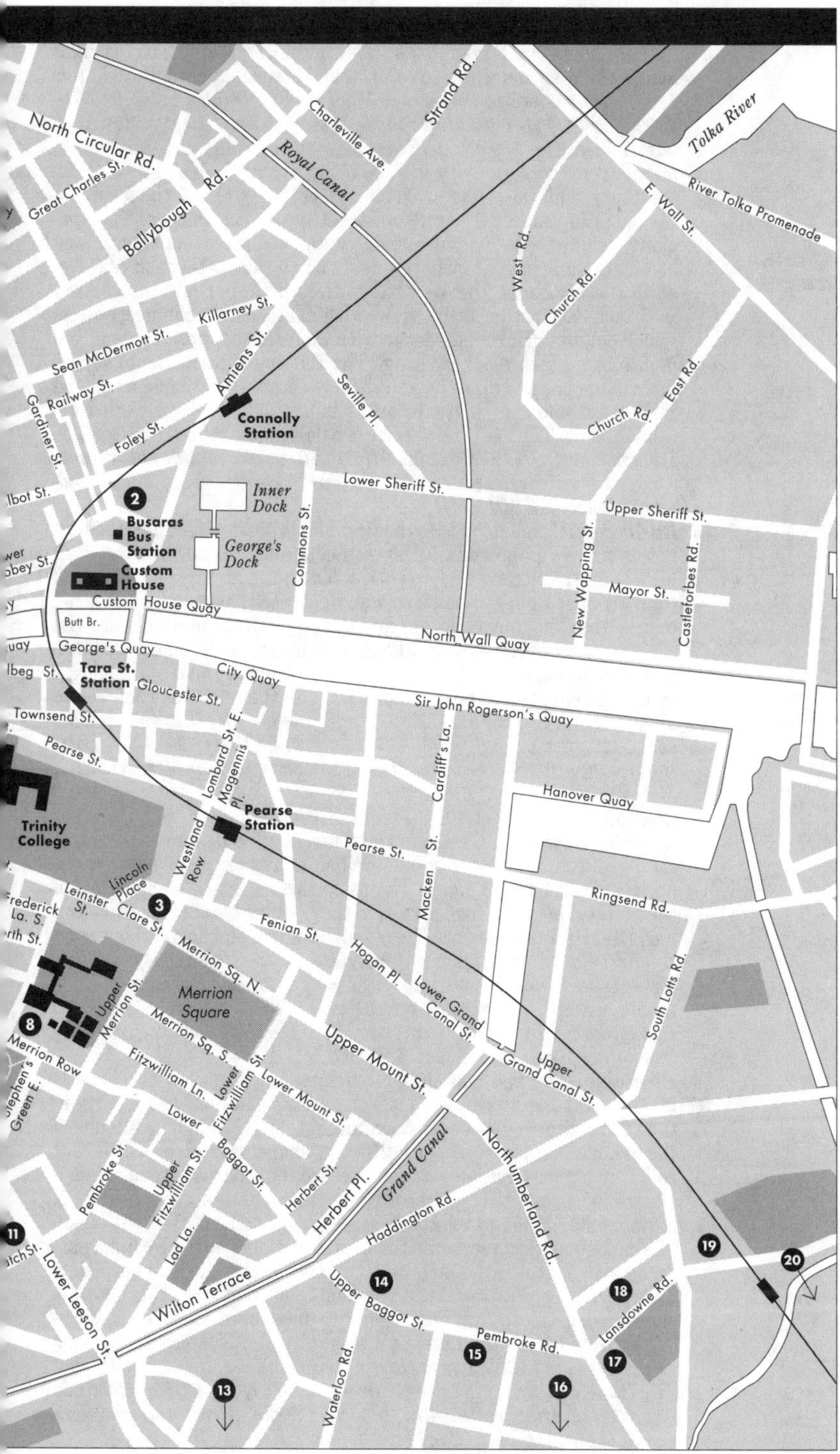

Tolka River
River Tolka Promenade
E. Wall St.
North Circular Rd.
Great Charles St.
Ballybough Rd.
Royal Canal
Charleville Ave.
Strand Rd.
West Rd.
Church Rd.
East Rd.
Killarney St.
Sean McDermott St.
Railway St.
Gardiner St.
Amiens St.
Connolly Station
Seville Pl.
Foley St.
Talbot St.
Busaras Bus Station
Custom House
Inner Dock
George's Dock
Commons St.
Lower Sheriff St.
Upper Sheriff St.
New Wapping St.
Castleforbes Rd.
Mayor St.
Custom House Quay
Butt Br.
North Wall Quay
George's Quay
Tara St. Station
Gloucester St.
City Quay
Townsend St.
Sir John Rogerson's Quay
Pearse St.
Lombard St. E.
Magennis Pl.
Cardiff's La.
Hanover Quay
Trinity College
Westland Row
Pearse Station
Pearse St.
Macken St.
Lincoln Place
Leinster St.
Frederick La. S.
Clare St.
Fenian St.
Ringsend Rd.
Merrion Sq. N.
Hogan Pl.
Lower Grand Canal St.
Merrion Square
Upper Merrion St.
Merrion Sq. S.
South Lotts Rd.
Upper Mount St.
Merrion Row
Fitzwilliam Ln.
Lower Fitzwilliam St.
Lower Mount St.
Upper Grand Canal St.
Lower Baggot St.
Northumberland Rd.
Grand Canal
Pembroke St.
Upper Fitzwilliam St.
Herbert St.
Herbert Pl.
Haddington Rd.
Lad La.
Wilton Terrace
Lower Leeson St.
Upper Baggot St.
Lansdowne Rd.
Pembroke Rd.
Waterloo Rd.
2
3
8
11
13
14
15
16
17
18
19
20

gian style. The comfortable bar is the ideal place to relax for a few quiet drinks. The Davenport's sister hotel, the Mont Clare, is right across the road and was also refurbished in recent years. Both hotels are fully air-conditioned. *Lower Merrion St., Dublin 2, tel. 01/661–6800, fax 01/661–5663. 120 rooms, 2 suites. Facilities: restaurant, bar, TV, radio, tea and coffee maker, direct-dial phone in room, hair dryer, room security safe, parking. AE, DC, MC, V.*

$$$ **Westbury.** This hotel has an excellent location, right off the fashionable shopping mecca of Grafton Street in the city center. The spacious main lobby is furnished with attractive antiques and comfortable armchairs where guests sit to take afternoon tea. Despite these efforts, the Westbury offers little period atmosphere. Bedrooms are rather utilitarian, with pastel color schemes; suites, which combine European decor with tasteful Japanese screens and prints, are much more inviting. The flowery Russell Room serves formal lunches and dinners, and the downstairs Sandbank, a seafood restaurant and bar, features decor imitating a Joycean-period establishment. The food and service can be disappointing. *Grafton St., Dublin 2, tel. 01/679–1122, fax 01/679–7078. 206 twin/double rooms, 8 suites. Facilities: 2 restaurants; shops in Westbury Mall beside hotel entrance. AE, DC, MC, V.*

$$ **Burlington.** Opened in 1969, the first and largest of Dublin's modern hotels has an impersonal glass-and-concrete facade, but the staff here is quite friendly and attentive. The hotel attracts a number of tour groups. Public rooms are well decorated, especially the large bar, with mahogany counters and hanging plants that enhance the conservatory-style setting. The generous-size bedrooms have large picture windows. For such a big hotel, the Burlington is surprisingly lacking in sports and health facilities, and the pool was removed to make way for the bar extension. *Upper Leeson St., Dublin 4, tel. 01/660–5222, fax 01/660–8496. 477 rooms. Facilities: 2 restaurants, nightclub, gift shop/newsagent, Irish cabaret in summer. AE, DC, MC, V.*

$$ **Grafton Plaza.** Just off St. Stephen's Green, this modern hotel is set within a traditional Georgian town house. The medium-size guest rooms, either doubles or twins, are bright and cozy; the bathrooms, however, can be a bit small. The room service snack menu avails of the tasteful Mexican food served in the popular hotel restaurant and bar, Break for the Border. There's also a warm and hospitable bar on the first floor. Many inner city attractions are within easy walking distance and a public multistory car park is around the corner. *Lower Stephen St., Dublin 2, tel. 01/475–0888, fax 01/475–0908. 75 rooms. Facilities: restaurant, bar, TV, direct-dial phone in room, tea/coffeemaker, blowdryer. AE, DC, MC, V.*

$$ ★ **Hibernian.** The red-and-amber brick exterior of this hotel dates from Edwardian times when it was built as a nurses' home early in the 20th century. The conversion to a hotel in 1993 makes full use of the original plan, each room a different shape, each floor a different color. A period-style library on the ground floor is now used as a lounge for guests to converse after an intimate dinner in the hotel's restaurant. Although relatively small, each room is fitted with deep pile carpets and comfortable furniture, complemented by light pastel shades. But it is the attention to finer details, such as potpourri and chocolates, that creates a personal touch and gives this hotel its characteristically warm and friendly atmosphere. Secure car parking is provided by the hotel and most city center attractions are a relatively short walk away. *Eastmoreland Place, off Upper Baggot St., Dublin 4, tel. 01/668–7666 or 800/414243, fax 01/660–2655. 30 rooms. Facilities: restaurant, bar, TV, radio, direct-dial phone in room, tea and coffee maker, hair dryer. AE, DC, MC, V.*

$$ **Jury's Christchurch Inn.** This new venture on behalf of the Jury's Group has proved popular in both Dublin and Galway, offering functional accommodation at reasonable prices and value for your money. The rather spartan rooms are decorated in pastel colors with utilitarian furniture and have a fixed price whether occupied by one, two, or three adults, or by two adults and up to two children. A bar offers a pub lunch, and the restaurant serves breakfast and dinner. Its advantage is its pleasant location facing Christchurch cathedral near the medieval part of Dublin and a public multistory car park at the very back of the hotel. *Christ Church Pl., Dublin 8, tel. 01/475–0111, fax 01/475–0488. 183 rooms. Facilities: restaurant, bar, TV, direct-dial phone in room. AE, DC, MC, V.*

$$ **Jury's** and **The Towers.** These two hotels offer striking contrasts in decor and design. Jury's is a seven-story, concrete-and-glass blocklike building; it adjoins The Towers, which is the same height with a light finish to its facade. Jury's, the older hotel, dating from 30 years ago, offers large, plainly decorated bedrooms with light walls and brown drapes; furnishings are functional but uninspired, especially for an expensive hotel. The Towers' bedrooms are a third larger than those of Jury's, with subtle, sand-colored decor, complemented by natural built-in wooden furniture. Both the large beds and the armchairs are blissfully comfortable. Rooms also have plenty of storage space. Suites are even grander, with their own sitting rooms and kitchenettes. Entry to the Towers is restricted to guests, who can enjoy their own lounge and well-stocked reading room. All shop and restaurant facilities are located in Jury's: The Kish serves only fish and features an elaborate bar; the Embassy Room has a green garden-theme decor; and the Coffee Dock, serving light fare, is open 23 hours a day (closed 4 AM–5 AM). The Dubliner's Bar, in a setting reminiscent of a farmhouse kitchen, has a collection of memorabilia, old photographs, and newspaper clippings, as well as a century-old printing press. Although both hotels are popular with businesspeople and vacationers, you'll probably be happier at the Towers, if you can afford the extra cost. *Ballsbridge, Dublin 4, tel. 01/660–5000, fax 01/660–5040. Jury's, 300 rooms, 8 suites; the Towers, 100 rooms, 4 suites with kitchenettes. Facilities: 2 restaurants, coffee shop, bar, pool, shop/boutique, Irish cabaret in summer. AE, DC, MC, V.*

$$ ★ **Lansdowne.** In the leafy suburb of Ballsbridge, convenient to the city center, this small establishment offers a very friendly ambience. The cozy, modest rooms are painted in pastel shades, and they have all the basics. The basement bar is a popular hangout for local businesspeople and fans of the international rugby matches held at nearby Lansdowne Road; photos of sports personalities hang on the walls. Next to the bar is Parker's Restaurant, which serves lunch and dinner, specializing in seafood and grilled steaks. *27 Pembroke Rd., Dublin 4, tel. 01/668–4079 or 01/668–2522. 28 rooms. Facilities: restaurant, bar, TV. AE, DC, MC, V.*

$$ **Stauntons on the Green.** Three late 18th century houses were joined together and converted into this new well-appointed guest house. All the guest rooms are en suite, and although the decor is unexceptional, no two rooms are the same shape, making the layout rather interesting. The rooms at the front of the house look out across St. Stephen's Green, and there can be a lot of traffic noise. Rooms at the back overlook very attractive walled gardens. The two-century-old Iveagh Gardens, a well-kept secret in Dublin, abut the hotel. The hotel is a convenient five-minute walk from the city center. *83 Stephen's Green, Dublin 2, tel. 01/478–2133, fax 01/478–2263. 30 rooms. Facilities: breakfast room, sitting room. AE, DC, MC, V.*

$$ **Stephen's Hall.** This is a new venture on the Dublin hotel scene: All

accommodations are suites consisting of a sitting room, kitchen, bathroom, and one or two bedrooms. This arrangement is proving popular with both business travelers and tourists. The hotel is in a tastefully modernized Georgian town house just off St. Stephen's Green. Rooms are comfortably equipped with quality modern furniture, and are far more spacious than the average hotel room. *14–17 Lower Leeson St., Dublin 2, tel. 01/661–0585, fax 01/661–0606. 37 suites. Facilities: restaurant, bar, basement bar, parking. AE, DC, MC, V.*

$$ **Temple Bar.** Don't let the plain facade of this hotel fool you. Inside, the lobby surprises, with its imaginative decor complete with art deco touches and large old-fashioned cast-iron fireplace, complemented by natural-wood furniture and numerous plants. Off the lobby is a small cocktail bar and the glass-roofed Terrace Restaurant, which serves sandwiches, pastas, omelets, and fish dishes all day long in a bright and open setting. There's also Buskers Bar, with modern decor and a traditional Irish whiskey bar, which offers a buffet. Nearly all of the rooms have double beds and are fairly big, with pastel wallpaper and natural wood furnishings. The hotel is conveniently located only 100 yards from O'Connell bridge and the new Temple Bar district. *Temple Bar, Dublin 2, tel. 01/872–4655, fax 01/873–3163. 108 rooms. Facilities: restaurant, 2 bars, TV, radio, hair dryer, garment press, tea and coffee maker in room. AE, DC, MC, V.*

$ ★ **Ariel House.** This redbrick Victorian guest house, dating from 1850, stands conveniently near bus routes and the DART line, a five-minute ride to the center of Dublin; it is also just down the road from the Berkeley Court and Jury's (*see above*). Michael O'Brien, the amiable owner, returned to Ireland from San Francisco and London, and he turned his home into this immaculate lodging with an extension in the back. The lobby, lounge, and restaurant are graced with Victoriana and lace curtains in the Irish style; the lounge features comfortable leather chairs, a white marble fireplace, lovely oil portraits, a Waterford crystal chandelier, and an exquisite Japanese doll. In the afternoon, Victorian tea is served. The bedrooms are plain with light walls and contemporary furniture, though some rooms in the main house have high ceilings. A well-prepared breakfast is served in the cozy dining room with a special glass-roofed area and fine wood furnishings. This is a good economical alternative to the more expensive hotels. *52 Lansdowne Rd., Dublin 4, tel. 01/668–5512, fax 01/668–5845. 30 rooms. Facilities: light refreshments, TV and phones in rooms. MC, V.*

$ **Dublin International Youth Hostel.** Housed in a converted convent, it offers dormitory accommodations (up to 25 people per room) and also family-size rooms that can take up to four people. This is a spartan, low-cost alternative to hotels; nonmembers of the international youth hosteling organization can stay for a small extra charge. The hostel is located north of Parnell Square, near the Mater Hospital. *51 Mountjoy St., Dublin 1, tel. 01/830–1766. 500 beds. Facilities: restaurant. No credit cards.*

$ **Isaac Tourist Hostel.** This cheap alternative for young people has bunk beds in a dormitory situation. Bathrooms are also shared. You can't get any cheaper (around £5 a night), but if you're prepared to pay around £12 a night, you can get a private room. The hostel is close to the Busaras bus station and the city center. *2 Frenchman's La., Dublin 1, tel. 01/836–3877. 21 private rooms, 16 dormitory rooms. No credit cards.*

$ ★ **Kilronan House.** This guest house, only a five-minute walk from St. Stephen's Green, remains a longtime favorite with vacationers, perhaps because of the friendly welcome they receive from the Murray family, who have run the place for 30 years. The large, late-19th-century terraced house, with a white facade, was carefully converted, and the owners can be commended for updating decor and furnishings each year. Bedrooms are pleasantly furnished, with plush carpeting and pastel-colored walls. Another welcome plus for visitors, and rather rare in Dublin hotels, let alone guest houses, is the orthopedic beds, which guarantee a restful night's sleep. *70 Adelaide Rd., Dublin 2, tel. 01/475–5266, fax 01/478–2841. 12 rooms. Facilities: TV, radio, direct-dial phone in room, tea-making equipment. AE, DC, MC, V.*

$ **Montrose House.** On a secluded road near Herbert Park in Ballsbridge, this small 19th-century redbrick B&B features lovely gardens that rival the floral splendor of the nearby park. Mrs. Ryan's welcome will be warm, but the clean, no-frills rooms have no individual bath or shower facilities. Breakfast is the only meal served. *16 Pembroke Pk., Ballsbridge, Dublin 4, tel. 01/668–4286. 4 rooms. No credit cards.*

$ **Mount Herbert.** This rather sprawling guest house, derived from combining a number of large Victorian-era houses, overlooks fine rear gardens in the residential Ballsbridge district, right near the main rugby stadium and a 10-minute bus ride from Dublin center. The simple rooms are painted in light shades with little furniture besides the beds, but all of them have bathrooms and TVs. Guests can relax in the lounge, and a large restaurant, overlooking the back garden, serves three meals a day, with unpretentious dinners of steaks and stews. The place is a great favorite with budget-minded visitors from all over the world who seek comfortable accommodations. *7 Herbert Rd., Dublin 4, tel. 01/668–4321, fax 01/660–7077. 144 rooms. Facilities: restaurant, shop. AE, DC, MC, V.*

Suburbs and County Dublin

$$$ ★ **Killiney Castle.** A 13-kilometer (8-mile) drive from the Dublin city center, this hotel is more agreeably situated than any lodging in the capital, for its lofty location allows guests sweeping views over south Dublin and parts of Dublin Bay. The original part of the hotel is a 19th-century stone castle, with a substantial modern addition where you'll find the bedrooms. Although some of these rooms are narrow, many are furnished with antiques and four-poster beds; they also feature large bathrooms and plenty of storage space. Ask for a room at the front of the building; the nighttime view over the lights of Dublin is spectacular. Restaurants include Jesters, in the basement disco, which has a mediocre grill menu, and Truffles, on the ground floor, which serves more formal breakfasts, lunches, and dinners. The health center is equipped with treadmills, bicycles, a sauna, squash and tennis courts, and a 25-meter (82-foot) indoor heated pool, and the hotel is convenient to golfing, horseback riding, and fishing. At the side of the hotel stands Killiney Hill, a viewpoint in a public park; the seaside village of Dalkey and Killiney Beach are both within comfortable walking distance. *Killiney, Co. Dublin, tel. 01/284–0700, fax 01/285–0207. 88 rooms. Facilities: 2 restaurants, indoor pool, tennis court, squash, parking. AE, DC, MC, V.*

$$ **Doyle Tara.** A seven-story minitower in the Doyle chain, this unpretentious, informal hotel is not far from the Booterstown bird sanctuary. An extension was recently built onto the main building with a slightly more modern decor. Still, its best rooms are in the original section facing Dublin Bay, stretching to the Howth peninsula. On the ground floor, you'll find a large bar and a restaurant attractively refurbished with rustic woodwork. The menu includes grilled fish, steaks, and omelets, but the food quality varies. The hotel service,

though, is very personable. *Merrion Rd., Dublin 4, tel. 01/269–4666, fax 01/269–1027. 114 rooms. Facilities: restaurant, bar, gift shop/newsagent. AE, DC, MC, V.*

$$ **Forte Crest.** The only hotel at Dublin Airport, this low-rise redbrick structure with a plain exterior has roomy but characterless sleeping accommodations. The lively bar features music during the weekends, while the usually crowded dual-level Garden Room restaurant serves mostly fish and meat entrées, as well as a good selection of vegetarian dishes. Some of the public rooms display interesting photographs from the early days of Irish aviation. *Dublin Airport, Dublin 1, tel. 01/437–9211, fax 01/842–5874. 195 rooms. Facilities: restaurant, bar, gift shop/newsagent. AE, DC, MC, V.*

$ **Montrose.** This well-designed hotel, located near the Irish TV and radio studios (RTE) and across the road from University College's Belfield campus, features large, relaxing bedrooms. It is only a 15-minute cab ride from the city center. *Stillorgan Rd., Dublin 4, tel. 01/269–3311, fax 01/269–1164. 190 rooms. Facilities: restaurant, bar, gift shop/newsagent, hairdresser. AE, DC, MC, V.*

$ **Royal Marine.** This 19th-century seaside hotel has been totally overhauled in recent years, and its public areas, bar, and restaurant have been completely modernized. The comfortable, capacious bedrooms have also been refurbished with contemporary decor; the eight suites with four-poster beds and separate sitting rooms preserve the lofty ceilings of the original building. Ask for a room at the front of the hotel, facing a gorgeous view of Dun Laoghaire harbor. *Dun Laoghaire, Co. Dublin, tel. 01/280–1911, fax 01/280–1911. 104 rooms. Facilities: restaurant. AE, DC, MC, V.*

$ **Skylon.** This modern five-story hotel, designed as a square box, with a concrete-and-glass facade, is on the main road into the Dublin city center from the airport. The generous-size rooms have been plainly decorated in cool pastel shades; they have little furniture other than double beds and a couple of easy chairs. The ground-floor area has been substantially renovated, with a large bar and a restaurant. The cooking is adequate but uninspired, with dishes such as grilled steak, poached cod, and omelets. *Upper Drumcondra Rd., Dublin 9, tel. 01/437–9121, fax 01/437–2778. 92 rooms. Facilities: restaurant, bar, gift shop/newsagent. AE, DC, MC, V.*

The Arts and Nightlife

Compared with most large cities, nightlife in Dublin may seem distinctly unglamorous, though it begins around 10 PM and runs until 4 AM. The plethora of pubs, some 900 in the city, is one source of entertainment, and many in the city center offer musical performances, often folk or jazz. For a good listing of cultural and evening events, consult *The Irish Times*, which has a daily guide to what's happening in Dublin and in the rest of the country, as well as complete film and theater schedules; *The Evening Herald* and *Evening Press*, with useful listings of theaters, cinemas, and pubs offering live entertainment; and *In Dublin*, a fortnightly guide to all film, theater, and musical events around the city.

The Arts

Classical Music The main theater for classical-music performance is the **National Concert Hall** (Earlsfort Terr., tel. 01/671–1888), which stages orchestral concerts and smaller recitals throughout the year. The **Royal Hospital Kilmainham** (Military Rd., tel. 01/671–8666) also presents frequent classical concerts.

Films Dublin has two dozen cinema screens in the city center, and boasts large multiscreen cinema complexes in several of its suburbs, which show a selection of current releases made in Ireland and abroad. Two theaters popular with movie buffs are the **Lighthouse** (Middle Abbey St., tel. 01/679–2644) and the **Screen** (College St., tel. 01/671–4988). **The Irish Film Centre** (6 Eustace St., tel. 01/677–8788) has two theaters.

Theater For theatrical productions, the main venues are the **Abbey** (Lower Abbey St., tel. 01/478–7222), which stages mainstream traditional plays, mostly Irish, and its sister theater at the same address, the **Peacock,** which offers more experimental drama. The Abbey originally opened in 1904 and became an important center for the Irish cultural renaissance. Poet W.B. Yeats and Lady Gregory, an aristocratic writer and patron of the arts, were prominent in the early Abbey, encouraging young playwrights such as J.M. Synge. The original theater burned down in 1951, but it reopened with a modern design in 1966.

The **Gate** (Cavendish Row, Parnell Sq., tel. 01/874–4045; *see* Tour 2: North City Center, *above*) stages a range of contemporary plays, while the **Gaiety** (South King St., tel. 01/677–1717) and the **Olympia** (Dame St., tel. 01/677–8962) both provide family-style entertainment. The **Project Arts Centre** (39 E. Essex St., tel. 01/671–2321), the **Andrew's Lane Theatre** (9–11 Andrew's La., tel. 01/679–5720), and the **Tivoli** (Francis St., tel. 01/453–5998) present experimental productions.

Nightlife

Irish Cabarets/ Dance Clubs **Leeson Street,** off St. Stephen's Green, known as "the strip," is a main nightclub area from 10 PM to 4 AM. Dress at these places is informal, but jeans and sneakers are not welcome. Drink prices can be exorbitant, up to £20 for a mediocre bottle of wine, and these clubs are not licensed to sell beer or liquor. The up side is that most of these clubs don't charge to get in.

Abbey Tavern (Howth, Co. Dublin, tel. 01/839–0307) offers a rip-roaring cabaret with rousing Irish traditional songs.

Burlington Hotel (Upper Leeson St., tel. 01/660–5222) features a well-performed Irish cabaret, with dancing, music, and song.

Jury's Hotel (Ballsbridge, tel. 01/660–5000) stages a cabaret show similar to that at the Burlington Hotel.

The Kitchen (6–8 Wellington Quay, tel. 01/677–6359) one of the newest nightclubs in Dublin, is part of the Clarence Hotel, and its popularity owes much to its owners, the rock band U2. The crowd here is of mixed age groups.

Pink Elephant (S. Frederick St., tel. 01/677–5876), a noted night spot with a young crowd, has a full bar and books the latest rock stars.

The Pod (Harcourt St., tel. 01/478–0166) is Dublin's most reknowned dance club, especially among the younger set. A new addition to the Dublin night scene, entry is judged as much on clothing as on age.

Irish Music and Dancing **Comhaltas Ceoltóiri Éireann** (35 Belgrave Sq., Monkstown, tel. 01/280–0295) offers boisterous summer evenings of genuine Irish music and dancing.

Pubs **Bad Bob's Backstage Bar** (34 E. Essex St., tel. 01/677–5482) is a very popular pub with the young; the late-night crowd enjoys its live rock music.

Bowes (Fleet St., tel. 01/671–4038) is a small, cozy pub that's a favorite with journalists who hop over from *The Irish Times* newspaper just across the street.

Brazen Head (Bridge St., tel. 01/677–9549), Dublin's oldest pub, dates from 1688; with its stone walls and open fires, it has changed little over the years. The place is renowned for traditional-music performances, as well as for lively sing-along sessions on Sunday evenings.

Byrnes (Galloping Green, Stillorgan, tel. 01/288–7683) has the airy atmosphere of an old-fashioned country pub, even though it's only 8 kilometers (5 miles) from the city center. It's one of the few pubs that hasn't been renovated. Old prints enhance the decor.

Cafe en Seine (40 Dawson St., tel. 01/677–4369), is a recent conversion to a Parisienne style "locale," with art deco furniture and a vaulted ceiling. Café au lait and licensed drinks are served all day until closing.

Dockers (5 Sir John Rogerson's Quay, tel. 01/677–1692) is a trendy riverside establishment, just round the corner from Windmill Lane Studios, where U2 and other noted bands record. Bono of U2 is a frequent visitor here. You'll find sing-alongs here by the piano.

Doheny & Nesbitt (5 Lower Baggot St., tel. 01/676–2945), a traditional spot with dark wooden decor and smoke-darkened ceilings, has hardly changed over the years.

Dubliner's Bar (Jury's Hotel, Ballsbridge, tel. 01/660–5000) is a busy meeting place at lunch and after work. Pick a quiet time to explore its great selection of old newspaper photographs, ancient front pages, and a 100-year-old newspaper printing press that was once used for the *Wexford People* newspaper.

Foxes (Glencullen, Co. Dublin, tel. 01/295–5647), 12 kilometers (8 miles) from the city center, sits 300 meters (1,000 feet) up in the Dublin mountains and is approached by a winding and steeply climbing road that turns off the main Dublin–Enniskerry road at Stepaside. It's packed with ancient artifacts and character. They serve lunch and dinner, and there's traditional Irish music in the evenings.

The Globe (S. Great George's St., tel. 01/671–1220), is a quiet place to enjoy its relaxing atmosphere and rich cappuccinos during daylight hours, but becomes a thriving social scene for young local artisans once the sun sets, and well into the night.

Horse Shoe Bar (Shelbourne Hotel, St. Stephen's Green, tel. 01/676–6471) has comparatively little space for drinkers around the semicircular bar; it's a popular meeting place for Dublin's smart social set, including politicians.

Kiely's (Donnybrook Rd., tel. 01/283–0208), at first glance, appears to be just another modernized pub, but go up the side lane, and you'll find a second pub, **Ciss Madden's,** in the same building. Even though it was built in 1992, it's an absolutely authentic and convincing reconstruction of an ancient Irish tavern, right down to the glass globe lights and old advertising signs.

Kitty O'Shea's (Upper Grand Canal St., tel. 01/660–9965) is decorated with pre-Raphaelite-style stained glass, complementing its lively, sports-oriented atmosphere. Its sister pubs are in Brussels and Paris, but this is the original.

McDaid's (3 Harry St., tel. 01/679–4395) attracted boisterous Brendan Behan and other leading writers in the 1950s; its wild literary reputation still lingers, although the bar has been discreetly modernized, and the atmosphere is altogether quieter.

Mother Redcap's Tavern (Back La., tel. 01/453–8306) is an authentic re-creation of a 17th-century Dublin tavern, with stone walls from an old flour mill, beams, and plenty of old prints of the city, as well as trendy Victorian posters.

Neary's (1 Chatham St., tel. 01/677–7371), with an exotic Victorian-style interior, was once the haunt of music-hall artists, as well as of a certain literary set. Today, actors and actresses from the adjacent Gaiety Theatre enliven the scene.

O'Brien's (Sussex Terr., tel. 01/668–2594), beside the Burlington Hotel, is a little, antique gem of a pub, scarcely changed in 50 years. The snugs (small, enclosed sections traditional in Irish pubs for male drinkers) are still good conversational enclaves, but for both sexes.

O'Donoghue's (15 Merrion Row, tel. 01/676–2807), a cheerful, smoky hangout, offers impromptu musical performances that often spill out onto the street.

Palace Bar (Fleet St., tel. 01/677–9290), scarcely changed over the past 60 years, is tiled and rather barren looking, but popular with journalists and writers. The walls are hung with cartoons drawn by the old-style illustrators who used to spend time here.

Ryan's Pub (28 Parkgate St., tel. 01/677–6097) is one of Dublin's last genuine late-Victorian-era pubs, and has changed little since its last (1896) remodeling. Its dark mahogany counters, old-fashioned lamps, and snugs create a marvelously restful setting.

Slattery's (129 Capel St., tel. 01/872–7971) has an undistinguished decor, but it remains one of the city's best traditional-music showcases, with performances held almost every night.

Stag's Head (1 Dame Ct., tel. 01/679–3701) dates from 1770 and was rebuilt in 1895; it has a smoky atmosphere and an unusual counter, fashioned from Connemara red marble.

Toner's (139 Lower Baggot St., tel. 01/676–3090), though billed as a Victorian bar, actually goes back 200 years, with an original flagstone floor to prove its antiquity, as well as wooden drawers running up to the ceiling, a relic of the days when bars doubled as grocery shops.

5 Dublin Environs

County Wicklow, the Boyne Valley, and County Kildare

By Hugh Oram

Updated by Giuliano Davenport

Only an hour or two from Dublin, you can find yourself deep in the countryside, with landscape ranging from County Wicklow's magnificent rugged mountain scenery to County Kildare and County Meath's flat pastoral lands rich in historical remains. Newgrange in County Meath is perhaps Ireland's most important prehistoric site. Astride the River Boyne in County Louth is Drogheda, a fascinating town settled by the Vikings in the early 10th century. The Dublin environs also have an impressive eastern coastline stretching from Counties Wicklow to Louth, punctuated by delightful harbor towns and fishing villages. The coast is virtually unspoiled for its entire length.

Essential Information

Important Addresses and Numbers

Tourist Information To answer questions on travel in the Dublin environs and for help in making lodging reservations, contact one of the following tourist information offices: **Dublin City Center** (Upper O'Connell St., tel. 01/874–7733), **Dublin Airport** (tel. 01/844–5387), **Dun Laoghaire** (tel. 01/280–6984), **Dundalk** (tel. 042/35484), or **Mullingar** (tel. 044/48650).

Mullingar is the head office of tourism covering the counties of Wicklow, Louth, Meath, and Kildare. During the summer, temporary Tourist Information Offices are open throughout the environs, in towns such as Arklow, Bray, and Wicklow Town, in County Wicklow; Drogheda, in County Louth; Trim, in County Meath; and Athy, Kildare, Naas, and Newbridge, in County Kildare.

Emergencies For **police, fire,** or **ambulance,** dial 999.

Getting Around

By Car The easiest and best way to tour Dublin's environs is by car, because public transportation to the more outlying areas is infrequent. Dublin Airport offers a choice of a dozen car rental companies, and all the main national and international firms have branches in Dublin's city center. Some reliable car rental firms in the Dublin vicinity include **Avis** (Hanover St., tel. 01/677–4010; Dublin Airport, tel. 01/844–4466), **Budget** (151 Lwr. Drumcondra Rd., tel. 01/37–98–02; Dublin Airport, tel. 01/844–5919), **Hertz** (Leeson St. Bridge, tel. 01/660–2255; Dublin Airport, tel. 01/842–9333), and **Murray's Rent-a-Car** (Baggot St. Bridge, tel. 01/668–1777; Dublin Airport, tel. 01/844–4179).

By Bus Bus services link Dublin with main and smaller towns in the environs. All bus services for the region depart from Busaras, the central bus station, at Store Street. For bus inquiries, contact **Bus Éireann** (tel. 01/836–6111).

By Train Train services run the length of the east coast, from Dundalk to Arklow, with many intervening stops, including Dublin, where the main stations are Connolly Station (Amiens St.) and Pearse Station (Westland Row). From Heuston Station, trains run westward to Newbridge, The Curragh, and Kildare Town. Contact **Iarnród Éireann (Irish Rail,** tel. 01/836–6222).

Guided Tours

Bus Éireann (tel. 01/836–6111; information available Mon.–Sat. 9–7, Sun. 10–7) runs guided bus tours to many of the historic and scenic locations throughout the Dublin environs on a daily basis during the summer. Visits include trips to Glendalough in Wicklow, Boyne Valley and Newgrange in County Louth, and a scenic drive through Counties Meath and Cavan. Most tours depart from Busaras Station, Dublin, but some leave from regional destinations, such as Dun Laoghaire.

Gray Line (tel. 01/661–9666), a privately owned touring company, also runs many guided bus tours throughout the Dublin environs between May and September.

Exploring the Dublin Environs

Numbers in the margin correspond to points of interest on the Dublin Environs map.

County Wicklow

East Wicklow Begin your tour of the eastern part of County Wicklow, often called the Garden of Ireland, in its main town and administrative center, 1 **Wicklow Town,** 51 kilometers (32 miles) south of Dublin on the N11, about one hour's driving time. Frequent train services to Wicklow Town run about every two hours from Connolly and Pearse stations in Dublin. Buses leave from Dublin about every two hours. Train and bus times are both about 1¼ hours.

The English name of Wicklow derives from the Danish words *Wyking alo* (Viking meadow). The town's Main Street is attractive, divided into two levels and framed by trees. On this street at the entrance of the town are the extensive ruins of a 13th-century Franciscan friary, which was closed down under the 16th-century dissolution of the monasteries in the area. Inquire at the nearby priest's house (Main St., tel. 0404/67196) to view the ruins. Also on Main Street is a statue in honor of the town's most famous resident, Captain Robert Halpin (1836–1894). Wicklow has long had a strong seafaring tradition, but Halpin's career culminated in his commanding the *Great Eastern,* the pioneer mid-19th-century ironclad steamship that laid the first transatlantic cable. A grateful British government awarded Halpin a substantial pension, and he used the money to build Tinakilly House, 3 kilometers (2 miles) on the Dublin side of the town, which is now a hotel and restaurant (*see* Dining and Lodging, *below*).

The most appealing area of Wicklow Town lies around the harbor. Harbour Road leads down to the pier; several alleyways connect this road to Main Street. A bridge across the River Vartry leads to a second, smaller pier, at the northern end of the harbor. From this end, follow the shingle beach, which stretches for 5 kilometers (3 miles); behind the beach is the broad Lough, a lagoon noted for its wildfowl. Immediately to the south of the harbor, perched on a promontory that is a good viewing point for much of the Wicklow coastline, is the ruin of the **Black Castle.** This structure was built in 1176 by Maurice Fitzgerald, an Anglo-Norman lord who arrived with the English invasion of Ireland in 1169. The freely accessible ruins extend over a

Dublin Environs

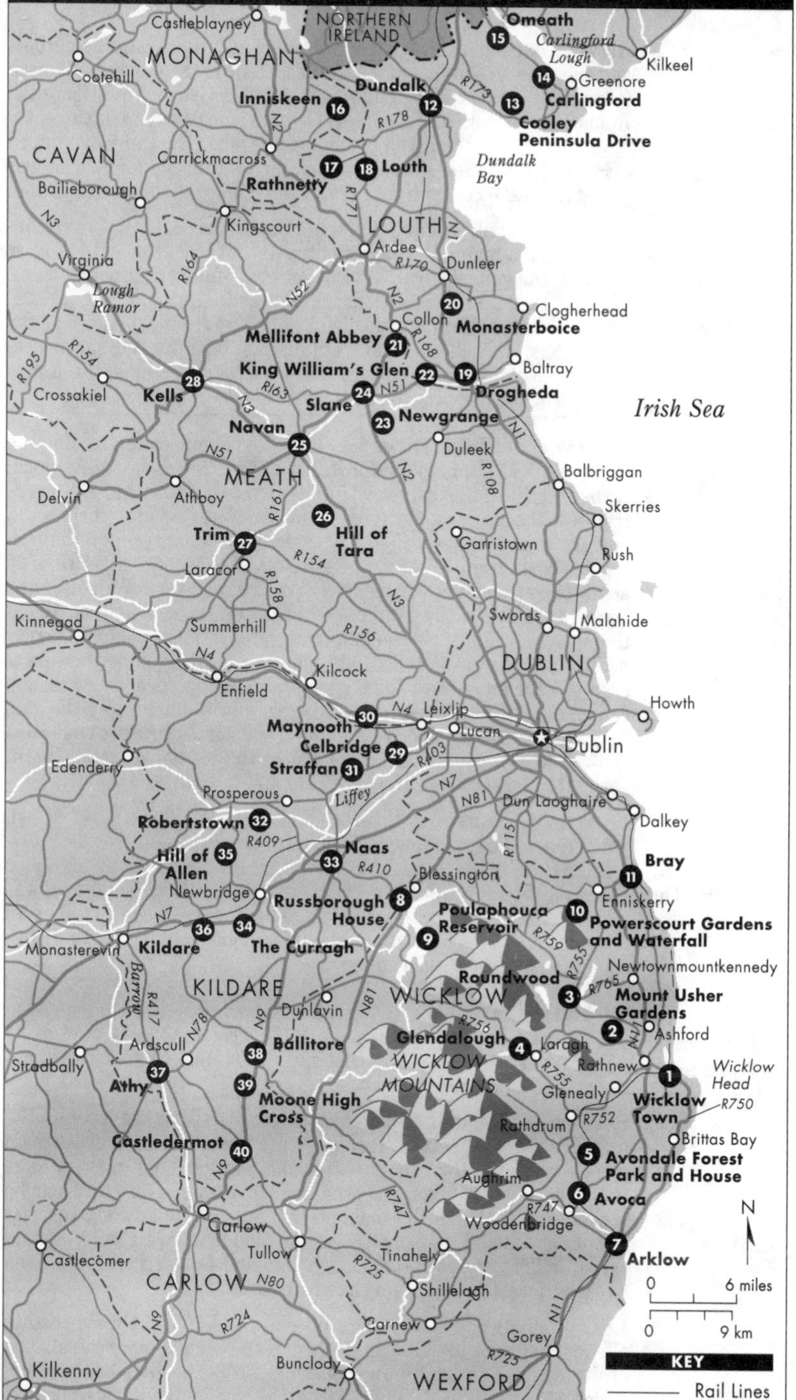

large area; with some difficulty, you can climb down to the water's edge.

Between one bank of the River Vartry, which flows into the harbor, and the road to Dublin stands the 18th-century **St. Lavinius Church** (Church of Ireland). The building is worth a visit to investigate the Romanesque door from a medieval church, the pews, the 12th-century stonework, and the atmospheric graveyard. The church is topped off by a green onion-shaped cupola, made from copper, which was added as an afterthought in 1771. *Admission free. Open daily 10–6.*

The old town jail, just above Market Square, recently has been converted into a major **Heritage Centre** (tel. 0404/67324, ext. 126); at present, the genealogical service it offers is fully operational.

Time Out **Pizza del Forno** (Main St., tel. 0404/67075) serves inexpensive pizzas and steaks, as well as vegetarian dishes. With its red-and-white-check tablecloths, low lighting, and pizza oven blazing away, it provides an agreeable stop for the whole family.

From Wicklow Town, travel 6½ kilometers (4 miles) north along the R750 and N11 roads to **Ashford.** Just before the village of Ashford,
2 turn directly off the main road into **Mount Usher Gardens.** At the entrance to the gardens, you'll find a cluster of crafts shops, including a pottery workshop, as well as a bookshop. You pass through the self-service restaurant to reach the gardens, which cover more than 20 acres on either side of the River Vartry. Edward Walpole, who owned a Dublin textile firm, took over the mill in 1868 and converted the site to gardens. Succeeding generations of the Walpole family maintained the grounds so that today the gardens, under new ownership, have more than 5,000 species, including eucalypti, azaleas, camellias, and rhododendrons. Visitors can wander along the garden paths, through woodland glades, and across bridges that span the river. *Tel. 0404/40116. Admission: £2 adults, £1.30 children. Open Mar. 17–Oct. 31, Mon.–Sat. 10:30–6, Sun. 11–6.*

From Ashford, drive north on the N11; after 11 kilometers (7 miles), you'll reach the small town of **Newtownmountkennedy.**

Time Out **Harvey's Bistro** (tel. 01/281–9203), on the Dublin end of Newtownmountkennedy, is a two-story cottage that has been converted into a restaurant; it specializes in tasty Irish home cooking, with dishes such as corned beef and cabbage.

Turn off by the Catholic St. Joseph's Church on Newtownmountkennedy's main street and take the R765 west for 9½ kilometers (6 miles)—past the reservoirs that supply Dublin's drinking water—as far as Roundwood.

3 **Roundwood,** standing 279 meters (900 feet) above sea level, is the highest village in Ireland. It consists of little more than a broad main street, although the Sunday-afternoon market held in the village hall, where cakes, jams, and other homemade goods are sold, can be a lively affair. From the main street, by the Roundwood Inn (*see* Dining and Lodging, *below*), a minor road leads west for 8 kilometers (5 miles) to two lakes, **Lough Dan** and **Lough Tay,** lying deep between forested mountains like Norwegian fjords.

Leave Roundwood by driving south on the R755, the main road to
4 **Glendalough,** for 9½ kilometers (6 miles). (Glendalough can also be easily reached from Dublin by taking the St. Kevin's bus service, which departs daily at 11:30 AM from the front of the Royal College of

Surgeons on St. Stephen's Green; cost: £7 round-trip.) This valley with two lakes, situated between forested mountains, is the setting of some of Ireland's most significant monastic ruins. The 6th-century missionary St. Kevin, a descendant of the royal house of Leinster, came to the valley to live as a hermit. According to one tale, St. Kevin was pursued here by a stunning redhead named Kathleen, whom he threw from a cliff into one of the nearby lakes. Whether or not the story is true, St. Kevin did indeed found a monastery here. Despite the attacks of the Vikings in the 9th and 10th centuries, the religious settlement continued to develop, only waning when English forces overran it in 1398. Substantial ruins were left behind and can be viewed today. Most of the buildings among the ruins are open all day and are freely accessible. The best introduction to the glories of the valley and lakeside is the **visitor center,** which has models of Glendalough and an audiovisual presentation that tells its whole history. *Tel. 0404/45325. Admission: £1 adults, 70p senior citizens, 40p children. Open Mar.–May and Sept.–Oct., daily 10–5; June–Aug., daily 10–7; Nov.–Feb., Tues.–Sun. 10–4:30.*

The **Teampaill na Skellig** (Church of the Oratory), on the south shores of the Upper Lake in Glendalough, is probably the oldest building on the site, dating from St. Kevin's time. A little to the east of this oratory is **St. Kevin's Bed,** a tiny cave in the rockface, about 9¼ meters (30 feet) above the level of the lake, where St. Kevin lived his hermit's existence in the 6th century. It is not easily accessible; you approach the cave by boat, but climbing the cliff to the cave can be dangerous and is not recommended. At the southeast corner of the Upper Lake is **Reefert Church,** also dating from the 6th century, whose ruins consist of a nave and a chancel. The saint also lived in the adjoining ruined beehive hut with five crosses, which marked the original boundary of the monastery. Here, you'll have a superb view up the valley.

The ruins by the edge of the Lower Lake are the most important part of the whole Glendalough site. The gateway, beside the Royal Hotel, is the only surviving entrance to an ancient monastic site anywhere in Ireland. Inside, you'll observe an extensive graveyard, with many elaborately decorated crosses. The perfectly preserved, six-story **Round Tower,** which was built around the 11th or 12th century, stands 31 meters (100 feet) high. The entrance to the first story stands 8 meters (25 feet) above ground level. The largest building here, and on the entire Glendalough site, is the 7th- to 9th-century **Cathedral,** which is substantially intact, with the nave, chancel, and ornamental oolite limestone window, which may have been imported from England. The nave is small for a large church, only 9 meters (30 feet) wide by 15½ meters (50 feet) long.

South of the cathedral is the 3½-meter- (11-foot-) high Celtic **St. Kevin's Cross.** Made of granite, it is the best-preserved such cross on the site. **St. Kevin's Church,** an early barrel-vaulted oratory with a high-pitched stone roof, is also worth a visit. Besides exploring all the ruins, you can also take extensive walks around the lakes; the scenery around the Upper Lake is particularly awesome.

South of Wicklow Town

From Glendalough, drive for 1½ kilometers (1 mile) to the crossroads of Laragh, then 8 kilometers (5 miles) on the R755 to Rathdrum. South of here, signposted off the R752 to Woodenbridge, 5 is the entrance to **Avondale Forest Park,** the location of **Avondale House.**

Avondale House resonates Irish history, for this was the home once owned by Charles Stewart Parnell, the 19th-century nationalist leader, who fell in love with a married woman named Kitty O'Shea; when her husband instituted divorce proceedings in 1890, the revelation of Parnell's affair during court hearings ruined his political career. The house, built in 1779, was acquired by John Parnell, great-grandfather of Charles Stewart, in 1795; Charles was born here in 1846. The two-story dwelling was used by the political leader as a residence and for social occasions, until his premature death in 1891.

The whole house has been flawlessly restored, with the reception and dining rooms on the ground floor filled with Parnell memorabilia, including many political cartoons of his time, which portray his efforts to secure home rule for Ireland. The surrounding estate and forest park are equally impressive. The park, which extends 523 acres, mainly on the west bank of the Avondale River, was the first forest in Ireland to be taken over by the state, in 1904; in subsequent years, a forestry school has been active here. Visitors can take a 5½-kilometers (3½-miles) walk along the river or stroll along a pine trail and an exotic tree trail. They may also observe the ruins of a teahouse and the stump of a 350-year-old beech tree, with all the rings marked in relation to historic events in Ireland and the world. *Tel. 0404/46111. Admission: £2 adults, £1 senior citizens and children. Car park fee: £1. Open Mar.–Oct., daily 11–5:30, Nov.–Feb., daily 11–5.*

Return to the main road, the R752, and continue south for a further
6 6½ kilometers (4 miles) to **Avoca,** a small hamlet set amid heavily forested hills at the confluence of the Rivers Avonbeg and Avonmore. At this deeply peaceful setting, beneath a riverside tree, the great poet Thomas Moore (1779–1852) composed his 1807 poem "The Meeting of the Waters." You can take some pleasant forest walks here, with scenic views of the valley, and visit **Avoca Handweavers** (tel. 0402/5105), the oldest handweaving mill in Ireland, with colorful tweed fabrics for sale.

Three kilometers (2 miles) south of Avoca is another attractive village, **Woodenbridge,** situated at a meeting of the Rivers Aughrim and Avoca. Continue for 8 kilometers (5 miles) on the R747 to
7 **Arklow,** the only industrialized town in County Wicklow; it has a fertilizer factory. The town is also an important fishing and maritime town in the county; though much of its appearance is somewhat grim, you can take restful walks along the river bank and around the harbor area. At the **Arklow Pottery Factory** on the quays, you can take guided tours and look at its crafts shop. *Tel. 0402/32401. Open weekdays 9:30–1 and 2–4:45, weekends 10–4:45.*

Arklow has a small **Maritime Museum,** set in the public library building by the railway station; it traces the town's distinguished seafaring traditions. *Tel. 0402/32868. Admission: £1 adults, 50p children. Open June–Sept., weekdays 10–1 and 2–5.*

To the immediate north of Arklow, off the R750 coastal road, are sandy beaches and quiet coves. The largest beach on **Brittas Bay** is popular in the summer with those on holiday from Dublin.

From Arklow, drive on the R747 road, passing Aughrim, a lovely little town, after 14½ kilometers (9 miles). From Aughrim, take the R747, passing another small village, Tinahely; continue 8 kilometers (5 miles) south of Tinahely on the R749 road, as far as **Shillelagh,** an attractive one-street village lined with stone cottages. About 3 kilometers (2 miles) to the east of Shillelagh is **Coolattin Wood,** one of the last original native woods left in Ireland, with impressively tall oak trees. The timber for the roof of Dublin's St. Patrick's Cathedral came from here.

West Wicklow

8 **Russborough House** is one of the highlights of the western part of County Wicklow; it is just off the N81, 3 kilometers (2 miles) south of Blessington, which can also be reached from Dublin by bus. To reach Russborough House from Wicklow Town by car, drive in the direction of Ashford on the main N11 road (in the direction of Dublin); then take the minor road that leads to Glendalough. From here, take the R756 across the Wicklow Gap as far as the main N81 road. When you reach the N81, turn right in the direction of Dublin; this road will lead directly to Russborough. To reach Russborough House from Shillelagh, head west on the R725, then turn right (north) at Tullow onto the N81 and drive toward Blessington.

Faced in gray Wicklow granite, this outstanding Palladian structure, built between 1740 and 1750, was designed by the architect Richard Castle, the first earl of Milltown. From the main block of the house, two semicircular loggias reach out to embrace the wings.

The main rooms of the building are decorated in baroque-style plasterwood, with lavishly ornamented ceilings executed by the Francini brothers, Italian craftsmen who were active in Dublin in the mid-18th century. The house belongs to Sir Alfred Beit, the nephew of a German entrepreneur, and the Beit art collection that is on display includes works by Gainsborough, Goya, Guardi, Metsu, Reynolds, Rubens, and Velázquez, as well as bronzes and porcelain. In 1988, after several robberies of the house, some of the more important works were donated to the National Gallery of Ireland. Russborough looks out over an impressive artificial lake to the mountains of Wicklow; the extensive woodland on the estate is open to visitors. *Tel. 045/652329. Admission: £2.50, upstairs £1. Open June–Aug., daily 10:30–5:30, Apr.–May and Sept.–Oct., Sun. and public holidays 10:30–5:30.*

Leave the grounds of Russborough House, turn right onto the main N81 road, and travel north for 3 kilometers (2 miles) to **Blessington,** with its very wide main street lined on both sides by tall trees. This small market town, founded in the second half of the 17th century, used to be a stop on the Dublin–Waterford mail-coach service in the mid-19th century, and until 1932 a quaint steam train ran from here to Dublin, along the side of the main road. Near Blessington is the
9 great **Poulaphouca Reservoir,** which provides water for Dublin. At the southern end of the reservoir lie two glens of outstanding natural beauty, Poulaphouca and Hollywood. Near the latter glen are fine views from the summit of Church Mountain. You can drive around the entire perimeter of the reservoir on minor roads.

From Blessington, drive north on the N81 for 8 kilometers (5 miles), then turn right onto the R759 and continue through wild upland country for 25½ kilometers (16 miles) to the Sally Gap, a bleak crossroads. At this junction, turn left onto the R115 for a further 13 kilometers (8 miles) to Glencree; from here drive another 25½ kilometers (16 miles) east along minor roads to Enniskerry.

The village of **Enniskerry** is a pretty spot, built around a central square and surrounded by the wooded Wicklow Mountains. (Enniskerry can also be reached directly from Dublin by taking the No. 44 bus from the Dublin quays area.) The main reason to visit
10 here, however, is the estate of the **Powerscourt Gardens and Waterfall.** The grounds were originally granted to Sir Richard Wingfield, the first viscount of Powerscourt, by King James I of England in 1609. Richard Castle, the architect of Russborough House (*see*

above), designed the grand Powerscourt House in the Palladian style; it was constructed between 1731 and 1740. In 1974 the house burned down, but there are now plans to restore it to its original splendor, complete with antique furnishings and paintings. However, the Powerscourt Gardens, which were laid out from 1745 to 1767 and redesigned from 1843 to 1875, survived beautifully and are considered among the finest in Europe. The gardens were originally planned by Daniel Robertson, who drew his inspiration from two sources: the Villa Butera in Sicily, and copious amounts of sherry.

The gardens comprise sweeping terraces, antique sculptures, and a circular pond and fountain flanked by winged horses; you have a magnificent view of the Italianate patterned ramps, lawns, and pond across the Dargle Valley, a beautiful, heavily wooded valley, to Sugar Loaf Mountain, one of Ireland's most dramatic vistas. The grounds include many specimen trees, an avenue of monkey puzzles, a parterre of brightly colored summer flowers, and a Japanese garden. The kitchen gardens, with their modest rows of flowers, are a striking antidote to the classical formality of the main sections. The gardens also offer a restaurant, a crafts center, and a children's play area. *Tel. 01/286–7676. Admission: £2.50 adults, £1.50 children. Open Mar.–Oct., daily 9–5:30.*

The equally renowned Powerscourt Waterfall, with a great height of nearly 124 meters (400 feet), is 5 kilometers (3 miles) south of the gardens; it is the highest falls in the British Isles. *Admission: £1 adults, 50p children. Open daily 10:30–7, or until dusk in winter.*

From Enniskerry, travel 8 kilometers (5 miles) along the road that
11 skirts the River Dargle toward **Bray,** one of Ireland's oldest seaside resorts. A sand and shingle beach stretches 2 kilometers (1⅛ miles) and is fronted by an esplanade—popular for strolling, especially on summer evenings. A recently opened National Aquarium (tel. 01/286–4688) along the esplanade is worth a visit. Watch out for Bray Head, rising 241 meters (791 feet) from the sea and visible from the DART train as it makes its way into Bray from Dublin.

In the old courthouse on Lower Main Street, opposite the Royal Hotel, the Heritage Center in the town hall houses many artifacts from Bray's history, such as old photographs and household items. *Tel. 01/286–8205. Admission free. Open Mon., Fri. and Sat. 10–5.*

Bray is perhaps better known for **One Martello Terrace** (tel. 01/286–8407), immediately by the harbor, where James Joyce (1882–1941) lived between 1887 and 1891. The writer used this house as the setting for the Christmas dinner in *A Portrait of the Artist as a Young Man.* Today the house is privately owned, but if you catch the owners on a good day, you may persuade them to show you the dining room; they recommend calling on Thursdays 10 AM–1 PM. Although the residence has been renovated, the dining room portrayed in Joyce's novel still maintains the spirit of his time. *Bray Tourist Information Office, tel. 01/286–7128.*

Immediately off the Bray–Greystones road just south of Bray, the **Kilruddery Gardens,** dating from the 17th century, have fine beech hedges, Victorian statuary, and a parterre of lavender and roses. *Tel. 01/286–3405. Admission: £1. Open May, June, Sept., daily 1–5; groups by appointment Apr.–Sept.*

County Louth

Dundalk and the Cooley Peninsula

12

The first stop on our tour of County Louth, Ireland's smallest county, is **Dundalk,** which lies 83 kilometers (52 miles) from Dublin on the N1, about a 1½-hour drive. Frequent train services run to Dundalk from Dublin's Connolly Station, departing at roughly 1½-hour intervals. The fastest express train is one hour. Buses to Dundalk leave Dublin about every 1½ hours; the trip takes about two hours.

The history of Dundalk, the main town of County Louth, dates from the early Christian period, around the 7th century. The area near the town is closely connected with Cuchulainn, a renowned figure in Irish mythology. Today, it is a frontier town, only 9½ kilometers (6 miles) from the Northern Ireland border, and few traces of its past remain. The remnants of two early religious foundations do survive, however; on Mill Street, the **bell tower** of a Franciscan monastery with Gothic windows dates from the 13th century, while the Church of Ireland's **St. Nicholas,** on Market Square, incorporates a 15th-century tower. The church was rebuilt in 1707 and has a large, early 19th-century transept. In the graveyard lies the tomb of Agnes Galt, sister of Robert Burns, the 18th-century Scottish poet. The church is open only during services.

In the town center stands the Catholic **St. Patrick's Cathedral,** built between 1835 and 1847 when the Gothic revival was at its height. It is modeled on the 15th-century King's College Chapel, at Cambridge in England, with its buttresses and mosaics lining the chancel and the side chapel walls. The fine exterior was built in Newry granite and the high altar and pulpit are of carved Caen stone. *Open daily 8–6.*

Other 19th-century buildings in Dundalk include the **Market House,** the **Town Hall,** and the **Courthouse,** which is the most impressive of these, built in the 1820s in a severe Greek Revival style, with Doric columns supporting the portico. The Courthouse stands north of St. Patrick's Cathedral.

Dundalk became known for many of its industries that grew to be quite profitable, but have since diminished. Opened in 1994, on Jocelyn Street, a **town museum** through relics, tools, and descriptions is dedicated to preserving the history of these major local industries, such as beer brewing, cigarette manufacturing, shoe- and bootmaking, and railway engineering. For details, call the tourist information office at 042/35484.

On the seaward side of Dundalk, extensive salt marshes and mud flats lie on the edge of Dundalk Bay. This area is one of the largest bird sanctuaries in Ireland: Species such as Brent geese, curlews, and oystercatchers are regular visitors. Leave Dundalk by the N1 road, driving northward for 6½ kilometers (4 miles) to Ballymascanlon. Behind the Ballymascanlon Hotel (*see* Dining and Lodging, *below*), you'll find the neolithic **Proleek Dolmen,** a huge mushroomlike stone structure that dates from the third millennium BC. Its capstone weighs nearly 50 tons.

13

From Ballymascanlon, you can begin the **Cooley Peninsula Drive.** Continue for 9½ kilometers (6 miles) along the R173 road to **Gyles Quay,** a small coastal village with a clean, safe beach. From the village, you'll have excellent views southward along the County Louth coast to Clogher Head. The R175 continues round the east of the peninsula to **Greenore,** a distance of 11 kilometers (7 miles). The town was built in Victorian times as a ferry-boat terminal, and today it has become a port for container traffic.

Continue 5 kilometers (3 miles) eastward from Greenore along the
14 R176 to **Carlingford,** a small fishing town dating from medieval times. **King John's Castle,** a massive 13th-century fortress, still dominates the entrance to Carlingford Lough. An unusual feature of this structure is the west gateway, which is only wide enough to admit one horseman. At present, out of the historic buildings in the town, only the castle is freely accessible to the public. Other remnants from the medieval days include a tower from the town wall and one of its gates, which later became the town hall. The 15th-century **Mint Tower House** with mullioned windows also survives. The final survivor from the Middle Ages is **Taaffe's Castle,** a 16th-century fortified town house.

Carlingford also has some striking thatched cottages, but what makes it particularly attractive is its natural setting; the mountains of the Cooley Peninsula rise up from behind the town, the Carlingford Lough lies at its front, and the Mountains of the Mourne rise only 5 kilometers (3 miles) away across the lough.

From Carlingford, drive for 6½ kilometers (4 miles) northwest along
15 the R173 to reach **Omeath,** the final town on the peninsula.

Omeath was until recently the last main *Gaeltacht* (Irish-speaking) village in this vicinity. On the eastern side of the village, you'll find the open-air Calvary and Stations of the Cross at the monastery of the Rosminian Fathers. Jaunting cars (traps pulled by ponies) take visitors to the site from the quayside, which has stalls selling all kinds of shellfish from the nearby lough, including oysters and mussels. A ferry service runs from the quay to Warrenpoint, across the lough in Northern Ireland.

A narrow road climbs the mountains behind Omeath; as you climb higher, the views become ever more spectacular, stretching over the Mountains of Mourne in the north and as far south as Skerries, 32 kilometers (20 miles) north of Dublin. This narrow road leads back to Dundalk.

16 At **Inniskeen,** 14½ kilometers (9 miles) west on the R178 from Dundalk and just over the county boundary in Monaghan, the area's most famous poet is commemorated at the **Inniskeen Folk Museum,** in a converted church next to a round tower. Patrick Kavanagh (1906–1969), born and raised here, became one of Ireland's leading poets and was brought back to the village for burial. *Tel. 042/78102. Donations appreciated. Open May–Aug., Sun. 2–5; other times, call for an appointment.*

17 In **Rathnetty,** 4.8 kilometers (3 miles) southwest of Dundalk on the R171, the landmark known as **Cuchulainn's Stone** is said to be the place where the ancient hero threw away his swords. He is reputed to have bound himself to this stone, so that even in death, he would face his enemies standing. Not until a bird perched on his shoulder could his adversaries be sure that Cuchulainn was really dead.

Continue for 1.6 kilometers (1 mile) southwest on the R171 to the
18 small village of **Louth,** set on a hill affording commanding views of the surrounding countryside. St. Patrick, Ireland's patron saint, was reputed to have built his first church in this village in the 5th century. He made St. Mochta the first bishop of Louth; still standing in the village is the excellently preserved **St. Mochta's House,** an oratory dating from the 10th century, with a high-pitched stone roof. The house is freely accessible, but visitors should watch out for cattle in the surrounding field.

From Louth, continue on the R171 passing **Ardee,** a market town with a broad main street. Ardee features two 13th-century castles that are presently closed to the public. **St. Mary's Church of Ireland** on Main Street incorporates part of a 13th-century Carmelite church. Proceed south from Ardee to Drogheda, taking the N2 and the N51 for a total of 20 kilometers (12½ miles).

19 **Drogheda** is one of the most enjoyable historic towns to visit on the east coast of Ireland. It was colonized in 911 by the Danish Vikings; two centuries later, the town was taken over by Hugh de Lacy, the Anglo-Norman lord of Trim, in the neighboring county of Meath. At first, two separate towns existed on the northern and southern banks of the River Boyne. By the 14th century, Drogheda was not only heavily walled and fortified but also unified, making it one of the four most important towns in Ireland. Today it is an industrial town, with cement-making one of its key industries, but its setting on the River Boyne dispels any grim industrial feeling. Even the new ring road, which runs along the southern bank of the river, has not done too much to mar the urban landscape.

Originally, Drogheda had 10 gates in its town walls, but only one survives today: **St. Laurence's Gate,** with two four-story drum towers, is one of the most perfect examples in Ireland of a medieval town gate. Nearby, on Chord Road, is the **Siena Convent,** with a delightfully peaceful little chapel, well worth a visit. *Admission free. Open daily 8–8.*

From St. Laurence's Gate, walk down the steep incline to the dock area, 400 yards away. The northern bank of the river is lined with the imposing warehouses built in the 18th century; this modern port is one of the busiest on the east coast. Towering over the river is the great length of the railway viaduct. Built around 1850 as part of the railway line from Dublin to Belfast, it is still used and is a splendid example of Victorian engineering; because of its height above the river, the viaduct remains the most prominent landmark in the town.

The center of the town, around West Street, is the historic heart of Drogheda. The bank building on the corner of West and Shop streets, called the **Tholsel,** is an 18th-century square granite edifice with a cupola; it used to house the town hall. Further along West Street is **St. Peter's,** a Roman Catholic parish church, built in striking Gothic style. It features a rather macabre point of interest for visitors: The preserved head of St. Oliver Plunkett is on display. He was a primate of Ireland who was martyred at Tyburn in London, in 1681. At the far end of West Street, where it becomes Narrow West Street, turn left toward the river, where you'll reach a well-preserved 13th-century tower. Rising 31 meters (100 feet), it is the only remaining portion of an Augustinian foundation.

On the heights above West Street, approached by streets and laneways that climb upward, you'll reach Fair Street. The 19th-century gray stone **Courthouse** displays 17th-century municipal charters and a sword and mace presented to the town council by William III after the Battle of the Boyne in 1690. *Admission free. Open weekdays 9–5:30.*

At the eastern end of Fair Street, turn left into the grounds of **St. Peter's Church of Ireland,** built in a severe 18th-century style, with a tower and a steeple. The building is rarely open except for Sunday services, but it has an impressive interior, with wooden pews, memorial tablets, an organ loft, and statuary. However, if the church is closed, you'll still have access to the fine views over the town from the churchyard. From this vantage point, Drogheda, despite all its recent development, still looks very much like a medieval town, with its uneven lines of slate roofs and chimneys.

The most striking feature on the horizon, seen from here, is the great mound of Millmount, on the other side of the river. You can reach this landmark off the Dublin road, immediately south of town. The tower on top of this mound was built comparatively recently—two centuries ago—but the mound is said to be the site of an 11th-century BC burial place. The gateway to the top of the mound is usually open during the day; if you go to the top, you'll have more extensive views across Drogheda.

The old British Army barracks forming a square at the foot of the tower have been renovated and contain crafts workshops, including a weaver's shop, a pottery and picture gallery and studio, and the recently refurbished **Millmount Museum.** The museum houses many relics of eight centuries of Drogheda's commercial and industrial past, including painted banners of the old trade guilds; a circular, leather-covered coracle (the traditional fishing boat on the River Boyne); and many instruments and utensils from domestic and factory use. Rather surprisingly, the museum does not have many mementos of the most infamous episode in Drogheda's history, when the English leader Oliver Cromwell sacked the town in 1649, killing 3,000 people. *Tel. 041/36391. Admission free. Open May–Oct., Tues.–Sun. 3–6, Nov.–Apr., Wed., Sat., and Sun. 3–6. Crafts shops open all year, Mon.–Sat. 9:30–6.*

Time Out The **Buttergate** restaurant (tel. 041/34759) in the Millmount complex is good for a lunch or dinner of stuffed chicken, pork chops, or seafood pancakes, but the real draw is the view over the town and the River Boyne, especially at dusk.

North of Drogheda From Drogheda's center, take the minor road north (R167) that follows the northern bank of the River Boyne estuary for 11 kilometers (7 miles) to **Baltray,** which still bears a close resemblance to an 18th-century Irish fishing village; from Baltray, continue north another 8 kilometers (5 miles) to the fishing village of **Clogherhead.** Take a walk above the local harbor to the heights of Clogher Head for outstanding views north to the Mountains of the Mourne and south to Skerries.

From Clogherhead, take the R170 for 23 kilometers (15 miles) to Dunleer, then turn south onto the N1 Dublin–Belfast road, returning in the Drogheda direction for 13 kilometers (8 miles) to the small,
20 secluded village of **Monasterboice,** with its fine collection of High Crosses. The 10th-century **Muireradach Cross,** a monolith which stands nearly 6 meters (20 feet) high, is considered to be the best-preserved example of a High Cross anywhere in Ireland; it features elaborate panels depicting biblical scenes, including a centerpiece of the Last Judgment. From the adjacent Round Tower, 34 meters (110 feet) high, the extent of the former monastic settlement at Monasterboice can be ascertained. The key to the tower door is held at the nearby gate lodge.

From Monasterboice, return to Dunleer and drive 9½ kilometers (6 miles) west, passing through the small village of **Collon,** laid out in the 18th century with just a single main street. Continue 8 kilometers (5 miles) south of Collon on the R168 and then take the
21 signposted right turn down the minor road to **Mellifont Abbey,** founded in 1142 as the first Cistercian monastery in Ireland; only fragments of the original ground plan survive. Some arches of the

Romanesque cloister still exist, and substantial portions of the abbey buildings can still be seen, including the two-story chapter house in the 12th-century English-Norman style. This structure was once a daily meeting place for the monks and now stores a collection of medieval glazed tiles. The lavabo is a curious structure, originally octagonal; it is now roofless, and only four walls are left. *Tel. 041/26459. Admission: free. Open May–mid-June, Tues.–Sat. 9:30–1 and 4–5:30; Sun. 2–5:30; mid-June–mid-Sept. daily 9:30–6:30.*

West of Drogheda

22 **King William's Glen** lies 6½ kilometers (4 miles) west of Drogheda, off the N51, following the northern bank of the River Boyne. A portion of King William's Protestant army hid here before the Battle of the Boyne (1690), which they won, and the nearby site of the battle is marked; many of the Protestant-Catholic conflicts in present-day Northern Ireland can be traced to the immediate aftermath of this battle. Part of the battle site is also incorporated in the nearby **Townley Hall Estate,** which offers forest walks and a nature trail. Continue on a farther 13 kilometers (8 miles) west, branching off the N51, onto the signposted minor road leading to the prehistoric sites at **Dowth, Knowth,** and **Newgrange.**

These sites have been under excavation since 1962, and while Dowth is still closed to the public, the partially excavated site at Knowth is open. It is far larger and more diversified than Newgrange, with a huge central mound and 17 smaller ones. About one-third of the site has been excavated, and there are seven passage tombs open to visitors. You can also watch archaeologists at work on the rest of the site. The earliest tombs and carved stones here date from the Stone Age (3000 BC), although the site was in use up until the early 14th century. In the early Christian era (4th–8th centuries AD) it was the seat of the High Kings of Ireland. *Tel. 041/24824. Admission: £1 adults, 70p senior citizens, 40p children and students. Opening times same as Newgrange,* below.

23 **Newgrange** is one of the most spectacular prehistoric tombs in Europe. It was built in the 4th millennium BC with some 250,000 tons of stones that were brought to the site by people with only a primitive knowledge of architectural technology. How they transported the thousands of stones to the site remains a mystery, but the grave may have been the world's earliest observatory. The mound above the tomb is more than 11 meters (36 feet) at the front; white quartz stones were used for the retaining wall. The tomb is so carefully constructed that on the day of the winter solstice, the rays of the rising sun hit a roof box above the entrance to the grave. Then the rays shine for about 20 minutes down the passageway that leads to the interior and illuminate the burial chamber. Visitors to the interior of this Bronze Age tomb may see the effect re-created artificially. The geometric designs on some stones at the center of the burial chamber continue to baffle experts. The entire history of the site is narrated in the adjoining interpretive center. *Tel. 041/24488. Admission: £1.50 adults, 60p children. Open mid-June–mid-Sept., daily 10–7; Apr.–mid-June and mid-Sept.–mid-Oct., Mon.–Sat. 10–5, Sun. 2–5. Rest of year, Tues.–Sat. 10–1 and 2–5, Sun. 2–5.*

Return to the N51 and continue westward for 5 kilometers (3 miles)
24 to the agreeable crossroads village of **Slane.** Here you can visit the **Slane Castle demesne** (estate) and take a fine walk to a 16th-century building known as the **Hermitage,** constructed on the site where St. Erc, a local man who was converted to Christianity by St. Patrick, led a hermit's existence. Another pleasant tree-lined walk takes you

along the River Boyne. The castle itself, badly damaged in a recent fire, is being restored.

About 1½ kilometers (1 mile) to the north of Slane is the 155-meter- (500-foot-) high **Slane Hill,** where St. Patrick proclaimed the arrival of Christianity in 433 by lighting the Paschal Fire. From the top of the hill, you'll have sweeping views of the Boyne valley; on a clear day, the panorama stretches from Trim to Drogheda, a vista extending for 40 kilometers (25 miles).

Ledwidge Cottage and Museum is about 1 kilometer (½ mile) east of Slane, on the road to Drogheda. This humble stone, slate-roofed cottage formerly belonged to Francis Ledwidge (1887–1917), a farm laborer who wrote lyric poetry. Just as he was beginning to win acknowledgment for his work, he joined the British Army and was killed in action in World War I. His cottage has now been furnished as it was in his time, a tribute to his short life. *Tel. 041/24285. Admission: £1. Open Mon.–Wed. 10–1 and 2–6; Sat. 10–1 and 2–7; Sun. 2–6.*

Time Out The **Conyngham Arms Hotel** (tel. 041/24155), at the crossroads in Slane, is an agreeable, family-run establishment with a self-service buffet during the day and set meals at dinner, including such entrées as chicken cooked in Irish-whiskey cream sauce and shrimp scampi.

County Meath

25 Begin your tour of County Meath at **Navan,** which is 48 kilometers (30 miles) from Dublin on the N3 or a short drive on the N51 from Slane. Allow one hour's driving time from Dublin. Navan is also 27 kilometers (17 miles) on the N51 from Drogheda, about a half-hour drive. No trains run from Dublin to Navan, but buses leave Dublin every 1½ hours; the journey takes about 1¼ hours.

Navan, in County Meath, is a busy market and mining town of considerable antiquity, with evidence of prehistoric settlements, but its real development did not begin until the 12th century, when Hugh de Lacy, Lord of Trim, had the place walled and fortified, making it a defensive stronghold of the English Pale in eastern Ireland. On the main thoroughfare, Trimgate Street, the Catholic **St. Mary's Church,** built in 1839, features an interesting late-18th-century wood carving of the Crucifixion, the work of a local artist, Edward Smyth, who at the time was the greatest sculptor Ireland had produced since the Middle Ages. On Fridays, the Fair Green, beside the church, is the site of a bustling outdoor market. *Church open daily 8–8.*

You'll have the best view of the town from the motte of Navan, an artificial hill that may have once been the tomb of a prehistoric queen, but was more likely an Ice Age gravel deposit; it was adapted for use by D'Angulo, a 12th-century baron. D'Angulo was responsible for the first fairs in Navan. He also built a defensive castle on the hill, and today from its summit, visitors have panoramic views of the area and the River Black. Navan also offers a tree-lined walk along the Ramparts, the towpath of the now disused Navan–Drogheda canal. With some difficulty, because of the undergrowth, you can walk along the canal for 13 kilometers (8 miles), as far as Slane.

26 The **Hill of Tara** is 13 kilometers (8 miles) south of Navan; follow the main N3 road in the direction of Dublin. The hill is signposted to the right; take the minor road for 1½ kilometers (1 mile). The site was

originally the location for an Iron Age Celtic hill fort, surrounded by multiple ring forts; some of these were ruined in the 19th century by religious zealots from England who thought that they would find the Ark of the Covenant here. The hill gained prominence when used as the residence of one of the high kings of Ireland until the 11th century; the site became an inspiration for many Irish legends. The last king to live here was Malachy II, who died in 1022. While the Hill of Tara was used as a royal residence, a great national assembly (*feis*) was held here every three years, when laws were passed and tribal disputes were settled. Tara's influence waned with the arrival of Christianity.

Today on the hill, you can only see a modern statue of St. Patrick and a pillar stone that may have been the coronation stone of the early kings. In the graveyard of the adjacent Anglican church, you'll find a pillar with the worn image of a pagan god and a Bronze Age standing stone. However, the main attraction of the Hill of Tara is its height: It stands more than 155 meters (500 feet) above sea level, and from its top on a clear day, you can see across the flat central plain of Ireland, with the mountains of east Galway rising nearly 160 kilometers (100 miles) away. In an old Church of Ireland church on the hillside, the new **interpretative center** tells the story of Tara and its legends. *Tel. 041/24824. Open daily May 10–5, June–Aug. 9:30–6:30, Sept. 10–5.*

Return from the Hill of Tara to Navan; 16 kilometers (10 miles)
27 south of Navan is **Trim,** which has some of the finest medieval ruins in Ireland. In 1359, the town was walled on the instructions of the English king and its fortifications strengthened; several parliaments were held here in the 15th century. Oliver Cromwell captured the town in 1649 and killed most of its inhabitants.

On the southern side of the town, **Trim Castle,** the largest Anglo-Norman fortress in Ireland, is by far the most imposing ruin in present-day Trim. In 1173, it was built by Hugh de Lacy on a site that slopes down to the placid waters of the River Boyne; it was soon destroyed and then rebuilt from 1190 to 1200. The ruins cover 2 acres and include an enormous keep with 21-meter- (70-foot-) high turrets, flanked by rectangular towers; the outer castle wall is almost 500 yards long, and five D-shaped towers survive. The castle remains are freely accessible at all times. Facing the river is another ruin, that of the Royal Mint, an indication of Trim's political importance in the Middle Ages.

The **Yellow Steeple** overlooks the town from a ridge opposite the castle. Dating from 1368, it is a remnant of the 13th-century Augustinian abbey of St. Mary's. Much of the tower was destroyed in 1649 to prevent its falling into Cromwell's hands, and today, only the striking, 38-meter- (125-foot-) high east wall remains. On Loman Street, the Church of Ireland cathedral, **St. Patrick's,** is of recent origin, dating from the early 19th century, but the square tower belongs to an earlier structure built in 1449. The town hall on Castle Street has records of Trim dating from 1659; these papers may be seen during business hours on weekdays. The nearby Education Centre (tel. 046/31158), also on Castle Street, has regular exhibitions of historical material.

Several places of interest lie on the outskirts of Trim. At **Newtown,** 1¼ kilometers (¾ mile) east of Trim on the banks of the River Boyne, is the ruin of what was the largest cathedral in Ireland, built by Simon de Rochfort, the first Anglo-Norman bishop of Meath, in 1210. At **Laracor,** 3 kilometers (2 miles) south of Trim on the R158, there is a wall left of the rectory where Jonathan Swift, the great 18th-century satirical writer, was rector from 1699 to 1714. Nearby are the walls of the cottage where Esther Johnson, the "Stella" who inspired much of Swift's writings, once lived. From Laracor, continue for 8 kilometers (5 miles) southeast along the R158 to **Summerhill,** one of the most pleasant villages of south County Meath; it has a large square and a village green with a 15th-century cross. Adjacent to Summerhill is **Cnoc an Linsigh,** an attractive area of forest walks with picnic sites, ideal for a half day's meandering. Many of the lanes that crisscross this vicinity of County Meath provide delightful driving between high hedgerows and afford occasional views of the lush pastoral countryside.

From Navan take the N3 northwest for 16 kilometers (10 miles) to
28 **Kells,** where St. Columba founded a monastery in the 6th century. In the 9th century, a group of monks from Iona in Scotland took refuge at Kells after being expelled by the Danes. Early in that century, these monks wrote and illustrated the Book of Kells, the Latin version of the four Gospels and one of Ireland's greatest medieval treasures. During the mid-17th-century Cromwellian wars, it was removed to Trinity College, Dublin, for safekeeping and remains there to this day, where it is on view in the Old Library (*see* Tour 1: South City Center in Chapter 4; Dublin). A facsimile copy is on display in the Church of Ireland **St. Columba's,** in Kells. In the church graveyard stand four elaborately carved High Crosses, while the stump of a fifth is in the marketplace; during the 1798 uprising, it was used as a gallows. Near the church is **St. Columba's House,** a small, two-story, 7th-century building measuring about 24 feet square; it is nearly 40 feet high with a steeply pitched stone roof, similar in appearance to St. Kevin's Church at Glendalough in County Wicklow (*see* County Wicklow, *above*) and Cormac's Chapel at Cashel in County Tipperary (*see* Chapter 7, The Southeast). Also adjacent to the church is the nearly 31-meter- (100-foot-) high Round Tower, in almost perfect condition, dating from before 1076. Unusually, its top story has five windows, each pointing to an ancient entrance to the medieval town.

County Kildare

North Kildare

Celbridge, the first stop on our tour of County Kildare, is 24 kilome-
29 ters (15 miles) from Dublin; take the N4 road out of Dublin. Between Lucan and Leixlip, turn onto the R403 and continue on the last 6½ kilometers (4 miles) to Celbridge. The drive from Dublin will take 30 minutes. No train service runs between Dublin and Celbridge. The Dublin City No. 67 bus leaves Middle Abbey Street, Dublin, at intervals of about one hour; the journey to Celbridge takes about one hour.

Celbridge is a rather nondescript market town, with a straggling main thoroughfare, but at the eastern end of this street, the gateway leads into one of Ireland's architectural glories, **Castletown House.** This immaculate Palladian-style house, with colonnaded wings at each side of the main building, was built in 1722 for William Conolly, the speaker of the Irish House of Commons. The house was designed by Alessandro Galilei, an Italian architect who created interiors as pleasing as the neoclassical facade. The intricate plasterwork in the halls was executed by the Italian Francini brothers; at the back of the house, the long gallery, painted in the blue Pompeian style and decorated with Venetian chandeliers, is the most notable of all the public rooms, which also include an 18th-century print room and a red drawing room. Downstairs, you'll find the nursery and the Victorian kitchen. The gardens are designed in the formal 18th-century style, with clipped hedges and neat lawns. The entire property is in an excellent state of preservation; the Irish Georgian Society was responsible for the renovation of both the house and the gardens. *Tel. 01/628–8252. Admission: £2.50 adults, £1 children. Open Apr.–Oct., weekdays 10–6, Sat. 11–6, Sun. 2–6; Nov.–Mar., Sun. and public holidays 2–6.*

From Celbridge, take the R403 west and turn north on the R406 to
30 **Maynooth.** This tiny university town houses St. Patrick's College, a center for the training of Catholic priests that also serves as a lay university, much expanded in recent years. The ruins of **Maynooth Castle** are at the entrance to the college; the oldest part of the castle is the keep, which probably dates from the 13th century; although the keep and the great hall are still in reasonable condition, much of the castle was destroyed in 1647. The key to the castle can be obtained from Castleview House, opposite. *Tel. 01/628–5222. Admission free. Open June–Sept., daily 3–6. At other times, by appointment.*

At the eastern end of Maynooth is **Carton House,** once the residence of the dukes of Leinster. The house was designed about 1740 in the classical style by Richard Castle, who also designed Russborough House, near Blessington. The grounds feature The Shell House, whose interior is decorated entirely with seashells. *Tel. 01/628–6250. Admission: £1.50 adults, 50p children. The house can be seen by appointment.*

From Maynooth, take the minor road due south for 13 kilometers (8
31 miles), to the village of **Straffan,** attractively situated on the banks of the River Liffey. It's here, as part of the Kildare Country Club (*see* Dining and Lodging, *below*), that Arnold Palmer designed one of Ireland's most reknowned 18-hole golf courses. The butterfly farm in Straffan is the only one of its kind in Ireland, featuring a tropical house with exotic plants, butterflies, and moths. Mounted and framed butterflies are available for sale. *Tel. 01/627–1109. Admission: £1. Open May–Aug., daily 10–6.*

Straffan's **Steam Museum** at Lodge Park covers the history of Irish steam engines. These handsome machines were often used agriculturally to help in such operations as churning butter and threshing corn. The steam engines stand in the courtyard of an 18th-century house; there is also a collection of model locomotives. If you want to be sure of arriving on a "live steam day," when one or more engines will be in operation, phone in advance to confirm. *Tel. 01/627–3155. Admission: live steam days—£4 adults, £2 children; otherwise £3 adults, £2 children. Open Easter–Sept., Tues.–Sun. 11–6.*

From Straffan, follow the R403 for 16 kilometers (10 miles) west-
32 ward; in Prosperous, take the signposted turn to **Robertstown,** 2½ kilometers (1½ miles) southwest. Here you can take scenic walks along the canal and boat trips on the water during the summer. The renovated late-18th-century canal hotel at Robertstown is now used for candlelighted dinners and musical entertainment. Dinners are preceded by an hour-long trip up and down the canal on the boat *Eustace. Tel. 045/60020. Canal trip and dinner cost about £21 per person. Canal trips and dinners are offered in May and Sept. on Sun. and public holidays; June, July, and Aug., they are offered daily.*

From Robertstown, drive eastward for 5 kilometers (3 miles) along the minor road, then turn right (heading southeast) onto the R409. Just past this junction is **Mondello Park,** where frequent motor races

33 are held; drive for a further 11 kilometers (7 miles) into **Naas,** a busy market town that St. Patrick is said to have visited more than once. Today, however, Naas is best known for the **Punchestown Racecourse,** 3 kilometers (2 miles) from the town. The racecourse has a wonderful setting amid rolling plains, and 16 kilometers (10 miles) away, the Wicklow Mountains form a spectacular backdrop. Although horse races are held regularly here, the most popular event is the April steeplechase festival.

About 8 kilometers (5 miles) south of Naas, past the uneventful town
34 of **Newbridge,** the **Curragh** starts; this broad plain, bisected by the main N7 road, is Ireland's major racing center, where each year several international horse races awarding substantial prize money are held. These meetings attract the upper echelons of Irish society, who enjoy intermingling four loves: horse racing, betting, champagne, and the social whirl. The Curragh is also the location for a large camp used by the Irish Army, whose main barracks are here; one of its prize relics is the armored car once used by Michael Collins, a leading Irish political leader who was assassinated in 1922. It can be seen with permission from the commanding officer (tel. 045/41301).

If time permits, a detour worth taking lies 8 kilometers (5 miles)
35 northwest of Newbridge: the **Hill of Allen,** which is an outstanding landmark in the vicinity, rising 209 meters (676 feet) high. Because it is one of the few high points on the surrounding plain, it offers wonderful views. The hill also has a special place in Irish mythology, since it was the site of one of three royal palaces in Leinster some 1,500 years ago; Fionn Mac Cumhaill, the hero of many Irish folk tales, also lived here.

From the Curragh, continue along the N7 for a further 5 kilometers
36 (3 miles) to **Kildare,** one of the most enjoyable towns to visit in this part of the country. **St. Brigid's Cathedral** (Church of Ireland), with its stocky tower, is immediately off the market square in the center of town. St. Brigid founded a religious settlement here in the 5th century; the present cathedral is a restoration of a building that dates from the 13th century. By the mid-17th century, the cathedral was in decline; it was partially rebuilt about 1686, but restoration work wasn't completed until much later, between 1875 and 1896. The stained-glass west window of the cathedral depicts three of Ireland's greatest saints: Brigid, Patrick, and Columba. *Admission free. Open daily 10–6.*

Outside, in the graveyard of the cathedral, but immediately adjacent to the main door, is the 33-meter- (108-foot-) high Round Tower, the second highest in Ireland, possibly dating from the 12th century. Energetic visitors can climb the stairs to the top, for extraordinary views across much of the Midlands. *Tel. 045/41654. Admission: 60p adults, 30p children. Open May–Sept., daily 10–6; Oct.–Apr., Sun. 2–5.*

South of the town about 2½ kilometers (1½ miles), clearly signposted to the left of the market square, are the **Japanese Gardens,** considered by many experts to be the finest in Europe. They were founded in the early years of this century by Lord Wavertree, a brewing millionaire, who also owned the National Stud (*see below*), immediately adjacent. A Japanese gardener, Tassa Eida, laid out the gardens between 1906 and 1910, and they have been kept in perfect condition ever since. The gardens symbolize the passage of humanity through life. With miniature lakes, little rivers spanned by bridges, and a profusion of Asian trees and flowers, the gardens form an absolute oasis. The section depicting eternity has been created in the Japanese Karesansui style, with emblematic features in sand and stone. Visitors can visit a small tearoom and also a garden center with a good selection of bonsai trees. *Tel. 045/21617. Admission: £1.50. Open Easter–Oct., Mon.–Sat. 10–5, Sun. 2–6.*

The **National Stud,** where breeding stallions are stabled, is a main center of Ireland's racing industry. On application, visitors can tour the Stud and its fine selection of Thoroughbred horses. You can also enjoy the **Irish Horse Museum,** a small, modern building where displays are devoted to the history of the horse in Ireland. Its most outstanding exhibit is the skeleton of Arkle, the Irish racehorse that won outstanding victories in races in Ireland and England during the late 1960s. The museum also contains medieval evidence of horses, such as bones from 13th-century Dublin, and also some early examples of equestrian equipment. Horses are kept in the stables, and also in the various paddocks easily accessible to visitors. *Admission and hours for the museum are the same as for the Japanese Gardens; the entrance fee to the Gardens covers the museum.*

Time Out The **Silken Thomas** (tel. 045/22232), a pub in the market square of Kildare Town, re-creates an Old World atmosphere with open fires, dark wood decor, and leaded lights.

South Kildare From Kildare Town, take the N7 for 11 kilometers (7 miles) to Monasterevin on the banks of the Grand Canal; then take the R417 for 19 kilometers (12 miles) south as far as Athy. For most of its distance, the road runs in close proximity to the River Barrow, one of Ireland's major waterways; from the road, you'll have fine views across the river to the low range of wooded hills on the County Laois side of
37 the river. **Athy** is an industrial and market town on the River Barrow, which widens considerably here. Overlooking the river, by the bridge, is a 16th-century castle, now a private house, that was built by the earl of Kildare to defend this strategic crossing. On the other side of the bridge from the castle is a pleasant park and the Catholic church, built in a pentagonal shape between 1963 and 1965; its striking interior features Stations of the Cross by George Campbell, a noted Irish artist; statues; and a crucifix on the high altar by local artist Brid ni Rinn. *Admission free. Open daily 8–6.*

Northeast of Athy, 6½ kilometers (4 miles) off the N78, is the **Motte of Ardscull,** a large hillock by the roadside; from the crossroads here, turn right onto the minor road that leads for 8 kilometers (5 miles)
38 eastward toward **Ballitore,** a former Quaker settlement in the 18th and 19th centuries. An old schoolhouse here has been converted into a small Quaker museum. Among the pupils at the school was Edmund Burke (1729–1797), the great orator and political philosopher. *Tel. 045/31109. Admission: £1. Open sporadically, usually Sun. afternoons.*

Ballitore also has the **Crookstown Heritage Centre,** an old mill that has been converted into a museum of the flour milling and baking industries. *Tel. 0507/23222. Admission: £2 adults, £1 children. Open Apr.–Sept., daily 10–7; Oct.–Mar., Sun. 10–5:30.*

From Ballitore go to the main N9 road and drive south for 3 kilometers (2 miles), as far as Timolin, where you'll reach the **Irish Pewter Mill,** a splendid tribute to an old Irish craft. Jugs, plates, and other pewter items are sold. *Tel. 0507/24164. Open weekdays 9:30–5; adjoining crafts center is also open weekends.*

Continue 1½ kilometers (1 mile) farther south on the N9, and at the Moone Post Office, take the signposted right turn, continuing for 3
39 kilometers (2 miles) to the **Moone High Cross,** an ancient Celtic cross that stands 5½ meters (17½ feet) high, with 51 sculptured panels showing scriptural scenes.

Time Out The **Moone High Cross Inn** (tel. 0507/24112) is an old pub packed with a cornucopia of local artifacts, newspaper clippings, and old photographs—all fascinating browsing while you enjoy delicious food such as bacon and cabbage and homemade apple pie.

From the main road at Moone, continue southward on the N9 for 3
40 kilometers (2 miles), as far as **Castledermot.** On the left-hand side of the village, you'll find an almost perfectly preserved 10th-century Round Tower together with two High Crosses, equally well conserved, on the grounds of the local church. From the church gate, you can walk back to the main road along the footpath that is totally enclosed by trees. On the right-hand side of the road in the village, the substantial ruins of a Franciscan friary, mostly dating from the 14th century, are freely accessible.

From Castledermot, you can return to Naas on the N9 (43 kilometers/27 miles).

Dining and Lodging

By Georgina Campbell and Hugh Oram

Updated by Georgina Campbell and Guiliano Davenport

Highly recommended restaurants and hotels are indicated by a star ★. For further information about dining and lodging, *see* Chapter 1, Essential Information, and Chapter 4, Dublin.

Dining

Category	Cost*
$$$$	over £25
$$$	£17–£25
$$	£12–£17
$	Under £12

**per person, without service or drinks*

Lodging

Category	Cost*
$$$$	over £100
$$$	£80–£100
$$	£60–£80
$	under £60

* *All prices are for a double-size room, except where stated, and include a 12½% local sales tax (VAT) and a 12% service charge.*

County Wicklow

Bray
Dining
★

The Tree of Idleness. This Greek-Cypriot restaurant, on the extreme southern stop on the DART line from Dublin, happens to be one of the best restaurants in the country. On the ground floor of a Victorian house near the seafront, this pleasant dining spot specializes in classic dishes and good hearty portions. Roast lamb stuffed with feta cheese and olives is highly recommended. The extensive wine list includes Greek and Cypriot house wines. *Bray, Co. Wicklow, tel. 01/286–3498. Reservations advised. Dress: casual but neat. AE, DC, MC, V. Dinner only. Closed Mon., Christmas, bank holidays, and first 2 wks of Sept. $$$*

Dunlavin
Dining and Lodging
★

Rathsallagh House. Joe and Kay O'Flynn's delightful home is well signposted, 56 kilometers (35 miles) southwest of Dublin on the edge of the Wicklow Hills not far from where the N756 meets the N81. Set in 500 acres of parkland in some of the most beautiful countryside in the east of Ireland, this large, comfortable farmhouse was converted from Queen Anne stables in 1798 when the original house burned down; it's now run as a Grade A country-house hotel. Double rooms are each decorated in different colors and have large bathtubs. The homey atmosphere is accentuated by the ample cupboard space and the good selection of books in each room. Kay's talents in the kitchen are legendary, and the equally famous relaxed atmosphere belies a high standard of professionalism. Although the dining room is small, tables are tastefully set with linen cloths and napkins, silver cutlery, enormous wine glasses, candles, and fresh flowers. French doors open onto the croquet lawn and, on cool evenings, guests have a welcoming fire blazing in the grate. In the kitchen, homegrown vegetables and fruit complement hearty roasts of local lamb or beef. Specialties include twice-baked cheese soufflé and warm salad of pigeon breast. Sports facilities include a golf course, a tennis court, an indoor heated swimming pool, and a sauna. *Near Dunlavin, Co. Wicklow, tel. 045/53112, fax 045/53343. 12 rooms with bath. Facilities: restaurant, bar. DC, MC, V. Closed Christmas week. $$$$*

Glendalough
Dining and Lodging

Glendalough Hotel. This old-fashioned 19th-century hotel, which sits in the glen at Glendalough, attracts an international clientele. Upstairs, the cozy bedrooms, all with private baths, are decorated in quiet pastel colors; four rooms are triples. Downstairs, the bar has been modernized and the main restaurant, a long room with grand windows, looks out onto the Glendalough monastery and wooded mountain scenery, with the sound of running water from the stream outside. The rather plain menu features fish and meat dishes, but helpings are hearty. *Glendalough, Co. Wicklow, tel. 0404/45135. 16 rooms with bath. Facilities: restaurant, bar, tennis court, fishing. AE, DC, MC, V. Closed Nov.–mid-Mar. $$*

Rathnew
Dining and Lodging
★

Tinakilly House. This impressive Victorian mansion, situated on 7 acres, was built in the 1870s by Captain Robert Halpin, a Wicklow man who made his fortune at sea. The great lobby at the entrance to the house stores mementos of Captain Halpin and his nautical exploits, including paintings and ship models. The house has been lovingly restored by William and Bee Power; the whole home is filled with impeccable Victorian antiques, and woods used originally in its construction, such as mahogany and pitch pine, have been meticulously replaced. Bedrooms have private baths, and some offer four-poster beds, Jacuzzis, and fine views of the Wicklow landscape. First-floor rooms are larger than the second-floor attic rooms, which are snug yet comfortable. A wing of 15 suites named after sea captains was opened in 1991. The 7 acres of Victorian gardens feature giant California redwoods at each end of the tennis court. The Irish country-house cuisine, with French influences in the presentation, uses fresh produce from the vegetable garden on the grounds. Specialties include roast breast of Barbary duck with fruit sauce, Wicklow lamb, and quail. *Rathnew, Co. Wicklow, tel. 0404/69274, fax 0404/67806. 29 rooms with bath. Facilities: restaurant, bar, tennis court, golf course and horseback riding nearby. AE, DC, MC, V. $$$$*

Hunter's Hotel. This old coaching inn, first opened in 1820, has a lovely rural setting on the banks of the River Vartry, only 1 kilometer (½ mile) east of Rathnew Village. A delightful Old World atmosphere has been maintained in the period prints, beams, and antique furnishings; the inn is a favorite place with local hunters and many foreigners. All bedrooms are furnished with old-fashioned Victorian-style flower-print wallpaper. Only 10 rooms have private tiled bathrooms; shared bathrooms for the remaining rooms can be rather Spartan. Ask about Room 17 on the ground floor, with a private garden entrance. Original Georgian furnishings have been extended to the dining room, where window tables are much in demand. In the summer, afternoon tea, with homemade scones and jams, is served in the magnificent garden that stretches down to the river. The restaurant serves traditional country-house cuisine using homegrown produce in such entrées as roast Wicklow lamb with herbs and mint sauce, and baked sea trout with herbs and parsley butter. *Rathnew, Co. Wicklow, tel. 0404/40106, fax 0404/40338. 18 rooms, 10 with bath. Facilities: restaurant ($$–$$$), bar. AE, DC, MC, V. $$*

Roundwood
Dining
★

Roundwood Inn. South of Dublin on the Glendalough road, amid spectacular scenery, you come to the highest village in the Wicklow Hills and this 17th-century inn. Furnished in a traditional style, with wooden floors and diamond-shaped windows, it is remarkable how little this place has changed over the years. Although the inn is best known for good, reasonably priced bar food—homemade broth, Irish stew, Galway oysters, or smoked Wicklow trout—eaten at sturdy tables beside an open fire, the more expensive restaurant offers a combination of Continental and Irish cuisines, reflecting the traditions of the German proprietor, Jurgen Schwalm, and his Irish wife, Aine. In the long dining room, the most coveted of the dark wooden tables are the ones in front of the big log fires. Local produce figures prominently on the menu, especially roasts like rack of Wicklow lamb, prime Irish beef, and local game in winter. Wiener schnitzel is a house special, and the feather-light fresh cream gâteau dessert is not to be missed. *Roundwood, Co. Wicklow, tel. 01/281–8107 or 01/281–8125. Reservations required. Dress: casual but neat. MC, V. Restaurant closed Sun. dinner and Mon. except on public holidays; bar closed Christmas Day, Good Friday only. $$$*

Wicklow Town
Dining and Lodging
★

Old Rectory Country House. Once a 19th-century rectory, this splendid country house in the Greek Revival style stands on a hillside just off the main road from Dublin on the approach to Wicklow Town. Owners Paul and Linda Saunders have successfully transformed the interior with dark marble fireplaces, bright colors, original oil paintings, and antique and contemporary furniture. The light, spacious rooms with private baths are decorated in white and pastel shades with Victorian antique furniture. In 1992 the dining room was moved into the new conservatory, built in the same period style as the house. Linda's innovative country-house cooking is based on pure ingredients, especially seafood and organic vegetables, and she specializes in salads and desserts, often including, or garnished with, edible flowers and herbs. Specialties include fillet of black sole stuffed with salmon and spinach terrine, and roast sea trout with a fresh herb sauce. Don't miss the house dessert, "Swan Lake" meringues, piped in the shape of swans and cygnets. *Wicklow Town, Co. Wicklow, tel. 0404/67048. 5 rooms, all with bath. Facilities: restaurant. AE, DC, MC, V. Closed Oct.–Easter. $$*

County Louth

Ardee
Dining

The Gables House and Restaurant. Just off the Dublin–Derry road (the N2), not far from the Dundalk junction, this restaurant was originally a 1940s house built on a school playground. The place features traditional decor, with antique mahogany furniture, deep-burgundy velvet curtains, and oil paintings by local artists. Mats on the polished tables, silver cutlery, linen napkins, lace coasters, and gleaming lead crystal glasses all contribute to the intimate atmosphere. Expect generous portions and a French-influenced cooking style; dishes include seafood from the Celtic Sea—poached wild salmon, turbot, hake, and prawns, finished in a sauce of carrots, celery, and chives (the colors of the Irish flag)—and a chocolate mousse with Frangelico liqueur and chopped hazelnuts layered with meringue. *Dundalk Rd., Ardee, Co. Louth, tel. 041/53789. Reservations advised. Dress: casual but neat. AE, MC, V. Dinner only. Closed Sun.–Mon.; first 2 wks of June and first fortnight of Nov. $$–$$$*

Collon
Dining

Forge Gallery Restaurant. This well-established restaurant is in a converted forge north of Dublin on the N2, just north of Slane. The reception area displays paintings by local artists for sale. Warm tones of rose and plum work well with the antique furniture; the old fireplace contributes warmth to the atmosphere. The cuisine is a mixture of French provincial with a strong hint of traditional Irish in winter, when old favorites like silversides or boiled mutton with caper sauce appear on the menu. Two popular specialties are salmon and crab in phyllo pastry, and the Rendezvous appetizer with prawns and scallops in a cream and garlic sauce. Be sure to try one of the seasonal homemade soups. *Collon, Co. Louth, tel. 041/26272. Reservations advised; weekend reservations required. Dress: casual but neat. MC, V. Closed Sun.–Mon.; 4 days at Christmas and all of Jan. $$$*

Drogheda
Dining and Lodging

Boyne Valley Hotel. Approached by a 1-kilometer- (½-mile-) long drive, this converted 19th-century mansion, which once belonged to a brewing family in Drogheda, is situated on extensive parkland. Bedrooms are adequately comfortable, with uninspired decor. The newer wing of the hotel has double rooms, all with private baths and contemporary furnishings. Other additions to the hotel include an attractive, plant-filled conservatory bar looking out over the parkland and the basement, which has been converted into the Cellar Restaurant. *Dublin Rd., Drogheda, Co. Louth, tel. 041/37737. 38 rooms with bath. Facilities: restaurant, bar, pitch-and-putt golf course. AE, DC, MC, V. $$*

Dundalk
Dining and Lodging

Ballymascanlon Hotel. This converted Victorian mansion standing on its own grounds, just north of Dundalk, has long had a fine reputation in the area for comfort and good cuisine. Bedrooms have private baths, and the hotel offers a sports complex with an indoor heated swimming pool, a gymnasium, and a sauna. Other sports facilities include two squash courts, two tennis courts, and a nine-hole golf course. The main restaurant, serving Irish and French cuisine, specializes in fresh seafood entrées, such as lobster in season; the menu also includes vegetarian platters. The hotel grounds also feature an unusual historical artifact, a prehistoric monument known as the Proleek Dolmen. *Dundalk, Co. Louth, tel. 042/71124. 36 rooms with bath. Facilities: restaurant, 2 bars, pool, table tennis, billiards, squash, tennis court, golf, gym. AE, DC, MC, V. $$*

County Meath

Kells
Dining and Lodging

Lennoxbrook. This fine country home, 5 kilometers (3 miles) north of Kells on the N3 road from Dublin to Cavan, is run by Paul and Pauline Mullan and dates back over 200 years. The Mullans are the fifth generation of the family to occupy the house, which is filled with antiques and family heirlooms. Upstairs, the five rooms, all with twins beds, are furnished with finely patterned wallpaper and period furniture and share two bathrooms. Dinner incorporates local produce, including lamb raised in the area. The house is convenient to Newgrange and provides a gate key to the prehistoric forts, passage graves, and other remains, dating from 2000 BC, on the Loughcrew Hills, a 15-minute drive away. *Kells, Co. Meath, tel. 046/45902. 5 rooms. Facilities: restaurant. No credit cards. $*

Kilmessan
Dining and Lodging

Station House Hotel and Restaurant. For anyone who likes the atmosphere of old railways, or simply good food served in unusual surroundings, the Flynn family's establishment is recommended. You reach the place by traveling up the N3 from Dublin to Navan and turning off the main road at the sign for the Hill of Tara, 9½ kilometers (6 miles) before Navan. Continue down the side road for 6½ kilometers (4 miles), past the Hill of Tara to Kilmessan. The railway station was once the junction for a hub of lines linking Dublin with County Meath, but it was closed down in 1952. The Flynns did a restoration job but kept the main features of the station. Diners can have their aperitifs on what was the old platform, while the old ticket office forms the dining room. The emphasis here is on local produce, including meat, vegetables, and fish, despite the inland location. Bedrooms are pleasantly decorated in a floral style; only half the rooms have private baths. Outside, the grounds have been well landscaped, but remnants of the old train station may still be seen, such as the signal box, the turntable for engines, and the engine shed (part of it used for bedrooms). *Kilmessan, Co. Meath, tel. 046/25239, fax 046/25588. 10 rooms, 3 with bath. Facilities: restaurant, bar. AE, MC, V. $$*

County Kildare

Castledermot
Dining and Lodging

Kilkea Castle. Built in the 12th century as a defensive Anglo-Norman castle, this was the home of the FitzGerald family for centuries. The castle is said to be haunted by apparitions and the sounds of battle, even in its new role as a luxury hotel. There are 11 rooms in the castle itself, while the rest are found around the adjacent courtyard. Renovations completed in 1994 have resulted in a smaller number of larger rooms, including six new suites; bedrooms in the castle tend to be more luxuriously furnished. The restaurant is now in what was the great hall of the castle; in these grand surroundings, appropriately decorative meals are served, with dishes based on fresh seasonal produce—some of it from the old walled gardens laid out below. The hotel features its own sports complex and river fishing. *Castledermot, near Athy, Co. Kildare, tel. 0503/45156, fax 0503/45187. 38 rooms with bath. Facilities: restaurant, 2 bars, heated indoor swimming pool, gymnasium, sauna, 2 tennis courts, river fishing for trout, clay-pigeon shooting, archery; horseback riding nearby. AE, DC, MC, V. $$$*

Maynooth
Dining and Lodging

Moyglare Manor. Just a half-hour drive southwest of Dublin, this imposing Georgian mansion, set on 16 pastoral acres dotted with cows and sheep, is renowned for its magnificent antique furnishings. The gracious drawing room has velvet chairs, oil paintings, and thickly draped windows. The grand bedrooms feature four-poster canopy beds, roomy wardrobes, marble fireplaces, and comfortable chintz armchairs. Some of the bathrooms are as large as a room in a modern home. A cocktail bar is decorated with portraits of residents of the house over the past 150 years. Despite the grandeur of the surroundings, the romantic dining room can be pleasantly intimate. The traditional French menu includes *crêpes au gruyère* and baked plaice stuffed with shrimps. Desserts tend to be rich and sophisticated. *Maynooth, Co. Kildare, tel. 01/628–6351 or 01/628–6469, fax 01/628–5405. 17 rooms with bath. Facilities: 2 bars, restaurant, tennis court; horseback riding nearby. AE, DC, MC, V. $$$$*

Naas
Dining and Lodging

Curryhills House Hotel. This Georgian farmhouse with modern additions and elegantly landscaped surroundings stands on the flat plain of Kildare, 11 kilometers (7 miles) northwest of Naas on the R403. The spacious bedrooms are unremarkably furnished but relaxing, and they all have either a bath or a shower. The basement restaurant serves local country-style specialties, such as turkey raised by the owners and served with mushrooms. The bar is a popular local meeting spot, and during weekends, traditional Irish music livens up the atmosphere. The hotel offers no sports facilities, but guests can participate in coarse angling, horseback riding, and golf nearby. *Prosperous, near Naas, Co. Kildare, tel. 045/68150. 10 rooms. Facilities: restaurant, bar. AE, DC, MC, V. $$*

Straffan
Dining and Lodging
★

Kildare Hotel and Country Club. Arnold Palmer designed the lush, wooded 18-hole golf course at the Kildare Country Club (affectionately known as the K-Club), which surrounds this French period former residence. It's enhanced by the manicured gardens and scenic views over the river Liffey, 27 kilometers (around 17 miles) from Dublin. Inside, the 45 rooms are spacious, well lighted, and very comfortable. The Byerly Turk Restaurant, named after a famous race horse, is well known in Dublin dining circles. Although chef Michel Flamme acknowledges the existence of an Irish cuisine with sophisticated versions of traditional dishes, his menu is unashamedly French; a three-course dinner might include roast duck confit with mixed beans, followed by guinea fowl with cream of girolles (dried mushrooms) and fruit tartlets on crème anglaise. *Straffan, Co. Kildare, tel. 01/6273333, fax 01/6273312. 45 rooms with bath. Facilities: 2 restaurants, 2 bars, 4 tennis courts, indoor swimming pool, 18-hole golf course, angling. AE, DC, MC, V. $$$$*

6 The Lakelands

By Pat Mackey

A resident of Waterford, Pat Mackey is the author of the travel guides Sunny South East by Hook and by Crook *and* Lakeland.

Updated by Alannah Hopkin

Irish schoolchildren were once taught to think of their country as a saucer with mountains around the edge and a dip in the middle. The dip is the Midlands—or the Lakelands, as the Bord Fáilte prefers to call it, and this often overlooked region comprises seven counties: Cavan, Laois (pronounced "leash"), Westmeath, Longford, Offaly, Roscommon, and Monaghan, in addition to North Tipperary.

Appropriately, a fair share of Ireland's 800 bodies of water speckle this lush countryside. Many of the lakes formed by glacial action some 10,000 years ago are quite small, especially in Cavan and Monaghan. Anglers who come to the area have learned to expect a lake to themselves, and many return year after year to practice the sport. The River Shannon, one of the longest rivers in Europe, bisects the Lakelands from north to south piercing a series of loughs (lakes): Lough Allen, Lough Ree, and Lough Derg. The Royal Canal and the Grand Canal cross the Lakelands from east to west, ending in the Shannon north and south of Lough Ree. Stretches of both canals are now being developed for recreational purposes.

Quiet and unspectacular, the Lakelands demand thorough and leisurely exploration—the rewards are many, but night owls and thrill-seekers should probably head elsewhere. The towns themselves—including Nenagh, Roscommon, Athlone, Boyle, Mullingar, Tullamore, Longford, and Cavan—are not especially interesting, but they appeal strongly to people hungry for a time when the pace of life was slower and every neighbor's face was familiar. Accommodations in the area are simple but offer good value. The Lakelands is an important cattle area, and the local cuisine reflects this. And since no place in Ireland is more than an hour and a half from the sea, you can also expect to find fresh ocean fish—not to mention salmon and trout from the many rivers and lakes. A town's main hotel is usually the social center, a good place from which to study local life. You might witness a wedding reception (generally a boisterous occasion for all age groups), a First Communion supper, a meeting of the local Lions Club, or a gathering of the neighborhood weight-watchers group. In the countryside around the small, friendly towns, you'll discover several well-maintained historic homes with carefully tended gardens; the impressive monastic remains at Clonmacnoise, Boyle, and Fore; excellent fishing and uncrowded parkland golf courses; and numerous lovely country walks along the water.

Essential Information

Important Addresses and Numbers

Tourist Information Offices Information is available from Tourist Information Offices in **Mullingar** (Dublin Rd., tel. 044/48650, fax 044/40413), **Athlone** (Church St., tel. 0902/94630), **Birr** (Emmet Sq., tel. 0509/20110), **Roscommon** (The Square, tel. 0903/26342), **Boyle** (Bridge St., tel. 079/62145), **Cavan** (Farnham St., tel. 049/31942), and **Monaghan** (Market House, tel. 047/81122).

Hospitals and Pharmacies For medical and ambulance service, contact Mullingar's **General Hospital** (tel. 044/40221). You can buy pharmaceutical supplies from **Fairgreen Pharmacy** (Quinnsworth Shopping Centre, Mullingar, tel. 044/48471).

Arriving and Departing by Plane

Airports The principal international airport serving the Lakeland region is **Dublin Airport** (tel. 01/844–4900). **Connaught International Airport** (tel. 094/67222) in Knock, County Mayo, is much smaller, and **Sligo Regional Airport** (tel. 071/68280) has daily flights from Dublin on Aer Lingus. Car rental facilities are available at Dublin and Knock Airports. For more information on these airports, *see* Chapters 4 (Dublin) and 10 (The Northwest).

Arriving and Departing by Car, Train, and Bus

By Car Mullingar, the regional capital, Longford, and Boyle are on the main N4 route between Dublin and Sligo. It takes one hour to drive from Dublin to Mullingar (55 kilometers/34 miles), and two hours from Mullingar to Sligo. To get from Mullingar to the southwest of the country, you can take the N52 to Nenagh where it meets the N7 and follow that into Limerick—a trip (150 kilometers/94 miles) of about two hours. The R390 from Mullingar leads you west to Athlone, where it connects with the N6 to Galway. The drive (120 kilometers/75 miles) takes about 2½ hours.

By Train A direct rail service links Mullingar to Dublin, with three trains every day making the 1½-hour journey. It costs £10.50 one-way and £12.50 round-trip. Contact **Irish Rail** (tel. 01/836–6222) for information.

By Bus **Bus Éireann** (tel. 01/836–6111) runs an express bus from Dublin to Mullingar in 1½ hours, with a round-trip fare of £9. Buses depart three times daily. A regular-speed bus, leaving twice daily, makes the trip in two hours.

Getting Around

By Car Most of the winding roads in the Lakelands are uncongested, although you may encounter an occasional animal or agricultural machine crossing the road. If you're driving in the north of Counties Cavan and Monaghan, be sure to avoid "unapproved" roads crossing the border into Northern Ireland. The approved routes into Northern Ireland connect the towns of Monaghan and Aughnacloy, Castlefinn and Castlederg, Swalinbar and Enniskillen, Clones and Newtownbutler, and Monaghan and Rosslea. Those driving a rented car should make sure it has been cleared for cross-border journeys. You can rent a car at **Hamill's Rent-a-Car** (Dublin Rd., Mullingar, Co. Westmeath, tel. 044/48682), **Hanlon Bros. Ltd.,** (Dublin Rd., Longford, Co. Longford, tel. 043/46421), or **O'Meara's Car Hire** (Baylough, Athlone, Co. Westmeath, tel. 0902/92325).

By Train Trains from Mullingar, departing twice daily every weekday and Sunday, stop at Longford (35 minutes), Carrick-on-Shannon (1 hour), Boyle (1¼ hours), and Sligo (2 hours).

By Bus The express buses leaving Dublin (*see* Arriving and Departing by Bus, *above*) make stops at Mullingar (1½ hours), Longford (2¼ hours), Carrick-on-Shannon (3 hours), Boyle (3¼ hours), and Sligo (4¼ hours). There is also a daily bus from Mullingar to Athlone, and an express service connecting Galway, Athlone, Longford, Cavan, Clones, Monaghan, and Sligo. Details of all bus services are available from Bus Éireann depots at the following locations: **Athlone Railway Station** (tel. 0902/72651), **Cavan Bus Office** (tel. 049/31353), **Longford Railway Station** (tel. 043/45208), **Monaghan Bus Office**

(tel. 047/82377), **Sligo Railway Station** (tel. 071/69888), and **Bus Éireann** (Dublin, tel. 01/836–6111).

Exploring the Lakelands

Numbers in the margin correspond to points of interest on the Lakelands map.

Highlights for First-Time Visitors

Birr Castle Demesne (*see* Tour 1)
Bord na Mona Bog Rail Tour (*see* Tour 1)
Clonmacnoise (*see* Tour 1)
Emo Court, near Portarlington (*see* Tour 3)
Shannon Boat Trip from Athlone or Banagher (*see* Tour 1)

Tour 1: North Tipperary and the West Lakelands

1 This tour starts in the southwest corner of the region, in **Nenagh,** a small town on the N7—the busy main road that crosses the country from Dublin to Limerick. Nenagh was originally a Norman settlement; it grew to a market town in the 19th century. All that remains of the original settlement is **Nenagh Castle Keep,** in the center of town; it is about 31 meters/100 feet high and 16 meters/53 feet across the base. Opposite the castle is the old county jail. Its gatehouse and governor's house now form the **Nenagh Heritage Centre,** which has permanent displays of rural life in the recent past before mechanization, as well as temporary painting and photography exhibits. *Tel. 067/32633. Admission: £1.50 adults, 75p children, students, and senior citizens. Open Easter–Oct., Mon.–Fri. 10–5, Sun. 2:30–5.*

2 Continue east on the N7 for 32 kilometers/20 miles to **Roscrea.** The main road cuts through a 7th-century monastery founded by St. Cronan; you'll pass the west facade of a 12th-century Romanesque church that now forms an entrance gate to a modern Catholic church. Above the structure's round-headed doorway is a hood-moulding enclosing the figure of a bishop, probably St. Cronan. Roscrea's main attraction is in the very center of town: **Damer House** and the **Roscrea Heritage Centre.** Damer House, a superb example of an early 18th-century town house on the grand scale, was used as a barracks during most of the 19th century; it was rescued from decay by the Irish Georgian Society. It was built in 1725 within the curtain walls of a Norman castle. In those days, homes were often constructed beside or attached to the strongholds they replaced. Damer House has a plain, symmetrical facade and a magnificent carved pine staircase inside. The house contains the collection of the Irish Country Furniture Society, supplemented by pieces from the National Museum—a treat for those interested in antiques. In the adjoining building, exhibits take up monastic settlements in the Midlands, the old Irish kitchen, and other local and national themes. *Tel. 0505/21850. Admission: £2 adults, £1.50 children, students, and senior citizens. Open June–Sept., daily 9:30–6; rest of year, Sat. and Sun. 10–5.*

Leave Roscrea on the N62 and head north for 19 kilometers (12
3 miles) to one of the most attractive towns in the region: **Birr,** a quiet, sleepy place with tree-lined malls and modest Georgian houses. All roads lead to the gates of **Birr Castle Demesne,** an imposing Gothic castle dating from the early 17th century that is still the home of the earls of Rosse. It is not open to the public; however, you can visit the

The Lakelands

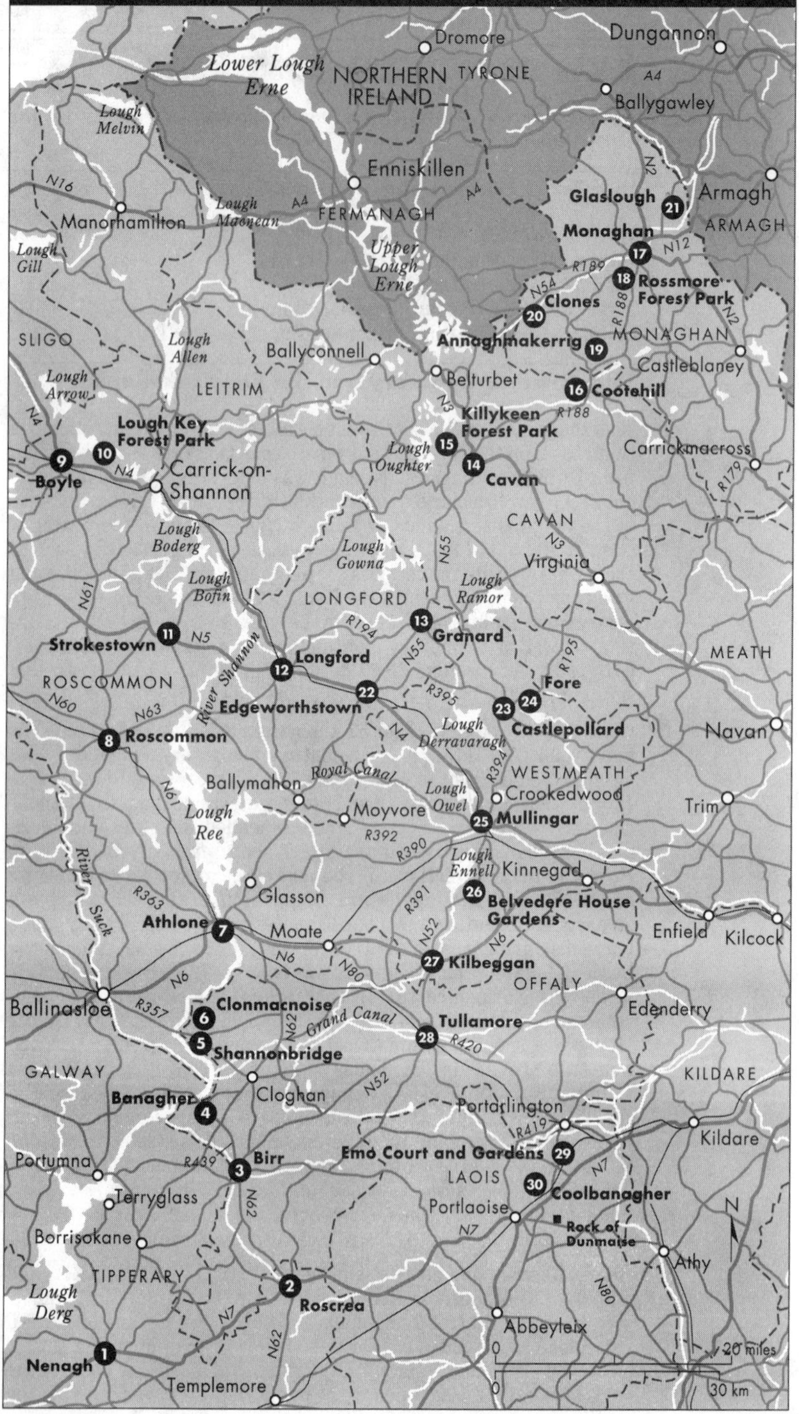

surrounding 100 acres of gardens, the oldest of which was planted three centuries ago. The present earl and countess of Rosse continue the family tradition of making botanical expeditions for specimens of rare trees, plants, and shrubs from all over the world. The formal gardens contain the tallest box-hedges in the world (10 meters/32 feet). In spring, you'll see a wonderful display of flowering cherries, magnolias, crab apple blossom, and naturalized narcissi; in autumn, the maples, chestnuts, and weeping beeches blaze red and gold. The grounds are laid out around a lake and along the banks of two adjacent rivers; above one of these stands the castle. The grounds also contain the remains of a giant (72-inch) reflecting telescope built in 1845, which remained the largest in the world for the next 75 years. Allow at least two hours to see all that's here. *Tel. 0509/20056. Admission: Apr.–Oct., £3 adults, £1.50 children; Nov.–Mar., £2 adults, £1 children. Open Apr.–Oct., daily 9–6; Nov.–Dec., daily 9–1 and 2–5.*

An optional excursion from Birr, recommended only in good weather, follows the R489 west to Portland for the **Lough Derg Drive.** Between Portland and Portumna the River Shannon widens into 32,000 acres of unpolluted water, known as Lough Derg, a popular center for watersports including water-skiing, yachting, and motor-cruising. Fishermen flock here as well for pike and coarse angling in particular. There are many excellent woodland walks around the shore of the Lough. The well-signposted scenic drive (approx 90 kilometers/50 miles) circles the lake passing through numerous attractive waterside villages from Portumna in the north to Kilaloe in the south. **Terryglass,** on the Tipperary shores of the Lough (on the R493 and well-signposted), is considered one of the prettiest villages in Ireland.

Alternately, from Birr take the R439 9.5 kilometers/6 miles north-
4 west to **Banagher,** a village on the Shannon that is a popular base for water-sports fans. If you happen to be in Banagher on a Thursday or a Sunday, you can take a two-hour Shannon Cruise on the *River Queen*, an enclosed launch that seats 54 passengers and has a full bar on board. *Silver Line Cruisers Ltd., The Marina, Banagher, Co. Offaly, tel. 0509/51112. Cost: £3.50 adults, £2 children. Departures mid-May–mid-Sept., 3 PM Thurs.; 2:30 and 4:30 PM Sun., weather permitting.*

Time Out **Flynn's** (Main St., Banagher, tel. 0509/51312), a light and spacious Victorian-style bar in the village center, offers a lunch menu of generously filled sandwiches, salad platters, a roast meat of the day, chicken, fish, or burgers and chips. It's a popular spot with the boating crowd and can be busy on weekends.

Leave Banagher by the R456, turning off after about 2 kilometers (1¼ miles), and follow signposts for Shannonbridge and Clonmacnoise. On either side of the road, you'll notice vast stretches of chocolate-brown boglands and isolated industrial plants for processing this area's natural resource. Bog is used in peat-fired electricity-generating stations, compressed into briquettes for domestic hearths, and made into moss peat and plant containers for gardeners. Ireland's liberal use of a resource that is scarce elsewhere in Europe provoked an indignant reaction from botanists and ecologists in the 1980s, which resulted in the setting aside of certain bog areas for conservation. Among these are the Clara Bog and Mongan's Bog in County Offaly, both relatively untouched, raised pieces of land with unique flora, and the Scragh Bog in County Westmeath. Because of the preservative qualities of peat, it is not unusual to come across bog timber 5,000 years old, or to dig up perfectly preserved domestic implements from more recent times—not to mention the occasional cache of treasure. Deer, badgers, and wild dogs inhabit the boglands, along with a rich bird and plant life. These areas are being preserved by Bord na Mona, the same government agency that makes commercial use of other boglands.

If you would like to have a close look at a bog, follow the signs in
5 **Shannonbridge** for the **Bord na Mona Bog Rail Tour,** which leaves from **Uisce Dubh,** 10 kilometers (6 miles) from Shannonbridge. A small green and yellow diesel locomotive pulls one coach across the bog at an average of 24 kilometers (15 miles) per hour while the driver provides commentary on a landscape unchanged for millennia. There are over 1,200 kilometers (745 miles) of narrow-gauge bog railway, and the section on the tour, known as the Clonmacnoise and South Offaly Railway, is the only part accessible to the public. *Uisce Dubh, near Shannonbridge, Co. Offaly, tel. 0905/74114. Admission: £3 adults, £2 children, students, and senior citizens. Tours on the hour, daily 10–5, Easter–Oct.*

6 **Clonmacnoise,** once one of Ireland's most important monastic settlements, is clearly signposted from Shannonbridge. The remaining buildings are on an esker, or natural gravel ridge, that overlooks a large marshy area beside the River Shannon. When the settlement was founded by St. Ciaran in 545, the Shannon was an important artery of communication, so that the site was not as remote as it appears now. Take time to survey the surrounding countryside from the higher parts of Clonmacnoise, and you'll get a good idea of the strategic advantages of its commanding riverside location.

In its heyday, Clonmacnoise was the burial place of the kings of Connaught and of Tara. It survived raids by feuding Irish tribes, Vikings, and Normans until 1552, when the English garrison from Athlone reduced it to ruin. Since then it has remained a prestigious burial place; among the ancient stones are many other graves of local people dating from the 17th to the mid-20th century, when a new graveyard was consecrated on adjoining land. The older surviving buildings include the shell of a small cathedral, two Round Towers, the remains of eight smaller churches, and several High Crosses, the best preserved of these being the Cross of the Scriptures, also known as Flann's Cross. Some of the treasure and manuscripts originating from Clonmacnoise are now housed in the National Museum in Dublin. *Co. Offaly, tel. 0905/74195. Admission: £1.50 adults, £1 senior citizens, 60p children. Open mid-June–Sept., daily 9–7; Oct.–May, daily 10–6 or dusk.*

Turn left out of the car park at Clonmacnoise, and signposts will lead you to the village of Ballynahown where you'll turn north onto
7 the N62 Athlone road. **Athlone** originated as a crossing point of the Shannon, at first as a ford. It marks the boundary between the old provinces of Leinster (to the east) and Connacht (to the west). **Athlone Castle** was built beside the river in the 13th century. After their defeat at the Battle of the Boyne in 1691, the Irish retreated to Athlone and made the Shannon their first line of defense. The castle was extensively renovated in 1991, the 300th anniversary of this rout. It remains an interesting example of a Norman stronghold and houses a small museum of artifacts relating to Athlone's eventful past. Admission includes access to an interpretative center depicting the siege of Athlone in 1691, the flora and fauna of the Shannon, and the life of the famous tenor John McCormack. *Town Bridge, Athlone, Co. Westmeath, tel. 0902/94360. Admission: £2.20 adults,*

80p children, £1.60 students and senior citizens. Open May–Sept., daily 10–5.

Athlone, the main shopping hub for the surrounding area, is an important road and rail junction, but it contains nothing of great interest to the visitor. Rather than explore its narrow, congested streets, take a ride on the *M.V. Avonree* riverboat up the Shannon to nearby Lough Ree. *The Strand, Athlone, tel. 0902/92513. Admission: £3.50 adults, £2.50 children. Sailings July–Sept. at 11, 2:30, and 4, except Wed. 4:30 only. 1½ hrs' duration; light refreshments on board.*

To explore the region west of the Shannon, take the N61 from
8 Athlone for 32 kilometers/20 miles to **Roscommon,** the capital of County Roscommon, where sheep and cattle raising is the main occupation. As you enter this pleasant little town on the southern slopes of a hill, you'll pass the remains of **Roscommon Abbey** on your right. The principal ruin is a church; at the base of the choir stand eight sculpted figures representing gallowglasses, or medieval Irish professional soldiers. The ruins are freely accessible. To the north of the town are the weathered remains of **Roscommon Castle,** a large Norman stronghold dating from the 13th century.

Those with an interest in fishing and walking will want to continue
9 north on the N61 for 43 kilometers/26 miles to **Boyle,** a delightful, old-fashioned town on the Boyle River midway between Lough Gara and Lough Key. The ruins of **Boyle Abbey** (on the N4), dating from the late 12th and early 13th centuries, still convey an impression of the splendor of this richly endowed Cistercian foundation. The nave, choir, and transept of the cruciform church are in good condition. The ruins are freely accessible. **King House,** in the center of Boyle not far from the Abbey, is a magnificent 16th-century house used at one time as a barracks for the famous Connaught Rangers. It was opened to the public in 1994 after extensive restoration and has exhibits on the Connaught Rangers, the Kings of Connaught, and the history of the house. *Tel. 0903/26100. Admission: £2.50 adults, £1.50 children. Open May–Sept., Tues.–Sun. 10–6; Apr. and Oct., Sat. and Sun. 10–6.*

Boyle is a mecca for anglers and walkers who can choose between the challenges of the Curlew Mountains to the north of the town, or
10 **Lough Key Forest Park** to the east, a popular base for campers and backpackers. The park consists of 840 acres on the shores of the lake, and contains a bog garden, a deer enclosure, and a cypress grove; boats can be hired on the lake. *Tel. 079/62214. Car park: £2. Freely accessible.*

The main tour leaves the N61 after about 12 kilometers/8 miles at Tulsk, turning right (east) onto the N5 for **Strokestown Park House.**
11 Like many villages near a "big house," **Strokestown** was designed to complement the house. The widest main street in Ireland—laid out to rival the Ringstrasse in Vienna—leads to a Gothic arch, the entrance to the house grounds. As you can see from its facade, this enormous house, seat of the Pakenham Mahon family from 1660 to 1979, has a complicated architectural history. The Palladian wings were added in the 18th century to the original 17th-century block, and the house was extended again in the early 19th century. The interior is full of curiosities, such as the gallery above the kitchen, which allowed the lady of the house to supervise domestic affairs from a safe distance. Menus were dropped from the balcony on Monday mornings with instructions to the cook for the week's meals. One wing houses lavish stables with vaulted ceilings and Tuscan pillars. There is also a distillery and a fully equipped nursery. In-

terested visitors are welcome to view the gardens, which are undergoing an ambitious restoration plan that will include the widest and longest herbaceous borders in Ireland. A museum documenting local events during the disastrous Famine (1845–1850) opened in 1994. *Strokestown, Co. Roscommon, tel. 078/33013. Admission: £3 adults, £2 senior citizens, £1 children. Open June 1–Sept. 15, Tues.–Sun. 12–5.*

From Strokestown, continue east on the N4 for 23 kilometers (14 miles) to Longford, the starting point of the next tour.

Tour 2: The Northern Lakelands

12 **Longford,** the county seat of County Longford, is a typical little market community on the main (N4) Dublin–Sligo road. Pick up the R194 Ballinalee–Granard road to visit **Carriglass Manor,** 5 kilometers (3 miles) outside town. The romantic Tudor-Gothic house was built in 1837 by Thomas Lefroy. His descendants still reside here, and they are proud that as a young man in England, Lefroy was romantically involved with the novelist Jane Austen. Just why they never married is a mystery, but it is believed that she based the character of Mr. Darcy in *Pride and Prejudice* on Mr. Lefroy. The house features some good plasterwork and many of its original mid-19th-century furnishings. A magnificent stableyard belonging to an earlier house on the site dates from 1790. Visitors also have access to a small costume museum. *Co. Longford, tel. 043/45165. Admission: £3 adults, £2 children. Open June 15–Sept. 15, Thurs.–Mon. 1–5:30, Sun. 2–6.*

13 Continue east from the manor on the R194 to **Granard.** This market town and fishing center stands on high ground near the Longford-Cavan border. The **Motte of Granard** at the southwest end of town was once the site of a fortified Norman castle. In 1932 a statue of St. Patrick was erected here to mark the 15th centenary of his arrival in Ireland. (At least a dozen statues of the patron saint, all virtually identical, were put up that year; see how many others you can spot on your travels.)

Leave Granard on the N55 and drive north for 30½ kilometers (19
14 miles) to **Cavan.** Cavan is an undistinguished little town serving the local farming community, but it has two attractions that you might like to visit. **Cavan Crystal** is an up-and-coming rival to Waterford in the cut-lead-crystal line; the company offers guided factory tours and access to their factory shop. This is a good opportunity to watch skilled craftspeople at work if you can't make it to Waterford. *Cavan Town, tel. 049/31800. Guided tours: weekdays 9:30, 10:30, 11:30, 12:30, 2:30.*

The **Cavan Folk Museum** holds what is called with pride "the Pig House Collection": costumes, kitchen and household goods, farmyard tools, machinery, and other bric-a-brac tracing the rural lifestyle from the 1700s to the present. At some quarters in the area, that way of life has changed so little that the "museum pieces" are still in use around the farm—which may be why the locals are so fond of this collection. *Cornafean, Cavan Town, tel. 049/37248. Admission: £1.50 adults, 50p children. Phone to confirm opening hours.*

Time Out **The Annalee Restaurant** (Hotel Kilmore, Dublin Rd., tel. 049/32288) is a bright two-tier room overlooking landscaped gardens. Fresh local produce is cooked in traditional Irish style, and vegetarian dishes are also available.

Traveling north from Cavan on the N3, you can follow signs to
15 **Killykeen Forest Park.** Organized within the beautiful mazelike network of lakes called **Lough Oughter,** this 600-acre park offers a series of planned and signposted walks and nature trails. *Tel. 049/32541. Admission free. Parking £1.50. Open Feb.–Dec., daily 9–5; closed Jan.*

Beyond Cavan you enter the heart of the northern Lakelands, with lakes both large and small on either side of the road. County Cavan and County Monaghan each have at least 180 lakes. The countryside is characterized by drumlins—small, steep hills consisting of boulder clay left behind by the glacial retreat 10,000 years ago. The boulder clay also filled in many of the pre-glacial river valleys, causing the rivers to change course and create shallow lakes, which provide excellent fishing.

16 The route then takes you northeast up the R188 to **Cootehill.** Fans of the songwriter Percy French (1854–1920) will recall the opening lines of his famous song "Come Back, Paddy Reilly, to Ballyjamesduff," which instruct the traveler in search of that little paradise to "turn to the left at the bridge of Finea, and stop when halfway to Cootehill." In fact, as locals will delight in telling you, if you follow these instructions you will not get to Ballyjamesduff at all—you'll get hopelessly lost.

Cootehill is one of the most underestimated small towns in Ireland. It has a lovely setting on a wooded hillside, and its wide streets, with their intriguing old shops, are always busy without being congested. Most of its visitors are anglers from Europe, the United Kingdom, and the rest of Ireland. Walk up to "the top of the town" (past the White Horse Hotel) and you will see the entrance gates to **Bellamont Forest.** Only pedestrians are allowed through the gates, which lead, after about a mile of woodlands, to an exquisite hilltop Palladian villa, small but perfectly proportioned, and virtually unaltered since it was built in 1728. It is now a private home but is occasionally opened to the public. If you are interested, inquire locally or at the Tourist Information Office in Cavan (tel. 049/31942).

Leave Cootehill for Monaghan on the R188, and enjoy the lack of traffic, which is typical of the undulating backroads in drumlin coun-
17 try. **Monaghan** is an attractive county town built around a central diamond. The old market house, dating from 1792, is now the **County Museum.** Its display tracing the history of Monaghan from earliest times to the present day is the winner of a European Community Heritage Award. *Tel. 047/82928. Admission free. Open Tues.–Sat. 11–1 and 2–5.*

Leave Monaghan on the R189 Newbliss road. Just outside the town
18 you will pass **Rossmore Forest Park,** 691 acres of low hills and small lakes with pleasant forest walks and signposted nature trails that are freely accessible. At Newbliss you can follow an optional excur-
19 sion (about 4.8 kilometers/3 miles) signposted **Annaghmakerrig.** Here you will find a small forest park with a lake, and above it Annaghmakerrig House, home of the stage director Sir Tyrone Guthrie until his death in 1971. He left it to the nation as a residential center for writers, artists, and musicians. It is not officially open to the public, but anyone with a special interest in the arts or in its previous owner can ask to be shown around.

20 Continue on the R183 from Newbliss to **Clones.** This is border country—also known as bandit country—and aimless exploring, especially on roads marked "Unapproved Road" (which lead to unmanned border crossings), is not recommended. In early Chris-

tian times, Clones was the site of a monastery founded by St. Tighearnach, who died here in AD 458. An Augustinian abbey replaced the monastery in the 12th century, and its remains can still be seen near the 23-meter/75-foot **Round Tower.** In the central diamond of the town stands a 10th-century Celtic High Cross, with carved panels representing scriptural scenes. Nowadays Clones, a small agricultural market town, is known chiefly for lace making. A varied selection of lace is on display around the town and can be purchased at the **Clones Lace Centre.** *Co. Monaghan, tel. 047/51051. Admission free. Open Mon.–Sat. 10–6, closed Tues. and Sun.*

Return to Monaghan on the N54 (21 kilometers/13 miles). If you have time for one more excursion in the area, leave Monaghan on the N12 11 kilometers (7 miles) out of town and take the first left (R185)
21 for **Glaslough,** which means "green lake." On the shores of its deep, beautiful waters is **Castle Leslie,** originally a medieval stronghold, which has been the seat of the Leslie family since 1664. The present castle was built in 1870 in a mix of Gothic and Italianate styles. The Leslie family, a mildly eccentric one known for its literary and artistic leanings, has many notable relations by marriage, including the duke of Wellington, who defeated Napoleon at Waterloo, and Sir Winston Churchill. Wellington's death mask is preserved at Castle Leslie, as is Churchill's baby dress, along with an impressive collection of Italian artworks. There are 14 acres of gardens with miniature golf and croquet; home-baked teas are served in the tearoom and conservatory. *Co. Monaghan, tel. 047/88109. Admission to house: £3 adults, £2 students and senior citizens, £1.50 children. Ghost tour daily 6 PM. Open June–Aug. daily 12–6; other times by appointment.*

Tour 3: The Eastern Lakelands

This tour takes Longford as its starting point, exploring the areas to the east and south. Those with literary interests may wish to stop in
22 **Edgeworthstown** (also known as Mostrim), 12 kilometers (8 miles) east of Longford on the N4. This town was the home of the novelist Maria Edgeworth (1769–1849), whose highly original satirical works, the best known of which is *Castle Rackrent,* were admired by such contemporaries as Sir Walter Scott and William Wordsworth, both of whom visited here. The family residence, Edgeworthstown House, at the eastern end of the village, is now a private nursing home and not open to the public. The Edgeworth family vault, where Maria and her father, Richard Lovell Edgeworth, an author and inventor, are interred, is in the churchyard of St. John's Church.

23 From Edgeworthstown take the R395 for **Castlepollard,** a pretty village of multicolored houses laid out around a triangular green. One and a half kilometers (1 mile) outside the village you'll find **Tullynally Castle and Gardens,** seat of the earls of Longford and the Irish home of the literary Pakenham family, whose members include the prison reformer and antipornography campaigner Frank Pakenham (the current earl of Longford); his wife Elizabeth and his daughter Antonia Fraser, both historical biographers; and his brother Thomas, a historian. The original 18th-century building was extended in the Gothic style in the 19th century, making it the largest castellated house in Ireland, with an elaborate facade of turrets and towers. In addition to a fine collection of portraits and furniture, the house contains many fascinating 19th-century domestic gadgets, as well as an immense kitchen. The grounds also include a landscaped park and formal gardens. *Co. Westmeath, tel. 044/61159. Admission to castle and gardens: £3.00 adults, £1.50 children and*

senior citizens; admission to gardens only: £1 adults, 50p children. Gardens open May–Oct., daily 10–5; castle rooms open July 16–Aug. 15, daily 2–6, and by appointment to groups.

24 From Castlepollard take the R195 and follow signposts to **Fore,** where you will find the remains of **Fore Abbey.** The oldest structure here is St. Fechin's Church, dating from the 10th century, with a massive cross-inscribed lintel stone. Nearby are the remains of a 13th-century Benedictine abbey, whose imposing square towers and loophole windows resemble a castle rather than an abbey.

Before leaving Fore, you might wish to visit the **Ben Breeze Open Farm,** just outside the village on the Kells road. The farm is basically a traditional dairy and pig farm, with 40 cows and 40 sows on 80 acres. There is also a large collection of fowl, including peacocks, quail, doves, and several varieties of hens and chicks; the most popular attraction is usually the baby pigs. *Fore, Co. Westmeath, tel. 044/66338. Admission £1. Open May–Aug., Mon.–Sat. 10–6. Closed Sun.*

25 Return to Castlepollard and take the R394 to **Mullingar,** a busy commercial and cattle-trading center on the Royal Canal midway between two large, attractive lakes, Lough Owel and Lough Ennel. This is an area of rich farmland, and the town is known as Ireland's beef capital; farmers all over Ireland describe a good young cow as "beef to the ankle, like a Mullingar heifer." The buildings in the town date mostly from the 19th century, with the exception of the large **Catholic Cathedral of Christ the King,** which was completed in 1939 in the Renaissance style. Finely carved stonework decorates the front of the cathedral, and the spacious interior has mosaics of St. Patrick and St. Anne by the Russian artist Boris Anrep. *Admission free. Open daily 9–5:30.*

The **Military and Historical Museum** is also worth a visit. On display here are weapons from the two World Wars, boats of oak from the 1st century AD, and uniforms and other articles of the old IRA. *Columb Barracks, tel. 044/48391. Admission free. Open to the public by appointment only.*

Time Out The **Bloomfield House Hotel** (Mullingar, Co. Westmeath, tel. 044/40894) is just outside Mullingar on the N52 Kilbeggan road on the shores of Lough Ennell. The castellated white building dates from 1837 and was previously a convent. A selection of salads and sandwiches is served in the bar, while the more formal Lakeview Restaurant offers classic French cuisine.

Leave Mullingar on the N52 heading south. You might like to stop 5
26 kilometers (3 miles) out of town to visit **Belvedere House Gardens,** remarkable for a beautiful setting on the northeast shore of Lough Ennel. Terraced gardens descend in three stages to the waters of the lake and provide a panoramic view of its islands. The estate also contains a walled garden with many varieties of trees, shrubs, and flowers, and parkland landscaped in the 18th-century style. *Mullingar, Co. Westmeath, tel. 044/40861. Open May–Sept., daily 12–6. Admission £1 adults, 50p children.*

27 **Kilbeggan,** 24 kilometers (15 miles) south of Mullingar on the N52, is known mainly for its distillery, which was established in 1757 to produce a traditional Irish malt whiskey. It closed down in 1954 and was re-opened in 1987 by Cooley Distillery. Cooley makes its whiskey in County Louth but brings it to Kilbeggan to be matured in casks. The Kilbeggan distillery has been restored as a museum of industrial ar-

chaeology illustrating the process of Irish pot whiskey distillation and the social history of the workers' lives. *Kilbeggan, Co. Westmeath, tel. 0506/32134. Admission: £2 adults, £1 students and children over 5. Open Apr.–Oct., Mon.–Sat. 9–6, Sun 10–6; Nov.–Mar., Mon.–Fri. 10–4. Guided tours every half-hour April–Oct.*

Just outside **Tullamore** (*see below*) on the N52 road to Birr is **Charleville Castle,** a castellated Gothic Revival manor house set on about 30 acres of woodland walks and gardens. This magnificent building dates from 1812 and is a fine example of the work of the architect Francis Johnston, who was responsible for many of Dublin's stately Georgian buildings. Guided tours of the interior are available. *Tullamore, Co. Offaly, tel. 0506/21279. Admission: £2.50 adults, £1.50 children. Open Apr.–May, Sat., Sun., and holidays 2–5; June–Sept., Wed.–Sun. 11–5.*

28 Continue on the N52 to **Tullamore,** the county seat of Offaly, on the Grand Canal. Turn left on the R420 and drive 27 kilometers (17 miles) until you reach **Portarlington,** a charming Old World town that until quite recently had a sizable bilingual (English/French) population of Huguenot origin. Next, proceed 8 kilometers (5 miles) south
29 of the town on the R419 to **Emo Court and Gardens.** The house was designed by James Gandon, architect of the Custom House and the Four Courts in Dublin, on a similarly grand scale. The domed rotunda, inspired by the Roman Pantheon, is one of the most impressive rooms in Ireland. This vast circular space is lit by a lantern in the coffered dome, which rests on gilded capitals and marble pilasters. The house has been magnificently restored by its present owner; it's a wonderful example of living on the grand scale. The grounds also include formal gardens with classical statuary and rare trees and shrubs. *Emo, Co. Laois, tel. 0502/26110. Admission to gardens: £2 adults, £1 children and senior citizens. Admission to house: £2.50. Gardens open daily 10:30–5:30; house open Apr.–mid-Oct., Mon. 2–6 and by arrangement.*

If Emo Court has turned you into an admirer of the work of James Gandon, you will enjoy a visit to the exquisite **Church of St. John the**
30 **Evangelist** in **Coolbanagher,** 1½ kilometers (1 mile) south on the R419. Gandon's original 1795 plans are on view inside the building, which also has an elaborately carved 15th-century font. *Open daily 9–6.*

The R419 joins the main N8 Cork–Dublin road about 1⅗ kilometers (1 mile) south of Coolbanagher.

Sports and the Outdoors

Bicycling

One of the best ways to immerse yourself in the Lakelands is to tour the region on a bicycle. But while the Lakelands may not offer the spectacular scenery of the more hilly coastal regions, it makes for less strenuous riding. Avoid the National Routes (N roads) and their heavy traffic. The twisting roads are generally in good condition, and there are picnic places in the state-owned forests just off the main road. As it is not considered a "must see" for most visitors to Ireland, a cycling tour of the Lakelands is a good choice for visitors who are interested in meeting the Irish rather than in comparing notes with other travelers. The rivers, canals, and the many lakes make it a popular recreational area for those who live in or near it. Bord Fáilte recommends two long tours: one of the

Athlone-Mullingar-Roscommon area, and another of the Cavan-Monaghan-Mullingar region. But part of the pleasure of traveling on bicycle is breaking away from the prescribed routes and making discoveries on your own. Shops that rent cycles in the Lakelands region include the following: **M.R. Hardiman** (Irishtown, Athlone, Co. Westmeath, tel. 0902/78669), **Brendan Sheerin** (Main St., Boyle, Co. Roscommon, tel. 079/62010), **E. Clerkin** (Main St., Monaghan, Co. Monaghan, tel. 047/81434), and **Leo Hunt** (Main St., Roscommon, Co. Roscommon, tel. 0903/26299).

Boating

There are 300 miles of navigable rivers and island-studded lakes in the region, and several companies rent out charter boats of varying sizes for vacations on the water. Most of these vessels hold from six to eight people, and all are operated by the parties who rent them: **Athlone Cruisers Ltd.** (The Jolly Mariner Marina, Athlone, Co. Westmeath, tel. 0902/72892), **Carrick Craft** (The Marina, Carrick-on-Shannon, Co. Leitrim, tel. 078/20236), **Celtic Canal Cruisers Ltd.** (24th Lock, Tullamore, Co. Offaly, tel. 0506/21861), **S.G.S. Marine** (Ballykeeran, Athlone, Co. Westmeath, tel. 0902/85163), and **Emerald Star Line** (47 Dawson St., Dublin 2, tel. 01/679–8166). **Shannon Sailing** (Dromineer, Nenagh, tel. 067/24295) offers cruises of scenic Longh Derg by water bus and also hires out cruisers and sailboards.

Fishing

Anglers from all over the world are attracted to the region's River Shannon and its abundance of lakes. General information can be obtained in most hotels, bed-and-breakfasts, and bars. Monaghan, Cavan, Boyle, and the small lakes to the east and west of Lough Derg are the best coarse fishing areas, while brown trout lakes and rivers can be found around Birr, Banagher, Mullingar, and Roscommon. For pike, you'll find the most fruitful areas around Cavan, Clones, Cootehill, Castleblaney, Kingscourt, Carrick-on-Shannon, Boyle, Belturbet, and Butlersbridge. Keep in mind, however, that certain laws have been passed to protect and conserve the dwindling population of Irish pike: You are forbidden to use live fish bait, to fish with more than two rods, to transfer live roach from one water to another, or to kill more than three pike in a day. For rudd fishing, the best places are the waters around Mullingar (Lough Patrick, Lough Analla, and the Royal Canal) and Monaghan (Lough na Glach, Lough Moynalty, and Lough Corcrin); and tench fishers seem to favor Carrick-on-Shannon, Boyle, Strokestown, Lanesborough, Athlone, Carrickmacross, and Shercock.

The Lakelands region hosts several angling festivals, with prize money and fringe events such as sing-alongs, dart games, and card competitions. Castleblaney has a tournament in March; Carrickmacross and Ballinsasloe, in May; Athlone, in July and October; and Cootehill, in September. Contact the Irish Tourist Board for more details on these tournaments.

For information on necessary licenses and permits, *see* Sports and Outdoor Activities in Chapter 1.

Golf

Six new, 18-hole courses have opened in the Lakelands in recent years, considerably reducing the pressure on facilities. While the parkland courses of the Lakelands may lack the spectacular challenge of Ireland's more famous scenic and coastal courses, they have a quiet charm all of their own, not the least of it being that, on weekdays at least, you are unlikely to have any trouble booking a tee time. Greens fees are generally moderate at £10 and under.

Delvin Castle Golf Club (Delvin, Co. Westmeath, tel. 044/64315), **Mount Temple Golf Club** (Campfield Lodge, Moate, Co. Westmeath, tel. 0902/81545), **Nuremore Country Club** (Carrickmacross, Co. Monaghan, tel. 042/61438), **Roscrea Golf Club** (Racket Hall, Roscrea, Co. Tipperary, tel. 0509/21130), **Rossmore Golf Club** (Rossmore Park, Near Cootehill, Co. Monaghan, tel. 047/81316), **Slieve Russell Hotel** (Ballyconnell, Co. Cavan, tel. 049/26444).

All of the following places also welcome visitors: **Athlone Golf Club** (Hodson Bay, Athlone, Co. Westmeath, tel. 0902/92073 or 0902/92235), **Birr Golf Club** (The Glens, Birr, Co. Offaly, tel. 0509/20082), **County Cavan Golf Club** (Arnmore House, Cavan, tel. 049/31283), **The Heath Golf Club** (Portlaoise, Co. Laois, tel. 0502/46533), **Longford Golf Club** (Glack, Longford, Co. Longford, tel. 043/46310), **Mullingar Golf Club** (Belvedere, Mullingar, Co. Westmeath, tel. 044/48629), **Nenagh Golf Club** (Graigne, Nenagh, Co. Tipperary, tel. 067/31476), **Tullamore Golf Club** (Brookfield, Tullamore, Co. Offaly, tel. 0506/21439).

Walking

Forest park trails (Killykeen, Lough Key, and Dun a Ri forest parks) and narrow country roads invite visitors to tour parts of the Lakelands on foot. One impressive walking trail to the east of Birr, called **the Slieve Bloom Way,** runs through the Slieve Bloom Mountains on a 50-kilometer (31-mile) circular route; its attractions include deep glens, rock formations, waterfalls, and views from mountain peaks.

Dining and Lodging

Dining

Category	Cost*
$$$$	over £20
$$$	£17–£20
$$	£12–£17
$	under £12

**per person, excluding drinks and service*

Lodging

Category	Cost*
$$$$	over £110
$$$	£85–£110

$$	£65–£85
$	under £65

**All prices are for a standard double room, including tax.*

Highly recommended restaurants and hotels are indicated by a star ★.

Athlone

Dining and Lodging

Hodson Bay Hotel. Instead of staying in Athlone's unremarkable town center, head 4 kilometers (2.5 miles) out of town on the Roscommon road (N63) to the shores of Lough Ree. A $5 million refurbishment has turned the bulky, pale-pink, four-story mansion—once an 18th-century family home—into a spacious modern hotel. Its good sporting facilities and attractive lakeside location have already made it popular with families. All guest rooms are coordinated in shades of deep pastel with cotton quilt coverlets and well-designed wooden furniture. The back ones overlook the roof of the conference center, so insist on a view of the lake when you book. The bar and L'Escale restaurant also overlook the lake. The latter is a romantic, candlelit room with well-spaced tables set with pink napery. Both the à la carte and set menus offer imaginative Irish cooking with a French accent: roast stuffed leg of lamb cooked over potatoes or veal escalope with tomato concasse, julienne of ham, and cheddar and Parmesan cheese are typical main courses. The hotel's central location also makes it a convenient touring base. *Roscommon Rd., Athlone, Co. Roscommon, tel. 0902/92444, fax 0902/92688. 46 rooms with bath. Facilities: 2 restaurants, bar, indoor heated pool, gym, sauna, Jacuzzi, 2 tennis courts, horseback riding, fishing, 18-hole golf course. AE, DC, MC, V. $$*

Ballyconnell

Dining and Lodging
★

Slieve Russell Hotel and Country Club. This magnificent hotel, 26 kilometers (16 miles) west of Cavan, makes a convenient break on the Dublin–Sligo journey. A fountain plays before the palatial floodlit neoclassical-style facade, and the spacious lobby gleams with polished marble. Most bedrooms have a Jacuzzi, super-king-size beds, floor-to-ceiling drapes, and chunky art deco–style furniture reminiscent of the great ocean liners. The sports and spa facilities are outstanding, but for many guests the excellent coarse and trout fishing—some of which is available within the hotel's 300-acre grounds—is the main attraction. The Conall Cearnach Restaurant is a formal spot with white napery and wrought-iron chandeliers. The extensive menu includes a variety of traditionally prepared seafood dishes, such as black sole on the bone or salmon hollandaise. The Brackley Buttery offers a more informal ambience. *Ballyconnell, Co. Cavan, tel. 049/26444, fax 049/26474. 151 rooms with bath. Facilities: 2 restaurants, 2 bars, indoor pool, gym, sauna, solarium, steam bath. 2 squash courts, 4 tennis courts, fishing, 18-hole golf course. AE, DC, MC, V. $$$$*

Birr

Dining

The Stables. People travel from miles around to dine in this small restaurant behind a Georgian town house opposite the castle gates. There's a tiny room, with a chaise longue and an open fire, where you can study the menu. The dining room—which was once the stables—is an open room with a high-beamed ceiling and plain whitewashed walls; the small tables have red napery and oak chairs. The Cordon Bleu–trained cook uses only fresh local produce. The menu features such old favorites as grilled sirloin steak *maître d'hotel* (with a spicy butter sauce), chicken Kiev, and stuffed paupiettes of pork with cider. *Oxmantown Mall, Birr, Co. Offaly, tel. 0509/20263. Reservations advised. AE, DC, MC, V. Open Tues.–Sat., dinner only. $$*

Lodging **County Arms.** Built in 1810, this small country house, just outside Birr on the Roscrea road (N62), was converted into a modest hotel in the late 1960s. Its last private owners were two elderly sisters, and the furnishings in the public rooms still recall an old-fashioned private home, with Victorian day couches, deeply cushioned armchairs, a grandfather clock, undistinguished paintings and brass bric-a-brac. The lovely walled garden to the left of the house has a small conservatory and gravel walks. The most attractive bedrooms, with tall Georgian windows, are found at the front of the house, but they overlook a dull suburban stretch of main road beyond the gardens. The more modestly proportioned back rooms have a better view of open countryside. All rooms have been refurbished recently in shades of dusty pink. *Roscrea Rd., Birr, Co. Offaly, tel. 0509/20791, fax 0509/21234. 18 rooms with bath. Facilities: restaurant, bar, fishing, tennis court. AE, DC, MC, V. $$*

Borrisokane

Dining and Lodging ★ **Ballycormac House.** This country hideaway is 11 kilometers (7 miles) southwest of Birr and 7 kilometers (3 miles) from Lough Derg. Leave Birr on the N52 Borrisokane road and turn right for Aglish after about 11 kilometers (7 miles). Signposts will direct you from there. Guests stay in a 300-year-old farmhouse whose owners now breed Irish hunting horses. Gardens surround the quaint cottage-style building, set amid 20 secluded acres. The cozy house features open fires and central heating and has been decorated with antiques and curios. Your hosts, the Paxman family, are known as much for their high standard of hospitality as for their equestrian pursuits. Dinner, prepared by a Cordon Bleu cook, is from organically grown produce and local meat and fish, and all breads, jams, and cakes are homemade. Each relaxing bedroom is pleasantly furnished in its own way. *Aglish, Borrisokane, Co. Tipperary, tel. 067/21129, fax 0509/20040. Advance booking essential. 5 rooms with bath. Facilities: evening meal (residents only), horseback riding, fox hunting, rough shooting, TV in one room only. AE, DC, MC, V. Closed Christmas week. $$*

Carrickmacross

Dining and Lodging **Nuremore.** This Victorian country house has been extended over the years and following a recent refurbishment is now a luxury hotel with excellent sporting facilities. It is 81 kilometers (50 miles) from both Dublin and Belfast, making it a popular weekend retreat. Built on the shores of Lough Naglach, which is stocked with trout, the 100-acre grounds include an 18-hole golf course. There are open fires in the large lounge, furnished with plump armchairs and Victorian tables. The bedrooms are decorated in the country-house style with Victorian mahogany furniture and coordinated color schemes. The restaurant serves a combination of French and Irish cuisine in formal surroundings amid a dusky pink decor. *Carrickmacross, Co. Monaghan, tel. 042/61438, fax 042/61853. 69 rooms with bath. Facilities: restaurant, bar, indoor pool, sauna, Jacuzzi, steamroom,* *gym, squash court, 2 tennis courts, snooker room, fishing, 18-hole golf course. AE, DC, MC, V. $$$$*

Clones

Lodging **Hilton Park.** Look for a large set of black gates with silver falcons 5 kilometers (3 miles) outside Clones on the R183 Ballyhaise road to find this large and stately early Georgian country house. It has three private lakes on its 500-acre grounds, which include 50 acres of gardens and parkland, a working sheep farm, and an organic market garden. Your friendly hosts, Johnny and Lucy Madden, run their magnificent house with stylish informality. All rooms are individually decorated with antiques and have lovely views; some have four-poster beds. Dinner, which consists of freshly prepared produce from their market garden and local meat and fish, is available for residents. *Clones, Co. Monaghan, tel. 047/56007, fax 047/56033. 5 rooms, 3 with bath. Advance booking essential. Facilities: trout and pike fishing, boating, lake swimming, croquet, golf, TV room (no TV or direct dial phones in rooms). MC, V. Closed Oct.–Mar. $$$$*

Cootehill

Dining and Lodging ★ **The White Horse.** This property typifies the better sort of market-town hotel, which serves as a focal point for the local community as well as providing a good grade of budget accommodation for the traveler. Some rooms in the rambling Victorian hotel building are on the small side; all of them are plainly decorated but well maintained, with a variety of town views. The quieter ones are in the back. The restaurant, a softly lit mahogany-furnished room in the interior of the hotel, is known far and wide for its very generous portions of simply cooked local meat and fish. *Main St., Cootehill, Co. Cavan, tel. 049/52124, fax 049/52407. 30 rooms, 24 with bath. Facilities: restaurant, bar, TV lounge. AE, MC, V. $*

Lodging **Riverside House.** The unpretentious, genuine old-fashioned Irish hospitality at Joe and Una Smith's farm is appreciated by both serious anglers and nonsporting guests. (The lodging is signposted 1 kilometer [½ mile] outside town off the R188 Cavan road.) You'll stay in a substantial Victorian house on 100 acres overlooking the River Annalee, which are worked as a dairy farm (bring your boots if you want to explore). All rooms have peaceful views and are individually decorated with modest antiques and family hand-me-downs. There is a play area for children, who are especially welcome. *Cootehill, Co. Cavan, tel. 049/52150, fax 049/52150. 6 rooms, 4 with bath. Facilities: evening meal by arrangement (BYOB), TV room, fishing, boats for hire. MC, V. $*

Kingscourt

Lodging **Cabra Castle.** This sprawling gray stone castle with its crenellated battlements and Gothic windows could have been designed in Hollywood. In fact, it was built in the 19th century as the centerpiece of a 1,000-acre estate, most of which now belongs to the Dun a Ri National Park. If you want the full treatment, ask for a "castle room," furnished with bigger and more elaborate Victorian antiques than the others. All the rooms are different shapes; some are around the courtyard, but most have pleasant views of the lightly wooded grounds. The Victorian-Gothic theme is carried through the bar and the restaurant with varying degrees of success; if you like that sort of thing, be sure to look at the castle gallery, which has hand-painted ceilings and leaded windows. *Kingscourt, Co. Cavan, tel. 042/67030, fax 042/67039. 29 rooms with bath. Facilities: restaurant, bar, bicycles, 9-hole golf course. AE, DC, MC, V. $$$*

Longford

Dining and Lodging

Longford Arms. Conveniently situated in the town center, this pleasantly refurbished Victorian hotel has spacious public rooms decorated in art nouveau style, with light woods, stained glass, and flounced drapes. Rooms are small, with plain modern furnishings, and most of them overlook an internal roof, but they are quiet and clean. The well-run restaurant serves generous portions of local meat (roasted or grilled) and a choice of fish dishes such as salmon hollandaise. *Main St., Longford, Co. Longford, tel. 043/46296, fax 043/46244. 51 rooms with bath. Facilities: restaurant, bar. AE, DC, MC, V. $*

Mullingar

Dining ★

Crookedwood House. This large old country house, 13 kilometers (8 miles) north of Mullingar on the R394 Castlepollard road, is something of a surprise in the area—well off the beaten track and yet producing the sort of food you would expect to find in a fashionable city restaurant. Orders are taken by the fire in a comfortable sitting room overlooking the lake, and served in the basement in three interconnecting rooms with whitewashed stone walls, an open fire, and a cozy dark-red color scheme. Starters may include a gâteau of homemade black pudding with apple fritter and onion marmalade or a selection of wild mushrooms with smoked bacon and garlic cream; main courses on the changing menu might be an island of seafood with two mousses in champagne sauce, a small and tasty Barbary duckling with crab apple sauce, or such vegetarian daily specials as rosti (potato pancake) with creamed mushrooms. The chef uses predominantly local produce and organically grown vegetables. *Near Mullingar, Co. Westmeath, tel. 044/72165. Reservations advised. AE, DC, MC, V. Open Tues.–Sat. 7–10 (last orders), Sun. 12:30–2. Closed 2 wks in Oct. $$$*

Dining and Lodging ★

Greville Arms. As you check into this old coaching inn, look out for the tall, bespectacled man in the glass case beside the reception desk, but do not be alarmed. He is a life-size wax effigy of James Joyce, who stayed here once in his youth and wrote about the visit in *Stephen Hero*. Deep carpets, dark paneled walls, and soft lighting give the public rooms an impression of luxury, while the spacious bedrooms are simpler in decor but have good modern amenities. The inn's dining room overlooks a pleasant stretch of the Royal Canal, and its walls are covered with photos and drawings of Joyce. The menu, though not exactly adventurous, is better than average, relying heavily on grilled or roast beef, pork, and lamb. Dishes prepared with local fish are also offered. *Pearse St., Mullingar, Co. Westmeath, tel. 044/48563, fax 044/48052. 39 rooms with bath. Facilities: restaurant, coffee shop, 2 bars, nightclub, fishing, bicycles for hire. AE, DC, MC, V. $$*

Terryglass

Dining and Lodging

Gurthalougha House. The house is approached by a mile-long wooded drive after which guests walk across a mossy cobbled courtyard to seek the small wooden door marked "Reception." The ample two-story Victorian house extends around three sides of the courtyard, and not until you enter the front wing do you realize that the waters of Lough Derg are only a stone's throw from the windows. Bessie and Michael Wilkinson encourage their guests to enjoy the outdoor life, including 5 kilometers (3 miles) of walks on the grounds, hunting and trekking nearby, and the use of their own fishing boats moored at their jetty. Guest rooms are various shapes and sizes, with spacious if idiosyncratic bathrooms, and are furnished with a modest selection of Victorian antiques. Michael does all the cooking, using the freshest ingredients in plain country-house style, and offers two choices for each course. The result is a simple, characterful, and cozy place to stay, quite devoid of formality and stuffiness. *Ballinderry, near Terryglass, Nenagh, Co. Tipperary, tel. 067/22080, fax 067/22154. 8 rooms with bath. Facilities: evening meal (book by midday), wine license, fishing, (fishing guide on request), 2 tennis courts, direct-dial phone in rooms. MC, V. $$*

Lodging **Riverrun House.** In the middle of Terryglass, what appears to be a rambling old farmhouse with a slated roof and dormer windows is in fact a newly built bed and breakfast. Typical of the very best of the newer B&Bs around the country, it combines country stylishness with practicality. The rooms are all admirably clean and clutter-free with duvet-covered king-size beds, framed botanical prints, one or two pieces of antique country pine, and throw rugs on stripped pine floors. A sunlit breakfast room has simple oilcloth-covered tables and a towering antique pine dresser. Evening meals are not available, but there is a choice of two pub restaurants in the village. A stream runs through the pretty south-facing garden, and small children are made especially welcome. *Terryglass, Nenagh, Co. Tipperary, tel. 067/22125. 6 rooms with bath. Facilities: tennis court, fishing boat for hire, free use of bicycles, direct-dial phone in rooms. AE, MC, V. $*

Tullamore

Dining and Lodging ★ **Moorhill Country House.** Surrounded by pretty gardens, this modest detached Victorian house (about 1 kilometer/.6 mile outside Tullamore on the N80) features large and comfortable rooms with wool carpets, floral drapes, and some antiques. Five new rooms in a separate wing on the ground floor have separate entrances and windows overlooking the garden. All the accommodations are maintained at a high standard. The expensive, award-winning restaurant in the converted stables is now a bright, whitewashed room looking onto a patio where barbecues are held in good weather. The four-course set menu includes such main courses as chicken in filo pastry, king scallops in saffron sauce, and fresh fish. *Clara Rd., Tullamore, Co. Offaly, tel. 0506/21395, fax 0506/52424. 11 rooms with bath. Facilities: restaurant, bar, tennis court, fishing, bicycles. AE, DC, MC, V. Dinner Wed.–Sat. from 6 PM, Sun. lunch. $$*

Virginia

Dining and Lodging **The Park Hotel, Deer Park Lodge.** This 18th-century hunting lodge on the shores of Lough Ramor is a fine place to take a few days' break from sightseeing. It has good sporting facilities and interesting walks nearby. While the exterior of the house has a certain charm, the decor inside is an uninspired mix of modern and reproduction-Victorian styles. The rooms are all different shapes and sizes; the four at the front have the best views of the lake. The expensive restaurant, in a pleasant Georgian room, serves classic French dishes—salmon, duck, and beef—featuring local produce. *Virginia, Co. Cavan, tel. 049/47235, fax 049/47203. 19 rooms, 16 with bath. Facilities: restaurant, bar, tennis court, 9-hole golf course, fishing, sauna. AE, DC, MC, V. Closed Nov.–Easter. $$*

7 The Southeast

Kilkenny Town, Wexford Town, Waterford City, Tipperary Town

By Alannah Hopkin and Pat Mackey

The Southeast will surprise visitors who expect Irish scenery to be rugged and wild. The coastal counties of Wexford and Waterford are low-lying and relatively flat, with long sandy beaches and low cliffs; inland, Counties Carlow, Kilkenny, and Tipperary consist of lush, undulating pastureland bisected by winding river valleys. This region has the mildest, sunniest, and also the driest weather in Ireland, with as little as 30 inches of rainfall per year—compared to an average of 80 inches on parts of the west coast.

The combination of sunshine and sandy beaches makes the Southeast's coast a popular vacation area with Irish families; but except for the resort of Tramore, it is relatively undeveloped. Its main attractions remain the natural beauty of its landscape and its small and charming fishing villages.

Both coastal and inland areas have a rich and interesting history. There is evidence of settlements from some 9,000 years ago in the Slaney Valley near Wexford. The Kings of Munster had their ceremonial center on the Rock of Cashel, which in the 7th century became an important monastic center and bishopric. There were other thriving early Christian monasteries at Kilkenny, Ardmore, and Lismore.

The quiet life of early Christian Ireland was disrupted from the 9th century onward by a series of Viking invasions. The Vikings liked what they found here—a pleasant climate; rich, easily cultivated land; and a series of safe, sheltered harbors—so they stayed and founded the towns of Wexford and Waterford. (Waterford's name comes from the Norse *Vadrefjord,* Wexford's from *Waesfjord.)* Less than two centuries later, the same cities were conquered by Anglo-Norman barons and turned into walled strongholds. The Anglo-Normans and the Irish chieftains soon started to intermarry, but the process of integration halted with the Statute of Kilkenny in 1366, for the English feared that if such intermingling continued they would lose whatever control over Ireland they had.

The next great crisis was Oliver Cromwell's Irish campaign of 1650, which in attempting to crush Catholic opposition to the English parliament brought widespread slaughter. The ruined or extensively rebuilt condition of most of the region's early churches is a result of Cromwell's desecrations. His outrages are still a vivid part of local folk memory, but not as vivid as the 1798 Rebellion, an ill-timed and unsuccessful bid for a united Ireland inspired by the French Revolution. The decisive "battle" took place at Vinegar Hill near Enniscorthy, where some 20,000 rebels, armed only with pikes, were cut down by British cannon fire. Songs commemorating these events of almost 200 years ago, such as "The Rising of the Moon" and "The Croppy Boy," are still sung in local bars.

Outside the months of July and August, the region is relatively free of traffic, making it ideal for leisurely exploration. Wexford, Waterford, and Kilkenny all have compact town centers best explored on foot, and they also make good touring bases. Wexford's narrow streets are built on one side of a wide estuary, and it has a delightful maritime atmosphere. The new National Heritage Park at nearby Ferrycarrig is well worth a visit, which will contribute enormously to an understanding of Irish history up to the 12th century. Waterford is less immediately attractive than Wexford, but it offers a richer selection of Viking and Norman remains, some good Georgian buildings, and also the famous Waterford Glass Factory, open to visitors. Kilkenny, an important ecclesiastic and political center up to the 17th century, is now a lively market town whose streets still contain many remains from medieval times, most notably the beautiful St. Canice's Cathedral and a magnificent 12th-century castle.

Among the inland riverside towns, Carrick-on-Suir and Clonmel each have a special quiet charm, while the village of Lismore has a hauntingly beautiful castle set in wooded gardens. Anglers will scarcely believe the variety of fishing and scenery along the Rivers Barrow, Nore, Suir, and especially in the Blackwater Valley area. County Tipperary is the location of the Rock of Cashel, ancient seat of the kings of Munster, which can be seen from miles around in all directions; this vast, cathedral-topped rock rising up above the plain is one of Ireland's most impressive sights.

Essential Information

Important Addresses and Numbers

Tourist Information Offices **Carlow** (Hadden Shopping Center, Tullow St., Carlow, tel. 0503/31554), **Cashel** (Town Hall, Cashel, Co. Tipperary, tel. 062/61333), **New Ross** (Harbour Centre, The Quay, New Ross, Co. Wexford, tel. 051/21857), **Tipperary** (3 James St., Tipperary, tel. 062/51457), **Kilkenny** (Rose Inn St., Kilkenny, tel. 056/51500, fax 056/63955), **Rosslare** (Rosslare Ferry Terminal, Kilrane, Rosslare Harbour, Co. Wexford, tel. 053/33622, fax 053/33421), **Tramore** (Railway Sq., Tramore, Co. Waterford, tel. 051/81572), **Waterford** (41 Merchant's Quay, Waterford, tel. 051/75788, fax 051/77388), **Wexford** (Crescent Quay, Co. Wexford, tel. 053/23111, fax 053/41743).

Emergencies **Waterford Regional Hospital** (Ardkeen, Co. Waterford, tel. 051/73321); **Gardai (Police) Emergency** (tel. 999); **Ambulance and Fire** (tel. 999).

Arriving and Departing by Plane

Airports and Airlines **Waterford Regional Airport** (tel. 051/75589) is located on the Waterford–Ballymacaw road in Killowen. **Manx Airlines** (tel. 01/260–1588) schedules flights out of this small regional airport daily to Stanstead, England.

Between the Airport and Center City Waterford City is 9½ kilometers (6 miles) from the airport. A hackney cab from the airport into Waterford will cost approximately £10.

Arriving and Departing by Car and Ferry

By Car Waterford, the regional capital, is easily accessible from all parts of Ireland. From Dublin, take the N7 southwest, change to the N9 in Naas, and continue along this highway through Carlow and Thomastown until it terminates in Waterford. The N25 travels east–west through Waterford, connecting it with Cork in the west and Wexford in the east. And from Limerick and Tipperary, the N24 stretches southeast until it, too, ends in Waterford.

Car Rentals The major car rental companies have offices at Rosslare Ferryport, and in most large towns rental information can be found through the local tourism office. Typical car-rental prices start at about £40 per day with unlimited mileage, and they usually include insurance and all taxes. **Budget** has offices in both Rosslare Harbour (The Ferryport, tel. 053/33318) and Waterford (41 The Quay, tel. 051/21670), as does **Murray's Europcar** (tel. 053/33634 in Rosslare Harbour; Cork Rd., tel. 051/73144, in Waterford).

By Ferry The region's primary ferry terminal is found just south of Wexford at Rosslare. **Stena Sealink** (tel. 053/33115) sails directly between Rosslare Ferryport and Fishguard, Wales. Pembroke, Wales, can be reached on the **B+I Lines** (tel. 053/33311), and there are three sailings weekly to France's Le Havre and Cherbourg on **Irish Ferries** (tel. 053/33158).

Getting Around

By Train Waterford is linked by **Irish Rail** (tel. 01/836–6222 in Dublin; 051/73401 in Waterford) service to Dublin. Trains run from Plunkett Station in Waterford to Dublin four times daily, making stops at Kilkenny, Thomastown, and Carlow. The daily train between Waterford and Limerick makes stops at Tipperary and Clonmel. The train between Rosslare and Waterford runs twice daily.

By Bus **Bus Éireann** (tel. 01/836–6111 in Dublin, 051/73401 in Waterford) makes the Waterford–Dublin journey four times daily for about £6. There are three buses daily between Waterford and Limerick, and three between Waterford and Rosslare. The Cork–Waterford journey is made twice daily. In Waterford the terminal is Plunkett Station.

By Car For the most part, the main roads in the Southeast are of good quality and are free of congestion. Side roads are generally narrow and twisting, and drivers should keep an eye out for farm machinery or animals on country roads.

Guided Tours

Walking tours of historic Wexford, arranged by the **Old Wexford Society,** meet at the Talbot Hotel on Trinity Street and at White's Hotel on George's Street every evening during the summer. (For details contact the tour guide, Mr. Sam Coe, tel. 053/41081.)

Walking tours of Kilkenny are arranged by **Tynan Tours** and operate from Monday through Saturday from the Kilkenny Tourist Information Office (tel. 056/65929 or 056/51500).

Burtchaell Tours lead a Waterford walk at 12 noon and 2 PM daily from March through September. It leaves from the Granville Hotel and costs £3 per person. For details and off-season information, call 051/73711.

Exploring the Southeast

Highlights for First-Time Visitors

Irish National Heritage Park (*see* Tour 1)
Kilkenny Castle (*see* Tour 1)
Lismore Castle Gardens (*see* Tour 3)
Monastic Remains at Ardmore (*see* Tour 3)
Rock of Cashel (*see* Tour 3)
Waterford Glass Factory (*see* Tour 2)

Tour 1: Carlow, Kilkenny and Wexford Towns

Numbers in the margin correspond to points of interest on the Southeast map.

This tour covers a region rich in historical and maritime attractions. From Carlow's small county seat you travel through the rich farmlands of the Barrow valley to the city of Kilkenny, pausing to explore the historic city center on foot. From Thomastown, just outside Kilkenny, another cross-country drive follows the River Nore to New Ross, where it meets the River Barrow, and on to John F. Kennedy's ancestral home and the Arboretum planted in his memory. The tour ends in the old Viking port of Wexford.

1 Begin at **Carlow Town** (83 kilometers/52 miles south of Dublin on the N9), which was established by the Anglo-Normans in the 12th century. Its position on the border of the English Pale—the small area around Dublin that was dominated by the English from Elizabethan times on—made it an important strategic center and hence the scene of many battles and sieges.

Today Carlow is a modern market town on the banks of the River Barrow, with a population of about 11,700 employed in such industries as sugar beet refining, flour milling, and malting. One of its most prominent sights is the Roman Catholic **Cathedral of the Assumption.** Completed in 1883, the Gothic-style cathedral is notable for its stained-glass windows and the magnificent monument on the tomb of its builder, Bishop James Doyle (1786–1834), a champion of Catholic emancipation; the monument was carved by the acclaimed Irish sculptor John Hogan (1800–1858). *Tullow St., tel. 0503/31227. Open daily 10–8.*

The ruins of the 13th-century **Carlow Castle** can be found near the bridge on the grounds of Corcoran's Mineral Water Factory. This castle withstood a siege by Cromwell's troops in 1650, only to be destroyed accidentally in the early 19th century when a Dr. Philip Middleton attempted to renovate the castle for use as a mental asylum. While setting off explosives to reduce the thickness of the walls, he managed to demolish all but the west wall and its two flanking towers.

One last stop is the **County Museum** in the town hall, whose exhibits include a reconstructed blacksmith's forge and a pre-industrial kitchen. *Centaur St., tel. 0503/31759. Admission: £1 adults, 50p children. Open Tues.–Sat., 9:30–5:30, Sun. 2:30–5:30.*

A brief 3¼-kilometer (2-mile) detour on the road to Tullow (R725) east of Carlow Town will bring you to the famous **Browne's Hill Dolmen.** This stone monument dates from 2000 BC and, with a capstone weighing in at 100 tons, is considered the largest in Ireland. Nineteenth-century historians thought that dolmens were Druidic altars, while the peasantry believed them to be giants' graves. They are, in fact, megalithic tombs dating from the Stone Age (c.3000–2000 BC). The dolmen is accessible through a field gate along the road; there is no admission fee.

Double back to Carlow Town and pick up highway N9 south for some
2 10 kilometers (6¼ miles) into **Leighlinbridge,** where the first bridge over the River Barrow was built in 1320. On the east bank lie the ruins of **Black Castle.** Built in 1181, this fortress was one of the earliest Norman defenses in Ireland, and has been the scene of countless battles and sieges over the centuries. Only one ruined 400-year-old tower stands today.

Just 4¾ kilometers (3 miles) west of Leighlinbridge, signposted to
3 the right off the N9, is the tiny village of **Old Leighlin,** site of a monastery founded in the 7th century by St. Laserian. It was rebuilt in the 12th century as **St. Laserian's Cathedral** and enlarged in the 16th

The Southeast

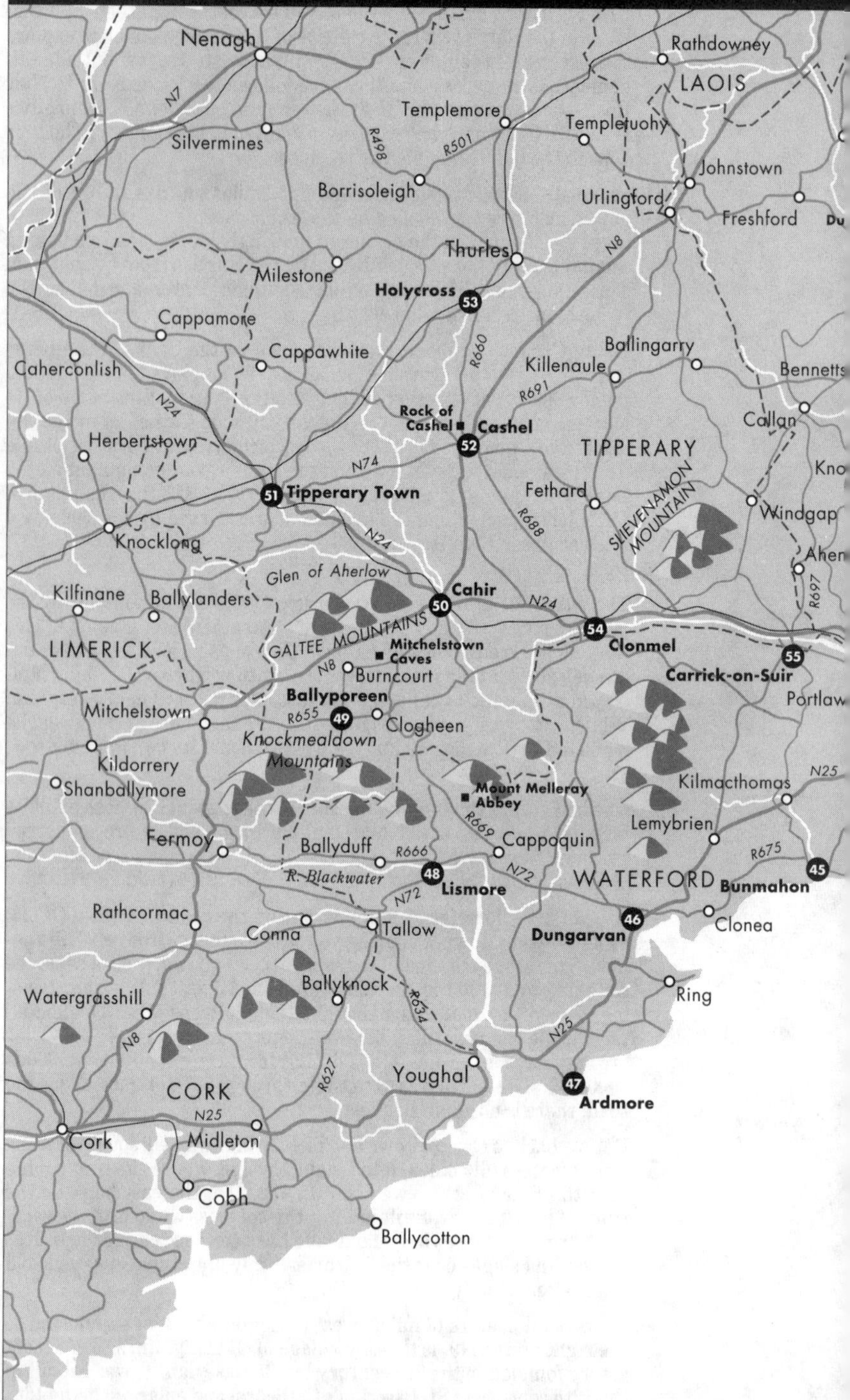

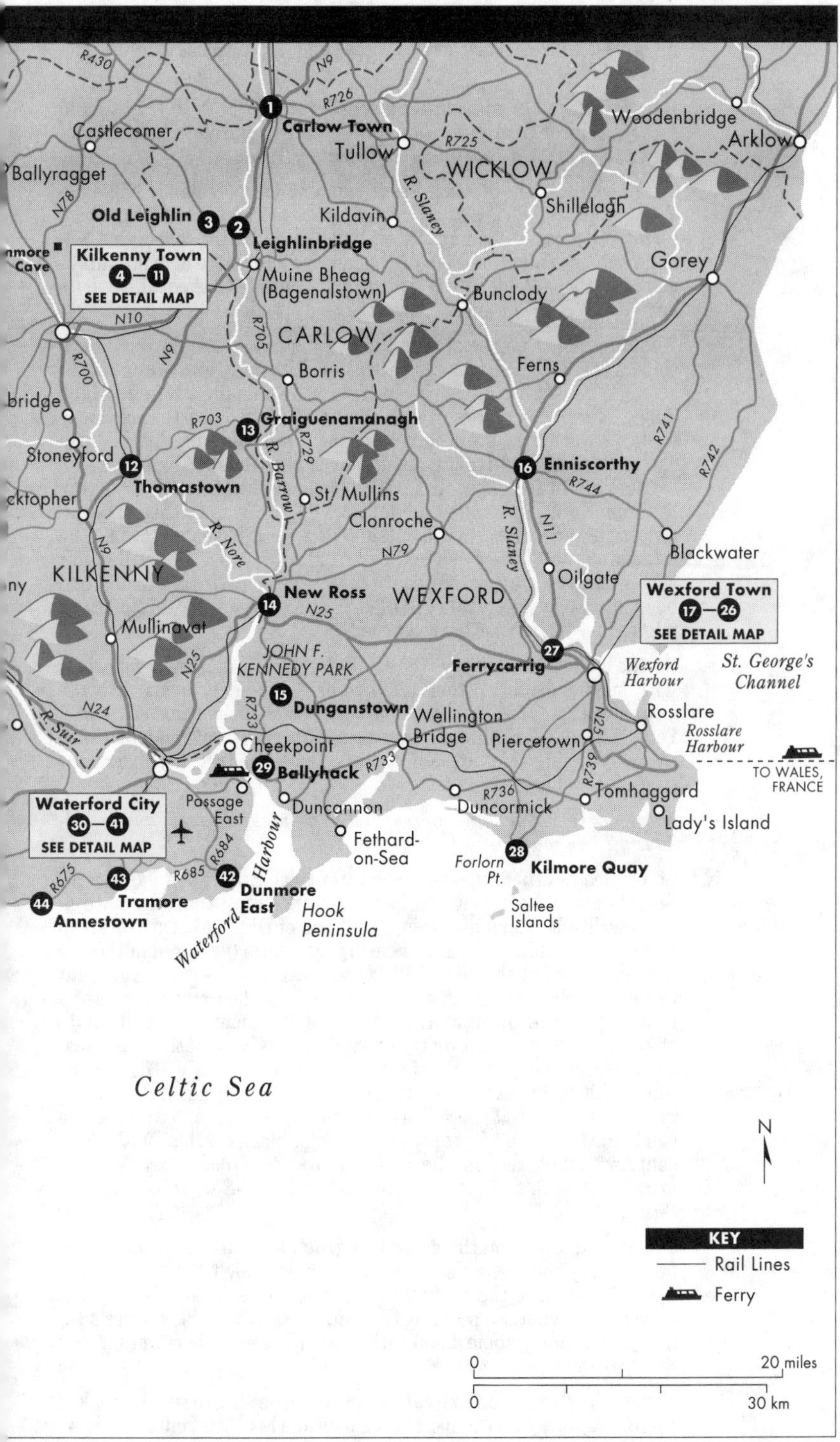
Carlow Town
Tullow
Woodenbridge
Arklow
WICKLOW
Castlecomer
Ballyragget
Old Leighlin
Leighlinbridge
Kildavin
Shillelagh
Kilkenny Town
4—11
SEE DETAIL MAP
Muine Bheag (Bagenalstown)
Bunclody
Gorey
CARLOW
Borris
Ferns
Graiguenamanagh
Stoneyford
Thomastown
Enniscorthy
St. Mullins
Clonroche
Blackwater
KILKENNY
Oilgate
New Ross
WEXFORD
Wexford Town
17—26
SEE DETAIL MAP
Mullinavat
JOHN F. KENNEDY PARK
Ferrycarrig
Wexford Harbour
St. George's Channel
Dunganstown
Wellington Bridge
Rosslare
Rosslare Harbour
Cheekpoint
Piercetown
Ballyhack
TO WALES, FRANCE
Waterford City
30—41
SEE DETAIL MAP
Passage East
Duncannon
Duncormick
Tomhaggard
Lady's Island
Fethard-on-Sea
Forlorn Pt.
Kilmore Quay
Tramore
Annestown
Dunmore East
Waterford Harbour
Hook Peninsula
Saltee Islands
R. Slaney
R. Barrow
R. Nore
R. Suir
Celtic Sea
N
KEY
Rail Lines
Ferry
0
20 miles
0
30 km

century. Worth noticing here are the Gothic doorway, some curiously carved 16th-century grave slabs, and St. Laserian's cross and holy well.

Return to the N9 and continue south, taking the N10 (right-hand fork) in Whitehall after 8 kilometers (5 miles), and continuing for another 16 kilometers (10 miles) to Kilkenny Town.

4 The best example of a medieval community in Ireland, **Kilkenny Town** (pop. 10,000) is attractively situated on the River Nore, which forms the moat of its magnificently restored castle. The name Kilkenny comes from the Irish for "Canice's Church," which nowadays refers to the splendid 13th-century St. Canice's Cathedral, with its ancient stone tower and imposing Gothic interior.

Kilkenny holds a special place in the history of Anglo-Irish relations. The infamous 1366 Statute of Kilkenny was intended to strengthen English authority in Ireland by keeping the heirs of the Anglo-Norman invaders from becoming absorbed into the Irish way of life. Intermarriage became a crime punishable by death. Irish cattle were barred from grazing on English land. Anglo-Norman settlers could forfeit their estates for speaking Gaelic, for giving their children Irish names, or for dressing in Irish clothes. The native Irish were forced to live outside town walls in shantytowns. The intermingling of the Irish and the Anglo-Normans was well under way when the statute went into effect; perhaps if this fusion had been allowed to continue, Anglo-Irish relations in this century might have been more harmonious.

By the early 17th century, the Irish Catholics had grown impatient with such repression; they tried to bring about reforms with the Confederation of Kilkenny, which governed Ireland for six years. Pope Innocent X sent money and arms. Cromwell responded in 1650 by overrunning the town and sacking the cathedral, which he used to stable his horses.

Numbers in the margin correspond to points of interest on the Kilkenny Town map.

5 **St. Canice's Cathedral,** on the corner of Dean Street and Parliament Street, is the best place to begin your walking tour. In spite of Cromwell's defacements, this is still one of the finest cathedrals in Ireland. The bulk of the 13th-century structure (restored in 1866) is in the early English style. Within the massive walls is an exuberant Gothic interior, given a somber grandeur by the extensive use of a locally quarried black marble. Many of the memorials and tombstone effigies represent distinguished descendants of the Normans, some depicted in full suits of armor. Look for a female effigy in the south aisle wearing the old Irish or Kinsale cloak; the 12th-century black marble font at the southwest end of the nave; and St. Ciaran's Chair in the north transept, also made of black marble, with 13th-century sculptures on the arms. *Dean St. Open Easter–Sept., Mon.–Sat. 9–6, Sun. 2–6; Oct.–Easter, Mon.–Sat. 10–1 and 2–4, Sun. 2–4.*

The Round Tower on the cathedral grounds is all that is left of the 6th-century monastic development around which the town developed. If you have the energy to climb the tower's 167 steps, you'll have a good vantage point at the top. Next door is **St. Canice's Library,** containing some 3,000 16th- and 17th-century volumes. *Dean St. Open daily 9–1 and 2–6.*

Across the street from the cathedral, you'll be able to see the back of
6 the **Black Abbey** on the next block south. This 13th-century friary,

named after the black capes of the Dominican friars, has recently been restored as a Dominican church. A museum displaying a number of historical artifacts is next door in the presbytery. From the Black Abbey, turn left and follow narrow Abbey Street—one of the town's more medieval-looking streets—to Parliament Street. Turn right. Two blocks down on your right, across the street from the
7 8 **Courthouse,** is the late-16th-century **Rothe House,** the restored home of a wealthy Tudor merchant and now the headquarters of the Kilkenny Archaeological Society, which mounts a number of special exhibitions here each year. *Parliament St., tel. 056/22893. Admission: £1.50 adults, £1 students and senior citizens, 60p children. Open Apr.–Sept., daily 10–12:30 and 3–5; Oct.–Mar., Sat. and Sun. 3–5 or by appointment.*

Time Out For a meal in an unusual setting, take the left fork off Parliament Street onto St. Kieran Street and try **Kyteler's Inn** (tel. 056/21064); this restaurant is in the cellar of a building notorious as the place where Dame Alice Kyteler, an alleged witch, was accused of poisoning her four husbands. The restaurant retains its 14th-century stonework and exposed beams. Its menu features a respectable French-influenced à la carte dinner and a fixed-price lunch. However, the owners can't resist serving witch's broth—really just a homemade vegetable soup.

Continue along Parliament Street, which is called High Street at this point. You'll notice as you walk through the town the many old-fashioned, brightly painted shop and bar facades, each with an individual color scheme and handcrafted details. The Victorian tradition of painting storefronts has nearly died out in many towns, but since the 1980s Kilkenny has led the field in its revival. You'll find the
9 town hall, or **Tholsel,** which was built in 1761 near the site of the medieval Market Cross, on the left.

Make a left off High Street onto Rose Inn Street to find the **Shee Alms House,** on the left side of the street. It was founded in 1582 by Sir Richard Shee as a hospital for the poor and served in that capaci-
10 ty until 1895. Today it houses the **Tourist Information Office** and CityScope, a sound-and-light show on 17th-century Kilkenny. *Rose Inn St., tel. 056/51500. Open May–Sept., Mon.–Sat. 9–6, Sun. 10–5; Oct.–Apr., Tues.–Sat. 9–5:15. CityScope admission: £1 adults, 50p children.*

High Street splits into Patrick Street and the Parade at Rose Inn
11 Street, and you should veer left onto the Parade to reach **Kilkenny Castle.** Kilkenny was the seat of the dukes of Ormonde, the powerful Butler family, for over 500 years. In 1967 they donated the present building, which dates from 1820, to the state. The gray stone building has two turreted wings and numerous chimneys poking over the battlements. It stands amid rolling lawns beside the River Nore in 49 acres of landscaped parkland. The newly restored west wing opened in 1994 and is included in the guided tour. There is also an impressive portrait gallery, 46 meters (150 feet) long, and a modern-art gallery with frequently changing exhibitions. *The Parade, Kilkenny, tel. 056/21450. Admission: £1 adults, 40p children; grounds free. Open Apr.–May, daily 10:30–5; June–Sept., daily 10–7; Oct.–Mar., Tues.–Sat. 10:30–12:45 and 2–5, Sun. 11–12:45 and 2–5.*

About 11 kilometers (7 miles) north of Kilkenny on the N78 (follow signposts for Castlecomer and Athy) is **Dunmore Cave,** a natural limestone cavern containing weird rock formations. The cave is mentioned in the ancient Book of Leinster as the dwelling place of Lord

Black Abbey, **6**
Courthouse, **7**
Kilkenny Castle, **11**
Rothe House, **8**
St. Canice's Cathedral, **5**
Tholsel (Town Hall), **9**
Tourist Information Office (Shee Alms House), **10**

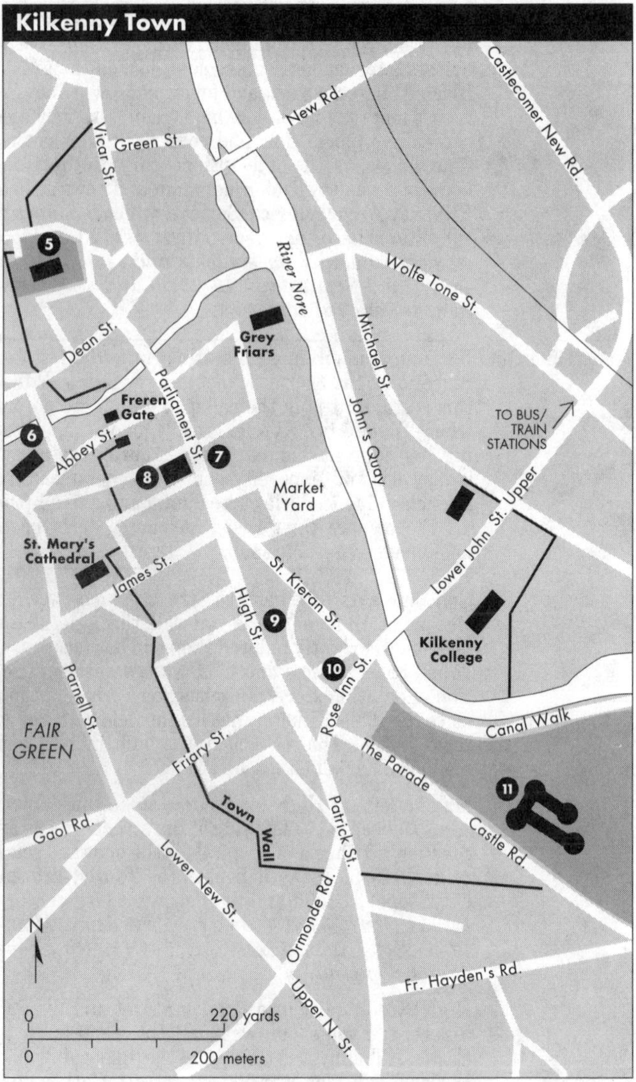

of the Mice, a giant cat killed by a female warrior named Aithbel. In the late 19th century, the bones of some 44 individuals, 25 of them children, were found here; they were probably seeking refuge from a Viking attack. Like many other Irish caves, Dunmore was considered the entrance to hell until well into the 17th century. Nowadays the cave is equipped with pathways, catwalks, and bridges to enable you to explore the eerie beauty of its formations in safety. *Dunmore, tel. 056/67726. Admission: £1 adults, 40p children. Open mid-Mar.–June, Tues.–Sat. 10–5, Sun. 2–5; mid-June–mid-Sept., daily 10–7; Oct.–mid-Mar., weekends 10–5.*

Numbers in the margin correspond to points of interest on the Southeast map.

Return to Kilkenny on the N78 and pick up the R700 for
12 **Thomastown,** a pretty, stone-built village 14½ kilometers (9 miles) to the south on the River Nore.

A short detour 2 kilometers (1 mile) to the south from Thomastown on the N9 will bring you to **Jerpoint Abbey,** a ruined Cistercian monastery dating from about 1180. Guide service is available from mid-June to mid-September, but interesting sculptures and restored Romanesque cloisters decorated with human figures are accessible year-round. *Tel. 056/21755. Admission: £1 adults, 40p children. Open Apr.–mid-June and mid-Sept.–mid-Oct., Tues.–Sun. 10–1 and 2–5; mid-June–mid-Sept., daily 9:30–6:30; otherwise, the key is with on-site caretaker.*

Return to Thomastown and pick up the R703 for 15 kilometers (9
13 miles) to **Graiguenamanagh,** a pretty, unspoiled village on the banks of the River Barrow at the foot of Brandon Hill. **Duiske Abbey,** which contains the largest Cistercian Church in Ireland, has been fully restored and is now used as the Catholic parish church. This is good walking country; ask locally for directions to the summit of Brandon Hill (516 meters/1,694 feet), a 7-kilometer (4.5-mile) hike.

From Graiguenamanagh take the R705 17 kilometers (11 miles) to
14 **New Ross,** a busy inland port on the banks of the River Barrow. Even though it is one of the oldest towns in County Wexford, only the most dedicated history buffs will be tempted to stop and explore the steep narrow streets above its unattractive docks.

Time Out The major attraction in New Ross is a cruise up the River Barrow on the **Galley Cruising Restaurant** (tel. 051/21723, Easter–Oct. only). You can take in the peaceful farmlands along the river bank while sampling lunch, afternoon tea, or dinner. The emphasis is on fresh local produce and seafood.

A short detour of 3 kilometers (2 miles) from New Ross on the Wexford N25 road will lead you to **Ballylane Farm.** These 200 acres offer an opportunity to experience a working farm firsthand and to add greatly to your appreciation of the Irish countryside as a working environment. The 1½-hour guided tour leads you through fields and woodlands where you will meet a wide variety of farm animals and observe the local wildlife. *New Ross, Co. Wexford, tel. 051/21315. Admission £2 adults, £1 children. Open May–Aug., daily 10–6; tours at 11:30, 2 PM, and 3:30. Otherwise, by appointment for groups.*

The **John F. Kennedy Memorial Forest Park** is clearly signposted from New Ross on the R733, which follows the banks of the Barrow southward. The cottage where the president's great-grandfather
15 was born may be found in **Dunganstown.** Kennedy relatives are still living in the house. About 2 kilometers (1 mile) down the road at Slieve Coillte is the entrance to the park, which features over 600 acres of forest, nature trails, and gardens, as well as an ornamental lake. The grounds contain some 4,500 species of trees and shrubs and serve as a training center for botanists and foresters. The top of the park offers fine panoramic views. *Dunganstown, tel. 051/88171. Admission: £1 adults, 70p senior citizens, 40p children. Open daily, May–Aug. 10–8; Sept. and Apr. 10–6; Oct.–Mar. 10–5.*

Return to New Ross and either pick up the N25 to go directly to Wexford (37 kilometers/23 miles) or join the N79 to take in Enniscorthy en route to Wexford (56 kilometers/35 miles).

16 **Enniscorthy,** a thriving market town with a rich history, is built on the steeply sloping banks of the River Slaney. Dominating the town

is its castle, built by a Norman knight in 1199 and once owned by the English poet Edmund Spenser, who gave us *The Faerie Queene*. The site of fierce battles against Oliver Cromwell in the 17th century and during the Uprising of 1798, the square-towered keep of Enniscorthy Castle now houses the **County Wexford Museum.** The museum contains thousands of historical items, including a reconstructed dairy and displays of pottery and military memorabilia; you'll find the curator eager to provide commentary on the exhibits. *Castle Hill, tel. 054/35926. Admission: £1.50 adults, 30p children. Open June–Sept., Mon.–Sat. 10–1 and 2–6, Sun. 2–5:30; Feb.–May and Oct.–Nov., daily 2–5:30; Dec.–Jan., Sun. 2–5.*

On the east side of town is the famous **Vinegar Hill,** where the most important battle in the Uprising of 1798 took place. Here some 20,000 rebels, armed only with pikes, made a last desperate stand against the continuous bombardment of the British Army's cannon fire.

St. Aidan's Cathedral stands on a commanding site overlooking the Slaney. This Gothic-revival building was built in the mid-19th century under the direction of Augustus Welby Pugin, the celebrated architect of London's Parliament building.

From Enniscorthy, take the N11 south for about 24 kilometers (15
17 miles) into the town of **Wexford,** an ancient place defined on maps by the Greek cartographer Ptolemy as long ago as the 2nd century AD. Its Irish name is Loch Garman, but the Vikings called it *Waesfjord*—the harbor of the mud flats—which became Wexford in English.

Numbers in the margin correspond to points of interest on the Wexford Town map.

The River Slaney empties into the sea at Wexford. The harbor has silted up since the days when the Viking longboats docked here; nowadays only a few small trawlers fish out of here. The town is on the south bank of the Slaney, with its main street running parallel to the quays on the riverfront. The opposite, or north, bank of the
18 Slaney, a short walk across the new bridge, forms the **Wexford Wildfowl Reserve.** The mud flats, known locally as slobs, are home to various species of ducks, geese, and swans. Screened blinds and an observation tower are provided for visitors, and a collection of the various species who live on the slobs has been established at the reception center. *Tel. 053/23129. Freely accessible.*

For a quick orientation and an introduction to Wexford's history, you might like to start your tour of Wexford by a visit to the audiovisual display, **The Wexford Experience,** in the town's Westgate Tower (*see below*). The early 13th-century gate tower forms part of the Norman and Viking walls of Wexford and has been sensitively restored. The audio-visual presentation lasts for about 30 minutes and is supplemented by seasonal exhibitions. *Tel. 053/46506. Admission £1 adults, 50p students and children. Open May–Sept., Mon.–Sat. 10–6, Sun. 2–6; Oct.–Apr., Mon.–Sat. 11–5.*

19 If you don't go there, the **Tourist Information Office** on the waterfront at Crescent Quay is a good place to start exploring Wexford's compact town center on foot. Here you can find out about guided walking tours organized by local historians.

20 In the center of Crescent Quay is a large bronze **Statue of Commodore John Barry,** the father of the American navy. Born in 1745 in nearby Ballysampson, he settled in Philadelphia by the age of 15 and became a brilliant naval fighter during the American Revolution.

Church of the Assumption, **22**
Church of the Immaculate Conception, **21**
Franciscan Church, **23**
Selskar Abbey, **26**
Statue of Commodore John Barry, **20**
Tourist Information Office, **19**
Westgate Tower, **25**
Wexford Bull Ring, **24**
Wexford Wildfowl Preserve, **18**

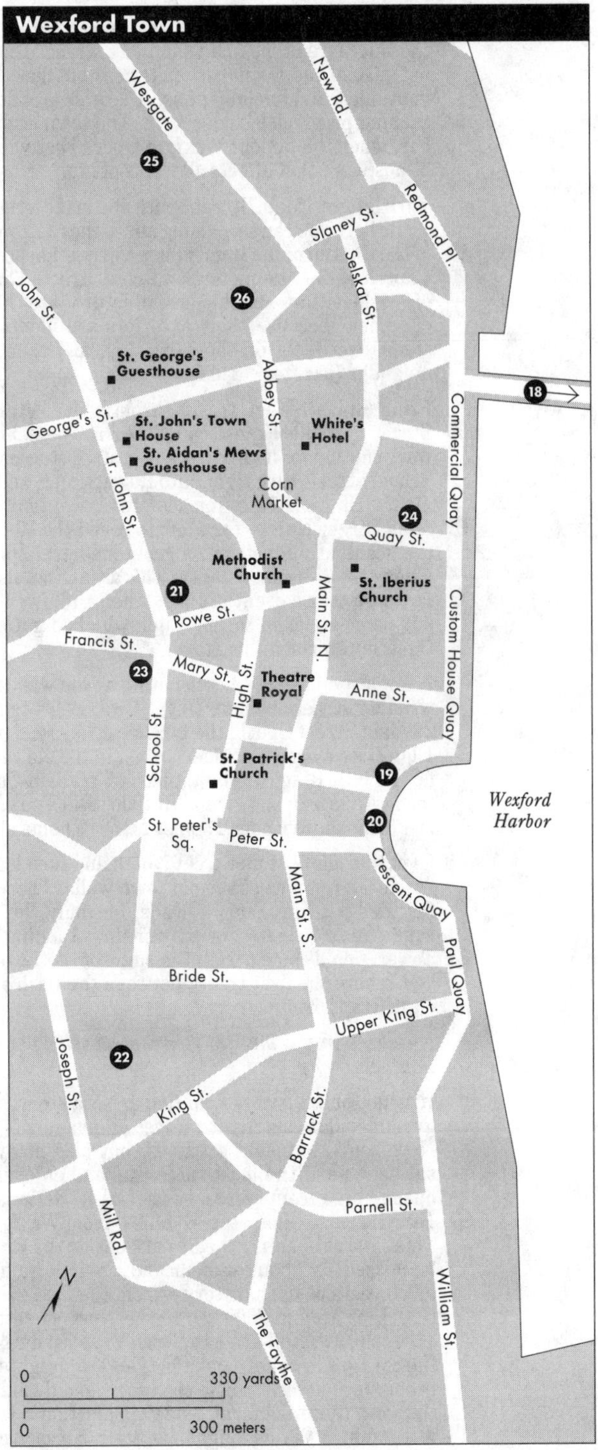

Walk up Peter Street from the quay to Main Street. This narrow thoroughfare is the main shopping street of the town, with a pleasant mix of old-fashioned bakeries, butchers, sweetshops, stylish boutiques, and friendly pubs. A browse around may delight visitors seeking provincial Irish charm. The town is at its best in late October, when the famous Wexford Opera Festival engenders a carnival atmosphere that affects all walks of life.

Turn left into Main Street South and make a right onto Bride Street. From here you can see, rising above the rooftops, the graceful spires
21 of the **Church of the Immaculate Conception** on Rowe Street, and the
22 **Church of the Assumption** on Bride Street. These elegant examples of 19th-century Gothic architecture are known as "the twin churches" because their exteriors are identical, their foundation stones were laid on the same day, and their spires both reach a height of 70 meters (230 feet).

From Bride Street travel through St. Peter's Square to School
23 Street and the **Franciscan Church.** The ceiling of this church is worth noting for its fine, locally crafted stucco work. Continue along School Street, turn right onto Rowe Street, and head downhill, passing the Church of the Immaculate Conception, mentioned above. At
24 Main Street North, turn left to reach the **Wexford Bull Ring,** once the scene of bullbaiting, a cruel medieval sport that was popular among the Norman nobility. This arena was also the site of another, far more tragic event in 1649, when Cromwell's soldiers massacred 300 panic-stricken townspeople who had gathered here to pray as the army stormed their town.

A few last addresses worth noting as you wander the town's narrow, winding streets include Oliver Cromwell's temporary residence at 29 Main Street South; the birthplace of Oscar Wilde's mother, Jane Elgee (who wrote as "Speranza"), in the old rectory on Main Street at the Bull Ring; the birthplace of William Cody, father of the famous American showman "Buffalo" Bill Cody, on King Street; and the 19th-century poet Thomas Moore's home at the Cornmarket.

Continue along Main Street North and turn left at Slaney Street to reach the remains of the old town walls. There were originally five fortified gateways in the walls, but only the largest one, the red
25 sandstone **Westgate Tower,** remains standing. South of Westgate
26 Tower, you'll come across the ruins of the 12th-century **Selskar Abbey,** where the first treaty between the Irish and the Normans was signed in 1169.

Numbers in the margin correspond with points of interest on the Southeast map.

It is not only visitors who find Irish history, with its Celtic background and its successive waves of invaders—Christians, Vikings, Normans—confusing at times, but also many of the Irish themselves. One of the most successful and enjoyable attractions to be opened in recent years is the **Irish National Heritage Park** at
27 **Ferrycarrig,** 5 kilometers (3 miles) from Wexford Town on the N25. This 35-acre open-air theme park beside the River Slaney should not be missed. In about an hour and a half, a guide takes you through 9,000 years of Irish history—from the first evidence of man on this island, at around 7000 BC, to the Norman settlements of the mid-12th century. Full-scale replicas of typical dwelling places illustrate the changes in beliefs and lifestyles. Highlights of the tour include a prehistoric homestead, a *crannóg* (lake dwelling), an early Christian *rath* (fortified farmstead), a Christian monastery, a horizontal water mill, a Viking longhouse, and a Norman castle. There are also

examples of pre-Christian burial sites and a stone circle. Most of the exhibits are "inhabited" by students in appropriate dress who will answer questions. Naturalists will enjoy the unspoiled riverside site, which includes several nature trails. *Ferrycarrig, tel. 053/41733. Admission: £3 adults, £2 children, students, and senior citizens. Open mid-Mar.–Oct., daily 10–7, last admissions at 5.*

Time Out Before heading back into town, stop for a pint and a plate of food at the **Oak Tavern** (Ferrycarrig, tel. 053/24922), a riverside bar about 2 kilometers (1 mile) from the gates of the park on the Enniscorthy road. Log fires blaze in the lounge, while in good weather you can relax on the riverside terrace of this charming Old World inn.

Return to Wexford on the N25, and follow it for 5 kilometers (3 miles) in the Rosslare direction until you reach the signpost for **Johnstown Castle Gardens** and **The Irish Agricultural Museum.** The castle itself, a massive Victorian Gothic building in gray stone, is now an agricultural college, but the attractive and well-maintained grounds, with ornamental lakes and over 200 different trees and shrubs, are open to the public. The main attraction is the museum, housed in the quadrangular stable yards. Extensive displays are devoted to rural transport, farming, and the activities of the farmyard and the farmhouse, with a special exhibit on dairying. The museum also contains an important collection of Irish country furniture. *Johnstown Castle, tel. 053/42888. Admission £1.50 adults, 75p children. Open Mon.–Sat. 9–12:30 and 1:30–5, Sun. 2–5.*

Tour 2: Coastal Drive from Wexford Town to Ardmore via Waterford City

This tour follows mainly minor roads along the prettiest parts of the coast in Counties Wexford and Waterford, pausing midway to explore Waterford City on foot. **Rosslare,** a seaside resort with a long sandy beach, lies 18 kilometers (11 miles) southwest of Wexford off the N25 on the R470. The terminus for car ferries from Fishguard, Pembroke, Le Havre, and Cherbourg is on the N25 8 kilometers (5 miles) south of the village. Instead of taking in Rosslare, this route leaves the N25 at Piercetown, 8 kilometers (5 miles) south of Wexford following the right-hand fork, R739, to **Kilmore Quay.** 28

This seaside village of thatched and whitewashed cottages, noted for its fishing industry, offers a pleasant view from the harbor over a flat coast that stretches for miles eastward. The village is the point of departure for day trips offshore to the **Saltee Islands,** Ireland's largest bird sanctuary. (From mid-May to the end of July, look for boats at the village waterfront to take you to the islands.) In late spring and early summer, several million sea birds nest among the dunes and on the rocky scarp on the south of the islands. Even if you are not an ornithologist, it's worth making the trip at these times to observe the sheer numbers of gulls, kittiwakes, puffins, guillemots, cormorants, and petrels.

On leaving Kilmore Quay, make your way northwest on the R736, then head west through Duncormick and on to Wellington Bridge. Past the bridge, head toward Fethard-on-Sea on the R733, following signs for the **Ring of Hook** drive. This is a strange and atypical part of Ireland, where the land is exceptionally flat and the narrow roads are straight. Except during July and August, when the many sandy beaches attract vacationing families, the roads are virtually empty, and the tiny hamlets appear eerily deserted. But the area has its own special charm, a peace and quiet enhanced by small thatched cottages with tiny but carefully tended gardens.

The Ring of Hook leads to **Duncannon,** a small resort with a good sandy beach and a delightful nautical atmosphere, on the north side of Waterford Harbor. Its history is marked by the visits of two kings; James II beat a hasty retreat out of Ireland through Duncannon port after his defeat at the Battle of the Boyne in 1690, and his successor, William III, also spent some days here before leaving for England.

From Duncannon, follow the signposts to Arthurstown and
29 **Ballyhack.** This attractive village on the upper reaches of Waterford Harbour, with its square castle keep and green hilly background, is much admired by painters and photographers. The castle was once owned by the Knights Templars of St. John of Jerusalem, who held the ferry rights by royal charter; traditionally they were required to keep a boat at Ballyhack to transport injured knights to the King's Leper Hospital at Waterford. Nowadays a small car ferry plies the same route in a five-minute crossing to Passage East.

A short detour 5 kilometers (3 miles) north of Ballyhack on the R733 New Ross road leads to **Dunbrody Abbey.** This ruined Cistercian abbey dates from the late 12th century and flourished until about 1539 when Henry VIII instigated the dissolution of the monasteries. Next to it lies **Dunbrody Castle,** property of the Marquess of Donegall, which now has a small visitor center comprising a tea shop, gift shop, and a small museum. There is an intricate yew-hedge maze containing 1500 yew trees and gravel paths. *Campile, Co. Wexford, tel. 051/88603. Car park £1 car, 50p bike. Admission free. Visitor Center open Apr.–Sept., Mon.–Fri. 10–6, Sat., Sun., and holidays 10–8.*

Time Out Seafood, renowned in this region, is the reason to drop in at Ballyhack's **Neptune Restaurant** (tel. 051/89284), just below the castle. If you aren't looking for a full meal, try a plate of local oysters or a fresh salmon sandwich in the conservatory, which overlooks the harbor.

Cross the estuary by ferry from Ballyhack to Passage East and fol-
30 low the R683 into the center of **Waterford City.** Like Wexford, Waterford was founded by the Vikings in the 9th century, and occupied by the Normans in the late 12th century. The city was overrun by Cromwellian forces in the 17th century and did not prosper again until the late 18th century. During this period, the city's famous glass-manufacturing industry was established. The best Waterford glass was produced from the late 1780s to the early 19th century. This early work, examples of which can be found in museums and public buildings all over the country, is characterized by a unique, slightly opaque cast that is absent from the modern product.

Numbers in the margin correspond to points of interest on the Waterford City map.

Initially, the slightly run-down commercial center doesn't look too promising. You'll need to park your car and proceed on foot to discover the heritage that the city has made admirable efforts over the past decade to preserve. Begin your tour at the corner of Greyfriar's Street and Custom House Parade down at the quays. (The **Tourist Information Office** is also down there at No. 41 Merchants Quay.) The city quays stretch for nearly a mile along the River Suir and were described in the 18th century as the best in Europe. Here you'll

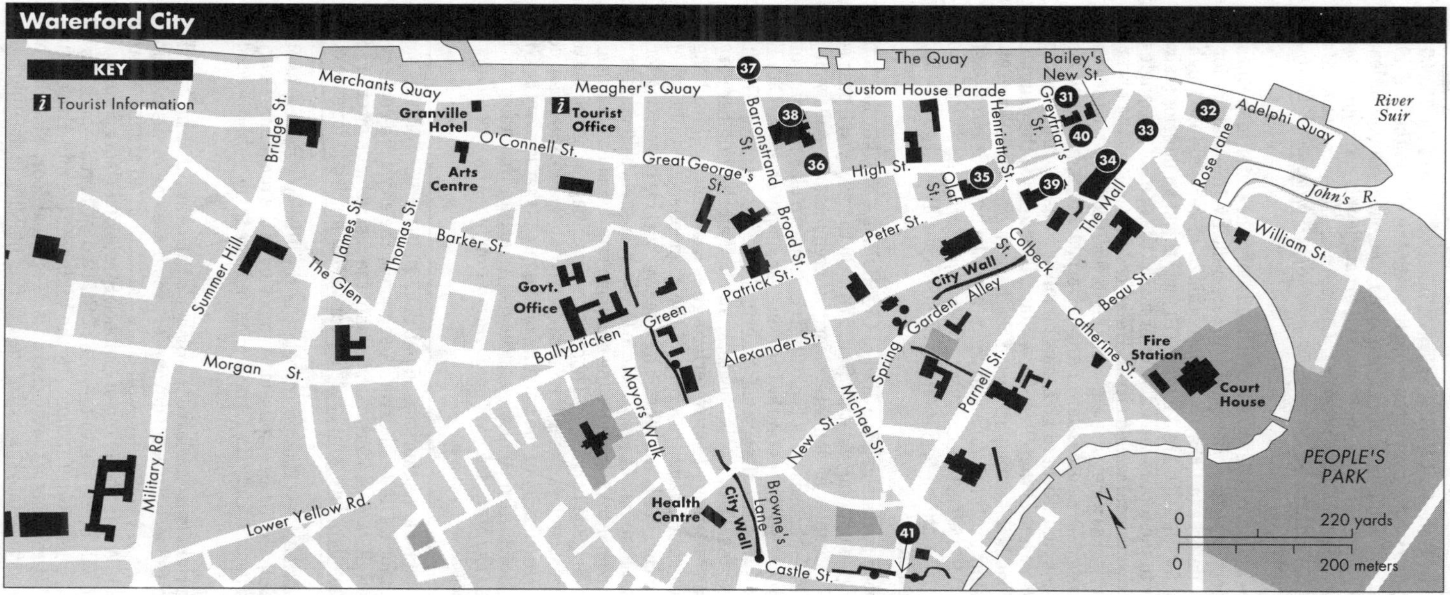

Bishop's Palace, **34**
Blackfriars Abbey, **36**
Christ Church Cathedral, **39**
City Hall, **33**
French Church, **40**
Holy Trinity Cathedral, **38**
Reginald's Tower, **32**
St. Olaf's Church, **35**
Victorian Clock Tower, **37**
Waterford Glass Factory, **41**
Waterford Heritage Centre, **31**

31 find the **Waterford Heritage Centre,** home to some of the 75,000 historical artifacts excavated from beneath the city in the mid-1980s. Parts of Viking houses are displayed alongside samples of leather work, bone carvings, pottery, and ornate jewelry. *Greyfriar's St., tel. 051/71227. Admission: £1. Open Apr., May, and Oct., Mon.–Fri. 10–1 and 2–6, Sat. 10–1; June–Sept., Mon.–Fri. 10–8, Sat. 10–1 and 2–5.*

Make a right on the Parade and head along the water to the massive
32 pepperpot-shaped **Reginald's Tower,** built by the Vikings for the city's defense in 1003. The walls of this 25-meter- (80-foot-) high circular fortification are 3 meters (10 feet) thick; an interior stairway leads to the top. Reginald's Tower marks the apex of a triangle that contains the old walled city of Waterford. Since 1955 the tower has been used as a civic museum, but historically it served in turn as the residence for a succession of Anglo-Norman kings, including Henry II, John, and Richard II; a mint for silver coins; a prison; and an arsenal. It is said that Strongbow's marriage to Eva, the daughter of Dermot MacMurrough, took place here in the late 12th century, thus uniting the Norman invaders with the native Irish. *The Mall, tel. 051/73501. Admission £1. Open Apr., May, and Oct., Mon.–Fri. 10–1 and 2–6, Sat. 10–1; June–Sept., Mon.–Fri. 10–8, Sat. 10–1 and 2–5.*

33 Proceed south along the Mall to **City Hall,** one of Waterford's finer Georgian buildings, dating from 1783. On the way you'll pass some good examples of domestic Georgian architecture—tall, well-proportioned houses with typically Irish semicircular fanlights above the doors. As you enter the imposing yet simply designed City Hall, be sure to notice the arms of Waterford over the entrance. The building contains two lovely theaters, an old Waterford dinner service, and an enormous 1802 Waterford-glass chandelier, which hangs in the Council Chamber; a copy of the chandelier hangs in Independence Hall in Philadelphia. The Theatre Royal is the setting for the annual Festival of Light Music in October. A small collection of military memorabilia includes the uniform, sword, and battle flag of the Irish Brigade carried by Thomas Francis Meagher at the battle of Fredericksburg. Meagher (1823–1867), an Irish-American hero, was born nearby in the building on the quays that is now the **Granville Hotel.** Also on display is the old American Union flag with 34 stars. *The Mall, tel. 051/73501. Admission free. Open weekdays 9–1 and 2–5.*

Time Out The **Reginald** restaurant and pub (The Mall, tel. 051/55087) is worth a look for its unusual decor: A section of the city's 9th-century Viking wall has been incorporated into the restaurant's interior. This is a popular place with locals for bar food at lunch and for snacks.

34 Alongside City Hall on the Mall is the **Bishop's Palace,** another building that is among the most imposing of the remaining Georgian town houses. Only the foyer is open and free to the public (weekdays 9–5).

Turn right once you leave the Bishop's Palace and then make a right on to Colbeck Street. On your left you'll see one of the remaining portions of the old city wall; there are sections all around the town center. A left at the top of Colbeck Street and then an immediate
35 right will bring you to the site of **St. Olaf's Church**—built, as you might guess from the name, by the Vikings in the mid-11th century. All that remains of the old church is its original door, which has been incorporated into the wall of the existing building (a meeting hall).

Continue north up St. Olaf's Street and make a left into High Street. 36 On your right is the ruined tower of **Blackfriars Abbey,** a Dominican abbey founded in 1226 and returned to the crown in 1541 after the dissolution of the monasteries. It was used as a courthouse until Cromwellian forces destroyed it in the 17th century.

From the crossroads ahead looking down Barronstrand Street to- 37 ward the quays, you can see the **Victorian Clock Tower** on Merchant's Quay, built in 1864 with public donations. Although it has no great architectural merit, it serves as a reminder of the days when Waterford was a thriving, bustling port with almost full employment. Now, as elsewhere in Ireland, the unemployment figure for its 38,500 inhabitants is high.

38 **Holy Trinity Cathedral** (Roman Catholic), on Barronstrand Street between High Street and the clock tower, has a simple, classic facade, but its interior is richly (some would say garishly) decorated with high vaulted ceilings and ornate Corinthian pillars. More interesting than its architecture is the fact that it was built in the late 18th century, when the Catholic religion was barely tolerated, on land granted by the Protestant city fathers.

Retrace your steps back along High Street until it joins Henrietta 39 Street. A right turn here brings you to **Christ Church Cathedral** (Church of Ireland). Although its facade is in a more ornate Renaissance style than the classic Catholic cathedral's, both buildings were designed by the same architect, a Waterford man named John Roberts. Christ Church Cathedral occupies the site of an 11th-century church, which was torn down in the 18th century and replaced with the current structure. Take note of the tomb of James Rice, an unusual *memento mori;* a high-relief effigy depicts him wrapped in his shroud in a state of decay, with all manner of frogs and bugs climbing out of his corpse.

Across Cathedral Square you can see the roofless ruins of the 40 **French Church,** a 13th-century Franciscan abbey, also known as Greyfriars, that was given to a group of Huguenot refugees (hence the "French") in 1695. A splendid east window remains amid the ruins. A short walk down Henrietta Street will bring you back to the quays, close to the starting point of the tour.

Time Out The **Olde Stand Victorian Pub and Restaurant** (Michael St., tel. 051/79488) serves lunch and snacks at reasonable prices. Old paintings, city maps, and a handcrafted wooden bar add touches of nostalgia.

If the weather is favorable you might consider a cruise along Waterford's harbor and the wide and picturesque estuary of the River Suir. A luxury river cruiser with refreshments departs from the quay beside Reginald's Tower and tours for 1 hour, 45 minutes. Tickets can be purchased at the Tourism Information Office. *Waterford Viking Cruises, tel. 051/75823. Admission: £5 adults, £2.50 children. Tours June–Aug., daily at noon, 3:30, and 8 PM; May and Sept., 3:30 and 8 PM.*

Last, but certainly not least, is the almost mandatory trip to the 41 **Waterford Glass Factory,** which lies about 2 kilometers (1 mile) from the Tourist Information Office. Take the N25 Waterford–Cork road south from the quay, or ask at the tourist office about the regular bus service.

On guided tours of the glass factory, you observe the specialized crafts of blowing, cutting, and polishing glass. Busy bare-armed workmen in leather aprons carry out their intricate tasks against a noisy background of glowing furnaces and ceaseless bustle. Children under 10 are not allowed on the tour, but they can watch videos of the process from the showroom. An extensive selection of crystal is on view (and for sale) in the showroom. Tours, which take 40 minutes, should be arranged in advance with the factory or through the tourist office. *Cork Rd., Kilbarry, tel. 051/73311. Admission free. Open weekdays 9–5. Tours between 10 and 3 only.*

Numbers in the margin correspond to points of interest on the Southeast map.

Leave Waterford on the R683, picking up the R684 after about 5 kilometers (3 miles). After another 8 kilometers (5 miles) you'll reach
42 **Dunmore East,** a fishing village of thatched cottages at the head of Waterford Harbour and the site of an attractive lighthouse. There are plenty of small beaches and cliff walks nearby, and you get a wonderful view of the estuary from the hill behind the village.

Double back on the R684 and take the R685 to the left, following
43 signposts for **Tramore.** The 5-kilometer- (3-mile-) long beach at Tramore is a popular escape for families from Waterford and other parts of the Southeast, as the many vacation homes and camper parks show. It is Ireland's biggest seaside resort and a dream-come-true for young children, but it is not to everybody's taste. One part of the seafront is taken over by a 50-acre amusement park, a miniature railway, and a boating lake, while the upper half of town is rather more quiet and reserved. Celtworld is a multi-media experience of the myths and legends of Celtic Ireland. Old hippies will find nostalgia in the pre-Raphaelite–style graphics by flower-power artist Jim Fitzpatrick, and children of all ages will enjoy the Marvel comic–style approach to Celtic mythology. Anyone with a serious interest in the subject, or even minimal intellectual pretensions, should probably keep well away. *Tramore, Co. Waterford, tel. 051/86166. Admission: £3.95 adults, £2.95 students and senior citizens, £2.75 children under 16. Apr., Mon.–Fri. 12–5, Sat. and Sun. 10–6; May, daily 10:30–6; June, daily 10–8; July and Aug., daily 10:30 AM–10 PM; Sept., daily 10:30–6; Oct.–Mar., weekends only. Call for hours. Last tickets sold 1 hr before closing time.*

At the western end of the beach the sand gives way to rocky cliffs guarded by the **Metal Man,** a giant cast-iron figure. He stands on top of a great pillar, and it is said that if a young woman hops on one foot around the base of the pillar three times, she will be married within a year. This custom, which is still observed in a lighthearted way, can be traced back to a stone that stood on the spot centuries ago and was used in ancient Celtic fertility rites.

Time Out **The Esquire** (Cross Market St., tel. 051/81324) is a quiet retreat where the internationally trained owner-chef applies his skills to fresh local produce. Originally built in 1937 as a "Gentleman's Bar," the establishment retains an air of gentility. A full à la carte menu with such dishes as smoked salmon, Irish peppered steak with brandy, and vegetarian specials is served in the restaurant, while a simpler—and faster—bar-food menu is also available.

Eleven kilometers (7 miles) west of Tramore on the R675, you join
44 the coast again at **Annestown,** a smaller, quieter resort town with a good sandy beach; 8 kilometers (5 miles) beyond this is the former
45 copper-mining center of **Bunmahon,** now a fishing village popular with holiday makers. This area offers a pleasant coastal drive with good views—unusual rock formations in the cliffs interspersed with sand dunes. Both towns are home to various rare flowers and birds.

You will find attractive and easily accessible beaches at Stradbally and Clonea.

Gradually the lowlands of Wexford and eastern Waterford, with their covering of soft grasses, give way to heath and moorland; the bog is created and maintained by the wetter climate of the hillier western Waterford countryside. You will see the mountains responsible for this change in climate rising up behind **Dungarvan,** a small town on Dungarvan Harbour and the administrative center for the part of the county outside Waterford City. It is a quiet town with good facilities for deep-sea fishing and sailboating, and is a popular base for climbers and hikers.

46

Time Out Dungarvan has several waterside bars with a relaxed, nautical atmosphere. One of the best is **The Moorings** (Davitt's Quay, tel. 058/41461), where you can feast on local seafood. **Merry's** (Lower Main St., tel. 058/41974), once a 17th-century wine merchant's establishment, is a reasonably priced restaurant with plenty of Old World atmosphere and decorated with unusual bygones.

Tour 3: The Blackwater Valley and County Tipperary

This tour takes you inland, through some of Ireland's lushest pasturelands, to some of its most romantic sites. The Blackwater Valley is famed for its beauty, its peacefulness, and its excellent fishing. Some of the finest racehorses in the world are raised in the fields of Tipperary, which is also the county in which you will find the magnificent monastic remains on the Rock of Cashel.

Leave Dungarvan on the N25 and head south, following signposts for Cork. The road climbs steeply past moorland interspersed with woodland. After about 16 kilometers (10 miles), look out for a signpost to Ardmore on the left. **Ardmore** is a delightful little resort at the base of a tall cliff, far more restrained in tone than Tramore. Follow the signs to the top of the cliff to reach Ardmore's monastic remains. The **Ardmore Tower** is 31 meters (97 feet) high, and is in exceptionally good condition. Such structures were built by the early Christian monks as watchtowers and belfries but came to be used as places of refuge for the monks and their valuables during Viking raids. This is the reason the doorway is 15 feet above ground level: Once inside, the monks could pull the ladder into the tower with them. Some 70 round towers remain in Ireland, but none has such a spectacular setting as this one's clifftop location.

47

Nearby is the ruined **Cathedral of St. Declan,** an ancient structure named after the founder of a monastic community; it has some weathered but interesting biblical scenes carved on its west front. The saint is said to be buried in **St. Declan's Oratory,** a small early Christian church that has been partially reconstructed in modern times.

Return to the N25 and turn left to cross over Youghal Bridge. After the bridge turn right onto the R634, and follow this road through Tallow to pick up the N72 into the lovely little town of **Lismore** on the banks of the Blackwater, a river famous for its trout and salmon. You will immediately be struck by a dramatic view of the magnificent **Lismore Castle,** a vast turreted gray stone building atop a wooded rock that overhangs the river. There has been a castle here since the 12th century, but the present structure, built by the sixth duke of Devonshire, dates from the mid-19th century. The castle still re-

48

mains in the same family, and was for many years the Irish home of Fred Astaire's sister, Adele, who married the duke of Devonshire. The upper and lower gardens, open to the public, consist of woodland walks, including an unusual yew walk said to be over 800 years old, and an impressive display of magnolias, camellias, and shrubs. *Tel. 058/54424. Admission: £2 adults, £1 children. Open May–Sept., Sun.–Fri. 1:45–4:45.*

Today, with a population of only 920, Lismore is a sleepy village, popular with anglers and romantics. From the 7th to the 12th century, however, it was an important monastic center, founded by St. Carthac (or Carthage), and one of the most renowned universities of its time. The only reminders of those days are the village's two cathedrals, a Roman Catholic one from the late-19th century, and the Church of Ireland St. Carthage's, which dates from 1633 and incorporates fragments of an earlier church. The latter cathedral also has some interesting tombs and effigies.

Leave Lismore, heading east on the N72 for 6½ kilometers (4 miles), for **Cappoquin,** a well-known coarse-angling center, and pick up the R669 north into the **Knockmealdown Mountains.** Your route is signposted as the **Vee Gap** road, the Vee Gap being its summit, from which you get superb views of the Tipperary plain, the Galtee Mountains in the northwest, and a peak called Slievenamon in the northeast. If the visibility is good, you should be able to see the Rock of Cashel, ancient seat of the kings of Munster, some 32 kilometers (20 miles) away. Just before you enter the Vee Gap, look for a 6-foot-high mound of stones on the left side of the road. It marks the grave of Colonel Grubb, a local landowner who liked the view so much that he arranged to be buried here standing up so that he could look out on the scene for all eternity.

As you travel on the R669, you might like to stop and visit the **Mount Melleray Abbey.** The monastery was founded in 1832 by the Cistercian Order in what was then a barren mountainside wilderness. Over the years the order has succeeded in transforming the site into more than 600 acres of fertile farmland. The monks maintain strict vows of silence, but visitors are permitted into most areas of the abbey. It is also possible to stay in the guest lodge by prior arrangement. *Tel. 058/54404. Admission free. Open daily 9–6.*

Continue north through Clogheen and pick up the R655 west to
49 **Ballyporeen,** a town best known as the ancestral home of Ronald Reagan. **Mitchelstown Caves** are clearly signposted from Ballyporeen to the right by the town church. Follow this road for 5 kilometers (3 miles) to explore one of the finest subterranean limestone formations in Ireland, created by the motion of water against the rock over millions of years. Some of the caves are massive, extending for miles. Although only a part of the system is open to the public, it is still an impressive and uncommercialized sight. *Tel. 052/67246. Admission: £2 adults, 50p children. Open daily 10–6.*

Rejoin the N8 about 1½ kilometers (1 mile) north of the caves and
50 turn right to reach **Cahir** (pronounced "care"). Cahir is a small market town on the River Suir, at the crossroads of the busy N24 and N8 roads. **Cahir Castle,** its main attraction, is a massive limestone structure dating from 1164 and built on rock in the middle of the river. There are regular guided tours and an audiovisual display in the lodge. *Tel. 052/41011. Admission £1 adults, 40p children. Open Apr.–June and late Sept., daily 10–6; June–mid-Sept., daily 9–7:30; Nov.–Mar., daily 10–1 and 2–4; closed Oct.*

Tipperary Town can be reached by following the N24 northwest from Cahir past the **Glen of Aherlow,** a lovely wooded stretch skirting the River Aherlow and its tributaries between the Galtee Mountains and the Slievenamuck Hills.

51 **Tipperary Town,** a dairy-farming center at the head of a fertile plain known as the Golden Vale, is a good starting point for climbing and walking in the hills around the Glen of Aherlow. Racehorses are County Tipperary's most famous export, and it has four racecourses—at Tipperary Town, Clonmel, Thurles, and Limerick Junction. Try to catch a meeting if you can: It makes an enjoyable and inexpensive day out.

52 Take the N74 east from Tipperary Town to **Cashel.** A visit to the **Rock of Cashel** will appeal to almost anyone who cares about the past. The rock itself rises as a giant circular mound 60 meters (200 feet) above the surrounding plain; it is crowned by a tall cluster of gray monastic remains. Cashel means "stone fort" in Gaelic. Legend has it that the devil, flying over Ireland in a hurry, took a bite out of the Slieve Bloom Mountains to clear his path (the gap, known as the Devil's Bit, can be seen to the north of the rock) and spat it out here in the Golden Vale.

The town of Cashel has a lengthy history as a center of royal and religious power. It was the pre-Christian seat of the kings of Munster and was probably at one time a center of Druidic worship. Here, according to legend, St. Patrick baptized King Aengus, who became Ireland's first Christian ruler. It was also at Cashel that St. Patrick is said to have plucked a shamrock to explain the mystery of the Trinity, thus giving a new emblem to Christian Ireland.

The best approach to the Rock is along the **Bishop's Walk,** a 10-minute hike from the Cashel Palace Hotel on Main Street. As you enter the monastic site, you'll see ahead a rough stone with an ancient cross; this is where, according to legend, St. Patrick baptized King Aengus. (Patrick was old then and drove his staff into the earth to support himself. After the ceremony, it was discovered that the staff had passed through the king's foot and the grass was soaked with blood. Aengus thought that this suffering was part of the Christian ceremony.) The stone at this site was also the Coronation Stone of the Munster kings; it dates from as early as the 4th century.

Actually, the stone that you see upon arrival is a replica; the real one is on display in the new museum across from the entrance. Although the museum with its 15-minute audiovisual display is an innovation that some find inappropriate and unnecessary, it does provide enthusiastic young guides, who will ensure that you do not miss the many interesting features of the buildings atop the Rock of Cashel.

The largest building on the summit is the shell of **St. Patrick's Cathedral,** while the best-preserved is **Cormac's Chapel.** The 13th-century cathedral was originally built in a flamboyant variation on Romanesque style, but was destroyed by fire in 1495; the restored building was desecrated during the 16th century. There is a series of sculptures in the north transept representing the Apostles and other saints and the Beasts of the Apocalypse. Look for the octagonal staircase turret that ascends beside the Central Tower to a series of defensive passages built into the thick walls. From the top of the Central Tower, you'll have a wonderful view of the surrounding plains and mountains. Another passage gives access to the Round Tower, a well-preserved building 30 meters (92 feet) high.

The entrance to Cormac's Chapel is behind the south transept of the cathedral. Note the high corbeled roof, modeled on the traditional covering of early saints' cells (as at Glendalough and Dingle); the typically Romanesque twisted columns around the altar; and the unique carvings around the south entrance. The chapel was built in 1127 by Cormac Macarthy, king of Desmond and bishop of Cashel (combination bishop-kings were not unusual in the early Irish church). *Rock of Cashel, tel. 062/61437. Admission: £1.50 adults, 60p children. Open mid-Mar.–June, daily 9:30–5:30; June–Sept., daily 9–7:30; Oct.–mid-Mar., daily 9:30–4:30.*

Take some time to linger at the Rock of Cashel, sitting on the short grass admiring the view of the plains of Tipperary, and absorbing the atmosphere of its pagan and Christian pasts. At the base of the rock is the **Bru Boru Heritage Center,** where Irish music, dancing, and culture are studied. Exhibits on aspects of Irish heritage change seasonally, and you can visit the crafts shop, genealogy center, and restaurant. *Cashel, Co. Tipperary, tel. 062/61122. Admission to Heritage Center: free. Open June–Oct., daily 9:30 AM–11 PM; Nov.–May, daily 9:30–5:30. Admission to evening song and storytelling (*see *The Arts and Nightlife,* below*): £5 adults, £2 children. Tues.–Sun. 9 PM, mid-June–mid-Sept. only.*

When you leave, you might want to look around the town of Cashel, which has a few interesting shops selling modern crafts and some well-preserved examples of the Victorian Irish shop front, with four-part windows divided by timber pilasters. Look for a run of six such windows on Main Street. The **GPA Bolton Library,** on the grounds of the St. John the Baptist Church of Ireland Cathedral, has a fascinating collection of rare books and manuscripts on display. *John St., tel. 062/61944. Admission: £1.50 adults, £1 students and senior citizens, 50p children. Open Mar.–Oct., Mon.–Sat. 9:30–5:30, Sun. 2:30–5:30.*

You can also visit the tiny **Cashel Folk Village,** which features a series of reconstructed 18th-century houses and shops as well as a range of antiques and tools from that period. *Main St., tel. 062/61947. Admission: £1.50 adults, 50p children. Open daily 9:30–8.*

Time Out The **Bishop's Buttery** (tel. 062/61411) in the Cashel Place Hotel on Main Street is an informal restaurant, adorned with elaborate Celtic-style hangings, in the cellar of a former bishop's palace. There are always such traditional Irish dishes on the menu as Irish stew (mutton, onion, carrots, and potatoes) and colcannon (a creamy combination of leeks, potatoes, butter, and nutmeg).

If the Rock of Cashel has left you in a mood for more ecclesiastical remains, make a detour on the R660, traveling 14 kilometers (9
53 miles) to the north of Cashel, to **Holycross,** site of **Holycross Abbey,** a Cistercian abbey church named after a relic of the True Cross. The abbey, which incorporates late-12th- and early 15th-century architecture, has been carefully restored and has some well-preserved stone carvings and window traceries. Part of the buildings are again occupied by priests who conduct pilgrimage services at 3 PM every Sunday from April to August. It is attractively situated on the banks of the River Suir. *Holycross, near Thurles, tel. 0504/43241. Shop and visitor center (admission free) open Easter–Sept., Mon.–Sat. 10:30–5:30, Sun. 2–5:30.*

54 Return to Cashel and pick up the R688 southeast to **Clonmel** (24 kilometers/15 miles), the county seat of Tipperary, set on the loveliest part of the River Suir, with wooded islands and riverside walks.

With a population of about 12,500, it is one of Ireland's largest and most prosperous inland towns. There has been a settlement here since Viking days; in the 14th century the town was walled and fortified as a stronghold of the Butler family. The novelist Laurence Sterne (1713–1768), author of *Tristram Shandy*, was born here, and the English novelist Anthony Trollope (1815–1882) served for a time in the post office. O'Connell Street, the main thoroughfare, runs east–west and close to the river. At one end is the West Gate, built in 1831 on the site of the medieval one. Among other notable buildings are the Court House (designed by Sir Richard Morrison), and the Franciscan Friary and St. Mary's Church of Ireland, both of which incorporate remains of earlier churches and some interesting tombs and monuments.

Clonmel is well-known in sporting circles, being the base of the Tipperary foxhounds and a greyhound-racing center. It is also the headquarters of the Irish Coursing Club. At greyhound races, the dogs chase an electronic "hare" around a fenced-in miniature racecourse; at a coursing meet they chase and kill a real hare in an open field. The latter, although an ancient sport with its own rules, is not for the squeamish, and meets are frequently disrupted by animal lovers. You will often see sleek, slim greyhounds in the area being exercised on leashes along the road. Some of them are worth thousands of pounds.

Time Out **Mulcahy's of Clonmel** (47 Gladstone St., tel. 052/22825) is an award-winning bar-restaurant. A selection of salads, snacks, and hot dishes is served from 10:30 to 7 in the Carvery Food Bar; from 6 PM an extensive à la carte menu is available in the Melleray Restaurant.

55 About 20 kilometers (12 miles) east of Clonmel on the N24 is a smaller riverside town, **Carrick-on-Suir.** This town is something of an oddity, as it lies partly in County Tipperary and partly in County Waterford. The beautifully restored **Ormonde Castle** is the main attraction here. The most interesting part of the castle is a Tudor manor house, one of the best-preserved Tudor buildings in Ireland; it was built in 1584 beside an older castle keep overlooking the river. The town is one of several claiming to be the birthplace of Anne Boleyn, and the house is said to have been built in order to entertain her daughter, Queen Elizabeth I, who never visited here. It contains some good early stucco work and many arms and busts of the English Queen. *Tel. 051/40787. Admission: £1 adults, 40p children. Open mid-June–Sept., daily 9:30–6:30.*

From Clonmel the N24 continues east to Waterford and west to Limerick. The Cork–Dublin road can be picked up by following the N24 west to Cahir for 16 kilometers (10 miles).

Shopping

Enniscorthy In Enniscorthy, stop by **Kiltrea Bridge Pottery** (Kiltrea Bridge, Caime, tel. 054/35107) and **Carley's Bridge Pottery** (Carley's Bridge, tel. 054/35312) for handcrafted pottery work.

Kilkenny Don't miss the **Kilkenny Design Centre** at Kilkenny Castle (tel. 056/22118) in the old stable yard opposite the castle. The establishment sells a range of goods that combine traditional crafts with modern design—ceramics, jewelry, sweaters, handwoven textiles, and so on. Also check out **The Sweater Shop** (High St., tel. 056/63405), and **P.T. Murphy** (85 High St., tel. 056/21127), which specializes in heraldic jewelry. **Richard Duggan and Sons Ltd., The Monster House**

(High St., tel. 056/22016) is a small department store with a good selection of Irish crystal and other souvenirs. **Nicholas Mosse Pottery** (Bennettsbridge, tel. 056/27105) stocks an attractive array of handmade spongeware.

Tipperary The **Tipperary Crystal factory** (Ballynoran, Carrick-on-Suir, tel. 051/41188) is a facility similar to that at Waterford, and purchases made at this showroom can also be shipped overseas with ease.

Waterford Outside of Waterford City, definitely pay a visit to the world-famous **Waterford Glass Factory** (Cork Rd., Kilbarry, tel. 051/73311). The showroom at the factory displays an extensive selection of both Waterford crystal and Wedgwood pottery, and overseas orders are handled promptly (*see* Tour 2, *above*). Numerous shopping arcades in Waterford provide ample opportunity for browsing. You'll notice an emphasis on tweeds, knitwear, and crystal in the arcades at Broad Street Centre and the new George's Court shopping mall, as well as along The Quay and on Barronstrand and Broad streets. Try **Quay Antiques** (128 The Quay, tel. 051/77784), **Kelly's** department store (75 The Quay, tel. 051/73557), and **Joseph Knox** (3 Barronstrand St., tel. 051/75307) for crystal and china.

Wexford County Wexford is a major center for pottery, leatherwork, weaving, silversmithing, and other crafts. In Wexford Town you'll want to visit the **Wool Shop** (39 S. Main St., tel. 053/22247) or **Casket Fabrics** (50 Patrick St., tel. 051/75304) for Aran sweaters, **John Hore's** (31 S. Main St., tel. 053/22200) for handmade Irish linen, and **Lowney Antiques, Ltd.** (61 S. Main St., tel. 053/23140) for your own small slice of Ireland's past.

Sports and the Outdoors

Participant Sports

Bicycling The Southeast is a relatively unchallenging area for cyclists, with the only seriously hilly parts in the Knockmealdown and Comeragh mountains to the south of the region. If you enjoy bird life and sea vistas, try planning a coastal route: Between Arklow and Wexford it is predominantly flat with long expanses of sandy beaches. The Hook Peninsula between Wexford and Waterford offers a network of small, quiet roads, many of them leading to small, quiet fishing villages. Traveling from Waterford to Dungarvan via Dunmore East and Tramore offers a variety of more typical scenery combining cliff-top rides with stretches of long sandy beaches. Be warned, however, that Irish families flock to this coast in July and August, leading to a significant increase in traffic both on and off the main roads. The Irish Tourist Board's Information Sheet No. 41C, "Cycling South East" (available free), outlines a series of cycling itineraries which take in all the main attractions of the area. Bikes can be rented through **Raleigh Cycle Centre** (5 St. John St., Kilkenny, tel. 056/62037), **Tony O'Mahony** (14 Sexton St., Abbeyside, Dungarvan, Co. Waterford, tel. 058/43346), or **The Bike Shop** (9 Selskar St., Wexford, tel. 053/22514).

Fishing Although most of Ireland's angling is concentrated in the northern center of the country around the counties of Leitrim, Cavan, and Monaghan, there is good fishing in the Southeast around Carlow Town and in parts of County Waterford. Carlow Town and Graiguenamanagh, both on the River Barrow, are also the sites of a popular angling festival held every May. Contact the **Southern Regional Fisheries Board** (Anglesea St., Clonmel, Co. Tipperary, tel.

052/23971) for further information. For deep-sea fishing, contact Cormack Walsh at the **Sea Angling Service** (29 Abbots Close, Sea Park, Dungarvan, Co. Waterford, tel. 058/43514).

Golf Some of Ireland's best parkland golf courses can be found in the Southeast. Among them are **Carlow Golf Club** (Deerpark, Co. Carlow, tel. 0503/31695), **Tramore Golf Club** (Tramore, Co. Waterford, tel. 051/86170), **Mount Juliet Golf Club** (Thomastown, Co. Kilkenny, tel 056/24725), **Kilkenny Golf Club** (Glendine, Co. Kilkenny, tel. 056/22125), **Waterford Castle Golf and Country Club** (The Island, Ballinakill, Co. Waterford, tel. 051/71633), **Rosslare Golf Club** (Rosslare Strand, Co. Wexford, tel. 053/32203), **Clonmel Golf Club** (Lyreanearle, Clonmel, Co. Tipperary, tel. 052/21138), **Tipperary Golf and Country Club** (Dundrum, near Cashel, Co. Tipperary, tel. 062/71116), and **Courtown Golf Club** (Kiltennel, Gorey, Co. Wexford, tel. 055/25166). Three new parkland courses opened in 1993: **Faithlegg Golf Club** (Faithlegg House, Checkpoint, Co. Waterford, tel. 051/382241), **St. Helen's Bay Golf Club** (St. Helens, Kilrane, Co. Wexford, tel. 053/33234), and **West Waterford Golf Club** (Coolcormack, Dungarvan, Co. Waterford, tel. 058/43216).

Hiking A number of hiking trails crisscrossing the Irish countryside have been designed and maintained by the National Sports Council, and several of these fine trails are in the Southeast. The relatively demanding trails attract serious walkers, and rain gear, windproof clothing, adequate food, a map, compass, and whistle should be taken along. The scenery on both trails is interestingly varied with wooded hills, rich farmland, and several water features. The **South Leinster Way** begins in the County Carlow town of Kildavin and makes its way southwest over Mt. Leinster and the River Barrow, terminating in Carrick-on-Suir. A second trail, the **Munster Way**, picks up where the first ends and leads through the Vee Gap in the Knockmealdown Mountains and on to Clogheen. Contact the tourist board for further information.

Horseback Riding If you have any equestrian skills at all, you will probably want to ride some of the fine horses bred in this part of Ireland. Inland, the terrain is mainly arable farmland, while the long sandy beaches of the coast are regularly used as gallops. The following places all offer riding by the hour or by the day; expect to pay about £12 for a two-hour trek, and about £32 for a full day, including packed lunch: **Carrigbeg Stables** (Carrigbeg, Bagenalstown, Co. Carlow, tel. 0503/21962), **Kilotteran Equitation Centre** (Kilotteran, near Waterford, tel. 051/84158), **Melody's Riding Stables** (Ballymacarberry, near Clonmel, Co. Tipperary, tel. 052/36147), **Horetown Equestrian Centre** (Horetown House, Foulksmills, Co. Wexford, tel. 051/63786), **Mount Juliet Equestrian Centre** (Thomastown, Co. Kilkenny, tel. 056/24455), **Warrington Riding School** (Warrington, Co. Kilkenny, tel. 056/22682), **Grangemore Riding Center** (Ardfinnan Rd., Cahir, Co. Tipperary, tel. 052/41426), **Boro Hill Equestrian Center** (Cloncroche, Enniscorthy, Co. Wexford, tel. 054/44117), **Laraheen Pony Trekking** (Laraheen House, Gorey, Co. Wexford, tel. 055/28289), and **Sheimalier Riding Stables** (Trinity, Taghmon, Co. Wexford, tel. 053/39251).

Spectator Sports

The people of the Southeast are a sporting lot, and on any given day in this region you're likely to find the stands at the races or the hurling matches full to brimming.

Dog Racing

Greyhound racing is extremely popular here, and Irish dogs are considered to be among the best in the world. Races are held at night, and the main dog tracks in the Southeast are **Clonmel Greyhound Racetrack** (Davis Rd., Clonmel, Co. Tipperary, tel. 052/21118), **Enniscorthy Greyhound Racetrack** (Showgrounds, Enniscorthy, Co. Wexford, tel. 054/33172), **Kilkenny Greyhound Racetrack** (St. James Park, Co. Kilkenny, tel. 056/21214), **Thurles Greyhound Racetrack** (Town Park, Thurles, Co. Tipperary, tel. 0504/21013), and **Waterford Greyhound Racetrack** (Kilcohan Park, Co. Waterford, tel. 051/74531).

Gaelic Football and Hurling

Tickets to Gaelic football and hurling matches are available through the **Gaelic Athletic Association** (GAA, Croke Park, Dublin, tel. 01/363222) or at the entrance to the local stadium. In the Southeast, games are played on Sundays at the following county grounds: **Clonmel GAA Grounds** (Western Rd., Clonmel, Co. Tipperary, tel. 52/21806), **Carlow GAA Grounds** (Dr. Cullen Park, Co. Carlow, tel. 503/32414), **Kilkenny GAA Grounds** (Nowlan Park, Co. Kilkenny, tel. 056/22841), **Waterford GAA Grounds** (Walsh Park, Co. Waterford, tel. 056/77798), and **Wexford GAA Grounds** (Wexford Park, Clonard Rd., Co. Wexford, tel. 053/24620).

Horse Racing

Horse races are held regularly at the following tracks in the Southeast: **Gowran Park** (Co. Kilkenny, tel. 056/26126), **Wexford Racecourse** (Bettyville, Wexford Town, tel. 053/42307), **Tramore Racecourse** (Tramore, Co. Waterford, tel. 051/81574), and **Clonmel Racecourse** (Powerstown Park, Clonmel, Co. Tipperary, tel. 052/22852).

Dining and Lodging

Dining

By Georgina Campbell and Pat Mackey

Category	Cost*
$$$$	over £23
$$$	£18–£23
$$	£15–£18
$	under £15

**per person, excluding drinks and service*

Lodging

Category	Cost*
$$$$	Over £130
$$$	£90–£130
$$	£65–£90
$	under £65

**All prices are for a standard double room.*

Highly recommended restaurants and hotels are indicated by a star ★.

Cahir

Lodging

Kilcoran Lodge. This handsome, 19th-century house sits amid beautiful countryside 6 kilometers (4 miles) outside Cahir beneath the Galtee Mountains on the main Cork–Dublin (N8) road. Rooms facing the front sport the best views of the beautiful heather-covered slopes. Guest rooms are pleasant and have Victorian-style furnishings and comfortable beds. The furnishing in the public areas is discreet and stately, and the entire hotel wears the ambience of a country manor house. *Co. Tipperary, tel. 052/41288, fax 052/41994. 23 rooms with bath. Facilities: restaurant, pool, health club, nearby fishing and horseback riding. AE, DC, MC, V. $$*

Cashel

Dining

★ **Chez Hans.** This small, converted Victorian church at the foot of the Rock of Cashel oozes Old World charm: Dark wood and tapestries provide an elegant background for tables dressed in beige linen. Traditional French cuisine with a hint of nouvelle has been adapted to take advantage of fresh Irish ingredients. Specialties include roast rack of spring lamb with a fresh herb crust and tarragon sauce, and free-range hot chicken, lightly smoked and served with a yogurt, apple, and Clonmel cider sauce. Steaks are always excellent here, as is the fish. Owner-chef Hans Matthia has compiled an unusual list of 11 house wines, including two exclusive whites from his sister's vineyard in Germany. *Rockside, tel. 062/61177. Reservations required. Dress: casual but neat. MC, V. Dinner only; closed Sun., Mon., Dec. 25–26, and the first 3 wks of Jan. $$$$*

The Spearman Restaurant. This small, front-parlor restaurant is hidden away in the center of Cashel, behind the Tourist Information Office. Two young local chefs are gaining a high reputation for imaginative, affordable food based on the best of fresh local produce. Start perhaps with a warm salad sprinkled with bacon and blue cheese or a cream of leek and mushroom soup; follow with stylish entrées such as baked chicken breast with a honey and whole-grain–mustard sauce and poached salmon in a creamy tarragon sauce. Stained-glass windows, hunting prints on the walls, art deco–style side lights, and tall-backed chairs disguise the fact that this was, until recently, a grocery store. *97 Main St., tel. 062/61143. Reservations advised. MC, V. Open daily 12:30–3 and 6–9:30. $$*

Dining and Lodging

★ **Cashel Palace.** Dramatically set at the foot of the Rock of Cashel, this 18th-century bishop's palace is an exquisite accommodation. The redbrick-and-stone manor house is set back from the street in its own garden, so despite its central location it is quite tranquil. The public rooms, paneled in pine and filled with Queen Anne antique furniture, are dominated by twin marble fireplaces and carved wood pillars. Perhaps the most striking feature is the sweeping, intricately carved red-pine staircase leading up to the second floor. The richly decorated guest rooms are equally luxurious, filled with four-poster canopied beds and antiques. Request a room facing the back so that you can enjoy the breathtaking view of the Rock of Cashel rising up behind the hotel. The Four Seasons restaurant in the hotel is an elegant dining room done in rich floral drapery, Waterford glass, and formal table settings. The menu here relies heavily on game in season, local lamb and beef, and fresh fish, while the less formal basement restaurant serves simple, light meals all day. *Main St., Co. Tipperary, tel. 062/61411, fax 062/61521. 17 rooms, 3 suites, all with bath. Facilities: 2 restaurants, bar, gardens, fishing, conference facilities. AE, DC, MC, V. $$$$*

Dundrum House Hotel. This magnificent four-story Georgian house is 12 kilometers (7.5 miles) outside busy Cashel and well worth the trek for the tremendous peace and quiet of the countryside. The River Muteen runs through the grounds right beside the house, which is surrounded by an 18-hole golf course. Fourteen high-ceilinged bedrooms take up the main house, with more in a three-story wing built during the house's previous incarnation as a convent. While smaller than those in the main house, they are still a generous size by most standards. All of the rooms have large pieces of early Victorian furniture, lovely views of the surrounding parkland, and relaxing pink and green decor. The cocktail bar in the old convent chapel has stained glass windows and a rather eerie atmosphere. The spacious dining room and lounge have elaborate plaster ceilings, attractive period furniture, and inviting open fires. *Dundrum, Cashel, Co. Tipperary, tel. 062/71116, fax 062/71366. 55 rooms with bath. Facilities: restaurant (dinner only), tennis court, fishing, golf course. AE, DC, MC, V. $$*

Clonmel

Lodging **Minella Hotel.** This bow-fronted Georgian manor hotel is found in a quiet neighborhood on the banks of the River Suir. The rooms afford fine views of the river, particularly those in the front and on the east wing. Old World charm is communicated through the comfortable Victorian furnishings and walls decorated with hunting prints. The dining room is oak-paneled. *Coleville Rd., Co. Tipperary, tel. 052/22388, fax 052/24381. 43 rooms with shower. Facilities: restaurant, 24-hr room service, bicycles, fishing. AE, DC, MC, V. $$$*

Dungarvan

Lodging **Clonea Strand Hotel.** This unpretentious, family-run hotel is on a scenic stretch of Waterford coastline overlooking Clonea Beach, about 3 kilometers (2 miles) outside Dungarvan. The hotel has direct access to a safe swimming beach. The rooms are comfortable and bright, with plenty of modern, natural-wood furnishings. Amenities include coffee/tea-making facilities and blow-dryers. *Clonea, Co. Waterford, tel. 058/42416, fax 058/42880. 58 rooms with bath. Facilities: restaurant, cable TV, pool, sauna, gym, 2 tennis courts, golf course, shore fishing. MC, V. $$*

Dunmore East

Dining **The Ship Restaurant.** Dinner is always delicious in this bar/restaurant found in a 19th-century house overlooking the bay. The dining room is casual and easygoing, with simple, sturdy furnishings; dark wood walls; and a nautical theme. The food is an imaginative mixture of French and Irish influences, and the emphasis is on fresh local seafood. Start off, perhaps, with deep-fried pastry parcels stuffed with fresh crabmeat, or pan-fried prawns with a lemon, verbena, and thyme mousseline. Entrées include grilled or pan-fried black sole, or kebabs of fresh prawns and scallops pan-fried in a chive and hyssop butter. Desserts, such as a chocolate boat filled with white-chocolate mousse on a raspberry *coulis*, are tempting, and there's a good selection of Irish farmhouse cheeses. *Tel. 051/83141 or 051/83144. Reservations accepted. Dress: casual. MC, V. Lunch served only June–Aug.; closed Sun. and Mon. Oct.–Apr. $$–$$$*

Foulksmills

Dining and Lodging

Horetown House. This is not for those who like bright lights and big cities. It is about 20 minutes' drive from the nearest town, Wexford, and the nightlife consists of a chat with the Young family beside the drawing room fire. It offers an ideal opportunity to sample a slower pace of life. The three-story, rambling Georgian house is furnished in the old-fashioned style with family hand-me-downs, and is fast becoming one of the few places of its kind that has not been done up by interior decorators. If you book in advance you can take afternoon tea in the house and sample the senior Mrs. Young's renowned home baking. Children are made welcome and good-value riding packages are a specialty. The stone-flagged Cellar Restaurant is rather more sophisticated than the house, serving a set five-course dinner with dishes like Wexford mussels in garlic, wild venison in mushroom sauce, and excellent salmon and steaks. *Foulksmills, Co. Wexford, tel. 051/63711, fax 051/63633. 12 rooms, 4 with bath. Facilities: restaurant, horseback riding. MC, V. Restaurant: reservations required; $$. Hotel: $*

Gorey

Dining

Marlfield House Hotel. A conservatory and an abundance of greenery create a light and airy garden atmosphere in this Regency-period house. Tables in this stylish restaurant are impeccably dressed with white linen, gleaming glasses, silver, and fresh flowers. The sophisticated cuisine is classical with modern leanings, and great emphasis is placed on the use of fresh local ingredients. Dishes include *salade tiède* made with a selection of salad greens and lambs' sweetbreads, duck livers, prawns or mussels, and wild local salmon served with a sorrel or watercress sauce. Chocolate is a specialty, and elegant desserts might combine white-chocolate mousse with dark-chocolate sauce. *Courtown Rd., Co. Wexford, tel. 055/21124. Reservations required. Jacket and tie suggested. AE, MC, V. Closed Dec. and Jan. $$$$*

Graiguenamanagh

Dining and Lodging

Corn Mill Lodge. This old, stone corn mill on the edge of the River Barrow has been stylishly converted into guest accommodations and topped off by a restaurant. All rooms have picturesque river views, simple black-wood furniture, sheepskin rugs, pitch pine beams, red window frames, and fully tiled bathrooms with either bath or shower. It is popular with outdoor types who enjoy hiking, mountain biking, canoeing on the river, and nearby riding and golf. The lodge also offers complimentary one-hour river-barge trips to introduce you to the area. Light lunches and snacks are available all day in El Patio Bar. The Loft Restaurant on the fourth floor has a high-pitched roof and black-wood tables on cast-iron bases and offers a five-course set menu or à la carte. Main course choices may include pan-fried lamb cutlets with rosemary butter, grilled sirloin steak, or poached salmon steak hollandaise. *The Quay, Graiguenamanagh, Co. Kilkenny, tel. 0503/24246, fax 0503/24733. 14 rooms, most with bath. Facilities: 2 restaurants, 2 bars, kayaks, canoes, bicycles, fishing. MC, V. $*

Kilkenny Town

Dining and Lodging

Lacken House Guesthouse and Restaurant. This well-known restaurant is in the cellar of a Georgian house on the edge of Kilkenny.

Owner-chef Eugene McSweeney and his wife Breda have maintained the period character of the house, using traditional furnishings throughout. Formally dressed waiters serve international dishes made with fresh local ingredients. Baked crab gâteau is a typical appetizer—crabmeat blended with a sole mousse, then baked in a *dariole* mold, turned out, and served with an herb and cream sauce. Salmon from the nearby River Nore is the star of the menu in dishes such as cutlet of Nore salmon with a galette of potato and celeriac served with sage butter sauce. For dessert try the homemade ice creams. (There are also 8 rooms with bath [$].) *Dublin Rd., tel. 056/61085, fax 056/62435. Reservations advised. Dress: casual but neat. AE, DC, MC, V. No lunch; closed Sun., Mon., and 1 wk at Christmas. $$–$$$*

Lodging **Butler House.** This elegant Georgian house, an integral part of the Kilkenny Castle complex, once belonged to the earls of Ormonde. It is now open to guests under the management of the Kilkenny Civic Trust. The best approach is through the crafts workshops opposite the castle and into its old-style walled back garden. Rooms are all decorated in good, modern taste, with plain oatmeal-colored carpets, off-white woolen spreads, large potted plants, and contemporary prints. Ask for a room with a bow window overlooking the garden and castle; those facing Patrick Street are noisier and generally smaller. *16 Patrick St., Kilkenny, tel. 056/22828, fax 056/65626. 13 rooms with bath. Facilities: evening meal (high season only), bar, TV and direct-dial phones in rooms. AE, DC, MC, V. $$*

The Newpark Hotel. Set back from the road in the rural suburbs of Kilkenny Town, this hotel is a popular base for businesspeople, tour groups, and independent travelers. At its core is a Victorian house, now surrounded by modern extensions. All the guest rooms are modern, bright, and airy, though you'll find that those in the rear have the best views. They are decorated in soft pastel colors and are brightened by floral-patterned drapes. The public spaces in the hotel are done in a country style and are accented with comfortable pine furnishings. *Castlecomer Rd., Co. Kilkenny, tel. 056/22122, fax 056/61111. 60 rooms with bath. Facilities: restaurant, pool, Jacuzzi, steam room, gym, 2 tennis courts, cable TV, 24-hr room service. AE, DC, MC, V. $$*

Leighlinbridge

Dining **The Lord Bagenal Inn.** This famous old pub beside the River Barrow is today a bar/restaurant with open fires and warm lighting. The bar menu is a basic selection of steaks, fresh fish, and some international dishes like chicken Kiev and spare ribs with sweet and sour sauce. The French-style restaurant's menu changes weekly and is considerably more sophisticated. A typical menu might include a homemade soup, avocado pear with prawn dressing, tournedos steak with *chasseur*, or poached or grilled salmon steak served with hollandaise or lime butter sauce. *Main St., Leighlinbridge, Co. Carlow, tel. 0503/21668. Reservations advised weekends. Dress: casual. DC, V. No dinner Sun. or Mon. Closed Dec. 25 and Good Friday. $$*

Nire Valley

Lodging **Hanora's Cottage.** Sixteen kilometers (10 miles) from Clonmel and 29 kilometers (18 miles) from Dungarvan, one of Ireland's premier B&Bs lies hidden away in an unfrequented river valley in Waterford's Comeragh Mountains. The cottage was built by owner Seamus Wall's great-grandparents John and Hanora in the late 19th century, and he and his wife Mary have been accommodating guests here since 1967. The guest rooms are a generous size by cottage standards and prettily decorated with chintz curtains and spreads. All have a TV and a phone, and there is one with a Jacuzzi. Nearby golf, riding, and walking are the main activities here, while the less energetic simply unwind in front of the open fire, which still has the bellows wheel and creel (for hanging pots) from the original cottage kitchen. The evening meal is prepared by their son Eoin, a promising young chef, and packed lunches are provided using Seamus's famous home-baked brown bread. *Nire Valley, via Clonmel, Co. Waterford, tel. 052/36134, fax 052/25145. 8 rooms with bath. Facilities: evening meal, packed lunch, guided walks by arrangement. Nearby horseback riding, fishing, and golf course: inclusive packages organized on request. MC, V. $*

Rosslare

Lodging ★ **Kelly's.** Owned and run by the Kelly family since 1895, this hotel is a traditional weekend retreat. The on-premises recreational facilities are extensive, including tennis and squash courts, pools, saunas, a golf course, and a health club—not to mention the beach and another golf course nearby. Guest rooms are done in comfortable, rustic decor, and those facing the front have lovely sea views. The lobby and public spaces employ cane furniture and pastel shades to set a relaxed atmosphere. *Co. Wexford, tel. 053/32114, fax 053/32222. 97 rooms with bath. Facilities: restaurant, solarium, tennis courts (2 indoor, 2 outdoor), squash, indoor and outdoor heated pools, croquet, jogging track, health club, saunas, cable TV, 24-hr room service. MC, V. Closed early Dec.–Feb. 28. $$*

Rosslare Harbour

Lodging **Great Southern Hotel.** Part of a popular Irish hotel chain, the Rosslare Great Southern is located on a rise overlooking the harbor, just a few minutes' walk from the ferry port. It's a modern two-story hotel—a stark, unimaginative structure on the outside. Its recently renovated interior is more cheerful, with a bright color scheme of blue, green, and white. The comfortable, modern guest rooms are done in a floral decor, and those facing the rear have views of the sea. *Co. Wexford, tel. 053/33233, fax 053/33543. 99 rooms with bath. Facilities: restaurant, bar, 2 tennis courts, nearby golf course, health club, saunas, pool, snooker room, children's playground, live entertainment during summer, cable TV, 24-hr room service. AE, DC, MC, V. Closed late Oct.–early Apr. $$*

Tuskar House Hotel. Found in a quiet area near the ferry port, this small, family-run hotel promises simple pleasures: comfortable rooms and good views of the sea (especially from the rear). The ambience of the public rooms is defined by lots of polished pine, glass, and greenery. In the guest rooms, you'll find functional, modern furniture and a bright, cheery decor. *St. Martin's Rd., Co. Wexford, tel. 053/33363, fax 053/33363. 20 rooms with bath. Facilities: restaurant, bar. AE, DC, MC, V. $*

Thomastown

Dining and Lodging **Mount Juliet.** One of Ireland's newest luxury hotels, this imposing Georgian mansion is within a walled estate of 1,400 acres on the River Nore (17 kilometers/11 miles south of Kilkenny City on the N9). The house has been sumptuously refurbished and incorporates many of the original features, including finely stuccoed ceilings, marble mantelpieces, and carved door trims. Its claim to be "a haven of tranquility" is all too true, but unless you are keen on the outdoor life, its rarified exclusivity and its isolation could quickly become tedious. The two great attractions here are horseback riding on the extensive trails within the estate (which is shared with the Ballyinch Stud) and golfing on the Jack Nicklaus–designed parkland course, which was inaugurated in 1991. The Lady Helen McAlmont Restaurant, a stately room in Wedgwood blue and white, its tables adorned with crystal, silverware, and fine linen, serves haute cuisine with Franco-Irish touches from succulent local produce. Bedrooms are large and individually decorated, with mahogany furniture, super-king-size beds, original fireplaces, and well-appointed bathrooms; all the rooms have peaceful views of the estate. *Co. Kilkenny, tel. 056/24455, fax 056/24522. 53 rooms with bath. Facilities: 2 restaurants, 2 bars, indoor heated pool, sauna, gym, clay pigeon shooting, fishing, hunting, tennis court, croquet, cricket, archery, 18-hole golf course, equestrian center, riding trails. AE, DC, MC, V. $$$$*

Waterford City

Dining ★

Dwyers of Mary Street. This unusual restaurant is in an old Royal Irish Constabulary barracks (the original bars are still on the downstairs windows). The pink, green, and cream color scheme is pretty and fresh, original paintings grace the walls, and the furnishings are a pleasing mixture of styles—antiques are offset by modern touches, such as Bauhaus chairs. The cuisine is French-influenced country house, and the menu changes every two weeks. A typical meal might begin with garlic prawns in a *rosti* nest, followed by boned stuffed quail with apple and sultana (raisin) stuffing and seasonal vegetables. Finish with brown bread ice cream—homemade ices are one of chef and co-owner Martin Dwyer's specialties. *Mary St., tel. 051/77478. Reservations advised. Dress: casual. AE, DC, MC, V. Closed Sun. in winter, holidays, first 2 wks in July and at Christmas. $$*

Dining and Lodging ★

Waterford Castle. If you've always dreamed of staying in a castle during your visit to Ireland, here's your opportunity. This luxury hotel occupies a genuine stone castle built by the Fitzgerald family in the 17th century. It's on a 300-acre island in the River Suir, 3 kilometers (2 miles) outside Waterford City, and can be reached only by car ferry. The main hall and drawing room are impressive, filled with ornate antique furniture and tapestries—be sure to notice the fine oak paneling and the great stone fireplace. The guest rooms are quite luxurious, featuring four-poster beds and a lavish decor. The traditional atmosphere in the Leinster Room restaurant is set by the ornate plastered ceiling, the oak furniture, and the deep burgundy Donegal carpet. The cuisine here is also traditional—country-style dishes include poached salmon, asparagus served in puff pastry, and bread and butter pudding. *The Island, Ballinakill, Co. Waterford, tel. 051/78203, fax 051/79316. 9 rooms with bath. Facilities: restaurant, tennis court, 18-hole golf course, pool, fishing, 24-hr room service. AE, DC, MC, V. $$$$*

Lodging

Jury's Hotel. Found on 35 acres of quiet parkland high above the River Suir, Jury's is a stylish modern hotel. All the rooms face south, toward Waterford City, and have panoramic views of the harbor and the surrounding countryside. The large foyer is impressive, with marble and brass trim, and the lobby seating is quite comfortable. Guest rooms are done in bright, pleasant colors, and the furniture is modern and functional. *Ferrybank, Co. Waterford, tel. 051/32111,* *fax 051/32863. 100 rooms, 4 suites, all with bath. Facilities: restaurant, 2 tennis courts, health club, saunas, Jacuzzis, pool, 24-hr room service. AE, DC, MC, V. $$$*

The Tower Hotel. This hostelry is right on The Mall, a quiet section of the city just 10 minutes from the train station by cab. The public rooms have recently been refurbished; they are filled with plenty of fresh flowers and greenery and accented with warm, polished wood trim. The bright, airy guest rooms are comfortable, with modern, functional furniture and a floral decor. Rooms in the rear have good views of the river. *The Mall, Co. Waterford, tel. 051/75801, fax 051/70129. 141 rooms with bath. Facilities: restaurant, indoor pool, sauna, gym, bicycles, 24-hr room service. AE, DC, MC, V. $$$*

★ **Diamond Hill Country House.** This creeper-covered modern guest house is found just 5 kilometers (3 miles) from Waterford City in a quiet cul-de-sac off the Waterford–Rosslare road. Its owners have won several awards for both the fine Irish breakfasts served here and the lovely gardens that surround the house. The country-house decor in the public spaces is comfortably accented with tweed fabrics, tapestries, and plenty of greenery. Bedrooms are bright and airy and are filled with modern furniture. *Slieverue, Co. Waterford, tel. 051/32855, fax 051/32254. 10 rooms with shower. Facilities: dining room, wine bar, crafts shop, gardens. MC, V. $*

Wexford Town

Dining

The Granary. Good restaurants are not abundant in Wexford, but you will be well looked after here by co-owners Paddy Hatton and his wife, Mary, a Ballymaloe-trained chef. The restaurant is opposite the Westgate in the heart of historic Wexford. It was originally a grain store, and the heavy beams and pillars have been retained, giving it an authentic ambience. The extensive menu offers a good range of local seafood including scallops in their shells with a white wine sauce. In winter, pigeon breast with juniper and cranberry sauce is a popular choice. *Westgate, tel. 053/23935. Reservations advised. Dress: casual but neat. AE, DC, MC, V. Open from 6 PM, closed Sun. and Dec. 25, 26. $$*

Dining and Lodging

★ **Ferrycarrig.** A pleasant alternative to Wexford town center is provided by this modern low rise (3 km/2 mi outside town on the N11 Enniscorthy road) on the banks of the River Slaney. Rooms are identically furnished, with relaxing pastel blue or pink color schemes and light-wood trim; they all overlook the well-kept riverside gardens. The restaurant, in a light and airy conservatory extension, is renowned locally for its fine cuisine and high standard of service. A singer and pianist entertain at dinner, which is worth lingering over. Typical dishes include boned guinea fowl with a fresh cranberry and orange sauce or poached turbot in a tomato and cucumber *vin blanc* sauce, surrounded by fresh mussels. *Ferrycarrig Bridge, Co. Wexford, tel. 053/22999, fax 053/41982. 40 rooms with bath. Facilities: restaurant, bar, fishing. AE, DC, MC, V. $$$*

Lodging

White's Hotel. Housed in a historic 19th-century building fronted by a modern conservatory, this property is a friendly, convivial place conveniently located in the center of town. Its numerous old-fashioned passageways, brass trim, and red velvet decor combine with candlelight and roaring log fires to create a warm ambience. The country-style guest rooms are furnished with Victorian reproductions. Rooms found in the new addition to the hotel are more spacious. *George's St., Co. Wexford, tel. 053/22311, fax 053/45000. 82 rooms with bath. Facilities: restaurant, 24-hr room service, nearby fishing and pony trekking. AE, DC, MC, V. $$*

McMenamin's Town House. Early breakfast by arrangement and an exceptional degree of comfort for its price range make this four-story Victorian villa, a short walk from the railway station in the town center, an ideal stop-over en route to or from the Rosslare ferries. Book months rather than weeks in advance if you want a room here during the Opera Festival (last two weeks in October). The bedrooms are spacious, warm, and immaculately clean, with glorious large pieces of highly polished Victorian furniture, and characterful antique beds, including a mahogany half-tester (with modern orthopedic mattresses). There are about eight choices at breakfast, including fresh fish of the day. Don't leave without tasting the McMenamin's homemade whiskey marmalade. *3 Auburn Terr., tel. 053/46442. 6 rooms with bath. Closed Dec. 18–29. MC, V. $*

The Arts and Nightlife

The Arts

Entertainment in the Southeast is largely confined to the tourist hotels during the summer. These programs of largely Irish entertainment are sponsored by the **Comhaltas Ceoltoiri Eireann (Irish Cultural Association,** 32 Belgrave Sq., Dublin, tel. 01/280–0295) for visitors. Live entertainment is held at their regional center, the **Bru Boru Heritage Center** (Cashel, Co. Tipperary, tel. 062/61122) at the foot of the Rock of Cashel. Folksinging, storytelling, and dance are enjoyed from May through September, Tuesday through Saturday. There is a *ceili* (Irish dance) held nightly during the summer at the Irish-language college, **Colaiste na Rinne,** at Ring in County Waterford (tel. 058/46104). One special performance you won't want to miss is that of the local mummers in County Wexford. Mumming, which combines a style of intricate wooden-sword dancing with spoken verse and incantations, was introduced into County Wexford in the 17th century by shipwrecked sailors from Cornwall, who could trace the dance back to their Moorish origins in North Africa. Contact the Wexford Tourist Information Office (tel. 053/23111) for further information.

Culture buffs won't want to miss the **Garter Lane Arts Centre** (O'Connell St., Waterford, tel. 051/55038), the largest such cultural center in Ireland. Call ahead for a schedule of upcoming concerts, exhibits, and theater productions at the center.

A number of popular cultural festivals are held in the Southeast on an annual basis. The **Waterford International Festival of Light Opera** (tel. 051/74402), the only competitive event of its kind, is a great draw for amateur musical societies from throughout Ireland and Great Britain. The festival runs for 17 nights every September at the Theatre Royal (The Mall, Waterford).

Also worth investigating is the **Wexford Opera Festival** (tel. 053/22141). For more than 30 years this season of professional operatic productions by famous artists from around the world has been held every October at the Theatre Royal in Wexford. Lastly, the **Kilkenny Arts Week** held in late August is a series of classical music performances, concerts, and readings at halls throughout Kilkenny. For more information, contact the Kilkenny Tourist Information Office (*see* Important Addresses and Numbers in Essential Information, *above*).

Nightlife

The neighborhood pub is an integral part of Irish life, and travelers who take time to visit some of them will be granted an unvarnished look at Ireland's people—not to mention one of Ireland's favorite pastimes. Wander in, ask the bartender to draw you a pint of Guinness, and strike up a conversation. The stories and local color you'll glean from a chat with your neighbor at the bar are sure to enrich your impressions of Ireland.

While you're traveling through the Southeast, there are a few establishments in particular that you might seek out for their fine entertainment. In County Wexford's Rosslare, visit the **Portholes Bar** at the Hotel Rosslare (Rosslare Harbour, tel. 053/33110) for lively traditional Irish music most evenings during the summer. **T&H Doolan's Bar** (George's St., tel. 051/72764) in Waterford City is another pub that hosts good traditional Irish music most summer nights and on weekends year-round. Also, the **Seanachie Pub** (Ballymacart, Ring, Co. Waterford, tel. 058/46285) is an award-winning place that features traditional music and dancing in the courtyard on Sundays during the summer.

Winner of the National Bar Catering and Pub of the Year Award on a number of occasions, **Langtons Bar** (69 John St., Kilkenny, tel. 056/65133) boasts old-style decor with an emphasis on sports memorabilia. Bar food, snacks, and full lunch or dinner are available. **The Bohemian Girl** (N. Main St., Wexford, tel. 053/24419) is also recommended for its bar food. In Dunmore East try the waterside **Strand Inn** (tel. 051/83174) which specializes in seafood.

8 The Southwest

Cork City, Killarney, the Ring of Kerry, Dingle

By Alannah Hopkin

A resident of Kinsale, Alannah Hopkin is the author of several books, including The Living Legend of St. Patrick *and* Inside Cork.

Cork, Kerry, Limerick, and Clare—the sound of these Southwest Ireland county names has an undeniably evocative Irish lilt. A varied coastline, spectacular scenery (especially around the famous lakes of Killarney), and a mild climate have long attracted visitors to this region. Although the Southwest contains Ireland's second and third largest cities—Cork and Limerick—its most notable attractions are rural: miles and miles of pretty country lanes meandering through rich but sparsely populated farmland. Even in the two main cities the pace of life is perceptibly slower than in Dublin. To be in a hurry in this region is to verge on demonstrating bad manners. It was probably a Kerryman who first remarked that when God made time, he made plenty of it.

As you look over thick fuchsia hedges at thriving dairy farms or stop off at a wayside restaurant to sample the region's seafood and locally raised meat, it is hard to imagine that some 150 years ago this area was decimated by famine. Thousands perished in the fields and the workhouses, and thousands more took "coffin ships" from Cobh in Cork Harbour to the New World. Between 1846 and 1849 the population of Ireland fell by an estimated 2½ million. Many small villages in the Southwest were wiped out. The region was battered again in the civil war that was fought with intensity in and around "Rebel Cork" between 1919 and 1921. Economic recovery only began in the late '60s, which led to a boom in hotel construction and renovation—not always, alas, in the style most appropriate to the area.

Outside of Killarney and Shannon, tourist development remains fairly low-key. The area is trying to absorb more visitors without losing too much of what attracts them in the first place: uncrowded roads, unpolluted beaches and rivers, easy access to golf and fishing, and unspoiled scenery where wildflowers, untamed animals, and rare birds (which have all but disappeared in more industrialized European countries) still thrive.

South of the city of Cork, the main business and shopping town of the region, the resort town of Kinsale is the gateway to a relatively unspoiled coastline containing Roaring Water Bay, with its many islands, and the magnificent natural harbor, Bantry Bay. The southwest coast of the region is formed by three peninsulas: the Beara, the Iveragh, and the Dingle; the road known as the Ring of Kerry makes a complete circuit of the Iveragh Peninsula. Killarney's sparkling blue lakes and magnificent sandstone mountains, inland from the peninsulas, have a unique and romantic splendor, though the area in July and August is packed with visitors. Around the Shannon estuary a traveler moves into "castle country," littered with ruined castles and abbeys as a result of Elizabeth I's attempt to subdue the old Irish province of Munster in the 16th century. Limerick City, too, bears the scars of history from a different confrontation with the English, the Siege of Limerick, which took place in 1691.

Although the Southwest offers several sumptuous countryhouse hotels, it is basically an easygoing, unpretentious region, where informality and simplicity are the keynotes of hospitality. As in the rest of Ireland, social life centers around the pub, and a visit to your "local" is the best way to find out what's going on. Local residents have not lost their natural curiosity about "strangers," as visitors are called. You will frequently be asked, "Are you enjoying your holiday?" "Yes" is not a good enough answer: What the locals are really after is your life story.

Essential Information

Important Addresses and Numbers

Tourist Information Bord Fáilte provide a free information service; their Tourist Information Offices (TIOs) also sell a selection of tourist literature. For a small fee they will book accommodations anywhere in Ireland. TIOs are located in the following places:

Cork City (Grand Parade, tel. 021/273251, fax 021/273504). **Killarney** (Town Hall, tel. 064/31633, fax 064/34506). **Limerick** (Arthur's Quay, tel. 061/317522, fax 061/315634). **Shannon Airport** (tel. 061/471664). **Skibbereen** (Town Hall, tel. 028/21766, fax 028/21353). **Tralee** (Ashe Memorial Hall, tel. 066/21288). They are open weekdays 9–6, Sat. 9–1.

Bantry (tel. 027/50229). **Clonakilty** (tel. 023/33226). **Dingle** (tel. 066/51188). **Kenmare** (tel. 064/41233). **Kinsale** (tel. 021/772234 or 021/774417 off-season, fax 021/774438). **Youghal** (tel. 024/92390). Their hours are weekdays 9–6, Sat. 9–1, July–Aug. only.

Emergencies **Police, Fire,** and **Ambulance:** all areas, tel. 999.

Doctor/Dentist **Southern Health Board** (tel. 021/545011).

Pharmacies **Cork: Hamilton Long** (66 Patrick St., tel. 021/270548). **Killarney: P. O'Donoghue** (Main St., tel. 064/31813). **Limerick: Roberts James** (105 O'Connell St., tel. 061/44414).

Arriving and Departing by Plane

Airports and Airlines The Southwest has two international airports: Shannon in the West, and Cork on the Southwest coast. **Shannon Airport** (tel. 061/471444), 26 kilometers (16 miles) west of Limerick City, is the point of arrival for all transatlantic flights; it also serves some flights from the United Kingdom and Europe. **Cork Airport** (tel. 021/313131), 5 kilometers (3 miles) south of Cork City on the Kinsale road, is used primarily for flights to and from the United Kingdom. Most U.K. flights to the Continent are routed via Dublin, apart from holiday charters. Regular 30-minute internal flights are scheduled between Shannon and Dublin, Shannon and Cork, and Cork and Dublin. **Kerry County Airport** (tel. 066/64644) at Farranfore, 16 kilometers (10 miles) from Killarney, mainly services small planes, but it is gradually increasing its commercial traffic with a daily flight from London via Dublin.

Flights from North America **Aer Lingus** offers direct flights to Shannon Airport from New York and Boston. **Delta** has direct flights to Shannon from Atlanta. **Aeroflot** flies to Shannon from Washington, DC, Chicago, and Miami. A number of charter flights also operate from the United States and Canada May–September; contact your travel agent and local newspapers for further details.

Flights from the U.K. **Aer Lingus** and **Ryanair** offer direct flights to Shannon and Cork City from most major U.K. airports.

Between Airports and Major Cities **By Bus.** From **Shannon Airport,** Bus Éireann (tel. 061/61311) runs a regular bus service to **Limerick City** between 8 AM and midnight. The ride takes about 40 minutes and costs £3.40.

A bus service runs between **Cork Airport** and the **Cork City Bus Terminal** (Parnell Pl., tel. 021/506066) every 30 minutes, on the hour and the half hour. The ride takes about 10 minutes and costs £1.70.

By Taxi. Taxis can be found outside the main terminal building at the Shannon and Cork airports. The ride from Shannon Airport to Limerick City costs about £16; from Cork Airport to Cork City costs about £4.

Arriving and Departing by Other Transportation

By Ferry/Car From the United Kingdom, the Southwest has two ports of entry: Rosslare (in County Wexford) and Cork City. (*See* Essential Information in Chapter 7, The Southeast for Rosslare ferry details.) From Rosslare Harbour by car, take the N25 to Cork (208 kilometers/129 miles) and allow 3½ hours for the journey. You can pick up the N24 in Waterford for Limerick City (211 kilometers/131 miles), which also takes about 3½ hours.

By Ferry/Bus Train connections between Rosslare Harbour and Cork City, Limerick City, or Tralee all involve changing at Limerick Junction, so the journey time is usually longer than by car or bus. It is quicker and cheaper, if less comfortable, to use the long-distance buses that service the ferries. **International Express Supabus** leaves London's Victoria Coach Station daily and travels overnight via Bristol to Fishguard, then on to Cork, Killarney, and Tralee. Timetables can be obtained from any National Express Coach Station or by calling Supabus (tel. 0582/404511). An Irish company, **Slattery's** (tel. 071/482–1604), also runs a bus service from London to Cork and Tralee. The journey to Cork via Rosslare by bus and ferry is an arduous one of about 18 hours.

Swansea–Cork Ferries (tel. 0792/456116) operates a 10-hour crossing between the two ports on a comfortable, well-equipped boat. Supabus (*see above*) will get you to the Swansea ferry from anywhere in the United Kingdom.

By Car The main driving access route from Dublin is the N7, which goes direct to Limerick City (192 kilometers/120 miles); from Dublin, pick up the N8 in Portlaoise for Cork City (257 kilometers/160 miles). The journey time between Dublin and Limerick runs just under three hours; between Dublin and Cork it takes about 3½ hours.

By Train From Dublin Heuston Station (tel. 01/836–6222), the region is served by three direct rail links to Limerick City, Tralee, and Cork City. Journey time from Dublin to Limerick is 2½ hours; to Cork, 2¾; to Tralee, 3¾. For passenger inquiries: in Limerick, tel. 061/315555; in Cork, tel. 021/506766; in Tralee, tel. 066/23522.

By Bus Bus Éireann operates Expressway services from Dublin to Limerick City, Cork City, and Tralee. Add approximately one hour to the journey time by train. Most towns in the region are served by the provincial Bus Éireann network (tel. 01/836–6111 in Dublin, 061/313333 in Limerick, 021/508188 in Cork, and 066/23566 in Tralee).

Getting Around

By Car A car is the ideal way to explore this region, packed as it is with scenic routes, attractive but remote towns, and a host of out-of-the-way restaurants and hotels that deserve a detour. The roads are generally small, two-lane affairs (one in each direction). You will find a few miles of two-lane highway on the outskirts of Cork City, Limerick

City, and Killarney, but much of your time will be spent on roads so narrow and twisty that it is not advisable to exceed 40 mph.

Getting around the Southwest is every bit as enjoyable as arriving, provided you set out in the right frame of mind—a relaxed one. There is no point in imposing a rigid timetable on your journey when you are visiting one of the last places in Western Europe where you are as likely to be held up by a donkey cart, a herd of cows, or a flock of sheep as by road construction or heavy trucks.

Car Rentals All the major car rental companies have desks at Shannon and Cork airports:

Shannon Airport: Avis (tel. 061/471094), **Euro Dollar** (tel. 061/472633), **Hertz** (tel. 061/471369), **Irish Car Rentals** (tel. 061/472649), and **Murray's Europcar** (tel. 061/471618).

Cork Airport: Avis (tel. 021/273295), **Budget** (tel. 021/314000), **Euro Dollar** (tel. 021/344844), **Hertz** (tel. 021/965849), and **Murray's Europcar** (tel. 021/966736).

In Killarney, try **Killarney Autos Ltd.** (Avis licensee) (tel. 064/31355).

By Train The rail network, which covers only the inner ring of the region, is mainly useful for moving from one touring base to another. Except during the peak season of July and August, only four trains a day run between Cork (or Limerick) and Tralee. More frequent service is offered between Cork City and Limerick City, but the ride involves changing at Limerick Junction—as does the journey from Limerick to Tralee—to wait for a connecting train. Be sure to ascertain the delay involved in the connection. (For passenger inquiries, *see* Arriving and Departing by Train, *above*.) The journey from Cork to Tralee takes 2¼ hours; from Cork to Limerick, about 2–2½ hours; from Limerick to Tralee, 3–3½ hours.

By Bus The provincial bus service, which is cheaper and more flexible than the train, serves all the main centers in the region. Additional services are available during the peak summer season. Express services are available between Cork City and Limerick City (twice a day) and between Cork and Tralee (high season only), and between Killarney, Tralee, Limerick, and Shannon (once a day; twice in peak season).

If you plan to travel extensively by bus, a copy of the Bus Éireann timetable (50p from bus terminals) is essential. As a general rule, the smaller the town, and the more remote, the less frequent its bus service. For example, Kinsale, a well-developed resort 29 kilometers (18 miles) from Cork, is served by at least five buses a day, both arriving and departing; Castlegregory, a small village on the remote Dingle Peninsula, has bus service only on Fridays.

The main bus terminals are at Cork (Parnell Pl., tel. 021/506066); Limerick (tel. 061/313333); and Tralee (Casement Station, tel. 066/23566).

Guided Tours

Orientation Tours **Bus Éireann,** part of the state-run public-transport network, offers a range of day and half-day guided tours from June to September. They can be booked at the bus stations in Cork or Limerick or at any Tourist Information Office (*see* Important Addresses and Numbers, *above*). A full-day tour costs £12; half-day, £7.50, exclusive of meals and refreshments.

Because distances are not great within the region, Blarney Castle, Killarney, Dingle, and Kinsale can all be visited on a full-day or half-day tour from either Cork City or Limerick City. From Cork, **Bus Éireann** offers orientation tours of the city and excursions to Youghal, Mitchelstown Caves, Gougane Barra National Park, and West Cork, as well as the previously mentioned destinations. They also offer open-top bus tours of the city on Tuesdays and Saturdays in July and August for £4 for adults and £2 for children.

Full-day and half-day coach tours of Killarney and the Shannon region (during mid-June–September only) are organized by **Gray Line Shannonway Tours** (c/o Tourist Office, Arthur's Quay, tel. 061/413088). **Shannon Castle Tours** (Limerick, tel. 061/61788) will escort you to an "Irish Night" in Bunratty Folk Park or take you to a medieval banquet at Bunratty or Knappogue Castle; although the banquet isn't authentic, it is a boisterous occasion that is full of goodwill.

Foremost among the Killarney tour operators is **Destination Killarney** (Scott's Gardens, Killarney, Co. Kerry, tel. and fax 064/32638). Besides offering day and half-day tours of Killarney and Kerry by coach or taxi, the group will prearrange your visit, lining up accommodations, entertainment, special-interest tours, and sporting activities in one package.

A full-day (10:30–5) tour costs from £10 to £13 per person, excluding lunch and refreshments. The Killarney Local Circuit tour is an excellent half-day orientation. The unique and memorable Gap of Dunloe tour at £13 includes a coach and boat trip. Add £10 for a horseback ride through the gap. More conventional day trips can also be made to the Ring of Kerry, the Loo Valley, and Glengarriff; the city of Cork and Blarney Castle; Dingle and Slea Head; and Caragh Lake and Rossbeigh.

The following companies will also organize day and half-day trips by coach or taxi: **Deros Tours** (Main St., tel. 064/31251), **Killarney & Kerry Tours** (Innisfallon, 15 Main St., tel. 064/33880), and **Castlelough Tours** (High St., tel. 064/32496).

Jaunting cars (pony and trap) that carry up to four people can be hired at a stand outside Tourist Information Offices. They can also be found at the entrance to Muckross Estate and at the Gap of Dunloe. A ride costs between £10 and £24, negotiable with the driver, depending on time (one–two hours) and route.

Special-Interest Tours

Special-interest tours of the region for small or large groups can be prearranged with Valerie Fleury of **Discover Cork** (Belmont, Douglas Rd., Cork, tel. 021/293873, fax 021/361358). Half-day and full-day tours are individually planned to satisfy each visitor's needs.

Walking Tours

Limerick City Tours (41 Meadow Vale, Raheen, Co. Limerick, tel. 061/301587) offers inexpensive walking tours of Limerick from June to September (and by arrangement other months). **Kerry Country Rambles** (53 High St., Killarney, Co. Kerry, tel. 064/35277) organizes theme walks, archaeology tours, and walking holidays.

Tourist Trails, which allow the visitor to follow a signposted route while reading an accompanying booklet (75p), have been set up in Cork City, Limerick City, Youghal, Kinsale, and Killarney Town. Booklets can be purchased at local Tourist Information Offices. History buffs should inquire at TIOs for details of guided walking tours, which are organized during the summer by local volunteers.

Exploring the Southwest

If you have only three or four days in the Southwest, you might consider skipping the cities and concentrating on the coast and the mountains. For a short visit, it makes sense to base yourself in Killarney. Reserve one day for an old-style trip through the Gap of Dunloe and the lakes by jaunting car and rowboat. If you have a car, several other attractions can be explored in a day.

If, on the other hand, your schedule allows a week or 10 days in the region, you might want to spend a night or two in the Cork City vicinity (taking in Blarney Castle and Cobh), a night in Kinsale, a night in a country-house hotel (such as the Park at Kenmare or Longueville House at Mallow), and two or three nights in Killarney. Then head west to the Ring of Kerry and the Dingle Peninsula if the weather is good, or north toward Limerick and the Shannon castles if it is not. But don't let passing showers deter you too much. In Killarney, especially, light showers are part of the experience and seldom last long; they can be followed within minutes by brilliant sunshine.

Highlights for First-Time Visitors

Blarney Castle (*see* Tour 1)
Bunratty Castle and Folk Park (*see* Tour 4)
Connor Pass (*see* Tour 3)
Cobh and the Queenstown Project (*see* Tour 1)
Gap of Dunloe (*see* Tour 3)
Garnish Island (*see* Tour 2)
Great Blasket Island (*see* Tour 3)
Kinsale (*see* Tour 2)
Skellig Islands (*see* Tour 3)
Slea Head (*see* Tour 3)

Tour 1: Cork City and Environs

Numbers in the margin correspond to points of interest on the Southwest and Cork City maps.

1 **Cork,** the major metropolis of the south, is Ireland's second-largest city. Its official population of 133,250 is misleadingly low because it doesn't include the many Corkonians who prefer to live outside the city limits, in pleasant rural areas 10 or 15 minutes' drive from town. In 1185, the city received its first charter from Prince John of Norman England. Major development occurred during the 17th and 18th centuries with the expansion of the butter trade, and many attractive Georgian-style buildings with wide bow-fronted windows were constructed during this time. Cork gets its name from the Irish (Gaelic) word *corcaigh,* which means "marshy place." When the marsh was drained, the River Lee was divided into two streams that now flow through the city, leaving the main business and commercial center on an island. As a result, the city features a number of bridges and quays, which, although initially confusing, add greatly to the port's unique character.

"Rebel Cork" emerged as a center of the nationalist Fenian movement in the 19th century. The city suffered great damage during the civil war in the early '20s, when much of its center burned. Dogged by economic slumps throughout this century, Cork is only now regaining some of its former glory through sensitive commercial development and an ongoing program of inner-city renewal. It is still something of a ghost town after 6 PM, when the business community has gone home.

Cork's main attractions are best visited on foot. Patrick Street is the
2 main thoroughfare; it's helpful to start at **Patrick's Bridge.** Look across the river to St. Patrick's Hill, where tall Georgian houses have mostly been converted to consulting rooms for doctors. The hill is so steep that steps are cut into the pavement. The slopes of the
3 hilly north city are dominated by the tower of **St. Mary's Pro-Cathedral** and the Shandon Steeple with its four-sided clock. If you're interested in tracing Cork ancestors, the presbytery at St. Mary's has records of births and marriages dating from 1784. *Cathedral Walk. Admission free. Open daily 9–6.*

The Bells of Shandon were immortalized in an atrocious but popular 19th-century ballad of that name. The pepper-pot **Shandon Steeple**
4 belongs to **St. Anne's Church** on Church Street, a three-minute walk downhill (toward the city center) from the Pro-Cathedral. Visitors who are prepared to climb the 120-foot tower can have the bells rung out over Cork at their request. *Admission: £1, £1.50 with bell tower. Open May–Oct., Mon.–Sat. 9:30–5; Nov.–Apr., 10–3:30.*

From Patrick's Bridge, you can't quite see the **bus station;** still facing the river, it is one block downstream on the right. The Brian Boru Bridge, in front of the bus station, leads to **Kent (Rail) Station,** which is north of the river two blocks to the right.

5 Turn your back on the river and head up **Patrick Street.** On the left is **Merchant's Quay,** where tall ships that once served the butter trade used to load up before heading downstream to the open sea. The design of the large, £30 million shopping center on the site (built in 1989) evokes the warehouses of old. **Roches Stores,** on the left, is the largest department store in town; **Cash's,** next door, is the most upscale.

Turn left into Winthrop Street, a pedestrian mall, which leads to the
6 **General Post Office,** a neoclassical building with an elegant colonnaded facade, built on the site of the Theater Royal. The post office is on Oliver Plunkett Street, a busy narrow road known for its fashion boutiques and jewelry stores.

Time Out Resist the temptation to nip in to McDonald's on Winthrop Street; try the **Long Valley** instead. This friendly old bar, popular with artists, writers, students, and other eccentrics, serves tea, coffee, and pints, as well as enormous sandwiches filled with salad and home-cooked meat.

Continue around the graceful curve of Patrick Street—and don't forget to look up. Above some of the standardized plate-glass and plastic shop facades are examples of the bow-fronted Georgian windows that are so typical of old Cork. Cross the street in front of
7 **Penney's** and take Academy Street, which leads to the **Crawford Art Gallery.** Here you'll find an excellent collection of landscape paintings depicting Cork in the 18th and 19th centuries. Look out for the work of Nathaniel Grogan (1740–1807). The gallery also mounts adventurous exhibitions by contemporary artists from Ireland and abroad; its cafeteria is one of the best places in town for a light lunch or a tasty home-baked cake. *Emmet Pl., tel. 021/273377. Admission free. Open weekdays 9–5, Sat. 9–1.*

8 The **Opera House,** an unfortunate concrete building dating from the '60s, is on the left of the Crawford, but turn right out of the front
9 door instead, crossing into the pedestrianized **Paul Street** area

The Southwest

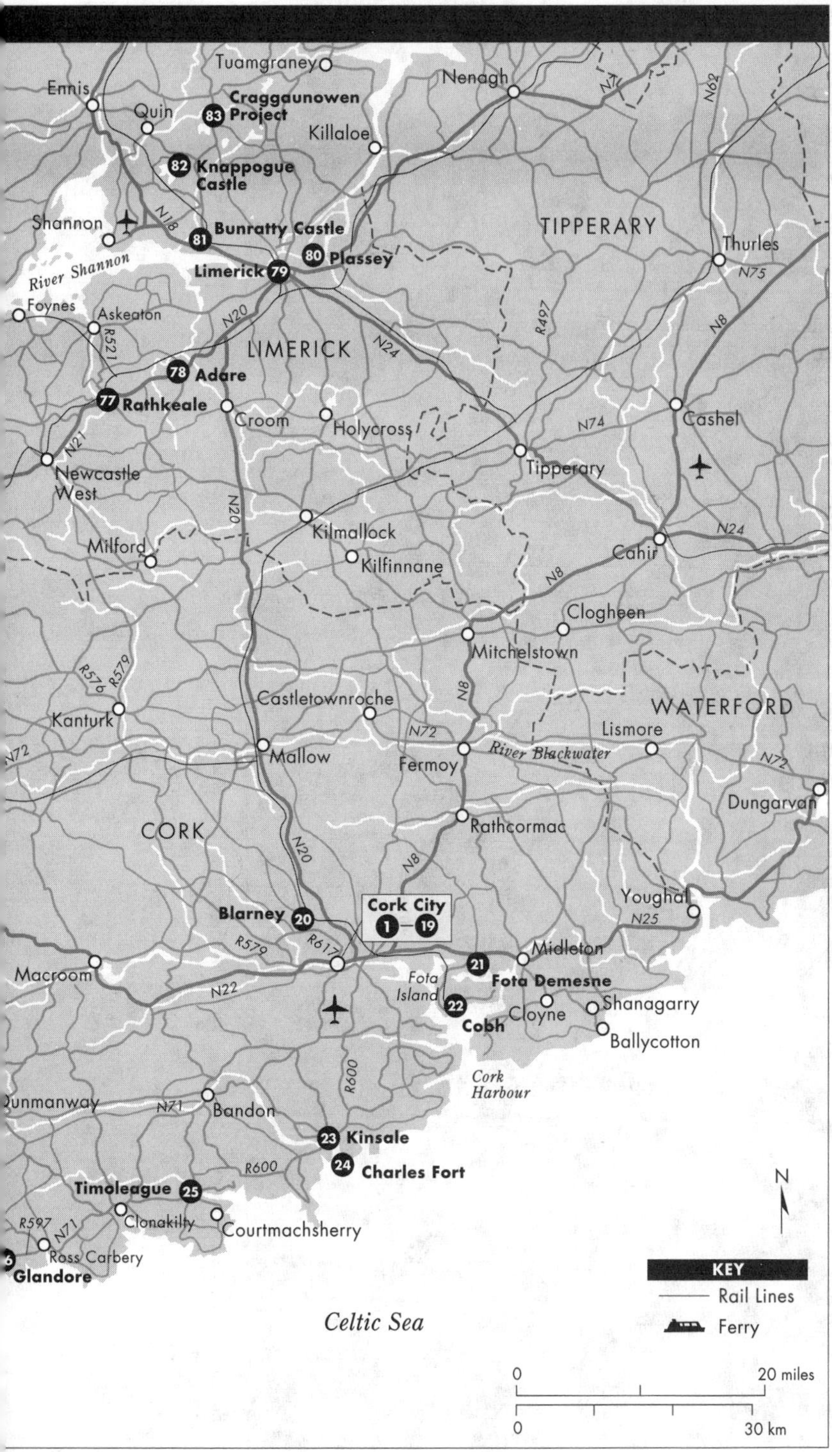
Tuamgraney
Nenagh
Ennis
Quin
83 Craggaunowen Project
Killaloe
82 Knappogue Castle
Shannon
N18
81 Bunratty Castle
80 Plassey
Limerick 79
TIPPERARY
Thurles
N75
River Shannon
Foynes
Askeaton
R521
N20
N24
R497
N8
LIMERICK
78 Adare
77 Rathkeale
Croom
Holycross
N74
Cashel
N21
Newcastle West
Tipperary
N20
Kilmallock
N24
Milford
Kilfinnane
Cahir
N8
Clogheen
Mitchelstown
R576
R579
N8
Castletownroche
WATERFORD
Kanturk
N72
Lismore
N72
Mallow
Fermoy
River Blackwater
N72
Dungarvan
CORK
Rathcormac
N20
N8
Youghal
Cork City
1—19
Blarney 20
N25
R579
R617
Midleton
Macroom
21
Fota Demesne
N22
Fota Island
22
Cloyne
Shanagarry
Cobh
Ballycotton
Cork Harbour
R600
Dunmanway
N71
Bandon
23 Kinsale
24 Charles Fort
R600
Timoleague 25
R597
N71
Clonakilty
Courtmachsherry
Ross Carbery
Glandore
N
KEY
Rail Lines
Ferry
Celtic Sea
0
20 miles
0
30 km

Cork City

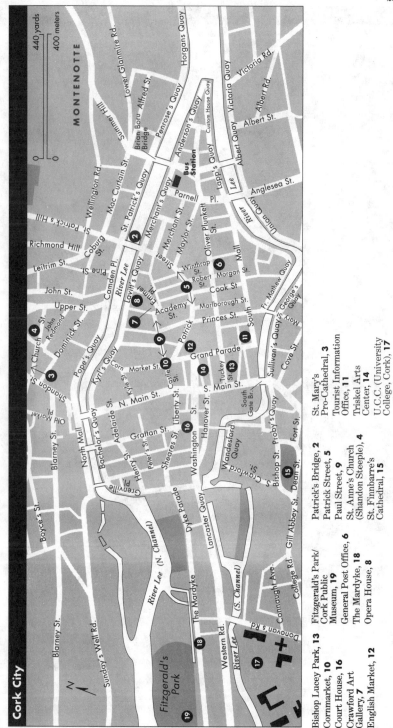

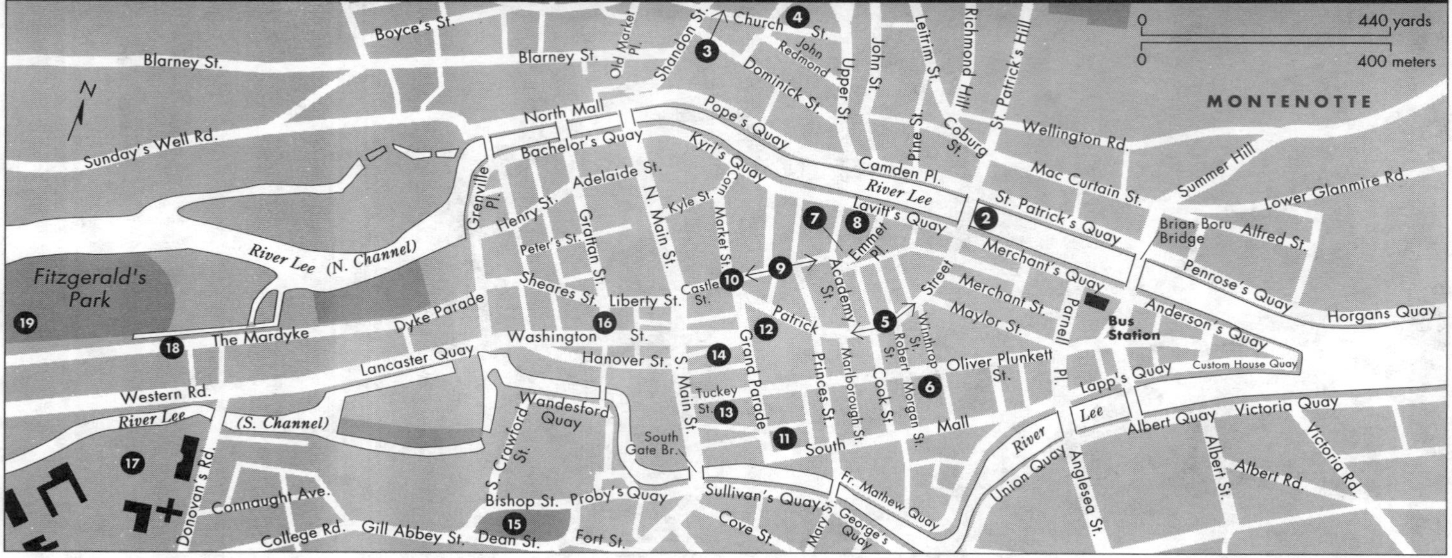

Bishop Lucey Park, **13**
Cornmarket, **10**
Court House, **16**
Crawford Art Gallery, **7**
English Market, **12**
Fitzgerald's Park/ Cork Public Museum, **19**
General Post Office, **6**
The Mardyke, **18**
Opera House, **8**
Patrick's Bridge, **2**
Patrick Street, **5**
Paul Street, **9**
St. Anne's Church (Shandon Steeple), **4**
St. Finnbarre's Cathedral, **15**
St. Mary's Pro-Cathedral, **3**
Tourist Information Office, **11**
Triskel Arts Center, **14**
U.C.C. (University College, Cork), **17**

whose development has transformed the city center. The piazza is a popular place for street theater and entertainment. The shops here offer the best in modern Irish design—from Donegal tweeds to hand-blown glass.

If you follow Paul Street in a westerly direction from the Crawford
10 Art Gallery, you'll reach the **Cornmarket,** once the site of a thriving outdoor market. This area has dwindled to a few secondhand clothes dealers, but the shops alongside are worth checking for antiques and crafts. Turn left at the crossroads at Paul Street for the Grand Pa-
11 rade, where you will find a **TIO** at the far end on your left-hand side. *Tourist House, Grand Parade, tel. 021/273251, fax 021/273504. Open weekdays 9–6, Sat. 9–1.*

If you're curious about food and not squeamish at the sight of it "in the raw," turn right out of the TIO, cross Oliver Plunkett Street,
12 and explore the **English Market.** Note the elaborate Victorian cast-iron construction and the old-fashioned displays of fresh country produce, the styles virtually unchanged since the turn of the century. The stall by the door sells a Cork specialty, tripe (cow's intestines) and *drisheen* (blood sausage). *Open weekdays 9–5:30, Sat. 9–1.*

Cross the Grand Parade by its central fountain and take a stroll
13 through the green space opposite, **Bishop Lucey Park.** Here you'll see works by contemporary Cork sculptors on permanent exhibi-
14 tion. Turn right at the top into South Main Street. The **Triskel Arts Center** is signposted down an alley on the right. It has a small auditorium, a coffee shop, and interesting exhibitions of contemporary arts and crafts. *Tobin St., tel. 021/272022. Admission free. Open weekdays 11–6, Sat. 11–5, and during advertised performances.*

15 If churches take your fancy, you will want to make a detour to **St. Finbarr Cathedral.** Turn left out of Bishop Lucey Park and cross the river at South Gate Bridge, turning right onto Proby's Quay. Pause awhile on the quay to savor the atmospheric views of the old quays from what was once the entrance to medieval Cork. The three spires of the 19th-century Gothic cathedral are visible up ahead on Bishop Street. St. Finbarr, the founder of Cork, established a monastery on this site around AD 650. The present cathedral belongs to the Church of Ireland. *Admission free. Open daily 9–6.*

Retrace your steps down South Main Street to the busy crossroads at Washington Street. The imposing classical portico across the road
16 belongs to the **Court House,** which dates from the 1830s and is still in use today.

From here, some may prefer to take a No. 5 bus to the Mardyke instead of walking. It is about a mile to the left up Washington Street and the Western Road. Alight near the Doric-porticoed gates of the University College campus.

17 **U.C.C.,** as **University College, Cork,** is known, has about 9,000 students. The main quadrangle is a fine example of 19th-century university architecture in the Tudor Gothic style, reminiscent of many an Oxford or Cambridge college. Several ancient Ogham stones (pre-Christian standing stones featuring an early form of writing) are on display, as well as occasional exhibitions of archival material from the old library. The Honan Collegiate Chapel, to the east of the quadrangle, was built in 1916 and modeled on the 12th-century Hiberno-Romanesque style (best exemplified by the remains of Cormac's Chapel at Cashel; *see* Tour 3 in Chapter 7, The Southeast). The college chapel contains stonework, textiles, and stained glass

executed earlier this century by craftsmen of the Irish revivalist school. *Tel. 021/276871. Admission free. Open weekdays 9–5, but phone ahead during school vacations.*

18 One block across Western Road beyond the campus entrance is **The Mardyke,** a popular riverside walk where cricket is played on sum-
19 mer weekends. It leads to **Fitzgerald's Park,** where a Georgian mansion, the **Cork Public Museum,** houses a well-planned exhibit of Cork's history from ancient times to the present day. *Tel. 021/ 270679. Admission free. Open weekdays 11–1 and 2:15–5, Sun. 3–5. Closed Sat. and bank holidays.*

Blarney

Numbers in the margin correspond to points of interest on the Southwest map.

20 **Blarney,** 8 kilometers (5 miles) northwest of Cork City on the R617, is a small community built around a village green dominated by the **Blarney Castle** to the north. In the peak season of July and August, or if en route to Killarney, follow the signposts off the main N22 Killarney road at Carrigrohane to avoid inner-city traffic tie-ups. Most first-time visitors wish to make the trip to Blarney Castle so they may acquire the "gift of the gab" by kissing its famous, lipstick-besmeared stone. Frankly, this is all a lot of blarney, but the kiss itself does make a good photograph.

To reach Blarney Castle, you'll need to climb 127 steep steps to the battlements. Expect a line from mid-June to September 1; while you wait, you can admire the views of the thickly wooded River Lee valley below. The ruined central keep is all that's left of this mid-15th-century MacCarthy stronghold. The efforts of Cormac MacCarthy to smooth-talk Elizabeth I of England gave the English language the term "blarney" to describe flattering and cajoling conversation. To kiss the stone, you must lie down on the battlements, hold on to a guard rail, and lean your head way back. It's good fun and not at all dangerous.

Visitors can also take pleasant walks around the castle grounds; Rock Close contains oddly shaped limestone rocks landscaped in the 18th century and a grove of ancient yew trees that is said to have been the center of Druid worship. *Blarney Castle, tel. 021/385252. Admission: £3 adults, £2 senior citizens, £1 children. Open May, Mon.–Sat. 9–6:30; June–Aug., 9–7; Sept., 9–6:30; Oct.–Apr., Mon.–Sat. 9–sundown, Sun. 9–5:30 year-round.*

Blarney Castle House, next door to the Castle, was built in 1784 in the style of a Scottish baronial mansion. The three-story gray stone building has picture-book turrets and fancy stepped gables. The interior features a fine stairwell and numerous family portraits. *Tel. 021/385252. Admission: £2 adults, £1.50 senior citizens, £1 children. Open June–mid-Sept., Mon.–Sat. noon–6.*

Blarney also probably has more crafts shops than anyplace else in Ireland. Most of these stores are concentrated on the south and west of the village green, a two-minute walk from the castle. A shopping visit here can be used profitably for price comparison and bargain hunting; in spite of appearances, these shops, in general, will not rip you off.

Time Out

Instead of braving Blarney's overcrowded bars and restaurants, take a break at the **Angler's Rest** (Leemount, Carrigrohane, tel. 021/ 871167), a delightful riverside inn with garden tables in the summer and a good choice of bar food. It is midway between Blarney and Cork, off the main N22 Killarney Road on the R579.

Cork Harbour–Fota Island and Cobh

To explore Cork Harbour, follow the signposts for Waterford on the N25 along the banks of the River Lee. Alternatively, a suburban rail service from Kent Station (tel. 021/506766 for timetable) has stops at Fota Island and Cobh (pronounced "Cove"), and it offers better harbor views than the road.

The turreted building on the opposite side of the Lee just outside town is **Blackrock Castle.** This 16th-century fortification was rebuilt in the 19th century and is now a restaurant and bar (tel. 021/357414). Shortly after you get a glimpse of Blackrock, the road leaves the river. The turning for Fota Island and Cobh (R624) is clearly signposted off the N25 on the right-hand side about 8 kilometers (5 miles) outside town. Turn right again at the gate lodge of the huge
21 **Fota Demesne,** on Fota Island.

The estate's 70-acre **Fota Wildlife Park** serves as an important breeding center for cheetahs and wallabies. It also contains free-ranging monkeys, zebras, giraffes, ostriches, flamingos, emus, and kangaroos. *Tel. 021/812678. Admission: £3.30 adults, £3 students, £1.90 children under 14 and senior citizens. Car park, including admission to arboretum and gardens, £1. Open Mar. 17–Oct. 31, Mon.–Sat. 10–6, Sun. 11–6.*

Turn right out of Fota and continue south on the R624 to Cobh. Fota Island is linked to Great Island by Belvelly Bridge. A signpost to the left here provides an interesting detour to **Barryscourt Castle,** a 13th-century structure, complete with courtyard and flanking towers. *Carrigtwohill, tel. 021/883864. Admission free. Open year-round, daily 11–6. Guided tours of castle keep are available June–Sept., £1.50.*

Cobh itself faces the open sea, which is some 8 kilometers (5 miles)
22 down the harbor at Roches Point. Both **Cobh** (previously known as Queenstown) and **Roches Point** are familiar landmarks for the many generations who left the port of Cork on immigrant ships for the New World. For a sense of their experience, and the best view of Cobh and St. Colman's Cathedral, an imposing 19th-century Gothic construction made of granite, take a one-hour harbor tour from Kennedy Pier. *Marine Transport, tel. 021/811485. Cost: £3 adults, £1.50 children. May–Sept., 10, 11, noon, 1:30, and 2:30.*

A new (1993) heritage center, **The Queenstown Project,** in the old railway station, re-creates the experience of emigrants who left Cobh between 1750 and the mid-20th century. It also tells the stories of the great transatlantic liners, including the *Titanic,* whose last port of call was Cobh, and the *Lusitania.* The *Lusitania* was sunk by a German submarine off this coast on May 7, 1915, with the loss of 1,198 lives. Many of the victims are buried in Cobh, with a memorial to them on the local quay. *Tel. 021/813591. Admission: £3.50 adults, £2 children and senior citizens. Open Feb.–Nov., daily 10–6.*

If you are heading for Kinsale and West Cork, take advantage of the new **Cork Harbour Crossing,** a car ferry that runs from Carrigaloe near Cobh to Glenbrook near Ringaskiddy, cutting out the traveling through Cork City. It operates continuously from 7:15 AM to 12:45 AM daily and costs £3 per car, 60p for pedestrians.

Tour 2: Kinsale to Glengarriff

This tour takes you on a meandering scenic drive of about 136 kilometers (85 miles) around the unspoiled coast of West County Cork. It starts at the historic old port of Kinsale and travels through a variety of seascapes to the lush vegetation of Glengarriff. The drive from Kinsale to Glengarriff can take about two hours nonstop, but the whole point of taking this tour is to linger anywhere that takes your fancy. The tour is most enjoyable between May and October, when the weather is still warm enough to explore the area on foot.

23 **Kinsale** is 29 kilometers (18 miles) from Cork City past the airport on the R600. This exceptionally beautiful town is built on the slopes of Compass Hill at the top of a wide fjordlike harbor. Its steep narrow streets and tall slated houses feature a Spanish accent that can be traced back to the Battle of Kinsale in 1601, when the Irish and Spanish joined forces here to fight the English—and lost. Subsequently an important fishing port, with the significant presence of a British army and navy, the town today attracts yacht owners and deep-sea anglers. It is also well known for its many fine restaurants, which definitely make a visit here worthwhile.

A signposted walking tour of the town, with an accompanying booklet (£1 from the Kinsale Tourist Information Office or Boland's on Pearse Street), will familiarize you with its interesting and varied history. Visit the **museum** in the town's 17th-century Dutch-style courthouse for more insight into the past, and take a look at its fascinating collection of cuttings and memorabilia from the wreck of the *Lusitania* (*see* Cobh, *above*). The museum staff will also give you details of free guided walks that take place regularly in the summer, or by appointment for groups. *The Old Courthouse, Market Pl., tel. 021/772044. Admission: 35p. Open Mon.–Sat. 11–5, Sun. 3–5.*

Leave the town center and return to the point where the main road from Cork City enters Kinsale. Follow the signpost at the water's
24 edge to Summer Cove and **Charles Fort.** This structure was built in the wake of the defeat of the Spanish and Irish forces, on the harbor shore 3 kilometers (2 miles) east of town. If the sun is shining, take the footpath that is signposted Scilly Walk; it winds along the edge of the harbor under tall overhanging trees and then through the village of Summer Cove. Charles Fort is one of the best preserved "star forts" in Europe, enclosing some 12 acres on a cliff top. It will remind some of Fort Ticonderoga in New York. In its heyday, it had a population of 2,000; it was in use until 1920, when it was burned out by the Irish Republican Army. *Tel. 021/772684. Admission: £1 adults, 40p children and senior citizens. Open mid-June–mid-Sept., daily 10–6:30; mid-Apr.–mid-June, Tues.–Sat. 10–5, Sun. 2–5. Guided tours on request. Mid-Sept.–mid-Apr., weekdays 8–4:30, except public holidays. No guides off-season.*

Time Out The **Spaniard Inn** (tel. 021/772436) looks over the town and harbor from a hairpin bend on the road to Charles Fort. Inside, sawdust-covered floors and a big open fire make this anglers' bar a cozy spot in the winter. In the summer, you can take a pint to the sunny veranda and watch the world go by on land and sea.

Next, leave town through its center by following the quays and drive west along the Bandon River toward the bridge. The route is signposted to **Ballinspittle** (R600). This grotto with a large statue of the Virgin Mary had a moment of fame in the summer of 1985 when tens of thousands saw the statue move nightly. Fundamentalists smashed the effigy, and its replacement remains immobile, although the pious still stop here.

The route takes you through **Garretstown Woods** (signposts for Clonakilty on the R600), which are carpeted with wild bluebells in April; then past the edge of Courtmacsherry Bay, running alongside a wide saltwater inlet that teems with curlew, plover, and other waders.

Time Out The **Pink Elephant** (Harbour View, Kilbrittain, tel. 023/49608) is an irresistible stopping place in good weather—a pink-painted, moderately priced bar and restaurant with sweeping sea views on its own grounds high above Courtmacsherry Bay. The bar serves soup and sandwiches on homemade brown bread; the restaurant features plain home cooking, including roast or grilled meat and a daily vegetarian special.

The pretty village of multicolored cottages glimpsed across the water is **Courtmacsherry,** where sandy beaches make it a popular holiday resort. It can be reached by following the signposts from Timoleague.

25 The R600 continues west to the head of the saltwater inlet (*see above*) and the village of **Timoleague,** which is dominated at the water's edge by a striking ruined abbey. Built in the mid-13th century, it is one of the best-preserved early Franciscan friaries in Ireland. You walk around the back to find the entrance gate. The abbey was sacked by the English in 1642, but like many ruins of its kind, it was used as a burial place until recent times. Ignoring the graves, you can trace the ground plan of the old friary—the chapel, refectory, cloisters, and wine cellar. At one time the friars were famous wine importers.

Timoleague Castle Gardens are signposted in the village. Although the castle is long gone—it has been replaced by a modest early 20th-century house in gray stone—the original gardens have survived. Palm trees and other frost-tender plants flourish in the mature shrubbery; there are two large, old-fashioned walled gardens, one for flowers and one for fruits and vegetables. *Tel. 023/46116. Admission: £1.20 adults, 60p children. Open Easter weekend and mid-May–mid-Sept., daily noon–6.*

The R600 now runs inland to **Clonakilty,** a small market town where many of the shops and businesses have abandoned chrome and plastic materials for traditional hand-painted signs and wooden facades—to very charming effect. Many fine sandy beaches are nearby; the best of them are found at Inchydoney, 3 kilometers (2 miles) outside of town.

This area is the heart of West County Cork, where small, twisted roads are overhung by tall hedges of *Fuchsia magellanica*. Originally imported as a garden shrub in the mid-19th century, it quickly adapted to the balmy sea air and is widely regarded as a weed used here for hedging—albeit a beautiful one with its delicate, drooping mauve-and-red trumpeted flowers. In June, the hedges are offset by tall purple foxgloves, and in August and September by bright purple heather.

The R600 joins the sea again at Rosscarbery, where you leave the main road by turning left at the signpost for Glandore at the end of the causeway. Glandore and Union Hall are twin fishing villages on
26 either side of the landlocked Glandore harbor. **Glandore,** with its steep hill and pretty church, is the more charming of the two; it is a popular spot for visitors from the United Kingdom and Germany. Glandore's influx of affluent visitors and expensive yachts has not been shared in **Union Hall,** where simple fishing trawlers still tie up at the quay.

Now you are truly in the back of beyond, where the tiny roads are
27 without route numbers. However, **Castletownshend** is clearly signposted from Union Hall via Rineen. Castletownshend's main street runs steeply down a hill to the sea. It has an unusual number of graciously designed large stone houses, mostly dating from the mid-18th century when it was an important trading center. Nowadays, this deliciously sleepy place comes alive in only July and August, when the activity centers on the waters of its sheltered harbor. It was the home of Edith Somerville and Violet "Martin" Ross, authors of the humorous "Resident Magistrate" (R.M.) stories, which in a good-natured manner show the differences between the British and the Irish ways of thinking; the stories were very popular during the early 20th century. The writers' graves can be visited by climbing the 52 steep steps to the cliff-top St. Barrahane's Church; the view is well worth the effort.

Time Out The place to go for a pint and a sandwich in Castletownshend is **Mary Ann's** (tel. 028/36146), one of the oldest bars in the country, whose low-beamed interior is frequented by a very friendly mix of visitors and locals. Writer Edna O'Brien claims that it is her favorite pub in the whole world.

You have only one way out of Castletownshend: the way you came in, up the hill, after which you take the Skibbereen road (the R596). If you have time for a side trip to Sherkin Island or Cape Clear Island, take the Baltimore road (the R595) by turning left at the entrance to
28 Skibbereen. **Baltimore,** once a small fishing village, is now a popular
29 sailing center. **Sherkin Island** is only a 10-minute ferry trip from Baltimore (seven ferries are scheduled daily; call 028/20125 for times). The island, with a population of 90, offers several safe sandy beaches and abundant wildlife.

30 **Cape Clear Island** is part of the West Cork Gaeltacht (Irish-speaking area). The ferry to the island takes about an hour (cost: £6 round-trip; call 028/39119 for sailing times), and it's exciting to watch the skipper thread his way through the many rocks and tiny islands of Roaring Water Bay. You have excellent views of the Fastnet Rock Lighthouse, focus of the famous yachting race. Cape Clear can be explored on foot in about an hour, but bird-watchers will want to stay longer. It is the southernmost point of Ireland, and its observatory is famous for records of rare songbird migrants. Large flocks of oceangoing birds can be seen offshore in the summer.

Baltimore, like Castletownshend, is the end of the road, and the visitor must double back to **Skibbereen,** a busy but uninteresting market town. From here take the N71 to Bantry. If you still have an appetite for lovely coastal villages, take a detour at Ballydehob on the R592 to Schull, then the R591 to Goleen and Crookhaven, returning to Bantry through Durrus.

31 On the right-hand side of the road as you enter **Bantry,** you will see the porticoed entrance to **Bantry House.** This magnificent mansion, set in Italianate gardens and overlooking the sea, was built in the mid-18th century. Giving the house a baroque, Continental air is an extensive art collection (including exquisite 18th-century tapestries and furniture) acquired by the second earl of Bantry during his European grand tour. Some of the rooms are now a little shabby, but the beauty of the location compensates for the lack of polish. Climb to the top of the rear garden for the best views. Next to the house is **The Bantry 1796 French Armada Exhibition Center,** a small but fascinating museum illustrating the abortive attempt by Irish national-

ist Wolfe Tone and his French ally General Hoche to land 14,000 troops in Bantry Bay to effect an uprising. *Bantry House, tel. 027/50047. Admission: house only or museum only: £3 adults, £1.75 senior citizens and students, children under 14 free; joint ticket £4.50. Open daily 9–6; till 8 on long summer evenings.*

It is not the town of Bantry that the balladeers celebrate, as a quick glance will confirm, but the glorious sweep of **Bantry Bay,** which is on your left as you climb out of town on the N71. This is a starker, more magnificent prospect than any encountered so far, and the sparse, windswept vegetation gives an idea of what the wet and windy winters are like on the more exposed part of this coast.

32 The descent into wooded, sheltered **Glengarriff** reveals yet another kind of landscape: It is mild enough down here for subtropical plants to thrive. You are also back on the beaten track with crafts shops, tour buses, and boatmen soliciting your business by the roadside.
33 Do not ignore the boatmen: They can row you over to **Garnish Island,** about 10 minutes offshore, which features beautiful formal Italian gardens, shrubberies with rare subtropical plants, and excellent views from the strange Grecian temple. (The boat trip is subject to negotiation—expect to pay about £4 round-trip.) *Tel. 027/63040. Admission £1.50 adults, 60p senior citizens and children. Open July–Aug., Mon.–Sat. 9:30–6:30, Sun. 11–6; Apr.–June and Sept., Mon.–Sat. 10–6:30, Sun. 1–6; Mar. and Oct., Mon.–Sat. 10–4:30, Sun. 1–5. Last landings 1 hr before closing.*

Tour 3: Killarney, the Ring of Kerry, and the Dingle Peninsula

Killarney, one of the region's most attractive locales, is a year-round, all-weather destination. Because of the area's topography, rain seldom lasts long among the mountains, and the passing showers, which can be watched approaching over the lakes, actually add to your enjoyment of the ever-changing scenery. However, rain can spoil the drive around the Ring of Kerry, blocking views across the water to the Beara Peninsula in the east and the Dingle Peninsula in the west. Dingle is also notorious for its heavy rainfall and an impenetrable sea mist that can strike at any time of year. If it does, sit it out in Dingle Town or the village of Dunquin, and enjoy the friendly bars, cafés, and crafts shops.

Killarney

34 The lakes and mountains of **Killarney** are perhaps the most celebrated—and the most commercialized—attractions in Ireland. Killarney's heather-clad mountains, lush subtropical vegetation, and deep-blue lakes dotted with wooded isles have left a lasting impression on innumerable visitors, beginning in the 18th century with the English traveler Arthur Young and Bishop Berkeley. Travelers in search of the natural beauty so beloved by the Romantic movement began to flock to the Southwest, among them writers Sir Walter Scott and William Thackeray. By the mid-19th century, Killarney's stunning scenery was considered as exhilarating and awe-inspiring as anything in Switzerland or England's Lake District.

The lives of Kerry's impoverished natives were transformed by the influx of affluent visitors that followed the 1854 arrival of the railway, and the locals became adept at inventing apocryphal legends and farfetched stories to impress the vacationers.

It is the combination of wild mountain scenery and lush subtropical vegetation that attracts today's visitors. The vegetation is splendid at any time of year. The red fruits of the Mediterranean strawberry

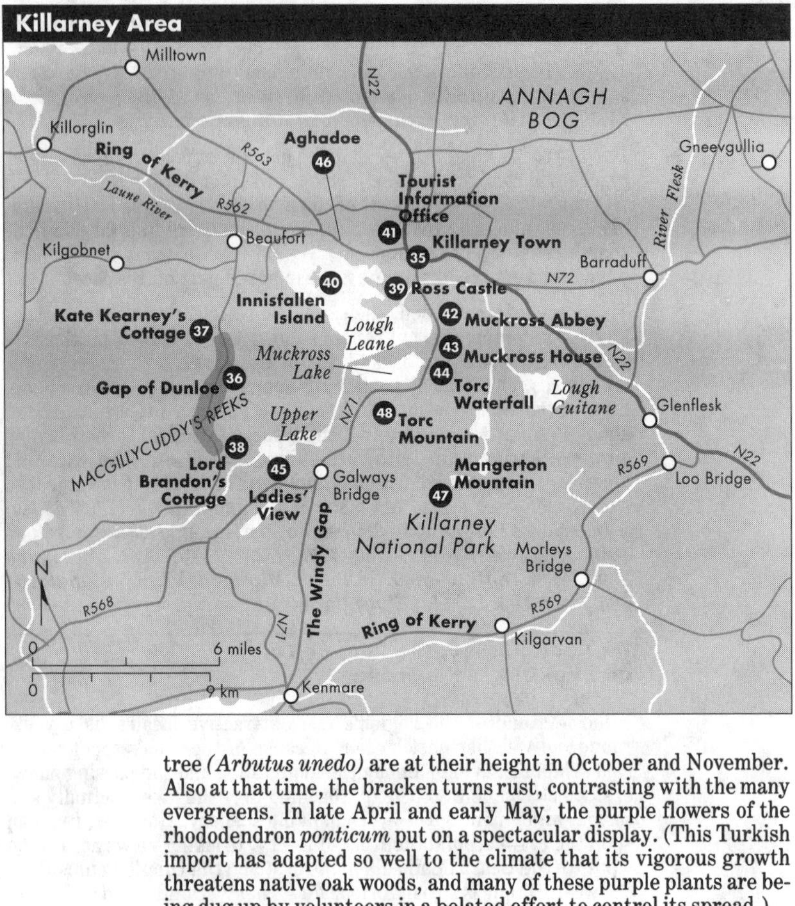

tree *(Arbutus unedo)* are at their height in October and November. Also at that time, the bracken turns rust, contrasting with the many evergreens. In late April and early May, the purple flowers of the rhododendron *ponticum* put on a spectacular display. (This Turkish import has adapted so well to the climate that its vigorous growth threatens native oak woods, and many of these purple plants are being dug up by volunteers in a belated effort to control its spread.)

Numbers in the margin correspond to numbered points of interest on the Killarney Area map.

35 **Killarney Town,** on a flat plain more than a mile from the lakes, is best regarded as a necessary evil in which little time should be spent. Overcrowded in July and August with Irish and European visitors, the peak season for Americans is September and October. At other times of year, particularly from November to mid-March, when many of the hotels are closed, the town is quiet to the point of being eerie. Given the choice, go to Killarney in April, May, or early October.

Limiting your time in Killarney should enable you to fit the Gap of
36 Dunloe and the Lower Lake into your itinerary. To reach the **Gap of Dunloe,** drive west 7 kilometers (4½ miles) from Killarney on the Beaufort road, R562, and follow the signs another 2½ kilometers
37 (1½ miles) to the Gap. You are advised to wait until you reach **Kate Kearney's Cottage** before hiring a jaunting car (pony and trap) or pony. Kate was a famous beauty who sold moonshine to visitors from her home, contributing greatly, one suspects, to their enthusiasm for the scenery.

Time Out **Kate Kearney's Cottage** (tel. 064/44116) is now, appropriately enough, a pub. It's a good place to pause for a glass of Irish coffee.

The trip through the Gap of Dunloe takes about 90 minutes. The road stretches for 6½ kilometers (4 miles) between MacGillicuddy's Reeks (to the west) and the Purple Mountains. If you are on an organized tour, you can walk or ride (on a pony or in a jaunting car) all the way through to Lord Brandon's Cottage at the head of the Upper Lake and continue by boat. Although cars are banned from the Gap, the first 3 kilometers (2 miles) are busy with horse and foot traffic in the summer, much of which turns back at the halfway point. Five small lakes are strung out beside the road, and massive glacial rocks form the side of the valley, creating strange echoes. (Test it out by giving a shout.) Parking is available near Kate Kearney's Cottage and Lord Brandon's Cottage.

38 At the head of the Gap, the **Upper Lake** comes into view, with the Black Valley stretching into the hills at the right. From **Lord Brandon's Cottage,** a tea shop serving soup and sandwiches (open Easter–September, 10–dusk), a path leads to the edge of the lake, and the journey is continued by rowboat. It is an old tradition for the boatman to carry a bugle and illustrate the echoes. Look out for caves on the left-hand side when passing through the narrow Middle Lake. The boat passes under Brickeen Bridge and into the **Middle Lake,** where 30 islands are steeped in legend, much of which, no doubt, will be recounted by your boatman.

39 The journey ends at **Ross Castle** a 14th-century stronghold. It has recently been fully restored and contains 16th- and 17th-century furniture. *Admission: £2 adults, £1 students and children. Open May and Sept., daily 9–6; June–Aug., daily 9–6:30; Oct., daily 9–5.*

40 You can take yourself to **Innisfallen Island** by hiring a rowboat at Ross Castle (cost: £1.50 per hour), or you can join a cruise in a covered, heated launch (cost: £5; also from Ross Castle a shuttle bus leaves from Scott's Gardens in Killarney Town to connect with ferry, £1). The romantic ruins on the island date from the 6th or 7th century. Between 950 and 1350 the *Annals of Innisfallen* were compiled here by the monks. (The book survives in the Bodleian Library in Oxford.) The launch and castle may be reached by car.

41 Another popular excursion from Killarney is a half-day trip to Muckross Abbey, Muckross House and Estate, and the Torc Waterfall. Cars are not allowed to tour the grounds of the estate, but you'll find a car park at the house. Some people choose to make the whole trip by jaunting car, hiring one at the stand near the **TIO** in Killarney. (The cost of a jaunting car is £10–£24, negotiable with the driver, for up to four people. Get an estimate from the TIO.) To save time and money, drive the 4 kilometers (2½ miles) to Muckross Abbey on the N71 Kenmare road, and pick up a jaunting car there. Or, hire a bicycle in town, pack a lunch, and make a day of it.

42 Though it was completely wrecked by Oliver Cromwell's British troops in 1652, the 15th-century Franciscan **Muckross Abbey** is still amazingly complete, although roofless. An ancient yew tree rises above the cloisters and breaks out over the abbey walls. Three flights of stone steps allow access to the upper floors and living quarters, where you can visit what was once their dormitory, kitchen, and refectory. *Admission free. Open daily daylight hours.*

43 **Muckross House,** a 19th-century Elizabethan-style manor, is about 1.6 kilometers (1 mile) farther west on the N71; it now houses the

Kerry Folklife Center, where bookbinders, potters, and weavers demonstrate their crafts. The informal grounds here are noted for their rhododendrons and azaleas, the water garden, and the outstanding limestone rock garden. In the park beside the house, **The Kerry Country Life Experience** comprises reconstructed farm buildings and outhouses, a blacksmith's forge, a carpenter's workshop, and a selection of farm animals. It is a reminder of the way things were done on the farm before the advent of electricity and the mechanization of farm methods. *Tel. 064/31440. Admission to farms or house only: £2.50 adult, £1 children; combined farm and house: £3.50 adult, £1.50 children. Open daily 9–5:30 (July and Aug. until 7).*

Another 1.6 kilometers (1 mile) west on the N71 (7 kilometers/4½
44 miles from Killarney) is the **Torc Waterfall,** about a 10-minute walk from the car park. After your first view of the roaring cascade, it's worth the climb up a long flight of stone steps to the second, less-frequented clearing. If the weather is fine, return to your car and
45 drive on west to **Ladies' View,** a panoramic vista. The N71 continues to Kenmare, from where you can complete the circuit by taking the shorter but very narrow Windy Gap route, or make a wide sweep via Kilgarvan on the R569 and N22, driving back through the town to
46 **Aghadoe,** 5 kilometers (3 miles) outside Killarney on the R562 Beaufort–Killorglin road. Here is another remarkable view of the Lower Lake with Innisfallen Island in the distance and the Gap of Dunloe away to the west. Stand beside Aghadoe's 12th-century ruined church and Round Tower and watch the shadows creep across the lake at dusk.

The Mangerton walking trail is reached by turning left off the N71 midway between Muckross Abbey and Muckross House (following
47 signposts). On foot you'll reach the summit of **Mangerton Mountain** (748 meters/2,756 feet) in about two hours—less should you choose
48 to hire a pony. **Torc Mountain** (537 meters/1,764 feet) can also be reached off Route N71; it is a satisfying 1½-hour climb. Do not attempt either in misty weather. The Kerry Way, a long-distance walking route, passes through the **Killarney National Park** on its way to Glenbeigh (detailed leaflet from the TIO). For the less adventurous, four safe and well-signposted nature trails of varying lengths are available in the National Park. Try Arthur Young's Walk (4 kilometers/2½ miles); it passes through old yew and oak woods frequented by Sika deer.

From May to September, Killarney offers visitors a lively nightlife, including discos, Irish cabarets, and singing pubs—the latter are a local specialty with a strong Irish-American flavor. But the real pleasure of Killarney is outdoors. Its mild, totally unpolluted air smells of damp woods and heather moors. Few people feel they have exhausted the area's natural resources in one visit. Most leave with the intention of one day returning to find the fascinating shifts of light, the varied scenery, and the peaceful solitude as seductive as ever.

The Ring of Kerry

Numbers in the margin correspond to points of interest on the Southwest map.

Because most tour buses travel the Ring of Kerry counterclockwise, we recommend that independent travelers take it clockwise, starting at Kenmare. This is equally convenient for those approaching from Glengarriff (on the N71) and Killarney (also on the N71). The trip covers 176 kilometers (110 miles) on the N70 (and briefly the R562) if you start and finish in Killarney; the journey will be 40 kilometers (25 miles) shorter if you only venture between Kenmare and Killorglin; from this latter point, people often choose to travel on to the Dingle Peninsula without returning to Killarney. Allow at least one full day for the Ring—and pray for sunshine, which makes all the difference.

49 **Kenmare** is a small market town at the head of the sheltered Kenmare River estuary and is a popular touring base.

As you drive down the Iveragh Peninsula, the Beara Peninsula and its blue-gray mountain ranges, the Caha and the Slieve Miskish, are 50 across the water to the south. The village of **Sneem** (from the Irish *an tSnaidhm*—the knot), on the estuary of the Ardsheelaun River, is one of the prettiest in Ireland, although its village green is atypically English-style. Look for "the pyramids" (as they are known locally) beside the parish church. These 4-meter- (12-foot-) tall traditional stone structures with stained-glass insets look as though they have been here forever. In fact, the sculpture park was completed in 1990 to the design of the Kerry-born artist, James Scanlon, who has won international awards for his work in stained glass. Another 3.2 kilometers (2 miles) south is the beautiful hotel and wooded estate of **Parknasilla.** The road then runs inland for a few miles before emerging at the coast again at **Castlecove.**

51 **Staigue Fort,** signposted 4 kilometers (2½ miles) inland at Castlecove, is one of the finest examples of an Iron Age stone fort in Ireland. Approximately 2,500 years old, this structure made from local stone is almost circular and about 23 meters (75 feet) in diameter, with only one entrance, on the south side. Between the Iron Age (from 500 BC to the 5th century AD) and early Christian times (6th century AD), such "forts" were, in fact, fortified homesteads within which several families of one clan and their cattle lived. The walls at Staigue Fort are almost 4 meters (13 feet) wide at the base, 2 meters (7 feet) at the top; they still stand at 5½ meters (18 feet) on the north and west sides. Within the walls stairs lead to narrow platforms on which the lookouts stood. (Private land must be crossed to reach the fort, and a nominal "compensation for trespass" is often requested by the landowner.)

52 Beyond the next village, **Caherdaniel,** is **Derrynane House.** This home once belonged to the famous politician Daniel O'Connell (1775–1847), "The Liberator," who campaigned for Catholic Emancipation (the granting of full rights of citizenship for Catholics), which became a reality in 1828. The house with its lovely garden and 320-acre estate now forms **Derrynane National Park.** The south and east wings of the house are open to visitors and still contain much of the original furniture and other items associated with O'Connell. *Derrynane House: tel. 066/75113. Admission: £1 adults, 40p children and senior citizens. Open mid-June–Sept., daily 10–1 and 2–7; Oct.–mid-June, Tues.–Sat. 10–1 and 2–5, Sun. 2–5. Park: admission free; open all year.*

53 The village of **Waterville,** 5 kilometers (3 miles) north, is famous for game fishing and its 18-hole championship golf course. Salmon and trout fishing are excellent at nearby Lough Currane.

Time Out **The Smuggler's Inn,** situated on a mile-long sandy beach, is a small, family-run guest house and restaurant with a good reputation for seafood. This is an ideal spot for a leisurely lunch or a quick pint and a sandwich. *Cliff Rd., Waterville, tel. 0667/4330. Closed Nov. 3–Feb. 15.*

Just outside Waterville, a scenic detour is signposted from the main Ring to Ballinskelligs, an Irish-speaking area with a fine sandy
54 beach, and **Valentia Island.** Some of the romance of visiting an island has been lost since Valentia was connected to the mainland by a road bridge in 1971. The island still gives its name to weather reports, but the station that monitors the Atlantic weather systems has now moved onto the nearby mainland.

55 From Valentia, you'll see the conical-shape **Skelligs** rising 217 meters (700 feet) out of the Atlantic. The larger rock, Skellig Michael (or the Great Skellig), which has the remains of a settlement of early Christian monks, is reached by climbing 600 increasingly precipitous steps. In spite of one thousand years' battering by Atlantic storms, the church, oratory, and beehive-shape living cells are surprisingly well preserved.

The Skellig Experience, situated where the road bridge joins Valentia Island, contains exhibits on local bird life, the history of the lighthouse and keepers, and the life and work of the early Christian monks. There is also a 15-minute audio-visual show that allows you to "tour" the monastery without leaving dry land. If, however, you're keen on seeing the Skelligs up close (landing is prohibited without a special permit), you can take a one-and-a-half-hour guided cruise with author and Skellig expert, Des Lavelle. Little Skellig is the breeding ground of more than 20,000 pairs of gannets, and Puffin island to the north has a large population of shearwaters, storm petrel, and puffins. Photographers will love the boat trip, but sailors are warned that these are choppy waters at the best of times. *Valentia, Co. Kerry, tel. 064/31633. Admission to center only: £3 adults, £1.50 children. Admission to center and cruise: £15 adults, £8 children. Open April–June and Sept., 9:30–5; July and Aug., 9:30–7. Phone to confirm cruise times or ask at Killarney TIO.*

56 The main road, the N70, is joined again just outside **Cahirciveen** (accent on the last syllable: Cah-her-sigh-*veen*), the main market town and shopping center for South Kerry, at the foot of Bentee Mountain. The impressive church that dominates the main street was built in 1888 to honor the local hero, Daniel O'Connell (*see* Derrynane House, *above*). Following the tradition in this part of the world, the town's modest terraced houses are painted in different colors—the brighter the better. The same sign writers who recently transformed Kenmare with their old-fashioned hand-painted signs have been at work here, too.

The road from Cahirciveen to Glenbeigh is one of the highlights of the Ring. To the north is Dingle Bay and the jagged peaks of the Dingle Peninsula, which will, in all probability, be shrouded in mist. If they are not, the gods have indeed blessed your journey. The road runs close to the water here, and beyond Kells it climbs high above the bay, hugging the steep side of Drung Hill before descending to Glenbeigh. Note how different the stark character of this stretch of the Ring is from the gentle, woody Kenmare Bay side.

57 **Glenbeigh** is a popular holiday base, offering excellent hiking in the Glenbeigh Horseshoe, as the surrounding mountains are known, and exceptionally good trout fishing on Lough Coomasaharn. If you have at least half an hour to spare you may enjoy a visit to the **Kerry Bog Village Museum,** a cluster of reconstructed, fully furnished cottages, which gives a vivid portrayal of the daily life of the region's working class in the early 1800s. *Beside the Red Fox Bar, tel. 066/69184. Admission: £2 adults, £1.50 senior citizens, £1 children. Open Mar.–Nov., daily 8:30–7; Jan.–Mar., on request. Closed Dec.*

58 **Rossbeigh,** 3 kilometers (2 miles) away, has about 3 kilometers (2 miles) of soft yellow sandy coastline backed by high dunes. It faces Inch strand, a similar formation across the water on the Dingle Peninsula.

A signpost to the right just outside Glenbeigh points to **Caragh Lake,** another tempting side excursion to a beautiful expanse of water set among gorse-and-heather-covered hills and majestic mountains. The road encircles the lake, hugging the shoreline much of the way.

59 **Killorglin,** which is perched atop a hill 9½ kilometers (6 miles) beyond Glenbeigh, is the scene of the famous Puck Fair, a three-day stint of merrymaking that takes place during the second weekend in August. A large billy goat with beribboned horns, installed on a high pedestal, presides over the fair. The origins of the tradition of King Puck are lost in time. Though some horse-, sheep-, and cattle-dealing still occurs at the fair, the main attractions these days are free outdoor concerts and extended drinking hours. The crowd is predominantly young and invariably noisy, so avoid Killorglin at fair time if you've come for peace and quiet. On the other hand, if you intend joining in the festivities, be sure to book accommodations well in advance.

The Dingle Peninsula

The landscape here is formed by rugged mountains and cliffs, interspersed with softly molded glacial valleys and lakes. The peninsula is outlined by long sandy beaches and rocky cliffs pounded by the Atlantic Ocean. On the coastal plains, dry stone walls enclose small, irregular fields. The whole area is exceptionally rich in antiquities, especially prehistoric and early Christian remains. The tip of the peninsula—**Corca Dhuibhne (Corcaguiny)**—is officially a Gaeltacht, although like all Gaeltacht communities, it is bilingual nowadays; English is the second language.

The peninsula can be covered in a long day trip of about 160 kilometers (99 miles). From Tralee, Killarney, or Killorglin, head for Castlemaine, and take the coast road (the R561 and R559) to the town of Dingle via Inch. If mist or continuous rain is forecast, postpone the trip until visibility improves.

The head of Dingle Bay is cut off by two sand spits that enclose Castlemaine Harbour. The sand spit on the Dingle side forms the
60 sheltered seaside resort **Inch,** which has a 6½-kilometer- (4-mile-) long sandy beach backed by dunes.

61 **Annascaul,** which is 8 kilometers (5 miles) down the coast road from Inch, near the junction of the Castlemaine and Tralee roads, was an important livestock center until the 1930s. This explains why such a small village has such a wide street (cattle trading was carried out in the streets), and also why it boasts so many pubs for so few residents.

Time Out

Photographers will be tempted to snap **Dan Foley's** (tel. 066/57257) flamboyantly painted pub. Wander in for a pint, and have a chat with Dan, who is also a magician, a farmer, and an expert on local history.

---

62 **Dingle,** the chief town of the peninsula, marks the start of the Irish-speaking area. It is backed by mountains and faces a sheltered harbor. In the summer months, its year-round population of 1,400 is more than doubled by visitors. Dingle offers a good selection of crafts shops and restaurants, but since 1985 its main attraction has been a very friendly and entertaining bottle-nosed dolphin who has taken up residence in the harbor. The Dingle dolphin, or Fungie, as

some people call him, will play for hours with swimmers (a wet suit is essential) and scuba divers, and he follows local boats in and out of the harbor. Being wild, it is impossible to predict whether he will stay, but boatmen have become so confident of a sighting that they offer trippers their money back if Fungie does not appear. Boat trips (cost: £5 adults, £2 children) leave the pier hourly in July and August between 11 and 6, weather permitting. At other times, call David Donegan at 066/51720.

Time Out Dingle has a wide choice of pubs, but **O'Flaherty's** (Bridge St. at the entrance to the town, tel. 066/51461) is something special. This simple stone-floored bar is a mecca for traditional musicians. Spontaneous music sessions occur most nights in July and August, less frequently at other times. Even without music, this pub provides a good spot to compare notes with fellow travelers.

---

63 **Ventry,** the next town along the coast, has a long sandy beach with safe bathing and ponies for hire. Between Ventry and Dunquin, you'll find several interesting archaeological sites on the spectacular cliff-top road along Slea Head. After you pass between two tall hedges of fuchsia bushes about 6 kilometers (3½ miles) outside
64 Ventry, the Iron Age promontory fort, **Dunbeg,** can be seen on the left below the road. A fortified stone wall cuts off the promontory, and the landward side is protected by an elaborate system of earthworks and trenches. Within the enclosure is a ruined circular building, with walls up to 6.35 meters (22 feet) wide. Unlike Staigue Fort on the Ring of Kerry, this was not a homestead but was probably used as a refuge in times of danger. *Freely accessible; follow signposts across fields.*

If you continue west along the coast road, you'll see signs indicating "Prehistoric Beehive Huts"—*clochâns* in Irish. These cells are built of unmortared stone on the southern slopes of Mt. Eagle. In the early Christian period, they were used by hermit monks. Some 414 of these huts exist between Slea Head and Dunquin. Due to the increase in traffic, some local farmers, on whose land these monuments stand, are charging a "trespass fee" of 50p from visitors.

The view of the Blasket Islands and the Atlantic Ocean from the top
65 of the towering cliffs of **Slea Head** stops most visitors in their tracks. The long sandy strand below, Coumenole, looks beautiful and sheltered, but swimming here is dangerous. This treacherous stretch of coast has claimed many lives in shipwrecks—most recently in 1982 when a large cargo boat, the *Ranga,* foundered on the rocks and sank. In 1588, four ships of the Spanish Armada were driven through the Blasket Sound; two made it to shelter, and two sank. One of these, the *Santa Maria de la Rosa,* was found only recently; it is currently being excavated by divers in the summer months.

66 The largest of the **Blasket Islands** visible from Slea Head, the **Great Blasket,** was inhabited until 1953. The Blasket islanders were great storytellers, and were encouraged by scholars of the Irish language to write their memoirs. *The Islandman,* by Tomás O Crohán, gives a vivid picture of a hard way of life. "Their likes will not be seen again" as O Crohán's catchphrase puts it. **The Blasket Centre** explains the heritage of these islanders and celebrates their use of the Irish language with videos and exhibitions. *Dunquin, Dingle Peninsula, tel. 066/56371. Admission: £2 adults, £1.50 senior citizens, £1 students and children. Open Easter–Sept., daily 10–6.*

67 **Dunquin** was once the mainland harbor for the islanders. No scheduled ferry service is available; inquire in Dunquin in June, July, and

So, you're getting away from it all.

Just make sure you can get back.

AT&T Access Numbers
Dial the number of the country you're in to reach AT&T.

*AUSTRIA†††	022-903-011	*GREECE	00-800-1311	NORWAY	800-190-11
*BELGIUM	078-11-0010	*HUNGARY	00◇-800-01111	POLAND†♦²	0◇010-480-0111
BULGARIA	00-1800-0010	*ICELAND	999-001	PORTUGAL†	05017-1-288
CANADA	1-800-575-2222	IRELAND	1-800-550-000	ROMANIA	01-800-4288
CROATIA†♦	99-38-0011	ISRAEL	177-100-2727	*RUSSIA† (MOSCOW)	155-5042
*CYPRUS	080-90010	*ITALY	172-1011	SLOVAKIA	00-420-00101
CZECH REPUBLIC	00-420-00101	KENYA†	0800-10	S. AFRICA	0-800-99-0123
*DENMARK	8001-0010	*LIECHTENSTEIN	155-00-11	SPAIN•	900-99-00-11
*EGYPT¹ (CAIRO)	510-0200	LITHUANIA♦	8◇196	*SWEDEN	020-795-611
*FINLAND	9800-100-10	LUXEMBOURG	0-800-0111	*SWITZERLAND	155-00-11
FRANCE	19◇-0011	F.Y.R. MACEDONIA	99-800-4288	*TURKEY	00-800-12277
*GAMBIA	00111	*MALTA	0800-890-110	UKRAINE†	8◇100-11
GERMANY	0130-0010	*NETHERLANDS	06-022-9111	UK	0500-89-0011

Countries in bold face permit country-to-country calling in addition to calls to the U.S. **World Connect**℠ prices consist of **USADirect**® rates plus an additional charge based on the country you are calling. Collect calling available to the U.S. only. *Public phones require deposit of coin or phone card. ◇Await second dial tone. †May not be available from every phone. †††Public phones require local coin payment through the call duration. ♦Not available from public phones. • Calling available to most European countries. ¹Dial "02" first, outside Cairo. ²Dial 010-480-0111 from major Warsaw hotels. ©1994 AT&T.

Here's a travel tip that will make it easy to call back to the States. Dial the access number for the country you're visiting and connect right to AT&T. It's the quick way to get English-speaking AT&T operators and can minimize hotel telephone surcharges.

If all the countries you're visiting aren't listed above, call **1 800 241-5555** for a free wallet card with all AT&T access numbers. Easy international calling from AT&T. **TrueWorld Connections.**

August for boats heading to Great Blasket during the day, depending on the weather (no phone available for the boats). At the pier (signposted from the main road), you will see curraghs (open fishing boats traditionally made of animal hide stretched over wooden laths and tarred) stored upside down. These light canoes (covered in canvas nowadays) are walked to the sea on the heads of three or four men, their legs beneath making each boat look like an enormous black insect. Similar boats are used in the Aran Isles, and when properly handled they prove extraordinarily seaworthy. The pier is surrounded by cliffs of colored silurian rock, which is more than 400 million years old and rich in fossils.

Dunquin is at the center of the Gaeltacht, and it attracts many students of Irish language and folklore. It will be familiar to film buffs, as it was around here that *Ryan's Daughter* was filmed by David Lean in 1969. The movie production gave tourism its first major boost in the area, and its shooting is recalled with affection. The ruins of the film's schoolhouse can be found about ⅘ kilometer (½ mile) outside Dunquin. You will notice that some of its cut-stone features are actually made of fiberglass. Ask for directions to the building at Kruger's Pub.

Time Out **Kruger's Pub,** well signposted in the town, is the main social center of Dunquin. It has always been frequented by artists and writers—including Brendan Behan—and still is.

Between Dunquin and Ballyferriter the road skirts **Clogher Strand;** this is not a safe spot to swim, but it's a good place to watch the ocean pounding dramatically on the rocks when a storm is approaching or a gale is blowing. Overlooking the beach is Louis Mulcahy's pottery studio. Mulcahy is one of Ireland's leading ceramic artists, producing large pots and urns that are both decorative and functional; he has trained several local people to work in the studio. Visitors are welcome to watch the work in progress and to buy items at workshop prices. *Clogher Strand, tel. 066/56229. Open daily 9:30–6.*

68 **Ballyferriter,** another Irish-speaking town, is mainly a holiday village and a popular center for self-catering vacationers, many of them German or Dutch. Like much of the peninsula, this area is great for walking. A footpath off the road north out of Ballyferriter,
69 signposted Béal Bán, will lead you past a long sandy beach to **Dún an Óir** (the walk is about 2½ kilometers/1½ miles). To reach this former fort by car, take the Dunquin road and turn right after about ⅘ kilometer (½ mile), following signposts. The site was originally an Iron Age promontory fort, within which an invasion force of about 600 Spaniards and Italians built another fort in 1580. They came to support the Catholic Irish against the Protestant English. The English successfully bombarded the fort from land and sea, and they then slaughtered all survivors, including many innocent local inhabitants. Dún an Óir—which means "fort of gold" in Irish—is now largely obliterated, but folk memory of the massacre is so strong that a memorial was erected on the site in 1980. *Freely accessible.*

Return to the main road and go back through Ballyferriter, following signs for Ballydavid, to visit two of the many important early
70 Christian sites in the area. **Gallarus Oratory,** on the right-hand side of the main road, is one of the best preserved early Christian churches in the country, dating from the 7th or 8th century. Note the ingenious use of corbeling—successive levels of stone projecting inward from both side walls until they meet at the top to form an

unmortared roof. The structure is still watertight after more than a thousand years. *Freely accessible.*

71 **Kilmakedar Church,** 3 kilometers (2 miles) northeast of Gallarus, is one of the finest examples of Romanesque (Early Irish) architecture surviving. Although the Christian settlement dates from the 7th century, the present structure was built in the 12th century. Note how the native builders integrated foreign influences with their own local traditions, keeping the blank arcades and round headed windows, but using stone roofs, sloping doorway jambs, and weirdly sculpted heads. Ogham stones and other interestingly carved, possibly pre-Christian stones can be examined in the churchyard. *Freely accessible.*

72 The summit of **Mt. Brandon** (953 meters/3,127 feet) is away on the left as you cross the Connor Pass (*see below*), and is accessible only to walkers. Do not attempt the climb in misty weather. The easiest way to make the climb is to follow the old pilgrims' path, the Saint's Road; it starts at Kilmakedar Church and rises to the summit from Ballybrack, which is the end of the road for cars. At the summit, visitors will reach the ruins of an early Christian settlement. The top can also be approached from a path that starts just beyond Cloghane (signposted left on descending the Connor Pass); the latter climb is longer and more strenuous.

From Kilmakedar, return to Dingle on the well-signposted main
73 road, then head north across the **Connor Pass,** a mountain route that passes over the center of the peninsula and offers magnificent views of Brandon Bay, Tralee Bay, and the beaches of North Kerry, with Dingle Bay in the south. It was from Brandon Bay that Brendan the Navigator (AD 487–577) is believed to have set off on his famous voyages in a specially constructed curragh. On his third trip it is possible that he reached Newfoundland or Labrador, then Florida. He was the inspiration for many voyagers, including Christopher Columbus.

The main road to Tralee is signposted right at Kilcummin, and runs just inland of Brandon Bay and Tralee Bay, giving glimpses of the latter's long sandy beach at Camp. One approaches Tralee across an uninteresting plain, distinguished only by the black and white sails
74 of the newly restored windmill at **Blennerville.** The surrounding buildings have been turned into an extensive visitors center with craft workshops, an audiovisual history of the windmill, and an exhibition recalling Blennerville's past as Kerry's major 19th-century emigration port. *Tel. 066/21064. Admission: £2.50 adults, £2 students and senior citizens, £1.50 children. Open Apr.–Oct., daily 10–5.*

There is also a very popular trip on a steam railway that departs from Blennerville every half hour and from Tralee every half hour from April through September. *Cost: £2.50 adults, £2 students and senior citizens, £1.50 children, £6.50 family ticket. Tel. 066/27777 for off-season timetable.*

Tour 4: North Kerry and Shannonside

Because of their proximity to Shannon Airport, the gateway to Ireland for transatlantic visitors, North Kerry and Shannonside have many more formally organized attractions than the rest of the Southwest. For the visitor, the area's well-restored castles help compensate for the lack of dramatic scenery. This tour takes in the north of County Kerry, the city of Limerick, and those parts of

Counties Limerick and Clare that border the estuary of the River Shannon.

75 **Tralee** is County Kerry's largest town, with a population of about 16,500. This busy yet unprepossessing place has long been associated with the popular Irish song "The Rose of Tralee," the inspiration for the annual Rose of Tralee International Festival. Irish communities from around the world send young women to join native Irish competitors; one of them is chosen as the "Rose of Tralee." Festival week, the last in August, attracts musicians and entertainers from all over the country, and it coincides with a horse race, so the town is always packed with people. Tralee is also the home of **Siamsa Tíre**—the folk theater of Ireland; it is worth stopping here to catch one of the theater's lively and colorful productions (*see* The Arts, *below*).

Kerry County Museum, in the Ashe Memorial Hall houses two exhibits. On the first floor, Kerry the Kingdom traces the history of Kerry's people from 5000 BC to the present using dioramas and an entertaining and informative audiovisual show. In the basement, Geraldine Tralee: The Irish Medieval Experience, enables the visitor to travel by "time-car" (an electric buggy), equipped with special lighting, sound, and odor effects, through a life-size reconstruction of Tralee in the Middle Ages (when it was under the Anglo-Norman Fitzgeralds, hence "Geraldine"). The time-car tour takes about 15 minutes; allow at least an hour for the first-floor exhibits. *Tel. 066/27777. Admission: £3.50 adults, £3 students and senior citizens, £2 children. Open Mon.–Sat. 10–6 (until 8 in Aug.).*

From Tralee, you can take the N69 road, which runs along a plain at the base of the Stack's Mountain, for 27 kilometers (16 miles) to **Listowel,** a small, sleepy market town that only really comes alive for its horse race during the third week of September.

Time Out Writer **John B. Keane** (author of *The Field,* which was made into a film starring John Hurt and Richard Harris) owns the bar that bears his name in the town center. As one would expect, Keane is a great raconteur.

A detour to the left at Listowel on the R553 will take you to the seaside resort of **Ballybunion,** famous for its long sandy beach and championship golf course. The main route along the N69 leads to **Tarbert** (18 kilometers/11 miles) on the Shannon estuary. This is the terminus for the ferry to Killimer in West Clare, a convenient 20-minute shortcut if you're heading for the west of Ireland. The **Shannon,** with a length of 273 kilometers (170 miles), is the longest river in Ireland or Britain. The magnificent estuary, in front of you at this point, stretches westward for a further 96 kilometers (60 miles) before reaching the sea.

76 The N69 continues up the Shannon estuary to **Glin** (5 kilometers/3 miles) and the first of several castles on the itinerary. A Fitz-Gerald castle at Glin, right on the banks of the Shannon, has been standing here for more than 700 years. The present knight of Glin, Desmond Fitzgerald, is a keen campaigner for the Irish heritage, and a well-known figure in the country's artistic circles. The current castle dates only from 1785; crenellations and Gothic details were added to the house in the 1820s to make it look more like an ancestral home. The neoclassical hall features elaborate plasterwork with a ceiling painted in the original red and green; the hall opens onto an imposing double staircase. The house also has a unique collection of 18th-century Irish furniture. *Tel. 068/34173. Admission: £2 adults, 50p*

children. Open May, daily 10–noon and 2–4; other times by appointment.

Foynes, which is 9 kilometers (5½ miles) up the N69, was the landing place for transatlantic air traffic in the 1930s and '40s. The famous flying boats landed here to refuel before heading on to their European destinations, carrying a diverse range of people, from celebrities to refugees. The town's museum, a must for aviation buffs, recalls the recent history of flying with a range of exhibits and an audiovisual show. *Tel. 069/65416. Admission: £2 adults, £1 children. Open Mar. 31–Oct. 31, daily 10–6.*

The N69 continues to Limerick through **Askeaton,** where the ruins of a 15th-century Desmond stronghold almost cover a rocky islet on the River Deel. On the banks of the river are the well-preserved ruins of a 15th-century Franciscan friary. *Freely accessible.*

Just beyond Askeaton, turn right on the R518 for Rathkeale and
77 Adare. **Castle Matrix,** in **Rathkeale,** dates from 1440, when it was in possession of the earls of Desmond. Confiscated by Elizabeth I, the castle served as a meeting place for the poet Edmund Spenser and Walter Raleigh when they were young and not yet famous. Raleigh subsequently brought the first potato tubers from North Carolina to Castle Matrix, from where they were distributed throughout south Munster (the old provincial name for the region). In 1962, the late Colonel Sean O'Driscoll, an American architect, bought Castle Matrix and restored it. The library, which serves as the headquarters of the Irish Heraldry Society, has an interesting collection of documents relating to the "Wild Geese," Irish mercenaries who served in European armies in the 17th and 18th centuries. *Tel. 069/64284. Admission: £3 adults, £1.50 children. Open May 15–Sept. 15, Sat.–Tues. 1–5.*

78 **Adare** is a lovely village with several thatched cottages amid wooded surroundings on the banks of the River Maigue. The village is also rich in ruins; on foot, you can locate the remains of two 13th-century abbeys, a 15th-century friary, and the keep of a 13th-century Desmond castle.

Beyond Adare, the N21 merges with the N20, which goes straight to
79 the center of **Limerick** (16 kilometers/10 miles), the third-largest city of the Republic, with a population of about 57,000. Oddly enough, no connection at all exists between the city and the facetious five-line verse form known as a limerick.

Like most Irish coastal towns, Limerick was originally a 9th-century Danish settlement. In 1691, the Irish retreated to the walled city of Limerick after the Battle of the Boyne. They were besieged by William of Orange, who made three unsuccessful attempts to storm the city but then raised the siege and marched away. A year later, another of William's armies overtook the city for two months, and the Irish opened negotiations. The resulting Treaty of Limerick was never ratified—it guaranteed religious tolerance—and 11,000 men of the Limerick garrison joined the French army rather than fight in a Protestant "Irish" army. These events and other colorful episodes from Limerick's history are the subject of a 45-minute son-et-lumière show at **St. Mary's Cathedral** on Bridge Street. The cathedral itself, once a 12th-century palace, features pilasters and a rounded Romanesque entrance that were part of the original structure. Take a close look at the grotesque black oak carvings on the 15th-century misericords in the choir stalls. *Admission to show: £2.50. mid-June–Sept. 15, nightly at 7 and 9:15. No advance booking needed.*

Nicholas Street, behind the cathedral, leads to Castle Street and the entrance to the newly restored **King John's Castle,** built by the Normans in the 13th century. Its north side still bears traces of the 1691 bombardment. If you climb the drum towers, you'll have a good view of the town and the Shannon. Inside, a 22-minute audiovisual slide show illustrates the history of Limerick and Ireland, an archaeology center has three newly excavated pre-Norman houses, and two exhibition centers display three-dimensional models of Limerick's history from its foundation in AD 922. *Tel. 061/411201. Admission: £3.20 adults, £1.60 students and children. Open Apr.–Sept., daily 9:30–5; Oct.–Mar., Sat. and Sun. 9:30–5.*

The old part of Limerick is in this area around the cathedral and the castle, dominated by mid-18th-century buildings with fine Georgian proportions. One of these structures, The Granary, built in 1774 for grain storage, is now the office of the **Limerick Regional Archives** (Michael St., tel. 061/410777), which, for a small fee, provides a genealogical research service. The main shopping area, which consists mostly of modest chain stores, lies a three- or four-minute walk to the south on O'Connell Street.

Time Out Just off O'Connell Street, on Honan's Quay, is the **Dolmen Gallery** (tel. 061/417929), which specializes in exhibits of contemporary Irish art; it also has a very pleasant restaurant that serves tasty, healthy, home-cooked food. *Open Mon.–Sat. 10–5:30.*

---

80 Limerick's university grounds are situated at **Plassey** on the outskirts of the city. The drive there is worth taking (five–10 minutes on the Ring road signposted Dublin N7) to visit the **Hunt Collection,** located on this small, but nicely landscaped campus. The museum, recently relocated to the new Foundation Building, contains the finest collection of Celtic and medieval treasures outside the National Museum in Dublin. European objets d'art are featured, as well as ancient Irish metalwork. There is also a good selection of Irish landscape paintings and the National Watercolour Collection. Note the full-scale copy of Leonardo da Vinci's *Flying Man* in the lobby. *Tel. 061/333644. Admission: £2 adults, £1 children. Open May–Sept., Mon.–Sat. 10–5.*

The N18 between Limerick and Shannon Airport is one of the best stretches of road in Ireland—but visitors will soon discover that four-lane highways are quite rare. Shannon Airport is 16 kilometers (10 miles) from Limerick. On the road to the airport is **Bunratty Castle and Folk Park** (16 kilometers/10 miles west of Limerick), one of those rare attractions that appeals to all age groups and manages to be both educational and fun.

81 **Bunratty Castle,** built in 1460, has been fully restored and decorated with 15th- to 17th-century furniture and furnishings. It gives a wonderful insight into the life of those times. As you pass under the walls of Bunratty, look for the three "murder holes," which allowed defenders to pour boiling oil on attackers below.

Bunratty Folk Park in the castle grounds, which re-creates a 19th-century village street, has examples of the traditional rural housing of the region. The park is every bit as quaint as some first-time visitors expect all of modern Ireland to be. The exhibits include a working blacksmith's forge; demonstrations of flour milling, bread making, candle making, thatching, and other traditional skills; and a variety of farm animals in reconstructed small holdings, complete with farmyard smells. An adjacent museum of agricultural machinery cannot compete with the furry and feathered live exhibits. *Tel.*

*061/361511. Admission: £4.10 adults, £3.75 students and senior citizens, £2 children. Open Sept.–May, daily 9:30–5:30 (last admission 4:15); June–Aug., daily 9:30–7 (last admission 6). Medieval banquets are held at the castle twice nightly (*see *Nightlife*, below*).*

Time Out No visit to Bunratty is complete without a drink in **Durty Nelly's** (tel. 061/364072) next door, a famous Old World pub that has inspired imitations around the world.

Shannon Airport is signposted to your left shortly after Bunratty, but if you have time before leaving, we suggest turning right at this crossroads. Take the R471 to Sixmilebridge and then turn left on to the R462 and left again at Kilmurry to the R469 for Quin and two more attractions.

82 **Knappogue Castle** at Quin is a 15th-century MacNamara stronghold that has been extensively restored and furnished in the 15th-century style. The castle, also a venue for medieval-style banquets, looks spectacular when floodlit. *Tel. 061/368103. Admission: £2.40 adults, £1.60 children. Open May–Sept., daily 9:30–4:30.*

Signposted off the road back to Sixmilebridge about 10 kilometers (6
83 miles) from Quin is the **Craggaunowen Project.** Craggaunowen Castle, a 16th-century tower house, has been restored with furnishings from the period. Especially notable are the two authentic replicas of early Celtic-style dwelling places that have been constructed on the castle grounds. On an island in the lake, reached by a narrow footbridge, is a clay-and-wattle *crannóg*, a fortified lake dwelling; it resembles what might have been built in the 6th or 7th century when Celtic influence was still predominant in Ireland. The reconstruction of a small ring fort shows how an ordinary farmer would have lived in the 5th or 6th century, at the time when Christianity was being established. Tools, cooking utensils, and a cooking pit are featured in this peaceful, open-air exhibit. Guides will explain the Iron Age (500 BC–AD 450) field system, which is stocked with animals, while crafts workers demonstrate skills from bygone ages. It is a strange experience to walk across the little wooden bridge above reeds rippling in the lake into Ireland's Celtic past as a jumbo jet passes overhead on its way into Shannon Airport—1,500 years of history compressed into an instant. *Tel. 061/367178. Admission: £3.10 adults, £1.80 children. Open Mar.–Oct., daily 10–6.*

Off the Beaten Track

Anne's Grove Gardens, near Castletownroche in north County Cork (midway between Mallow and Fermoy on the N72), were inspired by the ideas of William Robinson, a 19th-century gardener who favored naturalistic planting. Exotic foliage plants border paths winding down to the river; magnificent magnolias and vast numbers of naturalized primulas are among the plants on view. *Tel. 022/26145. Admission: £2 adults, £1 children and senior citizens. Open Easter–Sept., weekdays 10–5, weekends 1–6.*

The Beara Peninsula is the one part of the Southwest that most visitors leave out. For a wonderful whole-day scenic drive, turn left at Glengarriff and head south on R572 along the peninsula's edge. You'll have views across Kenmare Bay to the Sheep's Head Peninsula. Pass through Castletownbere, stopping just beyond it at the ruins of **Dunboy Castle and House** (open Easter–Oct., daily 10–7). Then follow signposts for **Dursey Island,** a bird-watcher's paradise, which is still inhabited, but only accessible by cable car. (Cost: 50p.

Open Mon.–Sat. 9, 11, 2:30, and 5; July–Aug., also 7 PM and 8 PM. For Sunday times, tel. 027/73016.) Return via **Allihies,** where a detour takes you along a precipitous and breathtaking coastal road to **Eyeries,** and then up the edge of the Kenmare River to Kenmare.

Riverstown House, 6 kilometers (4 miles) from Cork on the Dublin road (N20), has been restored with the help of the Georgian Society. It is mainly noted for allegorical plasterwork carried out by the Italian Francini brothers in 1734 and the rococo flowers and foliage adorning the dining room walls. The house is attractively furnished with period furniture. *Tel. 021/821205. Admission: £1.50. Open May–Sept., Thurs.–Sat. 2–6; other times by appointment.*

Shopping

Shopaholics risk severe withdrawal symptoms in the Southwest. Outside Cork City, visitors are faced mostly with crafts and sweaters, and most tourist-oriented crafts shops carry the same lines. The suggestions below should help you to find something a little different. (All shops are in Cork City unless otherwise stated.)

Specialty Stores

Antiques For country-style furniture, try **The Pine Pitch** (Emmet Pl., tel. 021/273131) or **Old Furniture Warehouse** (35 Hanover St. tel. 021/276082). For Georgian and Victorian furniture and objects, go to **Monica's** (24 Oliver Plunkett St., tel. 021/271118). Interesting jewelry, Victoriana, and period clothes can be found at **Victoria's** (2 Oliver Plunkett St., tel. 021/272752). For general bygones and curiosities, try **O'Regan's Antiques** (27 Lavitt's Quay, tel. 021/272902). In Bunratty, have a look at **Mike McGlynn Antiques** (tel. 061/364294); in Kinsale try **Victoria Murphy** (Market Quay, tel. 021/774317).

Clothing Oliver Plunkett Street and the Paul Street area remain the best bets for clothing in Cork. Try **Richard Alan** (63 Oliver Plunkett St., tel. 021/273759), **Monica John** (13 French Church St., tel. 021/271399), or **Betty Barclay** (64 Oliver Plunkett St., tel. 021/276323) for sophisticated and expensive styling. Younger and cheaper fashions can be found at **Red Square** (8 Paul St., tel. 021/271716) and **Moderne** (89 Patrick St., tel. 021/270266). In Kenmare, **Nostalgia** (27 Henry St., tel. 064/41389) has a good selection of antique lace and linen.

Rainwear **The House of Donegal** (6 Paul St., tel. 021/272447) carries classic rainwear for men and women that should last a lifetime. For more casual weatherproof clothing, try **The Tack Room** (Academy St., tel. 021/272704); for inexpensive rainwear, go to **Penney's** (27 Patrick St., tel. 021/271935) or the main street "drapery store" in any small town.

Sportswear **Matthews** (Academy St., tel. 021/277633) and **Great Outdoors** (23 Paul St., tel. 021/276382) cater to most needs.

Tweeds The best tweed comes from Donegal, and the **House of Donegal** (6 Paul St., tel. 021/272447) features a good stock of it. The shop sells both men's and women's ready-to-wear and made-to-measure, which they will ship home to you.

Crystal **Cash's** (18 Patrick St., tel. 021/276771) has a good selection of Waterford glass, as does **Blarney Woolen Mills** (Blarney, tel. 021/385280). **Kinsale Crystal** (Market St., Kinsale, tel. 021/774463) is a master cutter's studio that sells 100% Irish mouth-blown, hand-cut crystal.

For striking modern uncut crystal, try the **House of James** (10 Paul St., tel. 021/272324).

Irish Crafts For the very best in modern design, check out the **House of James** (10 Paul St., tel. 021/272324). This shop carries Stephen Pearce's tableware and bowls; you can also take a trip to his studio and buy at workshop prices (Kilmahon, Shanagarry, near Cloyne, Co. Cork, tel. 021/646807). **Blarney Woolen Mills** (Blarney, tel. 021/385280) has the largest stock and the most turnover of crafts in the country. The mills sell everything from Irish-made high fashion to Aran handknits to leprechaun key rings. They also have an outlet in Killarney (10–11 Main St., tel. 064/33222). **Boland's** (Pearse St., Kinsale, tel. 021/772161) features some unusual items, including exclusive sweaters, designer rainwear, and linen shirts. **Keane on Ceramics** (Pier Rd., Kinsale, tel. 021/772085) is a gallery that represents the best of the southwest's ceramic artists. Lisbeth Mulcahy at **The Weaver's Shop** (Green St., Dingle, tel. 066/51688) sells outstanding handwoven, vegetable-dyed woolen wraps, mufflers, and skirt lengths. **Louis Mulcahy**'s pottery (at Clogher, near Dingle, tel. 066/56229) sells tableware and decorative bowls and urns. **Peter Wolstenholme** (Pottery Workshop, Courtmacsherry, Co. Cork, tel. 023/46239) produces decorated tableware and witty ceramic objects. The most reliable crafts shops in Killarney are on Main Street and High Street; they all carry a standard range of crystal, handknits, T-shirts, sweatshirts, and tweed hats.

Sports and the Outdoors

Outdoor activities are very much a way of life in the Southwest, and, like everything else around the region, such activities are undertaken casually and informally, with a minimum of organization.

Participant Sports

Bicycling You'll find some of the most spectacular scenery in the country around Glengarriff, Killarney, and Dingle. The length of the hills—rather than their steepness—is the challenge here, but without the hills there wouldn't be such great views. A less strenuous option, equally scenic, but on a smaller scale, is the coast of West Cork between Kinsale and Glengarriff (*see* Tour 2, *above*). The Beara Peninsula proves very popular with cyclists who enjoy its varied coastal scenery and relative lack of traffic. (Avoid the long hairpin bends of the Healy Pass unless you are a committed thrill-seeker). Traffic can be a problem in July and August on the Ring of Kerry, where there is a lack of alternative routes to the one main circuit. Because of the various mountain ranges in the area, rain is never far off, except on the hottest summer days, so always carry a light waterproof jacket. Tours 2, 3, and 4 in this chapter are all suitable for cyclists. The Irish Tourist Board publication, *Cycling Ireland* (cost: £2), suggests six other bicycling circuits that can be made in the region.

For bicycle rentals, expect to pay about £7 per day, or £30 for seven days, with a £30 refundable deposit. Bicycles may be rented at the following establishments. **Blarney: Tony McGrath** (Stoneview, tel. 021/385658); **Cork: The Bike Store** (Isaac's, 48 McCurtain St., tel. 021/505339); **Dingle: John Moriarty** (Main St., tel. 066/51316); **Killarney: O'Callaghan Bros.** (College St., tel. 064/31465); **Limerick: Crescent Cycles** (St. Nessan Rd., tel. 061/227387); **Skibbereen: N.W. Roycroft** (Ilen St., tel. 028/21235); **Tralee: E. Caball** (15 Ashe St., tel. 066/22231).

Fishing Besides an abundance of facilities for sea angling and a wealth of salmon and trout rivers, the Southwest has the bonus of scenic surroundings—be it the black slate cliffs of the coast or the lush vegetation of Killarney and the Ring of Kerry. The deep-sea fishing season runs from April to October. Boat rental costs about £20 per person per day. Shore fishing is available all along the coast, from Cobh in the east to Foynes in the west. The whole region offers excellent opportunities for lake and river fishing, although most anglers head for Waterville or Killarney. Trout fishing has been disappointing recently, especially in the Waterville area, due to sea-lice infestation. Every effort is being made to ensure a good season in 1995, but check with Killarney's Tourist Information Office or the Irish Tourist Board if trout fishing is the prime purpose of your visit. Boats can be hired at Ballycotton, Cork Harbour in Cobh, Midleton, Passage West, Crosshaven, Kinsale, Courtmacsherry, Clonakilty, Castletownshend, Valentia Island, Fenit, and Dingle. Your hotel or the local Tourist Information Office can suggest places that rent boats. The latter will also recommend locations for coarse and game fishing. Coarse anglers will find pike at Macroom and coarse angling facilities at Mallow and Fermoy. Fishing tackle, bait, and licenses can be obtained at **The Cycle Center** (Thomond Shopping Center, Roxboro, Limerick, tel. 061/44900), **O'Neill's** (Plunkett St., Killarney, tel. 064/31970), and **T.W. Murray** (87 Patrick St., Cork, tel. 021/271089).

Golf The Southwest offers a great variety of 18-hole courses, many of them world-famous championship clubs set amid wonderful scenery. Greens fees average around £18 for a full day—£45 for the major championship courses. Professionals charge about £12 for 30 minutes of instruction. Bring your own clubs: They are not generally available for rental, and not all courses provide golf carts.

Cork Golf Club at Little Island is considered to be the most challenging in the county. The clubs in Waterville and Ballybunion in County Kerry are tricky but highly praised seaside links. Killarney Golf and Fishing Club is unsurpassed for its lake and mountain scenery. Because some clubs cannot welcome visitors on weekends or on competition days, it is best to phone ahead. The following is a selection of the available 18-hole courses.

Cork City: Douglas Golf Club (Douglas, tel. 021/891086); **Cork Golf Club** (Little Island, tel. 021/353451); **Harbour Point Golf Club,** (Clash Rd., Little Island, tel. 021/353094); **Lee Valley Golf Club** (Clashanure, Ovens, tel. 021/331721); **Monkstown Golf Club** (Parkgarriffe, Monkstown, tel. 021/841376); **Muskerry Golf Club** (Carrigrohane, near Blarney, tel. 021/385297). **County Cork: Macroom Golf Club** (Lackadue, Macroom, tel. 026/41072); **Mallow Golf Club** (Ballyellis, Mallow, tel. 022/21145); **Skibbereen and West Carbery Golf Club** (Licknavar, Skibbereen, tel. 028/21227); **Youghal Golf Club** (Knocknaveny, Youghal, tel. 024/92787). **County Kerry: Waterville Golf Club** (Ring of Kerry, tel. 066/74102); **Killarney Golf and Fishing Club** (Killorglin Rd., Killarney, tel. 064/31242); **Tralee Golf Club** (Barrow, Ardfert, Tralee, tel. 066/36379); **Ballybunion Golf Club** (Ballybunion, tel. 068/27146). **County Limerick: Adare Manor Golf Club** (Adare Manor, tel. 061/396204); **Shannon Golf Club** (near Shannon Airport, Co. Clare, tel. 061/471020); **Limerick Golf Club,** (Ballyneety, tel. 061/351881).

Health and Fitness Clubs Leisure centers are a new but fast-growing phenomenon in the region, and facilities are constantly being upgraded. Most hotels like to reserve their facilities for guests and local club members. Exceptions are listed below. Expect to pay up to £4 for the use of the pool, about £6 if access to a sauna and a gymnasium is included in the price. Aerobics classes cost about £2 an hour; tennis and squash courts start from £2.50.

Gleneagle Country Club (Muckross Rd., Killarney, tel. 064/31870) provides an indoor pool, a sauna, two tennis courts, and four squash courts. **Jury's Hotel Leisure Center** (Western Rd., Cork, tel. 021/507533) has an indoor/outdoor pool, a sauna, a Jacuzzi, two tennis courts, and one squash court open to the public until 5 PM. **Jury's Hotel Leisure Center** (Ennis Rd., Limerick, tel. 061/327777) features an indoor pool, a sauna, a Jacuzzi, a steam room, a gymnasium, and one tennis court. **Silver Springs Activity Center** (Silver Springs Hotel, Tivoli, Cork, tel. 021/507533) offers an indoor pool, a sauna, a steam bath, a Jacuzzi, two squash courts, and three tennis courts (two indoor, one outdoor and floodlit). **Brookfields Health and Leisure Complex** (College Rd., Cook, tel. 021/344032) is a new addition to the university's campus and has indoor pools, gym, sauna, and aerobics room. **Skellig Hotel** (Dingle, Co. Kerry, tel. 066/51144) has an indoor pool, a sauna, and one tennis court. **Westlodge Hotel** (Bantry, Co. Cork, tel. 027/50360) has an indoor pool, a sauna, two squash courts, one tennis court, and pitch and putt.

Hiking This is classic hiking country, particularly in the far southwest around Killarney and Dingle, with superlative scenery and a feeling of wilderness (even though you're never more than 2 or 3 miles away from civilization). On higher ground, fog can come down very quickly, so take local advice on weather conditions and adjust your schedule accordingly.

Two signposted long-distance trails for walkers are available in the region, the **Kerry Way,** which begins in Killarney and loops around the Ring of Kerry (209 kilometers/130 miles), and the **Dingle Way,** which loops from Tralee around the Dingle peninsula (153 kilometers/95 miles). Both routes consist of paths and "green roads" (unsurfaced) with some stretches linked by surfaced roads. In general, these routes, although rough underfoot, are suitable for families, particularly in summer. Details on the trails are available on free information sheets from the Irish Tourist Board, Sheet 26C for the Kerry Way and Sheet 26G for the Dingle Way. Other good off-the-highway walks can be found in **Killarney National Park; Gougane Barra** (northeast of Ballylickey off the R584), **Farran** (off the N22 about 10 miles west of Cork City), and **Doneraile Forest** (off the N20 about 5 miles north of Mallow) parks in County Cork; and **Currachase Forest Park** (east of Askeaton off the N69), County Limerick.

Horseback Riding Top quality racehorses and eventers are bred on the limestone pastures of Limerick and north Cork, and the serious equestrian will find some exciting and challenging animals in these counties. Hunts in Counties Cork and Limerick generally welcome visitors: Ask your riding stable for an introduction. In Kerry the bloodstock is traditionally more work-a-day. Horses and ponies can be hired by the hour; expect to pay from £6 per hour, increasing with the quality of the horse, about £12 if lesson is included. For trekking, the half-day rate is about £18 (rising to £30 in Killarney), which should include a guide or trek leader and the hire of a hat.

County Cork: Clonmeen Lodge (Banteer, tel. 029/56238); **Skevanish Riding Center** (Innishannon, tel. 021/775476); **Hitchmough Riding School** (Highland Lodge, Monkstown, near Cork City, tel. 021/371267); **Pinegrove Riding School** (White's Cross, near Cork City, tel. 021/303857). **County Kerry: Rocklands Stables** (Rockfield, Tralee Rd., Killarney, tel. 064/32592); **El Rancho Horse Holidays,** with four- and seven-day treks on Dingle Peninsula (Ballyard, Tralee, tel. 066/21840); **Killarney Riding Stables Ltd.**, with four- and seven-day treks in Killarney National Park, with accommodation (Ballydowney, Killarney, tel. 064/31686). **County Limerick: Adare Equestrian Center** (Clongownagh, Kidimo Rd., Adare, tel. 061/396373); **Clarina Riding Center** (Clarina, tel. 061/353087).

Jogging Most people use secondary roads because they have very little traffic, especially before 8 AM. The many long sandy beaches in the region are also popular with runners.

Water Sports

Bare-Boat Charters The sailing season runs from March to October for hardy souls (mainly into racing) who do not mind the need for full wet gear. More sybaritic types limit their season to June, July, and August, when the weather is more clement, and the sun more likely to shine. This is an excellent coast for yachting if you like the old-fashioned way of dropping anchor in a sheltered harbor without a previous booking. Marinas will be found only in Crosshaven, Kinsale, and East Ferry. Because of the demands of Irish insurance laws, boat charter is still in its infancy here, with only one company in business (*see below*). For the same reasons, dinghy hire is not very widespread, and you will need to demonstrate your competence. In comparison, sailboards are relatively easy to hire. Wetsuits are essential for sailboarding except on the hottest days in July and August and can also be hired.

The average cost of a four-berth yacht between 8½ meters and 10½ meters (28 and 35 feet) ranges from £120 per person per week (low season) to £150 (high season). Contact **Yachting International Ireland** (c/o Trident Hotel, Kinsale, Co. Cork, tel. 021/772927, fax 021/77470) for bare-boat charters.

Boardsailing and Dinghy Sailing The **Oysterhaven Boardsailing Center** (Oysterhaven, near Kinsale, Co. Cork, tel. 021/770738) offers tuition and hire of all equipment, including wet suits, from about £9 per hour. Sailing dinghies as well as sailboards can be hired by the hour (from about £6) or by the day (from about £20) from the following companies, which also offer tuition and residential courses: **Glénans Irish Sailing Club** (head office: 28 Merrion Sq., Dublin, tel. 01/611481) at Castletownbere, Co. Cork; **International Sailing Center** (5 E. Beach, Cobh, Co. Cork, tel. 021/811237); **Baltimore Sailing School** (The Pier, Baltimore, Co. Cork, tel. 028/20141).

Spectator Sports

Gaelic Games Gaelic football and hurling are fast-moving games that generate great excitement. The county finals are held early July in Cork City at Pairc Ui Chaiomh, but tickets are not easy to come by. Ask about more easily accessible local Gaelic Athletics Association (GAA) events at Tourist Information Offices.

Horse Racing The Southwest is good racing country and the breeding ground for many a National Hunt steeplechase winner. Plenty of small lively meetings provide a good day out. **Killarney** sponsors races that are held during early May and mid-July, **Tralee** has races in late August, and **Listowel** in late September. During the summer, two or three evening meetings a year take place at **Limerick** and **Mallow.**

Road Bowling Quite unrelated to 10-pin bowling, this outdoor sport, unique to Counties Cork and Armagh, is played on quiet stretches of back roads. Two players compete by throwing a heavy iron ball, either underhand or overhand, along the road for a distance of about a mile.

The lowest number of throws wins. Betting is complicated and the stakes can be high, which leads to much leaping and cheering, as well as a celebration afterwards in a nearby pub. Ask about bowling in any country pub, or look for listings in the classified ads of Saturday's *Cork Examiner*.

Sailboat Racing Small regattas, consisting of inshore and offshore sailing races, rowing races, swimming races, and local variations, such as curragh racing (Dingle) or salmon-boat racing (Kinsale), take place all along the coast during the summer. These lighthearted events are fun to watch and provide plenty of ad hoc entertainment. Kinsale and Dingle start the season on the August Bank Holiday (the first Monday in August), and Schull, Baltimore, Bantry, Cobh, Glandore, Lough Ine, and Castletownshend share the remaining August weekends. Details are available from local Tourist Information Offices.

Dining and Lodging

Dining

There was a time in southwest Ireland when diners could choose only between old-fashioned hotel restaurants serving plain roast meat or boiled fish, or unlicensed tearooms offering a high tea of cold meat, bread and butter, and cakes. Today the dining scene is diverse enough to suit all tastes. This region pioneered a phenomenon known as "the front parlour restaurant," which is typically operated by the owner-chef and his or her spouse. This kind of establishment usually begins in one room in the family home, often a room that was previously a shop or bar. The space is converted into a four- or five-table restaurant, with a small menu featuring fresh local produce cooked Continental style, accompanied by a small selection of wines. If the customer response is good, within a few years more rooms are converted for dining or larger premises are taken.

Some of the leading chefs in the region are French- or Swiss-trained, often having learned their trade in a fine restaurant abroad before setting up business at home. The result has become known as Hiberno-French or Franco-Irish cuisine; traditional Irish dishes are prepared using fresh local produce, influenced by both classical French cooking and nouvelle cuisine techniques.

The outstanding quality of local meat, game, and seafood is enhanced by sauces making subtle use of the rich cream and butter of the region in combination with leeks, mushrooms, sorrel and other herbs, and wines. Salads and vegetables still tend to be a weak point in the meal because most salad ingredients and vegetables must be imported. Similarly, desserts, apart from those making use of fresh cream, are often disappointing.

Very few restaurants in southwest Ireland require jacket and tie or fancy dresses at dinner. Unless it is specified below, rest assured that you will feel entirely at ease with your own interpretation of "casual but neat." In July and August and on weekends from May to October, these places operate under considerable pressure, and it is essential to book a table in advance. Be patient with delays and junior front-of-house staff, who are often catering students obtaining their first work experience.

Category	Cost*
$$$	over £25
$$	£15–£25
$	under £15

**per person for appetizer, main course, and dessert, excluding drinks and 10% tip*

Lodging

Accommodations in the Southwest include some of the best country-house hotels in the country, and many more modest establishments with spectacular seaside locations, where you'll receive excellent value. The region also offers reliable modern hotels with unremarkable decor and some delightfully renovated old-fashioned hotels.

Country-house hotels may appear very grand at first sight, but their main aim is to provide a relaxed stay in beautiful surroundings. A good pair of walking boots and a sensible raincoat are more useful here than a formal wardrobe. If you want to dress for dinner, as some people do, then an outfit suitable for a smart lunch in a large city is more than good enough. Elsewhere, informality is the order of the day.

Facilities have improved greatly over the last 10 years, but perhaps not enough to impress some first-time visitors. Only expensive hotels have fitness centers. However, most hotels can organize golf, deep-sea fishing, freshwater angling, and horseback riding. Bed-and-breakfasts are gradually introducing private bathrooms and, in the larger towns, televisions and direct-dial phones in rooms. The absence of a television or phone is indicated under *Facilities* below, as is the absence of an elevator in hotels with more than two stories.

Few hotels have coffee shops, but in general you can order tea or coffee and a sandwich or light snack at the bar. Bear in mind that, if you choose a B&B or guest house without a bar or restaurant, such provisions rest entirely on the goodwill of your host.

Accommodations in West Cork, Killarney, and Dingle are seasonal: Between November and March, choice is very limited. Outside these months, especially from July to mid-October, hotels are busy, so be sure to book well in advance. Hosts in this region are friendly, and there is a lack of cutthroat competition among them: If your first choice is booked up, ask the hotel to recommend some similar lodging nearby.

Category	Cost*
$$$$	over £140
$$$	£100–£140
$$	£70–£100
$	under £70

**All prices are for a standard double room.*

Highly recommended restaurants and hotels in a city or town are indicated by a star ★.

Adare

Dining ★

Mustard Seed. Fresh flowers adorn the tables of this chic little restaurant in a modest late-Victorian house among the thatched cottages of the village's main street. Chef-owner Dan Mullane's Irish kitchen produces imaginative, healthy cooking with such daily vegetarian specials as nut roast with fresh tomato *coulis*. Such unusual dishes as shark steak add variety to a menu that also includes roast free-range duckling and roast rack of lamb. *Main St., Adare, Co. Limerick, tel. 061/396451. Reservations advised. AE, DC, MC, V. Wine license only. Dinner only. Closed Sun.–Mon. and Feb. $$$*

Lodging ★

Adare Manor. This vast Victorian edifice, surrounded by a 1,000-acre riverside estate, is a short walk from the village. Until 1988, this enormous country-house hotel was the home of the earls of Dunraven. Its Gothic interior has vast stone arches, tall mullioned windows, heavy Flemish wood carvings, and elaborately decorated ceilings with hanging crystal chandeliers. Grandeur and opulence reign here on a large scale; it is well worth visiting just for a drink in the Tack Room (with music nightly in the summer) and a peek, if you can't pay the hotel rates. The bedrooms are every bit as splendid as the public rooms: More than 50 of them have individually carved fireplaces, and some of the "staterooms" are bigger than the entire ground floor of an ordinary hotel. All rooms have super-king-size beds, fabulous drapes and carpets, and enormous, mostly Victorian antiques that are painstakingly carved and ornamented. Try Room 203 with its elaborate vaulted, molded ceiling, or Room 301, which has 15-foot-tall stone-mullioned windows. *Adare, Co. Limerick, tel. 061/396566, fax 061/396124. 64 rooms with bath. Facilities: restaurant (jacket and tie preferred), 2 bars, indoor pool, sauna, gymnasium, horseback riding, tennis court, fox hunting by arrangement, clay-pigeon shooting, 9-hole golf course, fishing, helipad. AE, DC, MC, V. $$$$*

Dunraven Arms. This two-story Victorian inn in the village center positively oozes Old World charm. Adare is good hunting country, and an equestrian theme pervades the cozy bar and lounges where the dark walls are hung with paintings and prints of horseback riders. The bedrooms, though not large, are comfortably and tastefully decorated with antiques in the traditional style. Try Room 6, where Colonel Lindbergh stayed while working on the design of Shannon Airport. *Main St., Adare, Co. Limerick, tel. 061/396633, fax 061/396541. 45 rooms with bath. Facilities: restaurant, bar, horseback riding, fox hunting by arrangement, fishing, bicycling. AE, DC, MC, V. $$$*

Ballyferriter

Lodging

Granville Hotel. In the midst of some of the best scenery on the Dingle peninsula, this is a small, family-run hotel in a converted Georgian house. Rooms are all shapes and sizes and most are simply furnished with modest antiques. Ten of them have sea views and the rest overlook the wild Kerry mountains. It attracts independent-minded outdoor types, and your hosts Billy and Breege Granville will arrange a trip to the Blasket Islands and advise on local facilities for deep-sea fishing, horseback riding, guided walks, and mountaineering. *Ballyferriter, Dingle Peninsula, Co. Kerry, tel. and fax 066/56116. 14 rooms with bath. Facilities: restaurant, bar, table tennis. DC, MC, V. $*

Ballylickey

Lodging ★ **Ballylickey Manor House.** This modest 300-year-old whitewashed manor house, surrounded by gardens overlooking Bantry Bay, has a sophistication unusual for the area. The ambience here is more country-French than Irish—which can be a plus or a minus, depending on your taste. Four rustic chalets stand around the pool, but the best bet is one of the elegant rooms with bay windows in the main house, which was recently rebuilt and redecorated after a severe fire. The French cuisine in the candlelit restaurant is well above average for the region. *Ballylickey, near Bantry, Co. Cork, tel. 027/50071, fax 027/50124. 11 rooms with bath. Facilities: restaurant, bar, heated outdoor pool, fishing on grounds. AE, MC, V. Closed Nov.–mid-Mar. $$$$*

Baltimore

Dining **Chez Youen.** Youen Jacob, an exuberant Breton, owns and runs this small, rustic restaurant where copperware hangs from low beams above a simple tiled floor. It overlooks Baltimore Harbour and Sherkin Island and specializes in the best local seafood, bought directly from the town's fishing fleet. Lobster is available year-round; other treats on the menu include *coquilles St. Jacques* (poached scallops) and *moules marinières* (mussels in white wine). *Baltimore, Co. Cork, tel. 028/20136. Reservations advised on weekends. AE, DC, MC, V. Wine license only. Closed Nov. and Feb. Lunch, Easter–Sept. otherwise dinner only. $$*

Bantry

Lodging **Bantry House.** This magnificent mansion overlooking the bay is certainly the best place to stay in town. The Aubusson tapestries and other treasures are kept in the central section of the house, which is open to the public; newly refurbished rooms in both wings are available for bed-and-breakfast. Enjoy the view of Bantry Bay when you wake up—it is breathtaking on a clear day. *Bantry, Co. Cork, tel. 027/50047, fax 027/50795. 8 rooms with bath. Dinner by arrangement. No TV in rooms. AE, MC, V. $$$*

Caragh Lake

Lodging ★ **Ard na Sidhe.** ("Sidhe" is pronounced *Sheen;* it means "hill of the fairies.") This secluded Edwardian mansion, built in the style of an Elizabethan manor, is low and gabled with casement windows set in stone mullions and gray stone walls covered by creeper. The attractive large rooms have coordinated carpets and spreads, and lovely floral drapes on the bay windows. Rooms are best in the main building. Antiques and open fires adorn the traditionally furnished lobby and lounges. The hotel also offers delightful, award-winning lakeside gardens. Guests are entitled to use the sporting facilities at the Hotel Europe (*see* Killarney, *below*) and Dunloe Castle in Killarney. *Caragh Lake, near Killorglin, Co. Kerry, tel. 066/69105, fax 066/69282. 20 rooms with bath. Facilities: restaurant, bar, boating and fishing. No TV in rooms. AE, DC, MC, V. Closed Oct. 1–Apr. 30. $$$*

Castlelyons

Lodging **Ballyvolane House.** Approaching the Southwest from Dublin, Castlelyons is signposted off the N8 in Rathcormac, just south of

Fermoy. A true country-house atmosphere pervades this imposing 1728 stone mansion surrounded by extensive gardens, beyond which is a 100-acre dairy farm. The Green family treats guests as friends and gives them the run of the comfortably furnished downstairs rooms. Dinner is served at a large table in the elegant dining room; family silver is set on white napery. The rooms are exceptionally big, sitting areas generous, and decor consists of a rich assortment of antiques and family heirlooms. Both dinner and accommodation must be booked at least 24 hours in advance, but the pre-planning is well worth it. *Castlelyons, Co. Cork, tel. 025/36349, fax 025/36781. 6 rooms with bath. Facilities: private fishing, horseback riding, wine license only. MC, V. $$*

Cloyne/Midleton

Lodging **Ballymaloe House.** This place is a favorite hideaway for celebrities; although owner Myrtle Allen is too discreet to name any of them, it is well-known locally that Jeremy Irons is a regular guest. Originally the Allen family's home on a 400-acre farm, the rambling house, covered with creeping plants, has been developed into an informal, easygoing hotel over the past 20 years. The rooms here come in all shapes and sizes, but each one is decorated elegantly in variations on the country-house style. There are good options both in the main house and in the courtyard. Myrtle Allen has done much to revitalize Irish cookery, bringing in French undertones and insisting on using only fresh produce; the food at Ballymaloe remains as close as you can get in a restaurant to home cooking. The hotel is just 32 kilometers (20 miles) from Cork City, near the pretty fishing village of Ballycotton. Drive out and sample the buffet lunch if you're based in Cork. Turn off the N25 Waterford road at Midleton for Cloyne, then follow signposts down tiny back lanes for Shanagarry. The last 2 miles are the trickiest, especially in the dark. *Shanagarry, Midleton, Co. Cork, tel. 021/652531, fax 021/652021. 30 rooms with bath. Facilities: restaurant (jacket and tie preferred), bar, outdoor heated pool, tennis court, deep-sea fishing by arrangement. No TV in rooms. AE, DC, MC, V. $$$*

Cork City

Dining ★ **Arbutus Lodge.** The dining room in this solid Victorian villa is relatively small, ensuring that the highest standards are maintained. The tall ceiling, large bay window, polished mahogany sideboards, plush velvet chairs, original Irish paintings, and intricate fresh-flower arrangements on each table evoke the atmosphere of a luxurious private home, creating the ideal setting for a leisurely sampling of French-Irish haute cuisine. An eight-course "tasting menu" provides a perfect introduction to the restaurant's special cuisine. Imported ingredients are avoided as much as possible; local meat, fish, and game, which are lightly and appropriately sauced and garnished, are highlights. In winter, try the salmis of roast pheasant with lentils; in summer, the baked sea bass with sea urchin sauce is recommended. Two independent authorities, *The Wine Spectator* and the *Egon Ronay Guide*, recently declared the wine list here to be among the best in the world. If your budget is tight, sample the inexpensive buffet lunch (including tripe and onions, and beefsteak and kidney pie), which is served in the spacious Gallery Bar with panoramic views of the city. *Middle Glanmire Rd., Montenotte, Cork, tel. 021/501237. Reservations required. AE, DC, MC, V. Closed Sun. and Dec. 24–29. $$$*

★ **Clifford's.** Michael Clifford, once the head chef at the Arbutus Lodge (*see above*), now runs this small yet very fashionable restaurant on the western edge of the city center near the Jury's hotel. Although the interior of the Georgian town house has been modernized, it retains the old cornices and elaborate high ceilings. The high standard of cooking maintained here offers a limited number of choices on a fixed-price set menu. House specialties include spinach soup with miniature chicken quenelles (dumplings), medallions of veal garnished with apples and walnuts, and black sole and prawns in a pepper and lime sauce. *18 Dyke Parade, Cork, tel. 021/275333. Reservations advised. Jacket and tie required. AE, DC, MC, V. Wine license only. Closed Sun. and Mon., as well as Sat. lunch. $$$*

The Oyster Tavern. Under new ownership since 1992, this grand old Cork eatery, a venerable institution that has served the local population for more than 200 years, is still a favorite for business lunches and family celebrations. You now enter directly into the dark-paneled front bar, with the addition of a cocktail piano that some of the regulars resent. The main attraction of the Oyster is its traditional Old World atmosphere, redolent of a Victorian gentlemen's club with its dark woodwork, original 1790s mirrors, red plush upholstery, and waitresses dressed in black-and-white uniforms. Expect no surprises from the menu, but savor the exceptional quality of its basic ingredients. *Market Lane (off Patrick St.), Cork, tel. 021/272716. Reservations advised. AE, DC, MC, V. Closed Sun. and bank holidays. $$*

The Gallery Cafe. If you can't get out to the famous country-house hotel (*see* Cloyne, *above*), you can sample Ballymaloe cooking here. The large, airy room was, until recently, an integral part of Cork's municipal art gallery; it retains an artistic air, enhanced by several life-size statues. The food is prepared daily at Ballymaloe, and includes home-grown produce and fresh seafood. Open sandwiches on homemade brown bread are a popular lunchtime choice, and the cakes are also renowned. The evening menu is fashionably light; try seafood in a scallop shell or turkey breast baked with butter and watercress. *Crawford Art Gallery, Emmet Pl., tel. 021/274415. Open Mon.–Sat. 10:30–4:30, Wed.–Fri. 6:30–9:30. MC, V. Wine license only. $–$$*

Isaac's. Just across the street from the Everyman Palace, this stylish brasserie-style spot is the "in" place to see and be seen. It is a large, bright converted warehouse in a budget hotel of the same name (*see* Lodging, *below*) with the original cast-iron pillars still in place, a stunning collection of modern art on the walls, lively jazz on the sound system, and well-spaced, oilcloth-covered tables. It is run by Michael and Catherine Ryan of Arbutus Lodge fame (*see above*) and their young partner, chef Canice Sharkey. The very reasonably priced menu combines influences from the east and the Mediterranean. Start with Chinese fish soup or *crostini* with pâté, pesto, olives, and grilled peppers, followed by Madhur Jaffrey's Rogan Josh—lamb curry with *poppadums* and side dishes—or grilled king prawns with spices and garlic butter. Whatever your budget, this one is worth trying. *48 MacCurtain St., tel. 021/503805. Reservations advised weekends. MC, V. $*

Lodging

Fitzpatrick Silver Springs. Ten minutes outside town on the Dublin–Rosslare approach road, this 1960s glass-and-concrete hotel is set back from the busy main road among extensive lawns. The large and impersonal lodging is favored by tour buses in summer and business travelers in winter. The main recommendation is its recently added fitness center, which is the best in town. The fanciest and largest rooms, decked out in French-boudoir style in pink-and-gray plush, are located in the newest (1988) wing. *Tivoli, Cork, tel. 021/507533, fax 021/507641. 110 rooms with bath. Facilities: 2 restaurants, 2 bars, sauna, Jacuzzi, gymnasium, steam room, indoor pool, 2 squash courts, 3 tennis courts (1 outdoor, 2 indoor), bowling, 9-hole golf course. AE, DC, MC, V. Closed Dec. 25. $$$*

Imperial. From 1816 until the 1960s, this was Cork's premier hotel. Situated in the heart of the legal and banking district, just around the corner from the smartest shops, the building has an elegant classical facade with pilasters above a generous wrought-iron canopy that distinguishes it from the surrounding offices. The bar and the coffee shop, which are popular meeting places for business executives and affluent shoppers, have been spoiled by overenthusiastic modernization. To savor the Imperial's heritage, ask for an antique-style room with old mahogany furniture and velvet upholstery. The rest of the rooms, in various styles of hotel-modern, are spacious but undistinguished. *South Mall, Cork, tel. and fax 021/274040. 101 rooms with bath. Facilities: 2 restaurants, 2 bars, coffee shop. AE, DC, MC, V. $$$*

Jury's. This striking, modern, smoked-glass and steel structure beside the River Lee is a five-minute walk from the city center and a lively spot, which attracts a young, yuppie clientele. Its large, open lobby/restaurant area features a waterfall and hanging greenery—some of it plastic. Cork's Bar is popular with the locals at lunch and in the early evening. In the plain yet spacious rooms you'll find quilted spreads, small sofas, and floor-to-ceiling picture windows. Be sure to ask for a room that overlooks the interior patio garden and pool. *Western Rd., Cork, tel. 021/276622, fax 021/274477. 185 rooms with bath. Facilities: 2 restaurants, 2 bars, sauna, Jacuzzi, gymnasium, indoor/outdoor pool, 2 tennis courts, squash court. AE, DC, MC, V. Closed Dec. 25–26. $$$*

Morrison's Island. This luxury, modern hotel on the riverside is a two-minute walk from the Imperial Hotel. Spacious, modern one- or two-bedroom suites with kitchen are furnished with attractive, handcrafted light oak in a modern design. Polished marble floors and warm terra-cotta walls enhance the stylish mezzanine-level bar and restaurant overlooking the river. Four penthouses have terrace views of the city and the river as well. *Morrison's Quay, tel. 021/275858, fax 021/275833. 40 suites with bath. Facilities: restaurant, bar, bicycles. AE, DC, MC, V. $$$*

★ **Arbutus Lodge.** This two-story Victorian villa is the first choice in Cork for those who like the feeling of staying in a fancy private home; it is only a five-minute drive from the city center (well signposted from St. Luke's Cross) on a hill overlooking the River Lee and the city. The light, airy rooms have been individually decorated with fine antiques and original paintings. The rooms designated as "superior" have vast super-king-size beds (which can unzip into twins on request) and comfortable sofas. Ask for Room 14 with its magnificent bay window. The smaller "ordinary" rooms offer their surprises as well: Room 9, for instance, has a magnificent carved oak and walnut four-poster bed. The majority of guests are American, often on their third or fourth visit, but the bar and outstanding restaurant (*see* Dining, *above*) attracts a lively local clientele. *Middle Glanmire Rd., Montenotte, Cork, tel. 021/501237, fax 021/502893. 20 rooms with bath. Facilities: restaurant, bar, tennis court. AE, DC, MC, V. Closed Dec. 24–29. $$*

Moore's. An unpretentious establishment on a quiet inner-city stretch of the River Lee, Moore's many ardent fans praise the homey atmosphere and friendly staff. Others complain of the pervasive smell of cooking in the public areas and the twisted narrow corridors that resulted from combining three undistinguished town houses.

The cozy rooms have plain carpets and blue patterned drapes and spreads, but they vary greatly in size, shape, and outlook. The best bet is a room with a river view. *Morrison's Island, Cork, tel. 021/271291, fax 021/272485. 35 rooms with bath. Facilities: restaurant, bar. No elevator. AE, MC, V. $$*

Isaac's. This is a combined hostel and budget hotel, but far more pleasant than those words may suggest. It has quickly become a favored accommodation for both visitors and cost-conscious business people. The notice board in the reception area is the best place in town to get the low-down on concerts, tours, travel bargains, and off-beat activities. In a well-designed converted warehouse just north of the Lee, it's only a short walk from both bus and rail stations. The guest rooms are cheerful and attractively functional with lots of primary colors. If you want a private room with bath be sure to specify when booking. Its popular restaurant (*see above*) is under separate management, but the hotel has its own eating facilities, and the rates include Continental breakfast. *48 MacCurtain St., tel. 021/500011, fax 021/506355. 48 private rooms, 10 with bath, 18 dorms with 4–16 beds (200 beds in total). Facilities: cafeteria, TV lounge, table tennis. MC, V. $*

★ **Victoria Lodge.** This exceptionally well-appointed B&B, built originally in the early 20th century as a Capuchin monastery, is a five-minute drive from the town center; it is also accessible by several bus routes. Breakfast is served in the spacious old refectory with its polished benches and paneled walls still intact, and the common room is now a television lounge. The simple, comfortable bedrooms feature brown chenille spreads, cotton curtains, and mahogany bureaus. *Victoria Cross, Cork, tel. 021/542233, fax 021/542572. 20 rooms with bath. AE, MC, V. $*

Dingle

Dining

★ **Beginish.** Dingle is an oasis in a culinary desert, although this spot is outstanding by any standard. The small rooms feature pale green carpeting, fresh flowers on the blue linen tablecloths, and muted classical music. The food is an imaginative and generous interpretation of French nouvelle cuisine; specialties include brill fillets on leek fondue with white-wine sauce, and fillet of lamb in phyllo pastry with duxelles. The wine list, with about 100 choices, includes a good selection of half-bottles. *Green St., Dingle, Co. Kerry, tel. 066/51588. Reservations advised. AE, DC, MC, V. Closed Mon. and mid-Nov.–mid-Mar. $$*

Doyle's Seafood Bar. This establishment is more of a restaurant than a bar, but a sandstone-slated floor, rush-seated chairs, and pine tables create a very casual atmosphere. Because the seafood is fresh, John Doyle prefers to keep it simple: Fillets of plaice (flounder) stuffed with crab with prawn sauce is about the fanciest dish. Crab claws beurre blanc and scallops with a chive butter sauce are more typical options. The menu offers a good selection of seafood appetizers and irresistible homemade desserts. Eight very comfortable, moderately priced bedrooms are available in the adjoining town house—as long as you don't mind the pervasive odor of fish! *John St., Dingle, Co. Kerry, tel. 066/51174, fax 066/51816. Reservations advised. DC, MC, V. Closed Sun. and mid-Nov.–early Mar. $$*

★ **The Islandman.** The front of this dining spot consists of a bar and a bookshop that blend well with the dark wooden tables, bentwood chairs, and Tiffany lamps of the small restaurant. During the day, it is a popular café-bar. The dinner menu, which caters to more serious eaters, includes roast rack of Kerry lamb with red currant sauce;

fresh trout or salmon plainly broiled; or vegetarian pasta and a side salad. *Main St., Dingle, Co. Kerry, tel. 066/51803. Reservations advised for dinner. AE, DC, MC, V. $*

Lodging ★ **Benner's.** An American owner has restored this small town-center hotel to its former glory. It should be made a model for many similar establishments around Ireland still suffering from insensitive 1960s modernization programs. All the rooms are individually furnished with country-style stripped-pine antiques, plain pale cream wool carpets, and light green *eau de nil* paintwork. Rooms 2 and 3 have pine four-poster beds, but the largest rooms are 16 and 17 on the third floor. The atmosphere throughout is cheerful and uncluttered, with plump chintz sofas in the lobby and well-polished wood paneling on the ground floor. The front bar has a busy local trade, especially at lunchtime. *Main St., Dingle, Co. Kerry, tel. 066/51638, fax 066/51412. 25 rooms with bath. Facilities: restaurant, 2 bars, tennis court. No elevator. AE, DC, MC, V. $$*

Skellig. This is a product of Ireland's 1960s hotel boom, when novelty was prized at any cost. This movement has left us with a two-story, concrete-and-glass bedroom section joined to a spaceship-like lobby/bar/restaurant/pool complex meant to recall, of all things, *clochâns*, the local beehive-shape anchorite cells. Ask for a room in the new section, fresher than the original one. The hotel is on the water's edge, a five-minute walk from town; it is very popular with Irish families—who bring along swarms of children—in July and August. The spacious bar and lounge, which feature exposed stone work and wooden beams, are at their best when crowded and rather eerie when empty. *Dingle, Co. Kerry, tel. 066/51144, fax 066/51501. 100 rooms with bath. Facilities: restaurant, bar, tennis court, indoor pool, sauna. AE, DC, MC, V. Closed Nov. 16–Mar. 14. $$*

Cleevaun Country House. Follow the signs through Dingle Town toward Slea Head (R559) for 1½ kilometers (1 mile) to this newly built guest house. The modern, whitewashed building with a slate roof is set in 1 acre of landscaped gardens and overlooks Dingle Bay. The bright, well-equipped bedrooms have the same natural cottage-pine wood that is used throughout the rest of the inn. The breakfast menu offers a wide choice for those who are tiring of the ubiquitous "fry." *Lady's Cross, Dingle, Co. Kerry, tel. and fax 066/51108. 8 rooms with bath. MC, V. Closed Dec. 15–Jan. 15. $*

Durrus

Dining ★ **Blair's Cove House.** This restaurant, in the converted stables of a Georgian mansion overlooking Dunmanus Bay, has gleaming silverware, pink napery, and a large crystal chandelier, creating an element of elegance that contrasts sharply with the building's exposed beams and rough stone walls. In summer, you'll dine on the covered, heated terrace overlooking the rose-filled courtyard and fountain. The cuisine is French-Irish (the owners are French) with an emphasis on fresh local produce. Try rack of lamb cooked on the open oakwood grill, or a seafood special such as monkfish in Pernod sauce. *Blair's Cove, Durrus, Co. Cork, tel. 027/61127. Reservations advised on weekends. MC, V. Wine license only. Dinner only. Closed Sun. July & Aug., Sun. and Mon. rest of year. Closed Nov. 1–Feb. $$$*

Shiro Japanese Dinner House. One of the biggest surprises of West Cork's culinary world in recent years has been the success of this tiny, 12-seat restaurant, which serves authentic Japanese cuisine in an imposing Edwardian house surrounded by palm trees. The room is decorated with accomplished watercolors by the talented hostess, Tokyo-born Kei Pilz. A fixed-price four-course menu is available with a choice of main dishes such as yakitori (chicken roasted on the spit with a sweet sauce) and tempura (fried fish, squid, vegetables, and prawns). Shiro is more popular than ever, so book far in advance. *Ahakista, Durrus, Co. Cork, tel. 027/67030. Reservations required. AE, DC, MC, V. Dinner only. $$$*

Kanturk

Lodging **Assolas Country House.** This lovely 17th-century manor possesses the air of a dignified family home more than it does a hotel. It is immaculately furnished with period antiques in the individually designed bedrooms. The tableware in the dining room is old Bourke family silver. A large log fire is usually ablaze in the drawing room, where you can join the other guests for a predinner sherry. Both the well-manicured gardens and the cooking here have won awards. Kanturk is known for its good fishing and hunting, and it is within an hour's drive of Cork, Limerick, and Killarney. *Kanturk, Co. Cork, tel. 029/50015, fax 029/50795. 9 rooms with bath. Facilities: restaurant (dinner only; jacket and tie required), fishing, tennis court, boating. No TV in rooms. AE, MC, V. Closed Nov. 1–Mar. 11. $$$$*

Kenmare

Dining **D'Arcy's Old Bank House.** A short step from the gates of the Park Hotel and opposite the Lansdowne Arms, this L-shaped room, previously a bank, has been transformed into a front parlor restaurant with an open fire, white damask on the tables, dried flowers in the windows, and local paintings hanging on the white and terracotta walls. Owner/chef Matt D'Arcy's cooking is more highly accomplished than the simple surroundings might lead you to expect. The classic French menu offers excellent value and features the best of fresh local produce. Try, for example, *supreme de volaille et saumon* (breast of chicken and salmon with a creamy prawn sauce) or *filet de boeuf et champignon en croute* (pan-fried beef fillet with savory mushrooms in pastry). For dessert his wild heather, honey, and lavender ice cream is a must. *Main St., Kenmare, tel. 064/41589. Reservations advised weekends and mid-June–Sept. AE, DC, MC, V. Dinner only. Closed Dec. 24–29 and Sun.–Tues. Nov.–Feb. $$*

Dining and Lodging ★ **Park Hotel.** Formerly a bishop's palace, this establishment is now one of Ireland's premier country-house hotels. Set on extensive grounds with views of the Caha Mountains, the hotel property features terraced lawns that sweep down to the bay. The hotel is a favorite with affluent young executives from Germany and France as well as from Dublin. The thickly carpeted lobby features a black marble fireplace, a tall grandfather clock, and Victorian chaise longues. Sensuous watercolors of Kerry wildlife by Pauline Bewick, a well-known Irish painter who lives nearby, adorn the dining-room walls. The bedrooms are individually designed with late-Victorian furniture faithful to the house's original period; walnut or mahogany bedroom suites have matching wardrobes, chests of drawers, and headboards. A major renovation during the winter of 1990 doubled the size of rooms in the 1950s extension, and introduced stonework to the facade. "Superior deluxe" rooms are the smallest, but big by the standards of other places, with armchairs or sofas in the bedroom area. Park Suite rooms have an entrance hall and a separate sitting area; nine larger suites are also available. All bedrooms have finely equipped bathrooms with glossy Italian marble tiling. Be sure to sample the seafood on the nouvelle-cuisine menu of the renowned restaurant (jacket and tie required). *Kenmare, Co. Kerry, tel. 064/41200, fax 064/41402. 50 rooms with bath. Facilities: restaurant, bar, fishing, tennis court, horseback riding, 18-hole golf course, bicycles. TV in rooms on request. AE, DC, V. Closed Nov. 1–Dec. 23 and Jan. 3–Apr. 14. $$$$*

Sheen Falls Lodge. This rambling hotel opened in 1991 on the site of the former seat of the earls of Kerry. The magnificent setting—between Kenmare Bay and the fall of the River Sheen into the tidal estuary—has 300 secluded acres of lawns, semitropical gardens, and forest. The public rooms feature a mahogany-paneled library with over 1,000 books, mainly of Irish interest, and a billiard room adjacent to the bar. The bedrooms have a combination of new and antique furnishings; they all offer stunning views of either Kenmare Bay or the River Sheen. The restaurant, La Cascade, overlooking the falls, serves classic French cuisine using such local produce as lobster, salmon, oysters, mussels, quail, pheasant, lamb, and beef. Already it has won awards and high praises. Sheen Falls is the latest "in" place among high-flying Dubliners, and no doubt the international jet set will soon follow. *Kenmare, Co. Kerry, tel. 064/41600, fax 064/41386. 40 rooms with bath. Facilities: restaurant, bar, gym, sauna, steam room, salmon fishing, horseback riding, tennis court, croquet, bicycles, helipad. AE, DC, MC, V. Closed Jan.–Mar. 14. $$$$*

Foley's Shamrock. This family-run pub and restaurant has been offering lodging to visitors for over 30 years. Two stories of bedrooms rest above the town's pub—don't expect to get much sleep before midnight—all of which are spotlessly clean and simply decorated with plain carpets, white bedspreads, and odd little pictures. A recent renovation left all rooms with bath or shower, and, unusual for this part of the country, television. The ground-floor restaurant has Tudor-style wooden tables with mats, wooden dividers, and an extensive menu featuring generous portions of plain home cooking, including shellfish and lobster from the tank. Mrs. Foley, who stresses that everything is homemade right down to the bread, gives her guests the old-fashioned, warm-hearted welcome that has made Irish B&Bs world famous. *Henry St., Co. Kerry, tel. 064/41379, fax 064/41799. 10 rooms with bath. Facilities: restaurant, bar. MC, V. $*

Killarney

Dining ★ **Fredrick's.** The view of Killarney's lakes from the rooftop restaurant of the Aghadoe Heights Hotel (*see below*) is like a picture postcard, making it the ultimate romantic venue. And, as if that weren't enough, the food is outstanding. The restaurant has won numerous awards since reopening under new management in 1991. The tables are formally set with silver candelabra, white linen, pink napkins, and comfortable, fully upholstered chairs. Ask for a front table when you book. The English chef prepares a classic French menu, which varies according to season. Choose from the set menu or the small but comprehensive à la carte. Starters may include grilled squid with sesame prawns on young leeks or Dingle Bay oysters natural or Rockefeller. Main courses include classics such as black sole grilled or meunière, roast chateaubriand with sauce béarnaise, or more unusual dishes like medallions of veal with crab soufflé. This is one of the most expensive restaurants in Ireland, but the combination of its setting and haute cuisine makes it an unforgettable occasion. *Aghadoe Heights, Killarney, Co. Kerry, tel. 064/31766. Reservations advised. Jacket and tie preferred. AE, DC, MC, V. $$$*

★ **Foley's.** What appears to be a simple front-parlor restaurant behind a small bar with an open fire is in fact a warren of small rooms decorated with half-paneled walls, stained glass, and Tiffany lamps. The food is far superior to the decor; chef Carol Buckley, daughter of the original owners, trained in a superior French restaurant, and it shows. Typical dishes include roulade of trout stuffed with prawn mousse and grilled T-bone steak with garlic butter, accompanied by superb al dente vegetables. The chef's sauces make generous use of superior Irish cream and butter. The wine list offers over 200 choices, and a pianist entertains during the summer months. *23 High St., Killarney, Co. Kerry, tel. 064/31217. Reservations advised mid-June–Sept. AE, DC, MC, V. $$*

Gaby's Seafood. The tiled floors, pine booths, and red gingham cloths with matching lampshades at this town-center restaurant help create a cheerful, informal bistro atmosphere. The small dining room is usually crowded because of the good seafood. Try the seafood mosaic (seven or eight kinds of fresh fish in a cream-and-wine sauce) or lobster Gaby (shelled, boiled in a cream-and-cognac sauce, and served back in the shell). *17 High St., Killarney, Co. Kerry, tel. 064/32519. Reservations advised. AE, DC, MC, V. Closed Mon. lunch, Sun. $$*

Sheila's. Sheila's has fed the people of Killarney and its visitors for more than 30 years, and it was recently handed down from mother to daughter. Situated in the town center, it is brightly lighted and simply furnished with stripped pine tables and red paper mats. The unpretentious menu features such Irish specials as corned beef with cabbage and Irish stew (Kerry lamb stewed with barley, carrots, onion, and potatoes). In a town bedeviled by tourist traps, this friendly spot offers excellent value for the money. *75 High St., Killarney, Co. Kerry, tel. 064/31270. Reservations advised in high season. Wine license only. AE, DC, MC, V. $*

Lodging

Aghadoe Heights. This hotel reopened after a £4 million refurbishment in 1990 and has been carrying off awards ever since. Its marvelous lake view, from a bluff 4 kilometers (2.5 miles) outside town on the Tralee side, (signposted off the N22), will remain with you, and the 8 acres of grounds ensure absolute peace and quiet. The interior is a curious mix of very good taste—the owner's private collection of antiques and paintings adorn the public rooms—and rather odd taste, with the roof above the curved swimming pool supported by gilt-topped pillars. Two-thirds of the bedrooms have lake views, and all are relatively large with good-size bathrooms and matching floral drapes and spreads, lace-covered cushions, and fitted furniture in cherrywood, mahogany, or ash. The three suites are exceptionally spacious with romantic views of the lakes and a ruined abbey. *Aghadoe Heights, Killarney, Co. Kerry, tel. 064/31766, fax 064/31345. 57 rooms with bath. Facilities: restaurant, bar, heated indoor pool, sauna, Jacuzzi, tennis court, fishing. AE, DC, MC, V. $$$$*

Europe. The combination of a secluded lakeside location (a five-minute drive from town) and luxurious but unfussy decor gives this modern five-story hotel the edge over its competitors. Almost all the bedrooms feature solid pine trim, a lake view, and a private balcony. The spacious lounges and lobbies are rather large and impersonal, but they do have picture windows overlooking the lake and mountains and an imaginative display of old carved timber and valuable antiques. The sports facilities, including an Olympic-size pool, are among the best and most up-to-date in the district. *Killorglin Rd., Fossa, Killarney, Co. Kerry, tel. 064/31900, fax 064/32118. 205 rooms with bath. Facilities: 2 restaurants, 2 bars, indoor pool, sau-*

na, gymnasium, tennis court, fishing, horseback riding, bicycles. AE, DC, MC, V. Closed Nov.–Feb. $$$

Gleneagle. This lodging will appeal to sociable people who enjoy plenty of action but are unperturbed by bizarre decor; the main house and its three modern bedroom extensions combine clashing decorating styles and an apparently random selection of carpets and drapes. The hotel is on the main road to Kenmare, about a five-minute drive from town. It is popular with both Irish and American visitors, and serves mainly a younger crowd. Evening entertainment includes live music at the Eagles Whistle Singing Pub and, during mid-June through September, disco music and top Irish cabaret acts at the Wings Nightclub. Ask for a bedroom in the newest wing, which has a lake view; the rooms are the largest in the hotel, and all have private balconies. *Muckross Rd., Killarney, Co. Kerry, tel. 064/31870, fax 064/32646. 167 rooms with bath. Facilities: restaurant, bar, nightclub, 2 tennis courts, 4 squash courts, practice golf course, sauna, indoor pool. AE, DC, MC, V. $$*

Lake. Set well back from the main road opposite the Gleneagle, this vast 1820s house is a mildly eccentric place with a glorious location and excellent lake views. It appeals mainly to visitors from the United Kingdom and Germany. The authentic Victorian decor of the lobby, stairs, and corridors, including heavy wooden banisters and high ceilings, is diminished by the ill-chosen modern furniture, such as plastic stacking chairs in the restaurant and cheap cane tables and chairs in the sun lounge. Try Room 169, which offers polished mahogany furniture and a lake view. Rooms in the new wings have stripped oak trim and pretty print drapes, but you still reach them via long creepy corridors. *Muckross Rd., Killarney, Co. Kerry, tel. 064/31035, fax 064/31902. 65 rooms with bath. Facilities: restaurant, bar, tennis court, fishing. TV in rooms on request. No elevator. V. Closed mid-Nov.–Apr. $$*

★ **Arbutus.** Run by the friendly Buckley family since it was built more than 60 years ago, this is a good budget hotel in the town center; it is a short step from the bus and train station and a three-minute walk from the main shopping and dining area. The lobby has an open fire, and the bar is popular with locals. The rooms in the new second-story section are recommended for the space and recent furnishings. *College St., Killarney, Co. Kerry, tel. 064/31037, fax 064/34033. 36 rooms with bath. Facilities: restaurant, bar. No elevator. DC, MC, V. $*

★ **Kathleen's Country House.** Situated on the Tralee road a mile outside town, this imaginatively designed two-story guest house, incorporating traditional slate walls and roofing and large, modern windows, was built in 1979 to owner/manager Kathleen O'Regan-Sheppard's exacting specifications. The rooms are relatively spacious, light, and airy, with wooden trim, bright floral comforters, and matching floral curtains. Everything is spotlessly clean. The small second-floor lounge offers pleasant views of the wooded valley and Killarney Town below. The restaurant serves only fresh produce and organic vegetables. *Madam's Height, Tralee Rd., Killarney, Co. Kerry, tel. 064/32810, fax 064/32340. 16 rooms with bath. Facilities: restaurant (no smoking) for dinner only horseback riding, Wine license only or BYOB. AE, MC, V. $*

Lime Court. Budget accommodations have been springing up along the Muckross road between Killarney town and the national park, and this new one is only a five-minute walk from the town center. (Your hosts, the Moriarty family, will meet your train or bus if you ask when booking.) The modern building has two large bay windows at the front, with the rooms in an extension behind it, away from the cars and jaunting cars on the road. The reception area is furnished with antiques and large potted plants, and there is a baby grand piano in the spacious lounge. The relatively large guest rooms overlook green fields and are light, airy, and plainly but comfortably furnished with small sitting areas. *Muckross Rd., Co. Kerry, tel. 064/34547, fax 064/34121. 11 rooms with bath. Facilities: tea and coffee making facilities, wine license, table tennis. MC, V. $*

Linden House. On a busy road just off the main street, this family-run hotel is a plain, functional 1960s suburban home with uninspired olive-green drapes and carpeting and plywood decor; however, it offers an excellent value among the more inexpensive hotels. Its clientele consists mainly of independent travelers from Ireland, Europe, and the United States. The quietest rooms are in the back. The optional evening meal is a substantial, home-cooked affair. *New Rd., Killarney, Co. Kerry, tel. 064/31379, fax 064/31196. 20 rooms with bath. Facilities: restaurant (dinner only). MC, V. Closed Dec. and Jan. $*

Killorglin

Dining **Nick's Seafood and Steak.** Owner/chef Nick Foley trained as a veterinary surgeon but finds life in the kitchen more congenial. The old stone town house has a bar-cum-dining room at street level and a quieter dining room on the floor above. Seasonal specials include seafood and game; Foley is known for his cockle-and-mussel soup. In winter, sample the haunch of Kerry venison in red-wine and juniper sauce. All vegetables are grown locally. *Main St., Killorglin, Co. Kerry, tel. 066/61219. Reservations advised. AE, DC, MC, V. Bar food only at lunch. Closed Mon. and Tues. Dec.–Easter, and Nov. $$*

Kinsale

Dining ★ **The Vintage.** This charming, front-parlor restaurant, hidden away in a narrow back street one minute from the center of town, is the outstanding one of its kind. It is patronized equally by discerning locals and celebrities. The original front room has been extended without losing the impression that you are dining in a chic, antique-filled private home. Hot oysters in a sauce of dry white wine, cream, and sorrel, and guinea fowl with red cabbage and apples are among the unusual specialties on the sophisticated international menu. *Main St., Kinsale, Co. Cork, tel. 021/772502. Reservations advised. AE, DC, MC, V. Dinner only. Closed Sun. in winter, 2 weeks in Nov., 3 weeks in Jan.–Feb. $$$*

★ **Blue Haven.** This tastefully decorated old town house has received international acclaim for its seafood. Inexpensive bar food is served until 9:30 PM in the lounge bar, the patio, and the conservatory, which are all decorated with swagged curtains, hanging plants, and nautical brass. The quiet, pastel-colored restaurant overlooks a floodlit garden whose fountain is adorned by cherubs. For dinner, choose between something traditional, such as sole on the bone with lemon and parsley butter, or something more unusual, such as medallions of hake coated in a Pernod batter and served with a white butter sauce. There are also 10 moderately priced guest bedrooms. *3 Pearse St., Kinsale, Co. Cork, tel. 021/772209, fax 021/774268. Reservations advised. AE, DC, MC, V. $$*

Jim Edwards. One of the most succesful pub/restaurants in Ireland, this place is renowned for the quality of its steaks and seafood. The restaurant is unpretentiously decorated with dark wood tables, dark-green place mats, and red carpets and drapes. The staff, under the supervision of the owner and his wife, is friendly and efficient. Portions tend to be exceptionally generous, and children are welcome. Recommended dishes include the fricassee of seafood and the succulent char-grilled local steak fillet. (The separate bar serves inexpensive fare.) *Market Quay, Kinsale, Co. Cork, tel. 021/772541. Reservations advised weekends and summer. AE, DC, MC, V. $$*

Max's Wine Bar. More a small, chic restaurant than a wine bar, this establishment is run impeccably by owner Wendy Tisdall. In the low-beamed main room is a variety of small antique tables with equally varied chairs and benches. At the back is a small, flower-filled conservatory. Most menu choices can be ordered as either starters or main courses. Salads, which are not generally taken seriously in the Southwest, are especially good here, as is the homemade soup. Mussels in garlic breadcrumbs and salmon in sorrel sauce are among the seafood choices. *Main St., Kinsale, Co. Cork, tel. 021/772443. Reservations advised PM. MC, V. Closed Nov. 1–mid-Feb. $$*

Lodging

Trident. This modern low rise on the water's edge is popular with visitors who come to Kinsale for deep-sea fishing—mainly all-male Dutch or English groups. The cinderblock modern rooms feature tweed curtains and drapes and large windows overlooking the inner harbor. The Fisherman's Bar is a congenial spot for conversation between the locals and visiting anglers. *Pier Head, Kinsale, Co. Cork, tel. 021/772301, fax 021/774173. 58 rooms with bath. Facilities: restaurant, bar, sauna, Jacuzzi, gym, table tennis, bicycles, deep-sea fishing. AE, DC, MC, V. $$$*

The Bank House. This tall Georgian town house is owned and managed by a Swiss-Irish couple with sophisticated flair. The rooms are large, double-glazed against traffic noise, and have tall windows with classically draped curtains that match the pale yellow walls. Pretty touches like dried-flower arrangements and discreet modern prints add to the elegance. The honeymoon suite on the third floor has a magnificent harbor view, a large bathroom, and a super-king-size bed. *Pearse St., Co. Cork, tel. 021/774075, fax 021/774296. 9 rooms with bath. Facilities: wine license. AE, MC, V. $$*

The Moorings. Only yards from the water's edge in the fishing village of Scilly, this newly built accommodation has a panoramic view across Kinsale harbor, and yet is only a few minutes' walk from the town center. You'll be tempted to install yourself in the sunny conservatory, with its cane furniture and extrordinary cacti, and simply watch the boats go by. Hosts Pat and Irene Jones are full of friendly advice, and have furnished the house with characterful antiques. The rooms are all big with large tiled bathrooms, patchwork quilt spreads, and interesting prints and paintings by local artists. Rooms 1 and 5 are extra large, but all five rooms on the top floor have tiny balconies with two chairs. Only one ground-floor room lacks a view. *Scilly, Kinsale, Co. Cork, tel. 021/772376, fax 021/772675. 9 rooms with bath. Facilities: wine license. MC, V. $$*

★ **Scilly House.** Californian Karin Young has turned this lovely Georgian house set in an acre of mature gardens into a country inn, right on the edge of town opposite the Spaniard Inn. All the rooms offer wonderful views of the town, the harbor, and Charles Fort. They feature colonial furniture and old American quilts on the walls alongside Karin's watercolors. All the rooms are clean and fresh, with a restrained pink-and-white floral motif. In the evenings, host Bill Skelly often leads a sing-along around the grand piano in the library. *Scilly, Kinsale, Co. Cork, tel. 021/772413, fax 021/774629.*

7 rooms with bath. Facilities: wine bar, evening meal by arrangement. Wine license only. AE, MC, V. Closed mid-Nov.–April 1. $$

Limerick

Dining ★ **De la Fontaine.** Only a discreet black awning indicates the existence of this restaurant, which sits atop a former warehouse in the city center, a short walk to the east of O'Connell Street (turn right onto Roches Street). It offers both a cozy ambience and authentic French "cuisine moderne." The dining room, graced with pretty floral napery and heated by a glowing gas fire, has a high-pitched, oak-beamed ceiling. The cooking is chef/owner Alain Bras's interpretation of nouvelle cuisine; recommended dishes include a starter of the local specialty, venison—the thinnest slices marinated in red wine and juniper berries and served with a mild French mustard—or a main course such as *escalope* of salmon in its sea crust—wild salmon grilled in a crust of flour and sea salt and served with a sea urchin and saffron sauce. Among the light and imaginative desserts, the nougat glacé with Angelica and praline is irresistible. The restaurant also offers a good wine list. *12 Gerald Griffin St., Limerick, tel. 061/414461. Reservations advised. Wine license only. AE, DC, MC, V. Closed Sun., lunch served only on Fri. $$*

Lodging ★ **Castletroy Park.** The large, three-story redbrick and cut-stone hotel sits grandly atop a hill on the outskirts of town (follow signs for the N7 Dublin Road), overlooking the university campus and rolling countryside. The lobby, with its polished wood and oriental rugs, leads to a large conservatory that serves as a coffee shop and overlooks an Italian-style courtyard and the open country beyond. The relaxing atmosphere extends to the guest rooms, scented with potpourri and fitted with solid wood furniture, muted floral drapes and spreads, plain carpets, and rag-rolled walls. The bathrooms are well equipped with robes, slippers, and marble basins. Executive rooms have extra-large king-size beds, a large writing desk, two phones, fax and computer plugs. The fitness center is one of the best around, with a computerized gym and 20-meter pool. Mix with the locals in the Merry Pedlar Pub and Bistro, enjoy a formal meal in MacLaughlin's restaurant, or retire with a book to the library. This place is a real gem. *Dublin Rd., Limerick, tel. 061/335566, fax 061/331117. 107 rooms with bath. Facilities: 2 restaurants, bar, indoor pool, gym, sauna, steam room, Jacuzzi. AE, DC, MC, V. $$$$*

Jury's. Built around a garden overlooking the Shannon, this modern steel-and-glass hotel offers a quiet location only a four-minute walk from the traffic-filled city center. The bright, airy lobby and lounges are decorated with hanging greenery. Limericks Bar is a popular meeting place for local yuppies. Although the rooms have painted concrete walls, they are all spacious and feature floor-to-ceiling picture windows overlooking either the interior garden or the river. *Ennis Rd., Limerick, tel. 061/327777, fax 021/326400. 95 rooms with bath. Facilities: restaurant, bar, coffee shop, indoor pool, sauna, Jacuzzi, steam room, gymnasium, tennis court, fishing. AE, DC, MC, V. $$$*

Greenhills. This friendly, family-run hotel is a modern low rise in a quiet suburban area where the N18 meets the city-center route. Twenty minutes from Shannon and five minutes from the city center, it makes an excellent touring base. The elegant lobby with its black wood and brass trim has an oriental flavor. The best and newest rooms are in a quiet wing above the fitness center, and are big enough to have a small couch, tables, and chairs. All the rooms are color-coordinated in various styles with dark wood furniture and tiled bathrooms. The Jockey Club Bar is a lively spot that serves a buffet lunch, and there is also a coffee shop and restaurant. Children will love the 17-meter pool, and in high season they can avail of the hotel's kiddy club. *Ennis Rd., Limerick, tel. 061/453033, fax 061/453307. 55 rooms with bath. Facilities: restaurant, bar, coffee shop, indoor heated pool, sauna, Jacuzzi, steam room, gym, tennis court. AE, DC, MC, V. $$*

Mallow

Lodging **Longueville House.** A large early 18th-century house with Victorian wings and a magnificent conservatory, Longueville is an imposing edifice from the outside, with symmetrical two-story wings flanking the classic three-story central section featuring a porch supported by four pillars. The vast drawing rooms overlook the tranquil lawns of the estate (which is on the Blackwater River); they are decorated with large gilt-framed mirrors and oil paintings, and have a stately elegance. The bedrooms are comfortable and filled with antiques; the best rooms are the high-ceilinged ones on the first-story front. The President's Room restaurant serves highly acclaimed French-Irish cuisine. In summer it is possible, weather permitting, to dine in the magnificent conservatory. Don't forget to sample a glass of fruity white wine from the Longueville vineyard, which is believed to be the only commercial vineyard in Ireland. Mallow is at the crossroads of the Cork–Limerick and Waterford–Killarney roads, within an hour's drive of all four towns. *Mallow, Co. Cork, tel. 022/47156, fax 022/47459. 16 rooms with bath. Facilities: restaurant (jacket and tie required), bar, fishing. AE, DC, MC, V. Closed mid-Dec.–mid-Mar. $$$*

Parknasilla

Lodging **Parknasilla Great Southern.** A porter in a frock coat and striped gray pants typifies the elegant and slightly stuffy turn-of-the-century atmosphere of this grand old hotel. Previous guests include General de Gaulle, Princess Grace, and George Bernard Shaw, who wrote much of *Saint Joan* while staying here. Although some rooms are a bit plain, they have been tastefully decorated in soft pinks and blues. The sheltered coastal location and excellent sporting facilities make it an ideal retreat. *Parknasilla, near Sneem, Co. Kerry, tel. 064/45122, fax 064/45323. 85 rooms with bath. Facilities: restaurant (jacket and tie required), bar, tennis court, indoor saltwater pool, sauna, horseback riding, sailing, windsurfing, waterskiing, fishing, 9-hole golf course. AE, DC, MC, V. Closed Jan.–mid-Mar. $$$*

Shannon

Lodging For lodging convenient to Shannon Airport, *see also* listings for Adare and Limerick, *above*, and Ennis and Newmarket-on-Fergus in Chapter 9, The West.

Shannon Great Southern. This pleasant, modern low rise is conveniently located just across from the main terminal at Shannon Airport, making it an ideal first or last stopping place for transatlantic travelers. Try an Irish coffee in the circular bar overlooking the river; the drink was invented at Shannon Airport to fortify passengers on the fueling stopover that was inevitable in the early days of aviation. The bland yet comfortable rooms have unexceptional contemporary hotel decor. *Shannon Airport, Co. Clare, tel. 061/471122, fax 061/471982. 115 rooms with bath. Facilities: restaurant, bar. $$*

Skibbereen

Dining **West Cork Hotel.** Sometimes, plain cooking (just like Ma's) is just what you're in the mood for; this busy, family-run hotel is the place to find it. Forgive the vagaries of the decor, which range from fake Louis XV to nondescript modern, and concentrate on the vast portions of roast meat, potatoes, and vegetables, which are served by attentive waitresses. At dinner, hearty eaters will enjoy the mixed grill. *Bridge St., Skibbereen, Co. Cork, tel. 028/21277. Reservations advised for parties of more than 4. AE, DC, MC, V. $*

Tralee

Dining ★ **Skillet.** This is a friendly, relaxed bistro, with contemporary paintings, low beams, and red-and-white-check place mats. Backpackers and a generally young crowd are attracted by the generous portions and the low prices. Vegetarian lasagna and pan-fried trout with almonds are regular favorites. *Barrack La., Tralee, Co. Kerry, tel. 066/24561. No reservations necessary. Closed Sun. Oct.–May. MC, V. $*

Lodging **Ballyseede Castle.** Located 3 kilometers (2 miles) east of Tralee on the main Killarney road, this former Fitzgerald Castle is approached through an impressive granite gateway. Within easy reach of four of the best courses in the region, it's popular with golfers. Victorian additions complement this imposing three-story castle. The individually decorated rooms have been generously furnished with antiques and two magnificent drawing rooms with ornamental plasterwork and marble fireplaces complete the picture. Try the Yeats room, which is one of the fanciest. *Tralee, Co. Kerry, tel. 066/25799, fax 066/25287. 12 rooms with bath. Facilities: restaurant, bar. MC, V. $$*

Brandon. This five-story modern hotel in the center of town is not especially exciting, but it is the only place in Tralee with a pool and a fitness center, and, unlike some of its competition, it's clean and well run. The decent-size rooms are furnished plainly, with uninspiring urban views. The restaurant is reputable. Rates shoot up during the Rose of Tralee Festival (late August) and the Listowel races (third week in September). *Princes St., Tralee, Co. Kerry, tel. 066/23333, fax 066/25019. 154 rooms with bath. Facilities: restaurant, 2 bars, indoor pool, sauna, steam room, gymnasium. AE, DC, MC, V. $$*

Waterville

Dining **The Huntsman.** Locals agree that this is the best eatery in town, in spite of the overwhelming bordellolike decor: bright-red carpets, red chairs, and lampshades that tint the light red as well. The specialty here is fresh, plainly cooked fish: lobsters from the tank broiled and served with roe, salmon hollandaise, and scampi Newburg. *Waterville, Co. Kerry, tel. 066/74124. Reservations advised. AE, DC, MC, V. Closed Nov.–Feb. $$*

Lodging **Butler Arms.** The white castellated towers at the corners of this imposing but architecturally undistinguished hotel provide a familiar landmark on the Ring. The building has been in the same family for three generations; it has a regular clientele, predominantly male, who come back year after year for the excellent fishing and/or golf facilities nearby. It was a favorite base for Charlie Chaplin. Although the accommodations are neither smart nor chic, the solid comfort of the rambling old lounges with open turf fires is highly conducive to both conversation and relaxation. *Waterville, Co. Kerry, tel. 066/74144, fax 066/74520. 31 rooms with bath. Facilities: restaurant, 2 bars, tennis court, deep-sea and freshwater angling. AE, DC, MC, V. Closed Nov.–Easter. $$$*

Youghal

Dining and Lodging ★

Aherne's. This famous seafood bar and restaurant, under an hour's drive from Cork City, has been in the same family for three generations and has recently added 10 spacious well-equipped bedrooms. The rooms are behind the main dining area and have their own entrance and comfortable sitting room with an open fire burning all day. The whole wing is furnished with Victorian and Georgian antiques, and all the rooms have super-king-size beds. The restaurant serves memorable seafood: Start with hot creamed oysters or prawns in garlic butter; popular main courses include hot buttered lobster and imaginative creations like plaice stuffed with oysters in a red-wine sauce or crab rolled in brill with rosemary sauce. The inexpensive bar food includes homemade tagliatelle with seafood and seafood pie topped with mashed potato. *163 North Main St., Youghal, Co. Cork, tel. 024/92424, fax 024/93633. 10 rooms with bath. Facilities: restaurant, bar, bicycles, deep-sea fishing. AE, DC, MC, V. $$*

The Arts and Nightlife

The Arts

Arts Centers/Galleries

Some of Ireland's finest contemporary painters live and work in the Southwest—Pauline Bewick, Tim Goulding, Cormac Boydell, Barrie Cooke, and Maria Simonds-Gooding among them—but they often choose to exhibit mainly in Dublin and abroad. You may find some of the above artists' prints at the places mentioned below, but the bulk of the work on display is priced moderately and by lesser-known local artists, some of whom, no doubt, have a big future.

Cork Arts Society (16 Lavitt's Quay, Cork, tel. 021/277749) has a representative selection of fairly conservative oils and watercolors by local artists, all of which are for sale. For more adventurous work in all media, take a look at the **West Cork Arts Center** (North St., Skibbereen, tel. 028/22090), where works are also for sale. In Limerick, don't miss the **Dolmen Gallery** (Honan's Quay, tel. 061/417929). Offbeat exhibits can also be found at the **Triskel Arts Center** (Tobin St., off S. Main St., Cork, tel. 021/272022) and the **Belltable Arts Center** (69 O'Connell St., Limerick, tel. 061/319866). **J & R Forrester** (83 N. Main St., Bandon, tel. 023/41360) has a small gallery above its crafts shop showing well-selected, reasonably priced works.

A thriving community of ceramic artists resides in the Southwest (*see* Shopping, Irish Crafts, *above*). For a list and location map of potters who welcome visitors, drop in at or phone **J & R Forrester** (*see above*).

Film

Aside from the Cork Film Festival in Cork City, held annually in mid-September (details from the **Triskel Arts Center,** *see* Arts Centers/Galleries, *above*), the Southwest is not a good place for movie buffs. Such screens as there are are dominated by movies for the teenage market. If you want to catch up on the latest horror films, check the listings in the *Cork Examiner* or the *Limerick Leader*.

Theater **Cork Opera House** (Lavitt's Quay, Cork, tel. 021/270022) is the city's major hall for touring productions and variety acts. Smaller productions are staged at the **Everyman Palace** (MacCurtain St., Cork, tel. 021/501673), where the ornate Victorian interior has recently been restored.

The **Triskel Arts Center** in Cork and the **Belltable Arts Center** in Limerick (*see* Arts Centers/Galleries, *above*) have small auditoriums for one-person shows and experimental works.

In Tralee, try to catch the **National Folk Theater of Ireland (Siamsa Tíre).** Language is no barrier to this colorful entertainment, which re-creates traditional rural life through music, mime, and dance. *Godfrey Pl., Tralee, tel. 066/23055. Admission: £4 adults, £3 children. Shows July–Aug., Mon.–Sat.; May, June, and Sept., every Tues. and Thurs. at 8:30.*

Nightlife

Medieval Banquets Most first-time visitors will not want to miss the medieval banquets held at the Bunratty and Knappogue castles. Both events cater largely to overseas visitors, many of them on organized tours; they will have little appeal for independent travelers in search of "the real Ireland." Medieval banqueting may not be authentic, but it is fun. At Bunratty, you'll be welcomed by Irish colleens in 15th-century dress who bear the traditional bread of friendship; you are led off to a honey-and-mead reception. Before sitting down at the long tables in the candlelighted great hall, you don a bib: You'll need it, because you'll be eating the four-course meal medieval style—with your fingers! The serving wenches take time out to sing a few ballads or pluck the strings of a harp. This warmhearted evening of Irish hospitality can be taken in the lighthearted spirit in which it is offered. These banquets are so popular that they must be booked as far in advance as possible. *Bookings for both Bunratty and Knappogue can be made by calling 061/360788. Tickets, including 4-course meal, wine, mead, and entertainment: £29.50. Nightly (subject to demand) at 5:45 and 8:45.*

If you can't get a place for a banquet, the next best thing is a *Ceilí* at Bunratty Folk Park; this program features traditional Irish dance and song and a meal of Irish stew, soda bread, and apple pie. *Tel. 061/360788. Cost: £24.50, including wine. May–Sept., 5:45 and 9 PM.*

The **Killarney Manor Banquet** offers a five-course meal hosted by "Lord and Lady Killarney" in their 1860 castellated manor house. The food, with a choice of poached salmon or roast Kerry lamb for the main course, is served by waitresses in 19th-century costume. The entertainment here is excellent by any standards, with a team of professional singers and dancers presenting all your favourite Irish tunes and maybe a few ones new to you. *Loreto Rd., Killarney, Co. Kerry, tel. 064/31551. Tickets including 5-course meal and a mulled-wine reception: £26, entertainment only £9. Advance booking advisable. Banquets Apr.–Oct., nightly 8 PM. Entertainment from 8:45–10:45.*

Pubs, Cabarets, and Discos Pub entertainment is the key to the Southwest's nightlife and offers better value, variety, and authenticity than the package market–oriented Irish cabaret options. If the music is in the main bar, you'll seldom have to pay a cover charge. Dancing to a fully amplified band in a room adjacent to the bar costs anywhere from £1.50 to £8, depending on the performers. During mid-June through September, you'll find musical entertainment most nights; during other seasons, Thursday through Sunday are the busiest times. Dingle is the best place in the region for traditional Irish music; elsewhere, pubs and clubs offer a mix of traditional, Irish, and folk ballads; country and rock classics; and a touch of New Orleans jazz in Cork and Kinsale. Spontaneous music sessions can take off at any time, especially on the Dingle Peninsula; elsewhere, performances usually begin around 9. Discos and nightclubs are usually attached to hotels or bars; they are open from 10:30 PM until 1 or 2 AM. Expect to pay a £2.50–£5 cover fee.

Cork City **De Lacy House** (74 Oliver Plunkett St., tel. 021/270074) attracts a young crowd for rock and folk gigs. The best places for jazz are the bars at **The Metropole Hotel** (MacCurtain St., tel. 021/508122) and **Morrison's Island Hotel** (Morrison's Island, tel. 021/275858). Live music (rock and nostalgia) is featured at **Rearden's Mill** (25 Washington St., tel. 021/27169). Traditional musicians gather at **An Spailpin Fanach** (28 S. Main St., tel. 021/277949). The **Stradbally Village** (Grand Parade Hotel, tel. 021/274391) offers traditional music and dancing nightly in an indoor reconstructed village. In the same hotel, you'll find live rock music at **Chandra's Nightclub.**

County Cork Kinsale and Clonakilty are the liveliest towns for nightlife. Check out the **Spaniard Inn** (Scilly, tel. 021/772436) for live rock and folk groups. **The Shanakee** (Market St., Kinsale, no tel.) is renowned in the area for nightly sing-alongs and ballad sessions; dancing workshops are given every Thursday. The **Bacchus Brasserie** (Guardwell, tel. 021/772382) offers dining and dancing to the over-25s. Jazz buffs will enjoy **Creole** (Pearse St., Kinsale, tel. 021/774109), which features live New Orleans jazz sessions in summer.

Tigh de Barra in Clonakilty (Pearse St., tel. 023/33381) is a focal point for West Cork's traditional musicians, many of whom live in the nearby Irish-speaking area. **Dunmore House** (Muckross, Clonakilty, tel. 023/33352) features local artists in cabaret on Tuesdays and a family night with dancing and talent competitions on Thursdays, July to September.

Kerry Try the **Kingdom Bar** (Kenmare, tel. 064/41361) for traditional music; for folk music, head for the **Strand Hotel** (Waterville, tel. 066/74248). Just about every bar on the Dingle Peninsula offers music every night in July and August—or so it seems, if you're looking for a quiet one! **O'Flaherty's** (Bridge St., Dingle, no phone) is a fine place for traditional music. For sing-along and dancing, try **An Reált—The Star Bar** (The Pier, Dingle, no phone). In Tralee, ballad sessions are more popular than traditional Irish music. If you're looking for the latter, call 066/25965—the *seisún* (having a good time) hotline—which will tell you where the action is. **Horan's Hotel** (Clash St., tel. 066/21933) has disco music and cabaret acts nightly during July and August, on weekends only during the off-season.

Killarney Singing bars are popular in Killarney, where a professional leads the singing and encourages audience participation and solos. Try **The Laurels** (Main St., tel. 064/31149). Killarney is strict on "Over 21s, Neat Dress Essential," and this is the rule at the **Kenmare Rooms** in the East Avenue Hotel (East Ave., tel. 064/32522), which offers a live cabaret with big names in the summer. The charge here includes admission to **Revelles Disco. Scott's Hotel Gardens** (College Rd., tel. 064/31060) and **Gleneagles** (Muckross Rd., tel. 064/31870) are the summer hot spots, offering big-name cabaret acts, singing bars, and discos.

Limerick **Foley's Bar** (Lower Shannon St., tel. 061/418783) has a ballad or traditional session every night except Wednesday. Traditional music is featured at **Nancy Blake's Pub** (19 Denmark St., tel. 061/416443) on Tuesday and Sunday. The **Glory Hole Bar** (George Hotel, O'Connell St., tel. 061/414566) has sessions every night, and there is late-night disco at **Tropics** (also in the George Hotel) Friday through Sunday.

9 The West

Cliffs of Moher, the Burren, Galway City, County Mayo

By Alannah Hopkin

As any Dubliner will tell you, the West is distinctively different from the rest of Ireland. Within Ireland, the West refers to the region that lies west of the River Shannon; most of this area falls within the old Irish province of Connaught. The coast of this region is situated at the western extremity of Europe, facing its nearest neighbors in North America across 3,200 kilometers (2,000 miles) of Atlantic Ocean. While the East, the Southwest, and the North were influenced by either Norman, Scots, or English settlers, the West escaped systematic resettlement and, with the exception of the walled town of Galway, remained purely Irish in language, social organization, and general outlook for far longer than the rest of the country. The land in the West, predominantly mountains and bogs, did not immediately tempt the conquering barons. Oliver Cromwell was among those who found the place thoroughly unattractive, and he gave the Irish chieftains who would not conform to English rule the choice of going "to Hell or Connaught."

It was not until the late 18th century, when better transport improved communications, that the West started to experience the so-called foreign influences that had already Europeanized the rest of the country. The West was, in effect, dragged out of the 16th century and into the 19th. You will notice that all buildings of interest in the region date either from before the 17th century or from the late 18th century onwards.

Today, many people maintain that the West is the most typically Irish part of the country. It features the highest concentration of Irish-speaking communities and the best traditional musicians in the Republic. Many residents still live on small farms rather than in towns and villages (towns were unknown in pre-Christian Irish society); especially in winter, the smell of turf fires still pervades the region.

As in the Southwest, the population of the West was decimated by famine in the mid-19th century and by mass emigration from then until the 1950s. A major factor in the region's recovery from economic depression has been the attraction to visitors to its sparsely populated mountain landscape and long, indented coastline with its many lakes and rivers. Tourism's development, however, has been mercifully low-key. Apart from a seaside promenade and fun palace at Salthill, just outside Galway, the area has seen no major investment in public amenities. Instead, additional land has been acquired for the Connemara National Park. Despite the sufficient number of top-class accommodations and the many charmingly converted country-house hotels, nothing intrudes on the simple attractions of the region's rugged, unspoiled countryside. The existence of some of the best angling in Europe on the West's rivers, lakes, and seas accounts for many regular visitors. Most holiday cottages are built according to the model of the traditional thatched cabin. The residents of the West have encouraged the revival of such cottage industries as knitting, weaving, and woodworking; the provision of bed-and-breakfast in existing homes; and informal sessions of traditional music in small bars. The lack of razzmatazz makes the West an ideal destination for travelers on a tight budget. The place comes alive between June and September. April, May, and October are good times for an off-peak visit. Outside these months many places will be closed; nightlife options and restaurant choices become limited. During the winter, weather can be harsh, with gales and rain sweeping in day after day from the Atlantic.

Essential Information

Important Addresses and Numbers

Tourist Information Bord Fáilte provides free information service, tourist literature, and an accommodations booking service at its **Tourist Information Offices** (TIOs).

Main Offices **Ennis** (Clare Rd., tel. 065/28366), **Galway City** (Victoria Pl., Eyre Sq., tel. 091/63081, fax 091/65201), and **Westport** (The Mall, tel. 098/25711, fax 098/26709). These offices are open all year weekdays 9–6 and Saturday 9–1.

Other Offices **Achill** (tel. 098/45384), **Aran Islands (Inishmore)** (tel. 099/61263), **Ballina** (tel. 096/70848), **Castlebar** (tel. 094/21207), **Clifden** (tel. 095/21163), **Cliffs of Moher** (tel. 065/81171), **Kilkee** (tel. 065/56112), **Kilrush** (tel. 065/51047), **Lahinch** (tel. 065/81474), **Lisdoonvarna** (tel. 065/51577), **Salthill** (Galway City, tel. 091/63081), and **Thoor Ballylee** (near Gort, tel. 091/31436). These offices are generally open July and August only, weekdays 9–6 and Saturday 9–1.

Emergencies **Police, fire,** and **ambulance** in all areas: dial 999 toll-free.

Doctors and Dentists **County Clare: Mid-Western Health Board** (tel. 061/316655); **Counties Galway and Mayo: Western Health Board** (tel. 091/51131).

Pharmacies **Galway: Matt O'Flaherty** (39 Eyre Sq., tel. 091/62927). **Westport: O'Donnell's** (Bridge St., tel. 098/25163).

Arriving and Departing by Plane

Airports and Airlines The West's most convenient international airport is **Shannon** (tel. 061/471444), 25 kilometers (16 miles) east of Ennis in the Southwest (*see* Essential Information in Chapter 8, The Southwest). **Galway Airport** (tel. 091/755569), near Galway City, and **Horan International Airport** (tel. 094/67222), at Knock in County Mayo, are used mainly for internal flights, with steadily increasing U.K. traffic. A small airport for internal traffic only is also located at **Knockrowen,** Castlebar, in County Mayo (tel. 094/22853). Flying time from Dublin is 25–30 minutes to all airports.

Flights from the United States No scheduled flights run from the United States to Galway or Knock; use Shannon Airport (*see* Essential Information in Chapter 8, The Southwest).

Flights from the United Kingdom **Aer Lingus** offers daily flights from London's Heathrow Airport to Galway and Knock via Dublin; the trip takes about two hours. **Ryanair** flies to Knock daily from London's Luton Airport; flying time is 80 minutes. **Loganair** flies to Knock from Birmingham, Manchester, and Glasgow.

Between the Airport and the Cities Galway Airport is 6½ kilometers (4 miles) from Galway City. No regular bus service is available from the airport to Galway, but most flight arrivals are taken to Galway Rail Station in the city center by an airline courtesy coach. Inquire when you book. A taxi from the airport to the city center costs about £7.

If you're flying from Dublin to Horan International Airport in Knock, you can pick up your rental car at the airport. Otherwise, inquire at the time of booking about transport to your final destination: No regular bus service is available from Horan International Airport.

Arriving and Departing by Car, Train, and Bus

By Car Leave Dublin by the N4, picking up the N6 in Kinnegad for Galway City. The 204-kilometer (127-mile) journey between Dublin and Galway takes about three hours. From Cork City take the N20 through Mallow and the N21 to Limerick City, picking up the N18 Ennis–Galway road in Limerick. The drive from Cork to Galway lasts 209 kilometers (130 miles) and takes about three hours.

From Killarney the shortest and most pleasant route is the N22 to Tralee, then the N69 through Listowel to Tarbert and the ferry across the Shannon Estuary to Killimer in County Clare, joining the N68 in Kilrush, and then picking up the N18 in Ennis. The drive from Killarney to Galway is 193 kilometers (120 miles) on this route and takes just less than three hours. The ferry leaves Tarbert every hour on the half hour and takes 20 minutes, avoiding a 104-kilometer (65-mile) detour through Limerick City. It costs £6 one-way, £10 round-trip. (Ferries return from Killimer every hour on the hour.)

By Train Galway City, Westport, and Ballina are the main rail stations in the region. For County Clare, travel from Cork City, Killarney Town, or Dublin's Heuston Station to Limerick City (tel. 061/315555) and continue the journey by bus.

Trains for Galway, Westport, and Ballina leave from Dublin's Heuston Station (tel. 01/836–6222). The journey time to Galway is three hours; to Ballina 3¾ hours; and to Westport 3½ hours. For train passenger inquiries, call 091/64222 in Galway, 096/21011 in Ballina, 098/25253 in Westport.

By Bus **Bus Éireann** operates a variety of Expressway services into the region from Dublin, Cork City, and Limerick City to Ennis, Galway City, Westport, and Ballina, the principal depots in the region. Expect bus rides to last about one hour longer than the time by car.

For bus passenger inquiries, call 01/836–6111 in Dublin, 021/506066 in Cork, and 061/313333 in Limerick.

Getting Around

A car is essential in the West, especially during September through June. Although the main cities of the area are reached easily from the rest of Ireland by rail or bus, transport within the region is sparse and badly coordinated. If a rental car is out of the question, your best option is to make Galway your base and take day tours (available mid-June–September) west to Connemara and south to the Burren, and a day or overnight trip to the Aran Islands. It *is* possible to explore the region by local and intercity bus services, but you will need plenty of time.

By Car The West has good, wide main roads (National Primary Routes) and better-than-average local roads (National Secondary Routes), both known as "N" routes.

However, if you stray off the beaten track on the smaller Regional ("R") or unnumbered routes, particularly in Connemara and County Mayo, you may encounter some hazardous mountain roads. Narrow, steep, and twisty, they are also frequented by untended sheep, cows, and ponies grazing "the long acre" (as the strip of grass beside the road is called) or simply straying in search of greener pastures. If you find a sheep in your path, just sound the horn and the creature will scramble away. A good maxim for these roads is "You never know what's around the next corner." Bear this in mind, and adjust your speed accordingly. Hikers and cyclists constitute an additional hazard on narrow roads in the summer.

Within the Connemara Irish-speaking area, signs are in Irish only. The main signs to recognize are Gaillimh (Galway), Rós an Mhil (Rossaveal), An Teach Doite (Maam Cross), and Sraith Salach (Recess). A good map, available through newsagents and Tourist Information Offices, gives Irish and English names where needed.

If you haven't already picked up a rental car at Shannon Airport (*see* Getting Around by Car in Chapter 8, The Southwest), try the following:

Galway City and Vicinity: Avis (tel. 091/68886), **Budget** (tel. 091/66376), **Johnson and Perrott** (tel. 091/68886), **Murray's** (tel. 091/62222), **O'Mara's Rent-a-Car** (tel. 091/64663).

Horan International Airport, Knock: Avis (tel. 094/67252) and **Capitol Car Hire** (tel. 094/54805).

By Train Rail transportation is not good within the West. The major destinations of Galway City and Westport/Ballina are on different branch lines. Connections can only be made between Galway and the other two cities by traveling inland for about an hour to Athlone (for inquiries, *see* Arriving and Departing by Train, *above*).

By Bus In July and August, the provincial bus service is augmented by daily services to most resort towns. Outside these months, many coastal towns receive only one or two buses per week. Bus routes are often slow and circuitous, and service can be erratic. A copy of the Bus Éireann timetable (50p from any station) is essential. The main bus stations are located at **Ennis** (tel. 065/24177), **Galway City** (Ceannt Station, tel. 091/64222), **Westport** (Railway Station, tel. 098/25253), and **Ballina** (tel. 096/21011).

By Ferry to the Aran Islands Between June and September, **Aran Ferries** (TIO, Victoria Pl., Eyre Sq., tel. 091/68903 or 091/92447 outside office hours) has daily sailings from Galway Docks, a five-minute walk from Eyre Square, at 10:30 AM in June, July, and September, 9:30 and 1:30 in August. The crossing takes 90 minutes and costs £15 round-trip. The same company runs a boat from Rossaveal, 32 kilometers (20 miles) west of Galway City, that makes the crossing in 20 minutes and costs £12 round-trip. The shuttle bus from Galway costs £3. For £20 round-trip on the same route you can have one night at a B&B on the islands. Alternately, the TIO in Galway City (Eyre Sq., tel. 091/63081) will arrange accommodations. **Island Ferries** (tel. 091/61767), which has a booking office on Victoria Place opposite the TIO in Galway City, has a one-hour crossing from Rossaveal for £12 round-trip with up to five sailings a day in summer, weather permitting. Bicycles are transported free, and discounts are available for families, students, and groups of four or more. If you stay a night or two on the islands ask about accommodations when booking your ferry as there are some very competitive deals, including free nights in a hostel for backpackers.

If you are heading for Inishere, the smallest island, the shortest crossing is from Doolin in County Clare (*see* Tour 1, *below*).

Frequent interisland ferries are available in summer months, but tickets are not transferable, so ask the captain of your ferry about his interisland schedule if you plan to visit more than one island; otherwise, your trip can become expensive.

By Plane to the Aran Islands **Aer Arann** (tel. 091/93034) offers four flights daily on weekdays, and two flights on Saturday and Sunday during July and August. The flights call at all three of the Aran Islands and leave from

Connemara Airport (tel. 091/93034) near Galway. The flight takes about six minutes and costs £32 round-trip.

For £24, you can fly one-way and travel one-way by boat from the Galway City docks. Ask about other special offers at the time of booking.

Guided Tours

Orientation Tours The only full- and half-day guided tours in the region start from Galway. **CIE** offers a choice of full-day tours covering Connemara, the Burren and the Atlantic coast, Westport and Achill Island, Carraroe, and South Connemara (cost of all tours: £12 adults, £6 children), and half-day tours to Cong or South Connemara (cost: £8 adults, £4 children). Tours run from mid-June to early September only, with the widest choice available between mid-July and mid-August. Book in advance at Galway City's Ceannt Railway Station (tel. 091/64222) or the Salthill Tourist Information Office (tel. 091/63081), which also serve as departure points.

Galway Tours runs a day tour through Connemara and County Mayo, and another to the Burren in July and August and on certain bank holiday weekends. Tickets can be booked at the Tourist Information Office in Galway City (Victoria Pl., Eyre Sq., tel. 091/63081).

Walking Tours Galway City's **Tourist Information Office** (Victoria Pl., Eyre Sq., tel. 091/63081) has details of walking tours of Galway, which are organized by request.

Exploring the West

Allow at least four days for exploring the region, and six days if you aim to visit the Aran Islands and/or Achill Island. Although distances between sites are not great, most of the tours in this chapter use the scenic but slower national secondary routes, on which covering 80 kilometers (50 miles) to 112 kilometers (70 miles) a day is a comfortable target.

Highlights for First-Time Visitors

The Burren (*see* Tour 1)
Clifden (*see* Tour 3)
The Cliffs of Moher (*see* Tour 1)
Connemara National Park (*see* Tour 3)
Dun Aengus, Inishmore (*see* Tour 2)
Kylemore Abbey (*see* Tour 3)
Salmon Weir Bridge (*see* Tour 2)
Westport, Clew Bay (*see* Tour 3)

Tour 1: The Burren and Beyond—West Clare to South Galway

Numbers in the margin correspond to points of interest on the West map.

1 Start in **Ennis,** the county town of County Clare, 25 kilometers (16 miles) west of Shannon Airport on the main road (the N18) to Galway. **Ennis,** a pleasant if physically unremarkable town, is a major crossroads and a convenient stop between the West and the South-

The West

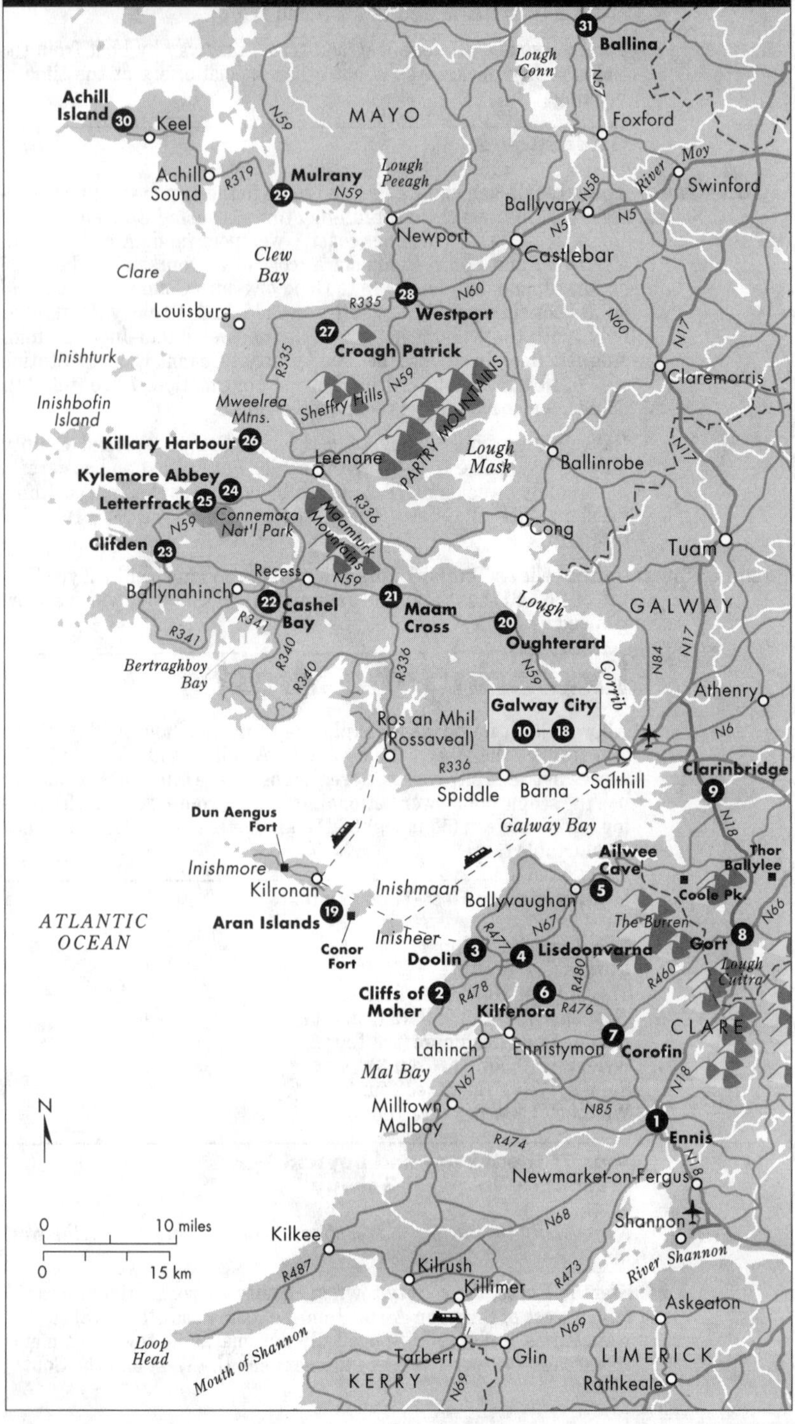

MAYO
Ballina
Lough Conn
Achill Island
Keel
Foxford
Achill Sound
Mulrany
Lough Peeagh
Swinford
River Moy
Ballyvary
Newport
Castlebar
Clew Bay
Clare
Louisburg
Westport
Croagh Patrick
Inishturk
Claremorris
Inishbofin Island
Mweelrea Mtns.
Sheffry Hills
PARTRY MOUNTAINS
Killary Harbour
Lough Mask
Leenane
Ballinrobe
Kylemore Abbey
Letterfrack
Connemara Nat'l Park
Maamturk Mountains
Cong
Clifden
Tuam
Recess
Ballynahinch
Cashel Bay
Maam Cross
Lough Corrib
GALWAY
Oughterard
Bertraghboy Bay
Athenry
Galway City
Ros an Mhil (Rossaveal)
Spiddle
Barna
Salthill
Clarinbridge
Dun Aengus Fort
Galway Bay
Ailwee Cave
Thor Ballylee
Inishmore
Kilronan
Inishmaan
Ballyvaughan
Coole Pk.
ATLANTIC OCEAN
Aran Islands
The Burren
Gort
Conor Fort
Inisheer
Doolin
Lisdoonvarna
Lough Cutra
Cliffs of Moher
Kilfenora
CLARE
Lahinch
Ennistymon
Corofin
Mal Bay
Milltown Malbay
Ennis
Newmarket-on-Fergus
Shannon
River Shannon
0 10 miles
0 15 km
Kilkee
Kilrush
Killimer
Askeaton
Loop Head
Mouth of Shannon
Tarbert
Glin
LIMERICK
KERRY
Rathkeale
N

west. It has always fostered traditional music, especially fiddle playing and step dancing (a kind of square dance). The Fleadh Nua festival in Ennis at the end of May attracts both performers and students of Irish music, who sing and dance in a series of concerts, workshops, and lectures.

Two statues in town bear witness to the role the people of Ennis have played in Irish democracy. On a tall limestone column above a massive pediment in the town center stands a statue of Daniel O'Connell (1775–1847), "The Liberator" (*see* Tour 3 in Chapter 8, The Southwest), who was a member of Parliament for County Clare between 1828 and 1831, the time at which he was instrumental in bringing about Catholic Emancipation. Outside the Courthouse (in the town park, beside the River Fergus, on the west side of Ennis) stands a larger-than-life bronze statue of Eamon De Valera (1882–1975), who successfully contested the election here in 1917 that launched his political career. Although De Valera was born in the United States, his maternal forebears were from County Clare. He was the dominant figure in Irish politics during this century, serving as prime minister for most of the years from 1937 until 1959, when he resigned as leader of Fianna Fáil, the party he founded; he went on to serve as president until 1973.

From Ennis, the main tour heads for the coast, which has been a playground for many generations of Irish people. If the season or the weather does not favor relaxing on sandy beaches and playing 18-hole golf courses, we suggest you take a shortcut, leaving Ennis on the N85 and joining the tour again at Lahinch, which is 32 kilometers (27 miles) from Ennis.

The main route follows the N68 from Ennis to Kilrush (43 kilometers/27 miles). (Those crossing from County Kerry by the Tarbert–Killimer ferry can join the tour at Kilrush, 5 kilometers/3 miles west of Killimer.) The N68 is a good stretch of relatively straight two-lane highway passing through a thinly populated region of small farms. Many visitors remark on the smallness of the farms in the West, the great majority being between 30 and 100 acres, and some no more than small holdings. In order to make a living, most of these farmers or their spouses (in some cases both) have a second job, such as fishing, running a B&B, or working seasonally. The rest rely on government subsidies or unemployment benefits, but few of them would trade their lives in western Ireland for more lucrative pursuits elsewhere.

Kilrush is a small market town based on a formal layout dating, like most towns in West Clare, from the mid-19th century. Streets radiate from a large central square, the widest street leading to the harbor and the docks. This plan creates the impression that the town (pop. 3,000) is bigger than it actually is. You'll find pleasant walks and picnic tables in the **Kilrush Woods,** a mature, freely accessible 420-acre forest on the east side of town.

Kilkee, which is 12 kilometers (8 miles) west of Kilrush on the N68, is a popular holiday resort with safe bathing both in the waters along its long sandy beach and in deep rock pools known as Pollock holes, which remain full at low tide. The latter attract scuba divers as well as swimmers. From Kilkee, you can take an excursion to Loop Head Lighthouse on the R487 (about 38 kilometers/24 miles round-trip). Loop Head is at the northern tip of the mouth of the Shannon, the very end of its long estuary.

The main route heads north up the coast on the N67. Sandy beaches and more Pollock holes can be found by taking a left off the main road at any sign that indicates "Strand" and traveling for about 2½ kilometers (1½ miles). The shortcut joins the main tour on the N67 at **Lahinch,** another resort village, which has two 18-hole golf courses. From here, take the R478 for the Cliffs of Moher. For the first time on this coast, the road narrows and starts to climb. It twists past small whitewashed farms and green fields with glimpses of the sea on the horizon.

❷ The best way to appreciate the magnificent **Cliffs of Moher** is to walk the short distance from the car park to O'Brien's Tower, at the cliffs' highest point. The car park is a favorite spot of performers, and if you're lucky you will find some free entertainment—perhaps step dancers, fiddle players, or even a one-man band. Next to the car park, take a look at the Visitor Center, at which leaflets explain various aspects of the cliffs' natural history, and visitors enjoy a crafts shop and tearoom. *Visitor Center, tel. 065/81171. Admission free. Open Apr.–Oct., daily 10–6.*

The cliffs rise vertically along 8 kilometers (5 miles) of coastline, at some points towering 185 meters (600 feet) above the sea. The stratified deposits of five different rock layers can be seen in the striations of the cliff face. The shelves of rock on the cliffs are home to numerous sea birds, including a large colony of puffins. On a clear day the Aran Islands and the mountains of Connemara are visible to the north, while the lighthouse on Loop Head and the mountains of Kerry may be seen to the south.

Follow the R478 from the cliffs inland toward Lisdoonvarna. A detour, signposted on the left as "Roadford/Doolin" on the R479, is a
❸ must for music lovers. **Doolin,** a tiny village consisting almost entirely of B&Bs, hostels, and pubs, claims three of the best pubs in Ireland for traditional music (*see* Nightlife, *below*). This village is a magnet for young musicians, some of whom camp out here for the whole summer learning from the resident virtuosos.

On Doolin Pier, about 1½ kilometers (1 mile) outside the village, local fishermen sell their catch fresh off the boat—lobster, crayfish, salmon, and mackerel. From mid-March until October (weather permitting), a regular ferry service takes visitors for a 30-minute ride to Inisheer, the smallest of the Aran Islands (*see* Tour 2, *below*). *Ferry, tel. 065/77086. Cost (round-trip): £12 adults, £6 children. Over 10 sailings daily mid-Mar.–Oct.*

❹ Retrace your route to the R478 and turn left for **Lisdoonvarna,** a small spa town featuring several sulfurous and iron-bearing springs with radioactive properties, all containing iodine. The town grew up in the late 19th century to accommodate visitors who wished to "take the waters." Its buildings reflect a mishmash of mock-architectural styles: Scottish baronial, Swiss chalet, Spanish hacienda, and American motel. Lovers of kitsch will find the town delightful, while others may condemn it as tacky.

Lisdoonvarna is the traditional vacationing spot for the West's bachelor farmers, who used to congregate here at harvest time in late September with the vague intention of finding wives. (Irish farmers are notoriously shy with women and reluctant to marry, often postponing the event until their mid- or late-fifties.) This tradition has been resurrected as the Matchmaking Festival, which takes place in Lisdoonvarna during late September and early October. Middle-aged singles dance to the strains of country-and-western bands, and a talent contest is held to find the most eligible bachelor. An increasing number of women from the United States are trying their luck at the festival and are all but guaranteed a good time, if not a husband.

By contrast, in July and August, the town is a favorite holiday spot with the Irish under-thirties, who dance the night away in a more contemporary style.

Lisdoonvarna Spa and Bath House has been renovated and is worth a visit if you're curious about health cures. The water offered here for drinking contains iron and magnesia and tastes quite as vile as does most spa water. The bathing water can be enervating but is comparatively pleasant. Electric sulfur baths, massage, and wax baths are available, as well as a sauna and a solarium. The spa complex is on the edge of town in an attractive parkland setting. *Tel. 065/74023. Admission free to complex. Sulfur baths: £5 (book in advance). Open early June–early Oct., daily 10–6.*

Lisdoonvarna is in the heart of the **Burren,** and as you travel 16 kilometers (10 miles) north on the N67 toward Ballyvaughan, the landscape becomes rockier and stranger. Instead of Irish green, gray is the prevailing color. The word Burren means "great rock." The Burren consists of fissured limestone known as *karst,* which is exposed in great irregular slabs known as pavements, with deep cracks between them. This plateau appears, from a distance, so dry that nothing could grow on it, and its landscape reminds many visitors of the surface of the moon. In fact, underneath the rough, scarred surface of the Burren are spectacular caves, streams, and potholes. "Turloughs"—seasonal lakes that disappear in dry weather—appear on the plateau's surface. In the cracks of the rocks, an amazing variety of wildflowers and plants can be found, which are at their best from mid-May to mid-June. Botanists are particularly intrigued by the cohabitation of Arctic and Mediterranean plants. Many of these plants are so tiny as to be invisible from the car window, so make a point of exploring some of this rocky terrain on foot.

5 Just outside Ballyvaughan, you'll see a signpost to the right for the **Ailwee Cave,** the only such chamber in the region accessible to those without spelunking expertise. This vast 2-million-year-old cave is illuminated for about 1,000 meters (3,300 feet) and contains an underground river and waterfall. *Tel. 065/77036. Admission: £3.50 adults, £2 children. Open early Mar.–early Nov., daily 10–6 (last tour 5:30); July and Aug., daily 10–7 (last tour 6:30).*

6 From the cave, return to the R480 and continue south, taking a right after about 16 kilometers (10 miles) on to the R476 for **Kilfenora.** Here, the tiny **Burren Display Center,** a modest audiovisual display with additional exhibits, explains all you'll want to know about the Burren's geology, flora, and archaeology. *Tel. 065/88030. Admission: £2 adults, £1 children. Open July and Aug., daily 9:30–6, Mar.–June and Sept.–Oct., daily 10–5.*

Have a look at the tiny church beside the Display Center before leaving. The ruins of a small 12th-century church, once the **Cathedral of St. Fachan,** have been partially restored as a parish church. There are some interesting carvings in the roofless choir, including an unusual life-size skeleton. In a field about 50 meters (165 feet) to the west of the ruins is an elaborately sculpted High Cross that is worth examining even though parts of it are badly weathered.

7 Retrace your route on the R476, carrying on for about 16 kilometers (10 miles) to **Corofin.** Here, those in search of their Irish roots will want to visit the **Clare Heritage Center,** which offers a genealogical service and do-it-yourself advice. It also features a display on the history of the West of Ireland in the 19th century, covering culture, traditions, emigration, and famine, as it exposes some grim statistics. In 1841, for example, the population of County Clare was

286,394. Fifty years later, famine and emigration had reduced this number to 112,334, and the population continued to decline, reaching an all-time low of 73,597 in 1956. (It is now heading for the 90,000 mark.) *Tel. 065/37955. Admission: £1.75 adults, £1 students and senior citizens, 75p children. Open Apr.–Oct., daily 10–6; Nov.–Mar., geneaology service only, weekdays 9–5; museum by appointment.*

Another site in Corofin that should appeal particularly to archaeology buffs is the **Dysert O'Dea Castle Archaeology Center,** a 15th-century castle on the edge of town, with an exhibition on the antiquities of the Burren. Twenty-five monuments stand within a 1½-kilometer (1-mile) radius of the castle; these date from the Bronze Age to the 19th century, and all of them are described at the center. *Tel. 065/37722. Admission: £1.80 adults, 80p children. Open May–Sept., daily 10–6.*

From Corofin, leave the Burren by taking the R460 north for 24 kilometers (15 miles) to Gort; turn left (north) on to the N18. In the
8 center of **Gort** (a dull little town), look out for a sign on the right for **Thoor Ballylee.** Admirers of the poet W.B. Yeats (1865–1939) will want to take the detour 5 kilometers (3 miles) up the N66 to visit the Norman tower that Yeats bought as a ruin in 1916 for the sum of £35. He repaired it and lived there intermittently until 1929. This handsome stone building beside a tranquil mill stream is now fully restored with Yeats's original decor and furniture. An audiovisual display is available on the Nobel Prize–winning poet and his works. *Tel. 091/31436. Admission: £2.50 adults, £1 children. Open Easter–Sept., daily 10–6.*

Return to the N18 and continue north for Galway City. Just outside Gort on the left-hand side is **Coole Park,** former location of the home of Yeats's patron, Lady Augusta Gregory (1859–1932). Once a center for the Irish literary revival, the house fell derelict after her death and was demolished in 1941. The park is now a national forest and wildlife park, with picnic tables. The only reminder of its literary past is the Autograph Tree, a copper beech on which many of Lady Gregory's famous guests carved their initials, including George Bernard Shaw, Sean O'Casey, and Douglas Hyde, the first president of Ireland. *Tel. 091/31804. Admission to Visitor Centre £1 adults, 70p senior citizens, 40p students and children. Open Apr.–mid-June and Sept., Tues.–Sat. 10–5; mid-June–Aug. 31, daily 9:30–6:30; Visitor Centre closed Oct.–mid-Apr.; Park open daily 10–dusk, freely accessible.*

As the road runs farther north you will see fields hedged by dry stone walls made of gray boulders piled on top of one another; mortar is not used in the walls' construction. They are a typical feature of the West of Ireland, as are the long evenings caused by the sun slowly sinking over the Atlantic on the western horizon. As you approach Galway City you will catch an occasional glimpse of the sea on your left. This is Oyster Country, where the famous Galway oyster grows.

9 **Clarinbridge,** 19 kilometers (12 miles) south of Galway City, is the place to stop and sample these shellfish, if there is an "R" in the name of the month of your travels. The new oyster season is launched with an Oyster Festival, a must for mollusk eaters, held annually in and around the town on the last weekend in September. From Clarinbridge, follow the signs for Galway City, which will take you to Eyre Square. Expect a few delays along the way in July and August, when traffic is at its peak.

Tour 2: Galway City and the Aran Islands

10 Many Irish people consider **Galway** to be the best city in the Republic. This compact, lively, and informal place possesses a distinctive cosmopolitan charm. Good road and rail links with the capital make Galway and the surrounding region a favorite weekend destination for jaded Dubliners. The city, which has always attracted writers and artists, features two small but internationally acclaimed theater companies (*see* The Arts and Nightlife, *below*). Its university is a center for Gaelic culture, where many students take their degrees in the Irish language. Galway's predominantly young and well-educated population has attracted several multinational companies to its industrial estates, and the town positively buzzes with energy.

Galway is the largest city in the West of Ireland, with about 47,000 residents; it is at the head of Galway Bay, where the River Corrib flows from the Lough down to the sea. Across the wide entrance to Galway Bay lie the three Aran Islands with their distinctive Irish-speaking communities. Galway has always been the chief trading post for the islands, and it is the most practical place from which to organize an excursion to them. The islands receive upward of 100,000 visitors per year, most of them between June and August, so do not expect to be a lone pioneer. However, a visit to these islands is still a unique experience and will be a topic of conversation long after your visit to Ireland is over. Such a trip will also greatly enhance your understanding of Irish folkways and Gaelic culture.

Galway celebrated the 500th anniversary of its charter as a city in 1984 with a great display of civic pride, which sparked an urban renewal scheme that has brought new life to the city's once-neglected docklands. The people here have plenty to be proud of. In the early 1980s, Galway was the first city in Ireland to discourage bland, international-style neon and plastic commercial signs and facades by reviving the old Irish tradition of hand-painted wooden shop signs with Gaelic lettering. The city has been further enhanced by the installation of well-designed modern sculptures, floral hanging baskets, and window boxes.

The founders of Galway were Anglo-Normans who arrived in the mid-13th century and fortified their settlement against "the native Irish," as local chieftains were called. Galway became known as the City of the Tribes because of the dominant role in public and commercial life of the 14 families who founded it. Their names are still common in Galway and elsewhere in Ireland and recur regularly in any account of Irish history and culture: Athy, Blake, Bodkin, Browne, D'Arcy, Dean, Font, French, Kirwan, Joyce, Lynch, Morris, Martin, and Skerret.

Numbers in the margin correspond to points of interest on the Galway City map.

Old Galway is best explored on foot—indeed, in July and August, when the tourist season is at its peak and traffic on its narrow streets becomes heavy, walking is virtually the only way to get
11 around. The major point of orientation for the visitor is **Eyre Square,** the center of the city. The square is dominated on its southeast side by the solid four-story limestone facade of the **Great Southern Hotel** (Eyre Sq., tel. 091/64041), built to coincide with the arrival of the railway in the mid-19th century. The bus station and Ceannt Rail Station are just behind the hotel on Station Road, on the left-hand side as you face the hotel. The **Tourist Information Office** is on Victo-

ria Place on the right-hand side of the hotel. *Tel. 091/63081. Open weekdays 9–6, Sat. 9–1.*

The grassy central area of Eyre Square is known as **Kennedy Park,** in honor of John F. Kennedy, who visited the city in 1963, five months before his assassination. The park is dominated by a beautiful 6-meter (20-foot) steel sculpture, which stands in the midst of a fountain pool. The work, installed in 1986, takes the form of brown sails that are seen on the traditional sailing boats, known as Galway hookers; these boats were used until the early part of this century to carry turf, provisions, and cattle across Galway Bay and out to the Aran Islands. The genial stone figure with a pipe, seated beside the steel sculpture, is Padraic O'Conaire, a pioneer of the Irish-language revival at the turn of the century. So ascetic was this great storyteller that when he died in a Dublin hospital in 1928 his only possessions were his pipe, his tobacco, and an apple. The monument beside the park fountain, known as the Browne Doorway, was taken in 1905 from a town house belonging to the family of that name. This doorway features the 17th-century coats of arms of both the Browne and Lynch families. Keep an eye out for similar if less elaborate versions of the entranceway as you walk around the old part of town. The bronze cannons in Kennedy Park were presented at the end of the Crimean War to the Connaught Rangers, recruits to a famous regiment of the British army from the West of Ireland.

Leave Eyre Square by Williamsgate, which is a small street on your left as you stand at the top of the square with your back to the Great Southern Hotel. The **General Post Office** is on Eglinton Street, the first street off Williamsgate to your right. Next, continue straight
12 ahead down William Street to **Lynch's Castle,** now a branch of the Allied Irish Bank, on the corner of Shop Street. This edifice is the best remaining example of a merchant's town-castle; a number of these fortified houses were inhabited by the leading families of Galway in the 16th and 17th centuries. Lynch's Castle features decorative details on its stone lintels that are usually found only in southern Spain; the building serves as a reminder of the close trading links that once existed, in the 16th and 17th centuries, between Galway and Spain.

To visit two of Galway's more famous sights, turn right at Lynch's Castle into Abbeygate Street, then take the first left, at Market
13 Street. Here you will find the **Lynch Memorial Window** embedded in a stone wall above a built-up Gothic doorway. At this spot, according to legend, James Lynch FitzStephen, mayor of Galway in the early 16th century, condemned his son to death after he had confessed to murdering a Spanish visitor. When no one could be found to carry out the execution, Judge Lynch hanged his son himself before retiring into seclusion.

Market Street leads to Lombard Street and the entrance to the
14 **Collegiate Church of St. Nicholas,** which was built by the Anglo-Normans in 1320 and enlarged in the 16th century. The church contains many fine carvings and gargoyles dating from the late Middle Ages. According to legend, Columbus once prayed here, because Galway was his last port of call before setting off on his voyage to discover the New World. The story, of course, is impossible to prove, but it's not totally implausible. On Saturday mornings, a traditional street market, held in the shadow of the church, enlivens the already busy city center. *Admission free. Open daily 8–dusk.*

If a browse around the shops is more enticing than the two previously mentioned attractions, continue from Lynch's Castle straight

Galway City

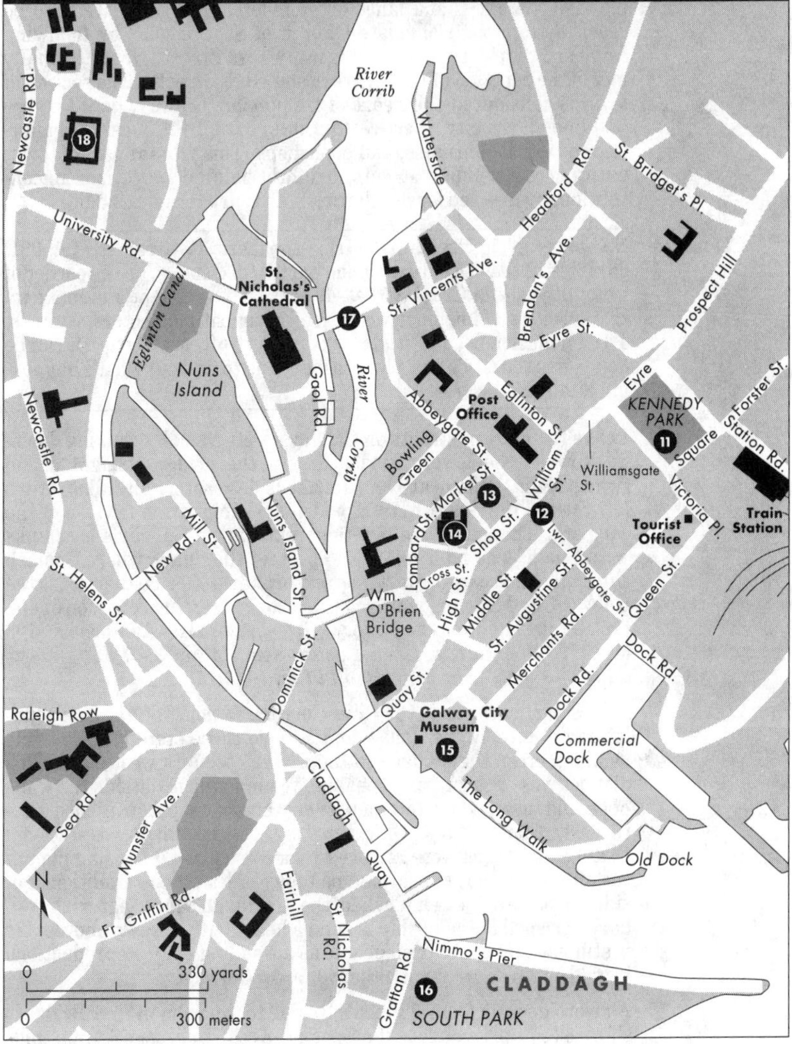

Claddagh, **16**
Collegiate Church of St. Nicholas, **14**
Eyre Square, **11**
Lynch's Castle, **12**
Lynch Memorial Window, **13**
Salmon Weir Bridge, **17**
Spanish Arch, **15**
University College, **18**

(south) down **Shop Street, High Street,** and **Quay Street,** investigating also the alleys and lanes on your left. (The same area can be reached from the Collegiate Church of St. Nicholas by following Lombard Street as it continues into Cross Street, where it finally meets the junction of Quay Street and High Street.) This section of town is considered the heart of fashionable Galway; here visitors will find all the city's best restaurants, bars, boutiques, art galleries, and crafts, antiques, and bookshops. This vibrant part of town, with narrow winding streets, brightly painted shops, and unconventionally dressed locals, charms both tourists and residents.

Time Out **Noctan's** (or **Tig Neactain,** to Irish speakers; 17 Cross St., tel. 091/66172) is a bar with old-fashioned partitioned snugs, on the corner of Quay Street and Cross Street. It serves an excellent and inexpensive selection of imaginative bar food at lunchtime. Actors, writers, artists, musicians, and students come here often; although it can be noisy, it is the city's "in" place to meet and to find out what's happening locally in the arts.

Leave the maze of streets on Galway's Left Bank by walking downhill toward the River Corrib. Ignore the bridge straight ahead (which leads to the nearby modern seaside resort, Salthill) and turn
15 left toward the **Spanish Arch,** which is visible at the far side of the car park. This structure, another reminder of Galway's past links with Spain, was built in 1594 to protect the quays where Spanish ships unloaded cargoes of wines and brandies. Beside the arch is the **Galway City Museum,** which contains an interesting selection of material relating to local history. *Tel. 091/67641. Admission: 50p adults, 30p children. Open Easter–Sept., daily 9–5; July–Aug., daily 9–8; Oct.–Easter, Wed. and Fri. 10–5:15.*

In this part of the city, the **River Corrib** is famous for its large population of mute swans. Pause and admire these stately birds while
16 looking across the estuary to the **Claddagh** on its west bank. This district was once an Irish-speaking fishing village outside the walls of the old town, which retained its own strong, separate identity until early this century. Unfortunately, the Claddagh's traditional thatched cottages were replaced by a conventional housing plan in the 1930s, and not much remains today of its unique traditions besides a piece of jewelry called the Claddagh ring, featuring two hands clasped in friendship around a heart with a crown above it. It is still used by many Irish people as a wedding ring. Reproductions in gold or silver are favorite souvenirs of Galway.

17 A riverside walk from O'Brien's Bridge to the **Salmon Weir Bridge** is signposted upriver from the Spanish Arch. In season—from mid-April to early July—shoals of salmon are visible from the bridge, lying in the clear river water before making their way upstream to the spawning grounds of Lough Corrib. This view is one of the most popular and memorable sights in Galway.

Galway's **Catholic Cathedral,** on an island forming the west bank of the River Corrib beside the Salmon Weir Bridge, was dedicated by Cardinal Cushing of Boston in 1965. The building features cut limestone with Connemara flooring, a copper dome, and all manner of expensive ornamentation. The 1960s was not a good period for Irish architecture, and its indelicate design lacks divine inspiration.

18 If an excursion to the campus of **University College** interests you, follow University Road to the west of the cathedral back on to the mainland, turning right into the quadrangle at the second corner after about ½ kilometer (¼ mile). The pleasant Tudor-Gothic-style quad-

rangle was completed in 1848, three years after the founding of the university. Its library boasts an important archive of Celtic-language materials, and it also hosts courses in July and August in Irish studies for overseas students.

The Aran Islands

Numbers in the margin correspond to points of interest on the West map.

For details on getting to the Aran Islands, *see* Getting Around in Essential Information, *above*.

Something very special about small inhabited islands creates a mag-
19 netic attraction for certain travelers. In the case of the **Aran Islands,** the attraction is enhanced by their geography—the same weird limestone rock that is found on the Burren (*see* Tour 1, *above*), lifted in great ramparts against the pounding Atlantic Ocean—and their Irish-speaking inhabitants, who have inherited the lands and traditions of a hardy, plain-living fishing and farming folk. All islands have their idiosyncrasies, but the Aran Islands are more unusual than most.

Over the years they have attracted a number of writers and artists, including J. M. Synge (1871–1909), who learned Irish on Inishmaan and wrote his play *Riders to the Sea* about its people. The film *Man of Aran,* made on Inishmore in 1932 by the American director Robert Flaherty, is a classic documentary recording the islanders' dramatic battles with sea and storm. Since those days the islanders have benefited enormously from 20th-century progress; they now have multichannel television, a daily air service to Galway (subsidized by the government), outboard motors on their currachs, and all the modern conveniences in their homes. Yet these island folk retain a certain distinctness from the mainland people, preferring a simpler kind of home decor, very plain food, and a strong sense of community. Crime is virtually unknown on the islands; you will find no locks on the doors of your B&B, and its front-door latch is left permanently open. Many of the islanders have sampled life in Dublin or the cities of the United Kingdom and the United States, but they often return home by choice, some of them in time to raise their families on the islands, where the population remains stable. The best time to visit the islands is May and early June when the unusual Burren-like flora is at its best, and before the bulk of the more than 100,000 annual visitors arrive.

Inishmore, the largest of the islands, with a population of 900, and the closest to the Connemara coast, is also the most commercialized, its appeal slightly diminished by the existence of some road traffic. In the summer, ferries arriving at **Kilronan,** its main village and port, are met by minibuses and pony and cart drivers, all anxious to show visitors "the sights." For the energetic, the best way to see the island is by bicycle. (Bring your own or hire one from the shed on the quay—no telephone.) The island is more than 8 kilometers (5 miles) long and about 3 kilometers (2 miles) wide at most points, with an area of 7,640 acres, making it just a little too large to explore comfortably on foot in a day. The **Aran Interpretative Center** will give you an insight into the history and culture of the island folk who lived for many years in virtual isolation from the mainland. *Tel. 099/61355. Admission £2 adults, £1.50 students, £1 children and senior citizens. Open Easter–late Sept., daily 10–6.*

Leaving Kilronan, you will notice the tall, dry (unmortared) stone walls, enclosing diminutive fields, which are a feature of the islands. The stone walls enabled the farmers to clear the land of rocks, while at the same time they created a buffer against the Atlantic gales.

The farmers then had to "manufacture" soil by combining sand and rotted seaweed—the only available materials. As the road climbs the hill beyond Kilronan, you have access to panoramic views of the Connemara coast. Footpaths lead across the fields to both stony and sandy beaches, most of them contained in small deserted coves.

The main attraction on Inishmore is **Dún Aengus,** one of the finest prehistoric monuments in Europe, dating from about 2000 BC. The fort sits spectacularly on the edge of a 90-meter- (300-foot-) high cliff overlooking a sheer drop. The defenses consist of three rows of concentric circles, but who were defending themselves against whom is a matter of conjecture. Visitors have a great view of the island and the Connemara coast from the innermost rampart. *Admission free. Freely accessible.*

Inishmaan, the middle island in both size and location, has a population of about 300 and can be comfortably explored on foot—in fact, you have no alternative! This island features several antiquities—Conor Fort, a smaller version of Dun Aengus; the ruins of two early Christian churches; and a chamber tomb known as the Bed of Diarmuid and Grainne, dating from about 2000 BC. Visitors can also take wonderful cliff walks above secluded coves.

On Inishmaan, the traditional Aran lifestyle is most evident. Until the mid-1930s or so, the women of Aran dressed in thick red woolen skirts to keep out the Atlantic gales, while the men wore collarless jackets, baggy trousers made of homespun tweed with *pampooties* (hide shoes without heels, suitable for walking on rocks), and a wide hand-plaited belt called a *críos* (pronounced "krish"). Most islanders still don the famous hand-knitted Aran sweaters, with their intricate designs and symbols, though nowadays they accompany them with jeans and sneakers. The origins of these designs gives an idea of the hardships endured by the islanders down the years: A body lost at sea could be identified by the pattern on its sweater, as each district had its own pattern. Often this design was the only means of identification.

It is possible to explore **Inisheer,** the smallest and flattest of the islands, on foot in an afternoon, though if the weather is fine you may be tempted to linger on the long sandy beach that lies between the quay and the airfield. In the summer, Inisheer's population of 300 is augmented by high school students from all over Ireland attending its language school. Only one stretch of road, about 450 meters (500 yards) long, links the airfield and the village.

The **Church of Kevin,** signposted to the southeast of the quay, is a small early Christian church that gets buried in sand by the storms every winter. Every year the islanders dig it out of the sand for the celebration of St. Kevin's Day on June 14. A pleasant walk through the village takes you up to **O'Brien's Castle,** a ruined 15th-century tower open free to the public, which sits on top of a rocky hill—the only hill on the island.

Nature lovers will enjoy a ramble to "the back of the island," as its uninhabited side facing the Atlantic is called. No beaches can be found on the back of the island, but people do swim off the rocks. It is worth making a circuit of the island to get a sense of its unique tranquillity. A maze of footpaths runs between the high stone walls that divide the fields. On Inisheer, the fields are so small that they can support only one cow each, or two to three sheep. Those that are not cultivated or grazed turn into natural wildflower meadows between June and August, overrun with harebells, scabious, red clover, oxeye daisies, saxifrage, and tall grasses. It seems almost a crime to walk here—but who can resist taking a rest in the corner of a sweet-smelling meadow on a sunny afternoon, sheltered by high stone walls with no sound but the larks above and the wind as it sifts through the stones? These singular moments make a visit to the Aran Islands worthwhile.

Tour 3: Through Connemara and County Mayo

Numbers in the margin correspond to points of interest on the West map.

Connemara is the name given to the western part of County Galway, which lies between Lough Corrib and the Atlantic. Its moorland is dominated by the Maamturk Mountains and the Twelve Bens range to the north and is fringed by a deeply indented Atlantic coastline with innumerable creeks, bays, and small harbors. Population in this area is sparse, even on the lowland plains, which are mainly bog. Connemara National Park, in the north of the region, covers some 4,900 acres.

Two main touring routes—inland and coastal—lead through Connemara. Those who have traveled out from Galway City to Rossaveal on the R336 coastal route through Salthill, Barna, and Spiddle will have noticed how this, once one of the most impressive and unspoiled coastal roads in Ireland (and in an Irish-speaking area), has been scarred by ill-sited and badly designed bungalows. The majority of traditional thatched cabins in the West are holiday homes; local residents prefer to live in garish concrete one-story homes—a strident Spanish hacienda style, totally out of keeping with the local climate, is particularly favored. These new buildings are deplored by most visitors, including leading architects and environmentalists, but are stoutly defended by the bungalow-dwellers themselves. To avoid a second look at these eyesores, those starting from Rossaveal should follow the continuation of the R336 northwards to Maam Cross, joining this tour there on the N59.

If you start from Galway City, get on the well-signposted outer-ring road and follow signs for the N59—Moycullen, Oughterard, and Clifden—the inland Connemara route.

After about 32 kilometers (20 miles), just past the village of Rosscahill, look for a signpost on the right side to **Aughnanure Castle.** This six-story stone tower house was built in the 16th century by the O'Flahertys, a ferocious Irish clan who frequently raided Galway City. The large square building stands beside the River Drimneen in the midst of a field often grazed by sturdy Connemara ponies—a local breed whose shaggy good looks and strong character have made them world famous. *No phone. Admission: 60p adults, 25p children and senior citizens. Open mid-June–mid-Sept., daily 10–6. Key with caretaker rest of year.*

20 Return to the main road and continue on the N59 to **Oughterard** (pronounced "Ook-ter-ard"), a small and pretty village close to the shore of **Lough Corrib.** The lough is signposted to the right in the village center, less than 1½ kilometers (1 mile) up the road, which explains why Oughterard is one of Ireland's leading angling resorts. In the summer from mid-June to early September, local boatmen offer trips on the lough, which has several islands. It is also possible to take a boat trip to **Cong** on the other side of the lough. This unusual village of small Gothic-style cottages was the location of the John Ford movie *The Quiet Man*, starring John Wayne, which was filmed in 1951. The boat docks beside **Ashford Castle,** now a luxury hotel

where President Reagan stayed during his visit in 1984. **Inchagoill Island** (the Island of the Stranger), midway between Oughterard and Cong, is a popular destination for a half-day trip; it features several early Christian church remains. *Cost of boat rides subject to negotiation—expect to pay about £6 per person.*

Pick up the N59 again in Oughterard, where it continues west beside a string of small lakes. The sudden appearance of their shining blue water reflecting the blue sky is a typical Connemara sight on a sunny
21 day. **Maam Cross** (where the Rossaveal road joins this tour) is literally just a crossroads, apparently in the middle of nowhere. It was once an important meeting place for the people of north and south Connemara, and is still the location of a big monthly cattle fair. Walkers will find wonderful views of Connemara by heading for any of the local peaks visible from the road.

Between Maam Cross and Recess (a distance of 16 kilometers/10 miles), you will find some of the best scenery in Connemara. A short walk to either side of the main road will lead you to the shores of one of the many small loughs in the area: Stop and linger if the sun is out—even intermittently. It is the quality of the light filtering through the clouds that gives such splendor to the distant, dark-gray mountains and creates fascinating patterns on the brown-green moorland below. In June and July, the light lasts in the sky until almost 11, and it is worth taking a late-evening stroll to observe the sun's reluctance to set.

If the weather is allowing the light to play its tricks, try to take a 26-kilometer (16-mile) detour to the left about 3 kilometers (2 miles) beyond Recess, following signposts for Cashel Bay (first right on the R340, second right on the R342) and then Ballynahinch (third right on the R341). If it is raining, however, stay on the main road for 19 kilometers (12 miles) from Recess to Clifden.

22 **Cashel Bay** is a quiet, extremely sheltered angling center at the head of Bertraghboy Bay. General de Gaulle is among the many people who have sought seclusion here. Take it easy on the narrow mountain roads—stray sheep and bolting Connemara ponies are regular hazards, along with cyclists and reckless local drivers. The final turn on to the R341 takes you along the shores of **Ballynahinch Lake** and into more wooded country. Woodland in this part of the world indicates the proximity of a "big house" whose owner can afford to plant trees for pleasure and prevent them from being cut down for fuel. You will see a sign on the left-hand side for **Ballynahinch Castle,** now a small hotel but once the home of the Martin family, one of whom, Richard Martin (1754–1834), known as Humanity Dick, was the founder of the Royal Society for the Prevention of Cruelty to Animals.

Time Out Drive through the gates of **Ballynahinch Castle** (Ballinafad, Co. Galway, tel. 095/31006) and slowly up its well-kept driveway. Nonresidents are welcome here, and the **Fisherman's Bar** in the castle basement serves inexpensive bar lunches year-round. You can also take scenic walks through the woodlands by the lake on the castle's 350-acre estate.

A left turn back onto the N59 will take you for 16 kilometers (10
23 miles) to **Clifden,** far and away the prettiest "town" in Connemara. In most places, Clifden, with 1,381 residents, would be called a village, but out here it is looked on as something of a metropolis. Clifden offers a good selection of small restaurants, lively bars with music most nights in the summer, some very pleasant accommoda-

tions, and excellent walks. These features, as well as its location between the mountains and the sea, have made it a popular base for touring Connemara by car.

The town, perched high above Clifden Bay with its back to the mountains, has a profile enhanced by the tapering spires of its two churches. At first glance, however, it does not appear to lie beside the sea at all. The seashore is, in fact, best discovered on foot, by taking a short (2-kilometer/1¼-mile) walk along the quay road through the grounds of the ruined **Clifden Castle.** The castle was the home of John D'Arcy, who founded the town in 1815, giving it its distinctive layout of a wide main street on a long ridge with a parallel street below it. The town is sleepy out of season but teems with visitors in July and August, when the **Clifden Connemara Pony Show** (equestrian events and sales accompanied by exhibits of Irish arts and crafts) is a main attraction.

To appreciate Clifden's almost Alpine location, take the aptly named **Sky Road,** signposted at the west end of town, a high narrow circuit of about 5 kilometers (3 miles) via Kingstown; you'll enjoy the breathtaking scenery above the precipitous shores of Clifden Bay.

Time Out Try the **D'Arcy Inn** (Main St., tel. 095/21450), a Tudor-style bar in the center of town, for a quick pub lunch or a light evening meal. Inexpensive, plain Irish fare—Irish stew or poached salmon, accompanied by plenty of spuds—is served either in the upstairs restaurant or in a small room at the back of the bar.

Next, continue on the N59 from Clifden toward Letterfrack (14 kilometers/9 miles) through the **Inagh Valley,** which is flanked by two impressive mountain ranges with distinctive conical-shape peaks, which rise almost directly to over 600 meters (1,968 feet) without any foothills.

Kylemore Valley, between the Twelve Bens and the Dorruagh Mountains, the latter naturally forested, is one of the more conventionally beautiful stretches of road in Connemara. The road passes over
24 three lakes; if you have not already stopped at the sign for **Kylemore Abbey,** you will certainly do so ¾ kilometer (½ mile) later to look back at this fantastic turreted gray stone building, which is visible across a reedy lake with a backdrop of wooded hillside. The abbey was built as a private home in 1864 by Mitchell Henry, a member of Parliament, and is now a convent of Benedictine nuns, who run a girls' boarding school here. The location is sheer heaven, almost enough to tempt one to take up the religious life.

The nuns welcome visitors to their well-stocked crafts center and simple cafeteria, and the grounds are freely accessible most of the year. Ask at the crafts shop for directions to the Gothic Chapel, a tiny replica of Norwich Cathedral built by Mitchell Henry on the abbey grounds. *Tel. 095/41113. Admission free. Crafts shop open Mar. 17–Nov. 1, daily 10–6; cafeteria open Easter and May–Oct. 15, daily 10–6; grounds open Feb.–Dec. 24, daily 10–6.*

About 8 kilometers (5 miles) beyond Kylemore, signposted in the
25 village of **Letterfrack,** is the **Connemara National Park Visitor Center.** Drop in for details of the many excellent walks and beaches in the area. Some of the shorter (under 2-kilometer/1¼-mile) walks can be followed from the main road on carefully laid-out gravel paths, though most visitors will want to venture farther afield. *Tel. 095/41054. Admission free. Car park: £1. Open Apr.–Oct., daily 10–6.*

Beyond Letterfrack the road travels for some miles alongside
26 **Killary Harbour,** a narrow fjordlike inlet that runs for 16 kilometers (10 miles) between the mountains, with its northern shore located in County Mayo. The harbor offers an extremely safe anchorage, 13 fathoms (78 feet) deep for almost its entire length and sheltered from storms by mountain walls. The rafts floating in Killary Harbour belong to fish-farming consortia who are artificially raising salmon and trout in cages beneath the water. This is a matter of some controversy all over the West, with some people fearing the long-term effect of pollution from certain fish-farming practices on wild salmon and trout, and others welcoming the employment opportunities.

At **Leenane,** another tiny village, you will find an exhibition center with the theme of "Sheep and Wool," illustrating the traditional industry of North Connemara and West Mayo. There are live demonstrations of carding, spinning, weaving, and the dyeing of wool with natural plant dyes. *Tel. 095/42231. Open year-round, Tues.–Sat. 10–5, Sun. 2–5. Admission: £2 adults, family tickets available.*

From Leenane we leave Killary Harbour and County Galway to head up into County Mayo. If the weather is good and you're seeking more mountain scenery, take a detour to the left about 1½ kilometers (1 mile) beyond Leenane on the R335, through the Doolough Valley between Mweelrea Mountain and the Sheeffry Hills and on to Westport via Louisburgh. Many lovers of the West claim that this section is the region's most impressive and unspoiled stretch of scenery. It will add about 24 kilometers (15 miles) to your journey. Otherwise take the N59 from Leenane direct to Westport, a distance of 32 kilometers (20 miles).

27 Look out on either road for the great bulk of **Croagh Patrick,** a 762-meter (2,500-foot) mountain with a conical tip. On clear days a small white building is visible at its summit; a wide path ascends to it. The latter is the Pilgrim's Path, which about 25,000 people, many of them barefoot, follow each year in order to pray to St. Patrick in the oratory on its peak. The traditional date for the pilgrimage is the last Sunday in July, but the climb can be made in about three hours (round-trip) on any fine day and is well worth it for the magnificent views of the islands of Clew Bay. The climb starts at **Murrisk,** a village about 8 kilometers (5 miles) outside Westport on the R335 Louisburgh road.

28 **Westport** is by far the most attractive town in County Mayo, situated on an inlet of Clew Bay, a wide expanse of sea dotted with islands and framed by mountain ranges. It is unusual in that it was planned by an architect, James Wyatt, in the late 18th century when he was employed to finish nearby Westport House (*see below*). Streets radiate from the central Octagon, and a charming riverside mall is lined with tall lime trees. The town remains a popular fishing center and has several good beaches close by. An old-fashioned farmers' market is held on Thursday mornings on the Octagon; work clothes, harnesses, tools, and children's toys are for sale. You will discover some equally old-fashioned shops—ironmongers, drapers, and the like—by wandering around the streets that lead to the Octagon.

Time Out For a picnic that's a little different, try the takeouts offered at the inexpensive German-owned **Continental Cafe** (High St., Westport, no phone), or sit at an outside table on the sidewalk and sample the home-baked goods, soups, and salads. Health-food lovers will regard this place as an oasis in the wilderness.

The Quay is clearly signposted from the Octagon, about 2 kilometers (1¼ miles) outside town. Visitors will find some good bars down here, as well as a choice of decent restaurants (*see* Dining, *below*). The main attraction on the Quay is **Westport House,** a stately home built on the site of an earlier castle and completed in 1788 by architect James Wyatt for the marquess of Sligo. The rectangular three-story house is furnished with late-Georgian and Victorian pieces. Family portraits by Opie and Reynolds, old Irish silver, and a collection of old Waterford glass are all on display. The home is situated superbly beside a lake with a small formal garden. However, its charm is sadly diminished for some visitors by rampant commercialization that extends even to video games in the old dungeons, which belonged to the earlier castle. The once tranquil grounds have given way to a small amusement park for children and a children's zoo. Sensitive souls should try to arrive early, when it is less likely to be busy. *Tel. 098/25430. Admission to house only: £5.50 adults, £2.50 children. Family day ticket to all attractions: £17.50. House only: open Apr.–May and Sept., daily 2–5; Grounds and house: June, Mon.–Fri. noon–5, Sat. and Sun. 2–6; July–Aug. 21, Mon.–Sat. 10:30–6, Sun. 3–6; Aug. 22–Aug. 31, daily 2–6.*

If the weather does not favor a visit to **Achill Island,** which offers cliff walks, sandy beaches, and deep-sea fishing, take the N60 from Westport House to Castlebar, the inland county seat, then the N5 to Ballavary, the N58 to Foxford, and the N57 to Ballina. The total drive from Westport House to Ballina is 50 kilometers (31 miles).

For Achill Island, take the N59 to **Newport,** a pleasant village on the Beltra River, which is popular from March to September with salmon fishermen. The N59 follows the shores of Newport Bay (the
29 northern shore of Clew Bay) to **Mulrany,** where the R319 branches off to the left for Achill.

30 **Achill Island** is one of those places that can be heaven on earth in good weather because of its splendid scenery. Accommodations and facilities, however, are very basic, so if the weather is too cold or wet to enjoy the outdoors, you'll probably be bored. A short causeway leads from the mainland to Achill Sound, the first village on the 147-square-kilometer (57-square-mile) island. Achill, the largest island off the Irish coast, is mainly bogland and wild heather. The main road runs through rhododendron plantations to Keel, which has a 3-kilometer (2-mile) beach with amazing cathedral-like rock formations in the cliffs at its east end. Alternatively, take the longer scenic route signposted "Atlantic Drive." Until a few years ago, the people of Achill made a very poor living. Even as recently as the 1960s, some families were reliant on "remittances" from family members who had emigrated to the United States or England. Tourism has improved things, as has the establishment of cottage industries (mainly knitting) and shark fishing, which is popular from April to July.

To reach Ballina, retrace your steps to Mulrany and turn left onto the N59. The road runs for about 24 kilometers (15 miles) across desolate, almost uninhabited bog, some of which has had its turf cut away down to rock level by successive generations' searching for fuel. The road then takes a right at Bangor across another long (32-kilometer/20-mile) stretch of bog to Ballina.

31 **Ballina,** with a population of about 7,500, is the largest town in County Mayo and has quite a bit of light industry. Fishing for salmon and trout on the River Moy and nearby Lough Conn is its chief attraction. The town center is untidy and generally uninteresting; unless you plan to stay here for the fishing, you will probably want to

drive straight through Ballina and continue for 59½ kilometers (37 miles) on the N59 to Sligo Town.

Off the Beaten Track

While in Galway City, admirers of the writer James Joyce (1882–1941) will want to visit **Nora Barnacle House,** home of his Galway-born wife. The building is in Bowling Green, adjacent to the Collegiate Church of St. Nicholas (*see* Tour 2: Galway City and the Aran Islands, *above*). Joyce stayed in the house many times. It contains memorabilia of the Barnacle family and papers relating to Joyce. *Tel. 091/64743. Admission: £1. Open May–Sept., Mon.–Sat. 10–5, off-season by appointment.*

A **Corrib Cruise** from Wood Quay at the Galway City Docks is a lovely way to spend a fine afternoon; it makes a welcome change from the car if you're touring. It lasts 1½ hours and travels 8 kilometers (5 miles) up the River Corrib and about 6 kilometers (3½ miles) around Lough Corrib. *Tel. 091/63081; ask for Aran Ferries. Cost: £5 adults, £2.50 children. Cruises May–Sept., daily at 2:30 and 4:30.*

If you are driving from Westport to Ballina, **Foxford Woollen Mills Visitor Center** makes a good stopping point. Besides looking at the crafts shop and enjoying the restaurant, you can visit "The Foxford Experience" which tells the story of the woollen mill (famous for its tweeds and blankets) from the time of the Famine, when it was founded by the Sisters of Charity to combat poverty, to the present day. *Foxford, Co. Mayo, tel. 094/56756. Admission: £2.50 adults, £1.50 children. Open Mon.–Sat. 10–6, Sun. 2–6. Tour every 20 mins.*

If you like small, peaceful islands, take a trip to **Inishbofin,** which is 12 kilometers (7½ miles) off the coast of Connemara. The island is about 6 kilometers (3½ miles) by 8 kilometers (5 miles), and has a population of 180. Cliffs, sandy beaches, small lakes, and a sheltered harbor are its main attractions. Inishbofin is popular with walkers, botanists, and naturalists. The Galway City Tourist Information Office (tel. 091/63081) will book your lodging on the island. Ferries (tel. 095/45806 for times and prices) leave daily from Cleggan, a small fishing village near Clifden, 1½ hours from Galway City.

Shopping

Shoppers hunt for crafts, Irish-made clothing, jewelry, antiques, and memorabilia in the West. The major shopping areas are Galway City and Ennis, and their most interesting shops carry the above-mentioned items. Connemara offers a large concentration of crafts shops; it is the best place in Ireland to buy an Aran sweater—either a traditional off-white design, or plain linen and cotton Aran-style knits in jewellike red, green, or blue.

Galway City is the place to buy a Claddagh ring (*see* Tour 2: Galway City and the Aran Islands, *above*). On the Aran Islands, sally rods are woven into attractive baskets (once used for potatoes or turf); colorful woven belts, known as críoses, are hand-plaited from strands of wool. Handwoven woolen or mohair shawls or rugs provide an affordable touch of luxury. Musical instruments, traditionally made furniture, Connemara marble jewelry, modern lead crystal, batik, handmade beeswax candles, tweed place mats, and dried flower arrangements are among the many other attractive and interesting items—apart from tweeds and sweaters—to be found in the West. The majority of crafts shops mentioned below will mail items for overseas visitors.

County Clare (West)

Doolin **Design Ireland Plus** (beside the cemetery and church, tel. 065/74309) carries only Irish-made goods, including sweaters, modern lead crystal, linen, lace, and tweed. A jeweler's workshop and a resident batik maker are also available.

Ennis **The Belleek Shop** (36 Abbey St., tel. 065/29607) carries Belleek china, Waterford crystal, and Donegal Parian china, as well as Lladro, Hummel, and other collectible china. **Flax In Bloom** (Abbey St., tel. 065/20833) offers women's and teenagers' fashions with an emphasis on Irish design and classic fabrics. **The Sweater Shop** (41 O'Connell St., tel. 065/20950) sells designer knitwear. At **Clare Business Center** (Francis St., tel. 065/20166) you'll find a variety of craft workshops that sell to the public. **Carraig Donn** (29 O'Connell St., tel. 065/28188) stocks Waterford glass and other Irish crystal, Belleek and other fine china, and their own array of knitwear. Stop off at **Honan Antiques** (Abbey St., tel. 065/28137) for Victorian items and mementos.

Lahinch **Design Ireland** (tel. 065/81480) is a small shop that carries Irish-made goods, including sweaters, linen, tweed, and other fine gift items.

County Galway

Clifden **Millar's Connemara Tweeds** (Main St., tel. 095/21038) is a general crafts and art gallery with a good selection of traditional tweeds and handknits. **The Celtic Shop** (tel. 095/21064) features good-quality general crafts. **The Woolen Store** (tel. 095/21282) specializes in knitwear.

Galway City **Cobwebs** (7 Pury Lane, tel. 091/64388) stocks small antiques and gifts with an accent on nostalgia. Try **House of James** (Castle St., tel. 091/67776) for the best in modern household items, as well as high-fashion (Irish-made) clothing. Browse in **Treasure Chest** (William St., tel. 091/67237) for china, crystal, gifts, and classic clothing. **Padráic O'Máille** (Dominick St., tel. 091/62696) carries Aran sweaters, handwoven tweeds, and classically tailored clothing. Stop at **Claddagh Jewellers** (Eyre Sq., tel. 091/62310) for jewelry; the store has a wide selection of traditional Claddagh rings. **The Galway Woolen Market** (21–22 High St., tel. 091/62491) offers good value in sweaters and sheepskin rugs. **Kenny's Bookshop** (High St., tel. 091/62739) offers five floors of books of Irish interest, mainly secondhand and antiquarian, as well as prints, maps, and a small art gallery. Check out **The Cornstore** (Middle St.), a stylish new shopping mall across from the back door of Kenny's. **Design Ireland Plus** (Unit 14, tel. 091/67716) has an excellent range of Irish-made crafts and clothing.

Kylemore **Kylemore Abbey** (tel. 095/41113) sells sweaters, gifts, and general crafts items.

Letterfrack **Connemara Handcrafts** (tel. 095/41058) is a large roadside shop with an extensive selection of crafts and women's fashions made by Avoca Handweavers.

Recess **Joyce's** (tel. 095/34604) is a roadside shop carrying an imaginative selection of modern ceramics, handwoven shawls, and other good-quality crafts, in addition to books of Irish interest and a gallery of original paintings and small sculptures.

Spiddle **Mairtín Standún** (tel. 091/83108), a family-run drapery store, has expanded into a well-stocked crafts shop specializing in local handknits and tweeds.

County Mayo

Ballina **De Danaan Antiques** (Teeling St., tel. 096/21063) stocks old and antique country pine furniture. Try **Maguire Martin Showrooms** (Tone St., tel. 096/22598) for Victorian and Edwardian furniture, porcelain, paintings, and memorabilia. **Victorian Village Antiques** (Pearse St., tel. 096/22127) carries Victorian furniture and bric-a-brac.

Foxford **Woolen Mills and Craft Shop** (tel. 094/56756) is a factory outlet for top-quality blankets, rugs, and tweeds.

Westport **O'Reilly and Turpin** (Mill St., no phone) features knitwear, handwoven items, and pottery. **Carraig Donn** (Ponise St., tel. 098/26287) have their own range of knitwear and a good selection of crystal, jewelry and ceramics. **Satch Kiely** (Westport Quay, tel. 098/25775) carries fine antique furniture and decorative pieces.

Sports and the Outdoors

Participant Sports

Bicycling County Clare and the Burren provide relatively easy terrain, with few hills over 300 meters (984 feet), and amazing sea views out to the Aran Isles from the west coast. Northwest of Galway, the rugged Connemara district provides some real challenges through countryside that is not only hilly but also very often wet and windy. However, in general, the roads follow passes between the mountains so the uphill stretches are not all that frequent, and hopefully, the wild scenery will compensate for the damp. Mayo offers similar terrain, combined with some amazing long flat roads crossing stretches of bog in the north and west. Just pray that the wind is not against you here. All Tourist Information Offices in the West provide lists of suggested cycle tours. The Irish Tourist Board publishes a leaflet, *Cycling Ireland* (£2), that describes four circuits in the West.

Bicycle Rentals **County Clare—Doolin: Patrick Moloney, Doolin Hostel** (tel. 065/74006); **Ennis: Michael Tierney** (17 Abbey St., tel. 065/29433); **Kilkee: Williams Ltd.** (Circular Rd., tel. 065/56041); **Kilrnsh: Korner Shop** (Henry St., tel. 065/51037).

County Galway—Clifden: John Mannion (Railway View, tel. 095/21160); **Galway City: Celtic Cycles** (Queen St., Victoria Pl., Eyre Sq., tel. 091/66606); **Renvyle: Renvyle Stores** (Tully, tel. 095/43485).

County Mayo—Achill Island: Achill Sound Hotel (tel. 098/45245); **O'Malley's Island Sports** (Keel P.O., tel. 098/43125); **Ballina: Gerry's Cycle Center** (Crossmolina Rd., tel. 096/70455); **Cong: O'Connor's Garage** (tel. 092/46008); **Westport: J.P. Breheny & Sons** (Castlebar St., tel. 098/25020).

Board Sailing and Dinghy Sailing The sailing season is short here, running from June to early September for all but the hardiest, and even in those months wet suits are essential for board sailing and advisable for dinghies.

Galway Sailing Center (Renville, Oranmore, tel. 091/94527) offers dinghy sailing and board sailing on Lough Corrib or on coastal waters. Instruction is also available. **Little Killary Adventure Center** (Salruck, Renryle, Co. Galway, tel. 095/43411) provides sailing and windsurfing instruction on sheltered coastal waters. One- and two-week courses in sailing and board sailing are available at the **Glénans Center,** based on an otherwise uninhabited island in Clew Bay near Westport. Contact the Center's head office (28 Merrion Sq., Dublin, tel. 01/611481).

Fishing Game fishing for wild Atlantic salmon, wild brown trout, and sea trout is one of the main attractions of the West. The salmon and brown trout season runs from March through September, closing earlier in some waters. Generally, fishing is at its best between mid-May and mid-June. The sea trout season starts in late May and also ends at the end of September; it has been disappointing in some places in recent years due to the infestation of sea lice. Every effort is being made to ensure a good season in 1995. Details of the numerous fisheries in the area are available from the local Tourist Information Offices, or consult the Irish Tourist Board leaflet *Angling Ireland* (£1.80). Similar leaflets are available on coarse angling and sea angling.

Shore fishing is available all along the coast. Boats can be hired from April to October for deep-sea fishing (about £18 per person per day) from the following ports: **County Clare:** Doonbeg, Liscannor, Ballyvaughan; **County Galway:** Roundstone, Spiddle, Clifden, Cleggan, Inishbofin Island; **County Mayo:** Westport, Ballina, Belmullet, Killala.

Fishing tackle, bait, and licenses can be obtained at **Freeny's** (High St., Galway City, tel. 091/62609), **Murt's** (7 Daly's Pl., Wood Quay, Galway City, tel. 091/61018), **John Walkin** (Tone St., Ballina, Co. Mayo, tel. 096/22442), and **Patrick Kelly** (Bridge St., Lower Westport, Co. Mayo, tel. 098/25982).

Fitness Clubs Only two hotels in the region allow nonresidents to use their fitness facilities.

The **Connemara Gateway** has an unusual indoor pool beneath a glass-topped dome. *Oughterard, Co. Galway, tel. 091/82328. Admission: £3 adults, £2 children; sauna £2, tennis court £1. Open daily 10–8.*

The **Downhill Hotel** features a sports complex with a 12-meter (39-foot) indoor oval pool, a sauna, a Jacuzzi, a gym, two squash courts, and three tennis courts. *Ballina, Co. Mayo, tel. 096/21033. Admission: £4 per day for use of all facilities. Open weekdays 3–11, Sat. 10–9, Sun. 10–7.*

Golf The West features some of the most challenging and ruggedly scenic courses in the country. Greens fees vary from £6 for a nine-hole course to £45 for a championship course, averaging about £15 per round for 18 holes. Courses are geared to visitors and are generally uncrowded, but it is always advisable to call beforehand.

County Clare The championship course at **Lahinch Golf Club** (Lahinch, tel. 065/81003) offers challenging links following the natural contours of the dunes. The 6,017-meter (6,613-yard) course has hosted many great golfing occasions since it opened in 1892. The new Lahinch course, known as the **Castle Course** (same tel.), offers a more carefree round of seaside golf, with shorter holes than the championship course. **Dromoland Golf Course** (Newmarket-on-Fergus, tel. 061/71144) is one of the most scenic in the country, set in a 700-acre estate of rich woodland in the grounds of the Dromoland Castle Hotel. It has a natural lake that leaves little room for error on a number of holes. **Ennis** features an 18-hole parkland course (Drumbiggle Rd., tel.

065/24074) overlooking the town. An exhilarating nine-hole course overlooks the sea at **Spanish Point** (Miltown Malbay, tel. 065/84198); **Kilrush** (Ennis Rd., tel. 065/51138) and **Kilkee** (East End, tel. 065/56048) also overlook the sea and have recently been extended to 18 holes.

County Galway The **Connemara Golf Club** (Ballyconneely, near Clifden, tel. 095/23502), which opened in 1973, is situated on a dramatic stretch of Atlantic coastline; the course measures 6,528 meters (7,174 yards), and its par of 72 is rarely matched. The **Galway City Golf Club** (Blackrock, Salthill, tel. 091/22169) is situated inland, although some of the fairways run close to the ocean. **Oughterard Golf Club** (tel. 091/82620) features a parkland course suitable for novices and those who wish to improve their games. **Tuam** (Barnacurra, tel. 093/24354) and **Ballinasloe** (Rosgloss, tel. 0905/42126) also offer 18-hole courses. **Galway Bay Golf and Country Club** (Renville, Oranmore, tel. 091/90500) is a new par-72, parkland course designed by Christy O'Connor, Jr., on the shores of Galway Bay.

County Mayo **Westport Golf Club** (Carrowholly, tel. 098/25113), beneath Croughpatrick Mountain, overlooks Clew Bay; designed by Fred Hawtree in the early 1970s, it has twice been the venue for the Irish Amateur Championship. **Castlebar Golf Club** (Rocklands, tel. 094/21649) is a moderately challenging parkland course. The new **Clann Lir Golf Course** (Carn, Belmullet, tel. 097/82123) provides 18 holes of links built particularly for visitors to the area. Nine-hole courses are at **Achill** (tel. 098/43202), **Ballina** (tel. 096/21050), and **Mulrany** (tel. 098/36262).

Hiking This is excellent hiking country if you like challenging hills and relatively rough terrain. The Burren in County Clare provides an unusual, almost lunar landscape, and is less demanding than Connemara. Here, and in the country to the north of Connemara in South County Mayo, the countryside is sparsely populated and subject to sudden changes in weather—usually associated with the onset of rain. For off-the-road walking, consult "Irish Walk Guides—The West," a pamphlet available at local TIOs, and take local advice on weather conditions.

There are only two signposted trails in the area. **The Burren Way** runs from Ballinalacken, just north of Doolin, to Ballyvaughan on the shores of Galway Bay, a distance of about 20 kilometers (12½ miles). The trail runs through the heart of the limestone landscape of the Burren, with ever-changing views of the Aran Islands and Galway Bay. The 73-kilometer (45-mile) **Western Way** extends from Oughterard on Lough Corrib through the mountains of Connemara and South County Mayo past Killary Harbour to Westport on Clew Bay; this trail includes some of the finest mountain and coastal scenery in Ireland.

Horseback Riding There is spectacular scenery to enjoy on horseback in this part of the world. The best-bred and most exciting horses will be found in the inland, eastern parts of Counties Galway, Clare, and Mayo. Along the more mountainous coastal areas, it is a matter of trekking at slow to medium paces and enjoying the view, rather than exercising your equestrian skills. Horses and ponies can be hired by the hour. Expect to pay about £7 for a hack, and about £10 if instruction or the use of indoor facilities is included.

County Clare **Castlefergus Farm Riding Stables** (Quin, tel. 065/25914) offers trekking over scenic countryside. **Ballyshannon Riding Establishment** (Ballyshannon House, Quin, Ennis, tel. 065/25645) has woodland trail riding and beginners' lessons and will provide riding equipment.

County Galway **Pine Lodge Equestrian Centre** (Peterswell, tel. 091/35399) offers residential riding holidays, day-long treks through forest paths and mountains, and riding by the hour. **Cashel House Hotel Riding Center** (Cashel, Connemara, tel. 095/31001) offers scenic treks. **Errislannan Manor Connemara Pony Stud and Riding Center** (Clifden, Connemara, tel. 095/21134) provides mountain treks, instruction, and courses for children.

County Mayo **Claremorris School of Equitation** (Lisduff, Claremorris, tel. 094/71684) features show jumping and forest riding. **Drummindoo Stud and Equitation Center** (Castlebar Rd., Westport, tel. 098/25616) welcomes beginners and children.

Tennis The West isn't a popular place for playing tennis because of its wet and windy climate. Some hotels have one or two courts (*see* Lodging, *below*). Nine courts at the **Galway Lawn Tennis Club** (Threadneedle Rd., Salthill, tel. 091/22353) are available to nonmembers at £4 per hour. Nonmembers can also use the facilities at the **Tennis and Badminton Club** (Ennis, Co. Clare, tel. 065/21430). A public court is situated on Newport Road in Westport in County Mayo, and four public courts may be found in Ballina beside the River Moy on the N59 Sligo road.

Spectator Sports

Hooker Racing No longer used as working boats to carry turf and provisions, a small fleet of hookers is maintained and raced by enthusiasts. These solid, heavy broad-beamed sailing boats with distinctive gaff-rigged, brownish-red sails participate in frequent races on Galway Bay in July and August. The main events take place in Carraroe in County Galway on the last weekend in July, and in Kinvara in County Galway (on the opposite southern shore of Galway Bay) on the third weekend in August.

Horse Racing Many small events are held throughout the year in the West, including trotting races, pony races, beach derbies, and the like. Local Tourist Information Offices can provide details. The main event is the **Galway Races,** which start on the last Monday in July and continue until the following Saturday. This boisterous, full-scale festival attracts a massive crowd; all manner of sideshows are set up, featuring entertainers, card sharps, Gypsy fortune-tellers, rifle ranges, and open-air concerts.

Dining and Lodging

Dining Because the West has a brief high season—from mid-June to early September—and a quiet off-season, it does not offer as big a choice of small owner-operated restaurants as other parts of Ireland. Often the best place to eat is a local hotel—Sheedy's Spa View in Lisdoonvarna, for example, which has one of the few excellent chefs in County Clare, or Rosleague Manor in Letterfrack. Hotel dining is described in Lodging, below.

The dominant style of cuisine in the West is best described as "country-house cooking"; it relies on dishes that could be prepared by an enthusiastic host for a private dinner party at home—for instance, homemade pâté or seafood cocktail, followed by tournedos or salmon hollandaise, and chocolate mousse for dessert. Even at Drimcong House (near Galway City), home of one of Ireland's most acclaimed chefs, the emphasis is on fresh local produce prepared in relatively simple ways, albeit with the perfection that only a master can achieve.

Restaurants in this region are less expensive than elsewhere and portions are extremely generous. You'll find it hard to stick to a diet here and salads and fresh fruit are scarce. But the quality of the meat (especially spring lamb, steak, chicken, and duck) and the seafood (especially oysters, salmon, and sea trout) is truly outstanding. Lobster, crayfish, crab, scallops, and mussels are available throughout the summer. Galway Bay's famous oysters are at their best when there is an "R" in the month; the oyster season officially runs from September to late April.

The majority of restaurants in the West are happy with a "casual but neat" appearance, so dress code is not indicated. Exceptions are the grander (i.e., $$ and $$$) country-house hotels, where any man in the cocktail bar or dining room after 7 PM should wear a jacket and tie.

Category	Cost*
$$$	over £25
$$	£15–£25
$	under £15

**per person for appetizer, main course, and dessert, excluding drinks and 10% tip*

Lodging The West features some of Ireland's best country-house and castle hotels, some distinguished regular old and new hotels, and a good choice of inexpensive B&Bs. Ashford and Dromoland castles are undoubtedly the stars of the region, but lesser-known (and less expensive) places such as Ballynahinch Castle and Cashel House Hotel, both in Connemara, offer similar comfort on a smaller, more intimate scale.

The region is short on moderately priced hotels (particularly Galway City), but to compensate, there are wonderful bargains in the lower price range. One of the great attractions of staying in the West, whatever the price range, is the restful atmosphere of so many of the hotels and guest houses, often situated in the middle of a large private estate beside a lake or river, overlooking the sea or distant mountains.

Accommodations are busy July and August, and the best places also get full in May, June, and September, particularly on weekends. Book well in advance. Many visitors enjoy outdoor activities, such as fishing, golfing, walking, and horseback riding; facilities for other sports, such as tennis courts or indoor pools, are scarce. So are television sets in bedrooms, even in upscale hotels. Rooms also do not always have direct-dial phones.

Category	Cost*
$$$$	over £125
$$$	£85–£125
$$	£60–£85
$	under £60

**All prices are for a standard double room, excluding service.*

Highly recommended restaurants and hotels are indicated by a star ★.

Achill Island

Lodging **Ostan Gob A'Choire (Achill Sound Hotel).** This small waterside hotel is in the first village you approach arriving from the mainland. The solid two-story town house has a brick-and-plate-glass bedroom extension. All bedrooms offer a sea view, but the nicer ones, with tweed curtains and reproductions of Georgian furniture, are in the old building. The smaller new rooms are already a little worn, but they are spotlessly clean and have pleasant views of the sound. *Ceilís* (Irish dancing and song) are staged in the bar most weekends. *Achill Sound, Co. Mayo, tel. 098/45245, fax 098/45621. 36 rooms with bath. Facilities: restaurant, bar. MC, V. Closed Nov.–Easter. $*

The Aran Islands

The only hotel on the islands is on Inisheer (*see below*). However, you'll find no shortage of B&Bs—most of them in simple family homes—even at peak times. The best way to book is through the Galway City Tourist Information Office (Victoria Pl., Eyre Sq., Galway, tel. 091/630081). Each island has at least one restaurant with a wine license that serves plain home cooking. Most B&Bs will provide a packed lunch and an evening meal (called high tea) on request.

Inisheer *Lodging* **Hotel Inisheer.** This pleasant modern low rise in the middle of the island's only village is a few minutes' walk from the quay and the airstrip. The simple whitewashed building with a slated roof and half-slated walls offers bright, plainly furnished rooms. A section of five rooms was added in 1990; they are slightly larger than the other 10 rooms. The restaurant (open to nonresidents) is the best bet on the island, although most of the food is imported frozen. *Lurgan Village, Inisheer, Aran Islands, Co. Galway, tel. 099/75020. 15 rooms, 6 with bath. Facilities: restaurant, bar, bicycles. No TV or direct-dial phone in rooms. AE, DC, MC, V. Closed Oct.–April 1. $*

Inishmore *Lodging* **Johnston Hernon's Kilmurvey House.** Situated in the island's second village about 6½ kilometers (4 miles) from the quay and the airport (accessible by minibus), this rambling stone 200-year-old farmhouse is the first choice of many visitors (about 60% of them American) to the island. Four large rooms in the old house are furnished with hand-me-downs, and four modern rooms in a new extension have built-in furniture. *Kilmurvey, Inishmore, Aran Islands, Co. Galway, tel. 099/61218. 8 rooms, 4 with bath. Facilities: restaurant with wine license, residents only. No TV or direct-dial phone in rooms. MC, V. Closed Oct.–May 1. $*

Ballina

Lodging **Downhill Hotel.** Delightfully situated on 40 wooded acres beside a gushing tributary of the River Moy (just off the N59 Sligo road), this hotel is a popular spot with anglers and outdoor types. The late-Victorian main house feels a little gloomy downstairs, but it is comfortable. Rooms in the new wing tend to be smaller than those in the main house, but the former have good views of the river across the garden. Rooms in the main house feature Georgian-style furniture with tastefully coordinated quilts and drapes. The sporting facilities are the best for miles. *Ballina, Co. Mayo, tel. 096/21033, fax 096/21338. 50 rooms with bath. Facilities: restaurant, 2 bars, indoor* *heated pool, gym, sauna, Jacuzzi, solarium, 2 squash courts, snooker, 3 tennis courts, fishing. AE, DC, MC, V. $$$*

Mount Falcon Castle. This rambling Victorian Gothic country-house 5 kilometers (3 miles) outside town is within easy reach of several beautiful small beaches. Owner-manager Constance Aldridge is renowned for putting guests at ease and encouraging them to mingle. Children are especially welcome. An excellent holiday base, the hotel features good walks and salmon fishing on the River Moy within the extensive grounds, with horseback riding, sea fishing, and golf nearby. Rooms are furnished comfortably with a mix of antiques and heirlooms, and overlook the wooded grounds. Local produce is usually served, and the country-style home-cooking has a fine reputation. *Ballina, tel. 096/21172, fax 096/21172. 10 rooms, 8 with bath. Facilities: restaurant (wine license only), tennis, fishing. No TV or phone in rooms. AE, DC, MC, V. Closed Jan.–Mar. $$$*

Ballyvaughan

Dining ★

Claire's. Look for a crafts shop with the name Manus Walsh over the door. He's Claire's husband, and her pretty little restaurant, overlooking a leafy garden, is behind his shop. This dining spot has pine walls covered with greenery and batiks, rush-seated pine chairs, and a bright yellow candle in a bottle on each table. You can taste the freshness in the simple but imaginatively prepared food. Try a rack of Burren lamb with fresh rosemary or a fresh Ballyvanghan lobster with melted butter. *Ballyvaughan, Co. Clare, tel. 065/77029. Reservations advised. AE, MC, V. Wine license only. Open Easter–Oct., dinner only. $$*

Lodging ★

Gregan's Castle Hotel. This quiet, well-run large Victorian country house, surrounded by award-winning gardens, is at the base of the aptly named Corkscrew Hill (on the N67, midway between Ballyvaughan and Lisdoonvarna) and overlooks the gray mountains of the Burren and Galway Bay. All bedrooms are individually furnished with Georgian and Victorian antiques and William Morris wallpaper; older ones feature molded plaster ceilings. The spacious new rooms on the ground floor have private patio gardens but lack the splendid views of the first-floor rooms. *Ballyvaughan, Co. Clare (via Galway), tel. 065/77005, fax 065/77111. 22 rooms with bath. Facilities: French restaurant (jacket and tie preferred), bar, croquet. No TV in rooms. MC, V. Closed Nov.–early Apr. $$$*

Cashel Bay

Lodging ★

Cashel House. This place has more antiques and curios per square foot than any other hotel in Ireland. Dermot McEvilly claims that he acquired his extensive collection when it was cheaper than buying new pieces; you'll admire the intricately carved oak tables, Biedermeier bureaus, gilt mirrors, Georgian bookcases, ormolu clocks, and other knickknacks scattered liberally around the lobby, lounge, library, and downstairs corridors. A favorite hideaway for sophisticated French and American guests, as well as Ireland's elite, this luxurious country house also features an award-winning 50-acre garden of exotic flowering shrubs, woodland walks, and Connemara ponies grazing out back. Bedrooms are furnished with a generous mix of antiques and curios and have king-size beds, which are canopied in the 13 minisuites. Each room overlooks a stretch of the richly planted garden and has plain wool carpets, pink-and-green drapes and spreads, and brass bedside lamps. For a sea view, ask for a front room. *Cashel Bay, Co. Galway, tel. 095/31001, fax 095/31077. 32* *rooms with bath. Facilities: horseback riding, tennis court, private beach, bicycle rental, fishing. AE, MC, V. $$$$*

Zetland House. This mid-Victorian hunting lodge was built for the earl of Zetland and is on a hill overlooking the secluded Cashel Bay. The hotel is popular with anglers, hunters, and townsfolk in search of a rural retreat. Bedrooms are decorated in floral chintz and overlook the garden. The minisuites with a sea view in the old house are twice as large as the other rooms and are furnished with late-Victorian antiques. Your best bet is one of the middle-grade "superior" rooms in the converted coach house: All offer sea views, highly polished mahogany antiques, velvet armchairs, and fully tiled bathrooms with decorated washbasins. *Cashel Bay, Co. Galway, tel. 095/31111, fax 095/31117. 19 rooms with bath. Facilities: restaurant, bar, fishing, shooting, horseback riding, tennis, bicycle hire. AE, DC, MC, V. Closed Oct. 15–Apr. 1. $$$$*

Clarinbridge

Dining

Paddy Burke's. Once a simple village bar on the main Ennis–Galway road, this long, low-ceilinged, 200-year-old thatched cottage, divided into three separate eating areas, is now a world-famous seafood restaurant. The bar itself verges on dingy; ask for a table in the restaurant's adjoining room, furnished with oak-topped tables and solid chairs. Copper pans and sporting prints adorn the walls. Oysters are a specialty; if they're not in season, try king scallops Mornay or monkfish in a garlic, cream, and white-wine sauce. *Clarinbridge, Co. Galway, tel. 091/96226. Reservations advised; essential in July and Aug. AE, DC, MC, V. $$*

Moran's of the Weir. Signposted off the main road on the south side of Clarinbridge, this waterside thatched cottage, the home of the Moran Family since 1760, houses a simply furnished restaurant at the back that serves only seafood. If oysters are not in season, try the seafood special (smoked salmon, crab, prawns, and crab claws with homemade brown bread) or a bowl of garlic mussels. *The Weir, Kilcolgan, Co. Galway, tel. 091/96113. Reservations advised. AE, MC, V. $*

Clifden

Dining

Doris's. Owned and run by a young German couple, this establishment occupies two small floors of one of the oldest houses in town. At this restful place with plain white walls, lots of natural wood, tweed drapes, and dark-red carpets and napery, you'll find upstairs both a harpist (most evenings) and an open turf fire. There is an eclectic menu including steak, pasta, pizza, and seafood fresh from the Atlantic; traditional Irish dishes, such as Irish stew; and Asian specials, which include Thai chicken, pork vindaloo, and Indian-style spicy prawns. *Clifden, Co. Galway, tel. 095/21427. Reservations advised weekends and July–Aug. AE, DC, MC, V. $$*

Lodging

★ **Rock Glen Manor House.** Cross the bridge at the west end of town and go 2½ kilometers (1½ miles) down the Roundstone road (the R341) to find this beautifully converted shooting lodge, built in 1815. On windy days, a tiny Connemara pony, Gregory, stands sentinel at the entrance gates and enjoys the breeze. Riding boots and tennis rackets in the hall make this feel more like a private home than a top-class hotel, as does the warm welcome from owner-manager Evangeline Roche. The ground floor is generously furnished with Victorian antiques; the large sunny drawing room, with plump white armchairs, magazines, books, and board games, offers a turf fire. Rooms vary in size and appeal; the best are on the first-floor front with sea views, but all the rooms are nicely furnished in the Georgian style, with fluffy mohair or chintz bedspreads, brass curtain rods and bedside lamps, and fully tiled bathrooms. Small-paned teak windows provide restful scenic views. Most guests are fly/drive tourists and others who appreciate the sedate and leisurely atmosphere of traditional country life that has been carefully re-created here. The Victorian-style restaurant, which serves fresh local produce, is worth a visit. *Clifden, Co. Galway, tel. 095/21035, fax 095/21737. 29 rooms with bath. Facilities: bar, restaurant (dinner only) snooker, tennis court. AE, DC, MC, V. Closed Oct.–mid-Mar. $$$*

Abbeyglen Castle. Perched on a hilltop about 1 kilometer (½ mile) outside Clifden overlooking the town and bay, this white-turreted fake castle (the crenellations were added only a few years ago) on 12 acres of steep grounds provides a stunning view over the church spires of Clifden to mountains, lakes, and the sea. A large dining room looks out to the wonderful view. Try to get a front room; the back rooms face an overgrown garden. Bedrooms are comfortable, with side tables and matching chintz spreads and drapes, but in some rooms the modern veneered furniture shows signs of wear. The bar is a lively and romantic spot on summer evenings. *Sky Rd., Clifden, Co. Galway, tel. 095/21201, fax 095/21797. 46 rooms with bath. Facilities: restaurant, bar, outdoor heated pool, tennis court, pitch-and-putt, sauna, solarium, snooker, bicycles, horseback riding, helipad. AE, DC, MC, V. $$*

Dun Aengus. A B&B only a few minutes up the road from the Abbeyglen, this is the highest house in Clifden, with a positively vertiginous view over the bay and town, which has to be seen to be believed. The large modern building has a weather-slated roof and a top story above the whitewashed ground floor. Simply fitted rooms are decorated with modern pine and candlewick spreads, and they have fully tiled bathrooms. Rooms numbered 1 to 4 share the singular view, as does the breakfast room. *Mrs. M. Ryan, Dun Aengus, Sky Rd., Clifden, Co. Galway, tel. 095/21069. 6 rooms with bath. Facilities: snooker, TV lounge (no TV or direct-dial phone in rooms). Evening meal June–Aug. subject to demand (BYOB). No credit cards. $*

Cong

Lodging

Ashford Castle. This American-owned and -managed large gray stone turreted castle on the edge of Lough Corrib, surrounded by neatly manicured lawns and gardens, will fulfill every first-time visitor's dream of a genuine Irish castle. The high-ceilinged interior is lavishly furnished with priceless antiques and top-quality reproductions. Large 19th- and 20th-century oil paintings in gilt frames hang from the castle's carved stone walls above polished wood paneling, illuminated by crystal chandeliers. However, as old hands will tell you, the place is a far cry from the unpredictable charms of the "real Ireland." The only Irish people you'll meet here, apart from the staff, are the gold Rolex set. The bedrooms in the discreetly added new wing are disappointingly like any other luxury hotel rooms; although they're beautifully furnished in the Georgian style, they have low ceilings and are boxy. Among the 20 "deluxe" rooms and six suites are the sunny ground-floor rooms occupied by President Reagan on his 1984 state visit; they still feature the extra-long bed especially made for him, and gold bath taps. "Deluxe" rooms have wonderful views of the river, lake, or gardens, generous sitting areas, heavily carved antique furniture, and extra-large bathrooms. The suites are vast and faultless, furnished with Georgian antiques and blissfully comfortable. *Cong, Co. Mayo, tel. 092/46003, fax 092/*

46260. 83 rooms with bath. Facilities: 2 restaurants, 2 bars, fishing, 9-hole golf course, horseback riding, jaunting car, bicycles, 2 tennis courts, clay-target shooting. AE, DC, MC, V. $$$$

Doolin

Dining

Bruach na Haille. The name means "the bank of the river Aille," and the river can be seen from the side windows of this charming little cottage restaurant. It was the first eatery to open in Doolin and has been run by the same owner-manager couple for 18 years. The various interconnecting rooms are low-beamed and cozy with stone-flagged floors, old dressers laden with colorful delft china, and open turf fires. Lobster from Doolin Pier is usually on the menu along with starters, such as warm salad of monkfish and scallops in lime and coriander dressing or roulade of smoked salmon with horseradish mayonnaise. Main courses may include baked seafood au gratin—cod and shellfish in a rich creamy sauce baked in individual portions, or supreme of chicken stuffed with crab meat and pimento nuts. Their sirloin steak with Irish whiskey sauce is renowned. *Roadford, Doolin, Co. Clare, tel. 065/74120. Wine license only. AE, DC, MC, V. Dinner only from 6 PM. Closed Nov.–mid-March. $$*

Ennis

Lodging

The Old Ground. This rambling creeper-clad building in the town center, dating from the early 18th century and much added to over the years, is a comfortable, well-established hotel that has retained its past elegance. The lodging serves as a popular base for Americans, especially golfers. The old house's attractive bedrooms offer pine headboards, brass bedside lights, and candy-striped wallpaper. Some rooms overlook the busy main street, so try to get one facing the gardens. Smaller rooms in the new wing have the same tasteful combination of pine and brass. Be sure to look at the lovely old silver and the large Georgian sideboards in the dining room. *Ennis, Co. Clare, tel. 065/28127, fax 065/28112. 58 rooms with bath. Facilities: restaurant, bar. AE, DC, MC, V. $$$*

West County. A striking, glass conservatory runs the length of the facade of this modern low-rise hotel on the edge of town (on the N18 Limerick road). It's a lively place, geared to the tour-bus trade, yet its roomy, pleasantly decorated public area can handle the crowds. Bedrooms feature wood-veneer furniture, speckled carpet, and floral drapes and spreads. The best rooms are at the front overlooking the gardens; the rest have a view of the car park. *Ennis, Co. Clare, tel. 065/28421, fax 065/28801. 110 rooms with bath. Facilities: 2 restaurants, 2 bars, nightclub with live entertainment. AE, DC, MC, V. $$*

Fanore

Dining and Lodging

Admiral's Rest. You can guess from the nautical bric-a-brac on view that this place belongs to a retired naval man—one John Macnamara, who is an expert on the Burren's wildlife. (Ten inexpensive B&B rooms are available in the next-door bungalow.) The restaurant is housed in a modernized cottage on the coast road between Lisdoonvarna and Ballyvaughan, just across the road from the sea, which is visible through the large oval windows. Decor is rugged but stylish, including varnished stone floors, stone-topped tables, *sugán* (rope-seated) chairs, an open wood and turf fire, and posies of wildflowers on the tables. Seafood, such as lobster, mussels, or crab claws in garlic butter, is the mainstay of the simple menu, but you can also order a grilled T-bone steak, Irish stew, or a spicy vegetarian salad. *Fanore (near Ballyvaughan), Co. Clare, tel. 065/76105, fax 065/76161. Reservations advised. Wine license only. AE, MC, V. Closed Nov.–Easter. $*

Galway City

Dining ★ **Drimcong House.** To reach this exceptional country-house restaurant 19 kilometers (12 miles) out of town on the N59 Oughterard/Clifden road, drive through the village of Moycullen; you'll see the driveway on your right. Gerry Galvin, the owner-chef, is one of the best cooks in Ireland. His wife Marie supplies the kitchen with herbs and unusual vegetables, all organically grown on the Galvins' land and virtually unavailable elsewhere in the West. The restaurant is housed in a modest, symmetrical two-story farmhouse, probably dating from the late-17th century. Leather place mats are set on solid oak tables, and the dining room is decorated with prints, cartoons, and original paintings by contemporary Irish artists. Gerry's cooking is distinguished by its simplicity; the exceptional menu might include hot oyster broth; monkfish marinated in olive oil and spring herbs, and then panfried and served on a leek sauce; or rack of Connemara lamb with an herby port-wine sauce. *Moycullen, Co. Galway, tel. 091/85115. Reservations advised. AE, DC, MC, V. Open Tues.–Sat. dinner only. Closed Christmas–mid-Mar. $$$*

Oyster Room. The main restaurant of the Great Southern Hotel, this establishment is by far the most formal eatery in Galway, a city noted for its easygoing informality. The high-ceilinged connecting rooms off the lobby are suitably hushed, decorated in pale pink and green tones and featuring thick carpets, elegantly draped windows, tall gilt mirrors, and brass lamps. Tables with comfortable velvet-upholstered chairs are well spaced. The conservative French-Irish cuisine showcases the local seafood. Specialties include fresh salmon stuffed with leaf spinach, wrapped in puff pastry and baked, served with a white wine and butter sauce and garnished with red and black caviar; or mosaic of seafood with a lemon butter sauce: turbot, salmon, sea trout, and monkfish lightly steamed, garnished with fresh prawns, mussels, and lemon. *Great Southern Hotel, Eyre Sq., Galway, tel. 091/64041. Reservations advised. Jacket and tie required. AE, DC, MC, V. $$$*

de Burgos. In the heart of Galway's newly fashionable docklands, this labyrinthine basement restaurant was once a grain store. It is now a welcome addition to the local gourmet dining scene. The stone walls and vaulted stone ceilings are whitewashed and complemented by elegant art deco–style furniture with pink and black napery. De Burgos was the name of one of the influential Norman families (the Blakes) that settled in Galway in the 13th century, and the historic Continental link is reflected in the French-influenced menu. The seafood all comes from local waters and may include noisettes of monkfish with tomato and chive coulis, and the "catch of the day" sautéed and served with a garlic and mustard cream. Medallions of venison *grand veneur* come with a red-wine sauce finished with red-currant jelly and cream, or for plainer tastes charcoal-grilled sirloin *Foyott* is served with béarnaise sauce and flavoured with meat glaze. Desserts are also inventive. A simpler, less expensive bar-food menu is served in the bar-reception area at lunch and dinner time. *15–17 Augustine St., Galway, tel. 091/62188. Reservations advised PM, and July and Aug. AE, DC, MC, V. Closed Sun. $$*

Eyre House and Park Room Restaurants. There is a large Victorian bar just off Eyre Square beside the bus and rail stations that has recently been refurbished. Behind the bar, with its etched glass partitions and velvet banquettes, is a large, busy room with Tudor-style stick back chairs and wooden-top tables, the Eyre House Restaurant. Behind that again is a slightly more formal and smaller room with linen table settings, the Park Room Restaurant. The same menu is served in both, and their food has received several awards of excellence. This is a good family eatery, with generous portions of plainly cooked food at lunchtime (prime rib of beef with horseradish sauce, salmon mayonnaise, and salad) and slightly fancier dishes on the dinner menu (roast duckling with fresh herb stuffing and orange and pink peppercorn sauce, duet of salmon and scallops with chervil sauce). *Forster St., Galway, tel. 091/64924. Reservations advised for groups of 6 and over. AE, DC, MC, V. $$ (lunch $)*

The Malt House. This cheerful little pub-restaurant is hidden away in an alley off High Street in the center of old Galway. Under new ownership since 1993, it has long been popular with both locals and visitors for good food served in pleasantly informal surroundings. Choose between eating in the bar itself or in the cozy room leading off the bar, which has beamed ceilings, white rough-cast walls, and chintz curtains. The steaks are excellent here, as is the rack of lamb with a parsley crust and the duckling à l'orange. Fresh prawns panfried in garlic butter and salmon fillet stuffed with buttered leeks and shrimp and baked in phyllo are both popular seafood options. At lunchtime a range of lighter dishes is also available, for example, crabmeat and potato cakes with a light mustard sauce. *Olde Malte Mall, High St., Galway, tel. 091/63993. Reservations advised. AE, DC, MC, V. Closed Sun. Oct.–Apr. $$*

★ **Noctan's.** A small menu (with a choice of three fish and three meat dishes and one vegetarian main course, as well as appetizers and desserts) is served in the first-floor room above one of the most famous bars in the old town's Left Bank. The Swiss chef bases his menu on the freshest available produce; popular main courses include fillet of beef grilled with mushroom and herb butter, duck with cider and cinnamon, and catch of the day—a fish and shellfish platter with a choice of fresh sauces. The mildly bohemian ambience is created by an open fireplace, filled with dried grasses in the summer, and a tiny red-walled corner room, which is decorated with old theatrical prints. An odd assortment of Victorian chairs surround the different-size tables, which are likely to be occupied by leading lights in Galway's thriving performing arts and visual arts scenes. *17 Cross St., Galway, tel. 091/66172. Reservations advised. MC, V. Dinner only. Closed Sun. $$*

McDonagh's Seafood Bar. McDonagh's fish shop has been here since the last century. A few years ago they started selling seafood chowder and Galway oysters at a small bar. Nowadays, one half of the shop still sells fresh fish and shellfish at lunchtime while the other half is a small café-style restaurant, its walls draped with fishing nets, shells, and plaster fish. In the evening the whole room is filled, such is the demand for their fish—"leaping fresh," as they say, and simply prepared. Try a plate of their home-smoked salmon, the famous Galway oysters au naturel, or a bowl of mussels steamed in wine and garlic. Hearty eaters can seldom resist their traditional fish and chips—cod, whiting, mackerel, haddock, or hake, deepfried in a light batter and served with a great heap of freshly cooked chips. *Quay St., Galway, tel. 091/65001. Reservations advised. AE, MC, V. Wine license only. Closed Sun. lunch Oct.–Apr. $*

Lodging

★ **Ardilaun House.** This lovely 19th-century house lies at the end of a tree-lined avenue in a quiet suburb, midway between the city center and the Salthill promenade—about five minutes' drive from both.

The peaceful public rooms overlooking the gardens have open fires in the large marble chimneypieces, fresh flower arrangements, and Regency-style furniture. The original house has been discreetly extended to allow for additional lodging space. The individually designed bedrooms feature a pink, gray, or green color scheme and Irish-made mahogany furniture with brass trim. All the fully tiled bathrooms have heated towel racks and marble sinks. For views of the bay, book a top-floor even-numbered room. Other rooms, which are just as pleasant, overlook the flower garden, shrubberies, and a fountain. *Taylor's Hill, Galway, tel. 091/21433, fax 091/21546. 89 rooms with bath. Facilities: restaurant, 3 bars, sauna, tennis court, gym, Jacuzzi. AE, DC, MC, V. $$$*

★ **Galway Great Southern.** Built in 1845 to coincide with the arrival of the railway in the area, this imposing limestone-faced hotel overlooking the main square is still the best address in town. As soon as you walk into the large, thickly carpeted lobby through heavy glass-paneled wooden doors with large brass handles, you know that you've arrived at one of Europe's grandest old-fashioned hotels; this solid and luxurious establishment retains a great sense of tradition. Rooms are fairly big and combine the best of old and new, with tall ceilings and windows, tastefully muted coordinated color schemes, and Georgian-style tables and chairs. Ask for a back room on the fifth floor if you want a view of Galway Bay. It's worth visiting the rooftop swimming pool to enjoy an extraordinary panorama of the city and Galway Bay. In the evening, guests can sample French-Irish cuisine at the formal Oyster Room (*see* Dining, *above*) or have a drink in the lobby at the charming Railway Bar and Lounge. *Eyre Sq., Galway, tel. 091/64041, fax 091/66704. 115 rooms with bath. Facilities: restaurant, 2 bars, indoor heated pool, sauna, plunge pool. AE, DC, MC, V. $$$*

Glenlo Abbey. Four kilometers (2½ miles) outside the city on the N59 Clifden road, Galway's newest luxury hotel was until recently a monastery, dating from 1740. It is set well back from the road with views over the lower reaches of Lough Corrib and surrounded by its own newly built nine-hole golf course. A wide flight of stone steps leads to the entrance lobby in a cut-stone Victorian house. The lobby has something of the atmosphere of a gentleman's club with hand-loomed rugs on solid parquet floors, large leather Chesterfield sofas, and rows of old leather-bound books. The spacious bedrooms are in a new wing overlooking the golf course and have Georgian-style furniture in mahogany veneer and super-king-size beds. The bathrooms have marbled walls and some have whirlpool baths. The elegant and rather hushed Ffrench Room serves Irish and international cuisine in formal Regency-style surroundings. *Bushy Park, Co. Galway, tel. 091/26666, fax 091/27800. 42 rooms with bath. Facilities: restaurant, 2 bars, tennis court, 9-hole golf course, gymnasium, sauna. $$$*

Brennan's Yard. A stone-built four-story building in Galway's dockland area has been strikingly converted into a modern hotel of unusually strong character. It is just beside the historic Spanish Arch and an easy walk from all the best shops. The bar has a wall of windows the height of the hotel and looks across the sea to the Claddagh, once Galway's fishing village, as do some of the bedrooms (ask for a sea view when booking). The rooms are not large and have quite small windows due to the age of the building, but they are very well designed, color-coordinated in dark pastels, and individually furnished with antique pine, modern ceramic or wooden table lamps, and paintings by local artists. The bathrooms are small but fully equipped. The hotel staff are all immensely proud of the place, and you should find the service exceptionally friendly. *Lower Mer-*

chant's Rd., tel. 091/68166, fax 091/68262. 24 rooms with bath. Facilities: restaurant, bar. AE, DC, MC, V. $$

Anno Santo. Situated 300 meters (960 feet) from the sea on a residential road in Salthill (about an eight-minute drive from the city center), this small hotel has been run by the Vaughan family since 1950. A two-story bedroom wing has been added to the original, rather overdecorated bungalow. The upstairs rooms are smaller but brighter than the downstairs ones. Carpets with dizzying designs, plywood headboards and closets, and white candlewick spreads will not win any design awards, but the bedrooms are spotlessly clean. Guests of all nationalities stay here, and the Vaughans are friendly and full of helpful touring advice. *Threadneedle Rd., Salthill, Galway, tel. 091/23011, fax 091/22110. 14 rooms with bath. Facilities: restaurant, bar. AE, DC, MC, V. Closed Dec. 20–Jan. 20. $*

Jurys Inn. This newly built 3-story hotel offers good-quality budget accommodation with a fixed price per room, which accommodate 3 adults or 2 adults and 2 children. The atmosphere unavoidably tends toward anonymous-international, but the location is central and attractive, and the level of comfort is high for the price range. Guest rooms overlooking the bubbling River Corrib have less traffic noise than the front ones, which look past the Spanish Arch to Galway Bay. Rooms are light and airy with modern pine fittings, plain carpets and walls, double-glazed windows with pleasant views, and fully equipped bathrooms. *Quay St., Galway, tel. 091/66444, fax 091/68415. 128 rooms with bath. Facilities: restaurant, bar, multi-story car parking fee). $*

Knockferry

Lodging

Knockferry Lodge. A half-hour drive from Galway City (21 kilometers/13 miles—turn right off the N59 in Moycullen), this is an excellent base for visiting the city as well as Lough Corrib and Connemara. Owners Des and Mary Moran encourage visitors to this secluded fishing lodge on the lake to stay more than one night—the longer you stay, the lower the rate. The Morans like to share their local knowledge with guests and encourage them to get to know each other around the turf fire after dinner. Bedrooms are pretty and simple, with modest antiques, Laura Ashley curtains and drapes, and hanging ferns in the half-tiled bathrooms. *Roscahill, Co. Galway, tel. 091/80122, fax 091/80328. 10 rooms with bath. Facilities: restaurant (wine license only), bar, fishing (boats for hire), billiards. No TV or direct-dial phones in rooms. AE, DC, MC, V. Closed Oct.–May 1. $*

Lahinch

Lodging

★ **Aberdeen Arms.** This beautifully refurbished Victorian seaside hotel is a model of its kind, offering elegance and comfort in a friendly, easygoing setting. It is popular with golfers, and humorous golfing prints hang on the dark-paneled walls of the bar and grill room. Ask for one of the new rooms that face the sea and feature spectacular skylights and windows. All rooms are large and tastefully decorated with built-in, cream-colored melamine closets, plain carpets, and matching cream floral drapes and spreads; some offer Georgian-style tables and chairs. The main dining room offers an excellent and varied menu of French-Irish cuisine; the hotel also serves one of the best breakfasts in the county. *Lahinch, Co. Clare, tel. 065/81100, fax 065/81228. 55 rooms with bath. Facilities: 2 restaurants, 2 bars, snooker, minigym, sauna, Jacuzzi, 10 tennis courts, bicycles. AE, DC, MC, V. $$*

Letterfrack

Lodging **Rosleague Manor.** This pink, creeper-clad, two-story Georgian house stands amid wooded grounds overlooking Ballinakill Bay and the mountains of County Mayo and Connemara. The clutter of walking and shooting sticks beneath the grandfather clock in the hall sets the tone of this fairly informal, small, country-house hotel. The best rooms are located on the first-floor front, overlooking the bay. All the solidly comfortable bedrooms are furnished with well-used Victorian and Georgian antiques, fourposters or large brass bedsteads, and drapes that match the William Morris wallpaper. The expensive, award-winning restaurant features seafood and homegrown vegetables. *Letterfrack, Co. Galway, tel. 095/41001, fax 095/41168. 15 rooms with bath. Facilities: restaurant, bar, tennis court, sauna. No TV in rooms. AE, MC, V. Closed Nov.–Apr. 1. $$$*

Lisdoonvarna

Lodging **Ballinalacken Castle.** This is not a castle but a sprawling Victorian lodge with bow windows that stands beside the 16th-century O'Brien castle ruins. On a hill, 4 kilometers (2½ miles) outside Lisdoonvarna, it commands a panoramic view of the Atlantic, the Aran Islands, and, across Galway Bay, the Connemara Hills; the hotel is surrounded by 100 acres of wildflower meadows. The interior is much less impressive, yet the room rates are reasonable. Bedrooms come in all different shapes and sizes; some have marble fireplaces and high ceilings. There are six large rooms in a new wing; all have sea views and dark wood furniture. The furniture in the public rooms is a haphazard mix of hand-me-downs, modern stuff, lovely old Irish oak, and sumptuous inlaid bureaus. *Lisdoonvarna, Co. Clare, tel. 065/74025. 12 rooms with bath. Facilities: restaurant, bar. MC, V. Closed Nov.–Apr. 1. $*

Sheedy's Spa View. Originally a 17th-century farmhouse, this is now a small, friendly hotel that has belonged to the Sheedy family since 1855. It is only a short walk from both the town center and the spa wells. Rooms are well cared for, simple, and spotlessly clean; most of them offer a Georgian-style coffee table and chairs. The award-winning, moderately priced Orchid Room restaurant serves an outstanding five-course set menu featuring French-Irish cuisine prepared by Patsy Sheedy and her internationally trained son, Frankie. *Lisdoonvarna, Co. Clare, tel. 065/74026, fax 065/74555. 11 rooms with bath. Facilities: restaurant (dinner only, bar food at lunch), bar, tennis court, TV lounge. No TV in rooms. AE, DC, MC, V. $*

Newmarket-on-Fergus

Lodging ★ **Dromoland Castle.** Thirteen kilometers (8 miles) from Shannon and 9½ kilometers (6 miles) from Ennis, this luxury hotel is a popular first stop with affluent American and French visitors. The original 16th-century O'Brien castle was pulled down early in the 19th century and replaced with an impressive turreted Gothic-style stone building that is now the hotel. The castle stands beside a lake, surrounded by well-landscaped formal gardens in their own neatly kept park. The hotel interior was recently given a face-lift by New York interior decorator Carlton Varney. Wide, thick-carpeted corridors are flanked by stone walls graced with large ancestral portraits. Bedrooms overlook the old Queen Anne stable yard and feature Regency-style furniture and a pleasant pink or green color scheme. A cut-glass decanter of complimentary sherry awaits guests in every room. The vast suites have ruched drapes on the tall windows, great views over the park, and antiques, many of them Irish-Georgian. *Newmarket-on-Fergus, Co. Clare, tel. 061/368144, fax 061/363355. 73 rooms with bath. Facilities: 18-hole golf course, lake fishing, bicycles, shooting (Nov.–Jan.), 2 tennis courts, billiards, horseback riding. AE, DC, MC, V. $$$$*

Newport

Lodging **Newport House.** This Georgian mansion is strictly for those who will feel at ease in a rather grand and elegant private home. The handsome creeper-covered building beside the Newport River dominates the little town. Beyond a small, tidy lobby are spacious reception rooms furnished with gilt-framed family portraits, Regency mirrors and chairs, handwoven Donegal carpeting, and crystal chandeliers hanging from ornate stucco ceilings. The sweeping staircase, top-lighted by a lantern and a glass dome, leads to an airy gallery and the bedrooms. These are bright and less elaborate than the public rooms, with pretty chintz drapes and a mix of Victorian antiques and merely old furniture. Most bedrooms have sitting areas and good views of the river and gardens; others have such compensations as the enormous Jacobean four-poster in Room 10. *Newport, Co. Mayo, tel. 098/41222, fax 098/41613. 19 rooms with bath. Facilities: restaurant, bar, fishing, snooker. No TV in rooms and no TV lounge. AE, DC, MC, V. Closed Oct.–mid-Mar. $$$*

Oughterard

Lodging **Connemara Gateway.** An adventurously designed modern low-rise building with traditional gray slated roofs above whitewashed walls, this hotel, about 1 kilometer (½ mile) outside the village on the Galway side of the N59, combines the best of old and new. The traditional Irish cottage is the theme of the lobby and the bar, both of which are decorated with wooden and cast-iron artifacts, old country pine furniture, and chintz sofas. The modern room furnishings are enhanced by floral wall panels, matching floral drapes, and fluffy mohair coverlets; all bedrooms have small sitting areas beside the large teak framed windows affording views of the gardens and the distant hills. The plentiful tour-bus trade does not spoil its carefully fostered charm. *Oughterard, Co. Galway, tel. 091/82328, fax 091/82332. 62 rooms with bath. Facilities: restaurant, bar, fishing, indoor heated pool, sauna, tennis court. Closed Oct.–Jan 1. DC, MC, V. $$$*

★ **Currarevagh House.** Turn right in the village square and follow the twisting road signposted "Lakeshore" for about 6 kilometers (4 miles) to find this very special, secluded place, pronounced "Curra-reeva." It's a genuine, unspoiled, old-fashioned country house in which breakfast is still laid out Edwardian buffet–style on the dining room sideboard and the afternoon tea ritual is observed in the drawing room. A terrifying tiger skin hangs on the staircase, and other stuffed hunting trophies jump out at you from the dark wood paneling. Magnificent displays of fresh flowers, gathered from the 150 wooded acres, adorn the lobby and sitting rooms, where plump white armchairs tempt you to a seat in front of marble fireplaces with open turf fires. Rooms are furnished with modest antiques and family hand-me-downs (successive generations of the Hodgson family have lived here since they built the house in 1846). All bedrooms in the main house have different, slightly haphazard color schemes; the front ones overlook Lough Corrib, while others offer an equally pleasant view of the gardens (including rhododendrons, azaleas, camellias, and hydrangeas) and the mountains. The bedrooms in the new wing blend in successfully with the old house. They are more conventionally furnished, with built-in furniture in dark polished wood, and overlook both the lake and the garden. *Oughterard, Co. Galway, tel. 091/82312, fax 091/82731. 15 rooms with bath. Facilities: restaurant, bar, fishing (boats for hire), tennis court, private beach (lakeside), croquet, TV room. No TV or direct-dial phones in rooms. No credit cards. Closed Nov.–mid-Mar. except for parties of more than 8. $$$*

Recess

Lodging ★ **Ballynahinch Castle.** Turn left off the N59 at the sign for the castle between Recess and Clifden, and after about 3 kilometers (2 miles) look out for a fairy-tale green-and-white-painted gate lodge on the right. The castle is really a large house built in the late 18th century, on the site of an O'Flaherty castle beside the Ballynahinch River; it's a favorite retreat of statesmen and movie stars—including ex–U.S. President Gerald Ford and actor Alec Guinness. Visitors can walk in the property's 40 wooded acres, and they have access to excellent fishing and shooting facilities. Ballynahinch achieves great comfort without ostentation; the tiled lobby with Persian rugs, for example, has two inviting leather chesterfields in front of an open fire. The wide corridors, carpeted in Turkish red, feature prints and old photos of Connemara on the walls. The biggest bedrooms, in the discreetly added new ground-floor wing, have four-poster beds, Georgian-style mahogany furniture, and floor-to-ceiling windows overlooking the river. Rooms in the old house are equally comfortable and quiet (they do not have televisions). *Ballinafad, Recess, Co. Galway, tel. 095/31006, fax 095/31085. 28 rooms with bath. Facilities: restaurant, bar, fishing, shooting, tennis court, bicycles, croquet. AE, DC, MC, V. $$$*

Westport

Dining **The Asgard.** This restaurant is in a small room above a pub, but it has its own separate entrance and a small anteroom with an open fire for pre-dinner cocktails. White damask napery covers the tables in the red-carpeted and red-draped dining room, which is decorated with large nautical prints and cooled by a brass ceiling fan. Service is friendly and professional. Cream of nettle soup, roast stuffed duckling with orange sauce, and fillet of sole vermouth are typical items on the menu of this popular and reliable eatery. *The Quay, Westport, tel. 098/25319. Reservations advised. Dinner only (award-winning, inexpensive bar food at lunch). AE, DC, MC, V. $$*

Quay Cottage. A tiny waterside cottage has been gutted and cleverly converted into an atmospheric, informal wine bar and shellfish restaurant. Fishing nets, glass floats, lobster pots, and greenery hang from the high-pitched roof with exposed beams. The dining room features rush-seated chairs at the polished oak tables and an open fire on evenings. The lively place attracts a youngish crowd, in search of a good time as much as of good food. Try the chowder special (a thick vegetable and mussel soup), garlic butter crab claws, or a half-pound steak fillet, and be sure to sample the homemade brown bread. *The Quay (beside Westport House), Westport, tel. 098/26412. Reservations advised evenings and Sunday lunch. Wine license only. AE, MC, V. Closed Jan. 1–Feb. 1. $$*

Lodging **Hotel Westport.** This glass and aluminum hotel, a five-minute walk from the town center, is quiet and convenient, surrounded by lawns and overlooking the grounds of Westport House. The lobby, bar, and restaurant, decorated in an art-nouveau style, have heavy mahogany and stained-glass partitions. All bedrooms in the two-story bedroom wing are identical but pleasant, with Georgian-style mahogany bureaus and tables, off-white floral comforters, and fully tiled bathrooms. *Westport, Co. Mayo, tel. 098/25122, fax 098/26739. 49 rooms with bath. Facilities: restaurant (dinner only), bar, tennis court, bicycles. AE, DC, MC, V. $$*

Olde Railway Hotel. By far the best bet in the town center, this Victorian railway hotel offers both character and comfort. Fishing trophies, Victorian plates, framed prints, and watercolors brighten up the solidly furnished lobby and lounge. A mix of Victorian and old pieces furnishes the individually decorated bedrooms. Room 209 features a heavy Victorian bed and a river view. Room 114 has a Victorian chaise longue and a large Georgian wardrobe. All the bedrooms are sunny, with ruched Austrian blinds. The front bar can be lively with good, inexpensive lunches and live music in the evening in season and weekends. *The Mall, Westport, Co. Mayo, tel. 098/25605, fax 098/25090. 15 rooms with bath. Facilities: restaurant (dinner only), 2 bars, fishing. AE, DC, MC, V. $$*

The Arts and Nightlife

The Arts

Visual Arts/Galleries The following small galleries are worth checking out for exhibits of reasonably priced painting, sculpture, stonework, ceramics, prints, wall hangings, and batiks by local artists: **Clifden, Co. Galway: Stanley's** (tel. 095/21039); **Millar's** (tel. 095/21038). **Ennis, Co. Clare: De Valera Library** (tel. 065/21616). **Galway City: Kenny's** (High St., tel. 091/62739); **University College** (tel. 091/24411); **The Grainstore** (tel. 091/66620). **Recess, Co. Galway: Joyce's** (tel. 095/34604). **Spiddle, Co. Galway: Stone Art Gallery** (tel. 091/83355). **Westport, Co. Mayo: Westport House Antique Shop** (Westport House, tel. 098/25404).

Theater Galway City has two small but famous theaters. **An Taibhdhearc** (Middle St., tel. 091/62024), pronounced "Awn Tie-vark," was founded in 1928 by Hilton Edwards and Micheal Macliammoir as the national Irish-language theater. It continues to produce first-class shows, mainly of Irish works in both the English and the Irish languages.

The **Druid Theatre** (Chapel La., tel. 091/68617) houses a comparatively young group of actors who have built up an excellent reputation over the past 10 years for adventurous and accomplished productions, mainly of 20th-century Irish and European plays, that travel regularly to the Royal Shakespeare Company's small stage in London.

Nightlife

Pubs are more or less the only form of nightlife around. Most large towns have a disco (usually an annex of a hotel or bar) patronized mainly by the under-thirties on Saturday or Sunday night, starting at about 10:30 and finishing at 1 or 2. In Galway City, the discos are located in the Salthill area. Expect to pay a £2.50 to £5 cover charge.

In Ennis, an Irish cabaret evening is presented at the **West County Hotel** (tel. 065/28421) every Tuesday and Friday from early June to late September, with the option of dinner and show (about £18.50) or show only (about £6). Also in Ennis, **Cois Na hAbhna** (tel. 061/71166), a stage show featuring traditional music, song, and dance, takes place at 8:30 PM on Saturdays in June and September, and on Mondays, Thursdays, and Saturdays in July and August.

Pubs Traditional-music performances can take place spontaneously, but the pubs listed below have built up a reputation for music, and they foster it by engaging professional musicians to play for at least part of the evening. Such music sessions usually start at about 9:30. Saturday and Sunday are the busiest nights. In general (unless there's a special big-name act), there's no admission charge for these sessions.

Traditionally, all those present at a spontaneous session pay their dues by contributing to the entertainment in turn. In the larger pubs, it is impossible to observe this custom; instead, each musician, as in a jazz session, will take a solo turn. But if you're privileged enough to be included in a small session, try to have someone in your group ready to sing, play music, or tell a good joke. Your participation is an excellent way to make friends. The following places all feature traditional and folk music unless otherwise indicated:

County Clare **Ballyvaughan: Monk's Pub** (tel. 065/77059). **Doolin: Gus O'Connor's** (tel. 065/74168); **McDermott's** (no phone); **McGann's** (tel. 065/74133). **Ennis: Brogan's** (24 O'Connell St., tel. 065/29480); **Ciaran's Bar** (1 Francis St., tel. 065/40180); **May Kearney's Bar** (1 Newbridge Rd., tel. 065/24888). **Ennistymon: Nagle's** (Main St., tel. 065/71023). **Kilfenora: Vaughan's Pub** (tel. 065/88004). **Lahinch: O'Dwyer's 19th** (tel. 065/81440). **Lisdoonvarna: The Roadside Tavern** (tel. 065/74084).

County Galway **Aran Islands: American Bar** (Kilronan, Inishmore, tel. 099/61130). **Clifden: Abbeyglen Castle Hotel** (tel. 095/21070). **Letterfrack: The Bard's Den** (tel. 095/41042). **Galway City: Sally Long's Music Bar** (rock and disco; tel. 091/65756); **The Quays** (Quay St., tel. 091/61777); **Noctan's** (Cross St., tel. 091/66172); **Garravanes** (Shop St., no phone); **Murray's Piano Bar** (cocktail music, Hotel Salthill, Salthill, tel. 091/22448). **Oughterard: Faherty's** (tel. 091/82194).

County Mayo **Achill Island: Alice's Harbor Inn** (Achill Sound, tel. 098/45138); **Achill Sound Hotel** (tel. 098/45245). **Ballina: Downhill Hotel** (tel. 096/21033). **Claremorris: Dalton Inn** (live rock, folk, and disco; tel. 094/71408). **Mulrany: Campbell's Tavern** (tel. 098/36234). **Westport: Ardmore Pub** (The Quay, tel. 098/25994); **Hogan's** (The Octagon, no phone).

10 The Northwest

Yeats Country, Donegal Bay, the Northern Peninsulas

By Andrew Sanger

British travel writer Andrew Sanger is the author of several popular guidebooks; he contributes frequently to a variety of publications, including The Guardian, The Daily Telegraph, *and* The Sunday Times.

In the wild wet grass-and-heather hills of Donegal, Leitrim, and Sligo, the three counties in the remote Northwest, you'll find some of Ireland's most majestic scenery. Cool, clean waters from the roaring Atlantic Ocean slice the landscape into long peninsulas of breeze-swept rocky crests, each one remote from the next. The lower country, at least where it is covered by layers of moist bog, cuts open to reveal dark brown peat underneath; although this area may be thought less pretty than the rest of the region, it has a haunting, lonely appeal.

Tucked into the folds of the Northwest's hills, modest little market towns and unpretentious villages with muddy streets go about their business quietly. In the squelchy peat bogs, cutters working with long shovels pause to watch and wave as you drive past. Remember to drive slowly along the country lanes, for around any corner you may find a whitewashed thatched cottage with children playing outside, a shepherd leading his flock, or a bicycle-riding farmer wobbling along in the middle of the road.

Keep in mind, though, that the whole region—and County Donegal in particular—attracts a good share of visitors during July and August; this is a favorite vacation area for people who live in nearby Northern Ireland. To be frank, a few places are quite spoiled by popularity with tourists and careless development. The Rosses Peninsula on Donegal's west coast, still sometimes described as beautiful, is marred by too much building. Bundoran, on the coast between Sligo Town and Donegal Town, a cheap-and-cheerful family beach resort full of so-called "Irish gift shops" and "amusement arcades," is another place to pass by rather than visit. On the whole, though, the Northwest is big enough, untamed enough, and grand enough to be able to absorb all of its summer (and weekend) tourists without too much harm.

Something in the turbulent Atlantic air blows over these hills—a sense that the past is not so far away, a lilting half-heard Celtic tune that soothes the soul yet fires the imagination. County Donegal has the country's largest Gaeltacht (Irish-speaking area). Driving in this part of the country, you'll be amused, frustrated, and delighted by turns whenever you come to a crossroads: Signposts show only the Irish place names, often so unlike the English versions as to be completely unrecognizable. All is not lost, however—maps generally give both the Irish and the English names, and locals are usually more than happy to help out with directions (in English), sometimes with a yarn thrown in. County Donegal was part of the near-indomitable ancient kingdom of Ulster, which was not conquered by the English until the 17th century. By the time they were driven out in the 1920s, the English had still not eradicated rural Donegal's Celtic inheritance.

If the whole of Ireland is a land of seemingly infinite diversity, in the Northwest even the air, the light, and the colors of the countryside change like a kaleidoscope. Look once, and scattered snow-white clouds are flying above tawny-brown slopes. Look again, and suddenly the sun has brilliantly illuminated some magnificent reds and purples in the undergrowth. The inconstant skies brighten and darken at will, bringing out a whole spectrum of subtle shades within the unkempt gorse and heather, the rocky slopes merging into somber peat and grassy meadows of scintillating green.

Not only close to the bracing ocean shore but also farther inland, water in all its forms dominates the Northwest; countless lakes, running streams, and rivers wind through lovely pastoral valleys. Be prepared for plenty of rainfall as well; don't forget to carry a raincoat or umbrella—although, as a kind local may inform you, the "brolly" acts purely as a talisman: "For it's only when you *don't* have it with you that the rain will really come down" is a piece of local wisdom.

Essential Information

Important Addresses and Numbers

Tourist Information The main visitor information center for the whole Northwest region is the Tourist Information Office (TIO) in **Sligo Town** (Áras Reddan, Temple St., tel. 071/61201). Sligo is in the extreme south of the region; if you are traveling in County Donegal in the North, try the TIO at **Letterkenny** (Derry Rd., tel. 074/21160) in a small chalet-type modern building about 1.6 kilometers (1 mile) out of town. Both TIOs are open year-round: Sept.–May, weekdays 9–1 and 2–5; June, Mon.–Sat. 9–1 and 2–6; July–Aug., Mon.–Sat. 9–8, Sun. 10–2.

The following TIOs are open only during the summer months (usually the first week in June to the second week in September):

Bundoran, County Donegal (Main St., tel. 072/41350).

Carrick-on-Shannon, County Leitrim (on the river quay, tel. 078/20170). Information for County Leitrim and its county town.

Donegal Town, County Donegal (Quay St., tel. 073/21148).

Dungloe, County Donegal (in the village center, tel. 075/21297).

Emergencies Call 999 for **police, fire,** or **ambulance** services.

Main Police Stations **Carrick-on-Shannon** (tel. 078/20021), **Donegal Town** (tel. 073/21021), **Letterkenny** (tel. 074/22222), and **Sligo Town** (tel. 071/42031).

Hospitals **Letterkenny General Hospital** (High Rd., Letterkenny, Co. Donegal, tel. 074/22022) and **Sligo General Hospital** (Dromahair Rd., Sligo Town, Co. Sligo, tel. 071/42161).

Arriving and Departing by Plane

Airports The principal international air arrival point to the Northwest is the tiny airport at Charlestown, near Knock. Usually known simply as **Knock Airport,** the official name is **Horan International Airport** (tel. 094/67247). **Eglinton Airport** (tel. 0504/810784), at Derry City, a few miles over the border, receives flights from the U.K. airports of Manchester and Glasgow and from Dublin. Eglinton is a particularly convenient airport for reaching northern County Donegal. Small local airfields are also located at **Carrickfinn** (tel. 075/48232) near Dungloe and **Sligo Airport** (tel. 071/68280 or 071/68318) at Strandhill, 8 kilometers (5 miles) from Sligo Town.

Airlines from the United Kingdom **Ryanair** offers flights daily to Knock Airport from London and other British and Irish airports. **Aer Lingus** has direct flights daily to Knock Airport, Eglinton Airport, and Sligo Airport from Dublin. **Loganair** provides direct flights daily to Eglinton Airport from Manchester and Glasgow, and to Carrickfinn Airport near Dungloe (four flights weekly) from Glasgow.

Between the Airports and Your Destination
By Bus

If you aren't driving, Knock Airport becomes less attractive, as you'll have no easy public transportation link to your destination, except the once-a-day (in season) local bus to Charlestown (11 kilometers/7 miles away). Nor can you rely on catching a bus at the smaller airports, except at Sligo Airport, where buses run from Sligo Town to meet all flights.

By Car For car renters, Knock Airport, just 54½ kilometers (34 miles) south of Sligo Town, has a convenient car rental desk. You can also pick up rental cars at Sligo and Eglinton (Derry) airports.

By Taxi Cabs sometimes stand waiting outside Knock Airport to meet incoming flights, but passengers arriving at the other airports may have to phone a local taxi company. Phone numbers of taxi companies are available from airport information desks and are also displayed beside pay phones inside the airport terminals.

Arriving and Departing by Car, Train, and Bus

By Car Sligo, the largest town in the Northwest, is relatively accessible on the main routes. The N4 travels the 224 kilometers (140 miles) direct from Dublin to Sligo, but you need to allow at least four hours for this journey. The N15 continues from Sligo Town to Donegal Town and proceeds from Donegal Town to Derry City, just over the border in the province of Northern Ireland. The best approach for anyone driving up from the West and the Southwest is on the N17, connecting Sligo to Galway.

By Train Sligo Town is linked by a direct train line to Dublin. From Dublin three trains a day are available, and the journey takes three hours and 20 minutes. The fare for the trip is £11 one-way, £14 round-trip. The train stops at Ballymote (20 minutes from Sligo), Boyle (40 minutes), and Carrick-on-Shannon (50 minutes). However, if you want to get to Sligo Town by rail from other provincial towns, you'll be forced to make some inconvenient connections and take roundabout routes. The rest of the region has no railway services. Contact **Irish Rail** (tel. 01/836–6222).

By Bus **Bus Éireann** (tel. 01/836–6111) can get you from Dublin to Sligo Town in four hours for £8 one-way, £11 round-trip. Three buses a day from Dublin are available. Another bus route, three times a day from Dublin, gets to Letterkenny, in the heart of County Donegal, in 4¼ hours, via a short trip across the Northern Ireland border, for £10 one-way, £13 round-trip. Other Bus Éireann services connect Sligo Town to other towns all over Ireland; for these connections, call 071/2152.

Getting Around

By Car Roads are uncongested, but in some places they are in a poor state of repair. In the Irish-speaking areas, signposts are written only in the Irish (Gaelic) language, which can be confusing. You need to prepare beforehand for this by checking the Irish names of places on your route.

Car Rentals You can rent a car in Sligo Town from **O'Mara** (tel. 071/44068), or at Sligo Airport from **Johnson & Perrott** (tel. 071/68461). At Knock Airport, cars may be rented from **Avis** (tel. 094/67252). A medium-size four-door costs around £50 per day with unlimited mileage (inclusive of insurance and taxes), or around £240 per week. Avis rentals tend to be a little more expensive than other companies'. If you're planning to tour mostly northern County Donegal, you may find it more convenient to rent a car in Derry City from **Hertz** (tel. 0504/360420). If you're planning to take a rental car across the border to Northern Ireland, inform the company in advance and check the insurance position.

By Bus **Bus Éireann** services operate out of Sligo Town (tel. 071/60066) and Letterkenny (tel. 074/21309) to destinations all over the region, as well as to other parts of Ireland. From Sligo Town, you can reach almost any point in the region for under £10. Several other local bus companies link towns and villages in the Northwest, including **Funtrek** (tel. 01/730852) and **McGeehans** (tel. 075/46101).

Guided Tours

In July and August, walking tours of Sligo Town depart twice daily from the Tourist Information Office at 11 AM and 7 PM. They are free and last about one to 1½ hours. However, the guides are generally students, so a tip of 50p or £1 is welcome. Also in July and August, for a friendly, relaxed minibus tour of the area with a knowledgeable guide, call **John Houze** (tel. 071/42747) for his tour around Lough Gill (cost: £6 adults, £2.50 children under 16) and his tour north of Sligo Town to Drumcliff, Lissadell House, and Creevykeel (cost: £6 adults, £2.50 children under 16). **Bus Éireann** (tel. 071/60066 in Sligo, 074/21309 in Letterkenny) offers useful budget-priced one-day guided coach tours of the Donegal Highlands and to Glenveagh National Park. These tours start from Bundoran, Sligo Town, Ballyshannon, and Donegal Town.

Exploring the Northwest

Highlights for First-Time Visitors

Ardara (*see* Tour 2)
Donegal Town (*see* Tour 2)
Glenveagh National Park (*see* Tour 3)
Grianan Ailigh, for the view of Lough Swilly (*see* Tour 3)
Lough Gill (*see* Tour 1)
Sheephaven Bay, from Rosguill Peninsula to Horn Head (*see* Tour 3)

Tour 1: Yeats Country—Sligo Town and Environs

Numbers in the margin correspond to points of interest on the Yeats Country and Around Donegal Bay and the Sligo Town maps.

This tour, which covers the most accessible part of the Northwest, visits a pleasant, peaceful countryside of lakes, farms, and woodland on the border of Counties Sligo and Leitrim. If you are familiar with the romantic poems of William Butler Yeats, it will undoubtedly bring to mind some of his best writing. Yeats knew intimately all these villages and landscapes and eloquently celebrated many of them in verse. Often on this route, you'll have glimpses of "bare Ben Bulben's head," as he called flat-topped Ben Bulben Mountain, which looms over the western end of the Dartry range.

1 Begin this tour at **Sligo Town,** although you may not be staying in the town itself; the most interesting accommodations are located a few miles out. This busy marketplace is very much the region's principal community. With a population of about 17,000 inhabitants, it is the only sizable town in the whole of Northwest Ireland. Sligo is cen-

tered around two bridges across the River Garavogue, and its name in Irish, Sligeach, means "place of shells." This lovely riverside location, squeezed onto a patch of land between Sligo Bay and Lough Gill, often became a battleground in its earlier days. The community was attacked by Viking invaders in the 9th century and, later, by a succession of rival Irish and Anglo-Norman conquerors. In 1245, Sligo was fortified by the most successful of these victors, Maurice FitzGerald, earl of Kildare, although nothing is left now of his medieval castle.

Modern-day Sligo offers visitors only modest sights, but it does deserve a stroll, especially because of its close associations with W. B.
2 Yeats and his talented family. At the **Yeats Memorial Building** beside Hyde Bridge, an annual Yeats Summer School is conducted every August—guest speakers are invited to lecture on the world-renowned poet and his contemporaries. During the rest of the year, occasional exhibitions and other lectures on the writer are held in the area.

Yeats's brother, Jack, was a famous painter in his day; he once said, "I never did a painting without putting a thought of Sligo in it." Yeats's father, John, had a considerable reputation as a portraitist. Many of the works of these two artists, including portraits of W. B.,
3 are displayed with paintings by other Irish artists at the **Sligo County Library and Museum,** on Stephen Street. Several pictures with connections to the Yeats family were donated by a New York stockbroker, James A. Healey, whose mother emigrated to the United States in 1884. Other items at the museum that can be seen on request are a collection of Yeats's first editions and such intriguing memorabilia as the author's personal letters and the Irish tricolor flag that draped his coffin when he was buried at nearby Drumcliff. *Stephen St., tel. 071/2212. Admission free. Library open Tues.–Sat. 10–1 and 2–5, and also 7–9 on Tues. and Thurs. Museum open June–Sept., Tues.–Sat. 10:30–12:30 and 2:30–4:30.*

To find Sligo's only existing relic of the Middle Ages, walk down Bridge Street, nearly opposite the library and museum. Cross the river and turn left into Abbey Street, and here you'll find the rather
4 forlorn ruins of the **13th-century Abbey,** built for the Dominicans by Maurice FitzGerald. After a fire in 1414, it was extensively rebuilt, only to be destroyed again by Cromwell's Puritans in 1641. Some fine stonework remains, especially in the 15th-century cloisters. *Admission free. Usually open—if not, key with caretaker (currently Mr. A. McGuinn, 6 Charlotte St.).*

Retrace your steps, turning left into Teeling Street to see the
5 **Courthouse.** Compared with the generally simple style of most Irish country architecture, this Victorian Gothic building is distinctly elaborate with its flamboyant, turreted Gothic exterior; it is not open to casual visitors. After it was built, the structure became a symbol for English power. The Courthouse takes its inspiration from the much larger Law Courts in London.

Continue beyond the Courthouse into Old Market Street right onto
6 High Street, passing the new **Dominican Abbey,** and left onto Church Street. At the end of Church Street, turn right onto Charles Street. You will notice along these streets that Sligo has numerous churches of all denominations. Presbyterians, Methodists, and even Plymouth Brethren are represented here, as well as Anglicans (Church of Ireland) and, of course, Roman Catholics. According to the Irish writer Sean O'Faolain, "The best Protestant stock in all Ireland is in Sligo." The Yeats family were part of that stock. At the

Yeats Country and Around Donegal Bay

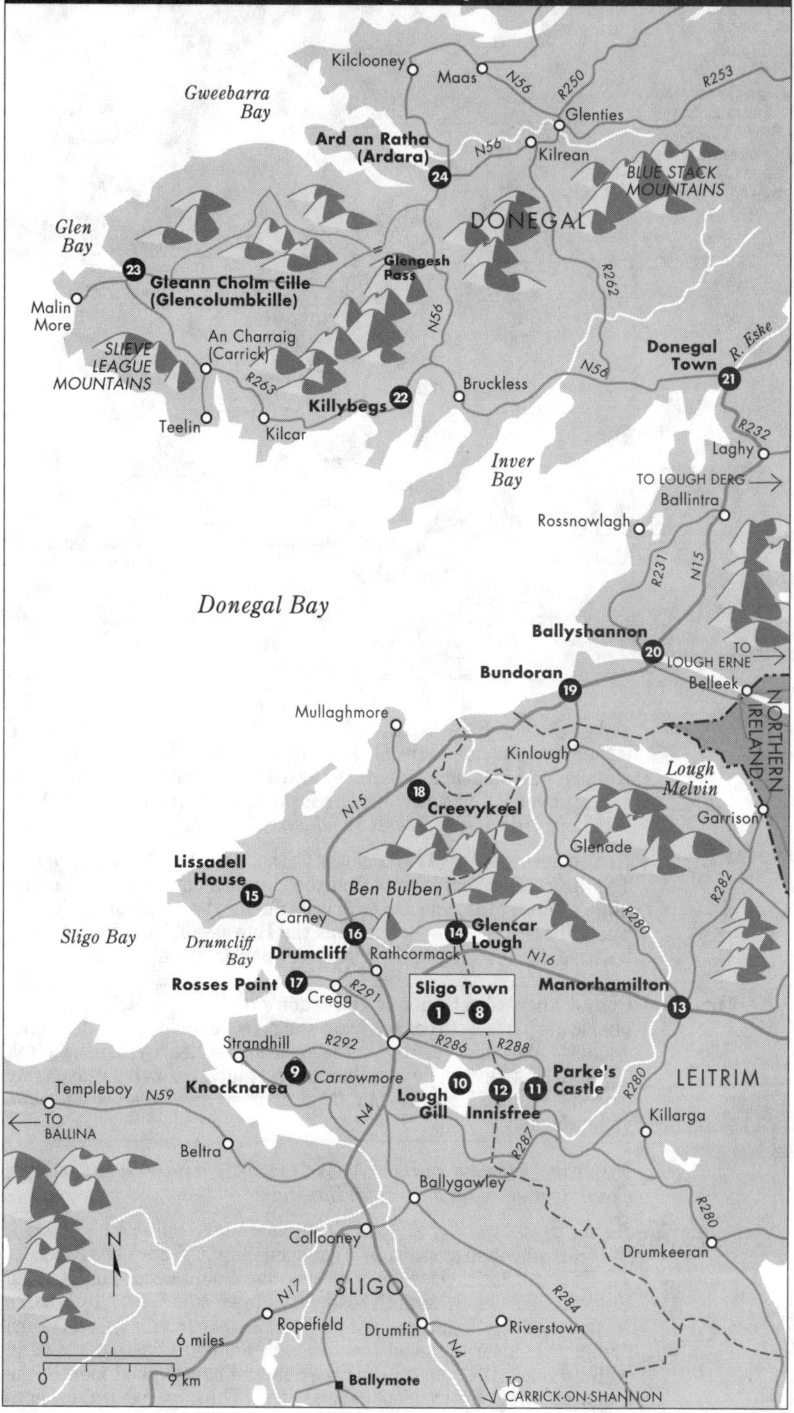
Kilclooney
Maas
N56
R250
R253
Gweebarra Bay
Glenties
Ard an Ratha (Ardara)
24
N56
Kilrean
BLUE STACK MOUNTAINS
DONEGAL
Glen Bay
Glengesh Pass
23
Gleann Cholm Cille (Glencolumbkille)
Malin More
R262
N56
SLIEVE LEAGUE MOUNTAINS
An Charraig (Carrick)
R263
Donegal Town
R. Eske
21
N56
Bruckless
Killybegs
22
Teelin
Kilcar
R232
Laghy
Inver Bay
TO LOUGH DERG
Ballintra
Rossnowlagh
R231
N15
Donegal Bay
Ballyshannon
20
TO LOUGH ERNE
Bundoran
19
Belleek
NORTHERN IRELAND
Mullaghmore
Kinlough
Lough Melvin
18
Creevykeel
N15
Garrison
Glenade
Lissadell House
15
Ben Bulben
R282
Carney
R280
Sligo Bay
16
14
Glencar Lough
Drumcliff Bay
Drumcliff
Rathcormack
N16
Rosses Point
17
Cregg
R291
Sligo Town
1 – 8
Manorhamilton
13
Strandhill
R292
R286
R288
9
Carrowmore
Parke's Castle
LEITRIM
Templeboy
N59
Knocknarea
10
12
11
R280
Lough Gill
Innisfree
N4
TO BALLINA
Killarga
Beltra
R287
Ballygawley
R280
N
Collooney
Drumkeeran
SLIGO
N17
R284
Ropefield
Drumfin
Riverstown
0
6 miles
N4
0
9 km
Ballymote
TO CARRICK-ON-SHANNON

Courthouse, **5**
Dominican Abbey, **6**
St. John's Cathedral, **7**
Sligo County Library and Museum, **3**
13th-century Abbey, **4**
Tourist Information Office, **8**
Yeats Memorial Building, **2**

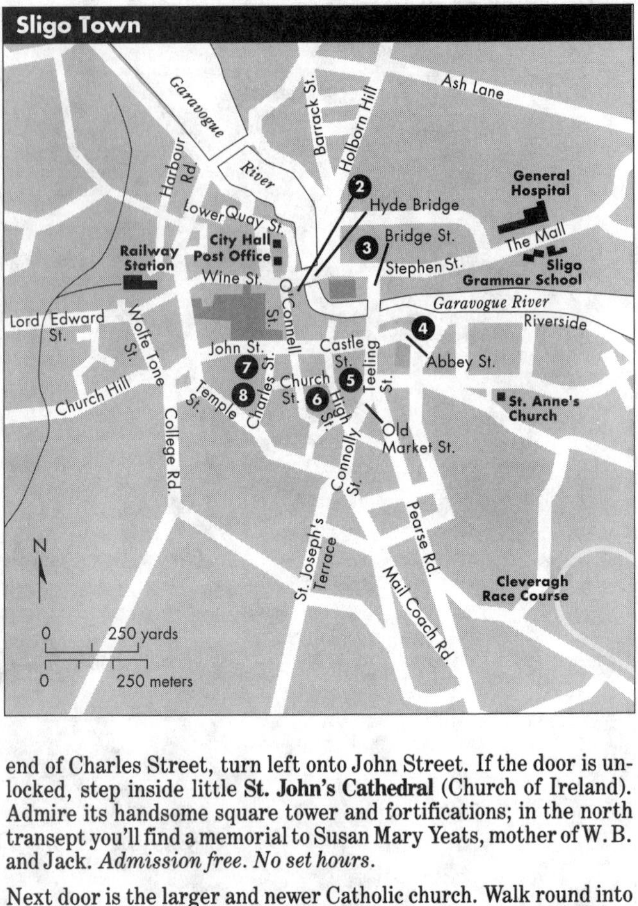

end of Charles Street, turn left onto John Street. If the door is unlocked, step inside little **St. John's Cathedral** (Church of Ireland). Admire its handsome square tower and fortifications; in the north transept you'll find a memorial to Susan Mary Yeats, mother of W.B. and Jack. *Admission free. No set hours.*

7

Next door is the larger and newer Catholic church. Walk round into Temple Street where you'll find the church's entrance and County Sligo's **Tourist Information Office,** useful for the whole of the Northwest. It's in the same building as the **Hawkswell Theatre,** an unattractive '60s low rise on the corner of Charles Street.

8

Time Out One of Sligo's best pubs is **Hargadon's** (O'Connell St.), an atmospheric old place with cozy private snugs (rooms)—try the fine sandwiches, cakes, and coffee. On the same street nearby, **Beezie's** (tel. 071/45239) is a lively, popular bar and restaurant serving reasonably priced "Tourist Menu" meals (typical Irish meat dishes with two vegetables).

Numbers in the margin correspond to points of interest on the Yeats Country and Around Donegal Bay map.

9 Rising to the west of Sligo is **Knocknarea** (328 meters/1,083 feet), the "cairn-heaped grassy hill" that once caught Yeats's imagination. To drive out for a closer look at this flat mountain not unlike Ben Bulben, take the Strandhill road out of town (the R292; it goes due west, following Sligo Bay). After 8 kilometers (5 miles), a left turn brings you closer to the hilltop—though you will have to get out and walk to reach the summit—where you will have a good view of the mountains of Counties Donegal and Sligo. The huge cairn at its sum-

mit, a heaped-stone monument made with 40,000 tons of rock, is traditionally believed to commemorate "passionate Maeve," as Yeats called her, a 1st-century AD Celtic queen of Connaught who is the heroine of many Irish legends. Archaeologists argue, though, that the cairn is more likely a 3,000-year-old tomb.

Strandhill, at the foot of Knocknarea, is an unremarkable seaside resort, though it does have a good sandy beach and one unusual attraction called Dolly's Cottage, a typical 19th-century rural dwelling that serves now as a folk museum in which members of the Irish Countrywomen's Association sell their homemade wares. Some evenings, folk music sessions are held here. *Admission free. Open July–Aug., daily 3–5.*

A short drive southeast of Knocknarea is **Carrowmore,** a site where several megalithic remains cover a broad area. Unfortunately, many have been badly damaged, but this is Ireland's largest single group of Stone Age monuments. Most are communal tombs dating from 4000 BC. You can reach Carrowmore on the minor road back to Sligo Town. The whole trip around Knocknarea and back into town is about 16 kilometers (10 miles).

Next, head from Sligo Town toward the shores of beautiful, gentle
10 **Lough Gill.** To leave Sligo, get onto Stephen Street and take the N16 out of town (signposted to Manorhamilton and Enniskillen). Turn right almost at once onto the R286. Within minutes you will find some gorgeous views of the lake so adored by the young Yeats. In fact, Lough Gill in Irish means simply "Lake Beauty." The legend is (there would have to be a legend about such a place) that the bell from Sligo's Abbey lies at the bottom of the lake and those who are without sin can hear it pealing. No one has ever reported hearing it.

As the road dips down to the lake, it changes to R288, where you'll
11 soon encounter **Parke's Castle,** on the right. This sturdy fortified house was constructed in the 17th century by an English gentleman settler who needed the strong fortifications to defend himself against a hostile populace. What made relations worse is that he obtained his building materials mainly by dismantling a historic fortress on the site, which had belonged to the clan leaders of the O'Rourkes of Breffni (this district used to be called Breffni). The entrance fee includes a short video show on the castle and local history. There's also a snack bar. *Tel. 071/64149. Admission: £1. Open June–Sept., daily 9:30–6:30; Apr.–May and Oct., daily 10–5.*

About 1.6 kilometers (1 mile) farther, the road twists away from the lake, following the River Bonet toward Dromahair. Just at the edge of the village, you can pause first to ponder the story behind **The Old Hall,** a fine riverside mansion on the river's right bank (signposted; not open to visitors). It was built in 1626 for another unwelcome English landowner, Sir William Villiers, who constructed his house from stones taken from the ruins of an important O'Rourke castle that stood right next door. In that old fort, in the year 1152, Tiernán O'Rourke lived with his pretty wife, Dervorguilla, until one day their castle was attacked by Dermot MacMurrough, king of Leinster, who managed to persuade Dervorguilla to run away with him. O'Rourke was furious and formed an alliance with all the other Irish chieftains to bring MacMurrough to justice.

O'Rourke did get his wife back, but MacMurrough then sought help from the Plantagenet king of England, Henry II, who sent one of his best men, Strongbow, to fight beside MacMurrough against the Irish kings. And so began the Anglo-Norman invasion of Ireland, the start of the long effort by England to conquer the Irish.

On the other side of the River Bonet stand the handsome remains of **Creevelea Abbey,** reached by a few minutes' walk along a footpath. In fact not an abbey but a friary, Creevelea was founded for the Franciscans in 1508 by a later generation of O'Rourkes. It was the last Franciscan community to be founded before the suppression of the monasteries by England's King Henry VIII. Like many such ruined abbeys, the place still has religious meaning for the local people, who treat it with reverence. One curiosity of this abbey is the especially large south transept; notice, too, its endearing little cloisters, with well-executed carvings on the pillars of St. Francis of Assisi. *Signposted at Dromahair. Admission free. Accessible all day.*

Real Yeats fans will want to cast eyes on nearby Innisfree, the "Lake Isle" around which the poet weaved his enticing imagery:

"I will arise and go now, and go to Innisfree . . .
And live alone in the bee-loud glade. . . .
I hear lake water lapping with low sounds by the shore;
While I stand on the roadway, or on the pavements grey,
I hear it in the deep heart's core."

To reach Innisfree, drive through the little village of **Dromahair** to take the R287, the minor road that heads back along the south side of Lough Gill toward Sligo Town. Turn right at a small crossroads, af-
12 ter 2 or 3 miles, where signposts point to **Innisfree** (pronounced *Inish Free*). A little road leads another couple miles down to the lakeside, where you can see the island just offshore. The small tree-covered island is not the haven of peace that it must have been when Yeats wrote those words—excursions arrive by boat from Sligo Town, and visitors traveling by car turn up throughout the day.

A little beyond the Innisfree turnoff lies **Dooney Rock,** across the water on the southwestern end of the Lough Gill; this is where the poet daydreamed, contemplated the lake's islands, and imagined a fiddler on the rock who made "folk dance like a wave of the sea."

Come back along the R287 toward Dromahair, but instead of turning into the village, continue driving (the road number changes to R280)
13 toward **Manorhamilton.** This small rural town was built in the 17th century for the Scottish Planter (colonist settling on Irish lands confiscated from Catholic owners) Sir Frederick Hamilton. Sir Frederick had been given the local manor house by Charles I of England (hence the town's name). The manor itself is now an ivy-covered ruin, and there's not much to see here. The surrounding scenery, however, is superb. Take the N16, signposted to Sligo Town, for about 9½ kilometers (6 miles) until you reach the little turning that
14 heads right to **Glencar Lough.** The turn is signposted "waterfall," and you'll discover several waterfalls here, with a parking lot and footpath leading to one of the highest. The lake is fed by the River Drumcliff and other streams at the foot of the Dartry Mountains: "Where the wandering water gushes/ From the hills above Glen-Car," as Yeats saw it.

Stay on Lough Glencar's right bank, and you'll reach a fork in the road: a left heads back to the N16 and Sligo Town, a right weaves across the country toward the N15 and the villages of Drumcliff and Carney. You want to take the right, but even if you miss it, almost any other right turn off the N16 will lead you in the same direction.

15 Next, stop at **Lissadell House** (signposted from the N15), near Carney, beside the Atlantic waters of Drumcliff Bay. This impressive aristocratic residence has belonged to the distinguished Gore-Booth family since it was built in 1834. The family became good

friends of W. B. Yeats, who recalled seeing the house often as a child from his grandmother's carriage. Later, in 1894, he was invited to visit the house and became acquainted with the two Gore-Booth daughters, Eva and Constance. He recalled their meeting in verse: "The light of evening, Lissadell,/ Great windows open to the south,/ Two girls in silk kimonos." Eva became a poet, while sister Constance went on to lead a dramatic political life as a fiery Irish nationalist, taking a leading role in the 1916 Easter Rising against the British.

Lissadell House is now open to the public, with tours of the house, a crafts shop, and refreshments. A copy of Yeats's poem "In Memory of Eva Gore-Booth and Con Markievicz" is displayed on a sign beside the main gate at the entrance, and aficionados of all things Yeatsian will find the house interesting if only for the associations with the poet. Others may prefer to wander the grounds. The interior is typical of 19th-century aristocratic country homes. The woods of the Lissadell estate have become a forestry and wildlife reserve—a fine place for bird-watchers, it serves as a home to Ireland's largest colony of the barnacle goose, along with several other species of wildfowl. *Tel. 071/63150. Admission: £2 adults, 50p children. Open June–Sept., Mon.–Sat. 10:30–12, 2–4:30.*

Double back from Lissadell, through Carney, in the direction of Drumcliff. Just north of Carney, by the way, the legendary Battle of the Book took place in AD 561, one of the earliest and most acrimonious cases in the whole history of copyright law.

St. Columba, a recluse and missionary who established Christian churches and religious communities in Northwest Ireland, is thought to have been the founder of a monastic settlement around AD 575 at
16 **Drumcliff,** east of Lissadell and Carney on the N15. The monastery flourished for many centuries, but all that is left of it now is the base of a Round Tower and a richly carved High Cross dating from around 1000. These remains stand close together by the road. More notable now is the fact that W. B. Yeats lies buried with his wife, Georgie, in an unpretentious grave in the grounds of Drumcliff's plain and simple Protestant church, opposite the High Cross. Yeats actually died on the French Riviera in 1939; it took almost a full decade for his body to be brought back to Drumcliff in accordance with his wishes. In the poem "Under Ben Bulben," he spelled out not only where he was to be buried but also what should be written on the tombstone: "Cast a cold eye/ On life, on death./ Horseman, pass by!" Today you can stand in the churchyard and read those words cut into the gray headstone. It is easy to see why the curious, flat-topped Ben Bulben (536 meters/1,730 feet) made such an impression on the poet; the mountain gazes calmly down upon the small rural church, and at the same time it faces the mighty Atlantic.

Before returning to Sligo Town, for another sight of the Atlantic breakers you can turn right off the N15 at Rathcormack and take a
17 trip, via Gregg, out to **Rosses Point,** where Yeats and his brother, Jack, often stayed during their summer vacations. This popular seaside and leisure area with good safe sandy beaches and fine views is around 6 kilometers (4 miles) from the N15 and is clearly signposted. Two popular sportsmen's havens, the County Sligo Golf Club and the Sligo Yacht Club, are also here. From Rosses Point, the drive is just 8 kilometers (5 miles) straight back to Sligo Town on the R291.

Tour 2: Around Donegal Bay

The soaring Donegal hills beckon from the horizon as you travel north to Donegal Town from Sligo Town. The rolling coastal fields break open here and there to give startling views across the waters of Donegal Bay. The whole stretch from Sligo Town to Donegal Town has become the Northwest's most popular vacation area, but this is certainly no French Riviera. You'll pass a few small and unremarkable seashore resorts, and, in some places, you may find that haphazard and fairly tasteless construction detracts from the scenery. In between these minor resort developments, the traveler encounters wide-open spaces free of traffic and full of fresh air. The most interesting part of this tour lies on the north side of the bay—all that rocky indented coastline due west of Donegal Town. That's where you'll breathe a sigh of relief and enter the true away-from-it-all world of County Donegal.

Take the N15 from Sligo Town in the direction of Donegal Town. The whole County Sligo coastal region is dotted with numerous prehistoric sites; 16 kilometers (10 miles) after you pass Drumcliff (*see*
18 Tour 1, *above*), you'll reach, at **Creevykeel,** one of Ireland's best megalithic court-cairns. The site (signposted) lies off the road, just beyond the edge of the village of Cliffony. You'll see a burial area and an enclosed open-air "court" where rituals were performed around 2500 BC.

Here you're crossing the county line into Donegal, but the first town
19 reached could hardly be less typical of the area. **Bundoran** is one of Ireland's most popular seaside resorts, yet it remains remarkably unsophisticated, with little to offer except a long seafront development favored by Irish and Northern Irish family vacationers. While its souvenir shops and amusement arcades are not very appealing, it does have certain attractions. You'll find first-class golf facilities available on the edge of town at Aughrus Head, as well as horseback riding, and good fishing is 6½ kilometers (4 miles) away at **Lough Melvin.** North of the town center you'll find another handsome beach at Tullan Strand, washed by the kind of waves that thrill surfers. Between the main beach and Tullan, some weird cliffside rock formations have been sculpted by the Atlantic's power. Something of a local spectacle, these natural creations have been given whimsical names such as the Fairy Bridges, the Wishing Chair, and the Puffing Hole (this last one blows wind and water from the waves pounding below).

Continue on the N15 for another 6½ kilometers (4 miles) to reach
20 **Ballyshannon,** which rises gently from the banks of the River Erne. On the left-hand side of the road as it reaches the town, you'll see the factory of **Donegal Parian China** (tel. 072/51826. Open May–Sept., 9 AM–6 PM daily), which produces exquisite chinaware and porcelain. At the factory's pleasant and spacious new visitor center, you can enjoy a 10-minute video showing how this delicate ware is produced and then join a free 15-minute tour. There's also an attractive showroom and shop and a tearoom serving light meals and snacks. (You may be more familiar with chinaware from the older **Belleek Pottery** [tel. 0365/65501], which straddles the Republic–Northern Ireland border 6½ kilometers/4 miles away. Both companies produce a delicate cream-colored pottery of great value and elegance.)

Lough Erne marks an ancient frontier, and the Ballyshannon River crossing was for centuries the gateway into the Ulster region. Through the medieval period Ballyshannon was the southern stronghold of the O'Donnell clan, whose lands eventually became

County Donegal. Today, Ballyshannon is a peaceful little town with mountain views; the surrounding area offers great opportunities for anglers because the local river and estuary are both teeming with fish. The town was also the birthplace of the prolific Irish poet William Allingham. Each year in early August, the normally quiet village springs to life with a grand festival of folk and traditional music (*see* The Arts and Nightlife, *below*).

Time Out In its triangular central area, Ballyshannon has several bars and places to grab a snack. The biggest and most popular pub is the green-shuttered **Seán Óg's,** which serves light Irish meals all day and features traditional music in the evenings.

Stay on the N15 toward Donegal Town, 21 kilometers (13 miles) away. About a mile before you arrive in town, a sign on the right points to **Donegal Craft Village** (shops are usually open 9 to 5), rather a grand name for a small roadside complex of crafts shops. You can shop for imaginative pottery, handwoven goods, and ceramics and stop off at a coffee shop that sells snacks. Then continue on into
21 **Donegal,** turning past the town's small harbor amid trees on the edge of Donegal Bay. Here you'll find a view across the water, with its tiny islands and wooded banks, that is tranquil and delightful. The road brings you into a triangular main area called the Diamond (a common name for the central square of a former Plantation town). Donegal is a small, carefully designed place with a population of fewer than 2,000. Rebuilt in the 17th century, it still preserves a touch of the dignity of that era. Its history actually goes back a lot farther than that Plantation period, when Protestant colonists were planted on Irish property confiscated from their Catholic owners. Donegal was previously known in Irish as *Dun na nGall,* or "Foreigners' Fort." The foreigners in question were Vikings, who in the 9th century set up camp here to facilitate their pillaging and looting. After they had been driven out, the town was taken over by the powerful O'Donnell clan (originally Cinel Conail), who made it the capital of Tyrconail, their extensive Ulster territories.

Near the north corner of the Diamond, clan leader Hugh O'Donnell built **Donegal Castle** (in fact, a fortified tower house rather than a castle) in the 1470s. More than a century later, this structure was the home of his descendant Hugh Roe O'Donnell, who faced the might of the invading English. He was to be the last clan chief of Tyrconail. As the English made steady gains, in 1602 he went to Spain to rally reinforcements from his allies there and died overseas. The Irish faction at Donegal Castle was defeated by English forces and it came into the possession of Sir Basil Brooke. In 1610, he reconstructed the little castle, making it much more lordly and luxurious, and adding the fine Jacobean fortified mansion with towers and turrets that can still be seen today. Inside, there are large ornate fireplaces carved with Brooke's crest. *Tirchonaill St. Admission free to view exterior.*

In 1474, Hugh O'Donnell founded a monastery by the waterside of Donegal Town for the Franciscans, but it was partially destroyed by gunpowder in 1601 during a war with English invaders. Despite the damage, it was probably in this monastery that the *Annals of the Four Masters* was written from 1632 to 1636. This important tome chronicles the whole Celtic history and mythology of Ireland from earliest times up to the year 1618. The Four Masters were four monks who believed (correctly, as it turned out) that Celtic culture was doomed after the English conquest, and they wanted to preserve as much of it as they could. At the National Library in Dublin, you may see facsimile pages of the monks' work (the original is kept under lock and key). The monastery's gaunt ruins, impressive more for the location than for what survives of the buildings, can still be seen on the bank of Donegal Bay, just a few paces from the town center and sheltered behind a sea wall. What remains is the choir, south transept, and two sides of the cloisters. *Freely accessible.*

A monument to the Four Masters is in the Diamond. Around the three sides of the Diamond, you'll find popular bars, a couple of good old-fashioned hotels, and several shops stocked with high-quality Donegal tweeds and knitwear. Donegal Town has long been one of two principal marketplaces where the county's handicrafts are brought down from the hills to be sold to the rest of the world (the other is the village of Ardara; *see below*). Spinning has almost disappeared now, but handweaving and knitting still contribute to the livelihoods of thousands of country people. In small workshops attached to their rural cottages, they produce top-grade handknits as well as what is regarded as the finest tweed in the world. Donegal Tweed is the name of a universally recognized style of cloth—a sturdy woolen fabric both soft and hard wearing, with distinctive mixed muted colors—that is still at its best when made in these Donegal mountains.

What makes the Donegal area so perfect for tweed making? The natural humidity of the air is important, as is the extremely soft water of the River Eske, which drains off the peat bogs and is used to wash the wool. If you've the time and inclination, and wish to judge the difference in quality, you might find it worthwhile to shop around the region for your handknits and tweed clothes—several village outlets have lower prices than in Donegal Town (*see* Shopping, *below*).

One well-known shop on the Diamond is **Magee's,** a general clothing store founded in 1866. The original Mr. Magee handed down his business in 1887 to his young cousin Mr. Temple, and the company, now providing suitings to top department stores and clothing manufacturers all over the world, is still owned and run by the Temple family. Much of the stock that carries Magee's label is made in the store's own factory beside the River Eske, only a short walk from the shop. Magee's tweed jackets are said to be among the best in the world, yet they are not expensive if you buy them here. A tour of the weaving factory is fascinating, if a little rushed. You'll see how old-fashioned handwork can be combined with the most modern electronic looms, the two complementing each other. Signs around the factory explain to visitors what is going on. *The Diamond, tel. 073/21100. Free factory tour (lasts around 10 min). No definite times: the first tour starts at about 11, the last at about 3.*

Time Out If you feel hungry before or after looking at **Magee's,** you won't need to leave the shop to find a bite to eat. The store has its own restaurant on the premises, serving snacks and simple dishes such as baked potatoes, quiches, and salads, or scones and cakes ideal for an inexpensive afternoon tea.

The main road west is the N56, which runs slightly inland from a magnificent shoreline of rocky inlets with great sea views; it's worthwhile turning off the road from time to time to catch a better sight of the coast. About 6½ kilometers (4 miles) out of Donegal Town, the N56 skirts **Mountcharles,** a bleak hillside village that looks back across the bay. Stay on the N56, which takes you through

Bruckless, where there is a good bed-and-breakfast accommodation, the 18th-century Georgian **Bruckless House** (*see* Dining and Lodging, *below*). Don't be too impressed by the Round Tower in the churchyard here, not an authentic medieval structure but a 19th-century belfry. Soon after Bruckless, the N56 turns inland across the bogs toward Ardara, but this tour stays by the shore.

The road now becomes the R263, which runs through attractive
22 heathland and wooded hills down to **Killybegs.** This thriving little fishing port takes one by surprise, with its big trawlers from Spain and France moored in its welcoming harbor. Although it is by far the most industrialized place along this coast, the village retains a certain charm because of its waterfront setting. Killybegs also used to serve as a center for the manufacture of Donegal hand-tufted carpets. Examples of this much-sought-after product have found their way into such varied places as the White House and the Vatican.

After Killybegs, the R263 narrows, climbs, and twists, giving even better views of Donegal Bay before descending again into pretty **Kilcar,** a traditional center of tweed making. The next village, signposted by its Irish name **An Charraig (Carrick),** clings to the foot of the **Slieve League Mountains,** whose dramatic color-streaked ocean cliffs are, at 2000 feet, the highest in Ireland and among the most spectacular. To see them, take the little road to the Irish-speaking village of Teelin, 1.6 kilometers (1 mile) south from Carrick. Then take the narrow lane (signposted to Bunglass) that climbs steeply to the top of the cliffs. For an even more thrilling perspective, some hardy folk walk on the difficult coastal path from Teelin.

After another 8 kilometers (5 miles), crossing barren moorland, the
23 road reaches **Gleann Cholm Cille (Glencolumbkille).** This tiny, spread-out hamlet clings to the rockbound harbor of Glen Bay, looking straight out to the pounding Atlantic. The name of this dramatic spot means St. Columba's Glen (or, alternatively, Columba's Glen Church), and the legend is that St. Columba, a Christian missionary (*see* Drumcliff in Tour 1, *above*), lived here for a while during the 6th century with a group of followers. Some 40 prehistoric cairns are scattered around the village, and these have become connected locally with the St. Columba myths. The **House of St. Columba,** on the clifftop rising north of the village, is a small oratory said to have been used by the saint himself. Inside, stone constructions are supposed to have been his bed and chair. Every year on June 9, starting at midnight, local people make a 2-mile barefoot procession called *An Turas* (the journey) around 15 medieval crosses and ancient cairns, collectively called the Stations of the Cross.

The **Folk Village** near the beach in Glencolumbkille is an imaginative museum of rural life. The exhibit is arranged as a group of traditional-style cottages—representative of three centuries—which are described on a guided tour. The dwellings are true to the old life, with bare earth floors and very basic living conditions. The complex also offers a crafts shop, where high-quality local handmade products can be bought. There's also a tea shop with snacks. *Tel. 073/30017. Admission: £1.50. Open May–Apr., Oct., Mon.–Sat. 10–6, Sun. 12–6; June–Sept., Mon.–Sat. 10–7, Sun. 12–7.*

From Glencolumbkille, if you drive 25½ kilometers (16 miles) up and over the scenic curves of **Glengesh Pass** with a succession of switch-
24 backs, you'll go down to the sea again at **Ard an Ratha** (**Ardara**—say it with the accent on the *last a*). This unpretentious, old-fashioned hamlet of low, pale cottages among the green and brown hills is for-

tuitously situated at the head of a lovely ocean inlet. For centuries, Ardara has been an important wool-trading center, where great cloth fairs were held on the first of every month. Nowadays, a Weavers' Fair and Vintage Weekend is held in July or August (but not every year), and it has more to do with music, dance, and having fun than with selling homespun. (For details of the Weavers' Fair, call the Secretary of the Ardara Tourism Committee at 075/41106.) Ardara actually enjoys traditional music all year round; it has a large number of charming and popular pubs, though several seem to be doubling as shops.

Though the cloth fairs have died out, cottage workers in the surrounding countryside still provide Ardara (and County Donegal) with very-high-quality handwoven cloths and, especially, handknits. If you fancy a chunky Aran sweater, you'll find few better or less expensive places to look for one than this area. You'll have several stores to choose from (*see* Shopping, *below*). During the summer, Ardara attracts quite a large number of visitors and verges on being overcrowded. Yet the tourists make little real impact: Ardara holds loyally to its own traditions and history.

Time Out The long-established **Nesbitt Arms** (tel. 075/41103) in the village center is a reasonable place for a drink and a snack.

The N56, the Donegal coast's narrow and unfrequented "main road," runs through Ardara. Heading south to return to Donegal Bay and Donegal Town (40 kilometers/25 miles), the road runs first across peat bogs—waterlogged grasslands of tawny, tweedy colors ruled across with black lines where the turf has been cut. North from Ardara, the road takes an erratic course up to **Dungloe** (40 kilometers/25 miles), where you can begin the next tour.

Tour 3: Northern Donegal

Numbers in the margin correspond to points of interest on the Northern Peninsulas map.

Traveling on northern County Donegal's country roads, you'll feel that you have escaped at last from all the world's hurry and hassle. True, the county's largest town, Letterkenny, is up here. And Letterkenny, with a population of 6,500, even has a set of traffic lights—the only traffic lights in the whole of the county. For the rest, you'll discover almost nothing but scenery: broad island-studded loughs of deep dark tranquillity; unkempt, windswept, sheep-grazed grasses on mountain slopes; ribbons of luminous greenery following sparkling streams; and the mellow colors of wide bog lands, all under shifting and changing cloudscapes. This tour, apart from Inishowen Peninsula, which is included as a separate excursion at the end, could take anywhere from one day to a week, depending on precisely how low a gear you slip into after a few breaths of Donegal air. You can cut the tour short if necessary, but try your best to catch the rewarding Fanad and Rosguill peninsulas and the drive around Sheephaven Bay.

25 We'll start from **Letterkenny;** although it may be the least attractive or interesting place on this whole tour, it is pleasingly down-to-earth. The bustling town center is just a single long street lined with an array of small shops and pubs and dominated by an imposing 19th-century church. The main Donegal **Tourist Information Office,** loaded with maps, literature, and advice, can be found 1.6 kilometers (1 mile) south on the Derry road, N13. *Tel. 074/21160. Open*

The Northern Peninsulas

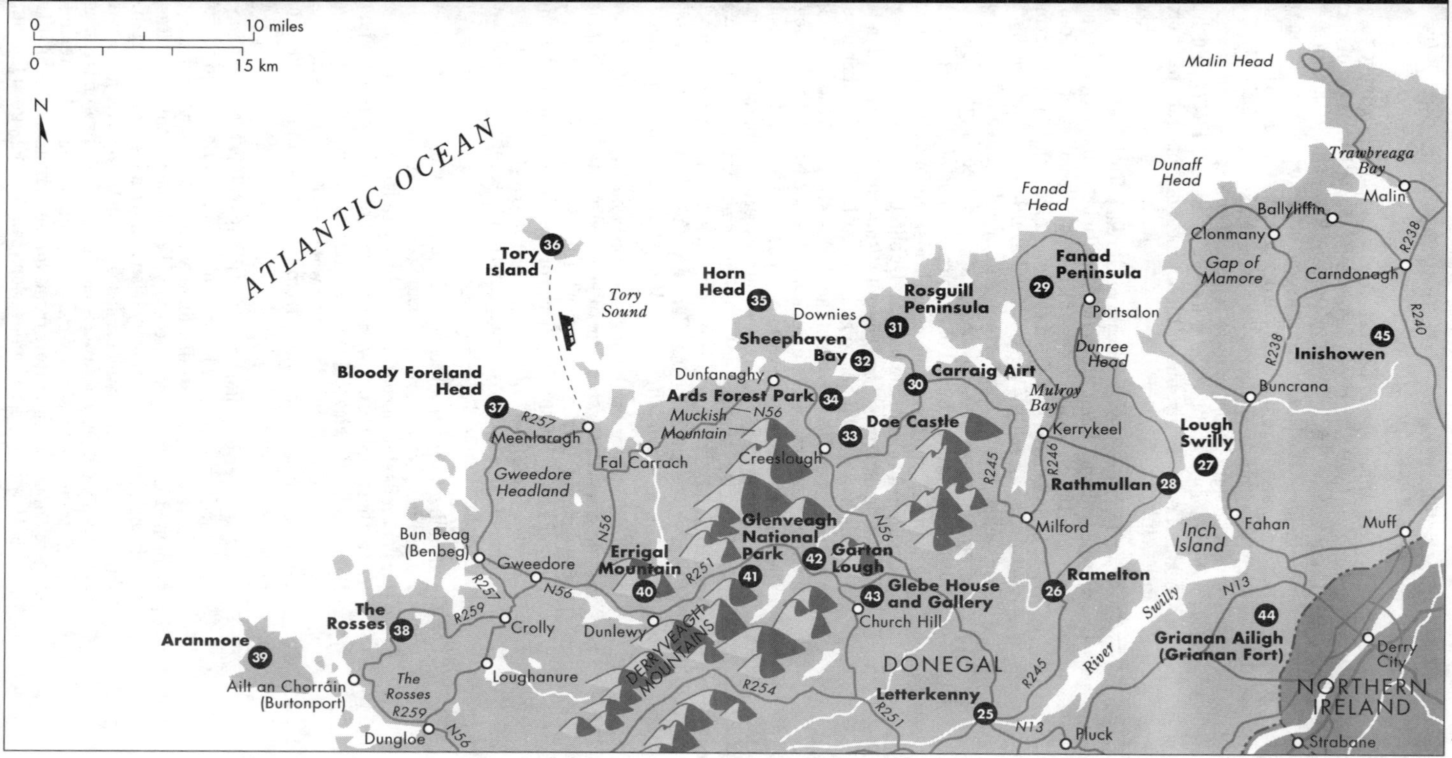

Sept.–May, weekdays 9–5; June, Mon.–Sat. 9–6; July–Aug., Mon.–Sat. 9–8, Sun. 10–2.

The best thing about Letterkenny is its close proximity to great
scenery in every direction. Take the R245 northward out of town for
26 13 kilometers (8 miles) to **Ramelton** (or Rathmelton, though the pro-
nunciation is the same). A handsome little former Plantation town,
it climbs uphill from a river harbor close to Lough Swilly. The village was the birthplace of Francis Makemie (1658–1708), who
preached here before emigrating and founding the American Presbyterian church. Take the waterside road (the R247), which runs
27 beside **Lough Swilly,** one of the loveliest of Donegal's big fjordlike
ocean inlets.

28 After 11 kilometers (7 miles), you'll reach **Rathmullan,** an ancient harbor village among green fields, with little houses looking across curving Lough Swilly to the Inishowen hills on the other side. The view is especially good from the ruins of a 16th-century Carmelite fortified priory at the top of the village. Rathmullan's modest harbor, below, was once important; here, English naval officers, posing as ordinary merchant seamen, captured Red Hugh O'Donnell in 1587. They invited him aboard to taste some of their "cargo of foreign wines," and the sociable clan leader fell for it. Once on board, he was shipped to imprisonment in Dublin Castle. After six years he escaped and returned to Donegal with added determination to defend his homeland—but to no avail. In 1607, Rathmullan's harbor was the scene of the Flight of the Earls—the great exodus of Ulster nobility that brought to an end the 13-year war with the English. The million-acre Ulster territories became part of the English domain, and two years later the Plantation era began, the root cause of the "Troubles" that are still continuing across the border in Northern Ireland. This rich history is explained at Rathmullan's little **Flight of The Earls Heritage Centre** *Rathmullan, tel. 074/58178. Admission: £1. Open May–Sept., Mon.–Sat. 10–6, Sun. 12–6:30.*

The old fort near Rathmullan dock is what remains of a Martello Tower. Six of the towers—fortified defenses built in case Napoleon's army should invade to support the Irish cause—were erected around Lough Swilly. Just north of the village, **Rathmullan House** (tel. 074/58188) is a top country-house hotel. It is one of the best accommodations in the Northwest and has an excellent restaurant (*see* Dining and Lodging, *below*).

29 Extending north from here is the barren and rock-strewn **Fanad Peninsula.** The signposted **Fanad Scenic Drive** takes you 27 kilometers (17 miles) up beside Lough Swilly to low-lying Fanad Head at its northern tip, then down again through the tiny resort village of **Kerrykeel,** with views of long and narrow Mulroy Bay twisting and turning on the other side. If you want to cut the journey short, you can take the back road direct from Rathmullen to Kerrykeel for 9½ kilometers (6 miles).

After another 6½ kilometers (4 miles) you'll reach sprawling Mil-
30 ford; turn right onto the R245 to follow Mulroy Bay round to **Carraig**
Airt (Carrigart). The small village, with a lot of charm and many old-
31 fashioned taverns, gives access via a slender isthmus to **Rosguill**
Peninsula, which is extremely beautiful with its rocky heart and its
fringe of sand dunes and beaches. The signposted **Atlantic Drive** circles the peninsula. This area is not as far off the beaten track as you
might think; you'll see several caravan sites and self-catering cottages, popular with visitors from Northern Ireland. At the little resort of **Downies,** visitors enjoy a long sandy beach, good fishing, and

a chance to buy directly from **McNutts Homespun Tweeds Factory.**
32 Westward are views of the shallow, meandering inlets of **Sheephaven Bay.**

The R245 follows round the sandy shores of the Bay, first running
33 down from Carraig Airt to the imposing waterside **Doe Castle,** a tall weather-beaten tower at the center of a complex structure enclosed within sturdy defenses. The castle occupies the southern end of Sheephaven Bay, at the foot of **Muckish Mountain** just inland. The building is further protected by the sea on three sides and by a rock-hewn moat on the fourth. Described by attacking English forces in 1587 as "the strongest fortress in all the province," the impressive edifice dates from at least 1440, when it became the home of MacSweeney Doe, one of the "gallowglasses" (from the Irish *gall o glach)*—foreign mercenaries employed by the O'Donnell clan. Despite the castle's present poor condition, it was still occupied by his descendants until 1890. MacSweeney Doe's curiously carved tombstone is fixed to the southwest tower of the outer wall. *Near Creeslough. Admission free. Usually open. If locked, inquire at caretaker's cottage on approach path.*

You'll pass through adjacent **Creeslough** (pronounced *creesh-la*),
34 where the road becomes the N56, to reach **Ards Forest Park** after a couple of miles. Clinging to Sheephaven Bay's southwest shore, the 1,188-acre national park is the former wooded estate of a Capuchin friary; the friary itself is still occupied by the Capuchins. Within the grounds are four prehistoric fortified sites and one dolmen. If the weather is fine, the park's forest trails and picnic sites provide a welcome opportunity to enjoy some air and exercise. *Tel. 074/53271. Admission: £1 adults or £3 per family; children under 12 free. Admission free in winter. Open daily 8 AM–9 PM.*

Another 8 kilometers (5 miles) on the N56 brings you into **Dun Fionnachaid (Dunfanaghy),** a tidy former Plantation village on the very edge of Sheephaven Bay. When the tide goes out, the vast sand flats of Killyhoey Beach are uncovered and the sea recedes into the far distance, but as it rises again the sands are submerged in double-quick time. On the west side of the village, the signpost to **McSwyne's Gun** (McSwyne is the old spelling of MacSweeney) leads to a huge natural blowhole that gives out a deafening bang when the tide rushes in during rough weather.

Time Out In Dunfanaghy, the **Carrig Rua** (tel. 074/36133)—the name's Irish for "red rock"—and **Arnold's** (tel. 074/36208) are both traditional village hotels on Main Street, offering decent unpretentious local fare at about £8 for lunch.

---

35 A little back road runs from Dunfanaghy up to **Horn Head,** the most spectacular of County Donegal's Atlantic headlands. From its sheer 186-meter (600-foot) cliffs, you have access to great views along the coast to the other headlands ranged one behind the other. And bird-watchers will love it here—the cliffs are home to hundreds of seabirds, including puffin and guillemot.

From this point westward, the terrain is rougher, wilder, and rockier; you're also likely to hear the Irish language being spoken. The N56 reaches round 11 kilometers (7 miles) to **Fal Carrach (Falcarragh),** the site of an Irish-language college.

Another 13 kilometers (8 miles) around the rugged seashore, in good weather, you can catch a ferry from **Meenlaragh** (near Gortahork) to
36 **Tory Island.** Though just 14½ kilometers (9 miles) offshore, Tory is

strangely inaccessible; the weather is rarely fair, and the currents are often difficult. Although the island is desolate, rocky, and barren—without a single tree—it has been inhabited since prehistoric times. The local people speak their own Irish dialect and refer to the mainland as "Ireland," considering themselves almost as a separate miniature nation. You'll find medieval and prehistoric relics scattered all over the ocean-battered landscape, notably the **Round Tower** of pink granite, partly ruined but still with its conical cap poised on the cliffs. At the island's eastern end, **Balor's Fort** is a prehistoric fortress, supposed to have been the residence of Balor, the terrifying one-eyed Celtic god of night and darkness. At the center of the island, the **wishing stones** have the power, it is said, to destroy enemies. Still talked about today is the time, in 1884, when the stones were turned against the British gunboat *Wasp* that came filled with police to collect taxes—which Tory Islanders are unaccustomed to paying. The ship sank, and all but six of the crew were lost. Most of the islanders don't earn enough to pay tax in any case and live simple lives as fishermen. Quite a few, however, have unexpected sidelines as artists, ever since 1968, when the well-known Irish painter Derek Hill chanced to meet islander James Dixon; Dixon felt that he could do a better job of painting than Hill. Many other Tory Island residents thought they could, too, and today the Tory Island artists, depicting their own life and landscape in a naive style, are widely acclaimed and have exhibited abroad.

Because no accommodation is available on Tory Island, be sure to ask before making the crossing to ensure that a return will be possible the same day. Returning to Meenlaragh on the mainland, you're on the edge of the **Gweedore** headland, which you can follow round on the R257, the coast road. Gweedore is rocky, sparsely covered with heather and gorse, and low-lying until you reach its farthest point,
37 **Bloody Foreland Head.** This dramatic name for once does not recall the slaughter of some historic battle but describes instead the vivid red hues of the gaunt rock face when lighted up at sunset.

Follow the shore road south another 13 kilometers (8 miles) to **Bun Beag (Benbeg)** and **Croithli (Crolly),** at the meeting between Gwee-
38 dore and the next distinctive headland, **The Rosses.** On both Gweedore and The Rosses, the bleak but dramatic terrain has not benefited from a liberal sprinkling of modern bungalows.

The Rosses, though similar to Gweedore, is more beautiful. The coast road, the R259, struggles over the unbelievably stony and inhospitable landscape, crisscrossed with water channels and strewn with myriad ponds. Yet quite a number of people manage to survive here, many of them Irish speakers. The decline of population and living standards was reversed by Patrick Gallagher (1873–1964), who became known as Paddy the Cope. Son of a poor local family, he left school at 10, went to Scotland as a farmhand, and saved enough money to return home in the 1950s and buy a small holding of his own. Gallagher, affectionately remembered throughout the area, persuaded the citizens around The Rosses to set up cooperatives to bring in new farming methods and machinery, as well as cooperatively owned stores to keep prices down.

Staying on the R259, after 16 kilometers (10 miles) you will reach **Ailt an Chorráin (Burtonport),** which claims to land more salmon and lobster than any other fishing port in Ireland. This village is the de-
39 parture point for a trip over to **Aranmore,** 6½ kilometers (4 miles) offshore. Aranmore means "big island," and it is indeed the largest and most populous of County Donegal's rocky offshore fragments. The ride out takes 25 minutes and costs £2 (seven crossings daily),

but although fairly accessible, the island still feels remote and ungoverned. It has been inhabited for thousands of years—witness the prehistoric fort on its south side—and offers good fishing, as well as striking cliff scenery and views back onto The Rosses.

If you drive 6½ kilometers (4 miles) farther round the coast, the R259 rejoins N56 at **An Clochan Liath (Dungloe),** a pleasant little fishing town regarded as the capital of The Rosses, though you'll find little to do or see here.

Next, start the journey back to Letterkenny. The N56 takes you direct to Croithli (Crolly) in 13 kilometers (8 miles), a quicker journey than going back along the coast road. Stay on the N56 north until you're a couple of miles beyond **Gaoth Dobhair (Gweedore)** village, on the little River Clady, and take the R251 to skirt the south side of
40 **Errigal Mountain** to the village of **Dunlewy,** altogether only about 13 kilometers (8 miles) from Crolly. This whole drive features great scenery, some of the best in County Donegal. Serene Errigal looks especially grand from Dunlewy. The **Lakeside Centre,** or Ionad Cois Locha, on the edge of Dunlewy Lough, is an interesting spot to pause for a look at a reconstructed 19th-century weaver's home where old-style weaving is demonstrated. There's also a café and crafts shop. *Tel. 075/31699. Admission free. Open Apr. and May, Sat. 11–6, Sun. 12–7, June–Sept., Mon.–Sat. 11:30–6, Sun. 12:30–7.*

Follow the R251 round as the road is edged northward by the **Derryveagh Mountains.** After 16 kilometers (10 miles), the road
41 brings you to the main gate of **Glenveagh National Park.** You must leave your vehicle at the entrance; a shuttle bus will take you farther into the park, or you may walk. Also at the gate, you'll see a visitor center with a permanent exhibition on the local way of life and on the influence of climate on the park's flora and fauna. The 24,000-acre protected wilderness has a thick carpet of russet-colored heath and dense woodland that rolls down the Derryveagh slopes into the broad open valley of the River Veagh (or Owenbeagh). At the center of the park is the dark and clear **Lough Beagh,** and on a ledge overlooking the long narrow lake stands the elaborately battlemented **Glenveagh Castle,** a most improbable edifice that looks exactly like what it is: a 19th-century folly. For all that, it's actually a grand, luxurious house inside, and its exotic, extensive gardens are also a sheer delight. Beyond the castle, footpaths lead into more remote sections of the park, where you may suddenly chance upon a herd of shy red deer or catch sight of a soaring falcon.

These Glenveagh lands were always known as a remote and beautiful region. They were brought together under single ownership by a ruthless gentleman farmer, John George Adair, who gradually acquired the estate, including its hundreds of poor tenants, between 1857 and 1859. In 1861, he evicted all the tenants without compensation and destroyed their cottages. Adair had the lakeside castle built in 1870, but immediately he went to live in Texas. Adair died in 1885 without returning to Ireland, but his wife, Cornelia, perhaps intrigued by the thought of her husband's castle, crossed the Atlantic to make Glenveagh her home. She lived extravagantly and spent a fortune to make the four different gardens and the walks as lovely as they are today; it was she who planted the luxuriant rhododendrons here. In 1984, the last owner of Glenveagh, U.S. millionaire Henry P. McIlhenny, generously presented the estate to the nation, after years of carefully maintaining and restoring the area. *Glenveagh National Park, Church Hill, Letterkenny, tel. 074/37088 or 074/37090. Admission: £1.50 adults, 60p children, £1 senior citizens.*

Several footpaths are available, including Derrylahan Nature Trail, a 1.6-km (1-mi) signposted trail. Guided walks can be arranged. Open Apr. 18–Oct. 26, daily 10:30–6:30 (until 7:30 in June–Aug.); closed Fri. in Apr. and Oct. Guided tours of the castle: £1.50 adults, 60p children, £1 senior citizens.

Time Out A cafeteria conveniently located in the park's visitor center serves such café food as fish and chips or tea and scones. A full meal will cost you about £5.

42 It is 13 kilometers (8 miles) from Glenveagh on the R251 to **Gartan Lough** (close to Church Hill village), although the lake is technically within the national park and is administered partly by the park authorities.

The lake and its surrounding mountain country are marvelously beautiful. St. Columba was supposedly born here in AD 521, and the legendary event is marked by a huge cross (at the beginning of a footpath into the national park). Nearby, you'll find other dubious "relics" of the saint that are popularly believed to possess magical powers, such as the Natal Stone, where he is thought to have first opened his eyes, and the Stone of Loneliness, where he is said to have slept.

43 More satisfying is a visit to **Glebe House and Gallery,** which consists of a fine Regency manor and 25 acres of gardens that sit on the northwest shore of the lake, just off the R251. The former home of the distinguished artist Derek Hill, it now serves as a remarkable gallery displaying Hill's extensive art collection, which includes works by Renoir and other great Impressionists and Picasso; paintings by Yeats's brother, Jack; and intriguing examples of the work of the Tory Islanders (*see above*). The decoration and furnishings of the house, including original William Morris wallpaper, are worth a look as well. In 1981, Derek Hill handed over this treasure trove of art to the nation. *Church Hill, tel. 074/37071. Admission: £1.50. Open Easter and May–Oct., Tues.–Sat. 11–6:30, Sun. 1–6:30.*

If you want to learn more about St. Columba and his times, return to the R251 and turn right almost at once onto the R254 in Church Hill. Straightaway you'll arrive at the **Colmcille Heritage Centre.** This exhibition and interpretation center features medieval manuscripts, stained glass, and displays tracing the decline of the Celtic religion and the rise of Irish Christianity. *Gartan, Church Hill, tel. 074/21160. Admission: £1.50. Open May, Sept.–Oct., Mon.–Sat. 11–6:30, Sun. 1–6:30; June–Aug., Mon–Sat. 10–6:30, Sun. noon–6:30.*

If you stay on the R251, you'll be back in Letterkenny after 16 kilometers (10 miles). One more major peninsula in the region is worth exploring—the huge Inishowen, the most northerly part of Ireland. This grandly wild piece of land remains unspoiled despite a string of small and untempting coast resorts. For the 160-kilometer (100-mile) Inishowen circuit, plus the 64-kilometer (40-mile) round-trip to reach it from Letterkenny, you would need to allow at least a whole day. If time is short, however, you can easily see the best of Inishowen in a much shorter time.

44 If nothing else, visit the Celtic fort **Grianan Ailigh (Grianan Fort).** Take the main Derry road, the N13, from Letterkenny. After 29 kilometers (18 miles), keep a lookout for signs to Buncrana, because the easy-to-miss sign for the fort is opposite. Instead of turning to Buncrana, take the narrow lane that climbs and turns for more than a mile to reach the fortress, on top of a 251-meter (810-foot) hill. The most striking thing here is the site itself, with an immense pano-

rama of the rolling Donegal and Derry landscape below. To the north, you're given an exquisite aerial view of the Swilly estuary, flowing around Inch Island into Lough Swilly. On either side rise the hills, often partly veiled by mists, of the Fanad and Inishowen peninsulas.

As for the fort, what you'll see is a circular stone enclosure—the diameter is about 23½ meters (76 feet)—that you can enter through a gate (open most of the year). Inside, you'll find further concentric defenses, with passages within the walls and earth ramparts that surround a sturdy central structure. No one knows when Grianan Fort was built, but it was probably an Iron Age fortress: Its position was accurately recorded in the 2nd century AD by the geographer Ptolemy of Alexandria. Later it became the seat of Ulster's O'Neill chieftains and remained so for many centuries, despite serious attempts by their enemies to destroy it, especially in the year 674 and again in 1101. The present-day fortress, however, owes a good deal to overzealous "restoration" in the 1870s; before that, it was in ruins. *Freely accessible.*

Go back to the N13 and cross straight over to take the Buncrana turning. When you meet the R238, another main road coming from Derry City—the town is only 8 kilometers (5 miles) away—turn
45 left. You're now on **Inishowen,** a green pastoral peninsula with a solid mountainous interior, enclosed by Lough Swilly on one side, Lough Foyle on another, and the battering Atlantic to the north. Following the R238, you come to **Fahan** (pronounced like "fawn"), with its monastic ruins. There's a good restaurant here, too, St. John's (evenings only). Just after the village, and opposite the North West Golf Club, signs on the right show the entrance to the IDA industrial estate. Turn in here, and you'll find the National Knitting Centre (residential courses in traditional Irish hand-knitting, tel. 077/62355 for details); the center has its own shop selling fine knitted goods. **Buncrana,** a popular downscale beach resort much favored by people from Derry City, has a 14th-century O'Docherty tower that gradually became part of an 18th-century mansion. Shortly after you pass Buncrana, turn left at the fork in the road away from the R238 to stay by the coast, driving past the 19th-century fort on **Dunree Head,** up and over the spectacular viewpoint of the **Gap of Mamore,** and down toward **Dunaff Head,** where Lough Swilly opens into the ocean. Rejoin the R238 at **Clonmany** and take it through **Ballyliffin,** another small resort town with an O'Docherty tower on the beach.

Time Out Ballyliffin is a convenient place for a snack or meal. Try **The Strand Hotel** (tel. 077/76107), a likable family-run establishment where you can get well-prepared home-cooked pub lunches.

By the junction of the R238 and the R240, you'll see a church with a curious remnant of early Christianity against one wall, the decorated 7th-century **Donagh Cross,** accompanied by a couple of pillar stones. The strange carvings on the stones clearly date from a pre-Christian period. Turn the corner into **Carndonagh,** a village featuring several more medieval monastic remains. The road then runs up beside **Trawbreaga Bay,** through picturesque **Malin** village on the waterside up to **Malin Head,** Ireland's most northerly point. Although it does have good views, Malin Head is not as dramatic a spot as some of the other headlands.

Take the signposted route across the peninsula from Malin Head to **Moville,** a sleepy waterside resort on the Lough Foyle side. The drive takes 8 kilometers (5 miles) from here to the peninsula's rocky eastern tip, **Inishowen Head.** On the way, at **Greencastle,** you'll see the fortifications of foreigners who tried to control the nine counties of Ulster: a 14th-century Anglo-Norman fortress and an English fort built five centuries later to defend against French support for the Irish. The drive along the lough shore toward Derry City is attractive but punctuated by small, uninteresting villages whose modernized pubs cater to day (or evening) visitors from Derry. If you want to turn away from Derry toward Letterkenny before reaching the border, take the R239 from **Muff** to **Bridge End,** where, incidentally, you can find one of the most attractive of Ireland's many new Catholic churches.

Off the Beaten Track

Ballymote Start out by traveling about 11 kilometers (7 miles) from Sligo Town south on the N4. Turn right onto the N17 and right again onto an unfrequented minor road, the R293, between meadows and woods for a farther 13 kilometers (8 miles) toward **Ballymote,** a most appealing village. Once a place of importance, the formerly imposing castle is now just a ruined shell, and the village is bustling, rustic, and has an extraordinary number of drinking holes—almost every business doubles as a bar! A powerful Anglo-Norman Ulster earl, Richard de Burgo, built the fortress in the 14th century, and for centuries afterward it stood firm against any English conquest of the Northwest. The castle's six towers still stand. Close by is another ruin, that of the Franciscan friary where the *Book of Ballymote* was written in 1391. This tome, now at the Royal Irish Academy in Dublin, holds tremendous significance to historians, because it enabled them to unravel the secrets of the old Ogham alphabet. This system of writing, with just 20 letters, was inscribed on Celtic standing stones, especially those dating from about the 4th and 5th centuries.

The Leitrim Lakes The hilly landscape of unspoiled County Leitrim is dappled with clean, cool lakes. Anglers love this area because its peaceful waters are filled with fish. Despite a liberal sprinkling of villages, in reality the county is almost uninhabited. Even its largest town, bright and bustling **Carrick-on-Shannon,** has a population of fewer than 2,000 people. The town has plenty of lively bars, and you can hire a boat here to tour the Shannon. From Sligo Town, take the N4 south to Carrick, which is a good base for a quick look around the vicinity. Take the R280 north from the town to **Drumshanbo** at the tip of huge **Lough Allen.** From here, the R208 turns back to **Drumcong** village and the small lakes **Scur** and **St. John.** Where the R208 meets the R202, turn right for Fenagh, and then right again onto the R209 to return along the south side of the lakes into Carrick. If you were to continue beyond Fenagh, you would reach **Mohill,** birthplace of Turlough O'Carolan, the 18th-century blind harpist regarded as the last of the Celtic bards. His most famous composition was adapted for "The Star-Spangled Banner." South of Carrick, labyrinthine back lanes meander across the broad **Shannon** and the lakes—**Boderg, Bofin,** and **Kilglass**—that straddle the river.

Lough Derg This site is really out of the way, yet tens of thousands determinedly beat a path to this lonely lake, ringed by heather-clad slopes, throughout the period from Whitsunday to the Feast of the Assumption (that is, from June to mid-August). In the center of the lough, Station Island, known as St. Patrick's Purgatory, is one of Ireland's most popular pilgrimage sites, even though it is also the most rigorous and austere of such sites in the country. Pilgrims stay on the island for three days, taking no sleep and no food except black tea and dry toast. They walk barefoot around the island, on its flinty stones, to pray at a succession of shrines. The pilgrimage has been followed since time immemorial; during the Middle Ages, it attracted large numbers of devotees from foreign lands.

You can reach the shores of Lough Derg by turning off the main Sligo–Donegal road (N15) in the village of Laghy onto the minor Pettigo road (R232), which hauls itself over the Black Gap and descends sharply into the border village of Pettigo, about 21 kilometers (13 miles) from the N15. From here, take the Lough Derg access road for 8 kilometers (5 miles). *If you would like to know more about St. Patrick's Purgatory in order to become a pilgrim, write: Reverend Prior, Lough Derg, Pettigo, Co. Donegal. Nonpilgrims may not visit the island June–mid-Aug.*

Shopping

The outstanding specialties of the Northwest are high-quality handwoven tweeds and handknits. Smart traditional tweed sports jackets, comfortable yet long-lasting, are one of the best buys. The region is also a good place to purchase Aran sweaters; they are knitted with distinctive crisscross patterns and are made of plain undyed wool. The sweaters are soft but durable. Not so long ago, these warm weatherproof pullovers were worn by every County Donegal fisherman, usually made to a design belonging exclusively to his own family. Patterns are not so restricted now, allowing greater variety in the knitwear, but all the sweaters have that unmistakable Aran look. High-quality machine-made tweeds are also available. All these wool-based items have been made here for centuries, and you'll find that prices are astonishingly low. You'll also want to look out for locally made parian china, a thin, fine, and pale product of very high quality and workmanship. Elaborate flower motifs and a basket-weave design are two distinctive features of this china, which has been a specialty of Belleek, on the Donegal–Fermanagh border, for more than 100 years. In recent years, it has also developed in and around Ballyshannon.

Ardara

This attractive village features several stores that sell handweaving and locally made knitwear. Nowadays the stores usually commission goods directly from cottage out-workers and provide them with the wool and patterns. Prices are about as low as you'll find anywhere. You can get an especially good deal on handsome, chunky Aran handknit sweaters (£45–£80). You'll find cardigans (similar prices) and scarves (£12) in the same style. You can pick up a pure wool handwoven tweed tie for about £6. A wide choice of ready-to-wear tweeds is carried in all the stores; good-quality tweed sports jackets for women (up to about £100) as well as men (about £95) are a bargain. The shops here also stock a selection of traditional Irish products from other parts of the country (glassware and linen, for example). The main stores, all recommended, are **Kennedy's** (tel. 075/41106), at the top end of the main street; **John Molloy** (tel. 075/41133), on the Killybegs road; and **C. Bonner & Son** (tel. 075/41196), on Front Street.

Ballyshannon and Belleek

Donegal Irish Parian China (tel. 072/51826), just south of Ballyshannon on the N15, is the Republic's largest manufacturer of parian china. A visitor center provides information on the manufacturing process. Visitors are welcome to take free tours of the workshops (May–Sept., daily 9:30–4:30) and can take advantage of lower factory prices. Traditional methods of manufacture are used, and most of the work is done by hand. The least expensive items (spoons or thimbles) cost around £4. A full tea set starts from about £205.

From Ballyshannon, the R230 runs along the south bank of the River Erne toward Belleek. Right beside the Garda (Irish police) checkpoint, 1.6 kilometers (1 mile) before the border to Northern Ireland, you'll find **Celtic Weave China** (tel. 072/51844), a small family business that produces high-quality parian china. The company specializes in the basket-weave design and in elaborate floral decoration, creating many one-of-a-kind pieces on commission for prestigious organizations around the world. A single piece of china will be made to your own specifications if you wish. Extremely delicate-looking handpainted china "flower baskets" are also available (though in fact this type of chinaware is not as fragile as it appears). Most pieces cost under £100.

Continue on the same road into Belleek in Northern Ireland, where **Belleek Pottery** (tel. 01365/65501) stands beside the Erne River. This is the best-known producer of Belleek chinaware. The visitor center here acts as a showroom for the company's wide range of elegant products. Although this is not within the limits of our Northwest region, you'll find Belleek china in the shops of Donegal and Sligo (*see* Chapter 11, Northern Ireland).

Donegal Town

Donegal Town has long been the principal marketplace for the region's wool products. There are several smaller shops retailing local handweaving and knits, but the town's principal store is **Magee's** (tel. 073/21100), which occupies a prime position on the Diamond, the town's central area. Look especially for items with Magee's own label; the store has its own factory in town making garments and fabrics for major clothing companies and big-name department stores. Tweed jackets cost around £135–£150 for men and £145 for women; men's suits are priced at £230, and ladies' suits at £200; skirts cost about £50. Aran sweaters are also available from around £80. You can even buy Magee's best-quality tweed by the roll at £20 per yard. For a smart handcrafted hat of tweed and Irish linen, stroll five minutes up Tirconaill Street, past the castle and the post office, to **Hanna's Hats** (tel. 073/21084). About 1.6 kilometers (1 mile) south of town, right beside the main N15, the **Donegal Craft Village** is a complex of new workshops where you can buy pottery, handweaving, and ceramics from local young craftspeople and watch the items being made.

Kilcar

For a fine selection of handwoven goods and other local crafts, stop off at **Studio** (tel. 073/38194). The store also features a tea shop on the premises.

Sligo Town

For a large selection of handknit and hand-loomed sweaters and all other woolen goods, try **P.F. Dooney & Son** (36 O'Connell St., tel. 071/2274). **Cosgrove's of Sligo** (32 Market St., tel. 071/42809), which retains its original 19th-century shop front, stocks fine foods to satisfy hungry tourists; it also has a crafts section with a selection of pottery, watercolors, and other works by local artists.

Sports and the Outdoors

Participant Sports

Bicycling The Northwest is mostly challenging but rewarding cycling country, with some steep climbs, occasionally strong winds, and sometimes quite a lot of rain, but with plenty of low-cost accommodations, marvelous scenery, and empty roads. These conditions are perfect for keen cyclists, but others may prefer to use a bike simply for some gentle meandering around a small area. Bicycle rentals are available in **Ardara** from **Donal Byrne** (West End, tel. 075/41156), in **Carrick-on-Shannon** from **Geraghty's** (Main St., tel. 094/31019), in **Donegal Town** from **C.J. Doherty** (Main St., tel. 073/21119), in **Ramelton** from **Hugh Whoriskey** (tel. 074/51022), and in **Sligo Town** from **Gary's Cycles** (Quay St., tel. 071/45418). Many of these rental shops have mountain bikes for cycling in rough hill country.

Bird-watching Bird-watchers have access to a large variety and population of bird life on County Donegal's northern headlands. Most of the bird species are not resident; huge numbers of winter and summer migrants land here. Bird sanctuaries are located on **Inch Island** in Lough Swilly (with a considerable number of whooper swan in the fall), on the **Lough Foyle** shore of Inishowen (with widgeon, waterfowl, and waders in the fall), at **Horn Head** (with Ireland's largest colony of razorbill, as well as puffin and guillemot), and at **Sheskinmore Lough** (with geese, ducks, and waders) near Ardara. The sand and mud flats of **Sligo Bay** attract geese, and in the grounds of **Lissadell House** at Rosses Point, you'll find flocks of barnacle geese. For more information, contact the **Irish Wildbird Conservancy** (Southview, Church Rd., Greystones, Co. Wicklow, tel. 01/875759).

Fishing The angling in Ireland's Northwest is of the highest class, attracting enthusiasts and connoisseurs from many countries. Yet there's so much space and so much water that it can feel as if you have the whole place all to yourself. There are a dozen sea-fishing festivals during the season, open to visiting anglers. Several hotels offer inclusive deals with bed, board, and lake, river, or sea angling (*see* Bay View Hotel, Killybegs, in Dining and Lodging, *below*).

No license is needed for sea fishing or for coarse and pike angling. For game fishing (salmon and sea trout), the license costs £3 for one day, £10 for 21 days, or £25 for a full season. The full-season license is valid throughout the whole country; there's also a local annual license, valid only in the Northwest, for £12. Senior citizens are exempt from these costs. The licenses can be obtained for County Donegal from the **Northern Regional Fishery Board** (Ballyshannon, tel. 072/51435) and for Counties Sligo and Leitrim from the **North-Western Regional Fisheries Board** (Ballina, Co. Mayo, tel. 096/22623). Some tackle shops are also permitted to sell licenses.

Anglers will find that the best area for brown trout is around Bundoran, including Lough Melvin. In western County Donegal, you'll have good opportunities for catching sea trout. Plenty of salmon and brown trout live in the rivers of southern County Donegal and northern County Sligo. More brown trout can be found in the loughs near Dunfanaghy in northern County Donegal, near Bundoran on the border of Donegal and Sligo counties, and in the border area of Sligo and Leitrim counties. Pike anglers and coarse anglers can cast their lines in the abundant County Leitrim lakes. If you want full information on fishing in these waters, suitable accommodations, details of boat hire, etc., ask the Irish Tourist Board (*see* Before You Go in Chapter 1, Essential Information) for the annual *Anglers' Guide*.

Tackle Shops **County Donegal: John McGill** (Main St., Ardara); **O'Doherty's** (Main St., Donegal Town); and **Pat Barrett** (Bundoran).

County Leitrim: The Creel or **Geraghty's** (both on Main St., Carrick-on-Shannon) and **Aodh Flynn** (Manorhamilton).

County Sligo: Barton Smith (Hyde Bridge, Sligo Town).

Golf The Northwest has a large number of nine- and 18-hole courses, most in seaside locations, and several of them are world-class. For a full list, you'll need to contact the Irish Tourist Board or local Tourist Information Offices. The Northwest's best 18-hole courses, which all welcome visitors, include **Bundoran Golf Club** (tel. 072/41360), on the cliffs above Bundoran beach; **Donegal Golf Club** (tel. 073/21262) at Murvagh; **County Sligo Golf Club** (tel. 071/77134) at Rosses Point, which has hosted just about every Irish championship; **The North West Golf Club** (tel. 074/61027), near Buncrana on Inishowen Peninsula; **Rosapenna Golf Club** (tel. 074/55301), 24 kilometers (15 miles) northwest of Letterkenny; and **Enniscrone Golf Club** (tel. 096/36297), in the midst of lovely scenery close to the Enniscrone resort on the County Sligo coast about 14½ kilometers (9 miles) north of Ballina. Expect to pay greens fees of around £10–£15 a day.

Hiking Trails in the Northwest provide the experienced walker with challenging opportunities. It helps to be able to read a map, and on high ground you're wise not to take any chances with the weather, which can suddenly become wet and misty. The mountain districts (such as the Blue Stacks, near Donegal Town) offer rough walks with dramatic views. There are long-distance footpaths across County Donegal, in County Leitrim, and around Lough Gill in County Sligo. For information about these walking routes, contact **Field Officer, Long Distance Walking Routes Committee** (Cospoir, 11th Floor, Hawkins House, Dublin 9). Good shorter trails are also accessible, clearly marked within Glenveagh National Park in northwest County Donegal.

Horseback Riding/Pony Trekking For hacking, trekking, and other horseback sport by the hour, the day, or longer periods, contact **Carrigart Riding Stables** (tel. 074/55114), at the foot of the Rosguill Peninsula; **Lenamore Stables** (tel. 077/84022), at Muff on Inishowen Peninsula; **Rockhill Trekking Centre** (tel. 074/50012), at Kerrykeel on the Fanad Peninsula; **Stracomer Riding School** (tel. 072/41787), at Bundoran on the south County Donegal coast; and the **Moneygold Riding Centre** (tel. 071/63337), at Moneygold Grange in County Sligo. Several other establishments offer full riding vacations including lodging; the details are shown in a leaflet from the Irish Tourist Board. For more information, contact **The Association of Irish Riding Establishments** (Mespil Hall, Kill, Co. Kildare, tel. 045/77208 or 045/77299).

Surfing There's great surfing along the Atlantic shores of County Donegal. Head to Strandhill, Rossnowlagh, and Bundoran on the south County Donegal coast (if you need to rent equipment), or to Marble Strand and Rosapenna in north County Donegal (if you have all your own gear). These areas offer excellent conditions for world-class surfing. Ask the **Irish Surfing Association** (Tigh-na-Mara, Rossnowlagh, Co. Donegal, tel. 073/21053) for more specific information.

Dining and Lodging

Dining

By Andrew Sanger and Georgina Campbell

The Northwest is not usually considered a great gastronomic center. You can expect meals to be generally plain and simple, but the servings are generous, with a filling portion of potatoes. Still, the ingredients used in dishes are of good quality and are locally produced. Fish, fresh from the sparkling clean rivers and loughs, could hardly be better. The region has only a few restaurants of distinction. In the rural districts, your best bet is to choose a hotel or guest house that can provide a decent evening meal as well as breakfast.

Category	Cost*
$$$$	over £30
$$$	£20–£30
$$	£10–£20
$	under £10

**per person for a typical three-course meal, including tax and service but excluding drinks*

Lodging

Although the Northwest is a far-flung corner of Ireland, the choice of good bed-and-breakfasts and small hotels in the region is excellent because of the constant influx of visitors, particularly in July and August. The traditional provincial hotels in Sligo Town, Donegal Town, and the small coastal resorts in between have been modernized and equipped with all the necessary comforts, yet they retain the charm that comes with older buildings and personalized service. However, away from these areas, your options are more restricted, and your best overnight choice, with some exceptions, is usually a modest guest house offering bed, breakfast, and an evening meal.

Many of the modern Irish guest houses recommended below are similar to one another in what they have to offer: They are often one-story buildings with undistinguished contemporary furniture and not much character. Many provide peat fires and merely adequate meals. For the most part, however, visitors will find hosts friendly, helpful, and concerned about keeping their properties clean and well-maintained.

A particular pleasure may be gained by staying in an Irish-speaking home. With a little bit of luck, the local Irish Tourist Information Offices can be helpful in making a booking with an Irish-speaking family. In Counties Donegal, Leitrim, and Sligo, you can also stay at some first-class country-house hotels where you are welcomed with gracious professionalism.

Category	Cost*
$$$$	over £95
$$$	£75–£95
$$	£45–£75
$	under £45

**All prices are for a standard double room, including breakfast and tax.*

Highly recommended restaurants and hotels are indicated by a star ★.

Ardara

Dining and Lodging

Bay View House. On the outskirts of the village, this modern, well-kept bungalow offers bed and breakfast, as well as a peaceful location with superb sea views. You can relax in front of a peat fire and picture windows in the guest lounge, and enjoy tasty traditional Irish home cooking in the dining room. *Mrs. Bennett, Bay View House, Portnoo Rd., Ardara, Co. Donegal, tel. 075/41145. 6 rooms with shower. Facilities: tea-making equipment in rooms, games room, dining room. V. Closed Nov. 15–Mar. 1. $*

Greenhaven House. Another good B&B, only a few minutes from the village, this modern family-run one-story home has its own gardens and marvelous views of the nearby mountains and bay. You'll be warmed by a peat fire in the lounge and wake up to a hearty breakfast. The owners can advise you on shopping for handknits and other items. *Mrs. Eileen Molloy, Greenhaven House, Portnoo Rd., Ardara, Co. Donegal, tel. 075/41129. 6 rooms with shower. No evening meal. No credit cards. Closed Nov.–Feb. $*

★ **Woodhill Guest House.** This spacious home of the Yeats family (no relation to the famous poet) stands on 4 acres of wooded grounds only ½ kilometer (¼ mile) from the village. The residence once belonged to the Nesbitts, former landlords of Ardara. The cream-colored exterior is Victorian, but parts of the interior date from the 17th century. The fine front public areas feature high ceilings and marble fireplaces; the hall has a lovely round table and stained-glass window. Bedrooms are less grand but large, with superb mountain views. You'll find this an amiable, relaxed place, with frequent Irish folk music sessions presented in the bar. The best feature here is the high-quality home-cooked food. The moderately priced restaurant, which seats 40, attracts visitors and locals alike with its Cordon bleu à la carte meals, in a French-Irish style. Relying upon fresh local ingredients, typical dishes include salmon with garlic and spinach sauce, accompanied by seasonal vegetables; or rack of lamb with herbs picked from the family garden. The elaborate desserts are all homemade. The Yeatses' own hens make the breakfast eggs as fresh as can be. *Mr. and Mrs. Yeats, Woodhill Guest House, Donegal Rd., Ardara, Co. Donegal, tel. 075/41112. 6 rooms with bath. Facilities: restaurant, bar, fishing, clay-pigeon shoots. AE, MC, V. $*

Ballymote

Dining and Lodging ★

Temple House. Well off the beaten track, and undoubtedly one of the most unusual B&Bs anywhere, this vast country mansion with a pillared entrance is outwardly gray and austere; the approximately 100 rooms are decorated and furnished in the Georgian and Victorian styles, with highly polished mahogany tables and sideboards, and the original rugs. This is not a country-house hotel but a working organic farm, surrounded by more than 1,000 acres of land. It's been in owners Sandy and Deb Perceval's family since 1665. Within the grounds, you'll find the ruins of the original fortified manor house, built to incorporate a historic Knights Templar castle; guests can also visit formal terraced gardens and a private lake with waterside footpaths. The huge bedrooms feature authentic Victorian curtains, marble-top washstands, polished floorboards, dressing tables, and huge shuttered windows. Deb Perceval prepares a good evening meal, using farm-fresh produce accompanied by top-class wines. The traditional Irish breakfasts are generous. The Percevals make no pretense of offering modern facilities—there are no televisions, for example—but they have done everything necessary to ensure that guests are comfortable. The five bedrooms include one with a little extra room attached, perfect for a child, and all rooms now have private bathrooms (although in one of the rooms, it's across the corridor). This is a remarkable place, full of character. *Mrs. D. Perceval, Temple House, Ballymote, Co. Sligo, tel. 071/83329. 5 rooms with bath or shower. Facilities: boating, shooting, fishing; golfing and horseback riding about 24 km (15 mi) away. MC, V. Closed Dec.–Mar. $$*

Bruckless

Dining and Lodging

Bruckless House. A two-story 18th-century farmhouse on the north side of Donegal Bay, within an easy drive of Glencolumbkille, Ardara, and Donegal Town, this unusual B&B stands on 19 acres of woods, gardens, and a meadow where Irish draft horses and Connemara ponies roam. Public rooms have a fine view of Bruckless Bay; their Asian decor reflects years spent in Hong Kong by the owners, the Evans family. The more conventional but comfortable bedrooms share a large bathroom upstairs. Wholesome dinners are prepared with fresh produce from the Evanses' garden, milk and cream from the resident cow, and seafood straight from the bay. *Mrs. C.J. Evans, Bruckless House, Bruckless, Co. Donegal, tel. 073/37071. 4 rooms, 1 with bath. DC, MC, V. Dinner must be booked by noon. Closed Oct.–Mar. $$*

Castlebaldwin

Dining and Lodging ★

Cromleach Lodge. Christie and Moira Tighe run this highly regarded small country hotel, situated on a hillside overlooking Lough Arrow, 5 kilometers (3 miles) off the N4 between Sligo Town and Carrick-on-Shannon at Castlebaldwin. The building is modern, but with a pleasant country-style interior. One of the two lounges is for nonsmokers. The spacious bedrooms, each with a king-size and single beds and a good-size bathroom, look out over the pretty Lough Arrow and are attractively decorated in relaxing pastel shades. If you stay here, take advantage of booking the cheaper half-board rate (which includes dinner at the hotel's excellent restaurant). There are three small dining rooms (two no-smoking), all with panoramic views, making each table equally desirable. An extensive six-course table d'hôte menu is priced according to the choice of the main course, and makes use of fresh ingredients in attractively presented dishes with light sauces. A typical meal could begin with grilled goat cheese, served with salad, followed by a soup such as fresh lobster bisque. Fresh fillet of turbot with chablis and chive sauce and salmon with saffron and lemon sauce are some of the seafood choices. Loin of lamb with rosemary juice and fresh breast of duck with juniper sauce are other favorites. A good choice of desserts includes a selection of fresh fruits individually marinated in different flavored syrups (such as apricots in Grand Marnier or kiwis in lemon and Pernod), a terrine of two chocolates layered with pistachio nuts, a selection of homemade ices, Irish farmhouse cheeses, and homemade petits fours. *Lough Arrow, Castlebaldwin, Co. Sligo, tel. 071/65155. 10 rooms with bath. Reservations advised. Dinner Mon.–Sat.; Sun. dinner fortnightly. Closed Dec. 23–31. AE, DC, MC, V. $$$*

Collooney

Dining and Lodging ★

Markree Castle. Fans of Knockmuldowney House (formerly at Strandhill, west of Sligo Town) will be pleased to learn that this huge, five-story gray stone castle, at the end of a long potholed dirt lane, is the family home of Charles Cooper, Knockmuldowney's onetime proprietor. Mr. Cooper and his wife, Mary, are again welcoming bed-and-breakfast guests, and they're also keeping the name Knockmuldowney Restaurant for evening meals. The 17th-century castle, on a 1,000-acre estate, features fine Edwardian and Victorian mahogany furniture throughout, an oak-paneled hall, and ornate Louis XIV plasterwork in the first-floor dining room. The comfortable bedrooms are furnished in the same rich, heavy period style, but the bathrooms have been modernized; rooms provide garden or river views. The dining room has been restored with 19th-century green and beige decor and plenty of gilding. Mrs. Cooper prepares the delectable French meals with Anglo-Irish touches. Two table d'hôte menus are offered; one is a reasonably priced set five-course menu, and the other has about five choices for each course. Recommended dishes include stuffed mushrooms Mornay and Egyptian lemon chicken, which is marinated in garlic, lemon juice, and oil and then baked in butter. Bailey's Blackberry Mist—a mousse made with blackberry puree and Bailey's Irish Cream liqueur—is a favorite dessert, served with homemade biscuits. On Sunday, a traditional lunch is available with a choice of two roasts or fish. Guests will also enjoy afternoon tea with biscuits, banana bread, and fruitcake. *Markree Castle, Collooney, Co. Sligo, tel. 071/67800 (11 km/7 mi south of Sligo Town on the N4). 11 rooms with bath. Facilities: restaurant. AE, DC, MC, V. $$$*

Donegal Town

Dining and Lodging

Harvey's Point. This Swiss-owned restaurant and comfortable 20-room hotel is at the foot of the Blue Stack Mountains. Guest rooms are in a building separate from the restaurant. Here you'll find good-size, well-equipped bedrooms with a light, simple, tasteful style: walls are warm pale colors, floors are polished wood. All rooms overlook Lough Eske. One end of the split-level wood-paneled dining room also overlooks the lake. The restaurant features warm peach decor, Tiffany lamps, and locally made granite-top tables. The French cuisine leans toward a nouvelle presentation, with several lobster entrées on the menu; it might be served whole with a choice of two sauces, alongside rice and mussels, or garnished with tomatoes and red cabbage. Fisherman's Platter, a selection of five kinds of fish, is also served with two sauces, and sirloin steak is served with a demiglaze sauce, topped with garlic butter. A special dessert is homemade ice cream with profiteroles and chocolate sauce. *Lough Eske, Donegal, Co. Donegal, tel. 073/22208. 20 rooms with bath. Facilities: restaurant (reservations required; jacket and tie advised), bar, gardens, conference facilities, tennis courts, bicycle rentals, boat rentals. MC, V. $$–$$$*

Hyland Central. Opening onto Donegal's central square, this family-run hotel offers a warm and friendly traditional atmosphere and a good location. Public areas retain a touch of Old World style, but the comfortable bedrooms (some of them quite spacious) lack character, with their rather ordinary modern furniture. Many rooms have a view of lovely Donegal Bay. The large dining room with its efficient staff serves good, filling food. The hotel is a favorite with business travelers, vacationers, and locals who come for a drink or a meal. *The Diamond, Donegal, Co. Donegal, tel. 073/21027. 74 rooms with bath or shower. Facilities: dining room, gardens, indoor pool, solarium, games room. AE, MC, V. $$*

★ **St. Ernan's House.** For a restful stay, it's hard to imagine anything better than this cream-colored, two-story, 19th-century hotel, built by a nephew of the duke of Wellington, on a wooded Donegal Bay island; the house is reached by a causeway only a short distance south of town. Its attractive bedrooms are furnished with antiques and have superb views of the bay. The grand dining room features silk drapes and wallpaper in a green-and-gold Regency stripe pattern. Tables are laid traditionally with white linen, and the entrées make use of fresh local produce, especially fish, prepared in the Irish country-house style. The five-course dinner changes nightly, but a typical menu might include white crabmeat in lime mayonnaise as an appetizer, followed by grilled salmon hollandaise, steamed cod with asparagus tips and Chablis sauce, or baked lamb with rosemary and apricot sauce. Desserts tend to be well-established favorites such as pears Bordeaux (poached in red wine) or crème caramel. *Brian and Carmel O'Dowd, St. Ernan's House, St. Ernan's Island, Donegal, Co. Donegal, tel. 073/21065. 12 rooms with bath. Facilities: dining room (dinner open to nonguests). MC, V. No children under 6. Closed Nov.–Easter. $$*

Dunfanaghy

Dining and Lodging

Arnold's Hotel. A favorite with Irish vacationers, this friendly hotel run by the Arnold family provides unassuming, relaxed accommodations and generous traditional Irish meals. The best rooms overlook the landscaped garden. The Arnolds offer to lead special-interest classes for guests, such as painting and bird-watching. *Main St., Dunfanaghy, Co. Donegal, tel. 074/36208. 34 rooms with bath and shower. Facilities: bar, baby-sitting, games room, tennis court. AE, DC, MC, V. Closed Nov.–Mar. $*

Carrig Rua Hotel. On the shore of Sheephaven Bay, this unpretentious, popular two-story white hotel is an ideal base for exploring northern Donegal and Glenveagh National Park. Friendly and modestly priced, the bed-and-breakfast establishment caters to the tastes of Irish family vacationers, especially those from across the border. Children are also made very welcome. The inviting rooms have new furniture and carpeting, and some offer bay views. Meals served here are plain and abundant in the traditional Irish style. *Main St., Dunfanaghy, Co. Donegal, tel. 074/36133. 22 rooms with bath or shower. Facilities: bar, baby-sitting. AE, V. $*

Fahan

Dining

Restaurant St. John's. This restored Georgian house sits on the lakeside. You'll find the atmosphere cozy and old-fashioned, with open fires, pictures of old Derry, and red decor in the dining room, although white Donegal linen is used for tablecloths and napkins. Owner-chef Reg Ryan specializes in uncomplicated home cooking, but he is fastidious about his ingredients and uses only local produce in the peak of its season and homegrown organic vegetables. Homemade bread is baked daily to serve with fresh garden soups and pâtés. The two six-course table d'hôte menus (one moderate, the other expensive) are both good values. Look for irresistible seafood appetizers, such as hot crab in garlic butter and cream, or monkfish, deep-fried in a very light batter and served with homemade mayonnaise. Fillets of brill with herbs and fennel sauce, or Donegal rack of lamb, served with apple and mint jelly, are typical main courses. Desserts include homemade ice creams and carrageen soufflé. *Fahan, Co. Donegal, tel. 077/60289. Reservations advised. Dress: casual. Dinner only. Closed Mon., Christmas Day, Good Friday, and 2 wks in Feb. DC, MC, V. $$–$$$*

Killybegs

Dining and Lodging

Bay View Hotel. The waterfront premises of the Bay View overlook the harbor of one of Ireland's busiest fishing ports. Its interior, including the bedrooms, is modern and functional, pleasantly decorated in relaxing pale colors. There's a comfortable, efficient dining room serving typical Irish table d'hôte and good à la carte meals. The hotel has extensive leisure facilities, and is well placed for touring the glorious north shore of Donegal Bay. Special rates include greens fees for golfers or sea trips for anglers. *Bay View Hotel, Main St., Killybegs, Co. Donegal, tel. 073/31950. 38 rooms with bath. Facilities: restaurant, bar, brasserie, indoor swimming pool, sauna, gym, conference facilities. AE, V. $$*

Letterkenny

Dining

Carolina House Restaurant. On the Ramelton Road 2½ kilometers (1½ miles) out of town, you'll find Charles and Mary Prendergast's pleasant restaurant, where the excellent and imaginative food is all freshly prepared to order. The emphasis is on traditional home-cooked dishes using fresh local meat and fish. Start, for example, with courgette (zucchini) mousse complemented with tomato and basil salad, followed by the seafood chowder. Main courses include spiced beef with a sauce of mango, melon, and papaya. Finish with homemade ice cream. Even the petit fours are homemade. *Loughnagin, Letterkenny, Co. Donegal, tel. 074/22480. Reservations advised. Dress: casual. MC, V. Dinner only. Closed Sun. and Mon. $$–$$$*

Dining and Lodging

Mount Errigal Hotel. One of County Donegal's smartest and most modern hotels, although not at all posh, this property appeals to both business and family-vacation visitors. Service here is friendly and professional. Private events and conferences are often staged here, and the bar remains a favorite for locals seeking a relaxed night out. The clean and comfortable bedrooms are efficiently arranged, with characterless, pale-colored furnishings. The Glengesh, the hotel's softly lit restaurant, serves popular Irish cooking; it features Edwardian-style brass and glass decor. *Ballyraine, Letterkenny, Co. Donegal, tel. 074/22700. 82 rooms* *with bath or shower. Facilities: restaurant, 2 lounge bars, disco, games room, facilities for guests with disabilities, video, sauna, baby-sitting. AE, DC, MC, V. $$*

Rathmullan

Dining

Water's Edge Restaurant. Dawn and Kevin Cairns run this restaurant set in a converted row of old cottages on the western shore of Lough Swilly. The cozy, romantic dining spot is two-tiered, with wooden beams, oak tables, deep burgundy-red decor, and linen tablecloths and napkins. The mixed international menu is influenced by the owners' travels but based squarely on fresh local ingredients and seasonal availability; fish is the main strength in summer, while steaks, chicken, duckling, and scallops appear more often in winter. If you like seafood, don't miss the Water's Edge Special, a mixture of fresh fish and shellfish—such as clams, lobster, salmon, and mussels—cooked in white wine and garlic and topped with Roquefort cheese. A popular dessert is Queen Sofia's Delight, a rich meringue-based sweet made with seasonal fruit and fresh cream. *The Ballyboe, Rathmullen, Co. Donegal, tel. 074/58182 or 58138. Reservations advised. Dress: casual but neat. Dinner year-round; light lunches in summer (June–Sept.) only. Closed Christmas Eve. DC, MC, V. $$–$$$*

Dining and Lodging

★ **Rathmullan House.** One of Ireland's most enticing and popular country-house hotels, this rambling, cream-colored, two-story mansion, dating from the 18th century, features large bay windows, fine antiques and oil paintings, and prize-winning gardens; its lawns stretch down to a deserted sandy beach. The public areas, including a drawing room, an impressive library, and a coffee room, are the height of elegance, and yet maintain an informal and friendly air. Bedrooms vary from old-fashioned basic to grand, but all of them feature antiques and light-colored wallpaper and curtains. Ask for a room facing Lough Swilly. The light-filled pavilion dining room, with a tented ceiling, has pink and green decor, silk drapes, and views of the gardens and the lake from the windows. Two table d'hôte menus—roasts and seafood with fresh produce—are available in the Irish country-house style. A typical menu might include poached salmon with black butter or roast lamb with herb stuffing and red currant jelly, followed by a sweet dessert or Irish farmhouse cheese. Breakfast, consisting of fresh fruit compotes, carrageen pudding, and other hot or cold dishes, is a specialty here. The hotel is well situated for visiting the Donegal coast, Glenveagh National Park, and the Glebe House and Gallery. *Rathmullen, Co. Donegal, tel. 074/58188. 23 rooms, 21 with bath or shower. Facilities: dining room, bar, gardens, heated indoor pool, sauna, steam room, tennis court, croquet. AE, DC, MC, V. Closed Nov.–Easter. $$$*

Fort Royal Hotel. On 18 acres of grounds beside Lough Swilly, this spacious, comfortable hotel, once an aristocratic private home, is a decent, less-expensive alternative to the Rathmullan House (*see above*). It attracts a regular clientele, who enjoy its relaxed professionalism and marvelous location. Rooms are clean and meals are satisfactory. *Rathmullen, Co. Donegal, tel. 074/58100. 15 rooms with bath or shower. Facilities: bar, gardens, golf course, tennis court, squash. AE, DC, MC, V. Closed Nov.–Mar. $$–$$$*

Riverstown

Dining and Lodging ★

Coopershill. A three-story Georgian farmhouse set on 500 acres of private woods and farmland, this fine stone abode has been home to seven generations of the O'Hara family since it was constructed in 1774. It provides an ideal place for a quiet vacation. Large public rooms are furnished with appealing period antiques and overstuffed furniture, and deer heads hang in the vast hallways. The spacious, beautifully furnished bedrooms reflect the same antique style (with no televisions), and most have four-poster or canopy beds. In the tranquil dining room overlooking the woods, Irish-style meals and a wide choice of wines are served by candlelight from a grand sideboard with family silver. The menu, which changes nightly, includes roast beef or lamb, fresh vegetables, and special soups. Guests can walk on the grounds amid undisturbed wildlife. *Coopershill, Riverstown, Co. Sligo, tel. 071/65108. 6 rooms with bath. Facilities: dining room, garden, private fishing, boating. AE, MC, V. Closed Nov.–mid-Mar. $$$*

Rossnowlagh

Dining and Lodging

Sand House Hotel. This large modern hotel, right on Donegal Bay (about 8 kilometers/5 miles northwest of Ballyshannon), makes a peaceful, well-positioned base for sightseeing the bay coastline. It has a mock manor-house exterior and access to a 3-kilometer (2-mile) stretch of sand. The renovated, well-kept bedrooms are beautifully decorated with antiques. Choose between a sea view at the front, or back rooms overlooking a golf course. You'll find the staff solicitous and cheerful. The efficient restaurant caters to the plain hearty appetites of Irish vacationers looking for something special. Fresh seafood, including Donegal Bay oysters and mussels, is the daily specialty, but meat dishes are also given careful attention. *Rossnowlagh, Co. Donegal, tel. 072/51777. 39 rooms with bath or shower. Facilities: restaurant, bar, baby-sitting, children's playroom, games room, golf course, surfing club, tennis court. AE, DC, MC, V. Closed Nov.–Easter. $$$*

Sligo Town and Environs

Dining and Lodging

Ballincar House Hotel. In its peaceful 6-acre wooded grounds between Sligo Town and Rosses Point, this out-of-town, leisure-oriented vacation hotel, formerly a private home, is convenient for exploring Yeats Country or the Donegal Bay coast. Its modern bedrooms with private baths and televisions may lack the charm of some other houses in the area, but the restaurant is highly recommended; it specializes in seafood, such as lobster Mornay and salmon. Because of the hotel's popularity, you're advised to reserve rooms well in advance. *Rosses Point Rd., Sligo, Co. Sligo, tel. 071/45361. 25 rooms with bath or shower. Facilities: restaurant, bar, gardens, tennis court, sauna, solarium, squash. AE, DC, MC, V. $$$*

Lodging

Silver Swan Hotel. Standing in the center of town on the Hyde Bridge, this popular hotel and restaurant has an impressive view of the Garavogue River rushing beneath the bridge. Within a rather bland '60s-style exterior, the comfortable mid-range hotel has been recently redecorated and the bedrooms refurnished with pleasing dark-wood modern fittings. There's traditional Irish music at the hotel every Wednesday night, and jazz every Sunday morning. *Hyde Bridge, Sligo, Co. Sligo, tel. 071/43231. 29 rooms with bath or shower. Facilities: restaurant, bar. AE, MC, V. $$*

Sligo Park Hotel. A mile out of town on the N4 (the main Dublin road), this modern, well-run property has undergone further upgrading and expansion, with the addition of a heated pool, a well-equipped gym, and a billiards room. Its predictable, reliable comforts appeal to business travelers, but it also makes a reasonable base for visitors to Yeats Country. Bedrooms, too, have been refurbished, and a new bar added, making this probably the best hotel in Sligo Town. The hotel offers dancing and piano entertainment on some evenings. *Pearse Rd., Sligo, Co. Sligo, tel. 071/60291. 89 rooms with bath or shower. Facilities: restaurant, bar, gardens, secretarial services, laundry services, gym, billiards room, heated swimming pool, tennis courts, room service. AE, DC, MC, V. $$*

The Arts and Nightlife

The Arts

The rustic and underpopulated Northwest features few serious arts activities and events. If you're in the right place at the right time, however, you can attend or participate in several entertaining festivals. Ask at the Tourist Information Offices for up-to-date advance booking information, or check announcements in the local press, including *The Donegal Democrat, The Leitrim Observer*, and *Sligo Champion*.

Theater In early June, during the **Ballyshannon Drama Festival,** the town hosts different drama companies for a program of mainly Irish plays. Sligo Town's **Hawk's Well Theatre** often features interesting programs. It brings in amateur and professional companies from all over Ireland (and occasionally from Britain) to stage a wide variety of shows. Most of the summer season is devoted to the works of popular Irish playwrights. *Temple St., Sligo, tel. 071/61526. Amateur shows: about £5; professional shows: about £6. Call for times. Box office open weekdays 10–6, Sat. 2–6.*

Music At the beginning of August, on the bank holiday weekend, the normally quiet town of Ballyshannon hosts one of Ireland's largest and best folk-music events, the **Ballyshannon Music Festival.** Visitors can hear both well-known and unknown folk and traditional musicians as they entertain in a riverside location. Impromptu performances occur at pubs. A party atmosphere prevails, attracting up to 12,000 visitors annually.

Hawk's Well Theatre in Sligo Town (*see above*) puts on concerts from time to time, including classical performances.

Nightlife

An evening out in the rural Northwest is generally an evening at a lively, popular pub with live music. Always ask locally or at your hotel if there is a nearby pub with "sessions," which are small-scale, informal performances of traditional folk music. For other entertainment, though, especially if you want something a little more sophisticated, you may have to look long and hard. Some hotels or large pubs, particularly at resort towns in season, put on a disco or dance on certain days of the week, or have performances by local groups with an emphasis on country-and-western music. These events generally don't deserve a special journey but can be entertaining if they are nearby.

For a small, old-fashioned village, Ardara in County Donegal offers a surprising number of pubs, many of them offering evenings of traditional music. **Peter Oliver's** bar provides music almost every night. **Nancy's,** which is perhaps one of the smallest pubs in the whole of the Republic, finds space for a folk group several nights a week.

In Donegal Town, **The Abbey Hotel** (tel. 073/21014), on the Diamond, features dancing on the weekend and Irish folk music during the week. Letterkenny, also in County Donegal, offers folk music, jazz, or dancing on weekends at the **Mount Errigal Hotel** (tel. 074/22700). Sligo Town's **Southern Hotel** (tel. 071/62101) and **Sligo Park** (tel. 071/60291) have bands, country-and-western shows, and discos during the whole week.

11 Northern Ireland

Belfast, the Antrim Coast, Derry City, the Mountains of Mourne

By Andrew Sanger

If Celtic legends are true, the giant Finn MacCool threw down the Giant's Causeway off the coast of Northern Ireland and marched across it in a few strides to reach the shores of Scotland, later returning to his homeland with equal ease. The story isn't entirely implausible. The channel between Scotland and Ireland, though turbulent, has never been much of a barrier to people moving in either direction, and the ancient Irish province of Ulster had close ties with its neighbor on the other side of the water.

Thanks largely to that strong Scottish influence, Ulster and its people have always been somehow separate from the rest of Ireland. Nearly 2,000 years ago the people of Ulster built the Black Pig Dyke—a great ditch and earth barrier—to mark the border between themselves and the other Irish regions to the south. To the southerners and to would-be conquerors, Ulster was known as a tough, indomitable land, home of a warlike people. The "Red Hand" at the center of its flag tells a typically ferocious tale: Two great Celtic warriors raced from Scotland to Ireland's northern coast to settle a dispute between them for possession of Ulster. The first to touch the foreign land could call it his own. In the last moments, one of the rivals cut off his own hand and threw it onto the shore and so, by blood and sacrifice, won Ulster.

Present-day Northern Ireland, a province under the rule of the United Kingdom, includes six of Ulster's nine counties (the others—Donegal, Cavan, and Monaghan—lie in the Irish Republic) and retains its sense of isolation. The hard-headed and industrious Scottish Presbyterians imported to make Ulster a bulwark against Ireland's Catholicism have had a profound and ineradicable effect on the place. Not least of the Scottish legacies are the North's distinctive accents. Northern Ireland has more factories, neater-looking farms, better roads, and more two-story redbrick houses (which are typical in Britain) than does the Republic. Of course, you'll also see, in Protestant districts, some of the odder manifestations of the pro-British Loyalists' zeal: curbstones and lamp posts painted in the British colors of red, white, and blue; entwined British and Ulster flags fluttering from tall poles raised in pocket-handkerchief front yards; and countless signs and crests declaring proud devotion to Ulster and the Queen.

For all that, the national frontier, which separates British Northern Ireland from the Irish Republic, is of little consequence to visitors, or even to residents, who may cross it freely at any time. The only inconvenience is that of waiting in line to be eyed warily by British soldiers, who are on the lookout for militant Republicans. No one should be deterred from traveling here on that account. The "Troubles"—almost always confined to a few city streets whose names come up again and again on news broadcasts—are not as bad in reality as they look on the screen. The truth is that Northern Ireland has a considerable number of attractions worth visiting and some of the very best of Irish scenery on its County Antrim coast and in the tranquil green lake country of County Fermanagh. It also maintains close links with the United States and Canada, to which many of its people have emigrated in the last century.

From the Norman period onward, the English made greater and greater inroads into Ireland, endeavoring to subdue what they believed (probably quite correctly) was a potential enemy and a collaborator with that great adversary of England's naval might, Catholic Spain. Ulster proved the hardest part to conquer, but in 1607 Ulster's Irish nobility were beaten and left their homeland in a great exodus known as the Flight of the Earls. Most went to Spain, abandoning their lands forever to confiscation by the English crown. The English distributed the territories among individuals called Planters—the name given to staunch Protestants from England and, even more often, from Scotland who came to Ireland to farm, work, and colonize. New Protestant towns were built, and Catholics became subjected to harshly repressive laws. Inevitably, tension between the two religious groups increased, often flaring into violence toward the end of the 19th century.

In the parliamentary elections of 1918, almost the whole of Ireland voted for Sinn Féin, the party that believed in independence for all of Ireland; in the six counties, however, the majority of votes went to the Nationalists (who were demanding Home Rule—local autonomy within the United Kingdom), and, especially in Counties Down and Antrim, to the Unionists (who wanted nothing less than to remain an integral part of the United Kingdom). In 1921, by a majority, leading Irish politicians in Dublin agreed to allow the North to remain in British hands, in exchange for complete independence for Ireland's remaining 26 counties. The North established its own parliament, housed in the imposing Stormont building just east of Belfast.

Although the "sectarian" conflict has clearly more to do with politics than religion, visitors may be surprised by the high degree of religious observance in the North. Protestants divide about equally into Anglicans and a variety of more or less austere nonconformists, especially Presbyterians. From the 1880s to the 1920s, the Nationalist movement included many Protestants. However, the passage of time caused positions to become more entrenched rather than less. The Unionists today are closely identified with the "planted" Protestant population, while the Nationalists or Republicans are inextricably associated with the native Irish community, which is almost entirely Catholic.

In the 1960s, after 40 years of living beneath the permanent Protestant majority, the Catholics launched a civil rights movement to demand equal rights in jobs, housing, and opportunities. The severity with which this was put down led to the return of direct rule from London and, at the same time, to a rebirth of the Irish Republican Army (IRA), which had lain dormant for decades. The war between the IRA and the British establishment has continued ever since. At the same time, Protestant paramilitary organizations wage their own war against the IRA. In an effort to undermine the extremism of both sides, in 1985 the London and Dublin governments signed the Anglo-Irish Agreement, which gives the Irish government a consultative voice in Northern Ireland's affairs.

The good news is that this tactic seems to be working, and in the last five years the political climate in Northern Ireland has become more relaxed. In 1990, a Fair Employment Commission was set up to integrate workplaces, and in the same year new legislation brought integration to schools, both of which institutions had traditionally segregated Protestants and Catholics. More and more people on both sides of the sectarian divide show a sincere willingness to make compromises and want only to live in peace with their neighbors. At the extremes, however, the violence between die-hard Nationalists and fanatically pro-British Loyalists still continues.

For this reason, visitors to Northern Ireland still have to exercise a little care. Certain areas have seen frequent frightening incidents, particularly the poor working-class districts—both Protestant and Catholic—in west Belfast, and similar neighborhoods in Derry. Yet apart from these easily identified danger spots, Northern Ireland (including these two cities) is as tranquil, inviting, and friendly as the rest of the country.

Essential Information

Important Addresses and Numbers

Tourist Information The main information center for the whole of Northern Ireland is the **Tourist Information Office** (TIO) in Belfast, which provides maps, advice, and information on every attraction in Belfast and the province, including upcoming events and festivals. *59 North St., tel. 01232/246609. Open weekdays 9–5:15; Easter–Sept., also open Sat. 9–2.*

Year-round local offices are located at **Armagh** (40 English St., tel. 01861/527808), **Carnlough** (Post Office, Harbour Rd., tel. 01574/85210), **Carrickfergus** (Town Hall, tel. 019603/51604), **Derry City** (Foyle St., tel. 01504/267284), **Downpatrick** (Down Leisure Centre, Market St., tel. 01396/613426), **Enniskillen** (Lakeland Visitor Centre, Shore Rd., tel. 01365/323110), **Giant's Causeway** (Visitor Centre, tel. 012657/31855), **Larne** (Larne Harbour, tel. 01574/70517), **Newcastle** (Central Promenade, tel. 013967/22222), **Newry** (Arts Centre, Bank Parade, tel. 01693/66232), and in more than a dozen other Northern Ireland towns. During June through August, many more towns and villages open Tourist Information Offices.

Emergencies For **police, ambulance, fire,** or **coast guard,** dial 999 in all of Northern Ireland. The **main police station** (tel. 01232/650222) in downtown Belfast is located at 6–10 North Queen Street.

Hospitals In Belfast, the main hospitals with emergency rooms are **Belfast City Hospital** (Lisburn Rd., tel. 01232/329241) and **Royal Victoria Hospital** (Grosvenor Rd., tel. 01232/240503). In Derry City, **Altnagelvin Hospital** (Belfast Rd., tel. 01504/45171) has an emergency room.

Weather Call Weathercall at 01891/500427 for a Northern Ireland weather forecast.

Arriving and Departing by Plane

Airports and Airlines **Aldergrove Airport,** or **Belfast International** (tel. 018494/22888), is Northern Ireland's principal air arrival point, situated 30½ kilometers (19 miles) from Belfast. **Belfast City (Harbour) Airport** (tel. 01232/457745) is the second airport, 6½ kilometers (4 miles) from Belfast. It receives flights from U.K. provincial airports and from Luton (near London). **Eglinton Airport** (tel. 01504/810784) is 8 kilometers (5 miles) from Derry City.

Flights from Britain **British Airways** (tel. 01232/240522) and **British Midland Airways** (tel. 01232/225151) operate most flights into Belfast. Other main airlines include **Loganair** (tel. 0141/889–3181) and **Air UK** (tel. 01345/666777).

Frequent services to Belfast are scheduled throughout the day from London Heathrow, London Gatwick, and 17 other U.K. airports. Flights take about 1¼ hours from London. British Airways' and British Midland Airways' shuttle services between London and Belfast are walk-on, no-reservation flights, and the airlines claim that no passenger will be turned away—another plane will be added if a scheduled flight is overbooked. Direct flights from Paris on Air

France and from Amsterdam on Schiphol also arrive in Belfast. Scheduled flights to Belfast from the United States and Canada are routed via London, but sometimes charter services fly direct to Belfast from New York and Toronto. Eglinton, Derry City's airport, receives flights from Manchester, England, and Glasgow, Scotland, via Loganair.

Between the Airports and the Cities **Belfast: Ulsterbus** (tel. 01232/320011) operates a shuttle bus every half-hour (cost: U.K.£3.50 one-way, U.K.£6 round-trip) between Aldergrove Airport and Belfast city center. From Belfast City Airport, you can travel into Belfast by train from Sydenham Halt to Central Station (East Bridge St.) or catch a taxi from the airport to your hotel.

Derry City: If you arrive at Eglinton Airport (8 kilometers/5 miles from Derry City), you will need to call a taxi (tel. 01504/811231 or 01504/263905) to get to your destination.

Arriving and Departing by Car, Ferry, Train, and Bus

By Car While many roads from the Irish Republic into Northern Ireland have been closed, drivers can choose from a score of legitimate crossing points; "unapproved" routes across the border also exist but are not recommended. Visitors should expect an army checkpoint at all approved frontier posts, but few formalities are practiced. The fast N1/A1 road connects Belfast to Dublin (160 kilometers/100 miles); sometimes you'll encounter delays at the border on this road (*see* Staying in Northern Ireland in Chapter 1).

By Ferry **Belfast Ferries** (tel. 0151/922–6234; nine-hour crossing) offers car ferries to Belfast from the English port of Liverpool. **Sealink Ferries** (tel. 0177/622620; 2½ hours) provides car ferries to Larne from Stranraer, Scotland, and **P&O European Ferries** (tel. 0158/12276; 2½ hours) has car ferries to Larne from Cairnryan, Scotland. An interesting new option is to cross on the **SeaCat** (tel. 01304/240241, May–Sept. only)—the world's largest catamaran—which carries cars and passengers from Stranraer to Belfast in just 1½ hours.

By Train The Belfast–Dublin Express train travels nonstop between the two cities in two hours. Six trains run daily in both directions (three on Sundays).

By Bus Northern Ireland's bus company, **Ulsterbus** (tel. 01232/32011), crosses the border to connect with the Republic's **Bus Éireann** (tel. 01/836–6111 in Dublin) services. The ride from Dublin to Belfast takes four hours, with a change at Monaghan. Buses to Belfast also run from London and from Birmingham, making the Stranraer ferry (tel. 0177/622620) crossing.

Getting Around

By Car In general, drivers will find that in Northern Ireland the roads are in much better shape, signposting is clearer, and gasoline is cheaper than in the Irish Republic. Northern Ireland visitors, however, must deal with army checkpoints; a soldier may ask you a few questions, or even wish to search your luggage; you'll pass through more quickly if you cooperate politely. Bad rush-hour delays can occur getting in and out of Belfast on highways A6 and A2. But on the whole, driving is quicker and easier in Northern Ireland than in areas south of the border.

Parking Always make sure you are not in a "control zone," where it is prohibited to leave a vehicle unattended. Most town centers are control zones, with free car parks situated within walking distance.

Car Rentals Visitors can choose among several local rental companies, but car rental isn't cheap. A compact car costs U.K.£150 to U.K. £180 per week (including taxes, insurance, and unlimited mileage). If you're planning to take a hired car across the border into the Republic, inform the company and check its insurance procedures. The following are some of the main rental offices. **Belfast: Avis** (Great Victoria St., tel. 01232/240404) and **Godfrey Davis** (58 Antrim Rd., 01232/757401). **Aldergrove Airport: Avis** (tel. 018494/22333) and **Hertz** (tel. 018494/22533). **Belfast City Airport: Avis** (tel. 01232/240404). **Derry City: Budget** (tel. 01504/360420).

By Train Northern Ireland Railways runs only three rail routes: Belfast–Derry via Coleraine, Belfast–Bangor along the shore of Belfast Lough, and Belfast–Dublin. Rail Runabout tickets allow seven days' unlimited travel from April–October only (cost: U.K.£25 adults, U.K.£12.50 children under 16;): For information contact **Northern Ireland Railways** (28 Wellington Pl., Belfast, tel. 01232/230310), **Belfast Central Station** (East Bridge St., tel. 01232/438220), and local rail stations.

By Bus Visitors can take advantage of frequent and inexpensive Ulsterbus links between all Northern Ireland towns. The main bus stations in Belfast are located behind the Europa Hotel on Great Victoria Street and on Oxford Street near the Central Railway Station. A good bet for touring by bus is a Freedom of Northern Ireland Ticket, which allows unlimited travel (cost: U.K.£9 a day or U.K.£28 for a week; children under 16 half price; prices subject to change). For all specific fare and schedule details, call **Ulsterbus** (tel. 01232/320011). Within Belfast, visitors have access to good city bus service. All routes start from Donegall Square; you'll find a kiosk there where you can pick up a timetable. For **Citybus** inquiries, call 01232/246485.

Banks and Money Exchange

Northern Ireland uses British currency. Irish *punts*, or pounds, are not accepted. Rates change rapidly, but the British pound is worth a little more than the Irish (*see* Currency in Chapter 1, Essential Information). You'll sometimes be given bank notes, drawn on Ulster banks, that are valid only in Northern Ireland; be sure not to get stuck with a lot of these when you leave, because they will be difficult to change at banks back home. As in the Irish Republic, credit cards are not widely accepted outside the main towns. Main banks are open weekdays 10–3:30. Changing money outside banking hours is possible at **Thomas Cook** branches at Belfast Airport (open weekdays 7 AM–8 PM, weekends 7 AM–10 PM) and 11 Donegall Place (open Mon.–Sat. 9–5:30).

Guided Tours

Orientation Tours **Citybus** offers a Belfast city orientation tour that takes in the shipyards and heads out from the city center as far as Stormont (9½ kilometers/6 miles east) and Belfast Castle on Cave Hill to the north. *Milewater Rd., tel. 01232/246485. Cost: U.K.£4.50 adults, U.K.£2.50 children, including afternoon tea. City tour leaves Castle Pl. June–Sept., Tues.–Thurs. at 2 PM.*

Ulsterbus (Milewater Rd., tel. 01232/320011) operates half-day or full-day trips during June to September from Belfast to the Glens of Antrim, the Giant's Causeway, the Fermanagh lakes, Lough Neagh, the Mourne Mountains, and the Ards Peninsula.

Special-Interest Tours

Giant's Causeway/Bushmills

If you're seeing the province without a car, you could have difficulty reaching the Giant's Causeway. Apart from a tour to that destination from Belfast, Ulsterbus has also teamed up with the Old Bushmills Distillery to run the **Bushmills Bus,** an opentop tour bus running from Coleraine to the Giant's Causeway via the coast resorts; you also visit Bushmills to observe whiskeymaking. *Tel. 01265/43334. Cost: U.K.£2.60 adults, U.K.£1.30 children and senior citizens. Bus leaves Coleraine Mon.–Sat. 9:20, 11:30, 2:10, and 4; Sun. 2:10 and 4 only.*

Lower Lough Erne

Kestrel is a 63-seat water bus operated by **Erne Tours** (tel. 01365/322882); it sets off from Round O pier at Enniskillen during the summer for a two-hour trip on beautiful Lough Erne. On weekdays, the boat makes a half-hour stop at Devenish Island to allow visitors to see Ireland's best Round Tower. From May to June there are Sunday trips at 3 PM, and occasionally at other times of the year. *Cost: U.K.£3 adults, U.K.£1.50 children.*

Exploring Northern Ireland

Along the shores of Northern Ireland's coasts and lakes, green gentle slopes descend majestically into hazy, dark-blue water, against a background of more slopes, more water, and huge cloud-scattered skies. If time is short, you might decide to skip Belfast. (If you arrive by plane, you can easily bypass Northern Ireland's capital, because the Belfast Airport is several miles from the city.)

You certainly won't need to stick rigidly to the route in this guide. Belfast and Derry, however, do deserve a visit, if possible. Belfast is a naturally lively, friendly city with plenty of attractions; it is testimony to the spirit of the place that the long years of sectarian violence have not dimmed its vivacity. Derry still has a few problems but is facing them with great energy. Much of the bad housing has been swept away; new developments are being built both in the suburbs and in the small city center. British fortifications remain much in evidence, though, and soldiers patrol in force. Derry's center is still enclosed by its medieval walls, making it one of Europe's best-preserved examples of a fortified town.

If you want to see only one small area with plenty of variety, the best choice would be a stay in or near Enniskillen, in County Fermanagh. The town itself is bright and bustling; Lough Erne nearby has magnificent lake views, as well as one of Ireland's most impressive Round Towers, on Devenish Island. On the other side of Enniskillen stands Castle Coole, one of the most graceful mansions of the 18th-century Anglo-Irish nobility.

Highlights for First-Time Visitors

The Giant's Causeway (*see* Tour 2)
The Glens of Antrim (*see* Tour 2)
Lower Lough Erne (*see* Tour 3)
Ulster Museum (*see* Tour 1)
Victorian (and older) pubs in Belfast (*see* Tour 1)

Tour 1: Belfast

Numbers in the margin correspond to points of interest on the Northern Ireland and the Belfast maps.

1 **Belfast** is quite unlike any other city, Irish or British. Its unique charisma derives from a curious mixture of identities, its sense of separateness, and, of course, the notoriety it has received as a center of conflict. Belfast combines the hard-headed proletarian quality of a large industrial town with the dignified self-confidence of a respectable and well-to-do provincial capital. It was a great Victorian success story, a boom town whose prosperity was built on trade: Linen and shipbuilding brought in most of the wealth. Now Belfast struggles against decline; linen is no longer a major industry here, and shipbuilding has suffered severe setbacks. The quaysides along the River Lagan, however, are still impressively active, and the dry dock is one of the world's largest.

The city's central district, lying west of the docks, extends from the City Hall to St. Anne's Cathedral. The area is alive with commerce, shops, cafés, pubs, and historic (but now modernized) streets. Large redbrick or white Portland stone Victorian banks, as well as offices and department stores, occupy this old heart, symbols of Belfast's high standing before the creation of the Irish Free State. Now the whole of this district is pedestrian for security reasons; the roads are closed to traffic by sturdy green railings with police checkpoints.

Perhaps the most astonishing thing about Belfast is its setting—high wild heath-green slopes rise abruptly at the end of the city-center streets. Until the Plantation period at the beginning of the 17th century, Belfast was an insignificant village called *Beal Feirste* (meaning "Sandbank Ford"). In the 1600s the district, formerly belonging to Ulster's ancient O'Neill clan, was granted to Sir Arthur Chichester, who was from Devon in southwest England. Chichester's son was made earl of Donegall, and he initiated the building of the town; he is remembered in many of the street names. A century later, French Huguenots (i.e., Protestants) fleeing persecution settled here, bringing their valuable skills in linen work. In the 18th century, Belfast saw a phenomenal expansion, with the population doubling in size every 10 years. The sectarian divide appeared during the 19th century when Presbyterian ministers began to preach bitterly against the town's Catholic residents. But the town's growth continued, factories were built, and industry expanded. In 1849, Queen Victoria paid a visit, and she is recalled in the names of buildings, streets, bars, monuments, and other places around the city. In the same year, the university opened and took the name Queen's College. Victoria granted Belfast full city status in 1888. Today its population is 400,000—one-third of all Northern Ireland's citizens.

When the working day is over, Belfast's central area closes down and the life of the town shifts south. Great Victoria Street down to Shaftesbury Square is known as the **Golden Mile,** though it is not at all as glittering as the name implies and is only about a third of a mile in length. Beyond it, down University Road to Stranmillis Road, is the **University Area.** Chances are that as well as drinking and eating in these two parts of the city, you'll also be staying nearby. The University Area is the safest part of town and features many good bed-and-breakfasts and guest houses.

Centrally located at the northern end of Great Victoria Street, 2 Belfast's best hotel, the **Europa** (tel. 01232/327000), makes a good starting point for a walking tour of the city center. Many Belfast residents trace an improvement in the atmosphere of their city, and especially an upsurge in evening entertainments, to the reopening in 3 1980 of the **Grand Opera House,** next door. This typical Victorian theater, built in 1895, retains its original, richly decorated auditorium, where heavy gilt moldings, ornamental plasterwork, and frescoes depict Asian themes. Although the city already had a lively theater with its own company, the Lyric in south Belfast, the Opera House attracted bigger, more diverse audiences upon its reopening. Today it mounts touring performances of all kinds: musicals, operas, and children's plays, as well as conventional theater. The best way to see and enjoy this immaculate example of Victoriana is to attend a performance. *Great Victoria St., tel. 01232/241919. Seats range from U.K.£3 to U.K.£20.*

Turn right from the Opera House onto Howard Street to reach Belfast's central Donegall Square, dominated by its columned and 4 domed **City Hall** (built in 1906). To appreciate the classical style and the setting of the building, first take a walk right around Donegall Square. In the gardens you'll see statues of Queen Victoria; a monument commemorating the unlucky ocean liner *Titanic,* which was built in Belfast; and a short column in honor of the U.S. Expeditionary Force, which landed in the city on January 26, 1942—the first contingent of the U.S. Army to land in Europe. Then step inside the City Hall; the public entrance is at the rear of the building. If it happens to be a Wednesday morning, you can join the weekly guided tour and be shown the Council Chamber, the Great Hall, and the Reception Room. If not, you may at least walk into the Entrance Hall, to the foot of the Grand Staircase. Here you'll discover a riot of ornamental marble inlays and decorative plasterwork reaching up toward the dome. *Donegall Sq., tel. 01232/320202. Admission free. Guided tours: Wed. 10:30.*

You'll notice many buses waiting on the western and eastern sides of Donegall Square. This is the terminus for all city buses. The gray building on Donegall Square's northwest corner (at the junction with Wellington Place) is the **Linen Hall Library.** This comfortable private library, founded in 1788, is not really a tourist attraction, but you may want to stop here. Besides being a perfect hideaway for relaxing with a newspaper, the library has an unparalleled collection of local historical documents. Paintings and prints that show Belfast views and landmarks adorn the walls. The artworks are for sale and make excellent and original souvenirs or gifts. Library members can now peruse books while having a coffee and snack at the coffee shop inside the reading room. *17 Donegall Sq. N, tel. 01232/321707. Membership costs U.K.£28 per year. Open Mon.–Wed. and Fri. 9:30–6, Thurs. 9:30–8:30, Sat. 9:30–4.*

Step round the corner of the library onto **Donegall Place,** Belfast's main shopping street. You'll pass through the security gates into the pedestrians-only zone. Stroll up to Royal Avenue, a continuation of Donegall Place.

Time Out Belfast offers dozens of intriguing pubs packed with relics of the Victorian and Edwardian periods. At the start of Royal Avenue, turn left into Bank Street to find **Kelly's Cellars,** a typical traditional bar with character. Specialties include Ulster fry (fried bacon, sausages, egg, etc., with potato bread) and champ 'n' sausages (champ is creamy mashed potatoes with chopped scallions), each for only

Northern Ireland

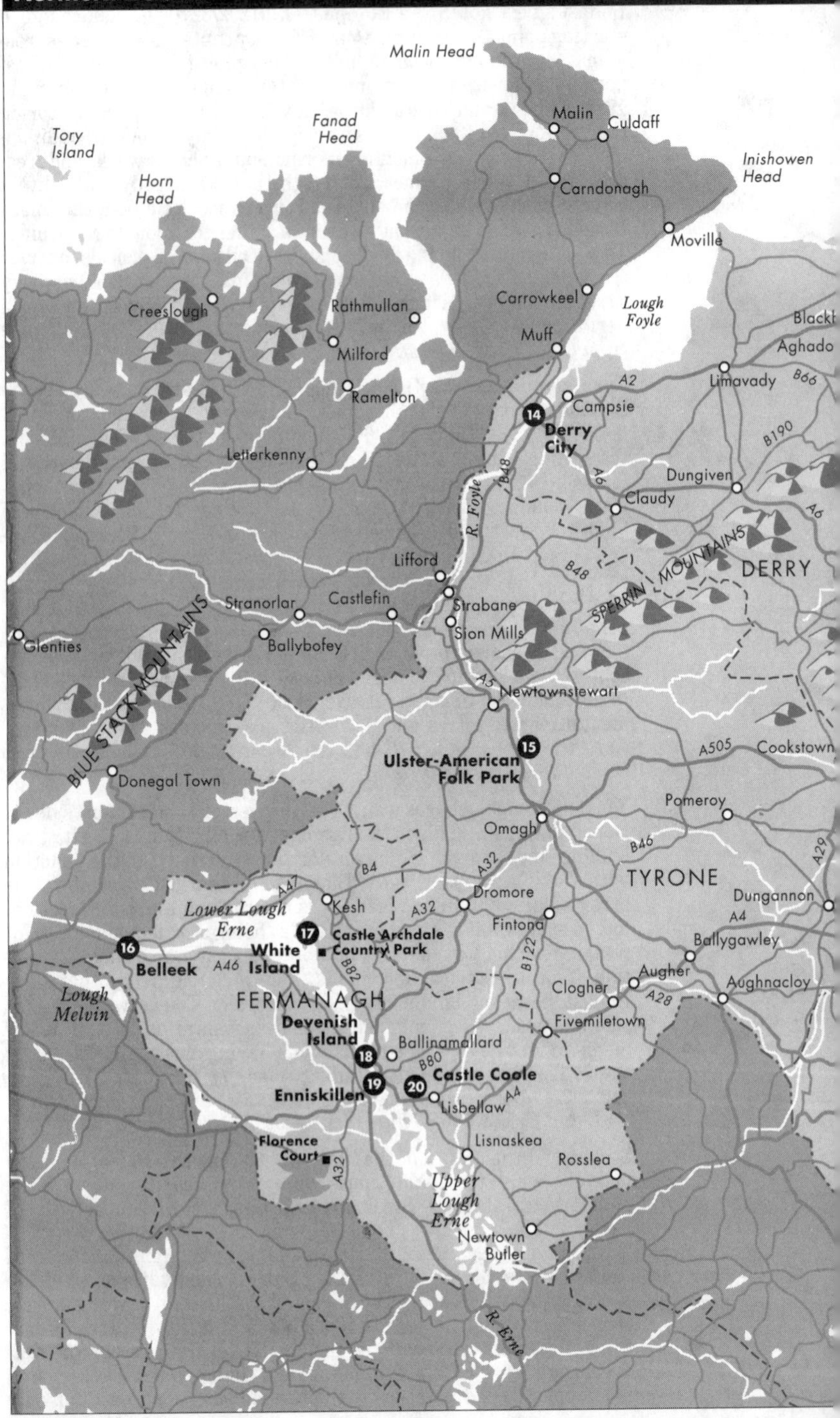

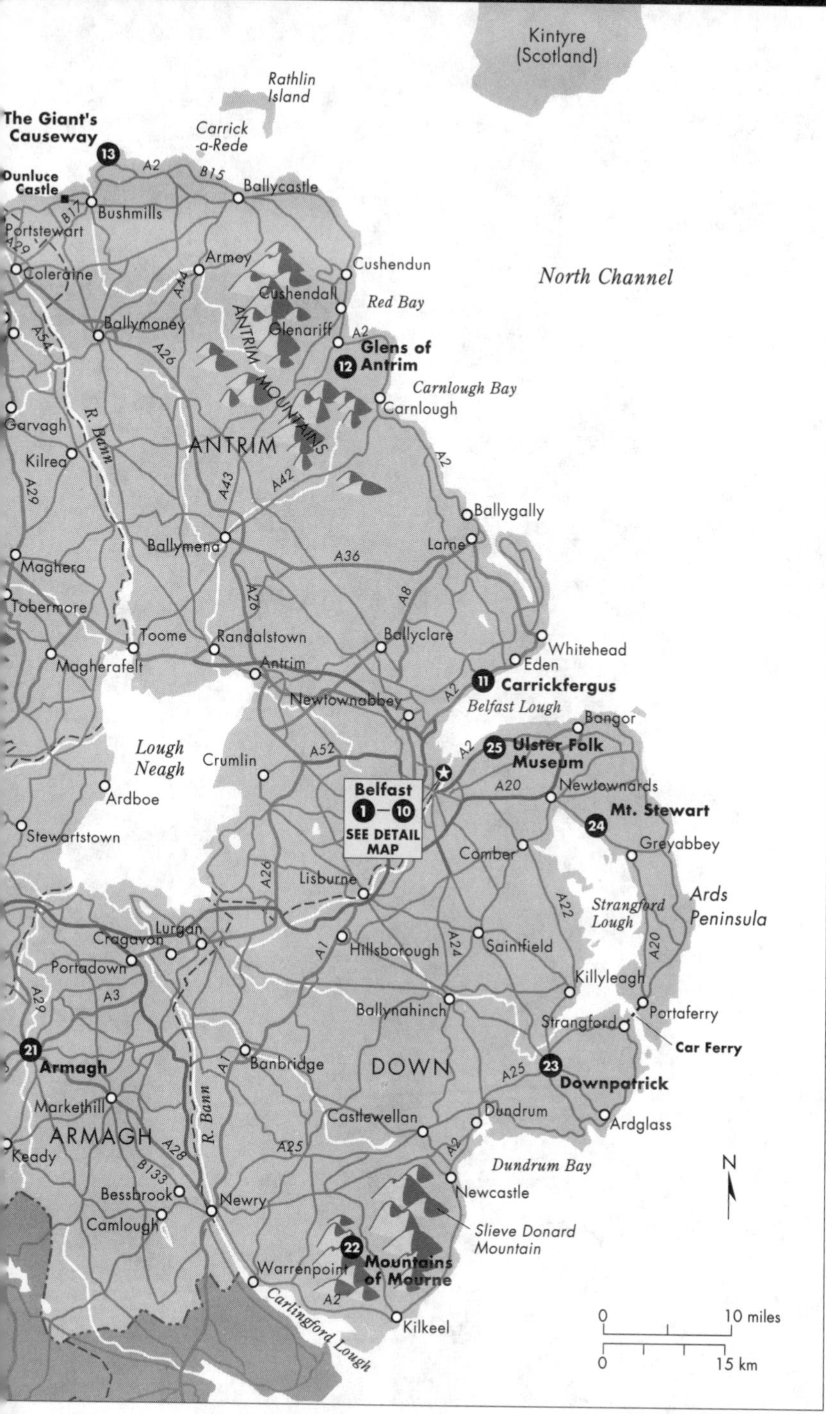

Kintyre (Scotland)
Rathlin Island
The Giant's Causeway
13
Carrick -a-Rede
Dunluce Castle
Bushmills
Ballycastle
Portstewart
Coleraine
Armoy
Cushendun
North Channel
Cushendall
Red Bay
Ballymoney
Glenariff
ANTRIM MOUNTAINS
12 Glens of Antrim
Carnlough Bay
Carnlough
Garvagh
R. Bann
ANTRIM
Kilrea
Ballygally
Ballymena
Larne
Maghera
Tobermore
Toome
Randalstown
Ballyclare
Whitehead
Magherafelt
Antrim
Eden
11 Carrickfergus
Newtownabbey
Belfast Lough
Bangor
25 Ulster Folk Museum
Lough Neagh
Crumlin
Belfast
1 — 10
SEE DETAIL MAP
Newtownards
Ardboe
Mt. Stewart
24
Stewartstown
Comber
Greyabbey
Lisburne
Strangford Lough
Ards Peninsula
Lurgan
Cragavon
Hillsborough
Saintfield
Portadown
Killyleagh
Portaferry
Ballynahinch
Strangford
Car Ferry
21
Armagh
Banbridge
DOWN
23
Downpatrick
Markethill
Castlewellan
Dundrum
Ardglass
ARMAGH
R. Bann
Keady
Dundrum Bay
Bessbrook
Newcastle
Newry
Camlough
Slieve Donard Mountain
22
Mountains of Mourne
Warrenpoint
Carlingford Lough
Kilkeel
N
0
10 miles
0
15 km
A2
B15
B17
A29
A44
A54
A26
A43
A42
A36
A8
A52
A20
A22
A24
A1
A3
A25
A28
B133

Albert Memorial Clock Tower, **7**
Botanic Gardens, **9**
City Hall, **4**
Europa Hotel, **2**
Grand Opera House, **3**
Northern Ireland Tourist Office, **6**
Queen's College, **8**
St. Anne's Cathedral, **5**
Ulster Museum, **10**

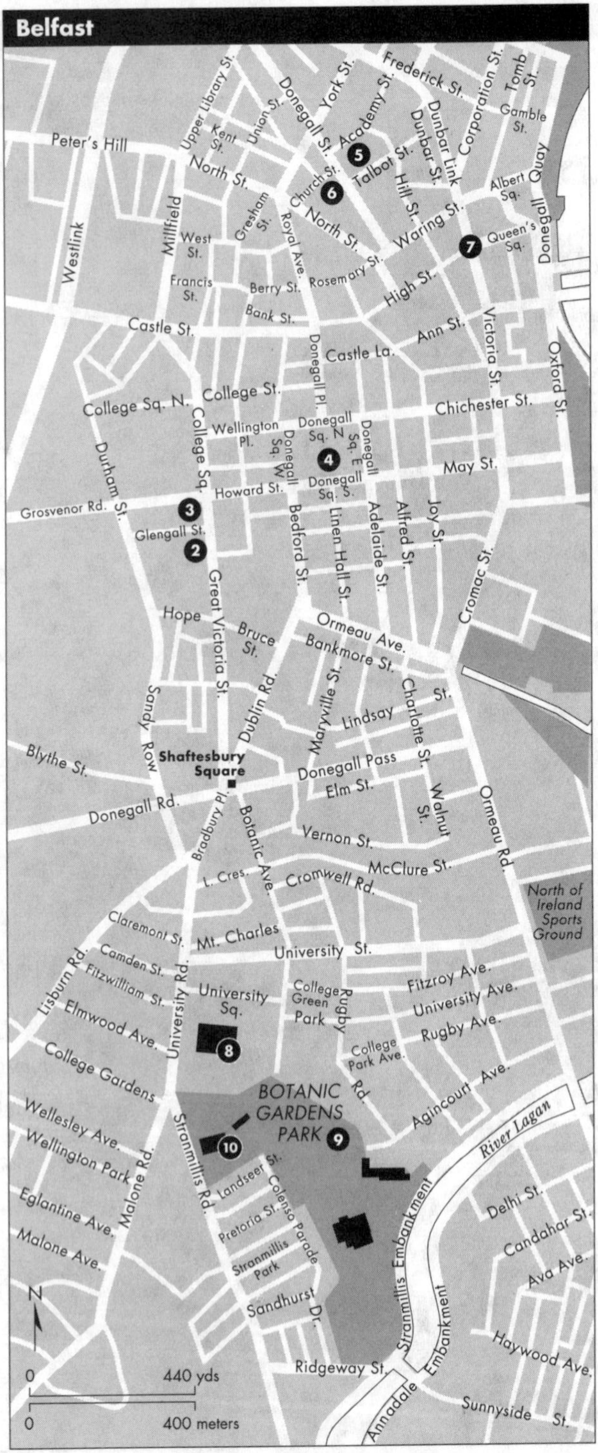

about U.K.£2. Two centuries ago, Kelly's Cellars was the regular meeting place of a militant Nationalist group, the Society of United Irishmen, whose leader, Wolfe Tone, is remembered as the founder of Irish republicanism.

---

5 To see **St. Anne's Cathedral,** continue to the end of Royal Avenue (crossing North Street), and then turn right onto Donegall Street. St. Anne's, a large edifice built at the beginning of this century, could almost be considered the spiritual headquarters of the province's Anglican establishment. Frankly, though, this is not an especially beautiful building. Its somber heaviness and deep rounded arches are hallmarks of the Irish neo-Romanesque style. Lord Carson, who was largely responsible for keeping the six counties inside the United Kingdom, is buried here beneath a suitably austere plain gray slab. Almost opposite the cathedral in St. Anne's Court, off
6 North Street, you will find the new premises of the main **Northern Ireland Tourist Office.** Behind St. Anne's Cathedral, you'll find an area of narrow cobbled back streets and abandoned warehouses; this district is undergoing a major overhaul, with new construction and businesses already promising to revive the neighborhood.

Walk south down to Waring Street (it runs at the bottom of both Hill Street and Donegall Street), turn left toward the River Lagan, then right into busy Victoria Street. From here, as you walk toward the
7 leaning **Albert Memorial Clock Tower,** you'll be able to see parts of Belfast's famous shipyards and two of the world's largest cranes, dubbed Samson (108 meters/350 feet high) and Goliath (143 meters/462 feet). At the clock tower, named for Queen Victoria's husband, Prince Albert (though he never came to Northern Ireland), turn right onto High Street.

Off High Street, and especially down to the parallel Ann Street, run narrow lanes and alleyways called entries. Though mostly cleaned up and turned into chic shopping lanes, they manage to hang on to something of their former raffish character. Wandering along these lanes you'll discover some unique pubs with authentic Victorian interiors. For example, take a look inside **The Morning Star** (Pottinger's Entry, off High St.) with its large windows and fine curving bar. **White's Tavern** (Winecellar Entry, off High St.) is Belfast's oldest pub, founded in 1630. Although it has been considerably updated, it still has a warm and comfortable ambience, with plush seats and a big open fire.

Follow Ann Street back to Donegall Place, then retrace your steps through Donegall Square to Great Victoria Street.

Time Out You might want a drink (and maybe a plate of oysters) in Belfast's best-preserved pub, the **Crown Liquor Saloon** (tel. 01232/325368), directly opposite the Europa Hotel on Great Victoria Street. The Crown, owned by the United Kingdom's official conservationist charity, The National Trust, dates from the end of the 19th century and has been kept in immaculate condition, with opulent ornamentation, richly carved woodwork around cozy snugs (private rooms), leather seats, colored tiles, and abundant mirrors.

The Europa and the Crown bar mark the start of **The Golden Mile,** so called because most of Belfast's evening life takes place in bars and restaurants here. The Crown is far from being the only impressive old pub on this stretch. Indeed, if you would like to try another Victorian bar with more locals and fewer visitors, you only have to walk into **Robinson's,** next door to the Crown. **The Beaten Docket,** on the other side of the Crown, is snazzier and appeals to a younger crowd.

8 The **University Area** is centered on **Queen's College** (set well back from University Rd.), which was constructed in the 1840s. Queen's is modeled on the colleges at Oxford University in England, with their spires, turrets, and fine stonework. **University Square,** adjacent to Queen's, is another architectural treasure with its Georgian terraces.

9 Spreading out beside Queen's, the 19th-century **Botanic Gardens** provide a welcome haven of quiet and greenery. A pretty highlight of the gardens is the 150-year-old curved iron-and-glass Palm House, the oldest such structure in the world. *Stranmillis Rd., tel. 01232/324902. Admission free. Gardens open daily dawn–dusk. Palm House open weekdays 10–5, weekends 2–5.*

10 Within the gardens, to the left of the main entrance, the **Ulster Museum** offers three floors devoted to the history and prehistory of Ireland and, in particular, Northern Ireland, together with a considerable collection of 19th- and 20th-century fine art. In the natural history section, you'll see, among other things, a skeleton of the now-extinct Irish giant deer. The museum's centerpiece is the fabulous jewelry and gold ornaments (as well as a cannon and other armaments) recovered from the Spanish vessel *Girona*, sunk off the Antrim coast in 1588. Perhaps the most imaginative, user-friendly sections are on the first floor—one colorfully traces the rise of Belfast's crafts, trade, and industry; the other tells the story of the Nationalist movement and explains the separation of Northern Ireland from the rest of the country. Visitors have access to a little café on level three. *Stranmillis Rd., tel. 01232/381251. Admission free. Open weekdays 10–5, Sat. 1–5, Sun. 2–5.*

The road south divides at the Botanic Gardens. Stranmillis Road leads into **Stranmillis,** a perfectly safe neighborhood with a cultured air and a choice of eateries. The community reaches over to the riverside towpath along the Lagan. **Malone Road** joins the river farther south, close to the out-of-town **Giant's Ring** (off Ballyleeson Road), a large, neolithic earthworks focused on an impressive *dolmen* (Celtic monument made of large stone slabs). To get this far, unless you're a keen walker (it's possible to come all the way on the Lagan towpath) you'll be happier driving in a car or taking a bus: Bus 22 passes close to the site, and on the return journey it will take you back to Donegall Square.

Tour 2: Around Counties Antrim and Derry

Numbers in the margin correspond to points of interest on the Northern Ireland map.

This circular route starts and finishes in Belfast, passing through some fair-sized towns, but most of the way you're driving in open country. Scenery is the best thing about Northern Ireland, but the region has much more to offer. For example, you'll discover the roots of several Ulstermen who became distinguished Americans. To follow the whole tour as described here could take an unhurried three or four days.

Begin this tour by heading north out of Belfast along the industrialized west shore of Belfast Lough. Cave Hill (*see* Off the Beaten Track, *below*), rising to the left, makes a popular day excursion for city dwellers.

11 Take the busy A2 toward **Carrickfergus.** This town on the shore of the lough grew up around **Carrickfergus Castle,** one of the first and one of the largest of Irish castles, which is still in good shape. Impressively standing on a rock ledge, it was built in 1180 by John de Courcy, provincial Ulster's first Anglo-Norman invader. The castle stood as a bastion of British rule right up until 1928, at which time it was still an English garrison. In fact, when Carrickfergus was enclosed by ramparts at the start of the 17th century, it was the only English-speaking town in Northern Ireland. Not surprisingly, this was the loyal port where William of Orange chose to land on his way to fight the Catholic forces at the Battle of the Boyne in 1690. However, the English did have one or two small setbacks, including the improbable victory in 1778 of John Paul Jones, the American naval hero, over the British warship HMS *Drake.* That, by the way, was America's first naval victory during the Revolutionary War. After the sea battle, the inhabitants of Carrickfergus stood on the waterfront and cheered Jones because they supported the American Revolution.

Walk through the castle's 13th-century gatehouse into the Outer Ward; continue into the Inner Ward, the heart of the fortress. Here stands the five-story Keep, a massively sturdy building with walls almost 2½ meters (8 feet) thick. Inside the Keep, you'll find a Cavalry Regimental Museum with historic weapons and an impressive vaulted Great Hall. These days, Carrickfergus Castle hosts entertaining medieval banquets (inquire at a local tourist office); if you're here at the beginning of August, you can enjoy the annual Lughnasa festival, a lively medieval costume entertainment. *Tel. 01960/351273. Admission: U.K.£2 adults, U.K.£1 children under 16. Open Apr.–Sept., daily 10–6; Oct.–Mar., daily 10–4 (closed all year Sun. AM).*

In the adjacent **Knight Ride and Heritage Plaza** (tel. 01960/366455), you can take a monorail "time trip" through the town's thousand years of history.

Structures that remain from Carrickfergus's past are St. Nicholas's Church, dating from the 13th and 14th centuries, and the handsomely restored North Gate in the town's medieval walls. **Dobbins Inn** (tel. 01574/51905) on High Street has been a popular hotel for more than three centuries. While in Carrickfergus, you might like to take a look at the **Andrew Jackson Centre,** in a thatched cottage a mile northeast of the town. This exhibit tells the tale of U.S. president Jackson, whose parents emigrated from Carrickfergus in 1765. This cottage was not their home, but it's thought to resemble it.

As you head away from the town on the A2, you'll pass through the village of **Eden,** where **Castle Dobbs** was the home of Arthur Dobbs, the 18th-century British governor of North Carolina. Signposted on the left, 2½ kilometers (1½ miles) off the road, **Dalway's Bawn,** built in 1609, is the best surviving example of an early *bawn,* or fortified farmhouse occupied by a Protestant Planter. Stay on the A2 to **Larne,** and pass through this workaday port town.

Soon after Larne, the coast of County Antrim becomes spectacular. Wave upon wave of high green hills curves down into the hazy sea, and the views are thrilling. The lower slopes are lush and intensively farmed, but rugged, too, while green moorland covers the rounded summits. Broad, rich glens, or valleys, cut through the hills toward the sea. In the 86 kilometers (54 miles) between Larne and
12 Ballycastle there are nine magnificent **Glens of Antrim.** The journey by these glens is mostly along a small, winding two-lane road close

to the sea. **Carnlough** (24 kilometers/15 miles out of Larne), a little resort made of white limestone, overlooks an endearing harbor within stone walls. There is a small tourist office inside the post office.

Time Out Carnlough's **Londonderry Arms** (20 Harbour Rd., tel. 01574/85255) is a fine old traditional inn by the harbor. It dates from the 17th century and once belonged to Winston Churchill. Fresh seafood is, of course, the specialty—try the seafood gratiné or the lobster—and substantial homemade wheat bread is served as well.

Beyond Carnlough the scenery becomes even more attractive. **Glenariff,** opening onto Red Bay at the village of Glenariff (also known as Waterfoot), is considered the loveliest of the glens. At neighboring **Cushendall,** you'll see a curious fortified square tower of red stone—a 19th-century jailhouse—standing at a crossroads in the middle of the village. If you would like a break from the Antrim coast, stay on the A2 direct to Ballycastle. But if you would prefer to stay by the sea, turn left at the tower in the direction of **Cushendun,** a tiny jewel of a village. From this part of the coast you can see the Mull of Kintyre on the Scottish mainland. The coast road rejoins the A2 after a few miles and descends—passing the ruins of the Franciscans' 16th-century **Bonamargy Friary**—into **Ballycastle,** the glens' main resort, at the northern end of the Glens of Antrim drive.

Every year since 1606, on the last Tuesday in August the town has hosted its **Oul' Lammas Fair,** a modern version of the ancient Celtic harvest festival Lughnasa. Ireland's oldest fair, this is a highly popular two-day event at which sheep and wool are still sold alongside the wares of more modern shopping stalls. If you're here at this time, treat yourself to the fair's traditional snacks, "dulse and yellow man" (edible seaweed and rock-hard yellow toffee). If you happen to be at Ballycastle in June, you might find yourself in the middle of the **Fleadh Amhran agus Rince,** a lively three-day music and dance folk festival.

From Ballycastle you have a view of L-shaped **Rathlin Island,** where in 1306 the Scottish king Robert the Bruce took shelter in a cave and was inspired to continue his armed struggle against the English by watching the patience of a spider spinning its web. It was on Rathlin in 1898 that Guglielmo Marconi set up the world's first radio link, from the island's lighthouse to Ballycastle. If the sea is not too rough (which it often is), a daily boat excursion journeys to the rocky windswept island; only 9½ kilometers (6 miles) away from shore, Rathlin can take an hour to reach. Make sure that you'll be able to return the same day.

Follow the shore road (B15) to **Carrick-a-Rede,** famous for one simple thing: a rope bridge. The bridge, swinging 25 meters (80 feet) above the crashing sea, is the precarious link between the mainland and a salmon fishery on a tiny island 18½ meters (60 feet) offshore. The walk across the bridge is pretty scary, but perhaps that's why almost every man, woman, and child passing this way likes to try it. *Admission free. Bridge open daily May–Sept.*

Another 8 kilometers (5 miles) along the coast brings you to
13 Ireland's strangest and most impressive geological curiosity, **The Giant's Causeway.** This bizarre sight consists of huge masses of mostly hexagonal pillars of volcanic basalt, clustered like honeycomb; about 37,000 of these columns extend down the cliffs, far into the sea. They were apparently created from boiling lava crystallizing as it burst into the sea; the lava came from an underground fis-

sure that stretched from Northern Ireland to the Scottish coast. According to legend, however, the columns were created when the giant Finn MacCool threw stepping-stones into the sea to make a causeway over to the Scottish island of Staffa.

Arriving by car, at first you'll reach a cliff-top parking lot beside the **Visitor Centre,** which provides displays about the area and an audiovisual exhibition explaining the formation of the causeway coast. Reaching the causeway itself requires a round-trip journey on foot of about 3 kilometers (2 miles). If you can't face such a trek, a minibus from the Visitor Centre will take you to the site. You can walk or scramble over the rocks (beware—they can be slippery and dangerous), some of which have been given whimsical names such as the Organ and the Harp. Farther out, Port-na-Spania is the spot where the 16th-century Spanish Armada galleass *Girona* went down on the rocks. The ship was carrying an astonishing cargo of gold and jewelry, some of which was recovered in 1967 and is now on display in the Ulster Museum in Belfast (*see* Tour 1: Belfast, *above*). Beyond that, Chimney Point is the name given to one of the causeway structures on which the Spanish fired, thinking that it was Dunluce Castle, which is 8 kilometers (5 miles) west. *Giant's Causeway Visitor Centre, Causeway Head, near Bushmills, tel. 012657/31855. Car park: U.K.£2. Audiovisual exhibition: U.K.£1 adults, U.K.50p children. Static exhibition: U.K.50p adults, U.K.30p children and senior citizens. Open July–Aug., daily 10–7. Closes earlier according to demand, rest of year.*

Time Out The pleasant little tearoom in the Visitor Centre provides wholesome snacks at moderate prices. Enjoy panoramic sea views while you enjoy the cakes and scones.

Just inland from The Giant's Causeway about 3 kilometers (2 miles) on the A2 is **Bushmills,** the village whose distillery produces the original, the best, and the most famous of Irish whiskeys. Enthusiasts of this elegant firewater who would like to see how it is made should call ahead at the Bushmills Distillery to join one of the guided tours. *Tel. 012657/31521. Admission free. Tours Mon.–Thurs. mornings and afternoons, Fri. mornings only.*

About 5 kilometers (3 miles) west of Bushmills, still on the A2, the **Dunluce Castle** ruin lies dramatically on a cliff top. Originally a 13th-century Norman fortress, it was captured in the 16th century by the indomitable local MacDonnell clan chiefs, who enlarged it, making it an important base for controlling the area. Maybe they expanded the castle a little too much, for in 1639 the kitchens and the cooks plummeted into the sea. Nearby is the new **Dunluce Centre,** an entertainment complex comprising rides, a show on myths and legends, a viewing tower, shops, and a restaurant. *Tel. 01265/824444. Admission to all attractions: U.K.£4 (U.K.£3.50 off-peak). Open Mar.–Sept., Mon.–Fri. noon–5, Sat.–Sun. 10 AM–9 PM (July and Aug., daily 10 AM–9 PM).*

To reach **Coleraine,** either take the A2 to the small resort of Portrush and turn inland on the A28 or turn back to Bushmills and take the B17 from there—either way, you'll drive about 13 kilometers (8 miles) to Coleraine from Dunluce Castle. At Coleraine, cross the River Bann into County Londonderry (or Derry). The Bann, which cuts through Northern Ireland, marks the boundary between the fiercely Protestant Counties Antrim and Down and the other four counties.

Take the A37 west from Coleraine through **Limavady,** with its Georgian main street. At No. 51, in the year 1851, Jane Ross noted down the tune played by a traveling fiddler and called it "Londonderry Air," better known now as "Danny Boy." While staying at an inn on Ballyclose Street, William Thackeray (1811–1863) wrote his rather lustful poem "Peg of Limavaddy," about a barmaid. Among the many Americans descended from Ulster emigrants was President James Monroe, whose relatives came from the Limavady area.

14 As the road turns toward **Derry City,** the neat terraces rising gently from the Foyle Valley come into view. The town appears attractive and inviting, which is astonishing because of its reputation as one of Europe's most troubled cities. In reality, here as in Belfast, the publicity is out of proportion to the actual situation, though as always, it is prudent to avoid wandering about in certain sections of town, notably Bogside and Creggan. The name of the city, by the way, is now officially Derry, although staunch Loyalists (including many government departments) still like to call it by its old Plantation period name, Londonderry. The county, though, is still called Londonderry. The "London" part of the name was tacked on in 1613 after the Irish nobility were thoroughly trounced and the city and county were handed over to the Corporation of London, which represented London's merchants. They brought in a large population of Protestants, built new towns for them, and reconstructed Derry within the **City Walls,** which survive almost unchanged to this day.

These substantial ramparts of gray stone, pierced by eight gates (originally four), are about 8 meters (25 feet) high and as much as 9 meters (30 feet) thick. The walls are only 1.6 kilometers (1 mile) all round, which indicates how small the walled area is. These days, Derry extends far beyond this fortified center; most of the life of the town actually takes place outside the walls. The best way to get the feel of Derry's history is to stroll along the parapet walkway atop the ramparts. You can do this on your own, or, in July and August, join one of the guided walks (cost U.K. £1.50) which depart from the town's new Tourist Information Office at 8 Bishop Street (tel. 01504/267284). Another good starting point is Shipquay Gate on the north side, beside the ornate Victorian **Guildhall;** convenient parking is close by. There are also guided walks of the walled area. Don't miss a visit to the excellent, informative, and entertaining Tower Museum in O'Doherty's Tower (*see below*) to understand the city and its story.

Over the centuries, the sturdy ramparts withstood many fierce attacks and were never breached, which explains Derry's coy sobriquet, "The Maiden City." The most celebrated siege occurred from 1688 to 1689, when James II (the Catholic king trying to regain the throne of England) reached the town with his army, expecting to be welcomed by Derry's governor, Colonel Lundy. But 13 Protestant apprentice boys had stolen the keys of the city gates; after throwing Lundy outside, these lads locked the gates to prevent James's entry. James, undeterred, blockaded the town with the intention of starving it into submission. Of the 30,000 people within the walls, a quarter of them died of hunger before reinforcements arrived from William of Orange (the Dutch Protestant claimant to the English throne). The blockade was broken, and James was forced to withdraw. The whole event is proudly recalled by Derry's Protestant community—now a minority of the population—who still hold colorful ceremonial marches in honor of the apprentice boys, reenacting the Protestants' triumph and annually burning an effigy of the hated Governor Lundy.

From Shipquay Gate, walk along Union Hall Street. You quickly reach **O'Doherty's Tower,** a sturdy bastion. Inside it, the **Tower Museum** houses the vivid and memorable Story of Derry exhibition, relating the history of the city from its beginnings as an oak grove right up to the present day. *The Tower Museum, Union Hall Pl., Derry BT48 6LU, tel. 01504/372411. Admission: U.K.£1.50 adults, U.K.50p children. Open Tues.–Sat. 10 AM–1 PM and 2–5.*

From here, turn up toward **Butcher Gate,** on the west side, which opens onto the Catholic Bogside district. The graffito "Doire Cholmcille" near this gateway is the old Irish name for Derry City—Columba's Oak. A five-minute walk downhill outside Butcher Gate into the Bogside will take you to **Free Derry Corner,** one of the city's compelling modern curiosities, a surviving gable wall, from a demolished terrace of houses, that is painted with the bold words YOU ARE NOW ENTERING FREE DERRY. From here you can see **Roaring Meg,** one of the original cannons from the 1688–89 siege, which still looks out from Double Bastion, a fortified corner on the ramparts. Go back inside Butcher Gate, and continue on Magazine Street to **Bishop Gate.** Here you'll discover one of the most extraordinary facts about the walls: The British army is still using them to defend the city. Bishop Gate, opening onto the Fountain Area, a Protestant quarter on the south side, is under exceptionally heavy guard.

Within the walls, Shipquay Street climbs steeply to the central square, the Diamond. On the way it passes an attractive new development lying to the right (look for a sign: THE VILLAGE). Beyond the Diamond, if you walk on Bishop Street, you'll pass **St. Columba's Cathedral.** Built in 1633 in simple Planter's Gothic style, the church is a treasure house of Derry Protestant emblems, memorials, and relics from the 1688–89 siege.

Time Out Among the several modest cafés suitable for a snack or lunch break in Derry City, one of the most agreeable is **The Boston Tea Party.** This small tea shop is in the new development called The Village, which is reached down an alley nearly opposite the Richmond Shopping Centre on Shipquay Street. Boston, by the way, has links with Derry dating from the 17th and 18th centuries, when many Derry residents escaped their hardships at home by emigrating to that U.S. city and other parts of the New World.

Tour 3: Around Counties Tyrone, Fermanagh, Armagh, and Down

From Derry City, head across County Tyrone toward Enniskillen. Take the A5 south via Strabane to Omagh. **Strabane** does not offer much to hold your interest, apart from the well-preserved 18th-century **Gray's Print Shop** (49 Main St., tel. 01504/884094). John Dunlap (1746–1812), who apprenticed here as a printer before emigrating to Philadelphia, founded America's first daily newspaper, *The Philadelphia Packet,* in 1771, and was also the man who printed and distributed the American Declaration of Independence. James Wilson, grandfather of President Woodrow Wilson, also emigrated. The original **Wilson family home,** a simple thatched cottage, still with much of the original 18th-century furniture, survives at Dergalt, 3 kilometers (2 miles) along the Plumbridge road. It can be visited by knocking at the farmhouse next door, still owned and worked by the Wilson family. For a delightfully rustic alternative route, drive along the minor road B48, which skirts the foot of the **Sperrin Mountains** and reaches all the way to Omagh.

About 27 kilometers (17 miles) south from Strabane on the A5, or 5 kilometers (3 miles) north if you're coming from Omagh, you'll reach 15 the **Ulster-American Folk Park,** which has been designed to re-create a Tyrone village of two centuries ago, a log-built American settlement of the same period, and the docks and ships that the emigrants to America would have used. The centerpiece of the park is an old whitewashed cottage, now a museum, which is the ancestral home of Andrew Mellon (1855–1937), the U.S. millionaire banker. Another thatched cottage is a reconstruction of the boyhood home of Archbishop John Hughes, founder of New York's St. Patrick's Cathedral. Exhibitions trace the contribution of the Northern Irish people to American history. The park also features a crafts shop and café. *Camphill, Co. Tyrone, tel. 01662/243292. Admission: U.K.£3 adults, U.K.£1.50 children. Open Easter–Sept., Mon.–Sat. 11–6:30, Sun. and holidays 11:30–7; Oct.–Good Friday, weekdays 10:30–5. Last admission 1½ hrs before closing.*

Drive south through **Omagh,** County Tyrone's capital, taking the A32 in the direction of Enniskillen. After 9½ kilometers (6 miles), turn right onto the B4 to the village of **Kesh,** beside **Lower Lough Erne.** The best of this highly scenic lake can be seen by driving from Kesh to Enniskillen on the shore road (B82). Lovers of Belleek pot- 16 tery should first skirt the northern edge of the lake to reach **Belleek,** where this distinctive fine porcelain is made. You can tour the **Belleek Pottery Ltd.** factory, where original methods of manufacture are still used; you can purchase some of the pottery, and enjoy a snack in the tea shop. *Tel. 01365/65501. Admission free. Tours Mon.–Thurs. 9:30–4:15; Fri. 9:30–3:15.*

Just a mile across the border, on the road to Ballyshannon in County Donegal, you can visit **Celtic Weave China** (tel. 072/51844), a small operation making handmade fine pottery similar to the items made in Belleek (*see* Shopping, *below*).

On the journey beside Lough Erne, apart from pausing to catch your breath at the lovely views of green hills extending down to the still lake water, you should also stop at **Castle Archdale Country Park,** signposted down a narrow road about 6½ kilometers (4 miles) from Kesh, where there's a lakeside marina, an open-air country museum, and a World War II exhibition featuring the Battle of the Atlantic. *Tel. 013656/21333. Admission free. No set hours.*

From Castle Archdale a June–September ferry (tel. 01365/22711; cost: U.K.£1; no boat Mon.) takes passengers to see the weird Celtic 17 carved figures on **White Island.** After you drive 13 kilometers (8 miles) farther from Castle Archdale Park, where the B82 joins the A32, a small sign shows the way to catch the little boat from April–September (tel. 01365/22711; cost: U.K.£2; no boat Mon.) over to 18 **Devenish Island.** The extensive but ruined 12th-century monastery on Devenish features Ireland's best example of a Round Tower and a richly carved High Cross.

Another 5 kilometers (3 miles) south along the A32 brings you to 19 **Enniskillen,** the pleasant capital of County Fermanagh, with its town center strikingly situated on an island in the River Erne between Upper and Lower Lough Erne. At the riverside, the 16th-century **Water Gate** is handsomely turreted, and part of the 15th-century **Castle Keep** contains the local history collection of the **Fermanagh County Museum** (tel. 01365/325050) and the polished paraphernalia of the **Royal Inniskilling Fusiliers Regimental Museum** (tel. 01365/23142). This year, a new Heritage Centre opens within the curtilage of the castle (tel. 01365/325000 for details). Beyond the West Bridge lies Portora Royal School, established in 1608 by King James I. Its grounds contain the ruins of Portora Castle. Writers Oscar Wilde and Samuel Beckett were both educated at Portora Royal School. The town's other sights are admittedly modest. Yet the spires of its 19th-century churches and town hall lend a certain charm to this friendly town. One satisfying journey to make from Enniskillen is a complete tour of Lower Lough Erne, allowing a full day to really enjoy it.

Time Out Among the several relaxed and welcoming old pubs in Enniskillen's town center, the one with the most appeal is **Blakes of the Hollow** on the main street, a place hardly altered since it opened in 1887. Its name derives from the facts that the heart of the town lies in a slight dip or hollow and the pub's landlord is named William Blake. Don't ask if he's related to the great poet of the same name—everybody does, and he isn't!

About 11 kilometers (7 miles) south from Enniskillen on the A4 and the A32, **Florence Court** deserves a visit if you have the time. One of the most impressive of Northern Ireland's grand Anglo-Irish mansions, it was built in the 18th century for John Cole, father of the first earl of Enniskillen. The house features abundant Rococo plasterwork, 18th-century furnishings, and a fine porcelain collection. You can stroll around the estate grounds, and have a snack and coffee at the tea shop. *Tel. 01365/82249. Admission: U.K.£2.40 adults, U.K.£1.20 children. Open June–Aug., Wed.–Mon.; Apr.–May, Sept., weekends only. Grounds open 10–1 hr before sunset; house open 2–6.*

Next, drive east from Enniskillen on the A4, the main Belfast road (from Florence Court, backtrack on the A32 to Enniskillen), and 3
20 kilometers (2 miles) from town, you'll see signs pointing to **Castle Coole** on the left. Another of the graceful mansions of the Anglo-Irish ruling class of the 18th and 19th centuries, this home is considered the finest of them all. The house stands in its own landscaped oak woods and parkland at the end of a long tree-lined driveway. In perfect Palladian symmetry, white colonnaded wings extend from either side of the white neoclassical mansion. In a recent restoration, anything not in keeping with the original design was removed. Inside, too, everything—from the lavish plasterwork to sumptuous period furniture—reflects the taste and wealth of its first owners, the earls of Belmore. Castle Coole is still the home of the present earl of Belmore. *Enniskillen, Co. Fermanagh, tel. 01365/322690. Admission: U.K.£2.40 adults, U.K.£1.20 children. Open Easter and June–Aug., Fri.–Wed. 2–6; May and Sept., weekends and holidays only; rest of year, grounds open, house closed.*

Continue in an easterly direction along the A4, through drumlin-dotted farmland (drumlins are tiny hillocks). At Augher village, pick up the A28 on the right.

After a 40-kilometer (25-mile) drive, the road reaches the small but
21 ancient ecclesiastical city of **Armagh.** Despite some pleasing Georgian streets (especially The Mall, east of the town center), the heart of Armagh can seem drab, and it suffers from having been a trouble spot in the religious conflict. Here St. Patrick founded a church, and the town has remained a religious center to the present day. In fact, *two* Armagh cathedrals are dedicated to Ireland's patron saint. Despite the 1921 partition of Ireland into two parts, the seat of the Catholic Archbishop of All Ireland remains in Armagh, as does the seat of the Archbishop of the Anglican Church of Ireland.

The pale limestone Victorian Gothic **Catholic Cathedral** with two pale spires, on a hill at the north end of town, is best seen from a distance. Nearer the town center, a squat battlemented tower identifies the **Protestant Cathedral,** in simpler early 19th-century Perpendicular Gothic style. It stands on the site of much older churches and contains several relics of Armagh's long history, including sculpted pre-Christian idols. This cathedral claims to be the burial place of Brian Boru, the great High King—that is, king of all Ireland—who drove the Vikings out of Ireland in the 11th century.

Walk down College Street, turning off English Street in the town center, to the broad Georgian esplanade called The Mall. At the north end of the green stands the 19th-century Courthouse, and at the other end, a dominating jailhouse. On the corner of The Mall East, the **Royal Irish Fusiliers Museum** (in Sovereign's House, tel. 01861/522911) features exhibits that illustrate part of the story of Britain's efforts to control this part of Ireland from the 1798 Rebellion onward.

On a completely different note, about 200 yards from the museum up College Hill—a continuation of College Street at the north end of The Mall—is Armagh's main attraction, the **Astronomy Centre and Planetarium.** The observatory here has been in continuous use since 1791. Nowadays it contains fascinating exhibits, including models of spacecraft, video shows of the sky, and hands-on computer displays. The Earthorium exhibition displays the world from three levels—its interior, surface, and atmosphere. The new AstroPark features a model solar system. *Tel. 01861/523689. Admission: Hall of astronomy and AstroPark, free. Special shows (Mon.–Fri. at 3 PM) and other exhibitions U.K.£3 adults, U.K.£2 children and senior citizens. Open Mon.–Fri. 11:30–5, Sat.–Sun. 1:30–5.*

Next, leave Armagh on the A28, driving toward Newry. Instead of going the entire way on the main road, after about 9½ kilometers (6 miles), you'll have a more enjoyable drive if you take the B133, on the right. This will lead you through a rustic drumlin landscape of vivid green pastures. The appearance of villages changes as you return toward the River Bann; houses and farms begin to resemble homes and farms in Britain rather than those in the Republic. **Bessbrook** is a "model village" built in 1846 by Quaker linen manufacturer John Grubb Richardson. It has a naive, dreamlike, toy-town quality, with its neat terraces and picture-book village stores. Richardson decreed that there would be no pubs at Bessbrook. Maybe that explains why there are no fewer than six in the neighboring village, Camlough. **Derrymore House,** a thatched cottage with a well-tended garden outside Bessbrook, is the place where in 1800 the fateful Act of Union was drafted.

From Bessbrook, the drive is only 3 kilometers (2 miles) to the middle of **Newry,** a town with a history of vigorous Irish nationalism, despite having the first Protestant church in Ireland, St. Patrick's. Though still standing, the church has been altered a great deal since it was put up in 1578, having been frequently damaged and repaired. Some 18th-century buildings in Newry survive, especially on Upper Water Street and Trevor Hill, notably the White Linen Hall. On weekends and market days, Irish citizens fill the town, coming from across the Northern Ireland border, only 6½ kilometers (4 miles) away, to take advantage of lower prices in the North.

Follow the east bank of industrialized Carlingford Lough via the A2 and then the wild Irish Sea to **Newcastle.** On the way you'll be circling the atmospheric and unspoiled **Mountains of Mourne,** which
22

"sweep down to the sea" (in the words of a popular song) from 620-meter (2,000-foot) summits. This area was long considered ungovernable, its hardy inhabitants living from smuggling contraband into the numerous rocky coves on the seashore. Much of the Mourne range is still inaccessible except on foot. The countryside of high windswept pasture- and moorland, threaded with bright streams, is perfect for away-from-it-all walkers. Newcastle is the main center for visitors to the hills. Looming above the town is **Slieve Donard,** its panoramic 870-meter (2,805-foot) summit grandly claiming views into England, Wales, and Scotland—"when it's clear enough," or, in other words, rarely!

23 **Downpatrick,** 19 kilometers (12 miles) away from Slieve Donard on the A2 and A25, used to be called plain and simple Down, but the town is proud of a suspected association with St. Patrick and changed its name in his honor. St. Patrick was a 5th-century Briton who, captured by the Irish, became a slave in the Down area; he escaped to France, where he learned about Christianity, and bravely returned to try to convert the local chiefs. Although it is not true that Patrick brought a new faith to Ireland (there was already a bishop of Ireland before Patrick got here), he must have been a better missionary than most because he did indeed win influential converts. The clan chief of the Down area gave him land at the village of Saul, near Downpatrick, to build a monastery.

Downpatrick's hilltop cathedral, built in 1790, preserves parts of some of the earlier churches and monasteries that have stood on the site since the 6th century. Even before that time, the cathedral site had long been an important fortified settlement (Down takes its name from the Celtic word "Dun," a fort). In the churchyard, a somber slab has been inscribed "Patric"—it's supposedly the saint's tomb, which is a bit of a fraud since no one knows where Patrick is buried. It might be here, at Saul, or, some scholars argue, more likely at Armagh. A lot of such mystery and legend surrounds Patrick. For some hard facts, visit the **St. Patrick Heritage Centre** next to the cathedral; it's housed, together with the **Down Museum,** inside a former 18th-century jail. *The Mall, tel. 01396/615218. Admission free. Open weekdays 11–5, weekends 2–5. Closed Sept.–June on Mon.*

From Downpatrick, head northeast on the A25 to **Strangford** (13 kilometers/8 miles) and the **Ards Peninsula.** At Strangford, **Castle Ward** is an 18th-century mansion in a bizarre mixture of styles—classical on one side, Gothic on the other. The 700-acre estate has a "Victorian pastimes center" for children, a wildfowl collection, a restaurant, an information office, and the old tower house, which once guarded the shore. Holiday cottages are available for rentals as well. *Located .8 kilometer (½ mile) west of Strangford on south shore of Strangford Lough, tel. 01396/86204. Admission: U.K.£2.50 adults, U.K.£1.25 children. House open May–Aug., Fri.–Wed. 1–6; closed Thurs. Estate open year-round, dawn–dusk.*

You'll have to cross Strangford Lough on the car ferry from Strangford to reach **Portaferry** (£2.40 per car, 60p per additional passenger, 30p for children and senior citizens), another quiet fishing village with old fortifications to guard this once-strategic channel, which joins the lough to the sea. The ferry crossing takes 10 minutes or less, and boats leave every half hour throughout the day all year long.

Time Out On the Portaferry waterside, **The Portaferry Arms** (tel. 012477/28231), an old, unpretentious bed-and-breakfast, has a full menu of inexpensive snacks and lunches. Take a window seat and watch the unhurried activity on the quay and the relaxed routine of the tiny ferry as it chugs to and fro across the lough.

Before moving on, you may want to take a look at Portaferry's unusual **Northern Ireland Aquarium,** renamed Explorer, which has models of the underwater environment in Strangford Lough and examples of 70 species that call the lough their home. Some of these creatures may not be what you expect—seals and some large, long-lived species of fish still live in the lake. *Northern Rope Walk, Portaferry, tel. 012477/28062. Admission: U.K.£2 adults, U.K.£1 children and senior citizens, children under 5 free; family ticket U.K.£4. Open Apr.–Aug., Mon.–Sat. 10–6; Sun., afternoons only. Sept.–Mar., Tues.–Sat. 10:30–5; Sun., afternoons only.*

The A20 makes its way north from Portaferry up the lakeshore. Strangford Lough is not really a lake; it is joined to the sea by the channel you crossed at Portaferry, and might be better described as a fjord. Although Strangford Lough is deep in the middle, it rises to shallow banks dotted with rounded islands (actually submerged drumlins). In fact, its original Norse name was *Strang Fjord* (Strong Fjord), referring to the powerful current that flows into and out of the water with every tide. Huge populations of wildfowl gather in and beside the water.

24 **Mount Stewart,** signposted on the right around 21 kilometers (13 miles) from Portaferry, is the grand 18th-century family home of the marquesses of Londonderry. The marvelous landscaped gardens give the impression that the owners had more money than they knew what to do with; they created luxuriant flower beds, elaborate hedges, and planned views, and they populated the grounds with surprising stone carvings of rare and extinct creatures. The octagonal Temple of the Winds is a copy of a similar little structure in Athens. *Newtownards, tel. 0124774/387. Admission: U.K.£3.30 adults, U.K.£1.65 children. Open June–Aug., Wed.–Mon. 1–6; May, Sept.–Oct., weekends and public holidays only.*

On the A20, from Newtownards west to Belfast direct is only 16 kilometers (10 miles), but it's worth detouring via Bangor (6½ kilome-
25 ters/4 miles from Newtownards on the A21) to visit the **Ulster Folk Museum,** which is also 11 kilometers (7 miles) from Belfast on the A2. Devoted to the province's social history, the open-air museum is set in some 70 acres around Cultra Manor and encircled by a larger park and recreation area. It brings Northern Ireland's past vividly to life with a score of reconstructed buildings brought here from around the region; these structures represent different facets of Northern Ireland life—a traditional weaver's dwelling, terraces of Victorian town houses, an 18th-century country church, a village flax mill, a farmhouse, and a rural school. You start your visit with the Folk Gallery, which explains the background of each building. Across the main road (by footbridge) is the Transport Museum, with exhibits showing every kind of transport, including a miniature railway on Saturdays during the summer. *Cultra, near Holywood, tel. 01232/428428. Admission: U.K.£2.60 adults, U.K.£1.30 children and senior citizens. Open May–Sept., Mon.–Sat. 11–6, Sun., afternoons only; Oct.–Apr., Mon.–Sat. 11–5, Sun., afternoons only. May–June, till 9 PM Wed.*

Off the Beaten Track

Belfast's Churches An amazing variety of religious denominations is represented in Belfast. The oldest house of worship is **Knockbreda Parish Church** (Church of Ireland), on Church Road, off the A24 on the south side of the city. This dark, sturdy, and atmospheric structure was built in 1737, the work of architect Richard Cassels, who designed many of Ireland's greatest mansions. It quickly became *the* place to be buried—witness the vast 18th-century tombs in the churchyard. The **First Presbyterian Church** (Rosemary St.) dates from 1783 and has an interesting elliptical interior. It hosts lunchtime concerts. **St. Malachy's** (Roman Catholic; Alfred St.), built in 1844, features some fine stonework, including an astonishing fan-vaulted ceiling. By the riverfront is one of the most appealing churches, **Sinclair Seamen's Church** (Presbyterian; Corporation Sq., off Donegall Quay). It was designed by Charles Lanyon, the architect of Queen's University, and has served the seafaring community since 1857. A maritime theme pervades the building; even the pulpit is shaped like a ship's prow.

Cave Hill On fine weekends, it seems that half of Belfast makes its way up to this airy hill north of the city center, where you'll find walks and fine views of the city spread out below. Up here visitors can also visit the zoo, the grand 19th-century baronial mansion **Belfast Castle** (now a restaurant), and, at the summit, the ancient earthworks of **MacArt's Fort.**

East Tyrone Tour 2 makes a quick dash across this large and most rural of Northern Ireland counties, but you may want to explore the area further. North of Omagh, the country is pretty and rustic, with small farm villages within sight of the bare Sperrin Mountains. Heading east from the town on the A505, you'll discover a pensive landscape of moist heath and bog. Left of the road, **Beaghmore** is a strange Bronze Age ceremonial site preserved for millennia beneath a blanket of peat: It has seven stone circles and 12 cairns. Farther along, the A505 reaches **Wellbrook Beetling Mill** (Corkhill, tel. 016487/51735; admission: U.K.£1.40 adults, 70p children), where locally made linen was first "beetled," that is, pounded with noisy water-driven hammers to give it a smooth finish. The mill is kept in working order by the National Trust. About 6½ kilometers (4 miles) beyond Wellbrook is **Cookstown,** an odd Plantation village with a single broad main street more than 1½ kilometers (1 mile) in length. From here, head down on the back lanes to **Lough Neagh,** the largest lake in the British Isles (396 square kilometers/153 square miles), noted for an abundance of eels. On its shore at **Ardboe** stands a remarkable 10th-century High Cross. It is huge—more than 5½ meters (18 feet) tall—and richly carved with biblical scenes.

Shopping

The best of Northern Ireland's traditional products, many made according to time-honored methods, include the exquisite linen and superior handmade woolen garments that are usually associated with the Republic of Ireland. Handmade lacework also remains a handicraft from the countrywomen of some Northern Ireland districts. Visitors should keep an eye out for hand-cut crystal from County Tyrone. Highly regarded as well is the mellow cream-colored parian china of Belleek, which is not only beautiful, but also a good investment.

At the other end of the price scale, handcrafted miniatures of the legendary leprechaun make an inexpensive and amusing (if predictable) souvenir. Blackthorn walking sticks are another popular memento from the province. Polished granite stones from the Mountains of Mourne provide a pretty reminder of a haunting corner of the province.

Belfast

Belfast's main shopping streets include Donegall Place, High Street, Royal Avenue, and several of the smaller streets connecting with them. The whole area is traffic-free (except for buses), so visitors will find it pleasant to wander and window-shop. **Anderson McAuley** (Donegall Pl., tel. 01232/326681) stocks a good selection of linen, Tyrone crystal, Belleek china, and miniatures. **Smyth's Irish Linens** (14 Callender St., behind Marks & Spencer, no phone) carries a great selection of handkerchiefs, tablecloths, napkins, and other linen goods, which make excellent souvenirs or presents. If you've an interest in bric-a-brac, visit the **Variety Market,** a flea market you'll find on May Street every Tuesday and Friday morning.

Gifts

China Anyone driving around Lower Lough Erne should pass through the village of Belleek, which sits right on the border with the Republic, beside the sparkling River Erne. On the riverbank stands the Visitor's Center of **Belleek Pottery Ltd.** (tel. 01365/65501), producers of world-famous Belleek chinaware and porcelain. Here a factory, a showroom, a permanent exhibition, a Belleek pottery museum, and a café are all under one roof. On weekdays, a tour of the factory starts every half hour. You'll find hardly any noise in the workshops, however—everything at Belleek is handmade, using the exact process that was invented in 1857. The showroom is filled with beautiful gifts, but prices are high: A cup and saucer costs about U.K.£25–U.K.£30, and a bowl in a basket-weave style (very typical of Belleek) could cost you several hundred U.K. pounds. *Tel. 013656/58501. Admission free. Tours Mon.–Thurs. 9:30–4:15, Fri. 9:30–3:15.*

Celtic Weave China Ltd. (Cloghore, Ballyshannon, Co. Donegal, tel. 072/51844) is a family-run outfit just across the border from Belleek on the Ballyshannon road. You'll find it on the left side of the road as you approach the garda (police) checkpoint on the Irish Republic side. Celtic Weave specializes in the intricate basket-style design, decorated with sprays of colorful china flowers. The company's work has an excellent reputation, and many pieces are made on commission.

Glassware Visitors can watch classic pieces of full lead crystal being mouth-blown and hand-cut at **Tyrone Crystal** (Killybrackey, Dungannon, Co. Tyrone, tel. 018687/25335). Tours are conducted on weekdays—phone ahead for tour times.

Sports and the Outdoors

Northern Ireland is a favorite destination for connoisseurs of the great outdoors. Despite its popularity, the province offers open spaces, few crowds, and perfectly tranquil waterways and countryside. A free brochure, *Holiday Breakaways,* available from the Northern Ireland Tourist Board, details hotels and guest houses that especially suit sports and outdoor enthusiasts. For more information, *see* Staying in Northern Ireland, in Chapter 1, Essential Information.

Participant Sports

Bicycling Roads are good and fairly traffic-free, so cycling is popular. There's no need to have a bike of your own—many towns have places to rent them. Bicycle rentals cost around U.K.£3.50–U.K.£7 a day, U.K.£27 for a week. In Belfast, rent from **Ernie Coates** (108 Grand Parade, tel. 01232/471912) or **Bike It** (4 Belmont Rd., tel. 01232/471141). Local Tourist Information Offices can offer suggestions for good cycling routes.

Bird-watching The province has as wide a range of habitats for birds as could possibly be packed into such a tiny area, and the wealth of species satisfies all bird lovers. The best time to come is winter, but even in summer visitors can participate in first-class bird-watching, especially on the Antrim uplands, all down the Antrim coast, and on the offshore islands. For wildfowl and wading birds, the shores of Lough Neagh and Strangford Lough are exceptional. For information, ideas, and details of field-study groups, contact Northern Ireland Tourist Information Offices and the **Royal Society for the Protection of Birds** (Belvoir Park Forest, tel. 01232/692547).

Fishing With a 606-kilometer (466-mile) coastline, part on the Atlantic and part on the Irish Sea, as well as major lakes and an abundance of unpolluted rivers, Northern Ireland is a great place for anglers. Set your rod for shark and conger off the Antrim coast, for big skate and tope in Strangford Lough, and for salmon and rainbow trout in the Glens of Antrim.

To catch fish, whether coarse or game, you'll need a license from the **Fisheries Conservancy Board** (1 Mahon Rd., Portadown, tel. 01762/334666), the **Foyle Fisheries Commission** (8 Victoria Rd., Derry, tel. 01504/42100), or the **Northern Ireland Tourist Board** (59 North St., Belfast, tel. 01232/246609), depending on where you're fishing, and you'll probably need a local permit as well. The license cost for 15 days is U.K.£10.65, for a whole season U.K.£15.35. In addition, you must get permission from the owner of the land where you plan to fish and you may have to pay a charge. If the landowner is the **Department of Agriculture** (Stormont, Belfast, tel. 01232/63939), you'll have to pay for an additional permit (cost: U.K.£17 for 15 days, or U.K.£7 a day). You don't have to approach these bodies individually: All licenses and Department of Agriculture permits are available from the Northern Ireland Tourist Board in Belfast (tel. 01232/231221) or the **Lakeland Visitor Centre** (Enniskillen, tel. 01365/323110), as well as from a number of tackle shops around the province.

Scores of tackle shops are situated around the province, and 10 of them are in Belfast. Here are a few useful addresses in main angling areas: **J. A. Knaggs** (Main St., Ballinamallard, tel. 0136581/321), **R. Bell** (38 Ann St., Ballycastle, tel. 012657/62520), **Carlton Park Fishing Centre** (Belleek, tel. 0136565/8181), **Smyth's** (1 Park St., Coleraine, tel. 01265/43970), **Lakeland Tackle and Guns** (Sligo Rd., Enniskillen, tel. 01365/323774), **Four Seasons** (80 Main St., Newcastle, tel. 013967/25078), **Hook, Line & Sinker** (43 South St., Newtownards, tel. 01247/811671).

Golf Northern Ireland features more than 70 golf courses—many in spectacular coastal settings—that welcome visitors. Greens fees vary from about U.K.£7 to U.K.£50. A course is nearly always within reach of your hotel, with a dozen golf clubs within 8 kilometers (5 miles) of Belfast. The **Royal County Down** (Newcastle, tel. 013967/23314) is considered by many golfers to be one of the finest courses in the world. Another championship course is at the **Royal Portrush Golf Club** (Portrush, Co. Antrim, tel. 01265/822311). All golf courses and clubs are listed in the Northern Ireland Tourist Board information guide No. 17, *Golf—Where to Play*, available from main tourist offices.

Hiking Northern Ireland has plenty of magnificent walking country. Ask at tourist offices for details of the newly marked walking and cycling trails of "The Linen Homelands"—the country south of Belfast. The **Ulster Way,** in particular, is for the serious hiker, an 896-kilometer (560-mile) trek right around the six counties. Apart from the ability to read a map, no special skills are needed, and the terrain never demands more than a pair of stout walking shoes. Of course, visitors do not have to walk the whole trail; some sections are easier than others, and some of the best stretches are clearly marked. More than 100 places to stay along the Ulster Way are listed in the Northern Ireland Tourist Board information guide, *Accommodation for Walkers on the Ulster Way*. The **Sports Council for Northern Ireland** (House of Sport, Upper Malone Rd., Belfast BT9 5LA, tel. 01232/381222) can also give advice about the Ulster Way; it sells books covering each section of the route. Anyone who would like to try a hand at tougher walks in the hills should obtain the excellent and informative little handbook in the Irish Walks series, No. 4, *The North East*, by Richard Rogers (published by Gill & Macmillan, 15-17 Eden Quay, Dublin; the book should be available in local book and sporting goods stores in Northern Ireland). It gives precise details of 45 hill walks, complete with descriptions of the wildflowers you'll see along the way. For hikes in the Mountains of Mourne, you can obtain maps and details of suggested routes from **The Mourne Countryside Centre** (91 Central Promenade, Newcastle, Co. Down, tel. 013967/24059).

Horseback Riding/Pony Trekking Sitting on the back of a horse or pony is a great way to travel into places that are out of bounds to motorists. Woodland, beaches, and rough country become accessible on guided rides, some suitable for complete beginners. Some 35 riding and trekking centers are located around the province, and several of them offer accommodations. Trekking rates are mostly U.K.£4–U.K.£5 an hour, with small reductions for children. The most convenient center in the Belfast area is **Lagan Valley Equestrian Centre** (172 Upper Malone Rd., Belfast, tel. 01232/614853). The center is open Monday through Saturday throughout the year, and it charges an hourly rate of U.K.£6 adults, U.K.£5 children (minimum age 7). The center runs pony treks through the Lagan Valley Regional Park, as well as residential summer camps. If you're over in the Enniskillen/Lough Erne area, **Drumhoney Stables** (Lisnarick, 5 kilometers/3 miles west of Irvinestown, tel. 013656/21892) can teach you to ride, take you on a pony trek through Castle Archdale Country Park, or even rent you a pony and trap (suitable for two adults and up to four children). Hourly rates are U.K.£7 for adults, U.K.£5 for children. The stables also have residential accommodations.

Lake and River Cruising Inland cruising on the Erne waterway—777 square kilometers (300 square miles) of lakes and rivers—is one of Northern Ireland's major treats. Upper and Lower Lough Erne are enclosed by some of Ireland's finest scenery and are studded with more than 100 little islands. Out on the lakes and the River Erne, which links them, you'll have all the solitude you want, but you'll find company at loughside hostelries. To hire a good standard-size boat, contact **Erne Charter Boat Association** (Lakeland Visitor Centre, Enniskillen, Co. Fermanagh, tel. 01365/323110). Expect to pay at least U.K.£300 to hire a four-berth cruiser for two or three nights.

Spectator Sports

Ask any tourist office for the leaflet of the year's *Events*, which shows the dates and times of major sports occasions. Look out especially for the **hurling** and **Gaelic football** events. Dates of local matches are listed in local newspapers. During the summer, you'll come across **cricket** matches being played throughout the province. One oddity is the ancient precursor of bowls, called **bullets,** which is still played in County Armagh. It involves throwing bowls (originally they were cannonballs, hence the name) along a narrow winding country lane; the first to cover 3 kilometers (2 miles) is the winner. The All-Ireland Championship for this sport is held in early August.

Dining and Lodging

Dining

Northern Ireland cuisine is similar to cooking in the Republic: Good-quality fresh local fish or meat is prepared in a simple style. Except in Belfast, acceptable Continental dishes are difficult to find. Vegetables receive an unimaginative treatment, and you'll find a heavy emphasis on potatoes, which are often served in two different ways on the same plate. Yet the hearty, unpretentious home cooking available is tasty, nourishing, and above all *filling*, because portions tend to be huge.

Visitors will not find much on the menu that is unfamiliar. Ulster fry, an inexpensive café and pub dish, is something like an Irish breakfast: a sizzling portion of bacon, sausages, tomatoes, and eggs, served with potato bread or soda bread. Champ is another potato dish, this time a creamy, buttery mash with scallions. Some other traditional favorites that remain popular include Guinness soup, oysters from Strangford Lough, Ardglass herring, and smoked salmon from Ballamena. Be sure to check out the variety of freshly baked breads, which you can sample at teatime. Tea, especially when described as high tea, is usually served around 6 PM; it's a full meal of breads and buns, accompanied with sandwiches or savory hot dishes, and followed by fruit cake. Among the delicious baked fare are scones (white or whole-meal), farls (triangular griddle cakes leavened with soda and buttermilk), potato bread (solid stuff, sometimes eaten fried), and wheaten bread (dark brown, very heavy). Most pubs will serve a pot of tea and a plate of scones.

Quite apart from cafés, pubs, and restaurants, Northern Ireland has discovered the convenience of fast food. Wine bars are another up-and-coming kind of eatery; in reality these are just inexpensive restaurants with good wine lists. Most diners, though, still prefer to take a pot of tea with their food.

Without being formal, the Northern Irish tend to dress soberly. Men often wear a jacket and tie when dining out; but if you prefer to dress more casually, that is quite acceptable at most establishments. By the standards of the Republic or the United States, or even the rest of the United Kingdom, restaurant prices are surprisingly moderate. Tax is usually included in the price of a meal. A service charge of 10% may be indicated on the bill; it is customary to pay this, unless the service was bad.

Category	Cost*
$$$$	over U.K.£25
$$$	U.K.£15–U.K.£25
$$	U.K.£10–U.K.£15
$	under U.K.£10

** per person for a typical three-course meal, including tax and service but excluding drinks*

Lodging

Northern Ireland has some good modern hotels but hardly any lodging in the more expensive categories. Travelers often find that the most enjoyable accommodations are low-cost guest houses (often family-run), offering bed and breakfast. Most B&Bs provide an evening meal as well, if needed. Visitors can choose from the humblest terraced town houses or farm cottages to the grandest country houses. Dining rooms of country-house lodgings frequently reach the standard of top-quality restaurants.

For details on Northern Ireland's six youth hostels, contact **Y.H.A.N.I.** (56 Bradbury Pl., Belfast BT7 1RU, tel. 01232/324733). All accommodations in the province are inspected and categorized by the Northern Ireland Tourist Board, which publishes all names, addresses, and ratings in the handbook *Where to Stay* (U.K.£3.50).

Category	Cost*
$$$$	over U.K.£135
$$$	U.K.£70–U.K.£135
$$	U.K.£40–U.K.£70
$	under U.K.£40

**All prices are for a standard double room, including breakfast and tax.*

Highly recommended restaurants and hotels are indicated by a star ★.

Belfast

Dining ★ **Roscoff.** This Golden Mile restaurant is now widely acclaimed as one of the best in the six counties or, indeed, the whole of Ireland. You're likely to hear the chat of barristers and government ministers at other tables. The curious decor is supposed to be reminiscent of the sea, with wave-shaped motifs, portholes, and a cloth-covered ceiling resembling billowing sails. The specialty is Breton fish and seafood all bought fresh each day (Roscoff is a port on the Brittany coast of France), though there are fine meat dishes as well. Portions are generous and accompanied by large quantities of vegetables. Among the starters is a toasted goat-cheese salad with avocado and walnut oil; as a main course try the excellent crispy duck confit. From the delicious desserts, sample the roast pears with freshly made chestnut and honey ice cream. *Shaftesbury Sq. (at the end of Great Victo-*

ria St.), tel. 01232/331532. Reservations advised. Jacket and tie advised. AE, DC, MC, V. Closed Fri. evening and Sun. $$$–$$$$

La Belle Epoque. Relaxed and intimate, this well-established restaurant offers a French charm, with Art Nouveau decor reminiscent of Paris. The menu features smoked salmon stuffed with fish mousse in a horseradish sauce as an appetizer, and a main course of fillet of beef with mustard and cream sauce. For dessert, you can't go wrong with the freshly made fruit sorbets. The set-price lunch menu is excellent value. *103 Great Victoria St., tel. 01232/323244. Reservations advised (required on weekends). Dress: casual. AE, DC, MC, V. Closed Sun. Lunch: $ Dinner: $$$*

★ **Restaurant 44.** This green-fronted establishment on a corner in the Golden Mile area is certainly one of the best and most agreeable eating places in Northern Ireland. Inside it has smart colonial decor, with green cane chairs, slatted shutters, a wooden ceiling fan, and a mural of elephants in India. The well-presented menu offers an imaginative, international array of dishes. Start with Stilton mousse with poached pears in port sauce, try a main course of paupiettes of salmon filled with a prawn mousse and served with lobster sauce, and end with an unusual floating island with fresh caramel. There are excellent vegetarian dishes (clearly marked on the menu) for every course, such as baked papaya with a rich tomato sauce and crispy noodles. *44 Bedford St., tel. 01232/244844. Reservations required. Dress: casual but neat. AE, DC, MC, V. Closed Sat. lunch and Sun. $$$*

Bananas. Adjoining Restaurant 44, with the same owners and kitchen, Bananas is as good as its neighbor. It features a similar but less opulent colonial style, with cane furniture, a plain wood floor, and ceiling fans. Palms grow in flowerpots that are made from old chimneys. The mixed international menu includes Continental and Asian cuisines, as well as many of the same dishes that are served next door. The choice ranges from Spanish tapas to Oriental stir-fry to pork escalope. There's a relaxed, brasserie-type atmosphere, and it's much brighter, noisier, and livelier than its neighbor. *44 Bedford St., tel. 01232/339999. Reservations required. Dress: informal. AE, DC, MC, V. Closed Fri. evening and Sun. $$*

Belfast Castle. Ben Madigan's is the name of the more stylish upstairs restaurant inside this grand Belfast landmark in the pleasant park on top of Cave Hill. The table in the bay window has a panoramic view over the city and lake. The Castle is not ancient but is imposing, with big rooms, paneled ceilings, and a huge stairway. The misspelled menu offers elaborate, generous, and vaguely French dishes. The restaurant is recommended for its setting. In the basement there's an atmospheric, old-fashioned bar and a wine bar with cheaper meals. *Cave Hill, tel. 01232/776925. Reservations advised. Jacket and tie advised. AE, DC, MC, V. $$*

The Strand. In the popular University Area, this dark and intimate bistro with candlelighted tables attracts students and professors with its adventurous and unusual menu. Recommended dishes include chicken pancakes, peanut plaice, or cod in coconut and apple sauce. For dessert try the cream-laden gâteaux. Several vegetarian entrées are available, such as broccoli and cashew-nut flan. *12 Stranmillis Rd., tel. 01232/682266. Reservations advised. Dress: casual. AE, DC, MC, V. $$*

Saints and Scholars. This University Area restaurant offers two distinct sections. The downstairs "library" has bookshelves on the walls, but the lively, noisy, and cheerful ambience could hardly be less studious. Upstairs, you'll find a calmer and more comfortable dining room. One of the special appetizers is deep-fried brie with gooseberry sauce. Main dishes include a hearty cassoulet (a rich, meaty stew with duck, sausages, and beans), wok-roasted monkfish, and Seafood Harmony (a selection of baked or poached fish with thermidor sauce). Many vegetarian dishes are available, such as mushrooms stuffed with cream cheese and avocado. The rich dessert crepes, supposedly made according to a recipe from the Danish royal court, are truly fit for a king. *3 University St., tel. 01232/325137. Reservations required. Dress: casual. AE, DC, MC, V. $*

Lodging

★ **Culloden Hotel.** Eight kilometers (5 miles) from the city center on the A2, this former 19th-century Scottish baronial mansion stands grandly amid 12 acres of woods and parkland. The public areas feature ornate woodwork, Louis XV chandeliers, decorative plasterwork, and stained glass. Bedrooms, both in the original section and in a newer wing, feature silk and velvet decor and fine views. The excellent dining areas include the large French Mitre Restaurant, with mahogany tables and a garden view, and a Grill Bar, which serves both snacks and meals. The hotel is in a peaceful part of town, close to the Ulster Folk Museum. *142 Bangor Rd., Holywood, Co. Down BT18 0EX, tel. 012317/425223. 91 rooms with bath. Facilities: restaurant, grill bar, tennis court, squash, croquet, games room, snooker, laundry, 24-hr room service. AE, DC, MC, V. $$$$*

Dukes Hotel. This delightful, modern hotel with a touch of style in the heart of the University area, though small, has a spacious lobby, good facilities, and an interesting restaurant (which leans toward healthy eating, with several vegetarian options). An unusual feature is the waterfall running down steps beside the stairs. Decor is smart gray, enlivened with plenty of greenery. The comfortable and well-laid-out rooms come with satellite TV, phones, and blow-dryers, and many have good views of the hills beyond the city. *65–67 University St., tel. 01232/236666. 21 rooms with bath. Facilities: restaurant, bars, conference rooms, sauna, gym. AE, DC, MC, V. $$$*

★ **Europa Hotel.** This popular modern high-rise city-center hotel has long attracted visiting journalists and business travelers. What it lacks in period charm is compensated for by the polite and efficient staff and the comfortable ambience. Bedrooms are blandly decorated, but they are warm, clean, and functional and offer all the modern conveniences. The hotel, conveniently near the Opera House, is only 1.6 kilometers (1 mile) from the train station and 6.5 kilometers (4 miles) from the airport. *Great Victoria St., Belfast BT2 7AP, tel. 01232/327000. 200 rooms with bath. Facilities: restaurant, café, bar, secretarial services, laundry, 24-hr security. AE, DC, MC, V. $$$*

Novotel Belfast. The reliable, well-established international Novotel chain, based in France, owns this comfortable modern hotel at Belfast (Aldergrove) International Airport. Rooms are generously equipped, with a double and single bed, satellite TV, and full bathroom. The location is particularly good for anyone planning a brief visit to the province and not wishing to stay within the city. *Belfast International Airport, tel. 018494/22033. 108 rooms with bath. Facilities: restaurant, bar, gym, sauna, conference rooms. AE, DC, MC, V. $$$*

Templeton Hotel. Midway between the city and the airport, this new hotel has an interior with distinctive woodwork. Bedrooms feature pastel fabrics and polished pine and are well equipped with blow-dryers, trouser presses, and cable TVs. There are three different places to dine; the main restaurant has good, hearty Irish cuisine and attractive blue and pink decor. *882 Antrim Rd., Templepatrick, Ballyclare (about 6 mi from Belfast), tel. 018494/432984. 20 rooms with bath. Facilities: restaurants, bar. AE, DC, MC, V. $$$*

Wellington Park Hotel. Formerly a private residence, this modernized establishment is among the best in the Queen's University area of town. Many evening visitors enjoy the relaxed bars, live music, and good food at this friendly family-run hotel. The quiet bedrooms are well-designed, with built-in wooden furniture; some of them feature loft sleeping areas. *21 Malone Rd., Belfast BT9 6RU, tel. 01232/381111. 50 rooms with bath or shower. Facilities: restaurant, bar, laundry. AE, DC, MC, V. $$$*

★ **Ash-Rowan Guest House.** Award-winning former restaurateurs Sam and Evelyn Hazlett own and run this outstanding B&B in a spacious Victorian home. Every bedroom has been decorated in a tasteful individual style, and each has a private bath and TV. Guests have access to a library. Breakfasts and dinners, prepared by the owners, are first-rate. This no-smoking house is on a tranquil residential street near Queen's University and the Ulster Museum. *Mrs. E. Hazlett, 12 Windsor Ave., Belfast BT9 6EE, tel. 01232/661758. 4 rooms with bath. MC, V. Closed Dec. $$*

Quality Plaza Hotel. This modern hotel, centrally located between Great Victoria and Bedford streets, has a decor of muted grays and pretty floral fabrics. Bedrooms and bathrooms are rather small and cramped, but all rooms have cable TV, a phone, a blow-dryer, and a trouser press. Room service can bring up a full three-course meal at any time of day or night. *15 Brunswick St., tel. 01232/333555. 83 rooms with bath. Facilities: restaurant, conference rooms. AE, DC, MC, V. $$*

Camera House. Mrs. Drumm runs this delightful B&B in a brick Victorian house with bay windows. Bedrooms are clean, cheerful, and simply furnished. You'll appreciate the friendly welcome and the generous breakfasts. *Mrs. A. Drumm, Camera House, 44 Wellington Park, Belfast BT9 6DP, tel. 01232/660026. 11 rooms, 7 with bath or shower. MC, V. $*

The Cottage. Aptly named, this lovely little B&B in Mrs. Muldoon's immaculate white home, 8 kilometers (5 miles) east of Belfast, has a charming flower-filled garden in the back. It's as rural a setting as you're likely to find so close to the city center. The traditional country-house decor combines beautiful antiques and modern comforts in the bedrooms. *Mrs. E. Muldoon, The Cottage, 377 Comber Rd., Dundonald, Belfast BT16 0XB, tel. 01247/878189. 3 rooms, 1 with bath. No credit cards. $*

Carrickfergus

Dining and Lodging

Dobbins Inn. Still thriving after more than three centuries, this modest family-run hotel on High Street attracts locals to its convivial bar, especially during live music performances on Sunday, Monday, and Tuesday evenings. The adequate bedrooms offer private baths, TVs, and tea-making equipment. High tea is available, and the DeCourcy restaurant serves an acceptable dinner. *6–8 High St., Carrickfergus, Co. Antrim, BT38 9HE, tel. 019603/51905. 13 rooms with bath. Facilities: restaurant, baby-sitting service. MC, V. $$*

Coleraine Area

Dining and Lodging

★ **Blackheath House.** Thirteen kilometers (8 miles) south of Coleraine, this fine country house, surrounded by magnificent countryside, was built as the home of the 18th-century bishop of Derry. The brown structure is within close driving distance of golf courses and the Causeway Coast beaches and cliff walks; the home retains a genteel character and stands amid 2 acres of landscaped gardens. Among its more modern comforts is an indoor swimming pool. The large bedrooms—including a four-poster room, a French Colonial room, and a pine room—have been individually decorated with a mixture of modern and antique furniture. The drawing room, with a fine marble fireplace, is filled with old pieces of furniture. Down in the cellars lies MacDuff's, a first-class expensive restaurant, open to nonresidents, where proprietors Joseph and Margaret Erwin provide excellent meals prepared with farm-fresh meats and local vegetables, game, and seafood. The menu offers steak in blue cheese sauce, sole in a sauce of tomato and herbs, and a good wine list. Breakfasts are filling, with a generous Ulster fry. *112 Killeague Rd., Blackhill, Coleraine, Co. Londonderry BT51 4HH, tel. 01265/868433. 6 rooms, 5 with bath. Facilities: restaurant (closed Sun. and Mon.), pool. No credit cards. $$*

Greenhill House. This charming Georgian country house about 13 kilometers (8 miles) south of Coleraine is run by Elizabeth and James Hegarty and provides a peaceful retreat. Guests enjoy the pleasantly decorated bedrooms, the substantial breakfasts, and the excellent dinners of locally caught fish, Ulster beef, and homemade bread and cakes. *24 Greenhill Rd., Aghadowey, Co. Londonderry BT51 4EU, tel. 01265/868241. 6 rooms with bath. No credit cards. Closed Nov.–Feb. $*

Lodging **Camus House.** Follow the road along the Bann valley south from Coleraine; 6½ kilometers (4 miles) out of town, you'll arrive at this appealing Georgian farmhouse that dates from 1685. Today it's a relaxed and gracious guest house, elegantly furnished, with a snug sitting room with a stone fireplace. Proprietor Josephine King provides a friendly atmosphere and a hearty breakfast. The pleasant bedrooms, decorated in pastel colors, have tasteful modern furnishings, reading lamps, and large closets. *27 Curragh Rd., Coleraine, Co. Londonderry BT51 3RY, tel. 01265/42982. 3 rooms without bath. No credit cards. $*

Derry City

Dining and Lodging **White Horse Hotel.** In the countryside overlooking Lough Foyle, yet only 8 kilometers (5 miles) northeast of Derry City on the road to Limavady, this former inn has been enlarged into a comfortable modern hotel that caters to business and vacation visitors and offers remarkable value. Bedrooms are clean and unpretentiously furnished, with TVs and tea-making equipment. Locals and guests alike enjoy the good Irish meals served at the relaxed grill bar or more formal restaurant. *68 Clooney Rd., Campsie, Co. Londonderry BT47 3PA, tel. 01504/860606. 50 rooms with bath. Facilities: restaurant, bar, 24-hr valet service. MC, V. $$*

Downpatrick/Ards Area

Dining and Lodging **Portaferry Inn.** Standing on the quayside (or "strand") overlooking the narrow channel that connects Lough Strangford to the sea, this centuries-old whitewashed inn offers well-kept, simply furnished double rooms. The main action takes place in the popular bar and restaurant, where unadventurous but competent breakfasts, lunches, and dinners are briskly served. *10 The Strand, Portaferry, Co. Down, BT22 1PE, tel. 012472/28231. 14 double rooms with bath or shower. Facilities: restaurant, bar/lounge, boat mooring, laundry. AE, DC, MC, V. $$$*

Enniskillen and Environs

Dining and Lodging ★

Jamestown House. Tucked away in lush, tranquil countryside near Lower Lough Erne and 11 kilometers (7 miles) from Enniskillen, this dignified country house dates from 1760 and is run by Arthur and Helen Stuart. The large, attractive bedrooms feature modern furnishings, and elegant drawing and dining rooms contain older fine polished mahogany pieces. Staying here is just like visiting friends in the country. A river runs through the grounds—Mr. Stuart is keen on angling and advises visitors on the best spots to fish in the area. Breakfasts and the expensive set dinners are generous and satisfying. *Magheracross, Ballinamallard, Co. Fermanagh, tel. 0136581/209. 3 rooms with bath or shower. No credit cards. $$*

Glens of Antrim

Dining and Lodging

Ballygally Castle. At the Larne end of the North Antrim coast drive, 40 kilometers (25 miles) from Belfast, you'll find an impressive little castle, complete with pointed turrets, facing the Ballygally Bay, which was built by a Scottish lord in 1625. After centuries of defending itself from invaders, the castle now cheerfully invites visitors to sample a good night's sleep and hearty breakfast within its substantial stone walls; modern plumbing and central heating have been skillfully integrated into the old Scottish-style design, but a recent extension, unfortunately, does not complement the castle architecture. Bedrooms, some of them in the castle turrets, have been individually decorated with comfortable furnishings. In the dining room a decent table d'hôte evening meal is served (to music, on Saturdays), and a Sunday high tea is also available. *Ballygally Castle, 274 Coast Rd., Ballygally, Co. Antrim BT40 2RA, tel. 01574/583212. 30 rooms with bath. Facilities: bar, dining room, baby-sitting, fishing on grounds. MC, V. $$*

Londonderry Arms. This ivy-covered traditional hotel by Carnlough Harbour, built as a coaching inn in 1848, features a lovely seaside garden, unique antique carved furnishings, regional paintings and maps, and Georgian period decor. The lodging once belonged to Sir Winston Churchill, and since 1947 it has been owned and run by the O'Neill family. A dozen of the bedrooms feature Georgian antiques, and the rest offer functional contemporary decor. Rooms 2, 8, and 9 are recommended for their spaciousness and good views. The hotel serves a substantial traditional Irish meal that relies on local seafood; bread and scones are homemade. Traditional Irish music is provided during the summer months. *Harbour Rd., Carnlough, Co. Antrim BT44 0EU, tel. 01574/885255. 21 rooms with bath. AE, DC, MC, V. $$*

Mountains of Mourne Area

Dining and Lodging

Slieve Donard Hotel. A lavish redbrick monument to Victoriana, this turreted hotel stands like a palace on spacious green lawns at one end of Newcastle's 6½-kilometer (4-mile) sandy beach. Guests will feel as if they are stepping back to the town's turn-of-the-century heyday as an elegant seaside resort, even though the rooms now have every modern comfort. Ask for a room overlooking the water. The relaxed gate-house pub/dining room serves adequate seafood dishes; folk music is presented every Saturday night. For daytime relaxation, walk the airy promenade or visit the Royal County Down Golf Club, right next door. *Downs Rd., Newcastle, Co. Down BT33 0AH, tel. 013967/23681. 120 rooms with bath. Facilities: pub/dining* *room, recreation center with 2 tennis courts and indoor pool. AE, DC, MC, V. $$$*

The Arts and Nightlife

The Arts

Just about all of Northern Ireland's arts and cultural activity is concentrated in Belfast. The *Belfast Telegraph* newspaper lists arts events. The high point of the province's cultural year is the **Belfast International Festival of Arts,** lasting a couple of weeks each November. It offers a full schedule of dramatic and musical events centered at Whitla Hall, at Queen's University. The **Belfast Folk Festival** in September is a weekend of traditional foot-tapping Irish music and dance at downtown locations.

Film **Cannon Cinema** (Great Victoria St., tel. 01232/322484), with four screens, and **Curzon Cinema** (Ormeau Rd., tel. 01232/641373), with three screens, are two of several city-center movie theaters showing new British and American releases and big box-office favorites.

Queen's Film Theatre is Belfast's art cinema, with two screens showing domestic and foreign movies. *University Sq. Mews, off Botanic Ave., tel. 01232/667687. Open during university semesters only.*

Music **The Ulster Hall** (Linenhall St., tel. 01232/241917) is the large city-center concert hall where classical orchestral pieces are performed; the center is the home base of the Ulster Orchestra. The hall has a splendid Victorian organ, so organ recitals are often held. Sometimes rock concerts are also scheduled here.

Whitla Hall (Queen's University, tel. 01232/245133) hosts classical concerts and recitals throughout the year.

Harberton Theatre (Harberton Park, Balmoral, tel. 01232/661302), in the southwest suburbs, is the home of the Ulster Operatic Society, which presents concerts and musicals.

Grosvenor Hall (Glengall St., tel. 01232/241917) is the place for some down-home music, including country-and-western, gospel, and folk concerts.

Theater and Opera **The Arts Theatre** (Botanic Ave., tel. 01232/324936), near the University Area, specializes in laugh-a-minute comedies and lightweight productions.

The Grand Opera House, a beautifully restored Victorian playhouse, has no company of its own but books shows from all over the British Isles and sometimes farther afield. It puts on a constant stream of plays of widely differing kinds, plus occasional operas and ballets. *Great Victoria St., tel. 01232/241919. Tickets: U.K.£4–U.K.£20.*

The Group Theatre is a showcase for Belfast's local dramatic societies. *Bedford St., tel. 01232/329685. Tickets: Mon.–Thurs. U.K.£2.50, Fri. and Sat. U.K.£3.*

The Lyric Theatre, in the south of Belfast, stages thoughtful drama played by its resident company and draws most of its inspiration from traditional Irish culture. *Ridgeway St., tel. 01232/381081. Tickets: Mon.–Thur. U.K.£6.50 or U.K.£8.50, Fri. and Sat. U.K.£7.50 or U.K.£9.50.*

Nightlife

A night out in Northern Ireland usually means an evening at a pub—that's where most entertainment takes place. The most popular pubs are those lively, convivial places where traditional Irish folk music is played frequently, and often quite spontaneously. They can be found in towns and villages all over the province, and the best way to locate them is to ask where to find a "singing pub." Pubs, by the way, close at around 11:30 PM.

Belfast
Golden Mile Area

Robinsons (next to the Crown Liquor Saloon, Great Victoria St., tel. 01232/329812) is a popular pub appealing to a young crowd. **The Beaten Docket** (also next to the Crown, tel. 01232/242926) is a noisier modern pub that attracts an even younger crowd than Robinsons; it features up-to-the-minute music. **Limelight** (Ormeau Ave., tel. 01232/325968) is a disco nightclub with cabaret on Tuesday, Friday, and Saturday, and music on other nights. **The Linenhall** (Clarence St., tel. 01232/248458) is a pub with a music lounge, where jazz is performed on Monday, Wednesday, and Saturday, and rock music on Thursday.

University Area

The Eglantine (tel. 01232/667994) and **The Botanic** (tel. 01232/660460), known as the Egg and the Bot to their student clientele, are two big, popular disco pubs facing each other across Malone Road.

City Center/Docks

Pat's Bar (Prince's Dock Rd., tel. 0232/744524) and **Maddens** (Smithfield, tel. 01232/244114) are popular pubs with first-rate sessions of traditional music. **The Rotterdam** (Pilot St., tel. 01232/746021) features folk, jazz, and blues performers. **Kelly's Cellars** (Bank St., tel. 01232/324835) offers blues on Saturday nights.

Index

Abbey Presbyterian Church, *96*
Abbeys. *See* Monasteries and abbeys
Abbey Theatre, *145*
Achill Island, *292, 311, 319, 332*
Adair, John George, *353*
Adare, *260, 270*
Aghadoe, *252*
Ailwee Cave, *299*
Albert Memorial Clock Tower, *383*
Allihies, *263*
Allingham, William, *345*
American Express, *10, 11*
Andrew Jackson Centre, *385*
Anglican Parish Church (Monkstown), *107*
Annaghmakerrig, *183*
Annals of the Four Masters, *345–346*
Annascaul, *255*
Anne's Grove Gardens, *262*
Annestown, *214*
Antiques, *9, 37, 263*
Apartment rentals, *43–44*
Aquariums, *394*
Aran Interpretive Center, *305*
Aran Islands
ferry service to, *34, 294*
hotels, *319*
plane travel to, *33, 294–295*
pubs, *332*
sightseeing, *305–307*
tourist information, *292*
Aranmore, *352–353*
Aran sweaters, *38*
Arbour Hill Cemetery, *97, 99*
Ardara
pubs, *370*
restaurants and hotels, *362*
shopping, *357*
sightseeing, *347–348*
Ardboe, *395*
Ardee, *159, 171*
Ardmore, *215*
Ardmore Tower, *215*
Ards Forest Park, *351*
Ards Peninsula, *393*
Arklow, *154*
Arklow Pottery Factory, *154*
Armagh, *374, 391–392*
Art galleries and museums
Dublin, *87, 93, 94, 95, 100, 106, 111*
Dublin environs, *155*
the Northwest, *338, 354*
the Southwest, *239, 243–244, 261, 286*
the West, *331*
Ashford, *152*
Ashford Castle, *307–308*
Ashtown Castle, *99*
Askeaton, *260*
Astronomy Centre and Planetarium, *392*
Athlone, *175, 180–181, 189*
Athlone Castle, *180–181*
Athy, *167*
ATMs (automatic teller machines), *11*
Aughnanure Castle, *307*
Avoca, *154*
Avoca Handweavers, *154*
Avondale Forest Park, *153–154*
Avondale House, *153–154*
Bailey Restaurant, *102, 104*
Baily Lighthouse, *111*
Ballina
hotels, *319–320*
pubs, *332*
shopping, *314*
sightseeing, *311–312*
tourist information, *292*
Ballinasloe, *8*
Ballinspittle, *246*
Ballitore, *167*
Ballsbridge
restaurants, *131, 134–135*
sightseeing, *106*
Ballybunion, *259*
Ballycastle, *8, 386*
Ballyclare, *8*
Ballyconnell, *189*
Ballydavid, *257*
Ballyferriter, *257, 270*
Ballyhack, *210*
Ballylane Farm, *205*
Ballylickey, *271*
Ballyliffin, *355*
Ballymote, *356, 363*
Ballynahinch Castle, *308*
Ballynahinch Lake, *308*
Ballyporeen, *216*
Ballyshannon
shopping, *358*
sightseeing, *344–345*
theater, *369*
Ballyvaughan, *320, 332*
Balmoral, *8*
Balor's Fort, *352*
Baltimore, *248, 271*
Baltray, *160*
Banagher, *179*
Bank of Ireland building, *87, 90*
Banks, *10, 11, 36*
Northern Ireland, *46, 376*
Bantry
hotels, *271*
sightseeing, *248–249*
tourist information, *234*
Bantry Bay, *249*
Bantry House, *248*
Bantry 1796 French Armada Exhibition Center, *248–249*
Barnacle, Nora, *312*
Barry, John, *206*
Barryscourt Castle, *245*
Battle of the Boyne
battle site, *161*
festival commemorating, *8*
Beaches, *40*
Dublin, *106, 119*
Dublin environs, *154*
Southeast, *215*
Wexford, *209*
Beaghmore, *395*
Beara Peninsula, *262–263*
Beckett, Samuel, *391*
Bed-and-breakfasts, *4, 43*
Bed of Diarmuid and Grainne (chamber tomb), *306*
Belfast
the arts, *406*
City Hall, *379*
climate, *6*
emergencies, *374*
festivals, *8*
guided tours, *376*
hotels, *402–403*
nightlife, *407*
pubs, *379, 383–384, 407*
restaurants, *400–402*
shopping, *396*
sightseeing, *378–379, 382–384, 395*
tourist information, *374*
transportation, *374–376*
Belfast Castle, *395*
Bella Cohen's Brothel, *102*
Bellamont Forest, *183*
Belleek, *8, 358, 390*
Belleek Pottery, *344, 358, 390, 396*
Belvedere College, *102*
Belvedere House Gardens, *185*
Benbeg, *352*
Ben Breeze Open Farm, *185*
Bessbrook, *392*
Bewley's Café, *91*
Bicycling, *38*
Dublin, *117*

Lakelands, *186–187*
Northern Ireland, *397*
the Northwest, *359*
the Southeast, *220*
the Southwest, *264*
tours, *4*
the West, *314*
Bird sanctuary, *157, 209*
Bird-watching, *8*
Northern Ireland, *397*
the Northwest, *359*
the Southeast, *209*
Birr, *177, 179, 189–190*
Birr Castle Demesne, *177, 179*
Bishop Lucey Park, *243*
Bishop's Palace, *212*
Bishop's Walk, *217*
Black Abbey, *202–203*
Black Castle (Leighlinbridge), *199*
Black Castle (Wicklow Town), *150, 152*
Blackfriars Abbey, *213*
Blackrock, *107, 114, 132, 133*
Blackrock Castle, *245*
Blankets, *38*
Blarney, *244*
Blarney Castle, *244*
Blarney Castle House, *244*
Blasket Centre, *256*
Blasket Islands, *256*
Blennerville, *258*
Blessington, *155*
Bloody Foreland Head, *352*
Bloomsday celebration, *7*
Boardsailing, *38, 267, 314–315*
Boating and sailing, *38, 39*
Lakelands, *187*
Northern Ireland, *47, 398–399*
the Southwest, *267*
the West, *314–315*
Bog tour, *180*
Bonamargy Friary, *386*
Book of Ballymote, *356*
Book of Kells, *87, 164*
Bookshops, *116*
Books on Ireland, *25–27*
Booterstown, *106*
Borrisokane, *190*
Botanic Gardens (Belfast), *384*
Botanic Gardens (Dublin), *108–109*
Bowling, *117, 399*
Boyle, *175, 181*
Boyle Abbey, *181*
Bray, *156, 169*
Brendan the Navigator, *258*
Breweries, *100*
Brian Boru, High King, *392*
Bridge End, *356*
Brittas Bay, *154*
Browne's Hill Dolmen, *199*
Bru Boru Heritage Center, *218*
Bruckless, *347, 363*
Brukless House, *347*
Bullets (game), *399*
Bull Island, *119*
Buncrana, *355*
Bundoran, *335, 444*
Bunmahon, *214*
Bunratty Castle and Folk Park, *261–262, 287*
Burke, Edmund, *167*
The Burren, *7, 299*
Burren Display Center, *299*
Burtonport, *352*
Bushmills, *377, 387*
Business hours, *36*
Northern Ireland, *46*
Bus travel, *32, 34*
Dublin, *84*
Dublin environs, *149*
Lakelands, *176–177*
Northern Ireland, *45, 375, 376*
the Northwest, *336, 337*
the Southeast, *198*
the Southwest, *235, 236*
the West, *293, 294*
Butterfly farm, *165*
Caherdaniel, *253*
Cahir, *216, 223*
Cahir Castle, *216*
Cahirciveen, *254*
Camping, *44*
Candle factory, *112*
Cape Clear Island, *248*
Cappoquin, *216*
Caragh Lake, *255, 271*
Carlingford, *158*
Carlow Castle, *199*
Carlow Town, *197, 199*
Carmelite Church, *91*
Carndonagh, *355*
Carnlough, *374, 386*
Car rentals, *18–19*
Dublin environs, *149*
Northern Ireland, *18, 376*
the Northwest, *336–337*
the Southeast, *197*
the Southwest, *236*
Carrick, *347*
Carrick-a-Rede, *386*
Carrickfergus, *374, 385, 403*
Carrickfergus Castle, *385*
Carrickmacross, *190–191*
Carrick-on-Shannon, *335, 356*
Carrick-on-Suir, *219*
Carrigart, *350*
Carriglass Manor, *182*
Carrowmore, *341*
Carton House, *165*
Car travel
border crossing, *32*
Dublin, *84*
Dublin environs, *149*
ferries for cars, *31–32*
Lakelands, *176*
Northern Ireland, *44–45, 375–376*
the Northwest, *336*
parking, *33–34*
road conditions, *33*
road signs, *33*
rules of the road, *33*
the Southeast, *197, 198*
the Southwest, *235–236*
the West, *293–294*
Casement, Sir Roger, *108*
Cashel, *197, 217–218, 223–224*
Cashel Bay, *308, 320–321*
Cashel Folk Village, *218*
Cash machines, *11*
Casino landmark (Dublin), *109*
Castle Archdale Country Park, *390*
Castlebaldwin, *363–364*
Castlebar, *292*
Castle Coole, *391*
Castledermot, *168, 172*
Castle Dobbs, *385*
Castlelyons, *271–272*
Castle Leslie, *184*
Castle Matrix, *260*
Castlepollard, *184*
Castles
Dublin, *90, 99, 107, 111*
Dublin environs, *150, 152, 158, 161–162, 163, 165*
Lakelands, *177, 179, 180–181, 184–185, 186*
Northern Ireland, *385, 387, 391, 393, 395*
the Northwest, *341, 345, 351, 353*
the Southeast, *199, 203, 206, 209, 210, 215–216, 219*
the Southwest, *244, 245, 251, 259–260, 261, 262*
the West, *300, 302, 306, 307–308, 309*
Castletown House, *164–165*
Castletownshend, *248*
Castle Ward, *393*
Cathedral of Glendalough, *153*
Cathedral of St. Carthage, *216*
Cathedral of St. Declan, *215*
Cathedral of St. Fachan, *299*
Cathedral of the Assumption, *199*

Catholic Cathedral (Armagh), *392*
Catholic Cathedral (Galway), *304*
Catholic Cathedral of Christ the King (Mullingar), *185*
Cavan, *175, 182*
Cavan Crystal, *182*
Cavan Folk Museum, *182*
Cave Hill, *395*
Caverns
the Southeast, *203–204, 216*
the West, *299*
Celbridge, *164*
Celtic Weave China, Ltd., *390, 396*
Celtword, *214*
Cemeteries
Dublin, *93, 97, 99, 108*
Dublin environs, *163*
Charles Fort, *246*
Charleville Castle, *186*
Cheeses, *37*
Chester Beatty Library, *106*
Children
Dublin attractions, *112*
traveling with, *22–23*
Chinaware, *344, 358, 390, 396*
Christ Church Cathedral (Dublin), *101*
Christ Church Cathedral (Waterford), *213*
Churches
Belfast, *383, 395*
Dublin, *90, 91, 95, 96, 97, 99, 100, 101, 107*
Dublin environs, *152, 153, 157, 159–160, 162, 163, 164, 166*
Lakelands, *185, 186*
Northern Ireland, *383, 389, 392, 395*
the Northwest, *338, 340*
the Southeast, *199, 202, 206, 208, 212, 213, 215, 216, 217–218*
the Southwest, *239, 243, 245, 257–258, 260*
the West, *299, 302, 304, 306*
Church of the Assumption (Wexford), *208*
Church of the Holy Trinity (Dublin), *90*
Church of the Immaculate Conception (Wexford), *208*
Church of Kevin, *306*
Church of St. John the Evangelist, *186*
Church of St. Theresa's (Dublin), *91*
City Hall (Belfast), *379*
City Hall (Waterford), *212*
Claddagh, *304*
Clare Heritage Center, *299–300*
Claremorris, *332*
Clarinbridge, *300, 321*
Clarke, Harry, *91*
Clifden
festivals, *7*
hotels, *321–322*
pubs, *332*
restaurants, *321*
shopping, *313*
sightseeing, *308–309*
tourist information, *292*
Clifden Castle, *309*
Cliffs of Moher, *292, 298*
Climate, *5–6*
Clogherhead, *160*
Clogher Strand, *257*
Clonakilty, *234, 247, 288*
Clones, *183–184, 191*
Clones Lace Centre, *184*
Clonmacnoise, *180*
Clonmany, *355*
Clonmel, *218–219, 224*
Cloyne, *272*
Cnoc an Linsigh (forest area), *164*
Cobh, *245*
Cody, "Buffalo" Bill, *208*
Coleraine, *387, 403–404*
Colleges and universities
Belfast, *378, 384*
Dublin, *86–87, 102*
Dublin environs, *165*
Northern Ireland, *378, 384*
the Northwest, *351*
the Southeast, *209*
the Southwest, *243–244, 261*
the West, *304–305*
Collegiate Church of St. Nicholas, *302*
Collon, *170, 171*
Collooney, *364*
Colmcille Heritage Centre, *354*
Columba, St., *343, 347, 354*
Computers, *16*
Concerts. *See* Music, classical
Cong, *307–308, 322–323*
Connemara National Park, *307*
Connemara region, *307–310*
Connolly, James, *97, 100*
Connor Pass, *258*
Conor Fort, *306*
Convents
Dublin environs, *159*
the West, *309*
Cookstown, *395*
Coolattin Wood, *154–155*
Coolbanagher, *186*
Coole Park, *300*
Cootehill, *183, 191*
Corca Dhuibhne, *255*
Cork
the arts, *286–287*
climate, *6*
festivals, *7, 8*
hotels, *273–275*
parking, *34*
pubs, *239, 288*
restaurants, *272*
shopping, *37–38, 239, 243, 244, 272–273*
sightseeing, *238–239, 243–245*
tourist information, *234*
Cork Public Museum, *244*
Cormac's Chapel, *217–218*
Corofin, *299–300*
Corpses, preserved, *97*
Costs of the trip, *12*
Cottages, *43*
County Antrim, *384–388*
County Armagh, *391–393*
County Clare, *295, 297–300, 313, 315–317, 332*
County Derry, *388–389*
County Down, *393–394*
County Dublin
hotels, *143–144*
restaurants, *131–136*
sightseeing, *106–112*
County Fermanagh, *390–391*
County Galway, *301–309, 313–314, 316, 317, 332*
County Kildare, *164–168, 172–173*
County Louth, *157–162, 171–172*
County Mayo, *292, 310–312, 314, 316, 317, 332*
County Meath, *162–164, 172*
County Museum (Carlow), *199*
County Museum (Monaghan), *183*
County Tipperary, *217–218*
County Tyrone, *389–390*
County Westmeath, *184–186*
County Wexford Museum, *206*
County Wicklow, *150, 152–156, 169–171*
Court House (Cork), *243*
Courthouse (Drogheda), *159*
Courthouse (Kilkenny Town), *203*
Courthouse (Sligo Town), *338*
Courtmacsherry, *247*
Crafts, Irish, *264*
Craggaunowen Castle, *262*

Crawford Art Gallery, *239*
Credit cards, *11, 48*
Creeslough, *351*
Creevelea Abbey, *342*
Creevykeel, *344*
Cricket, *399*
Croagh Patrick (mountain), *7, 310*
Crolly, *352*
Cromwell, Oliver, *208*
Crookstown Heritage Centre, *167*
Crosses. *See* High crosses
Cruises, *4*
Crystal, *37, 116, 182, 210, 213–214, 263–264, 396*
Cuchulainn's Stone, *158*
Cuisine of Ireland, *40–42*
Cultra, *8*
Cultural tours, *4*
Curragh plain, *166*
Currency exchange, *10–11*
Currency of Ireland, *11–12*
Cushendall, *386*
Cushendun, *386*
Custom House (Dublin), *97*
Customs, *13–15*

Dalkey, *108*
Dalkey Island, *108*
Dalway's Bawn (farmhouse), *385*
Damer House, *177*
Dance festivals, *7*
Davy Byrne's Pub, *104*
Department stores, *114*
Derry City
restaurants and hotels, *404*
sightseeing, *388–389*
tourist information, *374*
Derrymore House, *392*
Derrynane House, *253*
Derrynane National Park, *253*
Derryveagh Mountains, *353*
De Valera, Eamon, *108, 297*
Devenish Island, *390*
Dingle, *234, 255–256, 275–276*
Dingle Peninsula, *255–258*
Disabilities, hints for travelers with, *23–24*
Distilleries, *97, 185–186, 387*
Doctors. *See* emergencies *under cities and areas*
Doe Castle, *351*
Dog racing, *219, 222*
Dolemen Gallery, *261*
Dolly's Cottage, *341*
Dolphins, *255–256*
Dominican Abbey, *338*
Donabate, *111–112*
Donagh Castle, *345*
Donagh Cross, *355*
Donegal Craft Village, *345*
Donegal Parian China factory, *344, 358*
Donegal Town
hotels, *364–365*
nightlife, *370*
restaurants, *364–365*
shopping, *358*
sightseeing, *345–346*
tourist information, *335*
Donnybrook, *132*
Doolin, *298, 313, 323, 332*
Dooney Rock, *342*
Douglas Hyde Gallery of Modern Art, *87*
Downies, *350*
Down Museum, *393*
Downpatrick, *8, 374, 393, 404*
Drogheda, *159, 171*
Dromahair, *342*
Drumcliff, *343*
Drumcong, *356*
Drumshanbo, *356*
Drunk-driving laws, *34*
Dublin, *78–82*
airport, *28, 82–83*
the arts, *144–145*
beaches, *106, 119*
Brighton Square, *104*
business hours, *84–85*
children, attractions for, *112–113*
City Center, *86–96, 121–123, 126–131, 136–137, 140–143*
City Hall, *90*
climate, *6*
costs, *12*
crime, *85*
cultural heritage, *79*
Eccles Street, *102*
embassies, *82*
emergencies, *82*
festivals, *6, 7, 8*
Francis Street, *113–114*
free attractions, *112*
Grafton Street, *113*
guided tours, *85–86*
Henry Street, *113*
history of, *78–79, 82*
hotels, *136–144*
Irish Whiskey Corner, *97*
James Joyce's Dublin tour, *102–104*
lost and found, *82*
Marlay Park, *106, 112*
Merrion Square, *94*
Mountjoy Square, *95*
nightlife, *144, 145–147*
Northside, *108–112*
O'Connell Street, *96, 113*
parking, *34*
Phoenix Park, *99*
population, *78*
Prince's Street, *102*
pubs, *86, 90–91, 96, 99, 145–147*
restaurants, *90–91, 93, 96, 99, 107, 120–136*
St. Edna's Park, *104*
St. Stephen's Green, *93*
shopping, *37–38, 85, 113–117*
sightseeing, *86–113*
Southside, *104–108*
sports and the outdoors, *117–119*
tourist information, *82*
transportation in, *83–84*
transportation to, *82–83*
travel agencies, *82*
walking tours, *86*
Western section, *97–101*
Dublin Castle, *90*
Dublin Civic Museum, *91*
Dublin environs, *149*
beaches, *150*
emergencies, *149*
guided tours, *150*
hotels, *168–173*
pubs, *167, 168*
restaurants, *152, 160, 162, 167, 168–173*
sightseeing, *150–168*
tourist information, *149*
transportation, *149*
Dublin Experience (audiovisual presentation), *87*
Dublinia (audiovisual presentation), *101*
Dublin Writers Museum, *95–96*
Dublin Zoo, *99*
Duiske Abbey, *205*
Dun Aengus (prehistoric monument), *306*
Dunaff Head, *355*
Dún an Óir (fort), *257*
Dunbeg Fort, *256*
Dunboy Castle and House, *262*
Dunbrody Abbey, *210*
Dunbrody Castle, *210*
Duncannon, *210*
Dundalk, *7, 157, 171–172*
Dunfanaghy, *351, 365*
Dunganstown, *205*
Dungarvan, *215, 224*
Dungloe, *335, 348, 353*
Dun Laoghaire, *107–108, 131–132, 135, 144*
Dunlap, John, *389*
Dunlavin, *169*
Dunlewy, *353*
Dunluce Castle, *387*
Dunluce Centre, *387*
Dunmore Cave, *203–204*
Dunmore East, *214, 224*
Dunquin, *256–257*
Dunree Head, *355*
Dunsink Observatory, *112*
Durrus, *276–277*
Dursey Island, *262–263*

Duties, *13–15*
Dysert O'Dea Castle Archaeology Center, *300*

Earthorium, *392*
Eden, *385*
Edgeworth, Maria, *184*
Edgeworthstown, *184*
Electricity, *9*
Embassies, *82*
Emergencies
Dublin, *82*
Dublin environs, *149*
Lakelands, *175*
Northern Ireland, *374*
the Northwest, *335*
the Southeast, *197*
the Southwest, *234*
the West, *292*
Emmet, Robert, *100*
Emo Court and Gardens, *186*
Ennis
festivals, *7, 297*
hotels, *323*
nightlife, *331–332*
pubs, *332*
shopping, *313*
sightseeing, *295, 297*
tourist information, *292*
Enniscorthy, *205–206, 219*
Enniscorthy Castle, *205–206*
Enniskerry, *155–156*
Enniskillen, *374, 390–391, 405*
Ennistymon, *332*
Errigal Mountain, *353*
Eyeries, *263*

Fahan, *355, 366*
Falcarragh, *351*
Fanad Peninsula, *350*
Fanore, *323–324*
Farm vacations, *43*
Feast of the Assumption, *8*
Fermanagh County Museum, *390*
Ferries
from Britain, *31–32*
domestic travel, *34–35*
Northern Ireland, *375*
the Southeast, *198*
the Southwest, *235*
the West, *294*
Ferrycarrig, *208–209*
Festivals and seasonal events, *6–9*
Fiddle Stone Festival, *8*
Film
Belfast, *406*
Cork, *7, 286–287*
Dublin, *6, 145*
First Presbyterian Church (Belfast), *395*
Fishing, *38–39*
festivals, *7, 8*
Lakelands, *187*
Northern Ireland, *46–47, 397*
the Northwest, *359–360*
the Southeast, *220–221*
the Southwest, *265*
the West, *315*
Fitness centers
Dublin, *117–118*
the Southwest, *265–266*
the West, *315*
Fleadh Amhran agus Rince, *386*
Fleadh Nua festival, *7, 297*
Flight of the Earls Heritage Centre, *350*
Florence Court, *391*
Flying boats, *260*
Folk Village, *347*
Football, Gaelic, *7, 40*
Dublin, *7, 119*
Northern Ireland, *399*
the Southeast, *222*
the Southwest, *267*
Fore, *185*
Fore Abbey, *185*
Forts
Northern Ireland, *395*
the Northwest, *352, 354–355*
the Southwest, *246, 253, 256, 257*
the West, *306*
Fota Demesne, *245*
Fota Island, *245*
Fota Wildlife Park, *245*
Foulksmills, *225*
Four Courts building, *97*
Foxford, *312, 314*
Foynes, *260*
Franciscan Church (Wexford), *208*
Free Derry Corner, *389*
Freemasons Hall (Dublin), *92*
French Church, *213*
Fry Model Railway, *112*

Gaelic language, *16*
Gallagher, Patrick, *352*
Gallarus Oratory, *257–258*
Galway City
the arts, *331*
festivals, *7, 8*
hotels, *325–327*
pubs, *304, 332*
restaurants, *324–325*
shopping, *37, 313*
sightseeing, *301–305*
tourist information, *292*
Galway City Museum, *304*
Gap of Dunloe, *250*
Gap of Mamore, *355*
Garden of Remembrance, *95*
Gardens
Belfast, *384*
Dublin, *6, 95, 108–109, 111*
Dublin environs, *7, 152, 155–156, 165, 166–167*
Lakelands, *179, 182, 184–185, 186*
Northern Ireland, *384*
the Northwest, *353–354*
the Southeast, *209*
the Southwest, *247, 249, 252, 262*
Garnish Island, *249*
Garretstown Woods, *246–247*
Gartan Lough, *354*
Garter Lane Arts Centre, *230*
The Gate (theater), *95*
Gay and lesbian travelers, hints for, *25*
Genealogical Office, *92*
General Post Office (Cork), *239*
General Post Office (Dublin), *96*
General Post Office (Galway), *302*
Giant's Causeway, *374, 377, 386–387*
Giant's Ring, *384*
Glandore, *247*
Glaslough, *184*
Glasnevin, *108*
Glasnevin Cemetery, *108*
Glebe House and Gallery, *354*
Glenariff, *386*
Glenbeigh, *254*
Glencar Lough, *342*
Glencolumbkille, *347*
Glendalough, *152–153, 169*
Glengariff, *249*
Glengesh Pass, *347*
Glen of Aherlow, *217*
Glens of Antrim, *385–386, 405*
Glenveagh Castle, *353*
Glenveagh National Park, *353–354*
Glin, *259–260*
Golf, *39, 70–72*
Dublin, *118*
Lakelands, *187–188*
Northern Ireland, *8, 47, 75–76, 397–398*
the Northeast, *72*
the Northwest, *74–75, 360*
the Southeast, *221*
the Southwest, *73–74, 265*
tournaments, *7*
tours, *4–5*
the West, *315–316*
Gore-Booth family, *342–343*
Gorey, *225*
Gort, *300*
Government tourist offices, *2*
GPA Bolton Library, *218*
Graiguenamanagh,

205, 225
Granard, *182*
Grand Opera House (Belfast), *379*
Gray's Print Shop, *389*
Great Blasket, *256*
Grecian temple, *249*
Greencastle, *356*
Greenore, *157*
Gregory, Lady Augusta, *300*
Grianan Fort, *354–355*
Guest houses, *42–43*
Guinness Brewery, *100*
Guinness Hop Store, *100*
Gweedore, *352, 353*
Gyles Quay, *157*

Halpin, Capt. Robert, *150*
Health clubs. *See* Fitness centers
Health tips, *16–17*
Heraldic Museum, *92*
Heritage Center (Wicklow Town), *152*
Hermitage (Slane), *161*
High crosses
Dublin environs, *160, 164, 168*
Lakelands, *184*
Northern Ireland, *390*
the Northwest, *343*
the West, *299*
Hiking, *39*
Lakelands, *188*
Northern Ireland, *47, 398*
the Northwest, *360*
the Southeast, *221*
the Southwest, *266*
tours, *5*
the West, *316*
Hill, Derek, *354*
Hill of Allen, *166*
Hill of Tara, *162–163*
History of Ireland, *55–58*
Holycross, *218*
Holycross Abbey, *218*
Holy Trinity Cathedral (Waterford), *213*
Home exchanges, *43*
Homes, historic
Dublin, *92, 93, 94*
Dublin environs, *153–154, 155, 158, 164–165*
Lakelands, *177, 181–182, 183*
Northern Ireland, *391, 392, 393, 394*
the Northwest, *341, 342–343*
the Southeast, *203, 212*
the Southwest, *244, 248, 251–252, 262–263*
the West, *311*
Hooker racing, *317*
Hopkins, Gerard Manley, *108*
Horn Head, *351*
Horse auctions, *6, 8*
Horseback riding, *39*
Dublin, *118*
Northern Ireland, *47, 398*
the Northwest, *360*
the Southeast, *221*
the Southwest, *266–267*
tours, *5*
the West, *316–317*
Horse racing, *6, 7, 40*
Dublin, *119*
Dublin environs, *166*
the Southeast, *222*
the Southwest, *267*
the West, *317*
Horse shows, *7, 8, 309*
Hospitals, historic, *95, 99–100*
Hotels, *42–44. See also under cities and areas*
Northern Ireland, *47*
tipping, *36*
House of St. Columba, *347*
Howth, *109, 111, 132–134*
Howth Castle Gardens, *111*
Hugh Lane Municipal Art Gallery, *95*
Huguenot Cemetery, *93*
Hunt Collection, *261*
Hurling (Gaelic game), *40*
Dublin, *7, 119*
Northern Ireland, *399*
the Southeast, *222*
the Southwest, *267*

Inagh Valley, *309*
Inch, *255*
Inchagoill Island, *308*
Inishbofin, *312*
Inisheer, *298, 306–307, 319*
Inishmaan, *306*
Inishmore, *292, 305, 319*
Inishowen Head, *356*
Inishowen Peninsula, *355*
Innisfallen Island, *251*
Innisfree, *342*
Inniskeen, *158*
Inniskeen Folk Museum, *158*
Insurance, *17, 19*
Ireland's Eye (island), *109*
Irish Agricultural Museum, *209*
Irish Heraldry Society, *260*
Irish Horse Museum, *167*
Irish Museum of Modern Art, *100*
Irish National Heritage Park, *208–209*
Irish Pewter Mill, *167*
Irish Republican Army (IRA), *373*

Jackson, Andrew, *385*
Jails, *100*
James Joyce Cultural Center, *102*
James Joyce Martello Tower, *104, 108*
Japanese Gardens, *166–167*
Jazz festivals, *8, 9*
Jerpoint Abbey, *205*
Jewelry, *37–38, 116*
Jogging, *39*
Dublin, *118*
the Southwest, *267*
John F. Kennedy Memorial Forest Park, *205*
Johnstown Castle Gardens, *209*
Joyce, James, *7, 102, 104, 108, 156, 312*

Kanturk, *277*
Kavanagh, Patrick, *158*
Kells, *164, 172*
Kenmare, *7, 234, 253, 277–278*
Kennedy family, *199, 205*
Kennedy Park, *302*
Kerry, *288*
Kerry Bog Village Museum, *254*
Kerry County Life Experience, *252*
Kerry County Museum, *259*
Kerrykeel, *350*
Kesh, *390*
Kevin, St., *153*
Kilbeggan, *185–186*
Kilcar, *347, 358*
Kildare Town, *166*
Kilfenora, *299, 332*
Kilkee, *292, 297*
Kilkenny Castle, *203*
Kilkenny Town
the arts, *230*
festivals, *6, 7*
hotels, *225–226*
pubs, *231*
restaurants, *225–226*
shopping, *219–220*
sightseeing, *202–205*
tourist information, *197*
Killarney National Park, *252*
Killarney region, *249–252*
Killarney Town
festivals, *7*
hotels, *279–281*
nightlife, *288–289*
restaurants, *278–279*
sightseeing, *250*
tourist information, *234*
Killary Harbour, *310*
Killimer, *259*
Killiney, *119, 143*
Killorglin, *7, 255, 281*
Killybegs, *347, 366*
Killykeen Forest Park, *183*
Kilmainham Gaol, *100*
Kilmakedar Church, *258*

Kilmessan, *172*
Kilmore Quay, *209*
Kilronan, *305*
Kilruddery Gardens, *156*
Kilrush, *292, 297*
Kilrush Woods, *297*
King House (Boyle), *181*
King John's Castle (Carlingford), *158*
King John's Castle (Limerick), *261*
Kingscourt, *191–192*
King William's Glen, *161*
Kinsale
hotels, *282–283*
nightlife, *288*
restaurants, *281–282*
sightseeing, *245–246*
tourist information, *234*
Knappogue Castle, *262, 287*
Knitwear, *38*
Knockbreda Parish Church, *395*
Knockferry, *327*
Knockmealdown Mountains, *216*
Knocknarea (grassy hill), *340–341*
Kylemore Abbey, *309, 313*

Lace making, *184*
Ladies' View, *252*
Lahinch, *7, 292, 298, 313, 327, 332*
Lakelands, *175*
emergencies, *175*
hotels, *188–194*
restaurants, *179, 182, 185, 188–194*
sightseeing, *177–186*
sports and the outdoors, *186–188*
tourist information, *175*
transportation, *176–177*
Lakeside Centre, *353*
Lambert Puppet Theatre, *112*
Language, *16*
Laracor, *163–164*
Larne, *374, 385*
Ledwidge Cottage and Museum, *162*
Leenane, *310*
LeFanu, Sheridan, *94*
Leighlinbridge, *199, 226*
Leinster House, *92*
Leitrim Lakes, *356*
Letterfrack, *309, 313, 328, 332*
Letterkenny, *335, 348, 350, 366–367*
Libraries
Belfast, *379*
Dublin, *87, 91, 92, 101, 104, 106*
the Northwest, *338*
the Southeast, *202, 218*
the Southwest, *260*
the West, *305*
Lighthouses
Howth, *111*
the Southwest, *248*
Limavady, *388*
Limerick
the arts, *286, 287*
festivals, *6*
hotels, *283–284*
nightlife, *289*
restaurants, *283*
sightseeing, *260–261*
tourist information, *234*
Limerick Regional Archives, *261*
Linen, *38*
Linen Hall Library, *379*
Lisdoonvarna, *7, 292, 298–299, 328, 332*
Lisdoonvarna Spa and Bath House, *299*
Lismore, *215–216*
Lismore Castle, *215–216*
Lissadell House, *342–343*
Listowel, *7, 259*
Literature of Ireland, *25–27*
Londonderry. *See* Derry City
Long-distance calls, *12–13*
Longford, *182, 192*
Lough Allen, *356*
Lough Beagh, *353*
Lough Corrib, *307*
Lough Dan, *152*
Lough Derg, *179, 356–357*
Lough Erne, *344–345, 377, 390*
Lough Gill, *341*
Lough Key Forest Park, *181*
Lough Melvin, *344*
Lough Neagh, *395*
Lough Oughter, *183*
Lough Swilly, *350*
Lough Tay, *152*
Louth, *158*
Lower Lough Erne, *377, 390*
Luggage
airline rules, *9–10, 22*
insurance for, *17*
***Lusitania* memorial,** *245*
Lynch Memorial Window, *302*
Lynch's Castle, *302*

Maam Cross, *308*
MacArt's Fort, *395*
McSwyne's Gun (blowhole), *351*
Magee's (general clothing store), *346*
Mail service, *36*
Northern Ireland, *46*
Makemie, Francis, *350*
Malahide, *111–112, 133, 134*
Malahide Castle, *111*
Malin, *355*
Malin Head, *355*
Mallow, *284*
Mangerton Mountain, *252*
Manorhamilton, *342*
Mansion House (Dublin), *91–92*
Marino Casino, *109*
Maritime Museum (Arklow), *154*
Markets, open-air, *117, 243*
Marlay Park, *106, 112*
Marsh's Library, *101*
Martin, Richard, *308*
Matchmaking Festival, *7, 298*
Maynooth, *165, 173*
Maynooth Castle, *165*
Meagher, Thomas Francis, *212*
Medication, *9, 16–17*
Medieval banquets, *287*
Meenlaragh, *351*
Mellifont Abbey, *160–161*
Mellon, Andrew, *390*
Metal Man, *214*
Midleton, *272*
Military and Historical Museum, *185*
Millmount mound, *160*
Millmount Museum, *160*
Mint Tower House, *158*
Mitchelstown Caves, *216*
Mohill, *356*
Monaghan, *175, 183*
Monasterboice, *160*
Monasteries and abbeys
Dublin environs, *153, 158, 160–161*
Lakelands, *177, 180, 184, 185*
Northern Ireland, *386, 390*
the Northwest, *338, 342, 343, 345–346*
the Southeast, *199, 202–203, 205, 208, 210, 216, 218*
the Southwest, *247, 251*
the West, *309, 313*
Mondello Park, *165–166*
Money, *10–12*
Northern Ireland, *376*
Monkstown, *107*
Monkstown Castle, *107*
Moone High Cross, *168*
Moore, Thomas, *91, 154, 208*
Motte of Ardscull (hillock), *167*
Motte of Granard, *182*
Mountains of Mourne, *392–393, 405–406*
Mt. Brandon, *258*
Mountcharles, *346*
Mount Melleray Abbey, *216*
Mount Stewart (estate), *394*

Mount Usher Gardens, *152*
Moville, *355–356*
Muckish Mountain, *351*
Muckross Abbey, *251*
Muckross House, *251–252*
Muireradach Cross, *160*
Mulcahy, Louis, *257*
Mullingar, *175, 176, 185, 192*
Mulrany, *311, 332*
Murrisk, *310*
Museum of Childhood, *113*
Museums. *See also* Art galleries and museums
Belfast, *384*
Dublin, *85, 91, 92, 93–94, 95–96, 97, 100, 107, 108, 111, 113*
Dublin environs, *154, 157, 158, 160, 162, 165, 167*
Lakelands, *182, 183, 185–186*
Northern Ireland, *384, 389, 390, 392, 393, 394*
the Northwest, *338, 341*
opening and closing times, *85*
the Southeast, *199, 206, 209, 212*
the Southwest, *244, 246, 248–249, 254, 259, 260, 261*
the West, *299, 304*
Music, classical, *6, 7, 9*
Belfast, *406*
Dublin, *6, 144*
Music, traditional, *6, 7, 9*
Dublin, *6, 145*
the Northwest, *348, 369*
the West, *7, 297, 332*

Naas, *6, 166, 173*
National Botanic Gardens, *108–109*
National Gallery of Ireland, *94*
National Library, *92, 104*
National Maritime Museum, *107*
National Museum, *92*
National Museum Annexe, *92*
National Portrait Gallery, *111*
National Stud, *167*
National Wax Museum, *113*
Natural History Museum, *93–94*
Nature preserves
Dublin, *106, 109*
Dublin environs, *157*
Fota Island, *245*
Saltee Islands, *209*
Wexford, *206*
Navan, *162*
Nenagh, *177*
Nenagh Castle Keep, *177*
Nenagh Heritage Centre, *177*
New Berkeley Library, *87*
Newbridge, *166*
Newbridge House, *111–112, 113*
Newcastle, *374, 392–393*
Newgrange tombs, *161*
Newman House, *93*
Newmarket-on-Fergus, *328–329*
New Ormond Hotel, *102*
Newport, *311, 329*
New Ross, *197, 205*
Newry, *8, 374, 392*
Newtown, *163*
Newtownmount-kennedy, *152*
Nightlife. *See also under cities and areas*
business hours, *36, 46*
Nire Valley, *226–227*
Nora Barnacle House, *312*
North Bull Island, *109*
Northern Ireland, *372–374. See also* Belfast
the arts, *406*
banks, *46, 376*
border crossing, *32, 44*
business hours, *46*
bus travel, *32, 45, 375, 376*
car rentals, *18, 376*
car travel, *44–45, 375–376*
costs, *12*
currency, *12*
customs and duties, *14*
emergencies, *374*
ferries from Britain, *32, 375*
festivals and seasonal events, *8–9*
guided tours, *376–377*
history of, *372–373*
hotels, *47, 400–406*
mail service, *46*
money, *376*
nightlife, *407*
plane travel, *28, 31, 374–375*
pubs, *379, 383, 391, 407*
restaurants, *379, 383, 386, 387, 389, 393–394, 399–406*
safety concerns, *372, 373–374*
shopping, *46, 395–396*
sightseeing, *377–395*
sports and the outdoors, *46–47, 396–399*
telephones, *45*
tipping, *46*
tourist information, *2, 374*
train travel, *19–20, 45, 375, 376*
transportation, *44–45*
transportation in, *375–376*
transportation to, *374–375*
weather information, *374*
Northern Ireland Aquarium, *394*
the Northwest, *334–335*
the arts, *369*
emergencies, *335*
guided tours, *337*
hotels, *361–369*
nightlife, *369–370*
pubs, *340, 345, 348, 369–370*
restaurants, *340, 346, 348, 351, 354, 355, 361–368*
shopping, *357–359*
sightseeing, *337–357*
sports and the outdoors, *359–361*
tourist information, *335*
transportation, *335–337*
Number Twenty Nine (historic home), *94*

O'Brien, Edna, *248*
O'Brien's Castle, *306*
Observatories, *112*
O'Carolan, Turlough, *356*
O'Casey, Sean, *95*
O'Conaire, Padraic, *302*
O'Connell, Daniel, *94, 253, 297*
O Crohán, Tomás, *256*
O'Doherty's Tower, *389*
Older travelers, hints for, *24–25*
Old Hall (mansion), *341*
Old Leighlin, *199*
Old Library (Dublin), *87*
Omagh, *390*
Omeath, *158*
One Martello Terrace, *104, 156*
Opera, *7, 8, 9*
Belfast, *379, 406*
the Southeast, *230*
Ormond Castle, *219*
Oughterard, *307, 329–330, 332*
Oul' Lammas Fair, *8–9, 386*

Package deals, *4*
Parke's Castle, *341*
Parknasilla, *253, 284*
Parks, national and forest
Dublin environs, *153–154*
Lakelands, *181, 183*
Northern Ireland, *390*
the Northwest, *351, 353*

Parks, national and forest (*continued*)
the Southeast, *205*
the Southwest, *252, 253*
the West, *297, 300, 309*
Parnell, Charles Stewart, *100, 153–154*
Passage East, *210*
Passports, *13*
Patrick, St., *158, 162, 163, 182, 217, 391, 393*
Pearse, Patrick, *97, 100, 104*
Pewter, *167*
Phoenix Park, *99*
Photographic equipment, *15–16*
Planetariums, *392*
Plane travel
from Britain, *31*
with children, *22–23*
discount flights, *28–30*
domestic travel, *33*
Dublin, *82–83*
flight insurance, *17*
Lakelands, *176*
luggage insurance, *17*
luggage rules, *9–10, 22*
from North America, *27–30*
Northern Ireland, *28, 31, 374–375*
the Northwest, *335–336*
smoking rules, *30*
the Southeast, *197*
the Southwest, *234–235*
tips on, *30*
the West, *292, 294–295*
Plassey, *261*
Plunkett, St. Oliver, *159*
Portaferry, *393–394*
Portarlington, *186*
Poulaphouca Reservoir, *155*
Powerscourt Gardens and Waterfall, *155–156*
Powerscourt Townhouse, *91*
Prehistoric Beehive Huts, *256*
Prehistoric structures
Dublin environs, *157, 161*
Northern Ireland, *384, 395*
the Northwest, *341, 344, 347, 352, 354–355*
the Southeast, *199*
the Southwest, *253, 256*
the West, *306*
Prescription drugs, *9*
Pro-Cathedral (Dublin), *96*
Proleek Dolmen, *157*
Protestant Cathedral (Armagh), *392*
Pubs, *36, 41, 46. See also under cities and areas*
Puck Fair, *7, 255*
Punchestown Racecourse, *6, 166*

Quaker museum, *167*
Queen's College, *378, 384*
Queenstown Project, *245*

Rail passes, *19–20*
Raleigh, Sir Walter, *260*
Ramelton, *350*
Rathborne's Candle Factory, *112*
Rathkeale, *260*
Rathlin Island, *386*
Rathmullan, *350, 367*
Rathmullan House, *350*
Rathnetty, *158*
Rathnew, *169–170*
Reagan, Ronald, *216*
Recess, *313–314, 330*
Reefert Church, *153*
Reginald's Tower, *212*
Restaurants, *40–42. See also under cities and areas*
Northern Ireland, *47*
tipping, *36*
RHA Gallagher Gallery, *93*
Ring of Hook, *209–210*
Ring of Kerry, *252–255*
Ringsend Waterways' Centre, *106*
Riverstown, *368*
Riverstown House, *263*
Road bowling, *267–268, 399*
Roaring Meg, *389*
Robertstown, *165*
Roches Point, *245*
Rock of Cashel, *217–218*
Roscommon, *175, 181*
Roscommon Abbey, *181*
Roscommon Castle, *181*
Roscrea, *177*
Roscrea Heritage Centre, *177*
Rose of Tralee International Festival, *7, 259*
Rosguill Peninsula, *350*
Rossbeigh, *255*
Ross Castle, *251*
The Rosses (headland), *352*
Rosses Point, *343*
Rosslare, *197, 209, 227, 231*
Rosslare Harbour, *227*
Rossmore Forest Park, *183*
Rossnowlagh, *368*
Rothe House, *203*
Rotunda Maternity Hospital, *95*
Round Tower, *153*
Roundwood, *152, 170*
Royal Hospital, *99–100*
Royal Inniskilling Fusiliers Regimental Museum, *390*
Royal Irish Academy, *91*
Royal Irish Fusiliers Museum, *392*
Rugby, *6, 8, 119*
Rugs, *38*
Russborough House, *155*

Sailboat racing, *268*
Sailing. *See* Boating and sailing
St. Aidan's Cathedral, *206*
St. Anne's Cathedral (Belfast), *383*
St. Anne's Church (Cork), *239*
St. Anne's Park, *109*
St. Ann's Church (Dublin), *91*
St. Audoen's Church, *100*
St. Brigid's Cathedral, *166*
St. Canice's Cathedral, *202*
St. Canice's Library, *202*
St. Colman's Cathedral, *245*
St. Columba's Cathedral, *389*
St. Columba's Church, *164*
St. Columba's House, *164*
St. Declan's Oratory, *215*
St. Edna's Park, *104*
St. Fechin's Church, *185*
St. Finn Barre's Cathedral, *243*
St. Francis Xavier (church), *95*
St. John's Cathedral, *340*
St. Kevin's Bed, *153*
St. Kevin's Church, *153*
St. Kevin's Cross, *153*
St. Laserian's Cathedral, *199, 202*
St. Laurence's Gate, *159*
St. Lavinius Church, *152*
St. Malachy's Church, *395*
St. Mary's Cathedral (Limerick), *260*
St. Mary's Church (Navan), *162*
St. Mary's Church of Ireland (Ardee), *159*
St. Mary's Pro-Cathedral (Cork), *239*
St. Michan's Church, *97*
St.Mochta'sHouse, *158*
St. Nicholas (church), *157*

St. Olaf's Church, *212*
St. Patrick Heritage Centre, *393*
St. Patrick's Cathedral (Cashel), *217*
St. Patrick's Cathedral (Dublin), *101*
St. Patrick's Cathedral (Dundalk), *157*
St. Patrick's Cathedral (Trim), *163*
St. Patrick's College (Maynooth), *165*
St. Patrick's Day, *6, 8*
St. Patrick's Purgatory (pilgrimage site), *356–357*
St. Peter's Church (Drogheda), *159*
St. Peter's Church of Ireland (Drogheda), *159–160*
St. Stephen's Day, *8*
Salmon, smoked, *37*
Salmon Weir Bridge, *304*
Saltee Islands, *209*
Salthill, *292*
Sandymount Strand, *104, 106, 119*
Selskar Abbey, *208*
Shannon Airport, *27–28, 234, 261, 284–285*
Shannonbridge, *180*
Shannon River, *259*
Shawls, *38*
Shee Alms House, *203*
Sheephaven Bay, *351*
Shelbourne Hotel, *93*
Sherkin Island, *248*
Shillelagh, *154*
Ship travel from North America, *30–31*
Shopping, *36–38, 46. See also under cities and areas*
business hours, *36, 46*
Siamsa Tíre (folk theater), *259, 287*
Siena Convent, *159*
Sinclair Seamen's Church, *395*
Skellig Experience, *254*
Skelligs (archaeological site), *254*
Skibbereen, *234, 248, 285*
Sky Road, *309*
Slane, *161*
Slane Castle, *161–162*
Slane Hill, *162*
Slea Head, *256*
Slieve Donard, *393*
Slieve League Mountains, *347*
Sligo County Library and Museum, *338*
Sligo Town
emergencies, *335*
hotels, *368–369*
nightlife, *370*
restaurants, *368*
shopping, *359*
sightseeing, *337–338, 340–341*
summer school in, *7*
theater, *369*
tourist information, *335*
Sneem, *253*
the Southeast, *196–197*
the arts, *230*
emergencies, *197*
guided tours, *198*
hotels, *222–230*
nightlife, *231*
pubs, *231*
restaurants, *203, 205, 209, 210, 212, 213, 214, 215, 218, 219, 222–230*
shopping, *219–220*
sightseeing, *198–219*
sports and the outdoors, *220–222*
tourist information, *197*
transportation, *197–198*
the Southwest, *233*
the arts, *286–287*
emergencies, *234*
guided tours, *236–237*
hotels, *269–286*
nightlife, *287–289*
pubs, *239, 246, 247, 248, 251, 255, 256, 257, 259, 262, 287–289*
restaurants, *239, 244, 247, 248, 253, 261, 268–286*
shopping, *263–264*
sightseeing, *237–263*
sports and the outdoors, *264–268*
tourist information, *234*
transportation in, *235–236*
transportation to, *234–235*
Spanish Arch, *304*
Spenser, Edmund, *206, 260*
Spiddle, *314*
Sports, *38–40. See also specific sports; under cities and areas*
Northern Ireland, *46–47*
tours, *5*
Squash, *118*
Staigue Fort, *253*
Steam Museum, *165*
Sterne, Laurence, *219*
Stillorgan, *133, 135*
Strabane, *389*
Straffan, *165, 173*
Strandhill, *341*
Strangford, *393*
Strangford Lough, *393*
Strokestown, *181*
Strokestown Park House, *181–182*
Student and youth travel, *20–22*
Summerhill, *164*
Summer schools, *7*
Surfing, *361*
Sweny's Pharmacy, *104*
Swift, Jonathan, *101, 164*
Swimming, *118*
Swords, *135–136*
Synge, J.M., *305*

Taaffe's Castle, *158*
Tableware, *38*
Tailor's Hall (Dublin), *100–101*
Tara, Hill of, *162–163*
Tara's Palace (dollhouse), *113*
Tarbert, *259*
Taxis, *36, 84*
Teampaill na Skellig (Church of the Oratory), *153*
Teelin, *347*
Telephones, *12–13, 35*
Northern Ireland, *45*
Tennis, *40*
Dublin, *118–119*
the West, *317*
Terryglass, *179, 192–193*
Thackeray, William, *388*
Theater, *27*
Belfast, *406*
Dublin, *8, 90, 95, 145*
the Northwest, *369*
the Southwest, *287*
the West, *331*
Tholsel (Kilkenny Town), *203*
Thomastown, *205, 227–228*
Thoor Ballylee, *292, 300*
Timoleague, *247*
Timoleague Castle Gardens, *247*
Timolin, *167*
Tipperary, *6, 177, 179, 197, 217–219, 220*
Tipping, *36*
Northern Ireland, *46*
Torc Mountain, *252*
Torc Waterfall, *252*
Tory Island, *351–352*
Tours and Packages, *2–5, 22, 23, 25*
Tourist information, *2. See also under cities and areas*
Tower Museum, *389*
Townley Hall Estate, *161*
Train travel, *34*
Dublin, *84*
Dublin environs, *149*
Lakelands, *176*
Northern Ireland, *45, 375, 376*
the Northwest, *336*
rail passes, *19–20*
the Southeast, *198*
the Southwest, *235, 236*
the West, *293, 294*
Tralee, *7, 234, 259, 285, 287*
Tramore, *197, 214*

Transport Museum, *111*
Traveler's checks, *10*
Trawbreaga Bay, *355*
Trim, *163*
Trim Castle, *163*
Trinity College, *86–87*
Triskel Arts Center, *243*
Tullamore, *186, 193*
Tullynally Castle and Gardens, *184–185*
Tweeds, *38, 116, 263, 351, 357*
manufacture of, *346*
Tyrone Crystal, *396*

Uisce Dubh, *180*
Ulster-American Folk Park, *390*
Ulster Folk Museum, *394*
Ulster Museum, *384*
Union Hall, *247*
University College, Cork, *243–244*
University College, Galway, *304–305*

Valentia Island, *254*
Valentine, St., *91*
Value added tax (VAT), *37*
Vee Gap, *216*
Ventry, *256*
Victorian Clock Tower, *213*
Vinegar Hill, *206*
Virginia, *193–194*
Visas, *13*

Waterfalls
Dublin environs, *155–156*
Lakelands, *188*
the Northwest, *342*
the Southwest, *252*
the West, *299*
Waterford City
the arts, *230*
emergencies, *197*
festival, *7*
hotels, *228–229*
pubs, *231*
restaurants, *228*
shopping, *220*
sightseeing, *210–214*
tourist information, *197*
Waterford Glass factory, *213–214, 220*
Waterford Heritage Centre, *212*
Waterville, *253, 285–286*
Wax museums, *113*
Weather information, *6, 374*
Wellbrook Beetling Mill, *395*
the West, *291*
the arts, *331*
emergencies, *292*
guided tours, *295*
hotels, *318–331*
nightlife, *331–332*
pubs, *304, 308, 309, 332*
restaurants, *304, 308, 309, 310, 317–330*
shopping, *312–314*
sightseeing, *295–312*
sports and the outdoors, *314–317*
tourist information, *292*
transportation in, *293–295*
transportation to, *292–293*
Western Union, *11*
Westgate Tower, *208*
Westport, *292, 310–311, 314, 330–331, 332*
Westport House, *311*
Wexford
the arts, *230*
festivals, *8*
hotels, *229–230*
restaurants, *229*
shopping, *220*
sightseeing, *206–209*
tourist information, *197*
Wexford Bull Ring, *208*
Wexford Experience, *206*
Wexford Wildfowl Reserve, *206*
Whiskey, Irish, *37*
Whiskey-making, *97, 387*
White Island, *391*
Wicklow Town, *150, 152, 170–171*
Wilde, Oscar, *94, 391*
Wilson family home, *389*
Windmills, *258*
Wishing stones, *352*
Woodenbridge, *154*

Yeats, W.B., *94, 300, 337, 338, 342, 343*
Yeats Memorial Building, *338*
Yellow Steeple, *163*
Youghal, *234, 286*
Youth hostels, *21, 44*

Zoos
Dublin, *99*
the Southwest, *245*

Personal Itinerary

Departure *Date*

Time

Transportation

Arrival *Date* *Time*

Departure *Date* *Time*

Transportation

Accommodations

Arrival *Date* *Time*

Departure *Date* *Time*

Transportation

Accommodations

Arrival *Date* *Time*

Departure *Date* *Time*

Transportation

Accommodations

Personal Itinerary

Arrival *Date* *Time*

Departure *Date* *Time*

Transportation

Accommodations

Arrival *Date* *Time*

Departure *Date* *Time*

Transportation

Accommodations

Arrival *Date* *Time*

Departure *Date* *Time*

Transportation

Accommodations

Arrival *Date* *Time*

Departure *Date* *Time*

Transportation

Accommodations

Personal Itinerary

Arrival *Date* *Time*

Departure *Date* *Time*

Transportation

Accommodations

Arrival *Date* *Time*

Departure *Date* *Time*

Transportation

Accommodations

Arrival *Date* *Time*

Departure *Date* *Time*

Transportation

Accommodations

Arrival *Date* *Time*

Departure *Date* *Time*

Transportation

Accommodations

Personal Itinerary

Arrival *Date* *Time*

Departure *Date* *Time*

Transportation

Accommodations

Arrival *Date* *Time*

Departure *Date* *Time*

Transportation

Accommodations

Arrival *Date* *Time*

Departure *Date* *Time*

Transportation

Accommodations

Arrival *Date* *Time*

Departure *Date* *Time*

Transportation

Accommodations

Personal Itinerary

Arrival *Date* *Time*

Departure *Date* *Time*

Transportation

Accommodations

Arrival *Date* *Time*

Departure *Date* *Time*

Transportation

Accommodations

Arrival *Date* *Time*

Departure *Date* *Time*

Transportation

Accommodations

Arrival *Date* *Time*

Departure *Date* *Time*

Transportation

Accommodations

Addresses

Name

Address

Telephone

Name

Address

Telephone

Name

Address

Telephone

Name

Address

Telephone

Name

Address

Telephone

Name

Address

Telephone

Name

Address

Telephone

Name

Address

Telephone

Name

Address

Telephone

Name

Address

Telephone

Name

Address

Telephone

Name

Address

Telephone

Name

Address

Telephone

Name

Address

Telephone

Name

Address

Telephone

Name

Address

Telephone

Addresses

Name

Address

Telephone

Name

Address

Telephone

Name

Address

Telephone

Name

Address

Telephone

Name

Address

Telephone

Name

Address

Telephone

Name

Address

Telephone

Name

Address

Telephone

Name

Address

Telephone

Name

Address

Telephone

Name

Address

Telephone

Name

Address

Telephone

Name

Address

Telephone

Name

Address

Telephone

Name

Address

Telephone

Name

Address

Telephone

Notes

Notes

The only guide to explore a Disney World® you've never seen before:

The one for grown-ups.

0-679-02490-5 $14.00 ($18.50 Can)

This is the only guide written specifically for the millions of adults who visit Walt Disney World® each year without kids. Upscale, sophisticated, packed full of facts and maps, *Walt Disney World® for Adults* provides up-to-date information on hotels, restaurants, sports facilities, and health clubs, as well as unique itineraries for adults. With *Walt Disney World® for Adults* in hand, you'll get the most out of one of the world's most fascinating, most complex playgrounds.

At bookstores everywhere, or call **1-800-533-6478.**

Fodor's

Fodor's Travel Guides

Available at bookstores everywhere, or call 1-800-533-6478, 24 hours a day.

U.S. Guides

Alaska

Arizona

Boston

California

Cape Cod, Martha's Vineyard, Nantucket

The Carolinas & the Georgia Coast

Chicago

Colorado

Florida

Hawaii

Las Vegas, Reno, Tahoe

Los Angeles

Maine, Vermont, New Hampshire

Maui

Miami & the Keys

New England

New Orleans

New York City

Pacific North Coast

Philadelphia & the Pennsylvania Dutch Country

The Rockies

San Diego

San Francisco

Santa Fe, Taos, Albuquerque

Seattle & Vancouver

The South

The U.S. & British Virgin Islands

USA

The Upper Great Lakes Region

Virginia & Maryland

Waikiki

Walt Disney World and the Orlando Area

Washington, D.C.

Foreign Guides

Acapulco, Ixtapa, Zihuatanejo

Australia & New Zealand

Austria

The Bahamas

Baja & Mexico's Pacific Coast Resorts

Barbados

Berlin

Bermuda

Brittany & Normandy

Budapest

Canada

Cancún, Cozumel, Yucatán Peninsula

Caribbean

China

Costa Rica, Belize, Guatemala

The Czech Republic & Slovakia

Eastern Europe

Egypt

Euro Disney

Europe

Florence, Tuscany & Umbria

France

Germany

Great Britain

Greece

Hong Kong

India

Ireland

Israel

Italy

Japan

Kenya & Tanzania

Korea

London

Madrid & Barcelona

Mexico

Montréal & Québec City

Morocco

Moscow & St. Petersburg

The Netherlands, Belgium & Luxembourg

New Zealand

Norway

Nova Scotia, Prince Edward Island & New Brunswick

Paris

Portugal

Provence & the Riviera

Rome

Russia & the Baltic Countries

Scandinavia

Scotland

Singapore

South America

Southeast Asia

Spain

Sweden

Switzerland

Thailand

Tokyo

Toronto

Turkey

Vienna & the Danube Valley

Special Series

Fodor's Affordables

Caribbean

Europe

Florida

France

Germany

Great Britain

Italy

London

Paris

Fodor's Bed & Breakfast and Country Inns Guides

America's Best B&Bs

California

Canada's Great Country Inns

Cottages, B&Bs and Country Inns of England and Wales

Mid-Atlantic Region

New England

The Pacific Northwest

The South

The Southwest

The Upper Great Lakes Region

The Berkeley Guides

California

Central America

Eastern Europe

Europe

France

Germany & Austria

Great Britain & Ireland

Italy

London

Mexico

Pacific Northwest & Alaska

Paris

San Francisco

Fodor's Exploring Guides

Australia

Boston & New England

Britain

California

The Caribbean

Florence & Tuscany

Florida

France

Germany

Ireland

Italy

London

Mexico

New York City

Paris

Prague

Rome

Scotland

Singapore & Malaysia

Spain

Thailand

Turkey

Fodor's Flashmaps

Boston

New York

Washington, D.C.

Fodor's Pocket Guides

Acapulco

Bahamas

Barbados

Jamaica

London

New York City

Paris

Puerto Rico

San Francisco

Washington, D.C.

Fodor's Sports

Cycling

Golf Digest's Best Places to Play

Hiking

The Insider's Guide to the Best Canadian Skiing

Running

Sailing

Skiing in the USA & Canada

USA Today's Complete Four Sports Stadium Guide

Fodor's Three-In-Ones (guidebook, language cassette, and phrase book)

France

Germany

Italy

Mexico

Spain

Fodor's Special-Interest Guides

Complete Guide to America's National Parks

Condé Nast Traveler Caribbean Resort and Cruise Ship Finder

Cruises and Ports of Call

Euro Disney

France by Train

Halliday's New England Food Explorer

Healthy Escapes

Italy by Train

London Companion

Shadow Traffic's New York Shortcuts and Traffic Tips

Sunday in New York

Sunday in San Francisco

Touring Europe

Touring USA: Eastern Edition

Walt Disney World and the Orlando Area

Walt Disney World for Adults

Fodor's Vacation Planners

Great American Learning Vacations

Great American Sports & Adventure Vacations

Great American Vacations

Great American Vacations for Travelers with Disabilities

National Parks and Seashores of the East

National Parks of the West

The Wall Street Journal Guides to Business Travel

Fodor's

WORLDVIEW

TRAVEL UPDATE

Now there is a revolutionary way to get customized, time-sensitive travel information just before your trip.

Now you can obtain detailed information about what's going on in each city you'll be visiting before you leave home—up-to-the-minute, objective information about the events and activities that interest you most.

Travel Updates contain the kind of time-sensitive insider information you can get only from local contacts – or from city magazines and newspapers once you arrive. But now you can have the same information before you leave for your trip.

The choice is yours: current art exhibits, theater, music festivals and special concerts, sporting events, antiques and flower shows, shopping, fitness, and more.

The information comes from hundreds of correspondents and thousands of sources worldwide. Updated continuously, it's like having your own personal concierge or friend in the city.

You specify the cities and when you'll be there. We'll do the rest — personalizing the information for you the way no guidebook can.

It's the perfect extension to your Fodor's guide and the best way to make the most of your valuable travel time.

Use Order Form on back or call 1-800-799-9609

Your Itinerary: Customized reports available for 160 destinations

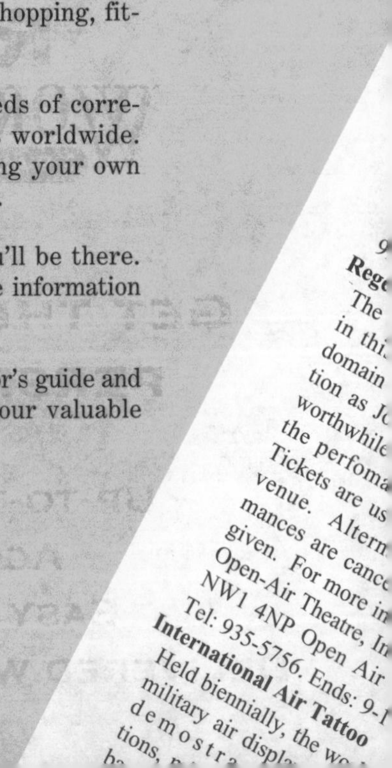

Personalized:
Prepared expressly for you.

Up-to-the-minute:
Includes the most current information available.

Your travel dates:
Covers only days when you will be there.

June 1

Fodor's/Worldview presents a Travel Update for:

Mr. Gavin Lynch
201 East 50th Street
New York, New York, 10022

Fodor's
WORLDVIEW

ARRIVE 23 Jun DEPART: 21 Jul

LONDON, UK

Your Interests:
Features only those categories that matter to you.

HIGHLIGHTS—EVENTS

Wimbledon Lawn Tennis Championships

Seats for the Wimbledon championships, especiall
those for the men's and women's finals on the
Centre Court, are the hottest tickets in Lon
ummer. Each winter there is a ballo
No. 1 Court seats for the fol
nt. Through this ballot, te
ance of securing a ticket.
r top matches are included
bining hotel accommodatio
ailable from the tourname
NAA Events Internation
4.

en Air Theatre Season

of open-air theater produ
lovely park, once the e
dandies, is as much of an
adway in the Park and e
bring your largest umbre
n interrupted by showe
e for the almost 1,200-seat
re offered when perfor-
ain, but refunds are not
ntact Sheila Benja
gent's Park

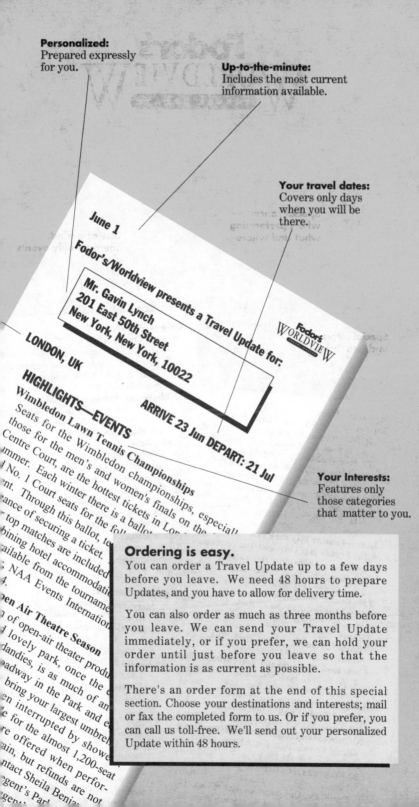

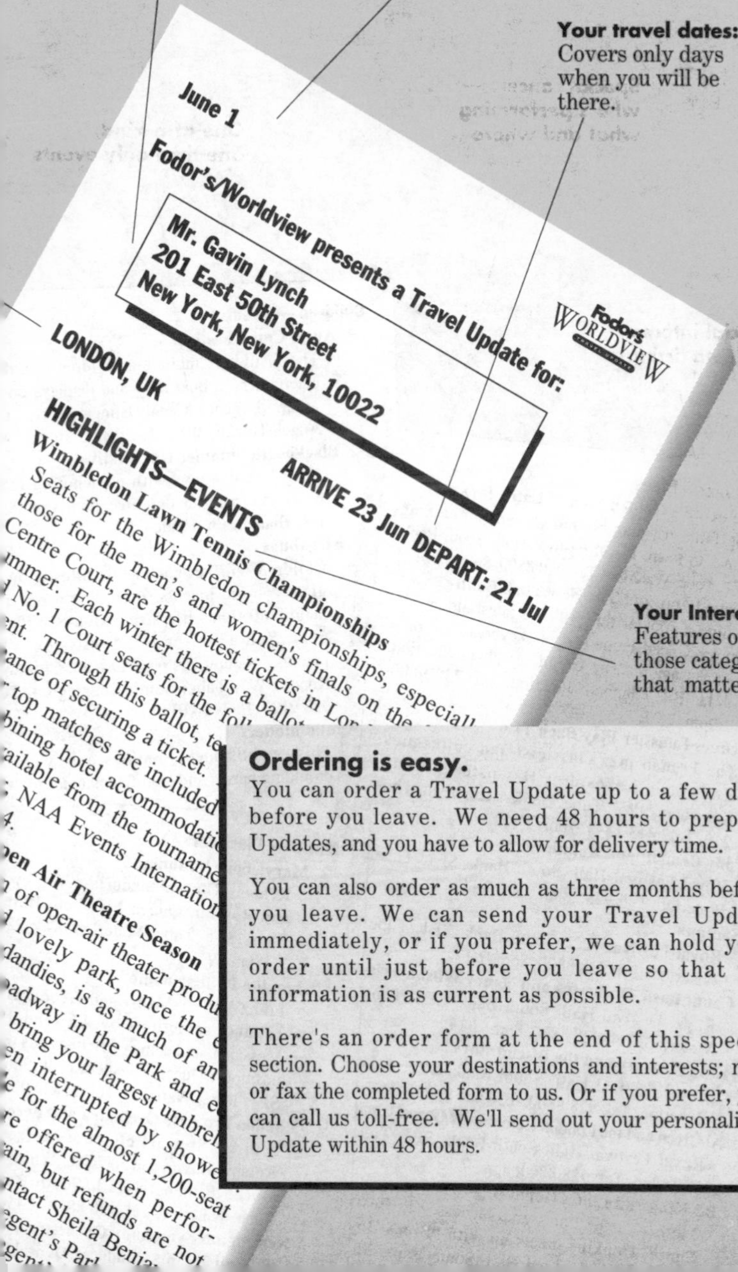

Ordering is easy.

You can order a Travel Update up to a few days
before you leave. We need 48 hours to prepare
Updates, and you have to allow for delivery time.

You can also order as much as three months before
you leave. We can send your Travel Update
immediately, or if you prefer, we can hold your
order until just before you leave so that the
information is as current as possible.

There's an order form at the end of this special
section. Choose your destinations and interests; mail
or fax the completed form to us. Or if you prefer, you
can call us toll-free. We'll send out your personalized
Update within 48 hours.

Here's what you get . . .

Detailed information about what's going on — precisely when you'll be there.

Show openings during your visit

Handy pocket-size booklet

Reviews by local critics

Exhibitions & Shows—Antique & Flower

Westminster Antiques Fair

Over 50 stands with pre-1830 furniture and other Victorian and earlier items. Thu-Fri 11am-8pm; Sat-Sun 11am-6pm. Admission 4 pounds, children free. Old Royal Horticultural Hall. Vincent Square. SW1. Tel: 0444/48 25 14. 6-24 thru 6/27.

Royal Horticultural Society Flower Show

The show includes displays of carnations, summer fruit and vegetables. Tue 11am-7pm; Wed 10am-5pm. Admission Tue 4 pounds, Wed 2 pounds. Royal Horticultural Halls. Greycoat Street and Vincent Square. SW1. Tube: Victoria. 7/20 thru 7/21.

mpton Court Palace International Flower Show

ajor international garden and flower show taking place in conjunction with

heater — Musical

Sunset Boulevard

In June, the four Andrew Lloyd Webber musicals which dominated London's stages in the 1980s (Cats, Starlight Express, Phantom of the Opera and Aspects of Love) are joined by the composer's latest work, a show rumored to have his best music to date. The 1950 Billy Wilder film about a helpless young writer who is drawn into the world of a possessive, aging silent screen star offers rich opportunities for Webber's evolving style. Soaring, aching melodies, lush technical effects and psychological thrills are all expected. Patti Lupone stars. Mon-Sat at 8pm; matinee Thu-Sat at 3pm. In-person sales only at the box office; credit card bookings, Tel: 344 0055. Admission 15-32.50 pounds. Adelphi Theatre. The Strand. WC2. Tube: Charing Cross. Tel: 836 7611. Starts: 6/21.

Leonardo A Portrait of Love

A new musical about the great Renaissance artist and inventor comes in for a London pre-... tested by a brief run at Oxford's Old ... The work explores

Spectator Sports — Other Sports

Greyhound Racing: Wembley Stadium

This dog track offers good views of greyhound racing held on Mon, Wed and Fri. No credit cards. Stadium Way. Wembley. HA9. Tube: Wembley Park. Tel: 902 8833.

Benson & Hedges Cricket Cup Final

Lord's Cricket Ground. St. John's Wood Road. NW8. Tube: St. John's Wood. Tel: 289 1611. 11am. 7/10.

usiness-Fax & Overnight Mail

Post Office, Trafalgar Square Branch

Offers a network of fax services, the Intelpost system, throughout the country and abroad. Mon-Sat 8am-8pm, Sun 9am-5pm. William IV Street. WC2. Tube: Chari...

Interest Categories

For your personalized Travel Update, choose the categories you're most interested in from this list. Every Travel Update automatically provides you with *Event Highlights* - the best of what's happening during the dates of your trip.

1.	**Business Services**	Fax & Overnight Mail, Computer Rentals, Photocopying, Protocol, Secretarial, Messenger, Translation Services
	Dining	
2.	**All Day Dining**	Breakfast & Brunch, Cafes & Tea Rooms, Late-Night Dining
3.	**Local Cuisine**	In Every Price Range—from Budget Restaurants to the Special Splurge
4.	**European Cuisine**	Continental, French, Italian
5.	**Asian Cuisine**	Chinese, Far Eastern, Japanese, Other
6.	**Americas Cuisine**	American, Mexican & Latin
7.	**Nightlife**	Bars, Dance Clubs, Casinos, Comedy Clubs, Ethnic, Pubs & Beer Halls
8.	**Entertainment**	Theater—Comedy, Drama, English Language, Musicals, Dance, Ticket Agencies
9.	**Music**	Country/Western/Folk, Classical, Traditional & Ethnic, Opera, Jazz & Blues, Pop, Rock
10.	**Children's Activities**	Events, Attractions
11.	**Tours**	Local Tours, Day Trips, Overnight Excursions, Cruises
12.	**Exhibitions, Festivals & Shows**	Antiques & Flower, History & Cultural, Art Exhibitions, Fairs & Craft Shows, Music & Art Festivals
13.	**Shopping**	Districts & Malls, Markets, Regional Specialities
14.	**Fitness**	Bicycling, Health Clubs, Hiking, Jogging
15.	**Recreational Sports**	Boating/Sailing, Fishing, Golf, Ice Skating, Skiing, Snorkeling/Scuba, Swimming, Tennis & Racquet
16.	**Spectator Sports**	Auto Racing, Baseball, Basketball, Boating & Sailing, Football, Golf, Horse Racing, Ice Hockey, Rugby, Soccer, Tennis, Track & Field, Other Sports

Please note that interest category content will vary by season, destination, and length of stay.

Fodor's WORLDVIEW TRAVEL UPDATE **Order Form**

THIS TRAVEL UPDATE IS FOR (Please print):

Name ____________________

Address ____________________

City ________ State ________ Country ________ ZIP ________

Tel # ( ) - Fax # ( ) -

Title of this Fodor's guide: ____________________

Store and location where guide was purchased: ____________________

INDICATE YOUR DESTINATIONS/DATES: You can order up to three (3) destinations from the previous page. Fill in your arrival and departure dates for each destination. **Your Travel Update itinerary (all destinations selected) cannot exceed 30 days from beginning to end.**

		Month / Day		Month / Day
(Sample) *LONDON*	*From:*	*6 / 21*	*To:*	*6 / 30*
1	From:	/	To:	/
2	From:	/	To:	/
3	From:	/	To:	/

CHOOSE YOUR INTERESTS: Select up to eight (8) categories from the list of interest categories shown on the previous page and circle the numbers below:

1 2 3 4 5 6 7 8 9 10 11 12 13 14 15 16

CHOOSE WHEN YOU WANT YOUR TRAVEL UPDATE DELIVERED (Check one):

❑ Please send my Travel Update immediately.

❑ Please hold my order until a few weeks before my trip to include the most up-to-date information.

Completed orders will be sent within 48 hours. Allow 7-10 days for U.S. mail delivery.

ADD UP YOUR ORDER HERE. ***SPECIAL OFFER FOR FODOR'S PURCHASERS ONLY!***

	Suggested Retail Price	Your Price	This Order
First destination ordered	~~$ 9.95~~	$ 7.95	$ 7.95
Second destination (if applicable)	~~$ 6.95~~	$ 4.95	+
Third destination (if applicable)	~~$ 6.95~~	$ 4.95	+

DELIVERY CHARGE (Check one and enter amount below)

	Within U.S. & Canada	Outside U.S. & Canada
First Class Mail	❑ $2.50	❑ $5.00
FAX	❑ $5.00	❑ $10.00
Priority Delivery	❑ $15.00	❑ $27.00

ENTER DELIVERY CHARGE FROM ABOVE: +

TOTAL: $

METHOD OF PAYMENT IN U.S. FUNDS ONLY (Check one):

❑ AmEx ❑ MC ❑ Visa ❑ Discover ❑ Personal Check (U. S. & Canada only)

❑ Money Order/ International Money Order

Make check or money order payable to: Fodor's Worldview Travel Update

Credit Card ____________________ **Expiration Date:** ________

Authorized Signature ____________________

SEND THIS COMPLETED FORM WITH PAYMENT TO:

Fodor's Worldview Travel Update, 114 Sansome Street, Suite 700, San Francisco, CA 94104

OR CALL OR FAX US 24-HOURS A DAY

Telephone **1-800-799-9609** • Fax **1-800-799-9619** (From within the U.S. & Canada)

(Outside the U.S. & Canada: Telephone 415-616-9988 • Fax 415-616-9989)

(Please have this guide in front of you when you call so we can verify purchase.)

Code: FTG

Offer valid until 12/31/95

Destinations

The Fodor's/Worldview Travel Update covers more than 160 destinations worldwide. Choose the destinations that match your itinerary from this list. (Choose bulleted destinations only.)

Europe
- Amsterdam
- Athens
- Barcelona
- Berlin
- Brussels
- Budapest
- Copenhagen
- Dublin
- Edinburgh
- Florence
- Frankfurt
- French Riviera
- Geneva
- Glasgow
- Istanbul
- Lausanne
- Lisbon
- London
- Madrid
- Milan
- Moscow
- Munich
- Oslo
- Paris
- Prague
- Provence
- Rome
- Salzburg
- * Seville
- St. Petersburg
- Stockholm
- Venice
- Vienna
- Zurich

United States (Mainland)
- Albuquerque
- Atlanta
- Atlantic City
- Baltimore
- Boston
- * Branson, MO
- * Charleston, SC
- Chicago
- Cincinnati
- Cleveland
- Dallas/Ft. Worth
- Denver
- Detroit
- Houston
- * Indianapolis
- Kansas City
- Las Vegas
- Los Angeles
- Memphis
- Miami
- Milwaukee
- Minneapolis/ St. Paul
- * Nashville
- New Orleans
- New York City
- Orlando
- Palm Springs
- Philadelphia
- Phoenix
- Pittsburgh
- Portland
- * Reno/ Lake Tahoe
- St. Louis
- Salt Lake City
- San Antonio
- San Diego
- San Francisco
- * Santa Fe
- Seattle
- Tampa
- Washington, DC

Alaska
- Alaskan Destinations

Hawaii
- Honolulu
- Island of Hawaii
- Kauai
- Maui

Canada
- Quebec City
- Montreal
- Ottawa
- Toronto
- Vancouver

Bahamas
- Abaco
- Eleuthera/ Harbour Island
- Exuma
- Freeport
- Nassau & Paradise Island

Bermuda
- Bermuda Countryside
- Hamilton

British Leeward Islands
- Anguilla
- Antigua & Barbuda
- St. Kitts & Nevis

British Virgin Islands
- Tortola & Virgin Gorda

British Windward Islands
- Barbados
- Dominica
- Grenada
- St. Lucia
- St. Vincent
- Trinidad & Tobago

Cayman Islands
- The Caymans

Dominican Republic
- Santo Domingo

Dutch Leeward Islands
- Aruba
- Bonaire
- Curacao

Dutch Windward Island
- St. Maarten/ St. Martin

French West Indies
- Guadeloupe
- Martinique
- St. Barthelemy

Jamaica
- Kingston
- Montego Bay
- Negril
- Ocho Rios

Puerto Rico
- Ponce
- San Juan

Turks & Caicos
- Grand Turk/ Providenciales

U.S. Virgin Islands
- St. Croix
- St. John
- St. Thomas

Mexico
- Acapulco
- Cancun & Isla Mujeres
- Cozumel
- Guadalajara
- Ixtapa & Zihuatanejo
- Los Cabos
- Mazatlan
- Mexico City
- Monterrey
- Oaxaca
- Puerto Vallarta

South/Central America
- * Buenos Aires
- * Caracas
- * Rio de Janeiro
- * San Jose, Costa Rica
- * Sao Paulo

Middle East
- * Jerusalem

Australia & New Zealand
- Auckland
- Melbourne
- * South Island
- Sydney

China
- Beijing
- Guangzhou
- Shanghai

Japan
- Kyoto
- Nagoya
- Osaka
- Tokyo
- Yokohama

Pacific Rim/Other
- * Bali
- Bangkok
- Hong Kong & Macau
- Manila
- Seoul
- Singapore
- Taipei

* Destinations available by 1/1/95